William Lilly's
CHRISTIAN ASTROLOGY
Book 1: An Introduction to Astrology
Book 2: The Resolution of All Manner of Questions and Demands
first published in 1647

Note: *Of the three books mentioned on the facsimile of the original title page (overleaf), this edition consists of the first two books only. The third book,* **Judgment upon Nativities,** *is available separately.*

GULIELMUS LILLIUS Astrologus *Natus Comitat: Leicest:*
1° Maÿ 1602.

Guliel: Marshall sculpsit . .

CHRISTIAN
ASTROLOGY
MODESTLY
Treated of in three Books.

The *first* containing the use of an EPHEMERIS,
the erecting of a Scheam of Heaven ; nature of
the twelve Signs of the Zodiack, of the
Planets ; with a most easie Introduction
to the whole Art of ASTROLOGY.

The *second*, by a most Methodicall way, Instructeth
the Student how to Judge or Resolve all manner of Questions contingent unto Man, *viz.* of Health, Sicknesse, Riches, Marriage, Preferment, Journies, &c.
Severall Questions inserted and Judged.

The *third*, containes an exact Method, whereby to
Judge upon Nativities ; severall wayes how to rectifie
them ; How to judge the generall fate of the Native by the
twelve Houses of Heaven, according to the naturall
influence of the STARS ; How his particular
and Annuall Accidents, by the Art of Direction, and its exact measure of Time
by Profections, Revolutions, Transits.
A Nativity Judged by the Method preceding.

By WILLIAM LILLY Student in Astrology.

Omne meum, nil meum :   *Nibil dictum, quod non dictum prius.*

✦✦✦✦✦✦✦✦✦✦✦✦✦
LONDON:
Printed by *Tho. Brudenell* for *John Partridge* and *Humph. Blunden,* in *Black-
friers* at the Gate going into *Carter-lane,* and in *Cornbil,* 1647.

On the cover: **La belle Strasbourgeoise** (1603), by Nicolas de Largilliere (1656 - 1746), at the Musee des Beaux Arts, Strasbourg. Extracts from pages 1, 25, 129 & 397 from the Regulus edition.

Back cover: The famous portrait of Lilly, from the Ashmolean Museum. And a blue shirt.

Printing History:
First edition, 1647
Second edition, 1659
As edited by Zadkiel no. 1 (Richard James Morrison), published as,
   "An Introduction to Astrology", 1852
Facsimile of the 1647 edition, published by Regulus Publishing Co. Ltd., 1985.
Retyped by Carol Wiggers, Just Us & Associates, 1985, revised 1997
Retyped, reset, by Deborah Houlding, Ascella, 1999

ISBN: 1 933303 02 6
Easter, 2004
Errata update, January 2006

Editor's Preface

While living in Santa Fe in 1998, I had a phone call from the late Olivia Barclay. She said the Regulus edition of **Christian Astrology** was going out of print (which I already knew), would I consider reprinting it myself? This was a tall order. The book is enormous, I had not previously published anything. I promised I would do what I could.

So I took my Regulus edition & put it on the copier. Adjusted the magnification to fill an 8.5 x 11 page, and set to it. I might not have been able to produce an 850 page hardcover book, but a cheap comb-bound version was possible, maybe. Before I was half done, I noticed an odd sort of headache. I finished the copy & phoned a friend in California. She confirmed my suspicion, whereupon we made a technical adjustment to the copying process. I have been thankful many times since that we did so.

Here published are Books 1 and 2 of Lilly's great classic. I have published Book 3, on Natal Charts, separately.

In planning this volume, I have reset the astrological matter, but used Lilly's original introductory pages, including his ephemeris and table of houses. It is useful, I think, to know what old books, old typesetting, looked like. It is also a way that modern readers may know Lilly's book as Lilly himself did. Lilly's layouts were very good, his tables often excellent. I have restored his layouts, including marginalia, and closely copied the tables. Those who have used the Regulus edition will find the contents of these pages to exactly match those in Regulus edition, in places, almost line for line.

As J. Lee Lehman has pointed out (I forget where), 17th century English was influenced by French, which, then as now, has gender. This may be the reason why, for example, one could find "cusp" and "cuspe" in the same sentence in Lilly's original. I have modernized his spelling, updated antique verb tenses (*has* for *hath*, etc.) and replaced abandoned words with their modern counterparts (*impeded* for *impedited*, etc.). I have left his use of second person singular (*thou*) and the verbs with it, strictly as is. As far as humanly possible, I have copied Lilly's use of italics, capitals and punctuation, even though his use of italics and capitals seems to be erratic, and the original punctuation results in very long sentences. I was not entirely pleased with the result: Lilly's book now reads as if it were by a contemporary writer, eg, it is much too easy too read. Casual readers may now think that when Lilly writes, "clown" he means a white-faced circus employee, "mechanic" someone who works in a garage, "match making" to be Carmen herself. None of these occupations, of course, existed in Lilly's day, he had other meanings in mind. I have glossed the most obvious of these, if readers find more I would appreciate hearing of them.

The first two books of Lilly's **Christian Astrology** are long and complex. No reprint, including the great Regulus facsimile, has been entirely free of mistakes. I have proofed and spell-checked - in places more than once - all that follows. Any mistakes found here are mine.

In reprinting Lilly I have tried to err on the conservative side, to let the author speak for himself. It is for readers to decide if I have been successful. We are slowly moving towards the translation of the most significant early astrological texts, as well as the reprinting of the great 17th century English classics, of which Lilly's were the greatest. The process involves many hard choices & should provoke debate. The result will be a library of astrological texts that will forever enrich the world.

I wish to thank Olivia Barclay for the suggestion, my wife Elizabeth for her patience, Margaret Cahill, at Wessex Astrologer, for encouragement, VBH, in California, for technical assistance, and, most of all, Mr. William Lilly himself. On more than one night I felt him peering over my shoulder. Hopefully he was pleased with what he saw.

David R. Roell
March 8, 2004

October 29, 2005: My thanks to Kevin Briggs for his errata.

To his moſt learned and vertuous friend
BOLSTROD WHITLOCK, Eſq. .
one of the Members of the honorable
Houſe of COMMONS in this
preſent PARLIAMENT.

Much honored Sir :

Hope this Dedicatory Epiſtle of mine publiſhed without your knowledge, ſhall beget no ſuch ſiniſter conſtructi-on in you, but that the fault ſhall be admitted as a veniall tranſgreſſion ; and this my preſumption finde eaſie remiſſion at your moſt gentle hands. I am now ſo well acquainted with your pleaſing native Diſpoſition, that in things of this nature where you are not in queſtion, I dare a little offend ; for its a fixed na-turall Maxime ingraffed in you, to love your friends ſin-cerely, and rarely to take offence upon ſlight failings.

Pardon this boldneſſe ; verily, ſo many, ſo number-leſſe are my engagements unto you, that I could doe no leſſe, having no other meanes remaining whereby to ex-

A 3   preſſe

vii

presse a gratefull heart, or to acquaint the present and future times, of your ardent and continuall promoting me and my poore labours, since first Divine Providence made me knowne unto you; so that I doe freely acknowledge, next unto Almighty God, your selfe have been the Instrumentall meanes of inabling me to performe, not onely what is already publique, but also this ensuing Treatise, which now I humbly offer unto your Patronage, as a thankfull testimony of my sincere respects due unto you : for had not you persevered all along a firme and an assured *Mecenas* unto me, my carkasse and Conceptions had beene buried in eternall silence ; so that the Students in this Art must acknowledge the Restauration of *Astrologie* unto your goodnesse. For, S I R, you have countenanced me your self ; you have commended me to your Friends ; you have never omitted to doe me, or my friends for my lake, any civill courtesies : And this I shall adde to your honour, that I no sooner at any time importuned your favour, but I was instantly sensible of your actual and reall performance of the thing I required.

Should I enumerate your vertues or curtesies in this kinde performed unto many besides my selfe, the day would faile me of time, and my hand grow weary of writing : but as in private you assist your friends, so have you most faithfully for almost seven yeeres served your Countrey in this present Parliament, even to the manifest decay of your health, to my owne knowledge, and consumption of many thousand pounds of your Estate : you have refused no paines to benefit this *Commonwealth*; and being ever delegated an honourable *Commissioner* upon all Treaties for Peace betwixt the King and Parliament, you have demeaned your selfe with
                                                                            such

ſuch candour, judgement and integrity in all of them, that the whole Kingdome are ſatisfied therewith, and we of the Commonalty ſtand indebted unto you.

Brevity beſt pleaſeth you, few words may become me; yet I cannot reſt in quiet untill I deliver thoſe excellent expreſſions of yours, which my owne eares heard from your mouth in 1 6 4 4. at what time this preſent Parliament was loe, and your ſelfe tampered withall to become Turncoat and renounce this Parliament ; *N O, I'le not remove from this preſent Parliament now ſitting at* Weſtminſter, *for unto this place was I called, and hither ſent by my Countrey for their ſervice , and if God have ſo decreed, that his Majeſty ſhall overcome us, yet am I reſolved to abide here, and to dye within the wals of that very Houſe; and I will take the ſame portion which God hath aſſigned to thoſe honourable Members that ſhall continue firme in this cauſe.* Theſe words you have made good even unto this day, to your eternall honour ; nor can the blacke mouthes of the moſt accurſed ſnarling Curs detract a graine from your worth.

I have now a large Field to walke in, and ſhould I further proceed, I am aſſured I ſhould move that ſweet diſpoſed temper of yours, which is not eaſily offended ; I am ſilent ; onely ;

Faveas (precor) primitiis creſcentis Indolis, quæ ſi ſub tuo ſole adoleverit, & juſtam tandem maturitatem conſequuta fuerit, non indignos fructus retributarum confido.

S I R, I hope you ſhall have no diſhonour to Patronize the Enſuing Worke, wherein I lay downe the whol

natu-

naturall grounds of the Art, in a fit Method : that thereby I may undeceive thoſe, who miſled by ſome Pedling
Divines, have upon no better credit then their bare
words, conceived Aſtrology to conſiſt upon Diabolicall
Principles : a moſt ſcandalous untruth, foyſted into both
the Nobility and Gentries apprehenſions, to deter them
from this Study, and to reſerve it intyre unto their owne
ſelves.

Wiſhing to you and your honourable Conſort all
happineſſe, I conclude in theſe laſt words, that
I am with all my heart,

Your moſt humble Servant,

Strand 16.
Aug. 1647.

WILLIAM LILLY.

To the READER.

Have oft in my former *Works* hinted the many *feares I had of that danger I was naturally like to be in in the yeer 1647. as any may read, either in my Epistle before the Conjunction of* Saturne *and* Jupiter, *printed 1644. or in page thereof 108. or in the Epistle of* Anglicus 1645. *where you shall find these words :* I have run over more dayes then fifteen thousand five hundred fifty and nine, before I am sixteen thousand four hundred twenty two dayes old, I shall be in great hazard of my life, but that yeer which afflicts me will stagger a Monarch and Kingdome, &c. *What concernes my selfe, hath almost in full measure proved true, in 1647. having in this untoward yeer been molested with palpitation of the Heart, with Hypocondry melancholy, a disaffected Spleen, the Scurvy, &c. and now at this present, viz.* August 1647. *when I had almost concluded this Treatise, I am shut up of the Plague, having the fourth of* August *buried one Servant thereof, and on the 28. of the same moneth another, my selfe and remainder of my Family enforced to leave my proper seat, and betake my selfe to change of ayre ; so that if either my present Epistles, or the latter part of the Book it selfe be any thing defective, as well they may, being written when my Family and selfe were in such abundant sorrow and perplexity ; I desire the Reader to be so civill, as to passe over those slight imperfections (if any be) with a candid censure.*

I thank almighty God, who hath prolonged my life to this present, and hath

hath been so gracious unto me, as to spare me so long, whereby I have been enabled now at length to perfect that Introduction so oft by me promised, so earnestly desired by many wel-wishers unto this learning.

The latter part of my prediction concerning Monarchy, is now upon the stage and eyes the of millions attending what shall become of it: let us leave the event hereof unto God, who is hastening to require a strict accompt of some people entrusted in the Kingdomes affaires ; fiat Justitia ; vivat Rex ; floreat Parliamentum.

The Citizens of London make small reckoning of Astrology ; there are in one of those Epistles of mine, words significant, and of which time will make them sensible (that they were not wrote in vaine) but now too
Use of the first Book. *late, actum est. To the work in hand, viz. the Book ensuing, which is divided into three Treatises ; the first whereof doth with much facility, and after a new method, instruct the Student how to begin his work, viz. it teacheth him the use of an Ephemeris, of the Table of Houses, &c. it acquaints him how to erect a figure of heaven, how therein to place the Planets, how to rectifie their motions to the hour of his Figure ; it unfolds the nature of the Houses, of the Planets, of the Signes of the Zodiack, their division, and subdivision, their severall properties, terms of Art, and whatever else is fit for the Learner to know before he enter upon judgment : unto whom and every one that will be studious this way, I give these cautions.*

Cautions for young Students. *First, that he be very exact in knowing the use of his Ephemeris, and in setting a Scheame of Heaven for all the hours of the day or night, and in reducing the motions of the Planets to the hour thereof when need requireth, and to know their characters distinctly and readily.*

Secondly, I would have the Student very perfect in knowing the nature of the Houses, that he may the better discover from what house to require judgment upon the question propounded, lest for want of true understanding he mistake one thing for another.

Thirdly, I would have him ready in, and well to understand the Debilities and Fortitudes of every Planet, both Essentiall and Accidentall.

Fourthly, he must be well versed in discovering the Nature of the Significator, what he signifies naturally, what accidentally, and how to vary his signification, as necessity shall require.

Fifily, let him well understand the nature of the Signes, their properties

ties

ties and qualities, and what forme, shape and conditions they give of them-selves naturally, and what by the personall existence of a Planet in any of them.

Sixtly, that he be ready in the shape and description which every Planet designes, and how to vary their shape as they are posited in Signe and house, or aspected of the Moon or any other Planet.

Seventhly, he must oft read the termes of Art, and have them fresh in his memory, and especially the twentieth and one and twentieth Chapters of the first Book.

If God almighty shall preserve my life, I may hereafter adde many things, and much light unto this Art, and therefore I desire the Students herein, that if they meet with any extraordinary casualty in their practice, they would communicate it unto me.

I have with all uprightnesse and sincerity of heart, plainly and honestly delivered the Art, and have omitted nothing willingly, which I esteemed convenient or fit, or what might any thing assist the yong Students herein; I have refused the Methods of all former Authors, and framed this De Novo, which I have ever found so easie and successfull, that as yet I never undertook the instruction of any, whom I have not abundantly satisfied, and made very capable of the Art, in lesse time then any could expect ; for although I am not yet six and forty yeers of age compleat, and have studied this Science *but since* 1632. *and have lived six yeers since that time in the Country, yet I know I have made more Schollers in this Profession, then all that professe this* Art *in* England.

It remaines, that I give every Author his due, and deale plainly, unto which of them I am engaged for such matter as they have assisted me with in the Introductory part : *verily the Method is my owne, it's no translation ; yet have I conferred my owne notes with* Dariot, Bonatus, Ptolomey, Haly, Etzler, Dietericus, Naibod, Hasfurtus, Zael, Tanstettor, Agrippa, Ferriers, Duret, Maginus, Origanus, Argol.

The second part of this Treatise judging of horary Questions, is very The second *large, and farre beyond my first intentions, hath exceeded its just pro-* Book. *portion : In building this Work I advised with* Bonatus, Haly, Dariot, Leupoldus, Pontanus, Avenezra, Zael : *I examined the*

B 2 *Manuscripts*

To the READER.

Manuscrips of Ancient and Reverend Professors in this Art, who lived more remote from these corrupt Times, (for unto the vulgar Professors now residing in this City, am I no wayes engaged ;) and though it was no small trouble unto me, to see the discrepancy of judgment amongst them and the more ancient printed Authors, yet I have with some trouble reconciled their disagreements, and reformed and corrected what might have led the Reader into an errour : for indeed the Writings of our Fore-fathers in the Language they did deliver their minds in, was found and solid, but the simplicity of such as undertook their translations was much and did beget mistakes, whilest they endeavouring to translate the Authors into Latin, or any other Language they thought fit, did not understand the Art or the Termes thereof ; so that of those their Labours, they rendred an ill accompt unto Posterity, as any may see in the translation of that we call the Judicium in Novem Judiciis, &c. and in other pieces of Alkindus, one whereof lately a learned Gentleman gave me, guilty of the same deficiency in the translation.

In this second Book I have omitted nothing which I could devise to be helpfull, and if my owne way of judicature please any, it being somewhat different from that of the Ancients, he may in many Chapters make use of it. I have illustrated every house with one or more Figures, and therein shewed the method of judgment, which I held very convenient for Learners, it being my whole intention to advance this Art, and make even a slender wit capable hereof.

The third Book.

You may in the third Book behold the entire Art of Nativities, I have made it plaine and significant : part of the Method, and much of the matter I had from Leovitius, who was the first that methodized the Art of Nativities, before his time extreemly defective in that point ; where he was not copious, I supplyed my selfe, or enlarged from Origanus, Junctine, Pezelius, Naibod, Cardan, Garceus, Schonerus, Albubater, Montulmo, Judeus, Ptolomey, Lindholt : Perhaps some will accuse me for dissenting from Ptolomey ; I confesse I have done so, and that I am not the first, or shall I that have done so, be the last ; for I am more led by reason and experience, then by the single authority of any one man, &c. I have inserted many judgments

ments of my owne, I could have added many more : but who am I ? being all errour, that should contradict the sayings of so many wise men, whose learnings and paines I so much esteem and reverence.

Little did I think this Work of Nativities would have swolen to so great a bulk; I assure you it exceeds my first intentions : the paines however hath been mine, and notwithstanding the importunities of some, and they not a few, who desired I should not deliver the Art in so plaine and easie a method;yet I professe,their words rather invited me to discover all I knew, then to conceale one sillable materiall.

Had I respected my owne private lucre, I need not have wrote at all; who could have compelled me ? my owne fortune is competent : but this thing we call the publick good, was ever, and shall be my maxime to guide me in such like actions : how shall I my selfe expect truth in any Author, if I my selfe, being an Author, play the knave in the same kind : Quod non vis tibi, ne facias alteri.

This Art of Astrology hath many more parts in it then at this present time I have handled, or indeed as yet have leisure to doe; yet I know it will be expected I should have wrote of Elections, of the Effects of the greater and lesser Conjunctions of the Planets, of Eclipses, Comets, prodigious Apparitions, the variation and inclination of the Weather, De generalibus Accidentibus Mundi, and by the ingresse of the Sunne into Aries, of every yeers particular Fate, of Monethly Observations, &c. Verily such things as these may justly be required at my hands ; for, unto God be the glory,they are all in a large measure knowne unto me, and I can performe them all, blessed be his name therefore : But as for Elections, me thinks he can be no ingenious Astrologian, that having studied or well entred into this my Book shall not be able (ad libitum) to frame his owne Figure of Elections, let the quere be what it will.

He that shall read my Discourse upon the Conjunction of ♄ and ♃, may make himselfe capable to write of the Major and Minor Conjunctions; I had no president for that, but wrought it out of the fire, at what time I had great leasure. I doe write Annually of Eclipses, as they happen in the yeer,of prodigious Appearances twiceI have Astrologically wrote, both time to good purpose, so did never any before that I read of.

Of Commets I have had no occasion as yet, but somewhat I began in

that

that *Tract of the ♂ of ♄ and ♃ , wherein I a little treated of the Com-
met in* 1618. *Posterity may know by that little, what Method I hold fittest to be followed, in that kinde of judgement. Of Weather, the knowledge thereof is so vulgar, yet withall the true Key so difficult, it requires
a long time of experience ; and besides, Master Booker hath promised
to undertake that burthen ; and indeed, he is onely able of all the* English
Nation I know to performe it : I have great hopes of Master Vincent
Wing, *but he is yet more* Mathematicall *then* Astrologicall; *there
may be many private men of great judgement therein, but its my unhap-
pinesse I know them not.*

*Annuall and Monthly judgements I have not yet digested into a Me-
thod, I hope to live and performe it ; I am the first of men that ever adventured upon Monethly Observations in such plaine language, yet is it
my harty desire to communicate hereafter what ever I know unto Posterity. Having been of late traduced by some halfe-witted fooles, I deliver
my selfe to Posterity who I am, and of what profession ; I was borne at*
Diseworth *in* Leicestershire May 1602. *in an obscure Village, and
bred a Grammer Scholler at* Ashby, *and intended for* Cambridge, &c.
1618. *and* 1619. *my Father decayed his Estate so much, that he was not
capable of sending me thither ; those two yeers I lived in some penury and
discontent ; in* 1620. *an Atturney sent me up unto* London *to wait on
a Gentleman, one* Gilbert Wright, *who lived and dyed in the House I
now live in ; he never was of any Profession, but had sometimes attended
the Lord Chancellour* Egerton, *and then lived privately.* 1624. *his
wife dyed of a Cancer in her left brest.* 1625. *I lived in* London *where
I now doe, during all that great Sicknesse, God be praised I had it not.*
February 1626. *my Master married againe ; he dyed May* 22. 1627.
*having before setled twenty pounds per annum of me during my life,
which to this day I thanke God I enjoy ; nor did I ever live so freely as
when I was his servant. Ere the yeer* 1627. *was quite run out my Mi-
stris was pleased to accept of me for her husband. During some yeers of her
life I passed my time privately and with much obscurity, yet we lived exceeding lovingly together ; but in* 1632. *I was strangely affected to* Astrology, *and desirous to study it, onely to see if there were any verity in it,
there being at that time some Impostors, that set out Bils publiquely what
they could doe. I met with a Master I confesse, but such a one, as of all*

was

was the verieſt Knave : This gave me ſmall encouragement ; after ſix weekes I caſt him off, nor to this day doe we converſe together. I was then forced to ſtudy hard, for rather then to intangle my ſelfe with another coxcombe, I was reſolved to lay all aſide ; but by diligence and hard ſtudy, and many times conference with ſome as ignorant as my ſelfe, I at laſt became capable of knowing truth from falſhood, and perceived the vulgar Aſtrologer that meerly lived of the Art, was a Knave.

In September 1633 *my wife dyed, not knowing any one in the world that had affinity unto her ; ſhe left me a competent fortune ; and this I ſhall acquaint Poſterity with, that having ſome Lands to diſpoſe of, rather then ſhe would ſuffer me to be at twentyNobles charges to convey it unto me, ſhe gave me the whole money, and ſold it for 200 ¹.*

In November 1634. *I married againe. In* 1635. *I was oppreſſed with the* Hypocondryack Melancholly *ſo ſorely, that I was enforced to leave* London, *and removed into* Surrey 1636. *where untill* September 1641. *I lived amongſt ſuch whom I may name the moſt rurall of all men living. I then came for* London, *ſtaggering in my judgement in point of Church-government ; and knowing that it is neceſſary, I ever loved Monarchy, but ſtill thought without a Parliament preſerved in their juſt rights, it would vaniſh to nothing. I was nothing knowne then, or taken notice of by any ; time produced me acquaintance, and amongſt theſe a good* Lady *in* 1643. *about* February, *deſired I would give judgement upon a moſt noble Gentlemans Urine a Councellor at Law, who then was not well ; I conſented, the Urine was brought, my judgement returned ; I viſited him, whom I no ſooner beheld, but I knew there was aboundance of gallantry in the man ; for indeed he is all Gentleman and a friend in very great earneſt ; my viſit of him was the happieſt day I ever ſaw in my whole life ; for by his alone generoſity and countenance, I am what I am, and* Aſtrology *is in deſpight of her enemies reſtored, and muſt call him her Reſtaurator.*

Being by his goodneſſe admitted to viſit him, I preſented him with a ſmall Manuſcript of my Aſtrologicall Judgment *of the yeer* 1644. *wherein I was free in delivering my opinion modeſtly of that yeers affaires : it pleaſed him to communicate it. Copies were obtained and diſperſed ; ſo that by his alone commendation of that poore Manuſcript unto his private friends, this noble* Art *at firſt had reſpect amongſt our*
Worthies

To the READER.

Worthies in the Parliament; since which time, the Judicious of the whole Kingdome had it in a better esteem; therefore let his name live unto Posterity in an honourable esteem, that upon so slender acquaintance with the Author, with the Art, hath been so advantagious unto both.

The Errataes perhaps are many, I desire the Student to correct them before he enter upon the Discourse; I wish they were lesse : but in a work of this nature, it's impossible.

All the Curtesies which either the Authors precedent to this Age, or at present living, have afforded me, I verily beleeve I have mentioned : I am heartily sorry if I have committed any errours, or omitted any corrections.

Corner house over against
Strand-bridge, August
21. 1647.

WILLIAM LILLY.

To his honored Friend the A u tho r.

WHat! *Perfian, Caldee, Arabick*, the *Greeke*,
  Latin Aftrologers, all taught to fpeake
In Englifh! *Trifmegiftus, Hercules,*
Pythagoras, Thales, Archimedes,
Great *Ptolomy*, and *Julius Firmicus,*
Albumazar, and *Albategnius,*
Hali, Bonatus, our owne *Efchuidus,*
And *John de Regiomonte, Ganivetus,*
Riffe, Leovitius, Michael Noftradame,
Cardan, and *Nabod, Ticho,* men of fame ;
All thefe, and more, are dead, all learned Men ;
Were they alive, they might come learn again.
But are they dead ? Behold Aftrologie,
Now *Phœnix* like, reviv'd againe in thee !
Queftions refolv'd, Nativities, Directions,
Tranfites, with Revolutions and Profections.
Saturne muft lay his fullen prankes afide,
And *Mars* his madneffe, left he be defcride ;
Venus her lufts ; his thefts muft *Mercury* ;
Sol his ambition ; *Jove* his jollity :
Luna her fickle and unconftant motion,
Is now notorious to each vulgar notion.
Aske what you will, VVould you refolved be ?
Obferve your time, learne your Nativitie :
Were *Picus, Chambers, Perkins, Melton, Geree,*
Vicars, to write againe, all men would jeer yee.
You durft not let us know when you were borne,
Your ignorance is brought to publick fcorn :
Our Latin *Lilly* is for Boyes are young ;
Our Englifh *Lilly* is for Men more ftrong.
The *Sybils* Books were burnt, they are all gone ;
I will preferve my choyce, This is that one :
Be you for or againft, or will ye, nill ye ;
I'm for the Art, and th'Author *William Lilly.*

(c)   JOHN BOOKER.

Upon the learned Worke of the
AUTHOR.

BEhold *Urania* with a *Lilly* deckt,
Prefents her felfe to *Englands* gracious view.
Let Envies fquare, or oppofite afpect
Not dare at her a frowning looke to fhew;
  Left it be faid, for fuch ungratefull fcornes,
  A *Lilly* late hath fprung among the thornes.

WILL. ROE.

To the Reader of CHRISTIAN
ASTROLOGY.

W onder you may! the volumes of the Skye
I n our owne Characters you here defcry.
L *una* and *Hermes*, *Venus* and the great
L ight of the World, and *Mars* in *Englifh* treat;
I *ove* and old *Saturne*; they their influence fend:
A nd their Conjunctions in our Tongue are penn'd.
M ay not *Apollo* then, the facred Bayes
L et fall upon his head, who cafts their Rayes
I nto the language of our *Albion* quill?
L oe! he hath taught great *Ptolom's* fecret skill.
L earning, that once in brazen piles did ftand,
Y ou now may fee is Printed in our Land.

R. L. *in Med. Studens &*

Philo-Mathemat.

On this unparalelled peece of Art.

NOt to commend the Author, 'tis the least
   Of all my thoughts, this Work will doe it best;
Nor yet to vex the prying Readers sence
   with bumbast words instead of Eloquence,
Doe I crowd in these rude unpolisht lines :
   But rather to informe the giddy times
How much they are his Debtors; what they owe
   To him, whose Labours freely doth bestow
On them his Art, his paines, his piercing sight,
   His lampe of life, to give their darknesse light.
Tis now a crime, and quite grown out of fashion,
   T'incourage Art amongst the *English* Nation.
Tell them of it, or Natures mysteries,
   Tush, cry they : Ignorance they idolize.
The glorious Stars, they think God doth not use them
   To doe his will : Lord ! how doe men abuse them ?
Nor will allow the Planets to fulfill
   (As instruments) Gods high decree or will.
Nay, some there are, though letter wise, they can
   Not yet beleeve that all was made for Man.
Barke black mouth'd Envie; carpe at what's well done,
   This Book shall be my choyce companion.

W. W.

(*b*) 2   *Anagram*

Upon this WORKE.

THe Author'sGod,Compoſer and theSetter
   Of all his works,and therin every letter.
Heaven is his Book;the Stars both great & ſmal
   Are letters Nonperill and Capitall
Diſperſt throughout;therin our learnings dull,
   In this thy Work it is compleat and full :
Could man compoſe or ſetHeavens letters right
   he would,like Printing,bring to publick ſight
All what was done,nay what was thought upó;
   For by this way, I ſee it may be done.

I. P.

The CONTENTS of the three *Books*.

The first Book.

The Contents.

The Contents of the second Book, containing the resolution of Questions.

Questions concerning the first House.

Judgments concerning the Second House, viz. of Riches.

Of the third house, viz. of Brethren, Sisters, Kindred, short Journeys.

The Contents.

Of The Fourth house, *viz.* of Parents, Lands, Tenements, Cities, Towns.

Of the fifth House, and its questions.

Other Judgments

The Contents.

Of the sixth House, and its Questions, *viz.* of Sickness, Servants, small Cattle.

Significations of the Seventh House, *viz.* of Marriage, Enemies, Law-suits, Contracts, Wars, Fugitives, Thefts

The Contents.

The Contents.

The Contents.

xxix

The Contents.

Eleventh House, *viz.* House of Friends, Hope, Substance of Kings.

Of the Twelfth House, *viz.* Imprisonment, Great Cattle, Witchery, private Enemies, Labour, banished Men.

MY Friend, whoever thou art, that with fo much eafe fhalt receive the benefit of my hard *Studies*, and doft intend to proceed in this heavenly knowledge of the Stars, wherein the great and admirable works of the invifible and alglorious God are fo manifeftly apparent. In the firft place, confider and admire thy *Creator*, and be thankful unto him, be thou humble, and let no natural knowledge, how profound and tranfcendent foever it be, elate thy minde to neglect that *divine Providence*, by whofe all-feeing order and appointment, all things heavenly and earthly, have their conftant motion; but the more thy knowledge is enlarged, the more do thou magnifie the power and wifdom of *Almighty God*, and ftrive to preferve thy felf in his faveur; being confident, the more holy thou art, and more neer to God, the purer *Judgment* thou fhalt give. Beware of pride and felf-conceit, and remember how that long ago, no irrational *Creature* durft offend Man, the *Microcofm*; but did faithfully ferve and obey him, fo long as he was Mr. of his own Reafon and Paffions, or until he fubjected his VVill to the unreafonable part. But alas! when iniquity abounded, and man gave the reins to his own *affection*, and deferted reafon, then every *Beaft, Creature* and outward harmful thing, became rebellious and unferviceable to his command. Stand faft, oh man! to thy *God*, and affured *principles*, then confider thy own noblenefs, how all created things, both prefent and to come, were for thy fake created; nay, for thy fake *God* became *Man*: thou art that *Creature*, who being converfant with *Chrift*, liveft and raigneft above the heavens, and fits above all power and authority. How many *pre-eminences, priviledges, advantages* hath God beftowed on thee? thou rangeft above the heavens by *contemplation*, conceiveft the *motion* and *magnitude* of the ftars; thou talkeft with *Angels*, yea with *God* himfelf; thou haft all *Creatures* within thy *dominion*, and keepeft the *Devils* in fubjection: Do not then for fhame deface thy *nature*, or make thy felf unworthy of fuch *gifts*, or deprive thy felf of that great *power*, *glory* and *bleffednefs* God hath alotted thee, by cafting from thee his fear, for poffeffion of a few imperfect *pleafures*. *Having confidered thy God, and what thy felf art, during thy being Gods fervant; now receive inftruction how in thy practice I would have thee carry thy felf.* As thou daily converfeft with the heavens, fo inftruct and form thy minde according to the image of *Divinity*; learn all the ornaments of *vertue*, be fufficiently inftructed therein; be humane, curteous, familiar to all, eafie of accefs, afflict not the *miferable* with terror of a harfh *judgment*; in fuch cafes, let them know their hard fate by degrees; direct them to call on *God* to divert his *judgments* impending over them: be modeft, converfant with the *learned, civil, fober man*, covet not an eftate; give freely to the *poor*, both *money* and *judgment*: let no wordly wealth procure an *erroneous judgment* from thee, or fuch as may difhonour the *Art*, or this divine Science: Love good men, cherifh thofe honeft men that cordially Study this *Art:* Be fparing in delivering Judgment againft the *Common-wealth* thou liveft in. Give not judgment of the death of thy Prince; yet I know experimentally, that *Reges fubjacent legibus Stellarum·* marry a *wife* of thy own, rejoyce in the number of thy friends, avoid law and controverfie: in thy Study, be *totus in illis* that thou maift be *fingulus in arte*; be not extravagant or defirous to learn every *Science*, be not *aliquid in omnibus*; be faithful, tenacious, betray no ones fecrets, no, no I charge thee never divulge either friend or enemies truft committed to thy faith. Inftruct all men to Live well, be a good example thy felf, avoid the fafhion of the times, love thy own Native *Country:* exprobrate no man, no not an enemy: be not difmaid, if ill fpoken of, *Confcientia mille teftes*; God fuffers no fin unpunifhed, no lye unrevenged.

B   WILLIAM LILLY.

JANUARY hath xxxi. dayes.

The daily Motion of the Planets and ☊.

		M ♄ ♈	D	M ♃ ♊	D	M ♂ ♑	A	☉ ♑		M ♀ ♓	D	M ☿ ♒	D	☽ ♏		☊ ♌	
1	a	27	48	28 R	12	10	5	21	34	5	7	5	29	21	23	12	34
2	b	27	50	28	6	10	51	22	35	6	17	7	8	3 ♐	17	12	45
3	c	27	52	27	59	11	37	23	36	7	26	8	44	15	8	12	42
4	D	27	54	27	53	12	23	24	37	8	35	10	18	26	59	12	24
5	e	27	56	27	46	13	9	25	38	9	44	11	49	8 ♑	54	11	52
6	f	27	58	27	40	13	55	26	39	10	53	13	18	20	54	11	10
7	g	28	0	27	34	14	41	27	41	12	2	14	45	3 ♒	1	10	24
8	a	28	2	27	28	15	27	28	42	13	10	16	10	15	17	9	24
9	b	28	4	27	22	16	17	29	43	14	18	17	33	27	44	9	9
10	c	28	6	27	17	17	0	0 ♒	44	15	26	18	50	10 ♓	23	8	50
11	D	28	9	27	11	17	46	1	46	16	34	20	2	23	14	8	49
12	e	28	11	27	6	18	32	2	47	17	42	21	7	6 ♈	18	9	6
13	f	28	14	27	1	19	19	3	48	18	50	22	6	19	38	9	36
14	g	28	17	26	56	20	5	4	49	19	57	23	0	3 ♉	15	10	17
15	a	28	20	26	51	20	51	5	50	21	4	23	47	17	9	10	59
16	b	28	23	26	46	21	37	6	51	22	11	24	25	1 ♊	22	11	34
17	c	28	26	26	42	22	2	7	52	23	17	24	47	15	52	11	55
18	D	28	29	26	37	23	10	8	53	24	23	24	57	2 ♋	34	11	54
19	e	28	32	26	33	23	56	9	54	25	29	25	0	15	23	11	29
20	f	28	36	26	29	24	43	10	55	26	35	24 R	53	0 ♌	11	10	44
21	g	28	39	26	24	25	29	11	56	27	41	24	33	14	50	9	49
22	a	28	43	25	21	26	15	12	57	28	47	23	53	29	12	8	58
23	b	28	46	26	17	27	2	13	58	29	52	23	9	13 ♍	18	8	22
24	c	28	50	26	13	27	48	14	58	0 ♈	57	22	21	26	59	8	5
25	D	28	54	26	10	28	35	15	59	2	2	21	29	10 ♎	15	8	8
26	e	28	58	26	7	29	21	16	59	3	6	20	33	23	9	8	27
27	f	29	2	26	4	0 ♒	8	18	0	4	10	19	33	5 ♏	36	8	58
28	g	29	6	26	2	0	54	19	1	5	14	18	26	17	49	9	33
29	a	29	11	25	59	1	41	20	2	6	18	17	14	29	48	10	9
30	b	29	15	25	57	2	28	21	3	7	21	15	58	11 ♐	39	10	38
31	c	29	20	25	55	3	4	22	4	8	24	14	50	23	27	11	1
lat	1	2	31	0	5	0	47			1	13	1	45				
of	10	2	29	0	4	0	51			0	39	0	26				
pla	20	2	26	0	2	0	55			0 S	9	2 S	10				

January 1646.

The Lunar Aspects.

		♄ Occid.	♃ Occid.	♂ Orient.	☉	♀ Occid.	☿ Occid.	The Planets Mutuall Aspects.
1	a				✱ 0			
2	b					□ 6	△ 9	
3	c							✱ ♄ ♃ 21
4	D	△ 2	☍ 2					☽ Apog.
5	e			☌ 9		✱ 2		[Eclip. ☉
6	f	□ 14			☌ 11:48			Vc ☉ ♃ SS ♂ ☿
7	g							□ ☉ ♄ 8 ☽ ☋
8	a		△ 23				☌ 2	
9	b	✱ 0						
10	c			✱ 14		☌ 11		
11	D		□ 7		✱ 17			
12	e			□ 23				☿ in Elong.Max
13	f	☌ 15	✱ 13				✱ 5	
14	g				□ 25			✱ ♂ ♀ 9
15	a			△ 6		✱ 7	□ 12	
16	b				△ 10			
17	c	✱ 20	☌ 17			□ 13	△ 15	
18	D							SS ♀ ☿ ☽ Perig
19	e	□ 21		☍ 14		△ 18		□ ♃ ♀ 22
20	f				☍ 18			
21	g	△ 23	✱ 19				☍ 15	SS ♄ ♀ ☽ ☊ E-
22	a							Vc ♃ ♂ [clip.totall
23	b		□ 23					
24	c			△ 1		☍ 8		
25	D				△ 11		△ 19	□ ♄ ♂ 11 Q ☉ ♄
26	e	☍ 11	△ 6	□ 13				
27	f						Orient.	☌ ☉ ☿ 17
28	g				□ 3.15		□ 1	
29	a			✱ 4		△ 13		
30	b				✱ 20		✱ 8	
31	c	△ 12	☍ 5					

A Table of Houses for the Latitude of 52. degrees.

☉ in ♈	10 House		11 House		12 House		1 House		2 House		3 House	
time from Noon.	deg.	min.	deg.	min.	deg.	min.	deg.	min.	deg.	min.	deg.	min.
Ho. Min.	♈		♉		Ⅱ		♋		♌		♍	
0 0	0	0	12	51	28	55	27	2	16	7	4	31
0 4	1	0	14	1	29	46	27	42	16	47	5	17
0 7	2	0	15	11	0 ♋	36	28	22	17	28	6	3
0 11	3	0	16	21	1	26	29	1	18	8	6	50
0 15	4	0	17	29	2	15	29	41	18	48	7	36
0 18	5	0	18	37	3	4	0 ♌	21	19	28	8	23
0 22	6	0	19	44	3	53	1	0	20	8	9	9
0. 26	7	0	20	51	4	42	1	39	20	48	9	56
0 29	8	0	21	59	5	29	2	18	21	27	10	42
0 33	9	0	23	6	6	18	2	58	22	8	11	30
0 37	10	0	24	12	7	6	3	38	22	48	12	17
0 40	11	0	25	16	7	53	4	17	23	27	13	3
0 44	12	0	26	22	8	40	4	56	24	8	13	51
0 48	13	0	27	26	9	27	5	35	24	48	14	37
0 52	14	0	28	30	10	12	6	14	25	28	15	24
0 55	15	0	29	34	10	59	6	54	26	9	16	11
0 59	16	0	0 Ⅱ	37	11	45	7	32	26	50	16	59
1 3	17	0	1	38	12	30	8	12	27	30	17	46
1 6	18	0	2	41	13	16	8	52	28	11	18	33
1 10	19	0	3	43	14	1	9	31	28	52	19	21
1 14	20	0	4	45	14	47	10	10	29	33	20	9
1 18	21	0	5	45	15	32	10	49	0 ♍	14	20	57
1 21	22	0	6	46	16	17	11	29	0	55	21	45
1 25	23	0	7	46	17	2	12	8	1	36	22	32
1 29	24	0	8	46	17	46	12	47	2	17	23	20
1 33	25	0	9	46	18	31	13	27	2	58	24	9
1 36	26	0	10	46	19	16	14	7	3	40	24	58
1 40	27	0	11	45	20	1	14	46	4	22	25	46
1 44	28	0	12	45	20	45	15	26	5	3	26	35
1 48	29	0	13	44	21	29	16	5	5	45	27	23
1 52	30	0	14	41	22	13	16	45	6	26	28	12

A Table of Houſes for the Latitude of 5 2. degrees.

☉ in ♉ Time frō Noon.		10 Houſe		11 Houſe		12 Houſe		1 Houſe.		2 Houſe.		3 Houſe.	
Ho.	Min.	deg.	min. ♉	deg.	min. ♊	deg.	min. ♋	deg.	min. ♌	deg.	min. ♍	deg.	min. ♍
1	52	0	0	14	41	22	13	16	45	6	26	28	12
1	55	1	0	15	38	22	57	17	25	7	8	29	1
1	59	2	0	16	36	23	42	18	5	7	50	29	50
2	3	3	0	17	33	24	27	18	45	8	33	0 ♎	40
2	7	4	0	18	29	25	10	19	25	9	14	1	29
2	11	5	0	19	26	25	55	20	5	9	57	2	19
2	15	6	0	20	23	26	38	20	45	10	39	3	8
2	19	7	0	21	20	27	23	21	26	11	23	3	58
2	22	8	0	22	17	28	7	22	7	12	6	4	48
2	26	9	0	23	13	28	51	22	47	12	48	5	38
2	30	10	0	24	9	29	35	23	27	13	31	6	28
2	34	11	0	25	5	0 ♌	19	24	8	14	14	7	19
2	38	12	0	26	1	1	4	24	49	14	58	8	9
2	42	13	0	26	56	1	47	25	30	15	41	8	59
2	46	14	0	27	51	2	32	26	12	16	25	9	50
2	50	15	0	28	46	3	16	26	53	17	8	10	40
2	54	16	0	29	41	4	1	27	34	17	52	11	32
2	58	17	0	0 ♋	38	4	46	28	17	18	36	12	24
3	2	18	0	1	33	5	30	28	58	19	21	13	14
3	6	19	0	2	27	6	15	29	40	20	5	14	6
3	10	20	0	3	22	7	0	0 ♍	23	20	50	14	57
3	14	21	0	4	17	7	45	1	5	21	34	15	49
3	18	22	0	5	11	8	30	1	47	22	19	16	40
3	22	23	0	6	5	9	15	2	29	23	4	17	32
3	26	24	0	6	59	10	0	3	12	23	49	18	24
3	30	25	0	7	53	10	44	3	54	24	35	19	16
3	35	26	0	8	48	11	30	4	37	25	20	20	8
3	39	27	0	9	43	12	15	5	20	26	6	21	1
3	43	28	0	10	36	13	1	6	3	26	51	21	53
3	47	29	0	11	30	13	46	6	46	27	31	22	46
3	51	30	0	12	24	14	31	7	29	28	23	23	38

A Table of Houſes for the Latitude of 52. degrees.

⊙ in ♊ time from Noon. Ho.Min.	10 Houſe deg. min. ♊		11 Houſe deg. min. ♋		12 Houſe deg. min. ♌		1 Houſe deg. min ♍		2 Houſe deg. min ♍		3 Houſe deg. min. ♎	
3 51	0	0	12	24	14	31	7	29	28	23	23	38
3 55	1	0	13	19	15	17	8	13	29	9	24	31
4 0	2	0	14	14	16	3	8	57	29	55	25	24
4 4	3	0	15	8	16	49	9	41	0 ♎ 42		26	17
4 8	4	0	16	2	17	35	10	25	1	28	27	0
4 12	5	0	16	56	18	21	11	9	2	15	28	2
4 16	6	0	17	50	19	7	11	53	3	1	28	56
4 21	7	0	18	44	19	53	12	37	3	48	29	49
4 25	8	0	19	38	20	40	13	22	4	35	0 ♏ 43	
4 29	9	0	20	31	21	25	14	6	5	21	1	36
4 33	10	0	21	25	22	11	14	51	6	9	2	29
4 38	11	0	22	19	22	58	15	35	6	56	3	23
4 42	12	0	23	14	23	45	16	21	7	44	4	17
4 46	13	0	24	8	24	31	17	5	8	31	5	11
4 50	14	0	25	2	25	18	17	50	9	18	6	5
4 55	15	0	25	57	26	5	18	35	10	6	6	59
4 59	16	0	26	51	26	53	19	21	10	54	7	53
5 3	17	0	27	44	27	39	20	6	11	41	8	47
5 8	18	0	28	38	28	27	20	51	12	28	9	40
5 12	19	0	29	32	29	14	21	37	13	16	10	34
5 16	20	0	0 ♌ 27		0 ♍ 2		22	22	14	3	11	28
5 21	21	0	1	21	0	50	23	8	14	51	12	22
5 25	22	0	2	15	1	37	23	53	15	39	13	17
5 29	23	0	3	9	2	24	24	39	16	20	14	11
5 34	24	0	4	4	3	12	25	25	17	14	15	6
5 38	25	0	4	57	4	0	26	10	18	2	15	59
5 42	26	0	5	52	4	47	26	56	18	50	16	53
5 47	27	0	6	47	5	35	27	42	19	38	17	47
5 51	28	0	7	41	6	23	28	28	20	25	18	42
5 56	29	0	8	35	7	10	29	13	21	13	19	36
6 0	30	0	9	29	7	58	0 ♎ 0		22	1	20	30

Table of houses, page 4

A Table of Houses for the Latitude of 52. degrees.

☉ in ♋ time from Noon. Ho. Min.	10 House ♋ deg. min.	11 House ♌ deg. min.	12 House ♍ deg. min.	1 House ♎ deg. min.	2 House ♎ deg. min.	3 House ♏ deg. min.
6 0	0 0	9 29	7 58	0 0	22 1	20 30
6 4	1 0	10 24	8 47	0 46	22 50	21 25
6 9	2 0	11 18	9 34	1 32	23 37	22 19
6 13	3 0	12 12	10 22	2 17	24 24	23 12
6 18	4 0	13 7	11 10	3 4	25 12	24 7
6 22	5 0	14 1	11 58	3 49	26 0	25 2
6 26	6 0	14 54	12 45	4 35	26 47	25 56
6 31	7 0	15 49	13 33	5 21	27 35	26 51
6 35	8 0	16 43	14 21	6 7	28 23	27 45
6 39	9 0	17 37	15 9	6 52	29 10	28 39
6 44	10 0	18 32	15 56	7 37	29 58	29 33
6 48	11 0	19 26	15 44	8 23	0 ♏ 45	0 ♐ 27
6 52	12 0	20 20	17 31	9 8	1 33	1 22
6 57	13 0	21 13	18 19	9 54	2 20	2 16
7 1	14 0	22 7	19 6	10 39	3 7	3 9
7 5	15 0	23 1	19 54	11 24	3 55	4 3
7 10	16 0	23 55	20 42	12 10	4 42	4 57
7 14	17 0	24 49	21 28	12 54	5 28	5 51
7 18	18 0	25 42	22 15	13 39	6 15	6 46
7 22	19 0	26 37	23 4	14 24	7 2	7 40
7 27	20 0	27 30	23 51	15 9	7 48	8 35
7 31	21 0	28 24	24 38	15 54	8 35	9 29
7 35	22 0	29 17	25 25	16 37	9 20	10 22
7 39	23 0	0 ♍ 11	26 12	17 22	10 6	11 16
7 44	24 0	1 4	26 58	18 7	10 53	12 10
7 48	25 0	1 57	27 45	18 51	11 39	13 3
7 52	26 0	2 51	28 21	19 35	12 25	13 57
7 56	27 0	3 43	29 18	20 19	13 11	14 51
8 0	28 0	4 36	0 ♎ 4	21 3	13 59	15 46
8 5	29 0	5 29	0 51	21 47	14 43	16 41
8 9	30 0	6 22	1 37	22 31	15 29	17 31

A Table of Houſes for the Latitude of 5 2. degrees.

⊙ in ♌ time from Noon. Ho. Min.	10 Houſe ♌ deg. min.	11 Houſe ♍ deg. min.	12 Honſe ♎ deg. min.	1 Houſe. ♎ deg. min.	2 Houſe. ♏ deg. min.	3 Houſe. ♐ deg. min.
8 9	0 0	6 22	1 37	22 31	15 29	17 35
8 13	1 0	7 14	2 23	23 14	16 14	18 29
8 17	2 0	8 7	3 9	23 57	16 59	19 23
8 21	3 0	8 59	3 54	24 40	17 44	20 17
8 25	4 0	9 51	4 39	25 23	18 30	21 12
8 30	5 0	10 44	5 25	26 6	19 15	22 7
8 34	6 0	11 36	6 10	26 48	20 0	23 1
8 38	7 0	12 28	6 55	27 31	20 44	23 55
8 42	8 0	13 19	7 41	28 13	21 29	24 49
8 46	9 0	14 11	8 25	28 55	22 15	25 43
8 50	10 0	15 2	9 10	29 37	23 0	26 37
8 54	11 0	15 54	9 55	0 ♏ 19	23 45	27 33
8 58	12 0	16 45	10 39	1 1	24 29	28 27
9 2	13 0	17 36	11 23	1 43	25 14	29 22
9 6	14 0	18 28	12 8	2 25	25 59	0 ♑ 18
9 10	15 0	19 20	12 52	3 7	26 44	1 14
9 14	16 0	20 10	13 35	3 48	27 28	2 8
9 18	17 0	21 1	14 19	4 29	28 12	3 4
9 22	18 0	21 51	15 2	5 10	28 56	3 59
9 26	19 0	22 41	15 45	5 51	29 40	4 54
9 30	20 0	23 32	16 28	6 32	0 ♐ 25	5 50
9 34	21 0	24 22	17 12	7 13	1 9	6 46
9 38	22 0	25 12	17 54	7 53	1 52	7 42
9 41	23 0	26 2	18 37	8 34	2 37	8 40
9 45	24 0	26 51	19 20	9 15	3 22	9 37
9 49	25 0	27 41	20 3	9 55	4 5	10 33
9 53	26 0	28 31	20 45	10 35	4 49	11 30
9 57	27 0	29 20	21 27	11 14	5 33	12 26
10 1	28 0	0 ♎ 9	22 9	11 55	6 18	13 24
10 5	29 0	0 59	22 52	12 35	7 2	14 22
10 8	30 0	1 48	23 33	13 14	7 47	15 19

A Table of Houses for the Latitude of 52. degrees.

⊙ in ♍ time from Noon. Ho.Min.	10 House. deg. min. ♍		11 House. deg. min. ♎		12 House. deg. min. ♎		1 House. deg. min. ♏		2 House. deg. min. ♐		3 House. deg. min. ♑	
10 8	0	0	1	48	23	33	13	14	7	47	15	9
10 12	1	0	2	37	24	15	13	54	8	31	16	16
10 16	2	0	3	25	24	56	14	34	9	15	17	15
10 20	3	0	4	13	25	38	15	14	9	59	18	14
10 24	4	0	5	2	26	20	15	53	10	44	19	14
10 27	5	0	5	50	27	1	16	33	11	28	20	14
10 31	6	0	6	39	27	42	17	12	12	13	21	14
10 35	7	0	7	27	28	23	17	51	12	57	22	14
10 39	8	0	8	15	29	4	18	31	13	42	23	14
10 42	9	0	9	3	29	46	19	10	14	28	24	15
10 46	10	0	9	51	0 ♏	27	19	49	15	13	25	15
10 50	11	0	10	38	1	8	20	29	15	58	26	17
10 54	12	0	11	26	1	49	21	8	16	44	27	19
10 57	13	0	12	14	2	30	21	48	17	29	28	21
11 1	14	0	13	1	3	10	22	27	18	15	29	23
11 5	15	0	13	49	3	51	23	6	19	1	0 ♒	26
11 8	16	0	14	36	4	32	23	46	19	47	1	30
11 12	17	0	15	23	5	12	24	25	20	33	2	33
11 16	18	0	16	9	5	52	25	3	21	19	3	37
11 20	19	0	16	57	6	32	25	43	22	7	4	43
11 23	20	0	17	43	7	12	26	22	22	54	5	48
11 27	21	0	18	30	7	52	27	1	23	42	6	54
11 31	22	0	19	18	8	32	27	41	24	30	8	1
11 34	23	0	20	4	9	12	28	21	25	18	9	8
11 38	24	0	20	51	9	52	29	0	26	7	10	16
11 42	25	0	21	37	10	32	29	39	26	56	11	23
11 45	26	0	22	24	11	12	0 ♐	19	27	45	12	31
11 49	27	0	23	10	11	52	0	58	28	34	13	39
11 53	28	0	23	57	12	32	1	38	29	23	14	48
11 56	29	0	24	42	13	12	2	18	0 ♑	14	15	59
12 0	30	0	25	29	13	53	2	58	1	5	17	9

C

A Table of Houſes for the Latitude of 5 2. degrees.

☉ in ♎ time from Noon. Ho.Min.	10 Houſe deg. min. ♎		11 Houſe deg. min. ♎		12 Houſe deg. min. ♏		1 Houſe. deg. min. ♐		2 Houſe. deg. min. ♑		3 Houſe. deg. min. ♒	
12 0	0	0	25	29	13	53	2	58	1	5	17	9
12 4	1	0	26	15	14	33	3	37	1	56	18	21
12 7	2	0	27	1	15	13	4	17	2	48	19	32
12 11	3	0	27	47	15	53	4	58	3	40	20	45
12 15	4	0	28	34	16	33	5	38	4	33	21	57
12 18	5	0	29	20	17	13	6	10	5	26	23	11
12 22	6	0	0 ♏	6	17	53	7	1	6	20	24	24
12 26	7	0	0	52	18	33	7	41	7	15	25	38
12 29	8	0	1	38	19	14	8	22	8	10	26	53
12 33	9	0	2	25	19	55	9	4	9	6	28	11
12 37	10	0	3	12	20	35	9	46	10	2	29	26
12 40	11	0	3	57	21	15	10	27	10	59	0 ♓	43
12 44	12	0	4	44	21	57	11	10	11	58	2	1
12 48	13	0	5	30	22	38	11	51	12	57	3	19
12 52	14	0	6	17	23	18	12	34	13	56	4	37
12 55	15	0	7	3	24	0	13	17	14	57	5	57
12 59	16	0	7	50	24	41	14	1	15	58	7	17
13 3	17	0	8	36	25	22	14	44	16	59	8	37
13 6	18	0	9	22	26	4	15	27	18	2	9	58
13 10	19	0	10	8	26	45	16	12	19	7	11	19
13 14	20	0	10	55	27	27	16	55	20	13	12	42
13 18	21	0	11	42	28	9	17	41	21	20	14	4
13 21	22	0	12	29	28	51	18	27	22	29	15	29
13 25	23	0	13	16	29	33	19	12	23	37	16	52
13 29	24	0	14	2	0 ♐	15	19	57	24	45	18	16
13 33	25	0	14	50	0	58	20	44	25	56	19	40
13 36	26	0	15	37	1	40	21	32	27	9	21	6
13 40	27	0	16	24	2	23	22	19	28	23	22	31
13 44	28	0	17	11	3	7	23	7	29	33	23	57
13 48	29	0	17	58	3	49	23	56	0 ♒	55	25	22
13 52	30	0	18	46	4	32	24	44	2	12	26	49

A Table of Houfes for the Latitude of 52. degrees.

☉ in ♏	10 Houfe		11 Houfe		12 Houfe		1 Houfe.		2 Houfe.		3 Houfe.	
Time fró Noon.	deg.	min.	deg.	min.	deg.	min.	deg.	min.	deg.	min.	deg.	min.
Ho. Min.	♏		♏		♐		♐		♒		♓	
13 52	0	0	18	46	4	32	24	44	2	12	26	49
13 55	1	0	19	33	5	16	25	34	3	32	28	15
13 59	2	0	20	21	6	1	26	25	4	54	29	43
14 3	3	0	21	9	6	45	27	16	6	19	1 ♈	11
14 7	4	0	21	57	7	29	28	7	7	42	2	37
14 11	5	0	22	44	8	14	28	59	9	7	4	6
14 15	6	0	23	32	8	59	29	52	10	35	5	33
14 19	7	0	24	22	9	45	0 ♑	46	12	6	7	1
14 22	8	0	25	11	10	31	1	41	13	38	8	30
14 26	9	0	25	59	11	16	2	36	15	10	9	57
14 30	10	0	26	48	12	3	3	32	16	45	11	25
14 34	11	0	27	38	12	49	4	29	18	23	12	52
14 38	12	0	28	27	13	37	5	26	20	3	14	20
14 42	13	0	29	16	14	24	6	25	21	45	15	48
14 46	14	0	0 ♐	6	15	12	7	25	23	30	17	16
14 50	15	0	0	55	16	0	8	26	25	14	18	44
14 54	16	9	1	45	16	48	9	28	27	3	20	10
14 58	17	0	2	36	17	38	10	33	28	54	21	38
15 2	18	0	3	26	18	28	11	38	0 ♓	45	23	6
15 6	19	0	4	16	19	17	12	43	2	37	24	31
15 10	20	0	5	7	20	8	13	51	4	33	25	58
15 14	21	0	5	58	20	59	15	0	6	31	27	24
15 18	22	0	6	50	21	51	16	10	8	31	28	50
15 22	23	0	7	41	22	43	17	21	10	32	0 ♉	15
15 26	24	0	8	33	23	35	18	33	12	35	1	39
15 30	25	0	9	24	24	29	19	48	14	39	3	4
15 35	26	0	10	17	25	23	21	5	16	47	4	28
15 39	27	0	11	9	26	17	22	23	18	56	5	52
15 43	28	0	12	2	27	12	23	43	21	4	7	15
15 47	29	0	12	54	28	8	25	5	23	12	8	36
15 51	30	0	13	47	29	3	26	30	25	21	9	59

C 2

xli

A Table of Houſes for the Latitude of 5 2. degrees.

☉ in ♐	10 Houſe	11 Houſe	12 Houſe	1 Houſe	2 Houſe	3 Houſe
Time frō Noon.	deg. min.	deg. min.	deg. min.	deg. min.	deg. min.	deg. min.
Ho. Min.	♐	♐	♐	♑	♓	♉
15 51	0 0	13 47	29 3	26 30	25 21	9 59
15 55	1 0	14 41	0 ♑ 1	27 57	27 33	11 21
16 0	2 0	15 35	0 59	29 26	29 49	12 43
16 4	3 0	16 30	1 58	0 ♒ 57	2 ♈ 2	14 4
16 8	4 0	17 25	2 57	2 31	4 14	15 24
16 12	5 0	18 20	3 57	4 8	6 26	16 43
16 16	6 0	19 15	4 58	5 46	8 35	18 1
16 21	7 0	20 10	6 1	7 29	10 47	19 19
16 25	8 0	21 7	7 4	9 13	13 0	20 38
16 29	9 0	22 2	8 7	11 0	15 10	21 55
16 33	10 0	22 59	9 11	12 51	17 21	23 12
16 38	11 0	23 56	10 16	14 42	19 30	24 28
16 42	12 0	24 53	11 24	16 41	21 39	25 45
16 46	13 0	25 50	12 32	18 41	23 44	27 0
16 50	14 0	26 47	13 41	20 44	25 48	28 14
16 55	15 0	27 46	14 51	22 52	27 52	29 28
16 59	16 0	28 45	16 2	25 0	29 57	0 ♊ 41
17 3	17 0	29 44	17 13	27 12	1 ♉ 49	1 53
17 8	18 0	0 ♑ 44	18 28	29 28	3 47	3 5
17 12	19 0	1 44	19 43	1 ♓ 49	5 44	4 17
17 16	20 0	2 44	21 1	4 11	7 28	5 28
17 21	21 0	3 45	22 19	6 35	9 31	6 34
17 25	22 0	4 46	23 38	9 2	11 22	7 47
17 29	23 0	5 47	24 57	11 32	13 10	8 57
17 34	24 0	6 50	26 20	14 7	14 57	10 6
17 38	25 0	7 53	27 44	16 42	16 38	11 14
17 42	26 0	8 56	29 11	19 21	18 21	12 23
17 47	27 0	10 0	0 ♒ 37	21 57	20 1	13 30
17 51	28 0	11 4	2 5	24 37	21 38	14 36
17 56	29 0	12 8	3 36	27 17	23 13	15 41
18 0	30 0	13 13	5 10	0 ♈ 0	24 50	16 47

A Table of Houfes for the Latitude of 52. degrees.

⊙ in ♑	10 Houfe		11 Houfe		12 Houfe		1 Houfe		2 Houfe		3 Houfe	
time from Noon.	deg.	min.	deg.	min.	deg.	min.	deg.	min.	deg.	min.	deg.	min.
Ho. Min	♑		♑		♒		♈		♉		♊	
18 0	♑ 0	0	13	13	5	10	♈ 0	0	24	50	16	47
18 4	1	0	14	19	6	47	2	42	26	24	17	52
18 9	2	0	15	24	8	22	5	22	27	54	18	56
18 13	3	0	16	29	9	58	8	2	29	23	20	0
18 18	4	0	17	38	11	40	10	40	0 ♊	51	21	4
18 22	5	0	18	45	13	21	13	17	2	16	22	7
18 26	6	0	19	54	15	3	15	52	3	39	23	9
18 31	7	0	21	3	16	50	18	28	5	2	24	12
18 35	8	0	22	13	18	38	20	58	6	21	25	14
18 39	9	0	23	22	20	29	23	24	7	40	26	15
18 44	10	0	24	32	22	22	25	49	8	59	27	16
18 48	11	0	25	42	24	16	28	11	10	16	28	16
18 52	12	0	26	54	26	13	0 ♉	32	11	32	29	16
18 57	13	0	28	7	28	11	2	47	12	46	0 ♋	16
19 1	14	0	29	19	0 ♓	7	5	0	13	58	1	14
19 5	15	0	0 ♒	31	2	8	7	8	15	9	2	13
19 10	16	9	1	46	4	11	9	15	16	19	3	12
19 14	17	0	3	0	6	15	11	19	17	28	4	10
19 18	18	0	4	15	8	21	13	19	18	36	5	7
19 23	19	0	5	32	10	30	15	17	19	43	6	4
19 27	20	0	6	48	12	39	17	9	20	49	7	1
19 31	21	0	8	5	14	49	19	0	21	53	7	50
19 35	22	0	9	22	17	0	20	47	22	56	8	53
19 39	23	0	10	40	19	12	22	31	23	59	9	50
19 44	24	0	11	59	21	25	24	14	25	2	10	45
19 48	25	0	13	17	23	34	25	52	26	3	11	40
19 52	26	0	14	36	25	45	27	28	27	3	12	35
19 56	27	0	15	16	27	58	29	3	28	2	13	29
20 0	28	0	17	17	0 ♈	13	0 ♊	34	29	1	14	24
20 5	29	0	18	39	2	27	2	3	29	59	15	19
20 9	30	0	20	1	4	39	3	30	0 ♋	56	16	13

xliii

A Table of Houſes for the Latitude of 5 2 . degrees.

☉ in ♒ time from Noon. Ho. Min.	10 Houſe deg. min. ♒	11 Houſe deg. min. ♒	12 Houſe deg. min. ♈	1 Houſe. deg. min. ♊	2 Houſe. deg. min. ♋	3 Houſe. deg. min. ♋
20 9	0 0	20 1	4 39	3 20	0 56	16 13
20 13	1 0	21 23	6 48	4 54	1 52	17 6
20 17	2 0	22 45	8 56	6 17	2 47	17 58
20 2	3 0	24 8	11 4	7 37	3 43	18 51
20 25	4 0	25 31	13 12	8 55	4 37	19 43
20 30	5 0	26 56	15 21	10 12	5 31	20 35
20 3	6 0	28 20	17 25	11 26	6 24	21 27
20 38	7 0	29 45	19 28	12 39	7 17	22 18
20 42	8 0	1 ♓ 1	21 29	13 49	8 9	23 10
20 46	9 0	2 36	23 29	15 0	9 1	24 2
20 50	10 0	4 1	25 27	16 9	9 52	24 53
20 54	11 0	5 28	27 23	17 16	10 42	25 44
20 58	12 0	6 54	29 15	18 22	11 32	26 34
21 2	13 0	8 21	1 ♉ 5	19 27	12 21	27 24
21 6	14 0	9 50	2 56	20 31	13 11	28 15
21 10	15 0	11 16	4 45	21 34	14 0	29 5
21 14	16 0	12 43	6 30	22 34	14 48	29 54
21 18	17 0	14 12	8 14	23 35	15 36	0 ♌ 44
21 22	18 0	15 39	9 56	24 33	16 23	1 33
21 26	19 0	17 7	11 37	25 31	17 10	2 22
21 30	20 0	18 35	13 14	26 27	17 56	3 12
21 34	21 0	20 3	14 50	27 23	18 43	4 1
21 38	22 0	21 30	16 21	28 19	19 29	4 48
21 41	23 0	22 58	17 54	29 14	20 15	5 38
21 45	24 0	34 27	19 24	0 ♋ 8	21 1	6 27
21 49	25 0	25 54	20 52	1 1	21 45	7 15
21 53	26 0	27 22	22 17	1 53	22 30	8 3
21 57	27 0	28 49	23 41	2 44	23 14	8 51
22 1	28 0	0 ♈ 16	25 6	3 35	23 59	9 31
22 5	29 0	1 44	26 28	4 26	24 44	10 27
22 8	30 0	3 11	27 47	5 15	25 27	11 14

A Table of Houses for the Latitude of 52. degrees.

⊙ in ♓	10 House	11 House	12 House	1 House	2 House	3 House
time from Noon.	deg. min.	deg. min.	deg. min.	deg. min.	deg. min.	deg. min.
Ho. Min.	♓	♈	♉	♋	♋	♌
22 8	0 0	3 11	27 47	5 15	25 27	11 14
22 12	1 0	4 37	29 5	6 4	26 10	12 1
22 16	2 0	6 3	0 ♉ 21	6 52	26 53	12 48
22 20	3 0	7 28	1 36	7 40	27 36	13 36
22 24	4 0	8 54	2 51	8 28	28 19	14 23
22 27	5 0	10 19	4 4	9 15	29 2	15 10
22 31	6 0	11 44	5 15	10 2	29 45	15 57
22 35	7 0	13 7	6 23	10 48	0 ♌ 27	16 44
22 39	8 0	14 31	7 30	11 33	1 9	17 31
22 42	9 0	15 55	8 39	12 19	1 51	18 18
22 46	10 0	17 18	9 47	13 4	2 33	19 5
22 50	11 0	18 41	10 53	13 47	3 15	19 52
22 54	12 0	20 1	11 58	14 31	3 56	20 38
22 57	13 0	21 23	13 1	15 16	4 38	21 24
23 1	14 0	22 42	14 2	15 59	5 18	22 10
23 5	15 0	24 3	15 3	16 43	6 0	22 57
23 8	16 0	25 23	16 4	17 26	6 41	23 43
23 12	17 0	26 40	17 3	18 8	7 22	24 29
23 16	18 0	27 58	18 2	18 50	8 3	25 16
23 20	19 0	29 17	19 1	19 32	8 44	26 2
23 23	20 0	0 ♉ 33	19 50	20 14	9 25	26 48
23 27	21 0	1 49	20 54	20 55	10 5	27 35
23 31	22 0	3 7	21 50	21 37	10 46	28 22
23 34	23 0	4 22	22 44	22 18	11 26	29 7
23 38	24 0	5 36	23 39	22 59	12 6	29 54
23 42	25 0	6 49	24 33	23 40	12 47	0 ♍ 40
23 45	26 0	8 2	25 27	24 21	13 27	1 26
23 49	27 0	9 15	26 20	25 2	14 7	2 13
23 53	28 0	10 27	27 12	25 42	14 47	2 59
23 56	29 0	11 39	28 4	26 22	15 27	3 45
24 0	30 0	12 51	28 55	27 2	16 7	4 21

A N
INTRODUCTION
TO ASTROLOGY.

CHAPTER I.

The number of Planets, Signs, Aspects,
with their several Names and Characters.

 N the first place you must know that there are seven Planets, so called and charactered:

Saturn ♄, *Jupiter* ♃, *Mars* ♂, *Sol* ☉, *Venus* ♀, *Mercury* ☿, *Luna* ☽. There is also the *Head of the Dragon*, thus noted ☊; and the *Tail* ☋. ☊ and ☋ are not Planets but Nodes.

There be also twelve Signs: *Aries* ♈, *Taurus* ♉, *Gemini* ♊, *Cancer* ♋, *Leo* ♌, *Virgo* ♍, *Libra* ♎, *Scorpio* ♏ *Sagittarius* ♐, *Capricornus* ♑, *Aquarius* ♒, *Pisces* ♓: Through these twelve Signs the Planets continually move, and are ever in one or other degree of them. It's necessary you can perfectly distinguish the character of every Planet and Sign before you proceed to any part of this study; and also the characters of these Aspects that follow, viz. ⚹ □ △ ☍ ☌.

You must know, every Sign contains in longitude thirty degrees, and every degree sixty minutes, &c.; the beginning is from ♈, and so in order one Sign after another: so the whole Zodiac contains 360 degrees; the second degree of ♉ is the two and thirtieth degree of the Zodiac, the tenth of ♉ is the fortieth, and so in order all throughout the twelve Signs; yet you must ever account the Aspects from that degree of the Zodiac wherein the Planet is, as if ♄ be in ten degrees of ♊, and I would know to what degree of the ecliptic he casts his sinister Sextile Aspect; reckoning from ♈ to the tenth degree of ♊, I find ♄ to be in the seventieth degree of the Zodiac, according to his longitude; if I add sixty degrees more to seventy, they make one hundred and thirty, which answers to the tenth degree of the Sign ♌, to which ♄ casts his ✳ Aspect, or to any Planet in that degree.

When two Planets are equally distant one from each other, sixty degrees, we say they are in a *Sextile* Aspect, and note it with this character ✳.

When two Planets are ninety degrees distant one from another, we call that Aspect a *Quartile* Aspect, and write it thus, □.

When two Planets are one hundred and twenty degrees distant, we say they are in a *Trine* Aspect, and we write it thus △.

When Planets are one hundred and eighty degrees distant, we call that Aspect an *Opposition,* and character the Aspect thus ☍.

When two Planets are in one and the same degree and minute of any Sign, we say they are in *Conjunction,* and write it thus ☌.

So then if you find ♄ in the first degree of ♈, and ☽ or any other Planet in the first degree of ♊, you shall say they are in a *Sextile* Aspect, for they are distant one from another sixty degrees, and this Aspect is indifferent good.

If ♄ or any other Planet be in the first degree of ♈, and another Planet in the first degree of ♋, you must say they are in a □ Aspect, because there is ninety degrees of the Zodiac between them: this Aspect is of enmity and not good.

If ♄ be in the first degree of ♈, and any Planet in the first degree of ♌, there being now the distance of one hundred and twenty degrees, they behold each other with a *Trine* Aspect; and this does denote Unity, Concord and Friendship.

If you find ♄ in the first degree of ♈, and any Planet in the first degree of ♎, they being now a hundred and eighty degrees each from other, are said to be in *Opposition:* A bad Aspect: and you must be mindful to know what Signs are opposite each to other, for without it you cannot erect the figure.

When ♄ is in the first degree of ♈, and any Planet is in the same degree, they are then said to be in *Conjunction:* And this Aspect is good or ill, according to the nature of the question demanded.

> *Signs opposite to one another are:*
> ♈ ♉ ♊ ♋ ♌ ♍
> ♎ ♏ ♐ ♑ ♒ ♓

That is, ♈ is opposite to ♎ and ♎ to ♈; ♉ to ♏; ♏ to ♉ and so in order as they stand.

I would have all men well and readily apprehend what precedes, and then they will most easily understand the Ephemeris; which is no other thing, than a book containing the true places of the Planets, in degrees and minutes, every of the twelve Signs both in longitude and latitude, every day of the year at noon, and every hour of the day, by correction and equation. *Ephemeris what, and its use.*

I have inserted an Ephemeris of the month of *January* 1646, and after it a Table of Houses for the latitude of 52 degrees, which will serve in a manner, all the Kingdom of *England* on this side of *Newark* upon *Trent*, without sensible error; and this I have done of purpose to teach by them, the use of an Ephemeris, and the manner and means of erecting a Figure of Heaven, without which nothing can be known or made use of in Astrology.

CHAPTER II.

Of the use of the Ephemeris.

The first line on the left-hand page, tells you, *January* has 31 days.

In the second line you find, The daily motions of the Planets and the Dragon's head.

In the third line and over the character of ♄ you have M.D. M signifying *Meridional*, D. *Descending*; that is, ♄ has Meridional latitude and is Descending.

In the next column you find M.D. and underneath ♃; that is, *Jupiter* has South or Meridional latitude, and is descending.

In the third column you find M.A. and under those letters ♂; that is, ♂ has Meridional latitude, and is ascending.

The ☉ has never any latitude.

In the next column to the ☉ you find ♀ and then ☿ with the title of their latitude: Now if over any of the Planets you find S.A. or D. it tells you that Planet has *Septentrional* or North latitude, and is either ascending or descending, as the letters A. or D. do manifest.

In the fourth line you see ♄, ♃, ♂, ☉, ♀, ☿, ☽, ☊; now you must observe ever, the ☋ is in the opposite Sign and degree to the ☊ though he is never placed in the Ephemeris.

In the fifth line you have ♈, ♊, ♑, ♑, ♓, ♒, ♏, ♌: Over ♈ you have ♄, that is to acquaint you, that ♄ is in the Sign of ♈: Over ♊ you have ♃, *viz.* ♃ is in the Sign of ♊: And so over ♑ stands ♂: And so of all the rest one after another.

In the sixth line you have figure 1, telling you it's the first day of *January*, and so underneath it to the lower end, you have the day of the month.

Next to the Figure *one*, you have the letter A, which is the letter of the day of the week; and if you run down under that column; you see the great letter to be D, which is the Sunday or Dominical letter of the year 1646.

Over against the first day of *January* under the character of ♄ you find 27.48, over those figures you see ♈; the meaning is, ♄ is the first day of *January* in 27 degrees and 48 minutes of ♈: now you must observe, sixty minutes make one degree, and that when any Planet has passed thirty degrees in a Sign, he goes orderly into the next, as out of ♈ into ♉, out of ♉ into ♊, &c.

In the fourth column, over against the first of the month, you find 28 R 12, over them ♊, and over it ♃; that is, ♃ the first of *January* is in 28 degrees of ♊ and 12 minutes: The letter R. tells you that he is retrograde; had you found Di. or D. it had told you he was then come to be Direct in motion. Of all these terms hereafter by themselves.

In the fifth column you find 10 05, over those figures ♑ ♂, *viz.* ♂ is the first of *January* in the tenth degree and five minutes of ♑.

And so by this order you find the ☉ to be in 21 degrees, and 34 minutes of ♑; and ♀ in 5 degr. 7 min. of ♓; ☿ in 5 degr. and 29 min. of ♒; the ☽ in 21 23 of ♏; ☊ in 12 degr. and 34 min. of ♌.

So that you see on the left-hand page, there are ten several columns; the first containing the day of the month; the second, the weekday letter; the third, the degree and minutes of ♄: the fourth contains the degrees and minutes ♃ is in; and so every column the like for the rest of the Planets.

Over against the tenth of *January,* under the column of the ☉, you find 0 ♒ 44 minutes, which only shows you the ☉ to be that day at Noon, in 0 degrees and 44 minutes of ♒, &c.

In the lower end of the left-side page, after the 31 of *January* you find Lat. of Pla. that is, the Latitude of the Planets.

Under the letter C you find 1 10 20.

Under the column of ♄ over against 1, you find 2 31; then continuing your eye, you have under ♃ 0 5; under ♂ 0 47; under ♀ 1 13; under ☿ 1 45. The meaning hereof is, that the first day of *January* ♄ has 2 degr. and 31 min. of latitude; ♃ 0 degr. 5 min; ♂ 0 degr. 47 min; ♀ 1 degr. 13 min; ☿ 1 degr. 45 min. of latitude: To know whether it is North or South, cast your eye to the upper column, and you may see over the character of ♄ stands M.D. that is, Meridional Descending, or South latitude; where you find N. it tells you the latitude is North; if you find A. the Planet is Ascending in his latitude; if D, then Descending.

CHAPTER III.

The right-hand page of the Ephemeris unfolded.

There are eight columns: the first contains the days of the month; the six next contains the manner, quality and name of those Aspects the ☽ has to the Planets; as also, the hour of the day or night when they perfectly meet in Aspect; the eighth column has only those Aspects which ♄, ♃, ♂, ☉, ♀, ☿ make to each other, and the time of the day or night when.

In the fourth line under ♄ you find *Occid.;* that is, ♄ is *Occidental* of the ☉ or sets after him; and so of ♃, or where you find *Occid.* it notes as much.

Under ♂ you find *Orient.* that is, ♂ is *Oriental,* or rises before the ☉. And so at any time.

For better understanding the true time when the ☽ comes to the Aspect of any Planet, you are to observe, that all those that write *Ephemerides,* compute the motion of the Planets for the noon time, or just at twelve: And you must know, we and they ever begin our day at Noon, and so reckon 24 hours from the noon of one day to the noon of the next, and after this manner you must reckon in the Aspects. As for example:

Over against the first day of *January* 1646, which is Thursday, and under the column appropriate to the ☉, you find ✶ 0. The meaning whereof is, that the ☽ is in ✶ aspect with the ☉ that first day of *January* at noon, or no hours P.M. or *Post Meridiem.*

Over against Friday the second of *January,* you find under the column of ♀ □ 6 and on the right hand over against the same day, under ☿ ✶ 9 which is no more than this, *viz.* the second of *January* at 6 o'clock after noon, the ☽ comes to the □ or Quartile aspect of ♀ and at nine o'clock she meets with the ✶ of ☿.

Over against the sixth day of *January,* being Tuesday, under ♄ you find □ 14, that is, fourteen hours after noon of that day, the ☽ comes to the □ of ♄: now you may easily find, that the fourteenth hour after noon of Tuesday, is two o'clock in the morning on Wednesday.

Again, under the column of the ☉ you find ☌ 11 48 which is no more but this, the ☽ comes to ☌ with the ☉ at 48 minutes after eleven o'clock at night: now you must know the ☽ her ☌ with the ☉ is her change, her next ☐ after ☌ with the ☉ is the first quarter, her ☍ with the ☉ is full ☽, her ☐ after ☍ is her last quarter.

If you understand but this, that thirteen hours is one o'clock the day subsequent, fourteen hours two o'clock, fifteen hours three o'clock in the morning, sixteen is four o'clock, seventeen hours is five in the morning, eighteen is six o'clock, nineteen hours is seven o'clock, twenty hours is eight in the morning, twenty one hours is nine o'clock, twenty two hours after noon is ten o'clock the next day, twenty three hours is eleven o'clock, &c. Now we never say twenty four hours after noon, for then it's just noon, and if we say 00.00 after noon that is just at noon, or then it's full twelve o'clock: Understand this and you cannot err.

In that column under the Planets mutual Aspects, over against the third of *January,* being Saturday, you find ✶ ♄ ♃ 21, that is ♄ and ♃ are in ✶ aspect 21 hours after noon of the Saturday; and that is, at nine o'clock on the Sunday morning following.

Over against the fourth day you find ☽ *Perigee,* that is, she is then nearest to the earth: over against the eighteenth day in the outmost column you find ☽ *Apogee,* that is, the ☽ is then most remote from the earth.

Over against the twelfth day, in the same outmost column, you find ☿ *in Elong. Max.* It should be ☿ *in Maxima Elongatione;* or that day ☿ is in his greatest elongation or distance from the ☉.

Over against the sixth of *January,* you find in the outside column Vc ☉ ♃ SS ♂ ☿; that is, the ☉ and ♃ are in a *Quincunx* aspect that day; now that aspect consists of five Signs, or 150 degrees.

SS is a *Semisextile,* and tells you, that day ♂ and ☿ are in *Semisextile* to each other: this aspect consists of 30 degrees.

Over against the 25 of *January,* you find in the outmost
column □ ♄ ♂ 11, and Q ☉ ♄; The meaning is, that at
eleven o'clock after noon, ♄ and ♂ are in a Quartile aspect;
and Q ☉ ♄ tells you, the ☉ and ♄ have a Quintile aspect to
each other that day: A Quintile consists of two Signs twelve
degrees, or when Planets are distant 72 degrees from each
other: we seldom use more aspects than the ♂, ✳, □, △, ☍:
to these of late one KEPLER, a learned man, has added some
new ones, as follows, *viz.*

A Semisextile, charactered **SS,** *consisting of thirty degrees.*
A Quintile **Q** *consisting of seventy two degrees.*
A Tredecile **Td** *consisting of* 108 *degrees.*
A Biquintile **Bq** *consisting of* 144 *degrees*
A Quincunx **Vc** *consisting of* 150 *degrees.*

I only acquaint you with these, that finding them any
where you may apprehend their meaning.

After those two sides of an Ephemeris, follows in order,
A Table of Houses; for without a present Ephemeris and
Table of Houses, it's impossible to instruct you to set a Figure, without which we can give no judgement, or perform
anything in this Art.

The use of   As there are twelve Signs in the Zodiac, through which
the Table the ☉ and all the Planets make their daily motion, so are
of Houses. there as you may see, twelve several great pages; and as ♈
is the first Sign of the Zodiac, so in the first line of the first
great page do you find ☉ in ♈; in the second grand page and
first line you find ☉ in ♉, in the third page and first line ☉
in ♊; and so in order according to the succession of Signs
one after another through the twelve pages: By help of these
Tables we frame a Figure, as I shall now acquaint you.

CHAPTER IV.

How to erect a Figure of Heaven by the Ephemeris and
Table of Houses, aforesaid.

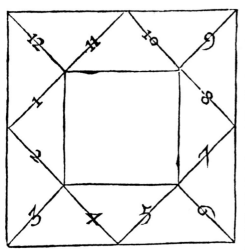

In the first place you are to draw the Figure thus; and to know that those twelve empty spaces are by us called the twelve Houses of Heaven, that square in the middle is to write the day, year, and hour of the day when we set a figure: the first house begins ever upon that line where you see the figure 1 placed, the second house where you see the figure 2 stand, the third house where you see the figure 3, the fourth house begins where you find the figure of 4, the fifth house where you see the figure 5, the sixth house where see the figure 6, the seventh house where you find the figure 7, the eighth house where you find the figure 8, the ninth house where you find the figure 9, the 10th house where you find the figure 10, the eleventh where you find the figure 11, the twelfth house where you find the figure 12: what space is contained between the figure one to the figure two, is of the first house, or what Planet you shall find to be in that space, you shall say he is in the first house; yet if he be within five degrees of the Cusp of any house, his virtue shall be assigned to that house whose Cusp he is nearest, &c. but of this hereafter. The Cusp or very entrance of any house, or first beginning, is upon the line where you see the figures placed; upon which line you must ever place the Sign and degree of the Zodiac, as you find it in the Table of houses, as if you find 10 degrees of ♈ for the tenth house, you must place the number 10 and Sign of ♈ upon the line of the tenth house, and that same tenth degree is the Cusp or beginning of that house, and so in the rest.

In erecting or setting your Figure, whether of a Question or Nativity, you are to consider these three things.

First, the year, month, day of the week, hour or part of the hour of that day.

Secondly, to observe in the Ephemeris of that year and day the true place of the ☉ in Sign, degree and minute at noon.

Thirdly, what hours and minutes in the Table of Houses do answer or stand on the left hand against the degree of that Sign the ☉ is in the day of the Question; for by adding the hour of the day, and hours and minutes answering to the place of the ☉, your figure is made, and this Sign where the ☉ is you must always look for in that great column under the title of the tenth house, where you find the ☉ and that Sign together; as if upon any day of the year when I set my figure, the ☉ is in ♈, then the first great page or side serves, for there you find ☉ in ♈; if the ☉ be in ♉, then the second page serves, and so in order: and as in the uppermost line you find ☉ in ♈ ♉ ♊, &c., so underneath those characters, and under the tenth house, you see 0 1 2 3 4 5 6, and so all along to 30 degrees; so that let the ☉ be in what degree he will, you have it exactly to degrees in the second lesser column, under the title of the tenth house; if any minutes adhere to the place of the ☉, as always there does, if those minutes exceed thirty, take the hours and minutes adhering to the next greater degree the ☉ is in; if less minutes than thirty belong to the ☉, take the same you find him with, for you must know it breeds no error in an Horary Question.

Example by one Figure following.

I would erect a Figure of Heaven the sixth of *January*, being Tuesday, 1646, one hour thirty minutes afternoon, or *P.M.* that is, *Post Meridiem*: First, I look in the Ephemeris over against the sixth of *January,* for the true place of the ☉ and I find it to be 26 39 ♑; then I look in the Table of Houses until I find the ☉ in ♑, which I do in the tenth great page, and under the number 10, which signifies the tenth house, I find

♑; I enter with the degree of the ☉, which being 26 39 I look for 27, and on the left hand against it, I find 19h 56m; in the head of the Table over them H.M. signifying Hours and Minutes: These hours and minutes, *viz.* 19.56, I add to the time of day in my Question, *viz.* 1.30 (and so I must always in every Question add both numbers to-

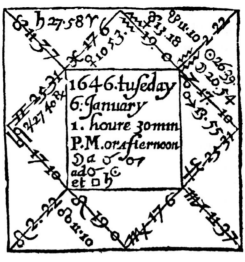

This chart in modern form, page A2

gether), and if they make more than 24 hours, I must cast away 24 hours, and enter the Table of Houses, under the title of *Time from Noon,* seeking for the remainder, or the nearest number to it, and on the right hand over against it, under the several columns, you shall have the Cusps of the tenth, eleventh, twelfth, first, second, third, fourth houses: but to my former purpose: I add 19.56 to 1.30 and they produce 21 hours, 26 minutes; which number I seek for in that column entitled, *Time from Noon,* or Hours, minutes, and which number I find precisely in the eleventh great page, under the ☉ in ♒; and over against 21.26 on the right hand under the column of the tenth house, I find 19, *Tenth house* and over its head upward, the Sign of ♒; so then I put the 19 degree of ♒ upon the Cusp of the tenth house.

In the third column, over against 21.26 I find 17.06, *Eleventh* over it the Sign of ♓, above ♓ the number 11, which ap- *house* points you 17 degrees, and 6 minutes of ♓ for the Cusp of the eleventh house.

In the fourth column you find over against the former *Twelfth* number 11.37, over that the character of ♉, at the upper *house* end 12, which tells you, that 11.37 degrees of ♉ must be placed on the Cusp of the twelfth house.

First house　In the fifth column over against the former number, you have 25 31, over it Ⅱ, over Ⅱ, 1 House, and directs you to place the 25 degrees and 31 minutes of Ⅱ upon the line or Cusp of the first house.

Second house　In the sixth column you find 17.10, over that ♋, 2 House, which tells you 17 10 degrees of the Sign ♋ must be placed on the Cusp or line of the second house.

Third house　In the seventh little column over against the former number you have 2 22, over it the Sign ♌ and in the upper line 3 House; so you are directed to put the 2 deg. and 22 minutes of ♌ upon the Cusp of the third house.

Having now perfected the tenth, eleventh, twelfth, first, second and third House, I must direct you how to perform the rest.

You must for understanding here know, that the first six Signs of the Zodiac are opposite to the six last, as formerly I told you.

♈	♉	Ⅱ	♋	♌	♍
♎	♏	♐	♑	♒	♓

Viz. ♈ is opposite to ♎, and ♎ to ♈; ♉ to ♏ and ♏ to ♉, and so all the rest in order.

The twelve houses also are opposite each to other: as thus

10	11	12	1	2	3
4	5	6	7	8	9

So that the tenth house is opposite to the fourth, the fourth to the tenth; the eleventh to the fifth, the fifth to the eleventh, and so all the rest as you find placed: The use you are to make of it is this, That if on the Cusp of the tenth house you find the Sign ♈, then must you place on the Cusp of the fourth the Sign ♎; and look what degree and minute possesses the Sign of the tenth house, the same degree and minute of the opposite Sign must be placed on the Cusp of the fourth house, and so of all the other Signs and Cusps of houses; and this is general, and ever holds true; without which rule observed, you cannot erect the Figure aright.

In our former Figure you see 19 ♒ on the Cusp of the tenth

house, ♌ is opposite to ♒, and the fourth house to the tenth; so then I place the 19 degree of ♌ upon the Cusp of that house.

Upon the line or Cusp of the eleventh house you see ♓ 17 6; ♍ is the Sign opposite to ♓, and the fifth house to the eleventh; so that I place the 17 degree and 6 minutes of ♍ upon the Cusp of the fifth house.

The Cusp of the twelfth house is the 11 37 of ♉, I see ♏ is opposite to ♉, and the sixth house to the twelfth; I therefore put the 11 degree and 37 minutes of ♏ on the Cusp of the sixth house.

I do so in the rest of the houses, and by this means I have framed the twelve houses, and placed the several Signs of the Zodiac upon the Cusps as they ought to be.

Having finished your twelve Houses by the Method preceding, you must now learn to place the Planets therein; which you must do by observing in the Ephemeris, the exact place of the Planet in Sign and Degree at noon the day of the Figure, and in what House you shall find the Sign wherein the Planet is, in that House must you place the Planet, within the house if the Planet be in more Degrees than the Cusp of the House; without the house, if his Degrees be less than those of the Cusp of the Houses.

Over against the sixth day of *January* aforesaid, I find ♄ to be in 27.58 of ♈: I look for ♈ in the figure, but find it not; I find ♓ on the Cusp of the eleventh, and ♉ on the Cusp of the twelfth House; so I conclude that the Sign ♈ is intercepted; for so we say when a Sign is not upon any of the Cusps of Houses, but is included between one house and another: I therefore place ♄ in the 11 house, as you may see.

In the next place I find the place of ♃ to be 27.40 ♊. I find 25.31 ♊ to be on the Cusp of the first House, because the Degrees adhering to ♃ are greater than the Cusp, I place ♃ within the House. And because he is noted Retrograde I place the letter R, the better to inform my judgement.

In the fifth column of the Ephemeris I find ♂ the sixth of *January* to be in the 13.55 ♑; which Sign in the figure is the Cusp of the eighth House: I therefore place ♂ as near the Cusp as I can, but his Degrees in the Sign being less than the Cusp of the House, I place him without the House.

I find the ☉ the sixth day of *January* to be in 26.39 ♑ whom I place beyond the Cusp of the 8th House, because the degrees of the ☉ in ♑ are more than the Cusp of the House.

In the same line, and over against the sixth of *January*, I find ♀ to be in 10 Degrees, and 53 minutes of ♓.

I find the Sign of ♓ on the Cusp of the eleventh House, and there I put ♀ in the tenth House, near the Cusp of the eleventh House, but not in the House, because the Degrees of the Sign she is in are not equivalent to the Degrees of the Cusp of the eleventh house, but are short of them.

In the eighth Column I find under the Character of ☿ 13.18, above it ♏. I therefore place ☿ near the Cusp of the tenth House, but not in the House; for you may see he is nearer in Degrees to the Cusp of the tenth House than the 9th; for by how much nearer he is in Degrees to the Cusp of any House, having the same Sign, by so much the nearer he ought to be placed to the Cusp of that House.

In the ninth Column, under the Column of the ☽ I find over against the sixth of *January* 20.54 and over the Figures ♑: so then I place the ☽ very near the ☉ in the eighth House, and between the Cusp of the House and the ☉; for you may see the ☽ has not so many Degrees as may put her beyond the ☉; nor has she so few to be without the eighth House. How to reduce the motion of the ☽ and other Planets to any hour of the day, you shall be instructed hereafter.

In the tenth column I find over against my said day 11.10, over against it ♌ and ♒: so you see the ☊ is in 11 degr. 10 min. of ♌; which I place in the middle of the third house, because ten degrees are very near as nigh the Cusp of the third house as fourth; the ☋ being always in the opposite Sign and degree to the ☊, I place in the ninth house, *viz.* in 11 degrees 10 minutes of ♒. This being done, I must observe how the ☽ separates and applies the same day; I find the sixth of *January* on the right-hand page of the Book, that the ☽ did last separate from a ♂ of ♂ and now is applying to a ♂ of ☉ at 11 48, that is, at eleven o'clock and 48 minutes after at night, then to a □

of ♄ at fourteen hours after noon, or at two o'clock the next morning.

Thus have you one Figure of Heaven erected, and the Planets therein placed, though not rectified to the hour of the day, for now to reduce their motion to any hour I shall show hereafter: But because I have by experience found, that many Learners have been much stumbled for want of sufficient directions in former Introductions to set a Scheme of Heaven, I shall be a little more copious, and show an example or two more.

I would erect a Figure on Saturday the 17 of *January* 1646, for eleven o'clock and twenty after noon: the ☉ that day at noon is in 7 degrees and 52 of ♒: in the eleventh page of the Table of Houses I find ☉ in ♒; under the column of the tenth house I look for the eighth degree of ♒, because 52 minutes want but little of a degree; over against the eighth degree on the left hand, under the title of *Time from noon*, I find 20 42, *viz.* 20 hours 42 minutes; so then I work thus:

Time of the day is 11 20

20 42

hours and minutes answering to the eighth degree of ♒, there being 62 min. *viz.* two min. more than one hour, I take that hour and add both numbers   hour min. together,   and they make   32   02 From 32 hours and 2 min. I subtract 24 hours, as I must ever do, if there be more than 24 hours, and then there remains as you see, 8 hours and 2 min.   32 02 which I find not precisely in   - 24 00 *Subtracted* the Table of Houses, but I find 8 0, which is near my   08 02 *Remains* number, and which serves very well; over against 8ʰ and 0ᵐ I find 28 0, and in the upper part I find ♋, and over it the tenth house, so then I have 28 degrees, 0 min. of ♋ for the Cusp of my tenth house: in the same line, on the right hand to this 28 degr. of ♋, you shall find 4 36, over it ♍, in the upper part of the eleventh house: so then 4 degr. 36 min. of ♍ are the Cusp of the eleventh house; then have you over against the said number of 8 hours 0 min. in the fourth

column, 0 ♎ 4, over its head the twelfth house, this tells you
the Cusp of the twelfth house is 0 degr. 4 min. of ♎: in the
fifth column over against the said former number, you have
21 3, over them figures at the top of the page, ♎, and then
the first house; which signifies, that you must place the 21
degr. and 3 min. of ♎ on the Cusp of the first house: adjoin-
ing to the 21 degr. and 3 min. of ♎ in the sixth column, I
find 13 57, over it the Sign ♏, in the upper part the second
house, by which I know, that 13 degr. and 57 min. of ♏ must
be placed on the Cusp of the second house. In the seventh
and utmost column over against my foresaid number of 8
hours and 0 min. I find 15 46, over them the Sign ♐, in the
upper column over their head the third house, pointing out
15 degrees 46 min. of ♐ for the Cusp of the third house; so
then your Cusps of houses stand thus:

> Tenth house 28 ♋
> Eleventh house 4 36 ♍
> Twelfth house 0 4 ♎
> First house 21 3 ♎
> Second house 13 57 ♏
> Third house 15 46 ♐

The Cusps of the other houses are found out by the opposite Signs and houses, as I formerly directed, *viz.* the fourth
house being opposite ever to the tenth, and the Sign ♑ to ♋, I
place the 28 degr. of ♑ on the Cusp of the fourth house: the
fifth is opposite to the eleventh, and ♓ is the opposite Sign to
♍, I therefore place the 4 degr. 36 min. of ♓ for the Cusp of the
fifth: the twelfth house is opposite to the sixth, so is ♈ opposite
to ♎, therefore I place 0 degr. 4 min. of ♈ on the Cusp of the
sixth house: the seventh house is opposite to the first house,
and ♈ to ♎, I therefore place the 21 degr. and 3 min. of ♈, the
opposite Sign to ♎, on the Cusp of the seventh house: the
eighth house is opposite to the second, and ♉ to ♏, I therefore
place the 13 degr. and 57 min. of ♉ on the Cusp of the
eighth house: the ninth house is opposite to the third, and
♊ to ♐, I therefore make the 15 degr. and 46 of ♊ the Cusp
of the ninth house: The Planets are to be placed in the

Figure as formerly directed; nor let it trouble you, if you find sometimes two Signs in one house, or almost three, or sometimes one Sign to be on the Cusps of three houses, ever place your Planets orderly as near the degree of the house, as the number of degrees your Planet is in will permit.

You must ever remember that if your hour of the day be in the morning, or as we say *Ante Meridiem,* or before noon, you must reckon the time, as from the noon of the day preceding: As for example:

I would erect a figure the 26 day of *January* 1646, being Monday, for 9 of the clock and 45 min. before noon.

My time stands thus: 9 ho. 45 min.

To this I add twelve hours, because it is properly in our account, the 21 hour and 45 minutes after noon of the Sunday preceding: so then you may say thus; the Figure is set for 9 hours and 45 minutes *ante meridiem,* or before noon of the Monday.

Or else 25 *January*, being Sunday, 21 hours and 45 min. *post meridiem,* or after noon, which is all one with the former time.

I find the ☉ at noon the same 26 day, to be in 16 degr. and 59 min. of ♒; I look in the Table of Houses what hours and min. correspond to the 17 degrees of ♒ in the tenth house; in the eleventh page I find the Sign ♒ and along in the column of the tenth 17 degr. 0 min, on the left hand I find over against them, 21 hours 18 min; to these I add the hours and min. of the day, *viz.* 21 45; added together, they make   43ʰ 03ᵐ· from which in regard they are more than 24 hours, I subtract 24.

$$43\ 03$$
$$-\ \underline{24\ 00}$$
$$\text{Rests}\ \ 19\ 03$$

With my 19 hours and 3 min. I enter the Table of Houses, and under the title of hours and minutes, or *Time from Noon,* I seek my number. In the tenth page I find 19 hours and 1 min. which is the next number to my desire, over against it I see 14 0, and in the upper part ♑ and tenth house, signifying the 14 degr. of the Sign ♑ is to be placed on the Cusp of the tenth house, the rest of the houses are found out in order as they stand in the Table of Houses over against my number of 19 hours and 1 min. I hope these examples will be sufficient for all young Learners; but that they may presently consider whether they have set their Figure right yea or no, let them take this general rule, that if the Figure be erected from noon to Sunset, the ☉ will be in the ninth, eighth or seventh house; if it be erected from Sunset till midnight, he shall find the ☉ in the sixth, fifth or fourth house; if it be set from midnight till ☉ rise, he shall find the ☉ in the third, second or first house; if the Figure be set from ☉ rise till noon, then he shall find the ☉ in the twelfth, eleventh or tenth house, &c.

CHAPTER V.

Of the daily motion of the Planets,
and how to reduce their motion to any hour
of the day, and to the Meridian of **London**.

We have seldom occasion to erect a Scheme of Heaven just at noon, to which time the motions of the Planets are exactly calculated, and need not any rectification; but usually all Questions are made either some hours before, or after noon; therefore it is needful you know how to take their diurnal or daily motion, or how many degrees or min. they move in 24 hours, that thereby you may have a proportion to add to the place of your Planets according to the hour of the day or night when you set your Figure: And although in horary Questions, it occasions no error (except in the motion of the ☽) yet I thought fit to instruct the Learner herewith, that so he may know how to do his work handsomely. *Example:*

You must set down the place of your Planet in Sign, degree and minute as you find him at noon; and if your Planet be direct, you must subtract him in degree and minute from the place he is in the day subsequent: but when a Planet is retrograde, you must do the contrary, *viz.* subtract the motion of your Planet the day subsequent from the day going before.

Example:

January 7 at noon, ♄ is   28 00 ♈   *Daily motion is 2 min.*
January 6 at noon, ♄ is   27 58

Here you see the daily motion of ♄ is only two minutes.

Jan 6 ♃ R   27 40 ♊   *Daily Motion is 6 min.*
Jan 7 ♃   27 34

Jan 7 ♂ is in 14 41 ♑
Jan 6 ♂ is in 13 55
           46

So the diurnal motion of ♂ is 46 min.

Jan 7 ☉ is in   27 40 ♑
Jan 6 ☉ is in   26 39
         1 01

The daily motion of the ☉ is one degr. and one min.

Jan 7 ♀ is in 12 02 ♓
Jan 6 ♀ is in 10 53
         1 09

The daily motion of ♀ is 1 degr. and 9 min.

Jan 7 ☿ is in 14 45 ♒
Jan 6 ☿ is in 13 18
         1 27

So the diurnal motion of ☿ is 1 degr. 27 min.

Jan 7 ☽ is in 03 01 ♒
Jan 6 ☽ is in 20 54 ♑

Subtract 20 degr. 54 min. of ♑ from 30 degr. the comple-
ment of a Sign, and there rest 9 degr. 6 min. which added
to 3 degr. 1 min. of ♒, make the diurnal motion of the ☽ to
be 12 degr. and 7 min. The work had been easier, but that
the ☽ was removed into another Sign before the day subsequent at noon.

Jan 6 ☊ is in　11 10 ♌
Jan 7 ☊ is in　<u>10 24</u>
　　　　　　　　00 46

　　The motion of the ☊ is 46 min. whom you must carefully observe, for he sometimes moves forward in the Sign, sometimes backward, which you may easily perceive by the Ephemeris, without further instruction.

How to find the quantity of the hourly motion of any Planet by the Table following.

In every Figure you set, the place of the Planets ought to be rectified to the hour of the setting the Figure, especially the place of the ☽, because of her swift motion; in the Planets you need not be scrupulous, but take whole degrees without sensible error, or indeed any at all: this I mean in Questions; but in Nativities, you are to have the places of them exactly to degrees and minutes; and above all, the motion of the Sun to minutes and seconds, because by his motion we set the yearly revolutions of Nativities.

　　I shall only deliver the practice of two or three Examples, and leave the rest to the diligence of every Learner. The Table follows.

de	mi	sec	th
mi	sec	th	4ʰ
1	0	2	30
2	0	5	0
3	0	7	30
4	0	10	0
5	0	12	30
6	0	15	0
7	0	17	30
8	0	20	0
9	0	22	30
10	0	25	0
11	0	27	30
12	0	30	0
13	0	32	30
14	0	35	0
15	0	37	30
16	0	40	0
17	0	42	30
18	0	45	0
19	0	47	30
20	0	50	0
21	0	52	30

de	mi	sec	th
mi	sec	th	4ʰ
22	0	55	0
23	0	57	30
24	1	0	0
25	1	2	30
26	1	5	0
27	1	7	30
28	1	10	0
29	1	12	30
30	1	15	0
31	1	17	30
32	1	20	0
33	1	22	30
34	1	25	0
35	1	27	30
36	1	30	0
37	1	32	30
38	1	35	0
39	1	37	30
40	1	40	0
41	1	42	30
42	1	45	0

de	mi	sec	th
mi	sec	th	4ʰ
43	1	47	30
44	1	50	0
45	1	52	30
46	1	55	0
47	1	57	30
48	2	0	0
49	2	2	30
50	2	5	0
51	2	7	30
52	2	10	0
53	2	12	30
54	2	15	0
55	2	17	30
56	2	20	0
57	2	22	30
58	2	25	0
59	2	27	30
60	2	30	0
61	2	32	30

In the preceding Scheme of the sixth of *Jan.* you find the diurnal motion of the Sun to be 61 min. or one degree one min. In the very last line of this Table I find 61, over the head of it *deg. min.* but over against 61 to the right hand, I find 2 32 30, which tells you, that the hourly motion of the Sun is, 2 min. 32 seconds, and thirty-thirds, as you may see in the upper part of the column over the heads of the figures.

The daily motion of ♂ is 46 min. in the Figure above named;

I enter down the first column, and find 46, against it I find 1 min. 55 seconds to be one hour's motion of ♂, when in 24 hours he moves 46 min.

You must note, if you enter with minutes, you must have minutes, if with seconds, seconds; and so in the rest: This in the motion of ♄, ♃, ♂, ☉, ♀, ☿; with the ☽ otherwise.

If the motion of your Planet be above 61 min. *viz.* 70 or 75 or 80 min. then enter the Table twice: as for example:

The motion of ☿ is, as you perceive, 1 degr. and 27 min. I would know what his hourly motion is, I enter first with 60 min. against which I find 2 30, *viz.* 2 min. 30 seconds, then I enter with 27, against which I find 1 7 30, *viz.* 1 min. 7 seconds, thirty-thirds, which I cast away, and add the two former sums together thus,

$$
\begin{array}{r}
2\ 30 \\
+\ \underline{1\ 07} \\
3\ 37
\end{array}
$$

added together they make 3 min. 37 seconds, and so much is the hourly motion of ☿, when his diurnal motion is 87 minutes.

The daily motion of the ☽ you see is 12 degr. and 7 min.

I enter down the first column with 12, against it I find 0 30 0, *viz.* 0 degrees 30 min. 0 seconds.

I enter with 7, over against it I find   00 17 30
I add the number to it   30 00 00

they produce 30 min. 17 seconds, and 30 thirds for the hourly motion of the ☽ in our figure: you may in her operation reject the seconds and thirds.

By this rule I would know where the true place of the ☉ is at that hour when we erected the Figure.

The hour of the day is 1 30, the time admitted by *Eichstadius* for reducing his Ephemeris to the *Meridian of London*, is 50 min. of an hour in motion, for they being more East than we, the ☉ comes sooner to them at their noon, than to us that are more Westward, by so much time: I add 50 min. to my former time, *viz.* 1 30, the whole is then 2 hours 20 min. Now if the motion of the ☉ in one hour be 2 min. 32 seconds,
then in two hours it will be   <u>2 min 32 seconds more.</u>
     added together they are   5 min. 4 seconds

Which being added to the place of the ☉ at noon, make the true place of the ☉ at time of erection of the Figure, 26 deg. 44 min. and 4 sec. of ♑; there is 20 min. of one hour more; but because they produce nothing of consequence, I omit further trouble herein.

The place of the ☽ the same day at noon is 20 54 ♑. If you add her motion in two hours, you shall see it will be twice 30 min. *viz.* one whole degree, and then her true place will be 21 54 ♑.

We that set many Figures, never care for this exactness, but use this general rule; In the motion of the ☉, ♀ and ☿, if the Figure be for six or seven hours after noon, we add about 15 min. to their places at noon, and so allowing for every six hours 15 min. motion.

Because the ☽ goes 12, 13 or 14 degr. in one day, we constantly add to her place at noon 3 degr. for every six hours, and some min. over; do so with the other Planets according to their diurnal motion: He that would do them more exact, may work them by multiplication and division, or procure some old Ephemeris, wherein there is usually large proportional Tables concerning this business.

Now as I have acquainted you, that in motion of the Planets you must in a Nativity or Question, if you please, allow the Planets so much to be added to their place at noon as can be got in 50 min. of an hour, so you must observe the contrary in the Aspects: As for example: The sixth of *January* you find ☽ in □ ♄ 14 P.M. *viz.* the ☽ comes to the □ aspect of ♄ at 14 hours after the noon of the sixth day of *January*, or at two o'clock the next morning on the seventh day: now you must subtract 50 min. of an hour from 14 hours, and then the true time of the ☽ her perfect □ to ♄ with us at *London*, is at 13 hours and 10 min. after noon: do so in all the Aspects, &c.

CHAPTER VI.
Of the twelve Houses of Heaven,
and some Names or Terms of Astrologie.

The whole Sphere of Heaven is divided into four equal parts by the *Meridian* and *Horizon*, and again into four

Quadrants, and every Quadrant again into three parts, according to other Circles drawn by points of Sections of the aforesaid Meridian and Horizon; so the whole Heaven is divided into twelve equal parts, which the Astrologers call Houses or Mansions, taking their beginning from the East.

The first Quadrant is described from the East to the Midheaven, or from the line of the first house to the line of the tenth house, and contains the twelfth, eleventh and tenth houses. It's called the *Oriental, Vernal, Masculine, Sanguine, Infant quarter.*

The second Quadrant is from the Cusp of the Midheaven to the Cusp of the seventh house, containing the ninth, eighth and seventh houses, and is called the *Meridian, Estival, Feminine, Youthful, Choleric quarter.*

The third Quadrant is from the Cusp of the seventh house to the Cusp of the fourth house, and contains the sixth, fifth and fourth houses, is called *Occidental, Autumnal, Masculine, Melancholic, Manhood, cold and dry.*

The fourth Quadrant is from the Cusp of the fourth to the Cusp of the first house, and contains the third, second and first house, is *Northern, Feminine, Old age, of the nature of Winter, Phlegmatic.*

The first, tenth, seventh and fourth houses here are called *Angles,* the eleventh, second, eighth and fifth are called *Succedents,* the third, twelfth, ninth and sixth, are termed *Cadents:* The Angles are most powerful, the Succedents are next in virtue, the Cadents poor, and of little efficacy: the Succedent houses follow the Angles, the Cadents come next *[after]* the Succedents. In force and virtue they stand so in order:

1 10 7 4 11 5 9 3 2 8 6 12

The meaning whereof is this, that two Planets equally dignified, the one in the Ascendant, the other in the tenth house, you shall judge the Planet in the Ascendant somewhat of more power to effect what he is Significator of, than he that is in the tenth: do so in the rest as they stand in order, remembering that Planets in Angles do more forcibly show their effects.

When we name the Lord of the Ascendant, or Significator

of the Querent, or thing quesited; we mean no other thing than that Planet who is Lord of that Sign which ascends, or Lord of that Sign from which house the thing demanded is required; as if from the seventh house, the Lord of that Sign descending on the Cusp is Significator, and so in the rest: but of this in the ensuing Judgements.

Cosignificator is when you find another Planet in aspect or conjunction with that Planet who is the principal Significator; this said Planet shall have signification more or less, and either assist or not in effecting the thing desired; and so has something to do in the Judgement, and ought to be considered: if a friendly Planet, he notes good; if an infortune the contrary, *viz.* either the destruction of the thing, or disturbance in it.

Almuten, of any house is that Planet who has most dignities in the Sign ascending or descending upon the Cusp of any house, whereon or from whence, you require your judgement.

Almuten of a Figure, is that Planet who in Essential and Accidental dignities is most powerful in the whole Scheme of Heaven.

The Dragon's Head we sometimes call   *Anabibazon.*
The Dragon's Tail   *Catabibazon.*

The Longitude of a Planet is his distance from the beginning of *Aries*, numbered according to the succession of Signs, to the place of the Planet.

Latitude is the distance of a Planet from the Ecliptic, either towards the North or South, by which means we come to say, a Planet has either Septentrional or Meridional Latitude, when either he recedes from the Ecliptic towards the North or South.

Only the Sun continually moves in the Ecliptic, and never has any latitude.

Declination of a Planet is his distance from the Equator, and as he declines from thence either Northward or Southward, so is his declination nominated either North or South.

CHAPTER VII.

Of the twelve Houses,
their Nature and signification.

As before we have said there are twelve Signs, and also twelve Houses of Heaven, so now we are come to relate the nature of these twelve Houses; the exact knowledge whereof is so requisite, that he who shall learn the nature of the Planets and Signs without exact judgement of the Houses, is like an improvident man, that furnishes himself with variety of Household stuff, having no place wherein to bestow them.

There is nothing pertaining to the life of man in this world, which in one way or other has not relation to one of the twelve Houses of Heaven, and as the twelve Signs are appropriate to the particular members of man's body; so also do the twelve houses represent not only the several parts of man, but his actions, quality of life and living, and the curiosity and judgement of our Forefathers in Astrology, was such, as they have allotted to every house a particular signification, and so distinguished human accidents throughout the whole twelve houses, as he that understands the Questions pertaining to each of them, shall not want sufficient grounds whereon to judge or give a rational answer upon any contingent accident, and success thereof.

Of the first House and its signification.

The first house, which contains all that part of Heaven from the line where the figure one stands, until the figure two, where the second house begins.

It has signification of the life of man, of the stature, colour, complexion, form and shape of him that propounds the Question, or is born; in Eclipses and great Conjunctions, and upon the ☉ his annual ingress into ♈; it signifies the common people, or general State of that Kingdom where the Figure is erected.

And as it is the first house, it represents the head and face of man, so that if either ♄, ♂ or ☋ be in this house, either at the time of the Question, or at the time of birth, you shall observe some blemish in the face, or in that member appropriate to the Sign that then is upon the cusp of the house; as if ♈ be in the Ascendant, the mark, mole, or scar is without fail in the head or face; and if few degrees of the Sign ascend, the mark is in the upper part of the head; if the middle of the Sign be on the cusp, the mole, mark or scar is in the middle of the face, or near it; if the later degrees ascend, the face is blemished near the chin, towards the neck. This I have found true in hundreds of examples.

Of colours, it has the White; that is, if a Planet be in this house that has signification of white, the complexion of the Party is more pale, white or wan; or if you inquire after the colour of the clothes of any man, if his significator be in the first house, and in a Sign corresponding, the party's apparel is white or grey, or somewhat near that colour, so also if the Question be for Cattle; when their Significators are found in this house, it denotes them to be of that colour or near it: The house is Masculine.

The Consignificators of this house are ♈ and ♄; for as this house is the first house, so is ♈ the first Sign, and ♄ the first of the Planets, and therefore when ♄ is but moderately well fortified, in this house, and in any benevolent aspect of ♃, ♀, ☉ or ☽, it promises a good sober constitution of body, and usually long life: ☿ does also joy in this house, because it represents the Head, and he the Tongue, Fancy and Memory: When he is well dignified and placed in this house, he produces good *Orators*: It is called the Ascendant, because when the ☉ comes to the cusp of this house, he ascends, or then rises, and is visible in our Horizon.

Questions concerning the second House.

From this house is required judgement concerning the estate or fortune of him that asks the Question, of his Wealth or Poverty, of all movable Goods, Money lent, of Profit or gain, loss or damage; in suits of Law, it signifies a man's Friends or Assistants; in private Duels, the Querent's second; in an Eclipse or great Conjunction, the Poverty or Wealth of the people: in the ☉ his entrance into ♈, it represents the Ammunition, Allies and support the Commonwealth shall have; it imports their Magazines.

It represents in man the neck, and hinder parts of it towards the shoulders, of colours the green.

So that if one make demand concerning any thing specified above in this house, you must look for signification from hence: It's a Feminine house and Succedent, called in some Latin Authors *Anaphora.*

It has Cosignificators ♃ and ♉; for if ♃ be placed in this house, or be Lord here, it's an argument of an estate or fortune; ☉ and ♂ are never well placed in this house, either of them show dispersion of substance, according to the capacity and quality of him that is either born or asks the questions.

The third House.

Has signification of Brethren, Sisters, Cousins or Kindred, Neighbours, small Journeys, or inland-Journeys, oft removing from one place to another, Epistles, Letters, Rumours, Messengers: It rules the Shoulders, Arms, Hands and Fingers.

Of Colours, it governs the Red and Yellow, or Croceal, or Sorrel colour: It has Cosignificators, of the Signs ♊, of the Planets ♂; which is one reason why ♂ in this house, unless joined with ♄ is not very unfortunate. It is a Cadent house, and is the joy of the ☽; for if she be placed therein, especially in a moveable Sign, it's an argument of much travel, trotting and trudging, or of being seldom quiet. The house is Masculine.

The fourth house.

Gives Judgement of Fathers in general, and ever of his Father that inquires, or that is born; of Lands, Houses, Tenements, Inheritances, Tillage of the earth, Treasures hidden, the determination or end of anything; Towns, Cities or Castles, besieged or not besieged; all ancient Dwellings, Gardens, Fields, Pastures, Orchards; the quality and nature of the grounds one purchases, whether Vineyards, Cornfields, &c., whether the ground be Woody, Stony or barren.

The Sign of the fourth denotes the Town, the Lord thereof, the Governor. It rules the Breast, Lungs.

Of Colours, the Red: Its Cosignificator is ♋, and of Planets the ☉; we call it the Angle of the Earth, or *Imum Coeli*; it is Feminine, and the North Angle: In Nativities or Questions, this fourth house represents Fathers, so does the ☉ by day and ♄ by night; yet if the ☉ be herein placed, he is not ill, but rather shows the Father to be of a noble disposition, &c.

The fifth House.

By this house we judge of Children, of Ambassadors, of the state of a Woman with child, of Banquets, of Alehouses, Taverns, Plays, Messengers or Agents for Republics; of the Wealth of the Father, the Ammunition of a Town besieged; if the Woman with child shall bring forth male or female; of the health or sickness of his Son or Daughter that asks the Question.

It rules the Stomach, Liver, Heart, Sides and Back, and is masculine.

Of Colours, Black and White, or Honey-colour, and is a Succedent house. Its Cosignificators are ♌ and ♀, who does joy in this house, in regard it's the house of Pleasure, Delight and Merriment; it's wholly unfortunate by ♂ or ♄, and they therein show disobedient children and untoward.

The Sixth house.

It concerns Men and Maidservants, Galley slaves, Hogs, Sheep, Goats, Hares, Conies, all manner of lesser Cattle, and profit or loss got thereby; Sickness, its quality and cause, principal humour offending, curable or not curable, whether the disease be short or long; Day-Labourers, Tenants, Farmers, Shepherds, Hogherds, Neatherds, Warreners; and it signifies Uncles, or the Father's Brothers and Sisters.

It rules the inferior part of the Belly, and intestines even to the Arse: this house is a Feminine and Cadent house, unfortunate, as having no aspect to the Ascendant.

Of Colours, black colour. ♂ rejoices in this house, but his Cosignificator is of the Sign ♍, of Planets ☿; we usually find that ♂ and ♀ in Conjunction in this house, are arguments of a good Physician.

The seventh House.

It gives judgement of Marriage, and describes the person inquired after, whether it be Man or Woman; all manner of Love questions, our public enemies; the Defendant in a Lawsuit, in War the opposing party; all Quarrels, Duels, Lawsuits; in Astrology the Artist himself; in Physic the Physician; Thieves and Thefts; the person stealing, whether Man or Woman; Wives, Sweethearts; their shape, description, condition, Nobly or ignobly born; in an Annual ingress, whether War or Peace may be expected: of Victory, who overcomes, and who worsted; Fugitives or runaways; Banished and Outlawed men.

It has cosignificator ♎ and ☽, ♄ or ♂ unfortunate herein, show ill in Marriage.

Of colour, a dark Black colour.

It rules the Haunches, and the Navel to the Buttocks; and is called the Angle of the West: and is Masculine.

The eighth House.

The Estate of Men deceased, Death, its quality and nature; the Wills, Legacies and Testaments of Men deceased; Dowry of the Wife, Portion of the Maid, whether much or little, easy to be obtained or with difficulty. In Duels it represents the Adversary's Second; in Lawsuits the Defendant's friends. What kind of Death a Man shall die. It signifies fear and anguish of Mind. Who shall enjoy or be heir to the Deceased.

It rules the Privy-parts. Of colours, the Green and Black.

Of Signs it has ♏ for cosignificator, and ♄. The Hemorrhoids, the Stone, Strangury, Poisons, and Bladder are ruled by this House; and is a succedent House, and Feminine.

The ninth House.

By this House we give judgement of Voyages or long journeys beyond Seas; of Religious men, or Clergy of any kind, whether Bishops or inferior Ministers; Dreams, Visions, foreign Countries, of Books, Learning, Church Livings, or Benefices, Advowsons; of the kindred of one's Wife, & *sic e contrario.*

Of colours it has the Green and White.

Of man's body it rules the Fundament, the Hips and Thighs. ♐ and ♃ are cosignificators of this House; for if ♃ be herein placed it naturally signifies a devout man in his Religion, or one modestly given; I have oft observed when the Dragon's tail, or ♂ or ♄ have been unfortunately placed in this House; the Querent has either been little better than an Atheist or a desperate Sectarist: The ☉ rejoices to be in this House, which is Masculine, and Cadent.

The tenth House.

Commonly it personifies Kings, Princes, Dukes, Earls, Judges, prime Officers, Commanders in chief, whether in Armies or Towns; all sorts of Magistracy and Officers in Authority; Mothers, Honour, Preferment, Dignity, Office, Lawyers; the profession or Trade any one uses; it signifies Kingdoms, Empires, Dukedoms, Countries.

It has of colours Red and White, and rules the Knees and Hams.

It's called the *Medium coeli* or Midheaven, and is Feminine. Its cosignificators are ♑ and ♂; either ♃ or the ☉ do much Fortunate this House when they are placed therein, ♄ or ☋ usually deny honour, as to persons of quality, or but little esteem in the world to a vulgar person, not much joy in his Profession, Trade or Mastery, if a Mechanic.

The eleventh House.

It does naturally represent Friends and Friendship, Hope, Trust, Confidence, the Praise or Dispraise of any one; the Fidelity or falseness of Friends; as to Kings it personifies their Favourites, Councillors, Servants, their Associates or Allies, their Money, Exchequer or Treasure; in War their Ammunition and Soldiery; it represents Courtiers, &c., in a Commonwealth governed by a few of the Nobles and Commons, it personifies their assistance in Council: as in *London* the tenth House represents the Lords Major; the eleventh the Common-Council; the Ascendant the generality of the Commoners of the said City.

Of members it rules the Legs to the Ankles.

Of colours, it rules the Saffron or Yellow.

It has of the Signs ♒, and ☉ of the Planets; for cosignificators ♃ does especially rejoice in this House; it's a succedent House, and masculine, and in virtue is equivalent either to the seventh or fourth Houses.

The Twelfth House.

It has signification of private Enemies, of Witches, great Cattle, as Horses, Oxen, Elephants, &c. Sorrow, Tribulation, Imprisonments, all manner of affliction, self-undoing, &c., and of such men as maliciously undermine their neighbours, or inform secretly against them.

It has cosignificators ♓ and ♀; *Saturn* does much joy in that House, for naturally *Saturn* is author of mischief; and it rules in Man's body the Feet.

In colour it presents the Green.

It's a Cadent House, Feminine, and vulgarly sometimes called *Cataphora,* as all Cadent Houses may be. This is the true Character of the several Houses, according to the *Ptolemaic* Doctrine, and the experience myself have had for some years: I must confess the *Arabians* have made several other divisions of the Houses, but I could never in my practice find any verity in them, wherefore I say nothing of them.

CHAPTER VIII.

Of the Planet Saturn, *and his signification.*

HE is called usually *Saturn*, but in some Authors *Names.* *Chronos, Phaenon, Falcifer.*

He is the supremest or highest of all the Planets; is placed between *Jupiter* and the Firmament, he is not very bright or glorious, nor does he twinkle or sparkle, but is of a Pale, Wan or Leaden, Ashy colour, slow in Motion, finish- *Colour.* ing his Course through the twelve Signs of the Zodiac in 29 years 157 days, or thereabouts; his middle motion is two *Motion.* minutes and one second; his diurnal motion sometimes is three, four, five, or six minutes, or seldom more; his great- *Latitude.* est North latitude from the Ecliptic is two degrees 48 minutes; his South latitude from the Ecliptic is two degrees 49 minutes; and more than this he has not.

In the Zodiac he has two of the twelve Signs for his *Houses.* Houses, *viz., Capricorn* ♑ his Night-house; *Aquarius* ♒ his Day-house. He is Exaltation in ♎, he receives his Fall in ♈; he rejoices in the Sign *Aquarius.*

He governs the Airy Triplicity by day, which is com- *Triplicity.* posed of these Signs; ♊, ♎, ♒; in all the twelve Signs he has these degrees for his Terms, allotted him by *Ptolemy*:

In ♈	27	28	29	30		
In ♉	23	24	25	26		
In ♊	22	23	24	25		
In ♋	28	29	30			
In ♌	1	2	3	4	5	6
In ♍	19	20	21	22	23	24
In ♎	1	2	3	4	5	6
In ♏	28	29	30			
In ♐	21	22	23	24	25	
In ♑	26	27	28	29	30	
In ♒	1	2	3	4	5	6
In ♓	27	28	29	30		

Term.

The meaning whereof is, that if ♄ in any Question be in *Face.*

any of these degrees wherein he has a Term, he cannot be said to be peregrine, or void of essential dignities; or if he be in any of those degrees allotted him for his Face or Decanate, he cannot then be said to be peregrine: understand this in all the other Planets.

He has also these for his Face or Decanate.

In ♉ 21 22 23 24 25 26 27 28 29 30
In ♌ 1 2 3 4 5 6 7 8 9 10
In ♎ 11 12 13 14 15 16 17 18 19 20
In ♐ 21 22 23 24 25 26 27 28 29 30
In ♓ 1 2 3 4 5 6 7 8 9 10

He continues Retrograde 140 days.

He is five days in his first station before Retrogradation, and so many in his second station before Direction.

Nature. He is a Diurnal Planet, Cold and Dry (being far removed from the heat of the Sun) and moist Vapours, Melancholic, Earthly, Masculine, the greater Infortune, author of Solitariness, Malevolent, &c.

Manners & Actions, when well dignified. Then he is profound in Imagination, in his Acts severe, in words reserved, in speaking and giving very spare, in labour patient, in arguing or disputing grave, in obtaining the goods of this life studious and solicitous, in all manner of actions austere.

When ill. Then he is envious, covetous, jealous and mistrustful, timorous, sordid, outwardly dissembling, sluggish, suspicious, stubborn, a contemner of women, a close liar, malicious, murmuring, never contented, ever repining.

Corporature. Most part his Body more cold and dry, of a middle stature; his Complexion pale, swarthy or muddy, his Eyes little and black, looking downward; a broad Forehead, black or sad Hair, and it hard or rugged; great Ears, hanging; lowering Eyebrows, thick Lips and Nose, a rare or thin Beard, a lumpish, unpleasant Countenance, either holding his Head forward or stooping, his Shoulders broad and large, and many times crooked; his Belly somewhat short and lank; his Thighs spare, lean and not long; his Knees and Feet indecent, many times shovelling or hitting one against another, &c.

You must observe, if *Saturn* be Oriental of the *Sun*, the stature is more short, but decent and well composed. ♄ *Oriental.*

The man is more black and lean, and fewer Hairs; and again, if he want latitude, the body is more lean; if he have great latitude, the body is more fat or fleshy; if the latitude be Meridional or South, more fleshy, but quick in motion. *Occidental.*

If the latitude be North, hairy and much flesh.

♄ in his first station, a little fat.

In his second station, fat, ill favoured Bodies, and weak; and this observe constantly in all the other Planets.

In general he signifies Husbandman, Clowns, Beggars, Day-labourers, Old men, Fathers, Grandfathers, Monks, Jesuits, Sectarists. *Quality of Men.*

Curriers, Night-farmers, Miners under ground, Tinners, Potters, Broom-men, Plumbers, Brick-makers, Malsters, Chimney-sweepers, Sextons of Churches, Bearers of dead corpses, Scavengers, Hostlers, Colliers, Carters, Gardeners, Ditchers, Chandlers, Dyers of black Cloth, a Herdsman, Shepherd or Cow-keeper. *Profession.*

All Impediments in the right Ear, Teeth, all quartan Agues proceeding of cold, dry and melancholy Distempers, Leprosies, Rheumes, Consumptions, black Jaundice, Palsies, Tremblings, vain Fears, Fantasies, Dropsy, the Hand and Foot-gout, Apoplexies, Dog-hunger, too much flux of the Hemorrhoids, Ruptures if in *Scorpio* or *Leo*, in any ill aspect with *Venus*. *Sicknesses.*

Sour, Bitter, Sharp; in man's body he principally rules the Spleen. *Savours.*

He governs Bearsfoot, Starwort, Wolf-bane, Hemlock, Fern, Hellebore the white and black, Henbane, Ceterach or Finger-fern, Clotbur or Burdock, Parsnip, Dragon, Pulse, Vervain, Mandrake, Poppy, Moss, Nightshade, Bythwind, Angelica, Sage, Box, Tutsan, Orage or golden Herb, Spinach, Shepherd's Purse, Cumin, Horsetail, Fumitory. *Herbs.*

Tamarisk, Savine, Senna, Capers, Rue or Herbgrace, Polypody, Willow or Sallow Tree, Yew-tree, Cypress tree, Hemp, Pine-tree. *Plants and Trees.*

Beasts, &c.   The Ass, Cat, Hare, Mouse, Mole, Elephant, Bear, Dog, Wolf, Basilisk, Crocodile, Scorpion, Toad, Serpent, Adder, Hog, all manner of creeping Creatures breeding of putrefaction, either in the Earth, Water or Ruins of Houses.

Fishes   The Eel, Tortoise, Shell-fishes.

Birds, &c.   The Bat or Blude-black, Crow, Lapwing, Owl, Gnat, Crane, Peacock, Grasshopper, Thrush, Blackbird, Ostrich, Cuckoo.

Places.   He delights in Deserts, Woods, obscure Valleys, Caves, Dens, Holes, Mountains, or where men have been buried, Churchyards, &c. Ruined Buildings, Coal-mines, Sinks, Dirty or Stinking Muddy Places, Wells and Houses of Offices, &c.

Minerals.   He rules over Lead, the Loadstone, the Dross of all Metals, as also the Dust and Rubbish of everything.

Stones.   Sapphire, Lapis Lazuli, all black, ugly Country Stones not polishable, and of a sad ashy or black colour.

Weather.   He causes Cloudy, Dark, obscure Air, cold and hurtful, thick, black and cadence Clouds: but of this more particularly in a Treatise by itself.

Winds.   He delights in the East quarter of Heaven, and causes Eastern Winds, at the time of gathering any Plant belonging to him, the Ancients did observe to turn their faces towards the East in his hour, and he, if possible, in an Angle, either in the Ascendant, or tenth, or eleventh house, the ☽ applying by a △ or ✶ to him.

Orb.   His Orb is nine degrees before and after; that is, his influence begins to work, when either he applies, or any Planet applies to him, and is within nine degrees of his aspect, and continues in force until he is separate nine degrees from that aspect.

In Generation he rules the first and eighth month after Conception.

Years.   The greatest years he signifies - 465.
His greater - 57.
His mean years - 43 *and a half.*
His least - 30.

The meaning whereof is this; Admit we frame a new Building, erect a Town or City, or a Family, or principality is begun when *Saturn* is essentially and accidentally strong, the Astrologer may probably conjecture the Family, Principality, &c. may continue 465 years in honour, &c, without any sensible alteration: Again, if in one's Nativity *Saturn* is well dignified, is Lord of the Geniture, &c. then according to nature he may live 57 years; if he be meanly dignified, then the Native but 43; if he be Lord of the Nativity, and yet weak, the child may live 30 years, hardly any more; for the nature of *Saturn* is cold and dry, and those qualities are destructive to man, &c.

As to Age, he relates to decrepit old men; Fathers, Grandfathers, the like in Plants, Trees, and all living Creatures.

Countries. Late Authors say he rules over *Bavaria, Saxony, Stiria, Romandiola, Ravenna, Constantia, Ingoldstad.*

Angel. Is *Cassiel*, alias *Captiel*.

His Friends are ♃, ☉ and ☿; his enemies ♂ and ♀.

We call *Saturday* his day, for then he begins to rule at ☉rise, and rules the first hour and eighth of that day.

CHAPTER IX.

Of the Planet Jupiter, *and his signification.*

*J*upiter is placed next to *Saturn* (amongst the Ancients) you shall sometimes find him called *Zeus, or Phaeton:* He is the greatest in appearance to our eyes of all the Planets (the ☉, ☽ and ♀ excepted): in his Colour he is *Colour.* bright, clear, and of an Azure colour. In his Motion he *Motion.* exceeds *Saturn*, finishing his course through the twelve Signs in twelve years: his middle motion is 4 min. 59 seconds: his Diurnal motion is 8 10 12, or 14 min, hardly any more.

Latitude. His greatest North latitude is 1 38
His greatest South latitude is 1 40

Houses. He has two of the twelve Signs of the Zodiac for his houses, *viz.,* ♐ his Day-house, and ♓ his Night-house.

He receives Detriment in Ⅱ and ♍: He is Exalted in ♋, has his Fall in ♑.

Triplicity.   He rules the Fiery Triplicity by night, *viz*, ♈, ♌, ♐.

Terms.   He has also these degrees allotted for his Terms, *viz.*

In ♈	1	2	3	4	5	6		
In ♉	16	17	18	19	20	21	22	
In Ⅱ	8	9	10	11	12	13	14	
In ♋	7	8	9	10	11	12	13	
In ♌	20	21	22	23	24	25		
In ♍	14	15	16	17	18			
In ♎	12	13	14	15	16	17	18	19
In ♏	7	8	9	10	11	12	13	14
In ♐	1	2	3	4	5	6	7	8
In ♑	13	14	15	16	17	18	19	
In ♒	21	22	23	24	25			
In ♓	9	10	11	12	13	14		

Face.   He has assigned him for his Face or Decanate,

Of Ⅱ	1	2	3	4	5	6	7	8	9	10
Of ♌	11	12	13	14	15	16	17	18	19	20
Of ♎	21	22	23	24	25	26	27	28	29	30
Of ♑	1	2	3	4	5	6	7	8	9	10
Of ♓	11	12	13	14	15	16	17	18	19	20

He is Retrograde about 120 days, is five days in his first station before retrogradation, and four days stationary before Direction.

Nature.   He is a Diurnal, Masculine Planet, Temperately Hot and Moist, Airy, Sanguine, the greater Fortune, author of Temperance, Modesty, Sobriety, Justice.

Manners & Actions, when well placed.   Then is he Magnanimous, Faithful, Bashful, Aspiring in an honourable way at high matters, in all his actions a Lover of fair Dealing, desiring to benefit all men, doing Glorious things, Honourable and Religious, of sweet and affable Conversation, wonderfully indulgent to his Wife and Children, reverencing Aged men, a great Reliever of the Poor, full of Charity and Godliness, Liberal, hating all Sordid actions, Just, Wise, Prudent, Thankful, Virtuous: so that when you find

♃ the Significator of any man in a Question, or Lord of his Ascendant in a Nativity, and well dignified, you may judge him qualified as abovesaid.

When ♃ is unfortunate, then he wastes his Patrimony, *When ill.* suffers every one to cozen him, is Hypocritically Religious, Tenacious, and stiff in maintaining false Tenets in Religion; he is Ignorant, Careless, nothing Delightful in the love of his Friends; of a gross, dull Capacity, Schismatical, abasing himself in all Companies, crouching and stooping where no necessity is.

He signifies an upright, straight and tall Stature; brown, *Corporature.* ruddy and lovely Complexion; of an oval or long Visage, and it full or fleshy; high Forehead; large grey Eyes; his Hair soft, and a kind of auburn brown; much Beard; a large, deep Belly: strong proportioned Thighs and Legs; his Feet long, being the most indecent parts of his whole Body; in his Speech he is sober, and of grave Discourse.

The Skin more clear, his Complexion Honey-colour, or be- *Oriental.* tween a white and red, sanguine, ruddy Colour; great Eyes, the Body more fleshy, usually some Mole or Scar in the right Foot.

A pure and lovely Complexion, the Stature more short, *Occidental.* the Hair a light Brown, or near a dark Flaxen; smooth, bald about the Temple or Forehead.

He signifies Judges, Senators, Councillors, Ecclesiasti- *Men & their* cal men, Bishops, Priests, Ministers, Cardinals, Chancel- *quality in* lors, Doctors of the Civil Law, young Scholars and Stu- *general.* dents in a University or College, Lawyers.

Clothiers, Woolen-Drapers.

Pleurisy, all Infirmities in the Liver, left Ear, Apoplex- *Diseases.* ies, Inflammation of the Lungs, Palpitations and Trembling of the Heart, Cramps, pain in the Backbone, all Diseases lying in the Veins or Ribs, and proceeding from corruption of Blood, Squinzies. Windiness, all Putrefaction in the Blood, or Fevers proceeding from too great abundance thereof.

He governs the Sweet or well scented Odours; or that *Savours.* Odour which in smell is no way extreme or offensive.

Sea-green or Blue, Purple, Ash-colour, a mixed Yellow *Colours.* and Green.

Herbs and Drugs. Cloves and Clove-Sugar, Mace, Nutmeg, Gillyflower, the Strawberry, the herb Balsam, Betony, Centaury, Flax, Arsesmart, Fumitory, Lungwort, Pimpernel, Wallwort, Oregano or Wild Marjoram, Rhubarb, Self-heal, Borage, Bugloss, Wheat, Willow-herb, Thorough-leaf, Violets, Laskwort, Liverwort, Basil, Pomegranates, Peony, Liquorice, Mint, Mastic, the Daisy, Feversend, Saffron.

Plants, Trees. Cherry-tree, Birch-tree, Mulberry-tree, Coral-tree, the Oak, Bayberries, Olive, Gooseberries, Almond tree, the Ivy, Manna, Mace, the Vine, the Fig tree, the Ash, the Pear tree, the Hazel, the Beech tree, the Pine, Raisins.

Beasts. The Sheep, the Hart or Stag, the Doe, the Ox, Elephant, Dragon, Tiger, Unicorn, those Beasts which are Mild and Gentle, and yet of great benefit to Mankind, are appropriate to him.

Birds. The Stork, the Snipe, the Lark, the Eagle, the Stockdove, the Partridge, Bees, Pheasant, Peacock, the Hen.

Fishes. The Dolphin, the Whale, Serpent, Sheath-fish or River Whale.

Places. He delights in or near Altars of Churches, in public Conventions, Synods, Convocations, in Places neat, sweet, in Wardrobes, Courts of Justice, Oratories.

Mineral. Tin.

Precious Stones. Amethyst, the Sapphire, the Smarage or Emerald, Hyacinth, Topaz, Crystal, Bezoar, Marble, and that which in *England* we call Freestone.

Weather. He usually produces serenity, pleasant and healthful North Winds, and by his gentle Beams allays the ill weather of any former Malignant Planet.

Winds. He governs the North Wind, that part which tends to the East.

Orb. His Radiation or Orb, is nine degrees before and after any of his aspect.

Generation. He governs the second and tenth Month; his proper seat in man is the Liver; and in the Elements he rules the Air.

Years. His greatest years are 428, his greater 79, his mean 45, least 12.

Age. Men of middle age, or of a full Judgement and Discretion.

He governs the second Climate.   *Climate.*

Babylon, Persia, Hungary, Spain, Cologne.   *Countries.*

The number of three is attributed to him.   *Number.*

Zadkiel.   *Angel.*

Thursday, and rules the first hour after ☉ rise, and the eighth; the length of the Planetary hour you must know by the rising of the ☉, and a Table hereafter following.   *Day of the week.*

All Planets except ♂ are friends to ♃. In gathering any Herb appropriated to ♃, see that he be very powerful either in Essential or Accidental Dignities, and the ☽ in some manner in good aspect with him, and if possible, let her be in some of his Dignities, &c.

CHAPTER X.

Of the Planet **Mars,** *and his several significations.*

MARS does in order succeed *Jupiter*, whom the Ancients sometimes called *Mavors, Ares, Pyroeis, Gradivus;* he is less in body than *Jupiter* or *Venus*, and appears to our sight of a shining, fiery, sparkling colour; he finishes his course in the Zodiac in one year 321 days, or thereabouts; his greatest latitude North is 4 31 min. his South is 6 degr. and 47.   *Colour in Element.*   *Latitude.*

His mean motion is 31 min. 27 seconds.   *Motion.*

His diurnal motion is sometimes 32, 34, 36, 38, 40, 42, 44 min. a day, seldom more.

He has ♈ for his Day-house, and ♏ for his Night-house; he is exalted in 28 degr. of ♑, and is depressed in 28 ♋, he receives detriment in ♎ and ♉; he is retrograde 80 days; stationary before he be retrograde, two or three days, &c. He is stationary before direction two days; after, but one day.

He governs wholly the Watery Triplicity, *viz.* ♋, ♏, ♓.   *Triplicity.*

In the whole twelve Signs, *Ptolemy* assigns him these degrees for Terms, *viz.*   *Terms.*

In ♈ 22 23 24 25 26
In ♉ 27 28 29 30
In ♊ 26 27 28 29 30
In ♋ 1 2 3 4 5 6
In ♌ 26 27 28 29 30
In ♍ 25 26 27 28 29 30
In ♎ 25 26 27 28 29 30
In ♏ 1 2 3 4 5 6
In ♐ 26 27 28 29 30
In ♑ 20 21 22 23 24 25
In ♒ 26 27 28 29 30
In ♓ 21 22 23 24 25 26

Face.   He has allotted him for his Face these degrees.

In ♈   1 2 3 4 5 6 7 8 9 10
In ♊   11 12 13 14 15 16 17 18 19 20
In ♌   21 22 23 24 25 26 27 28 29 30
In ♏   1 2 3 4 5 6 7 8 9 10
In ♑   11 12 13 14 15 16 17 18 19 20
In ♓   21 22 23 24 25 26 27 28 29 30

Nature.   He is a Masculine, Nocturnal Planet, in nature hot and dry, choleric and fiery, the lesser Infortune, author of Quarrels, Strifes, Contentions.

Manners when well dignified.   In feats of War and Courage invincible, scorning any should exceed him, subject to no Reason, Bold, Confident, Immovable, Contentious, challenging all Honour to themselves, Valiant, lovers of War and things pertaining thereunto, hazarding himself to all Perils, willingly will obey nobody; nor submit to any, a large Reporter of his own Acts, one that fights all things in comparison of Victory, and yet of prudent behaviour in his own affairs.

When ill placed.   Then he is Prattler without modesty or honesty, a lover of Slaughter and Quarrels, Murder, Thievery, a promoter of Sedition, Frays and Commotions; an Highway-Thief, as wavering as the Wind, a Traitor, of turbulent Spirit, Perjured, Obscene, Rash, Inhumane, neither fearing God or caring for man, Unthankful, Treacherous, Oppressors, Ravenous, Cheaters, Furious, Violent.

Generally Martialists have this form: they are but of *Corporature.*
middle Stature, their Bodies strong, and their Bones big,
rather lean than fat; their Complexion of a brown, ruddy
colour, or of a high colour, their Visage round, their Hair
red or sandy flaxen, and many times crisping or curling,
sharp hazel Eyes, and they piercing, a bold confident countenance, and the man active and fearless.

When ♂ is Oriental, he signifies Valiant men, some *Oriental.*
white mixed with their redness, a decent tallness of Body,
hairy of his Body.

Very ruddy Complexioned, but mean in Stature; little *Occidental.*
Head, a smooth Body, and not hairy; yellow Hair, stiff; the
natural humours generally more dry.

Princes Ruling by Tyranny and Oppression, or Tyrants, *Qualities*
Usurpers, new Conquerors. *men and*
Profession.

Generals of Armies, Colonels, Captains, or any Soldiers
having command in Armies, all manner of Soldiers, Physicians, Apothecaries, Surgeons, Alchemists, Gunners, Butch-
ers, Marshals, Sergeants, Bailiffs, Hangmen, Thieves, Smiths,
Bakers, Armourers, Watchmakers, Botchers, Tailors, Cut-
lers of Swords and Knives, Barbers, Dyers, Cooks, Carpen-
ters, Gamesters, Bear-wards, Tanners, Curriers.

The Gall, the left Ear, tertian Fevers, pestilent burning *Diseases.*
Fevers, Migraines in the Head, Carbuncles, the Plague and all
Plague-sores, Burnings, Ringworm, Blisters, Frenzies, mad
sudden distempers in the Head, Yellow-jaundice, Bloodyflux,
Fistulas, all Wounds and Diseases in men's Genitals, the Stone
both in the Reins and Bladder, Scars or small Pox in the Face,
all hurts by Iron, the Shingles, and such other Diseases as
arise by abundance of too much Choler, Anger or Passion.

He delights in Red colour, or Yellow, fiery and shining *Colours and*
like Saffron; and in those Savours which are bitter, sharp *Savours.*
and burn the Tongue; of Humours, Choler.

The Herbs which we attribute to ♂ are such as come *Herbs.*
near to redness, whose leaves are pointed and sharp, whose
taste is caustic and burning, love to grow on dry places, are
corrosive and penetrating the Flesh and Bones with a most
subtle heat: They are as follows: The Nettle, all manner of

Thistles, Restharrow or Cammock, Devils-milk or Petty spurge, the white and red Brambles, the white called vulgarly by the Herbalists Ramme, Lingwort, Onions, Scammony, Garlic, Mustard-seed, Pepper, Ginger, Leeks, Dittander, Horehound, Hemlock, red Sanders, Tamarinds, all Herbs attracting or drawing choler by Sympathy, Radish, Castoreum, Aresmart, Assarum, Carduus Benedictus, Cantharides.

Trees. All Trees which are prickly, as the Thorn, Chestnut.

Beasts and Animals. Panther, Tiger, Mastiff, Vulture, Fox; of living creatures, those that are Warlike, Ravenous and Bold, the Castor, Horse, Mule, Ostrich, the Goat, the Wolf, the Leopard, the wild Ass, the Gnats, Flies, Lapwing, Cockatrice, the Griffin, Bear.

Fishes. The Pike, the Shark, the Barbel, the Fork-fish, all stinking Worms, Scorpions.

Birds. The Hawk, the Vulture, the Kite or Glead, (all ravenous Fowl), the Raven, Cormorant, the Owl, (some say the Eagle) the Crow, the Pye.

Places. Smith's, Shops, Furnaces, Slaughterhouses, places where Bricks or Charcoals are burned or have been burned, Chimneys, Forges.

Minerals. Iron, Antimony, Arsenic, Brimstone, Ochre.

Stones. Adamant, Loadstone, Bloodstone, Jasper, the many coloured Amethyst, the Touchstone, red Lead or Vermilion.

Weather. Red Clouds, Thunder, Lightning, Fiery impressions, and pestilent Airs, which usually appear after a long time of dryness and fair Weather, by improper and unwholesome Mists.

Winds. He stirs up the Western Winds.

Orb. His Orb is only seven degrees before and after any of his aspects.

Years. In man he governs the flourishing time of Youth, and from 41 to 56; his greatest years are 264, greater 66, mean 40, less 15.

Countries. *Sarmatia, Lombardy, Batavia, Ferrara, Gothland,* and the third Climate.

Day of the week. He governs Tuesday, and therein the first hour and eighth from ☉ rise, and in Conception the third month.

Angel. *Samael.* His Friends are only ♀; Enemies all the other Planets.

CHAPTER XI.

Of the Sun, *and his general and particular significations.*

The *Sun* is placed in the middle of all the Planets, and is called amongst the Ancients, both Poets and Historians, *Sol, Titan, Ilios, Phoebus, Apollo, Pean, Osyris, Diespiter.* It's needless to mention his Colour, being so continually visible to all mortal men: He passes through all the twelve Signs of the Zodiac in one year, or 365 days and certain hours: His mean motion is 59 8; yet his diurnal motion is sometimes 57m 16 seconds, sometimes more, never exceeding 61 minutes and six seconds. *Sol.* *Motion.*

He always moves in the Ecliptic, and is ever void of latitude, so that it is very improper in any Astrologian to speak of the ☉ his latitude.

He has only the Sign of ♌ for his house, and ♒ for his detriment. *House.*

He is exalted in the 19 degree of ♈, and receives his fall in 19 ♎.

The *Sun* governs the fiery Triplicity, *viz.,* ♈, ♌, ♐ by day. *Triplicity.* *Terms.*

He has no degrees of the twelve Signs admitted him for his Terms, though some affirm, if he be in the six Northern Signs, *viz.* ♈, ♉, ♊, ♋, ♌, ♍, he shall be said to be in his Terms, but because there is no reason for it, I leave it as Idle.

In the twelve Signs he has these degrees for his Decanate or Faces.

In ♈,	the 11 12 13 14 15 16 17 18 19 20
In ♊,	the 21 22 23 24 25 26 27 28 29 30
In ♍,	the 1 2 3 4 5 6 7 8 9 10
In ♏,	the 11 12 13 14 15 16 17 18 19 20
In ♑,	the 21 22 23 24 25 26 27 28 29 30

The ☉ is always direct, and never can be said to be Retrograde; it's true, he moves more slowly at one time than another.

Nature.   He is naturally Hot, Dry, but more temperate than ♂, is a Masculine, Diurnal Planet, Equivalent, if well dignified to a Fortune.

Manners when well dignified   Very faithful, keeping their Promises with all punctuality, a kind of itching desire to Rule and Sway where he comes: Prudent, and of incomparable Judgement; of great Majesty and Stateliness, Industrious to acquire Honour and a large Patrimony, yet as willingly departing therewith again; the Solar man usually speaks with gravity, but not many words, and those with great confidence and command of his own affection; full of Thought, Secret, Trusty, speaks deliberately, and notwithstanding his great Heart, yet is he Affable, Tractable, and very humane to all people, one loving Sumptuousness and Magnificence, and whatever is honourable; no sordid thoughts can enter his heart, &c.

When ill dignified.   Then the Solar man is Arrogant and Proud, disdaining all men, cracking of his Pedigree, he is Purblind in Sight and Judgement, restless, troublesome, domineering; a mere vapour, expensive, foolish, endowed with no gravity in words, or soberness in Actions, a Spendthrift, wasting his Patrimony, and hanging on other men's charity, yet thinks all men are bound to him, because a Gentleman born.

Corporature.   Usually the ☉ presents a man of a good, large and strong Corporature; a yellow, saffron Complexion, a round, large Forehead: goggle Eyes or large, sharp and piercing; a Body strong and well composed, not so beautiful as lovely, full of heat, their hair yellowish, and therefore quickly bald, much Hair on their Beard, and usually a high ruddy Complexion, and their bodies fleshy, in conditions they are very bountiful, honest, sincere, well-minded, of great and large Heart, High-minded, of healthful Constitution, very humane; yet sufficiently Spirited, not Loquacious.

Oriental.   In the ☉, we can only say he is Oriental in the Figure, or in the Oriental quarter of the Figure, or Occidental, &c., all other Planets are either Oriental when they rise, or appear before him in the morning.

Occidental.   Occidental, when they are seen above the earth after he is set.

He signifies Kings, Princes, Emperors, &c. Dukes, Marquesses, Earls, Barons, Lieutenants, Deputy-Lieutenants of Counties, Magistrates, Gentlemen in general, Courtiers, desirers of Honour and preferment, Justices of Peace, Majors, High-Sheriffs, High-Constables, great Huntsmen, Stewards of Noblemen's houses, the principal Magistrate of any City, Town, Castle or Country Village; yea, though a petty Constable, where no better, or greater Officer is; Goldsmiths, Braziers, Pewterers, Coppersmiths, Minters of Money.

Quality of men and their professions:

Pimples in the Face, Palpitation or Trembling, or any Diseases of the Brain or Heart, Tympanies, Infirmities of the Eyes, Cramps, sudden swoonings, Diseases of the Mouth, and stinking Breaths, Catarrhs, rotten Fevers; principally in man he governs the Heart, the Brain and right Eye, and vital Spirit, in Women the left Eye.

Sickness.

Of Colours he rules the Yellow, the colour of Gold, the Scarlet or the clear Red, some say Purple. In Savours, he likes well a mixture of Sour and Sweet together, or the Aromatical flavour, being a little Bitter and Stiptical, but withal Confortative and a little sharp.

Colours and Savours.

Those Plants which are subject to the ☉ do smell pleasantly, are of good savour, their Flowers are yellow or reddish, are in growth of Majestic form, they love open and Sunshine places, their principal Virtue is to strengthen the Heart, and comfort the Vitals, to clear the Eyesight, resist Poison, or to dissolve any Witchery, or Malignant Planetary Influences; and they are Saffron, the Laurel, the Pomecitron, the Vine, Enula Campana, Saint John's Wort, Amber, Musk, Ginger, Herbgrace, Balm, Marigold, Rosemary, Rosa solis, Cinnamon, Celandine, Eyebright, Peony, Barley, Cinquefoil, Spikenard, Lignum Aloes, Arsenic.

Herbs and Plants.

Ash tree, Palm, Laurel tree, the Myrrh tree, Frankincense, the Cane tree or plant, the Cedar, Heletrepion, the Orange and Lemon tree.

Trees.

The Lion, the Horse, the Ram, the Crocodile, the Bull, Goat, Nightworms or Glowworms.

Beasts.

The Sea Calf or Sea Fox, the Crabfish, the Starfish.

Fishes.

Birds. The Eagle, the Cock, the Phoenix, Nightingale, Peacock, the Swan, the Buzzard, the fly Cantharis, the Goshawk.

Places. Houses, Courts of Princes, Palaces, Theatres, all magnificent Structures being clear and decent, Halls, Dining Rooms.

Minerals or Metals. Amongst the Elements ☉ has domination of fire and clear shining flames; over metals, he rules Gold.

Stones. The Hyacinth, Chrysolite, Adamant, Carbuncle, the Etites stone found in Eagle's nests, the Pantaure, if such a stone be the Ruby.

Weather. He produces weather according to the season; in the Spring gentle moistening Showers; in the Summer heat in extremity if with ♂; in Autumn mists; in Winter small Rain.

Winds. He loves the East part of the World; and that wind which proceeds from that quarter.

Orb. Is 15 degrees before any aspect; and so many after separation.

Years. In age he rules youth, or when one is at the strongest; his greatest years are 1460, greater 120, mean 69, least 19.

Countries. Italy, Sicily, Bohemia; and the fourth Climate, Phoenicia, Chaldea.

Angel. Michael.

Day of the Week. He rules Sunday the first hour thereof, and the eighth; and in numbers the first and fourth; and in conceptions the fourth month. His Friends are all the Planets except ♄, who is his Enemy.

CHAPTER XII.

Of the planet **Venus** *and her several significations and nature.*

Name. After the Sun succeeds *Venus;* who is sometimes called *Cytherea, Aphrodite, Phosphoros, Vesperugo, Erycina.*

Colour in the Element. She is of a bright shining colour, and is well known amongst the vulgar by the name of the evening Star or *Hesperus;* and that is when she appears after the Sun is set: common people call her the morning Star, and the learned *Lucifer,* when she is

Motion. seen long before the rising of the Sun. Her mean motion is 59 min. and 8 seconds: her diurnal motion is sometimes

62 min. a day 64, 65, 66 or 70, 74, 76 minutes; but 82 min. she never exceeds. Her greatest North or South latitude is nine degr. and two min. In *February* 1643 she had eight degr. and 36 min. for her North latitude. *Latitude.*

She has ♉ and ♎ for her houses, she is exalted in 27 ♓; she receives detriment in ♈ and ♏ and has her fall in 27 ♍. *Houses.*

She governs the Earthly Triplicity by day *viz.* ♉, ♍, ♑; she is two days stationary before retrogradation, and so many before direction, and does usually continue retrograde 42 days. *Triplicity*

She has these degrees in every Sign for her terms. *Her Terms.*

In ♈, 7 8 9 10 11 12 13 14
In ♉, 1 2 3 4 5 6 7 8
In ♊, 15 16 17 18 19 20
In ♋, 21 22 23 24 25 26 27
In ♌, 14 15 16 17 18 19
In ♍, 8 9 10 11 12 13
In ♎, 7 8 9 10 11
In ♏, 15 16 17 18 19 20 21
In ♐, 9 10 11 12 13 14
In ♑, 1 2 3 4 5 6
In ♒, 13 14 15 16 17 18 19 20
In ♓, 1 2 3 4 5 6 7 8

These degrees are allowed for her Face.

In ♈,　21 22 23 24 25 26 27 28 29 30
In ♋,　1 2 3 4 5 6 7 8 9 10
In ♍,　11 12 13 14 15 16 17 18 19 20
In ♏,　21 22 23 24 25 26 27 28 29 30
In ♓,　1 2 3 4 5 6 7 8 9 10

She is a Feminine Planet, temperately Cold and Moist, Nocturnal, the lesser Fortune, author of Mirth and Jollity; the Elements, the Air and Water are Venereal; in the Humours, Phlegm with Blood, with the Spirit and Genital seed. *Element.* *Nature.*

She signifies a quiet man, not given to Law, Quarrel or Wrangling, not Vicious, Pleasant, Neat and Spruce, loving *Manners & quality when well placed.*

Mirth in his words and actions, cleanly in Apparel, rather Drinking much than Gluttonous, prone to Venery, oft entangled in Love-matters, Zealous in their affections, Musical, delighting in Baths and all honest merry Meetings, or Masks and Stage-plays; easy of Belief, and not given to Labour or taking any Pains, a Company-keeper, Cheerful, nothing Mistrustful, a right virtuous Man or Woman, oft had in some Jealousy, yet no cause for it.

When ill. Then he is Riotous, Expensive, wholly given to Looseness and Lewd companies of Women, nothing regarding his Reputation, coveting unlawful Beds, Incestuous, an Adulterer; Fanatical, a mere Skipjack, of no Faith, no Repute, no Credit; spending his Means in Alehouses, Taverns, and amongst Scandalous, Loose people; a mere Lazy companion, nothing careful of the things of this Life, or anything Religious; a mere Atheist and natural man.

Corporature. A man of fair, but not tall Stature, his Complexion being white, tending to a little darkness, which makes him more Lovely; very fair Lovely Eyes, and a little black; a round Face, and not large, fair Hair, smooth, and plenty of it, and it usually of a light brown colour, a lovely Mouth and cherry Lips, the Face pretty fleshy, a rolling wandering Eye, a Body very delightful, lovely and exceedingly well shaped, one desirous of Trimming and making himself neat and complete both in Clothes and Body, a love dimple in his Cheeks, a steadfast Eye, and full of amorous enticements.

Oriental. When Oriental the Body inclines to tallness; or a kind of upright straightness in Person, not corpulent or very tall, but neatly composed. A right Venerian person, is such as we say, a pretty, complete, handsome Man or Woman.

Occidental. When she is Occidental, the Man is of more short stature, yet very decent and comely in Shape and Form, well liked of all.

Qualities of men & profession. Musicians, Gamesters, Silk-men, Mercers, Linen-Drapers, Painters, Jewellers, Players, Lapidaries, Embroiderers, Women-tailors, Wives, Mothers, Virgins, Choristers, Fiddlers, Pipers, when joined with the ☽, Ballad singers, Perfumers, Seamstresses, Picture-drawers, Engravers, Upholsterers, Limners, Glovers, all such as sell those Commodities which adorn Women either in Body (as Clothes) or in Face, (as Complexion-waters.)

Diseases by her signified, are principally in the Matrix and members of Generation; in the reins, belly, back, navel and those parts; the Gonorrhoea or running of the Reins, French or Spanish Pox; any disease arising by inordinate lust. Priapism, impotency in generation, Hernias, &c. the Diabetes or pissing disease. *Sicknesses.*

In colours she signifies White, or milky Sky-colour mixed with brown, or a little Green. In Savours she delights in that which is pleasant and toothsome; usually in moist and sweet, or what is very delectable; in smells what is unctuous and Aromatical, and incites to wantonness. *Savours colours.*

Myrtle always green; all herbs which she governs have a sweet savour, a pleasant smell; a white flower; of a gentle humour, whose leaves are smooth and not jagged. She governs the Lily white and yellow, and the Lilly of the valley, and of the water. The Satyrion or Cuckoopint, Maidenhair, Violet; the white and yellow Daffodil. *Herbs and Plants.*

Sweet Apples, the white Rose, the Fig, the white Sycamore; wild Ash, Turpentine-tree, Olive, sweet Oranges, Mugwort, Ladies' mantle, Sanicle, Balm, Vervain, Walnuts, Almonds, Millet, Valerian, Thyme, Amber, Ladanum, Civet or Musk, Coriander, French Wheat, Peaches, Apricots, Plums, Raisins. *Trees.*

The Hart, the Panther, small cattle, Coney, the Calf, the Goat. *Beasts.*

Stockdove, Wagtail, the Sparrow, Hen, the Nightingale, the Thrush, Pelican, Partridge, Ficedula, a little Bird Feeding on Grapes; the Wren, Eagle, the Swan, the Swallow, the Owsel or Black bird, the Pye. *Birds.*

The Dolphin. *Fishes.*

Gardens, Fountains, Bride-chambers, fair lodgings, Beds, Hangings, Dancing Schools, Wardrobes. *Places.*

Copper, especially the Corinthian and White; Brass, all Lattenware. *Metals and Minerals.*

Cornelian, the Sky-coloured Sapphire, white and red Coral, Marcasite, Alabaster, *Lapis Lazuli* because it expels Melancholy, the Beryl, Chrysolite. *Stones.*

Wind and Weather.	She governs the South-wind being hot and moist; in the temperament of the Air, she rules the *Etesia;* she foretells in Summer, Serenity or clear weather; in Winter, rain or snow.
Orb.	Her Orb is 7 before and after any aspect of hers.
Years.	Her greatest years are 151, her greater 82, her mean 45, her least 8. In Man she governs Youth from 14 to 28.
Countries.	*Arabia, Austria, Campagna, Vienna, Polonia* the greater, *Turing, Parthia, Media, Cyprus*, and the sixth climate.
Angel.	Her Angel is *Anael.*
Day of the week.	Her day of the week Friday, of which she rules the first and eighth hour; and in conception the fifth Month. Her Friends are all the Planets except ♄.

CHAPTER XIII.
Of Mercury, *and his signification, nature and property.*

Name.	HE is called *Hermes, Stilbon, Cyllenius, Arcas. Mercury* is the least of all the Planets, never distant from the Sun above 27 degrees; by which reason he is sel-
Colour.	dom visible to our sight. He is of a dusky silver colour; his mean motion is 59 min. and 8 seconds; but he is sometimes so swift that he moves one degree and 40 min. in a day, never more; so that you are not to marvel if you find him sometimes go 66, 68, 70, 80, 86 or 100 in a day: he is Stationary one day, and retrograde 24 days.
Latitude.	His greatest South Latitude is 3 degr. 35 min. His greatest North Latitude is 3 deg. 33.min.
House.	He has ♊ and ♍ for his Houses, and is exalted in the 15 of ♍; he receives detriment in ♐ and ♓, his fall is in ♓.
Triplicity.	He rules the airy triplicity by night, *viz.* ♊ ♎ ♒.
Terms.	He has these degrees in every Sign for his Terms.

In ♈ 15, 16, 17, 18, 19, 20, 21
In ♉ 9, 10, 11, 12, 13, 14, 15
In ♊ 1, 2, 3, 4, 5, 6, 7
In ♋ 14, 15, 16, 17, 18, 19, 20
In ♌ 7, 8, 9, 10, 11, 12, 13
In ♍ 1, 2, 3, 4, 5, 6, 7

In ♎︎ 20, 21, 22, 23, 24
In ♏︎ 22, 23, 24, 25, 26, 27
In ♐︎ 15, 16, 17, 18, 19, 20
In ♑︎ 7, 8, 9, 10, 11, 12
In ♒︎ 7, 8, 9, 10, 11, 12
In ♓︎ 15, 16, 17, 18, 19, 20

These subsequent degrees are his Faces or Decanate: *Face.*

In ♉︎ 1, 2, 3, 4, 5, 6, 7, 8, 9, 10
In ♋︎ 11, 12, 13, 14, 15, 16, 17, 18, 19, 20
In ♍︎ 21, 22, 23, 24, 25, 26, 27, 28, 29, 30
In ♐︎ 1, 2, 3, 4, 5, 6, 7, 8, 9, 10
In ♒︎ 11, 12, 13, 14, 15, 16, 17, 18, 19, 20

We may not call him either Masculine or Feminine, for *Nature.* he is either the one or other as joined to any Planet; for if in ♂ with a Masculine Planet, he becomes Masculine; if with a Feminine, then Feminine, but of his own nature he is cold and dry, and therefore Melancholy; with the good he is good, with the evil Planets ill; In the Elements the Water; *Elements.* amongst the humours, the mixed, he rules the animal spirit: he is author of subtlety, tricks, devices, perjury, &c.

Being well dignified, he represents a man of a subtle and *Manners* political brain, intellect, and cogitation; an excellent dispu- *when well* tant or Logician, arguing with learning and discretion, and *placed.* using much eloquence in his speech, a searcher into all kinds of Mysteries and Learning, sharp and witty, learning almost anything without a Teacher; ambitious of being exquisite in every Science, desirous naturally of travel and seeing foreign parts: a man of an unwearied fancy, curious in the search of any occult knowledge; able by his own *Genius* to produce wonders; given to Divination and the more secret knowledge; if he turn Merchant, no man exceeds him in a way of Trade or invention of new ways whereby to obtain wealth.

A troublesome wit, a kind of Phrenetic man, his tongue *Manners,* and Pen against every man, wholly bent to fool his estate and *when ill* time in prating and trying nice conclusions to no purpose; a *placed or* great liar, boaster, prattler, busybody, false, a tale-carrier, given *dignified.* to wicked Arts, as Necromancy and such like ungodly knowledges; easy of belief, an ass or very idiot, constant in no place or opinion, cheating and thieving everywhere; a newsmonger, pretending all manner of knowledge, but guilty of no true or solid learning; a trifler; a mere frantic fellow; if he prove a Divine, then a mere verbal fellow, frothy, of no judgement, easily perverted, constant in nothing but idle words and bragging.

Corporature.   Vulgarly he denotes one of a high stature and straight thin spare body, a high forehead and somewhat narrow long face, long nose; fair eyes, neither perfectly black or grey, thin lips and nose, little hair on the chin, but much on his head, and it a sad brown inclining to blackness; long arms, fingers and hands; his complexion like an Olive or Chestnut colour. You must more observe ☿ than all the Planets; for having any aspect to a Planet, he does more usually partake of the influence of that Planet than any other does: if with ♄ then heavy, with ♃ more temperate, with ♂ more rash, with ☉ more genteel, with ♀ more jesting, with ☽ more shiftier.

Oriental.   When he is Oriental, his complexion is honey colour, or like one well Sunburnt; in the stature of his body not very high, but well jointed, small eyes, not much hair; in very truth, according to the height of body, very well composed, but still a defect in the complexion, *viz.* swarthy brown, and in the tongue, *viz.* all for his own ends.

Occidental.   When Occidental, a tawny visage, lank body, small slender limbs, hollow eyes, and sparkling and red or fiery; the whole frame of body inclining to dryness.

Quality of men and professions: He generally signifies all literary men, Philosophers, Mathematicians, Astrologians, Merchants, Secretaries, Scriveners, Diviners, Sculptors, Poets, Orators, Advocates, Schoolmasters, Stationers, Printers, Exchangers of Money Attorneys, Emperor's Ambassadors, Commissioners, Clerks, Artificers, generally Accountants, Solicitors, sometimes Thieves, prattling muddy Ministers, busy Sectaries, and they unlearned; Grammarians, Tailors, Carriers, Messengers, Footmen, Usurers.

Sickness.   All Vertigos, Lethargies or giddiness in the Head, Madness, either Lightness, or any Disease of the Brain; Phthisis, all stammering and imperfection in the Tongue, vain and fond Imaginations, all defects in the Memory, Hoarseness, dry Coughs, too much abundance of Spittle, all snaffling and snuffling in the Head or Nose; the Hand and Feet Gout, Dumbness, Tongue-evil, all evils in the Fancy and intellectual parts.

Mixed and new colours, the Grey mixed with Sky-colour, such as is on the Neck of the Stockdove, Linsie-woolsie colours, or consisting of many colours mixed in one. Of Savours a hodgepodge of all things together, so that no one can give it any true name; yet usually such as do quicken the Spirits, are subtle and penetrate, and in a manner insensible.   *Colours and Savours.*

Herbs attributed to ☿, are known by the various colour of the flower, and love sandy barren places, they bear their seed in husks or pods, they smell rarely or subtlety, and have principle relation to the tongue, brain, lungs or memory; they dispel wind and comfort the Animal spirits, and open obstructions. Beans, three leaved-grass, the Walnut and Walnut-tree; the Filbert-tree and Nut; the Elder tree, Adders tongue, Dragonwort, Twopenny grass, Lungwort, Aniseeds, Cubebs, Marjoram. What herbs are used for the Muses and Divination, as Vervain, the Reed; of Drugs, Treacle, Hiera, Diambra.   *Herbs and Plants.*

The Hyena, Ape, Fox, Squirrel, Weasel, the Spider, the Greyhound, the Hermaphrodite, being partaker of both sexes; all cunning creatures.   *Beasts.*

The Linnet, the Parrot, the Popinian, the Swallow, the Pye, the Beetle, Pismires, Locusts, Bees, Serpent, the Crane.   *Birds.*

The Fork-fish, Mullet.   *Fishes.*

Tradesmen's shops, Markets, Fairs, Schools, Common Halls, Bowling Alleys, Ordinaries, Tennis Courts.   *Places.*

Quicksilver.   *Minerals.*

The Millstone, Marcasite or fire-stone, the Achates, Topaz, Vitriol, all stones of diverse colours.   *Stones.*

He delights in Windy, Stormy and Violent, Boisterous Weather, and stirs up that Wind which the Planet signifies to which he applies; sometimes Rain, at other times Hail, Lightning, Thunder and Tempests, in hot Countries Earthquakes, but this   *Winds and Weather.*

must be observed really from the Sign and Season of the year.

Orb.   His orb is seven degrees before and after any aspect.

Years.   His greatest years are 450; his greater 76; his mean 48; his little or least 20: in Conceptions he governs the sixth month.

Countries.   He has *Greece, Flanders, Egypt, Paris.*

Angel.   His Angel is named *Raphael.*

Day of the   He governs Wednesday, the first hour thereof, and the eighth.
week. His Friends are ♃ ♀, ♄, his Enemies all the other Planets.

CHAPTER XIIII.
Of the Moon, *her properties and significations.*

Name.   THE *Moon* we find called by the Ancients, *Lucina, Cynthia, Diana, Phoebe, Latona, Noctiluca, Proserpina.* She is nearest to the Earth of all the Planets; her colour in the Element is vulgarly known: she finishes her course through
Motion. the whole twelve Signs in 27 days, 7 hours and 43 min. or thereabouts: her mean motion is 13 degr. 10 min. and 36 seconds, but she moves sometimes less and sometimes more, never exceeding 15 degr. and two min. in 24 hours space.

Latitude.   Her greatest North latitude is 5 degr. and 17 min. *or there-*
Her greatest South latitude is 5 degr. and 12 min. *abouts*

She is never Retrograde, but always direct; when she is slow in motion, and goes less in 24 hours than 13 degr. and 10 min. she is then equivalent to a Retrograde Planet.

House.   She has the Sign ♋ for her house, and ♑ for her detriment; she is exalted in 3 ♉ and has her fall in 3 degr. ♏. She governs the Earthly Triplicity by night, *viz.* ♉ ♍ ♑.
Triplicity. The *Sun* and she have no Terms assigned them.

In the twelve Signs she has these degrees for her Decanate or Face.

In ♉ 11, 12, 13, 14, 15, 16, 17, 18, 19, 20
In ♋ 21, 22, 23, 24, 25, 26, 27, 28, 29, 30

In ♎︎   1,   2,   3,   4,   5,   6,   7,   8,   9,   10
In ♐︎   11, 12, 13, 14, 15, 16, 17, 18, 19, 20
In ♒︎   21, 22, 23, 24, 25, 26, 27, 28, 29, 30

She is a Feminine, Nocturnal Planet, Cold, Moist and Phlegmatic.

Nature.

She signifies one of composed Manners, a soft, tender creature, a Lover of all honest and ingenious Sciences, a Searcher of, and Delighter in Novelties, natural propensity to flit and shift his Habitation, unsteadfast, wholly caring for the present Times, Timorous, Prodigal, and easily Frightened, however loving Peace, and to live free from the cares of this Life, if a Mechanic, the man learns many Occupations, and frequently will be tampering with many ways to trade in.

Manners or Actions when well placed or dignified.

A mere Vagabond, idle Person, hating Labour, a Drunkard, a Sot, one of no Spirit or Forecast, delighting to live beggarly and carelessly, one content in no condition of Life, either good or ill.

When ill.

She generally presents a man of fair stature, whitely coloured, the Face round, grey Eyes, and a little louring; much Hair both on the Head, Face, and other parts; usually one Eye a little larger than the other; short Hands and fleshy, the whole Body inclining to be fleshy, plump, corpulent and phlegmatic: if she be impeded of the ☉ in a Nativity or Question, she usually signifies some blemish in, or near the Eye: a blemish near the eye, if she be impeded in Succedent Houses; in the Sight, if she be unfortunate in Angles and with fixed Stars, called *Nebulas*.

Corporature.

She signifies Queens, Countesses, Ladies, all manner of Women; as also the common People, Travellers, Pilgrims, Sailors, Fishermen, Fishmongers, Brewers, Tapsters, Vintners, Letter-carriers, Coachmen, Huntsmen, Messengers, (some say the Pope's Legats) Mariners, Millers, Alewives, Malsters, Drunkards, Oysterwives, Fisherwomen, Charwomen, Tripewomen, and generally such Women as carry Commodities in the Streets; as also, Midwives, Nurses, &c., Hackneymen, Watermen, Waterbearers.

Qualities Men and Women.

Apoplexies, Palsy, the Colic, the Bellyache, Diseases

Sickness.

in the left Side, Stones, the Bladder and members of Generation, the Menstrues and Liver in Women, Dropsies, Fluxes of
the Belly, all cold rheumatic Diseases, cold Stomach, the Gout
in the Wrists and Feet, Sciatica, Colic, Worms in Children and
men, Rheums or Hurts in the Eyes, *viz.*, in the Left of Men, and
Right of Women: Surfeits, rotten Coughs, Convulsion fits, the Falling sickness, Kings-evil, Apostems, small Pox and Measles.

Colours and Savours: Of Colours the White, or pale Yellowish white, pale Green,
or a little of the Silver colour. Of Savours, the Fresh, or
without any savour, such as is in Herbs before they be ripe,
or such as do moisten the Brain, &c.

Herbs, Plants and Trees. Those Herbs which are subject to the *Moon* have soft
and thick juicy leaves, of a waterish or a little sweetish
taste, they love to grow in watery places, and grow quickly
into a juicy magnitude; and are:

The Colwort, Cabbage, Melon, Gourd, Pompion, Onion,
Mandrake, Poppy, Lettuce, Rape, the Linden tree, Mush-
rooms, Endive, all Trees or Herbs who have round, shady,
great spreading Leaves, and are little Fruitful.

Beasts or Birds. All such Beasts, or the like, as live in the water; as
Frogs, the Otter, Snails, &c. the Weasel, the Cunny, all Sea
Fowl, Cuckoo, Geese and Duck, the Night Owl.

Fishes. The Oyster and Cockle, all Shellfish, the Crab and Lob-
ster, Tortoise, Eels.

Places. Fields, Fountains, Baths, Havens of the Sea, Highways
and Desert places, Port Towns, Rivers, Fishponds, standing
Pools, Boggy places, Common shores, little Brooks, Springs,
Harbours for Ships or Docks.

Minerals. Silver.

Stones. The Selenite, all soft Stones, Crystals.

Weather. With ♄ cold Air; with ♃ Serene; with ♂ Winds red
Clouds; with the ☉ according to the Season; with ♀ and ☿
Showers and Winds.

Winds. In Hermetical operation, she delights towards the North,
and usually when she is the strongest Planet in the Scheme,
viz. in any Lunation, she stirs up Wind, according to the
nature of the Planet she next applies to.

Is 12 degrees before and after any Aspect. *Orb.*

Her greatest years are 320, greater 108, mean 66, least *Years.*
25. In conceptions she rules the seventh month.

Holland, Zealand, Denmark, Nuremberg, Flanders. *Countries.*

Gabriel. *Angel.*

Her day is Monday the first hour and the eighth, after *Day of the*
the rise of the Sun are hers. Her enemy is ♄, and also ♂. *week:*

The Head of the Dragon [☊] is Masculine, of the *The Head of*
nature of ♃ and ♀, and of himself a Fortune; yet the An- *the Dragon.*
cients do say, that being in ♂ with the good he is good, and
in ♂ with the evil Planets they account him evil.

The Tail of the Dragon [☋] is Feminine by nature, *The Tail*
and clean contrary to the Head; for he is evil when joined
with good Planets, and good when in conjunction with the
malignant Planets. This is the constant opinion of all the
Ancients, but upon what reason grounded I know not; I
ever found the ☊ equivalent to either of the Fortunes, and
when joined with the evil Planets to lessen their malevolent signification; when joined with the good to increase
the good promised by them. For the Tail of the Dragon, I
always in my practise found when he was joined with the
evil Planets; their malice or the evil intended thereby was
doubled and trebled, or extremely augmented, &c., and when
he chanced to be in conjunction with any of the Fortunes
who were significators in the question, though the matter
by the principal significator was fairly promised, and likely
to be perfected in a small time; yet did there ever fall out
many rubs and disturbances, much wrangling and great
controversies, that the business was many times given over
for desperate ere a perfect conclusion could be had; and
unless the principal significators were Angular and well
fortified with essential dignities, many times unexpectedly
the whole matter came to nothing.

CHAPTER XV.

Another brief Description of the shapes and forms of the Planets.

ħ Signifies one of a swarthy colour, palish like lead, or of a
black earthly brown; one of rough skin, thick and very
hairy on the body, not great eyes, many times his complexion is between black and yellow, or as if he had a spice of
the black or yellow Jaundice: He is lean, crooked, or beetle-
browed, a thin whey Beard, great lips, like the black Moors;
he looks to the ground, is slow in motion, either is bow-
legged, or hits one leg or knee against another; most part a
stinking breath, seldom free from a Cough: He is crafty for
This where his own ends, seducing people to his opinion, full of revenge
he is per- and malice, little caring for the Church or Religion; it's a
egrine or foul nasty, slovenly knave, or a whore; a great eater, or one
unfortunate. of a large stomach, a brawling fellow, big great shoulders,
covetous, and yet seldom rich, &c.

4 We must describe 4 and a Jovialist, to be one of a
comely stature, full faced, full eyed, a sanguine complexion,
or mixed with white and red, a large space between his
eyebrows, usually his Beard is of a flaxen or sandy-flaxen
colour: sometimes also when 4 is combust very sad or black,
his hair thick, his eyes not black, his teeth well set, good
broad teeth, but usually some mark of difference in the two
fore-teeth, either by their standing awry, or some blackness
or imperfection in them. His hair gently curls (if he be in a
fiery Sign). A man well spoken, religious, or at least a good
moral honest man; a person comely and somewhat fat (if 4
be in moist Signs) fleshy; if in Airy Signs, big and strong; if
in earthly Signs, a man usually well descended; but if he be
significator, of an ordinary clown, as sometimes he may be,
then is he of more humanity than usually in such kind of men.

♂ A Martial Man, is many times full faced with a lively
high colour like Sunburnt, or like raw tanned Leather, a

fierce countenance, his eyes being sparkling or sharp and darting, and of yellow colour; his hair both of head and beard being reddish (but herein you must vary according to the Sign, in fiery signs and airy where ♂ falls to be with fixed Stars of his own nature, there he shows a deep sandy red colour, but in watery signs, being with fixed Stars of his own nature, he is of a flaxenish or whitish bright hair; if in earthly Signs, the hair is like a sad brown, or of a sad Chestnut colour). He has a mark or scar in his face, is broad-shouldered, a sturdy strong body, being bold and proud, given to mock, scorn, quarrel, drink, game, and wench: which you may easily know by the Sign he is in; if in the house of ♀ he wenches, if in ☿'s he steals, but if he be in his own house he quarrels, in *Saturn's,* is dogged; in the *Sun's,* is lordly; in the *Moon's,* is a drunkard.

☉ The Sun does generally denote one of an obscure white colour mixed with red; a round face, and short chin, a fair stature, and one of comely body; his colour sometimes between yellow and black, but for the most part more sanguine than otherwise: a bold man and resolute, his hair curling; he has a white and tender skin, one desirous of praise, fame and estimation amongst men; he has a clear voice and great head, his teeth somewhat distort or obliquely set, of slow speech but of a composed judgement; using outwardly a great *decorum* in his actions, but privately he is lascivious and inclinable to many vices.

♀ Who is signified by *Venus,* whether Man or Woman, has a goodly and fair round visage, a full eye, usually we say goggle-eyed, red ruddy lips, the nether more thick or bigger than the upper, the eyelids black, however lovely and graceful; the hair of lovely colour (but most part according to the Sign as before repeated) in some it's coal black, in others a light brown, a soft smooth hair, and the body extremely well shaped, ever rather inclining to shortness than tallness.

☿ We describe *Mercury,* to be a man neither white or black

but between both, of a sad brown or dark yellowish colour, long visaged, high-forehead, black or grey eyes, a thin long sharp nose, a thin spare beard (many times none at all) of an auburn sad colour next to black, slender of body, small legs, a prattling busy fellow, and in walking he goes nimbly, and always would be thought to be full of action.

☽ She by reason of her swiftness, varies her shape very often, but in the general, she personifies one having a round visage and full faced, in whose complexion you may perceive a mixture of white and red, but paleness overcomes; if she be in fiery signs, the Man or Woman speaks hastily; in watery signs, he or she has some freckles in his or her face, or is blub cheeked; no very handsome body, but a muddling creature, and unless very well dignified, she ever signifies an ordinary vulgar person.

The colours of the Planets and Signs.

♄ Gives black colour: ♃ a colour mixed with red and green: ♂ red, or iron colour: ☉ yellow or yellow Purple: ♀ white or purple colour: ☿ sky-colour or bluish: ☽ a colour spotted with white and other mixed colours.

♈ White mixed with red: ♉ white with Citrine: ♊ white mixed with red: ♋ green or russet: ♌ red or green: ♍ black speckled with blue: ♎ black or dark crimson, or tawny colour: ♏ brown: ♐ yellow or a green sanguine: ♑ black or russet, or a swarthy brown: ♒ a sky-colour with blue: ♓ white glistering colour.

CHAPTER XVIᴀ.
Of the twelve Signs of the Zodiac, and their manifold Divisions.

The whole Zodiac is divided into twelve equal parts, which we call Signs, and give them the names of living

Creatures, either for their properties they hold with living Creatures, or by reason of the situation of the Stars in those places which somewhat resemble the effigies and similitude of living creatures: Their names and characters follow.

1	2	3	4	5	6
♈	♉	♊	♋	♌	♍

7	8	9	10	11	12
♎	♏	♐	♑	♒	♓

Every one of these Signs contains thirty degrees or parts in longitude: Hence it comes to pass that the whole Zodiac does consist of 360 degrees, every degree contains 60 minutes, which we also call scruples, every minute contains 60 seconds, and so further if you please, &c., but in Astrology we only make use of degrees, minutes and seconds.

These Signs are again divided many ways; as first, into four Quadrants or quarters, answering to the four quarters of the year.

The Vernal or Spring quarter, is sanguine, Hot and Moist, and contains the first three Signs, *viz.* ♈ ♉ ♊.

The Estival or Summer quarter is Hot, Dry and Choleric, and contains the fourth, fifth and sixth Signs, *viz.* ♋ ♌ ♍.

The Autumnal or Harvest quarter is Cold, Dry and Melancholy, and contains the seventh, eighth and ninth Signs, *viz.* ♎ ♏ ♐.

The Hyemnal, Brumal or Winter quarter is Cold, Moist and Phlegmatic, and contains the tenth, eleventh and twelfth Signs, *viz.* ♑ ♒ ♓.

They are again divided in division of the Elements, for some Signs in nature are Fiery, Hot and Dry, *viz.,* ♈, ♌, ♐, and these three Signs constitute the *Fiery Triplicity.*

Others are Dry, Cold and Earthly, *viz.* ♉, ♍, ♑, and make the *Earthly Triplicity.*

Others are Airy, Hot and Moist, *viz.* ♊, ♎, ♒, which make the *Airy Triplicity.*

Others are Watery, Cold and Moist, *viz.* ♋, ♏, ♓, and are called the *Watery Triplicity.*

Again, some Signs are Masculine, Diurnal, and there-fore Hot, as ♈, ♊, ♌, ♎, ♐, ♒.

Some are Feminine, Nocturnal, therefore Cold, *viz.*, ♉, ♋, ♍, ♏, ♑, ♓.

The use whereof is this, That if you have a Masculine Planet in a Masculine Sign, it imports him or her more manly; and so if a Masculine Planet be in a Feminine Sign, the man or woman is less courageous, &c.

Some Signs again are called Boreal, Septentrional or Northern, because they decline from the Equinoctial North-ward, and these are ♈, ♉, ♊, ♋, ♌, ♍; and these six Signs contain half the Zodiac, or the first semicircle thereof.

Some Signs are called Austral, Meridional or Southern, for that they decline Southward from the Equinoctial, and these are ♎, ♏, ♐, ♑, ♒, ♓.

Moveable.   The Signs again are divided into Moveable, Fixed and Common, ♈, ♋, ♎, ♑ are called moveable and Cardinal: move-able, because when the ☉ enters into ♈ and ♎, the Weather and Season of the year quickly varies and changes; they are called Cardinal, because when the ☉ enters into any of those Signs from that time we denominate the Quarters of the year.

For from the ☉ entering into ♈ and ♎ the Equinoctial or the Spring and Autumn arise; from the ☉ his entrance into ♋ and ♑ rises the Solstice of Summer and Winter.

So then the Equinoctial Signs are   ♈ ♎.
Solstitial and Tropics   ♋ ♑.

Fixed Signs.   The Fixed Signs do in order follow the Equinoctial and Tropics; and they are called fixed, for that when ☉ enters into them, the season of the year is fixed, and we do more evidently perceive either Heat or Cold, Moisture or Dryness.

The fixed Signs are these, ♉, ♌, ♏, ♒.

Common.   Signs are constituted between moveable and fixed, and retain a property or nature, partaking both with the preced-ing and consequent Sign: and they are ♊, ♍, ♐, ♓.

They are called Bicorporeal or double bodied, because they represent two Bodies: as ♊ two Twins, ♓ two Fishes.

The right knowledge of these in Astrology is much, and you must understand it thus; In the Question or Figure of Heaven, if the Planet who is Lord of the Ascendant be in a moveable Sign, and the Sign ascending be also one, it denotes the person to be unstable, and of no resolution, easily mutable, perverted, a wavering inconstant man.

Let us admit the Ascendant to be fixed, and the Lord of that Sign also in a fixed Sign, you may judge the party to be of firm resolution, no changeling; or as we say, one that will stand to maintain what he has said or done, be it good or ill.

If the Sign ascending be common, and the Lord of that Sign also in a Common Sign, you may judge the man or woman to be neither very wilful or easily variable but between both.

The Signs also are divided into:

Bestial or Quadrupedian, in *viz.* ♈, ♉, ♌, ♐, ♑;these have representation of Four-footed Creatures.

Fruitful or prolific, *viz.* ♋, ♏, ♓.

Barren Signs, ♊, ♌, ♍.

Manly or human, courteous Signs, ♊, ♍, ♎, ♒.

Feral Signs are ♌ and last part of ♐.

Mute Signs or of slow Voice, ♋, ♏, ♓; the more if ☿ be in any of them, in ♂, □, or ☍ of ♄.

The use here is, that if your Significator or Lord of the Ascendant be in ♈, ♉, ♌, ♐, ♑, there's in the condition of that party something of the nature of that Beast which represents that Sign he is in; as if he be in ♈, the man is rash, hardy and lascivious; if in ♉, steadfast and resolved, and somewhat of a muddy condition, vitiated, with some private imperfection, &c. and so of the rest.

Let us admit, one propounds his Question, if he shall have children, then if the ☽ and principal Significators be in Prolific Signs, and strong, there's no question but he shall; the same do, if the Question concern Barrenness, *viz.* if the Ascendant or fifth house be of those Signs we call barren Signs, it generally represents few or no children.

In Questions, if ♊, ♍, ♎ or ♒ ascend, or the Lord of the

Ascendant be in human Signs, then we may judge the man to be of civil carriage, very affable and easy to be spoken with, &c.

Antiscion of the Planets.   Besides these and many other divisions of the Signs, I thought good to be plain in setting down the Antiscions of the Planets.

Ptol. Apho. Stelle irratio   The Antiscion Signs are those, which are of the same virtue and are equally distant from the first degree of the two Tropic Signs, ♋, ♑, and in which degrees whilst the ☉ is, the days and nights are of equal length; by example it will be plain; when the ☉ is in the tenth degree of ♉ he is as far distant from the first degree of ♋ as when in the twentieth degree of ♌; therefore when the ☉ is in the tenth of ♉ he has his Antiscion to the twentieth of ♌; that is, he gives virtue or influence to any Star or Planet that at that time either is in the same degree by Conjunction, or casts any Aspect to it.

But that you may more fully and perfectly know where your Antiscion falls in degrees and minutes, behold this following table.

A general Table of the Antiscions in Signs.

$$\left. \begin{array}{c} ♊ \\ ♌ \\ ♍ \\ ♎ \\ ♏ \\ ♐ \end{array} \right\} \qquad \left\{ \begin{array}{c} ♋ \\ ♉ \\ ♈ \\ ♓ \\ ♒ \\ ♑ \end{array} \right.$$

Any Planet in ♊ sends his Antiscion into ♋, or being in ♌ into ♉.

If you would know the exact degrees and minutes, you must work as follows.

Let us suppose ♄ in twenty degrees and thirty five minutes of ♌, I would know in what part of the Zodiac he has his Antiscion.

Over against ♌ I find ♉, so then I conclude his Antiscion is in ♉. To know the degree and minute, work thus:

See what degree and minute the Planet is in, subtract that

from 30 degrees, and the remainder tells you both the degree and minute.

As ♄ being in 20 degrees and 35 minutes of ♌, I subtracted from   30 00

         20 35

      9^{deg} 25   *Subtracted.*

Here I subtract 35 min. from one whole degr. or from 60 min. which I borrow, and there rests 25 min. One degr. I borrowed, taken from 10, and there rest 9 degr. One that I borrowed and two are three, taken from three, then nothing remains, so then I find my Antiscion of ♄ falls to be in 9 degr. & 25 min. of ♉, which Signs as you see is over against ♌; but this Table expresses the work more quickly.

The Antiscions in degr.		Antiscions of the Planets in minutes			
1	29	1	59	16	44
2	28	2	58	17	43
3	27	3	57	18	42
4	26	4	56	19	41
5	25	5	55	20	40
6	24	6	54	21	39
7 in	23	7	53	22	38
8	22	8 in	52	23 in	37
9	21	9	51	24	36
10	20	10	50	25	35
11	19	11	49	26	34
12	18	12	48	27	33
13	17	13	47	28	32
14	16	14	46	29	31
15	15	15	45	30	30

The use is easy if you enter with the whole degrees of your Planet, the two first columns serve you, as ♂ supposed to be 14 degr. of a Sign, look 14 in the first column, over against it is 16, to that degree he sends his Antiscion.

If you have minutes, enter the four last columns; as if you enter with 17 min. in the fifth column, over against it you find 43. or first look the Sign where the Antiscion falls, then subtract the number of degr. and minutes the Planet is in from 30, what remains is the degree and minute where the Antiscion is; and as there are

Antiscions, which of the good Planets we think are equal to
a ✶ or △; so are there Contrantiscions, which we find to be
of the nature of a □ or ☍: and to know where it is, you do no
more than observe in what Sign and degree the Antiscion is,
in the Sign and degree opposite to that place the Contrantiscion is: as in the former examples, the Antiscion of ♄ is in
nine degr. and 25 min. of ♉ his Contrantiscion must then be
in 9 degr. and 25 min. of ♏.

There are also many other divisions of the Signs: as into
Signs commanding, *viz.* ♈ ♉ ♊ ♋ ♌ ♍.

And Signs obeying ♎ ♏ ♐ ♑ ♒ ♓.
And into Signs of right or long ascension, *viz.* ♋ ♌ ♍ ♎ ♏ ♐.
And into Signs of short or oblique ascension, *viz.* ♑ ♒ ♓ ♈ ♉ ♊.

Signs of long ascension continue two hours and more in
the ascendant: and Signs of short ascensions, do arise in
little more than an hour, and some in less, as you may
experiment by the table of Houses:

*I would know how many hours the Sign of ♌ continues
in the Ascendant or Horizon?*

In the first page of the Table of Houses, I look for the
Sign ♌, under the title of the first House, and in the fourth
line, I find 00 ♌ 21, *viz.* no degree, 21 min. of ♌.

Over against that number on the left hand, under the
title of hours and min. or time from noon, I find 00 18 min.,
or no hours, 18 min. I then continue with my sign ♌ in the
same column until I find 29 40 by which I perceive that the
Sign ♌ is removing out of the Ascendant: I seek under the
title of hours and minutes from noon over against the said
29 40 of ♌: on the left hand, what hours and min. stand
there. I find the number of 3 ho. 6 min. I subtract my former
number of 00 18 min. from 3 hours and 6 min.

3 h   6
00   18
2   48   There remains two hours and 48 min. of an
hour, which is all the space of time that ♌ continues in the
Ascendant, and in this regard it is called a sign of long ascension.

You shall see the difference now in a sign of short Ascension.

I would know how long the sign of ♏ continues in the Ascendant. See in the ninth page, and under the title of the first house: in the third line I find 00 ♏ 57, *viz.* 0 degree, 57 min. of ♏, over against it under hours and min. I find 16ʰ 4 min. In the tenth line under the first house I find 29 28. against it on the left hand 17 8 *viz.* 17 hurs, 8 min. I subtract my former hours and min. from the latter

$$
\begin{array}{r}
17 \quad 8 \\
\underline{16 \quad 4} \\
1 \quad 4
\end{array}
$$

the difference is one hour and 4 min. and so long time the sign of ♏ rests in the Ascendant: without exact knowledge here, one cannot attain to any exactness in natural Magic, *viz.* in gathering Herbs, or perfecting many other rarities.

That which is most necessary for every Student in the Art is, that he know and be expert in the following Chapter.

CHAPTER XVIb.
The Nature, Place, Countries, general Description, and Diseases signified by the twelve signs.

In the original, both this & the preceding chapter were numbered XVI. (ed. note.)

♈ Is a Masculine, Diurnal Sign, moveable, Cardinal, Equinoctial; in nature fiery, hot and dry, choleric, bestial, luxurious, intemperate and violent: the diurnal house of ♂ of the Fiery Triplicity, and of the East.

Quality.

All Pushes, Whelks, Pimples in the Face, small Pox, hare Lips, Polypus, *(noli me tangere)* Ringworm, Falling-sickness, Apoplexies, Migraines, Toothache, Headache and Baldness.

Diseases.

Where Sheep and small Cattle do feed or use to be, sandy and hilly Grounds, a place of refuge for Thieves, (as some unfrequented place); in Houses, the Covering, Ceiling or Plastering of it, a Stable of small Beasts, Lands newly taken in, or newly ploughed, or where Bricks have been burned or Lime.

Places ♈ Signifies.

A dry Body, not exceeding in height, lean or spare, but lusty Bones, and the party in his Limbs strong; the Visage

Description of the Body shape ♈ presents.

long; black Eyebrows, a long Neck, thick Shoulders, the Complexion dusky brown or swarthy.

Kingdoms Subject to ♈.   Germany, Swevia, Polonia, Burgundy, France, England, Denmark, Silesia the higher, Judea, Syria.

Cities: Florence, Capua, Naples, Ferrara, Verona, Utrecht, Marseilles, Augusta, Casarea, Padua, Bergamo.

Qualities of the Sign ♉.   ♉ Is an Earthly, Cold, Dry, Melancholy, Feminine, Nocturnal, Fixed, Domestic or Bestial Sign, of the Earthly Triplicity, and South, the Night-house of *Venus*.

Diseases.   The Kings Evil, sore Throats, Wens, Fluxes of Rheums falling into the Throat, Quinzies, Impostumes in those part.

Places.   Stables where Horses are, low Houses, Houses where the implements of Cattle are laid up, Pasture or Feeding grounds where no Houses are near, plain grounds, or where Bushes have been lately grubbed up, and wherein Wheat and Corn is sowed, some little Trees not far off; in Houses, Cellars, low Rooms.

Shape and description.   It presents one of a short, but of a full, strong and well set stature, a broad Forehead, great Eyes, big Face; large, strong Shoulders; great mouth and thick Lips; gross Hands; black rugged Hair.

Kingdoms subject to ♉.   Polonia the great, North part of *Sweathland, Russia, Ireland, Switzerland, Lorraine, Campania, Persia, Cyprus, Parthia.*

Cities.   Novgorod, Parma, Bologna, Palermo, Mantua, Sienna, Brescia, Karlstad, Nantes, Leipzig, Herbipolis.

Quality and Property of ♊.   ♊ It's an aerial, hot, moist, sanguine, Diurnal, common or double-bodied human Sign; the diurnal house of ☿: of the airy triplicity, Western, Masculine.

♊ Diseases.   He signifies all Diseases or infirmities in the Arms, Shoulders, Hands, corrupted Blood, Windiness in the Veins, distempered Fancies.

Places.   Wainscot Rooms, Plastering and Walls of Houses, the Halls, or where Play is used, Hills and Mountains, Barns, Storehouses for Corn, Coffers, Chests; High Places.

Kingdoms Countries.   Lombardy, Brabant, Flanders, the West and Southwest of *England, Armenia.*

Cities.   London, Louvain, Bruges, Nuremberg, Cordova, Hasford, Mont, Bamberg, Cesena.

Description.   An upright, tall, straight Body: either in Man or Woman, the Complexion sanguine, not clear, but obscure and dark, long Arms, but many times the Hands and Feet short and very fleshy; a dark Hair, almost black; a strong, active Body, a good piercing hazel Eye, and wanton, and of perfect sight, of excellent understanding, and judicious in worldly affairs.

♋ Is the only house of the *Moon*, and is the first Sign of the Watery or Northern Triplicity, is Watery, Cold, Moist, Phlegmatic, Feminine, Nocturnal, Moveable, a Solstice Sign, mute and slow of Voice, Fruitful, Northern.

Quality and property of ♋.

It signifies Imperfections all over, or in the Breast, Stomach and Paps; weak Digestion, cold Stomach, Phthisis, salt Phlegms, rotten Coughs, dropsical Humours, Impostumations in the Stomach, Cancers which ever are in the Breast.

Diseases.

The Sea, great Rivers, Navigational Waters; but in the Inland Countries it notes places near Rivers, Brooks, Springs, Wells, Cellars in Houses, Wash-houses, Marsh grounds, Ditches with Rushes, Sedges, Sea banks, Trenches, Cisterns.

Places.

Generally a low and small stature, the upper parts of more bigness then the lower, a round Visage; sickly, pale, a whitish Complexion, the Hair a sad brown, little Eyes, prone to have many Children, if a Woman.

Shape and description.

Scotland, Zealand, Holland, Prussia, Tunis, Algeria, Constantinople, Venice, Milan, Genoa, Amsterdam, York, Magdeberg, Wittenberg, Saint *Lucas, Cadiz.*

Kingdoms, Countries and Cities.

♌ Is the only house of the *Sun*, by nature, Fiery, Hot, Dry, Choleric, Diurnal, Commanding, Bestial, Barren, of the East, and Fiery Triplicity, Masculine.

Quality and property of ♌.

All sicknesses in the ribs and sides, as Pleurisy, Convulsions, pains in the back, trembling or passion of the heart, violent burning fevers, all weakness or diseases in the heart, sore eyes, the Plague, the Pestilence, the yellow-Jaundice.

Diseases.

A place where wild Beasts frequent, Woods, Forests, Desert places, steep rocky places, inaccessible places, King's Palaces, Castles, Forts, Parks, in houses where fire is kept, near a Chimney.

Places.

Great round Head, big Eyes starting or staring out, or goggle-eyes, quick-sighted, a full and large body and it more than of middle stature, broad Shoulders, narrow Sides, yellow or dark flaxen hair and it much curling or turning up, a fierce

Shape and form.

countenance, but ruddy, high sanguine complexion, strong valiant and active.

Kingdoms, Countries, Cities. *Italy, Bohemia, the Alps, Turkey, Sicily, Apulia, Rome, Syracuse, Cremona, Ravenna, Damascus, Prague, Linz, Koblenz, Bristol.*

Quality and property ♍ ♍ It's an earthly, cold, melancholy, barren, feminine, nocturnal, Southern Sign; the house and exaltation of ☿, of the earthly triplicity.

Places. It signifies a Study where Books are, a Closet, a Dairy-house, Cornfields, Granaries, Malt-houses, Hayricks, or of Barley, Wheat or Peas, or a place where Cheese and Butter is preserved and stored up.

Diseases. The Worms, Wind, Colic, all Obstructions in the bowels and miseraicks, croaking of the Guts, infirmness in the Stones any disease in the belly.

Kingdoms, Countries, Cities. *Greece,* the South part thereof, *Croatia,* the *Athenian* territory, *Mesopotamia, Africa,* the Southwest of *France, Paris, Jerusalem, Rhodes, Lyons, Toulouse, Basil, Heidelberg, Brundusiam.*

Shape and form. A slender body of mean height, but decently composed; a ruddy brown complexion, black hair, well-favoured or lovely, but no beautiful creature, a small shrill voice, all members inclining to brevity; a witty discreet soul, judicious and excellently well spoken, studious and given to History, whether Man or Woman; it produces a rare understanding, if ☿ be in this Sign, and ☽ in ♋, but somewhat unstable.

Nature and property ♎ ♎ Is a Sign aerial, hot and moist, Sanguine, Masculine, Moveable, Equinoctial, Cardinal, Human, Diurnal, of the Aerial Triplicity, and Western, the chief house of ♀.

Diseases. All Diseases, or the Stone or Gravel in the reins of the Back, Kidneys, heats and diseases in the Loins or Haunches, Impostumes or Ulcers in the Reins, Kidneys or Bladder, weakness in the Back, corruption of Blood.

Places. In the Fields it represents ground near Windmills, or some straggling Barn or out-house, or Sawpits, or where Coopers work or Wood is cut, sides of Hills, tops of Mountains, grounds where Hawking and Hunting is used, sandy and gravelly Fields, pure clear Air and sharp; the upper rooms in Houses, Chambers, Garrets, one Chamber within another.

Shape and form. It personifies a well framed body, straight, tall and more subtle or slender than gross; a round, lovely and beautiful Visage, a pure sanguine colour; in Youth, no abundance or excess in either white or red, but in Age usually some pimples, or a very high Colour, the Hair yellowish, smooth and long.

The higher *Austria, Savoy* its Dukedom, *Alsace, Livonia, Lisbon* in *Portugal, Frankfort, Vienna, Placentia,* the Territory in *Greece* where sometimes the City *Thebes* stood, *Arles, Fribourg, Spires.* *Kingdom, Countries, Cities.*

♏ Is a cold, watery, nocturnal, phlegmatic, feminine Sign, of the watery Triplicity, fixed and North, the house and joy of *Mars,* feminine; usually it does represent subtle, deceitful men. *Quality and property of ♏.*

Gravel, the Stone in the Secret parts, Bladder, Ruptures, Fistulas, or the Piles in *Ano,* Gonorrhoea, Priapism, all afflicting the Privy parts either in man or woman; defects in the Matrix. *Diseases.*

Places where all sorts of creeping Beasts use, as Beetles, &c. or such as be without wings, and are poisonous; Gardens, Orchards, Vineyards, ruinous Houses near Waters; muddy, moorish Grounds, stinking Lakes, Quagmires, Sinks, the Kitchen or Larder, Wash-house. *Places.*

A corpulent, strong, able Body, somewhat a broad or square Face, a dusky muddy Complexion, and sad, dark Hair, much and crisping; a hairy Body, somewhat bow-legged, short necked, a squat, well-trussed Fellow. *Form and Description.*

North part of *Bavaria,* the Woody part of *Norway, Barbary,* the Kingdom of *Fez, Catalonia* in *Spain, Valencia, Urbino* and *Forum Julii* in *Italy, Vienne, Messina* in *Italy, Gaunt, Frankfurt an der Oder.* *Kingdom, Countries, Cities.*

♐ Is of the fiery triplicity, East, in nature fiery, hot, dry, Masculine, Choleric, Diurnal, Common, bicorporeal or double bodied, the House and joy of ♃. *Quality and nature of ♐.*

It rules the Thighs and Buttocks in the parts of man's body, and all Fistulas or Hurts falling in those members, and generally denotes blood heated, Fevers Pestilential, falls from Horses, or hurts from them or four-footed Beasts; also prejudice by Fire, Heat and intemperateness in Sports. *Diseases.*

Places.   A Stable of great Horses, or Horses for the Wars, or a House where usually great four-footed Beasts are kept; it represents in the Fields, Hills, and the highest places of Lands or Grounds that rise a little above the rest; in houses upper rooms, near the fire.

Shape and form of body.   It represents a well-favoured Countenance, somewhat long Visage, but full and ruddy, or almost like Sunburnt; the Hair light Chestnut colour, the Stature somewhat above the middle Size; a conformity in the Members, and strong able body.

Kingdoms, Countries, Cities.   *Spain, Hungary, Slavonia, Moravia, Dalmatia, Buda* in *Hungary, Toledo, Narbonne, Cologne, Stargard.*

Quality and nature of ♑.   ♑ It's the House of *Saturn* and is Nocturnal, Cold, Dry, Melancholy, Earthly, Feminine, Solstical, Cardinal, Moveable, Domestic, Four-footed, Southern; the exaltation of ♂.

Diseases.   It has government of the Knees, and all Diseases incident to those places, either by Strains or Fractures; it notes Leprosy, the Itch, the Scab.

Places.   It shows an Ox-house, or Cow house, or where Calves are kept, or Tools for Husbandry, or old Wood is laid up; or where Sails for Ships and such Materials are stored; also Sheep-Pens, and grounds where Sheep feed, Fallow-grounds, barren Fields Bushy and Thorny; Dunghills in Fields, or where Soil is laid; in houses low, dark places, near the ground or threshold.

Corporature.   Usually dry Bodies, not high of Stature, long, lean and slender Visage, thin Beard, black Hair, a narrow Chin, long small Neck and narrow Breast. I have found many times ♑ ascending, the party to have white Hair, but in the seventh ever Black, I conceive the whiteness proceeded from the nature of the Family rather than of the Sign.

Kingdoms, Countries, Cities.   *Thrace, Macedonia* in *Greece* now *Turkey, Albania, Bulgaria, Saxony* the Southwest part, *West-Indies, Styria,* the Isles *Orcades, Hassia, Oxford, Mecklenburg, Cleves, Brandenburg.*

Nature and property of ♒.   ♒ Is an aerial, hot and moist Sign, of the airy Triplicity, diurnal, sanguine, fixed, rational, human, masculine, the principal house of ♄, and house wherein he most rejoices; Western.

Sickness.   ♒ Governs the Legs, Ankles, and all manner of infirmities incident to those members, all melancholy Winds coagulated in the Veins, or disturbing the Blood, Cramps, &c.

Hilly and uneven places, places new digged, or where *Places.* quarries of Stone are, or any Minerals have been digged up; in Houses, the roofs, eaves or upper parts; Vineyards, or near some little Spring or Conduit-head.

It presents a squat, thick Corporature, or one of a strong, *Shape and* well composed Body, not tall; a long Visage, sanguine Com- *form.* plexion; if ♄ who is Lord of this house, be in ♑ or ♒, the party is black in Hair, and in Complexion sanguine, with distorted Teeth; otherwise, I have observed the party is of clear, white or fair Complexion, and of sandy coloured Hair, or very flaxen, and a very pure Skin.

Tartary, Croatia, Walachia, Muscovy, Westphalia in *Kingdoms,* *Germany, Piedmont* in *Savoy,* the West and South parts of *Countries,* *Bavaria, Media, Arabia, Hamburg, Bremen, Montferrat* and *Cities.* *Pisaurum* in *Italy, Trent, Ingolstadt.*

♓ Is of the Watery Triplicity, Northern, cold Sign, *Property* moist, Phlegmatic, feminine, nocturnal, the house of *Jupi-* *and quality* *ter,* and exaltation of *Venus,* a Bicorporeal, common or double *of ♓.* bodied Sign, an idle, effeminate, sickly Sign, or representing a party of no action.

All Diseases in the Feet, as the Gout, and all Lameness *Sickness.* and Aches incident to those members, and so generally salt Phlegms, Scabs, Itch, Botches, Breakings out, Boils and Ulcers proceeding from Blood putrefied, Colds and moist diseases.

It represents Grounds full of water, or where many *Places.* Springs and much Fowl are, also Fishponds or Rivers full of Fish, places where Hermitages have been, Moats about Houses, Water-Mills; in houses near the water, as to some Well or Pump, or where water stands.

A short Stature, ill composed, not very decent, a good *Corporature.* large Face, palish Complexion, the Body fleshy or swelling, not very straight, but incurvating somewhat with the Head.

Calabria in *Sicily, Portugal, Normandy,* the North of *Kingdoms,* *Egypt, Alexandria, Reims, Worms, Ratisbon, Compostella.* *Countries,* *Cities.*

CHAPTER XVII.

Teaching what use may be made of the former Discourse of the twelve Signs.

IF one demand of the *Artist*, of what condition, quality or stature the person quesited, or inquired of is, then observe the Sign of that house whereby he is signified, the Sign wherein the Lord of that house is, and wherein the *Moon* is, mix one with another, and by the greater testimonies judge; for if the Sign be human, aerial, that ascends or descends, and the Lord of that Sign or the ☽ in any Sign of the same triplicity or nature, you may judge the Body to be handsome, and the conditions of the party to be sociable, or he very courteous, &c.

If the *Quere* be concerning a Disease, and ♈ be either on the cusp of the Ascendant, or descending in the sixth, you may judge he has something in his Disease of the nature of ♈, but what it is, you must know by the concurrence of the other significators.

If a Country man or Citizen has lost or misses any Cattle, or any material thing in his house, let him observe in what Sign the Significator of the thing is in; if in ♈, and it be a Beast strayed, or the like, let him see what manner of places that Sign directs to, and let him repair thither to search, considering the quarter of the heaven the Sign signifies: if it be an immovable piece of Goods, that without man or woman cannot be removed, then let him look into such parts of his house, or about his house as ♈ signifies.

If one asks concerning Travel, whether such a Country, City or Kingdom will be healthful or prosperous to him, yea or no; see in the Figure in what Sign the Lord of the Ascendant is in, if the significator be fortunate in ♈, or if ♃ or ♀ be therein, he may safely travel or sojourn in such Cities or Countries as the Sign of ♈ represents, which you may easily discern in the above named Catalogue. Those Countries subject to the Sign wherein the *Infortunes* are placed, unless

themselves be significators, are ever unfortunate: where remember, that a Gentleman inquires usually, if he shall have
his health and live jocundly in such or such a Country or
City; the Merchant he wholly aims at Trade, and the increase
of his Stock, therefore in the Merchant's Figure you must
consider the Country or City subject to the Sign of the second
house, or where the *Part of Fortune* is, or Lord of the second
is, and which is most fortified, and thither let him Trade.

CHAPTER XVIII.
Of the Essential Dignities of the Planets.

The exact way of judicature in Astrology is, first, by
being perfect in the nature of the Planets and Signs.

Secondly, by knowing the strength, fortitude or debility of the Planets, Significators, and a well posing of them
and their aspects and several mixtures, in your judgement.

Thirdly, by rightly applying the influence of the position of Heaven erected, and the Planets aspects to one another at the time of the Question, according to natural (and
not forced) maxims of Art; for by how much you endeavour
to strain a judgement beyond nature, by so much the more
you augment your Error.

A Planet is then said to be really strong when he has
many Essential dignities, which are known, by his being
either in his House, Exaltation, Triplicity, Term or Face, at
time of the erecting the Figure. As for Example:

In any Scheme of Heaven, if you find a Planet in any
of those Signs we call his house or houses, he is then essentially strong, and we allow for that five dignities; as ♄ in
♑, ♃ in ♐, &c.

Essential dignity by House

In *judgment*, when a Planet or Significator is in his own
house, it represents a man in such a condition, as that he is
Lord of his own house, estate and fortune; or a man wanting
very little of the Goods of this world, or it tells you the man
is in a very happy state or condition: this will be true, unless the

significator be retrograde, or combust, or afflicted by any other malevolent Planet or aspect.

Exaltation.   If he be in that Sign wherein he is exalted, you may allow him four dignities essential, whether he be near the very degree of his exaltation, yea or not; as ♂ in ♑ or ♃ in ♋.

If the significator be in his exaltation, and no way impeded, but Angular; it presents a person of haughty condition, arrogant, assuming more to him than his due; for it's observed, the Planets in some part of the Zodiac do more evidently declare their effects than in others; and I conceive this to be in those Signs and degrees where fixed Stars of the same nature with the Planet are more in number, and nearer the Ecliptic.

Triplicity.   If he be in any of those Signs which are allotted him for his Triplicity, he has allowed him three dignities; but herein you must be cautious; as for example: In a Question, Nativity, or the like, if you find the ☉ in ♈, and the Question, or Nativity, or Scheme erected be by night, and you would examine the ☉ his fortitudes, he shall have four dignities for being in his exaltation, which continues through the Sign; but shall not be allowed any dignity, as being in his triplicity; for by night the ☉ rules not the fiery Triplicity, but ♃; who had he been in place of the ☉, and by night, must have had allowed him three dignities: and this do generally in all the Planets, ♂ excepted, who night and day rules the watery Triplicity.

A Planet in his triplicity, shows a man modestly endowed with the Goods and Fortune of this world, one prettily descended, and the condition of his life at present time of the Question, to be good; but not so, as if in either of the two former dignities.

Term.   If any Planet be in those degrees we assign for his Terms, we allow him two dignities; as whether day or night, if ♃ be in one, two, three or four, &c., degrees of ♈, he is then in his own Terms, and must have two dignities therefore, and so ♀ in any of the first eight degrees of ♉, &c.

A Planet fortified, only as being in his own Terms, rather shows a man more of the corporature and temper of the Planet

than any extraordinary abundance in fortune, or of eminency in the Commonwealth.

If any Planet be in his *Decanate, Decurie* or *Face*, as ♂   *Face.*
in the first ten degrees of ♈, or ☿ in the first ten degrees
of ♉, he is then allowed one essential dignity; for being in
his own Decanate or Face, cannot then be called peregrine.

A Planet having little or no dignity, but by being in
his *Decanate* or *Face*, is almost like a man ready to be
turned out of doors, having much ado to maintain himself
in credit and reputation: and in *Genealogies* it represents a
Family at the last gasp, even as good as quite decayed,
hardly able to support itself.

The Planets may be strong another manner of way,
viz. Accidentally; as when Direct, swift in Motion, Angular, in △ or ✶ aspect with ♃ or ♀, &c. or in ♂ with certain
notable fixed Stars, as shall hereafter be related. Here
follows a Table of Essential Dignities, by which only casting your Eye thereon, you may perceive what essential
dignity or imbecility any Planet has.

There has been much difference between *Arabians,
Greeks* and *Indians* concerning the *Essential* Dignities of
the Planets; I mean how to dispose the several degrees of
the Signs fitly to every *Planet*; after many Ages had passed,
and until the time of *Ptolemy*, the *Astrologians* were not
well resolved here; but since *Ptolemy* his time, the *Greeks*
unanimously followed the method he left, and which ever
since the other Christians of *Europe* to this day retain as
most rational; but the *Moors* of *Barbary* at present and
those *Astrologians* of their Nation who lived in *Spain* do
somewhat at this day vary from us; however I present thee
with a Table according to *Ptolemy*.

A Table of the Essential Dignities of the Planets according to *Ptolemy*														
Signs	Houses of the Planets	Exaltation	Trip. of the Plan. D	N	The Terms of the Planets					The faces of the Planets			Detriment	Fall
♈	♂ D	☉ 19	☉	♃	♃ 6	♀ 14	☿ 21	♂ 26	♄ 30	♂ 10	☉ 20	♀ 30	♀	♄
♉	♀ N	☽ 3	♀	☽	♀ 8	☿ 15	♃ 22	♄ 26	♂ 30	☿ 10	☽ 20	♄ 30	♂	
♊	☿ D	☊ 3	♄	☿	☿ 7	♃ 14	♀ 21	♄ 25	♂ 30	♃ 10	♂ 20	☉ 30	♃	
♋	☽ N/D	♃ 15	♂	♂	♂ 6	♃ 13	☿ 20	♀ 27	♄ 30	♀ 10	☿ 20	☽ 30	♄	♂
♌	☉ N/D		☉	♃	♄ 6	☿ 13	♀ 19	♃ 25	♂ 30	♄ 10	♃ 20	♂ 30	♄	
♍	☿ N	☿ 15	♀	☽	☿ 7	♀ 13	♃ 18	♄ 24	♂ 30	☉ 10	♀ 20	☿ 30	♃	♀
♎	♀ D	♄ 21	♄	☿	♄ 6	♀ 11	♃ 19	☿ 24	♂ 30	☽ 10	♄ 20	♃ 30	♂	☉
♏	♂ N		♂	♂	♂ 6	♃ 14	♀ 21	☿ 27	♄ 30	♂ 10	☉ 20	♀ 30	♀	☽
♐	♃ D	☋ 3	☉	♃	♃ 8	♀ 14	☿ 19	♄ 25	♂ 30	☿ 10	☽ 20	♄ 30	☿	
♑	♄ N	♂ 28	♀	☽	♀ 6	☿ 12	♃ 19	♂ 25	♄ 30	♃ 10	♂ 20	☉ 30	☽	♃
♒	♄ D		♄	☿	♄ 6	☿ 12	♀ 20	♃ 25	♂ 30	♀ 10	☿ 20	☽ 30	☉	
♓	♃ N	♀ 27	♂	♂	♀ 8	♃ 14	☿ 20	♂ 26	♄ 30	♄ 10	♃ 20	♂ 30	☿	☿

The Use of the Table.

Every Planet has two Signs for his Houses, except *Sol* and *Luna*, they but one apiece: ♄ has ♑ and ♒; ♃ ♐ and ♓; ♂ ♈ ♏; ☉ ♌; ♀ ♉ ♎; ☿ ♊ ♍; ☽ ♋. The one of these Houses is called *Diurnal*, noted in the second Column by the Letter *D*. The other is *Nocturnal*, noted by the Letter *N*. In these Signs the Planets have their Exaltations, which the third Column points out; as the ☉ in 19 ♈; ☽ in 3 ♉; ☊ in 3 degr. ♊, &c. are exalted.

These twelve Signs are divided into four Triplicities: The fourth Column tells you which Planet or Planets both night and day govern each Triplicity: As over against ♈, ♌, ♐, you find ☉, ♃, *viz.* ☉ governs by day in that Triplicity, and ♃ by night: Over against ♉, ♍, ♑, you find ♀ and ☽; *viz.* that ♀ has domination by day, and ☽ by night in that Triplicity: Over against ♊, ♎, ♒, you find ♄, ☿; which rule as aforesaid:

Over against ♋, ♏, ♓, you find ♂, who, according to *Ptolemy* and *Naibod*, rules only that Triplicity both day and night.

Over against ♈, in the fifth, sixth, seventh, eighth, ninth columns, you find ♃ 6, ♀ 14, which tells you, the first six degrees of ♈ are the Terms of ♃; from six to fourteen, the Terms of ♀, &c.

Over against ♈, in the tenth, eleventh and twelfth columns, you find ♂ 10, ☉ 20, ♀ 30, *viz.*, the first ten degrees of ♈ are the Face of ♂; from ten to twenty the Face of ☉; from twenty to thirty the Face of ♀, &c.

In the thirteenth column, over against ♈, you find ♀ *Detriment*; *viz.*, ♀ being in ♈, is in a Sign opposite to one of her own Houses, and so is said to be in her Detriment.

In the fourteenth column, over against ♈, you find ♄, over his head *Fall*; that is, ♄ when he is in ♈ is opposite to ♎ his Exaltation, and so is Unfortunate, &c. Though these things are expressed in the nature of the Planets already, yet this Table makes it appear more evidently to the eye.

CHAPTER XIX.

Of several Terms, Aspects, words of Art, Accidents, and other materials things happening amongst the Planets; with other necessary Rules to be well known and understood before any Judgment can be given upon a Question.

The most forcible or strongest Rays, Configurations or Aspects, are only these (nominated before): the Sextile ⚹, Quadrate □, Trine △, Opposition ☍, we use to call the Conjunction ☌, an Aspect, but very improperly.

A *Sextile* aspect is the distance of one Planet from another by the sixth part of the Zodiac or Circle; for six times sixty degr. do make 360 degr. This aspect you shall find called sometimes a *Sexangular* Aspect, or a *Hexagon*.

A Quadrate aspect, or *Quadranglar*, or *Tetragonal*, is the distance of two Points, or two Planets by a fourth part of the *Circle*, for four times ninety do contain three hundred and sixty degrees.

The *Trine* aspect consists of 120 degrees, or by a third part of the *Circle*, for three times a hundred and twenty degrees make the whole *Circle*, or 360 degrees. It's called a *Triangular* aspect, or *Trigonal,* and if you find sometimes the word *Trigonocrator,* it is as much as a Planet ruling or having domination in such a Triplicity or Trigon; for three Signs make one Trigon or Triplicity.

An *Opposition* or Diametral Radiation is, when two Planets are equally distant 180 degrees, or half the *Circle* from each other.

A *Conjunction, Coition, Synod or Congress* (for some use all these words) is, when two Planets are in one and the same degree and minute of a Sign. Other new Aspects I have formerly mentioned in the beginning of this Discourse. You must understand amongst these Aspects, the *Quadrate* Aspect is a sign of imperfect enmity; and that the *Opposition* is an aspect or argument of perfect hatred; which is to be understood thus: A Question is propounded, *Whether two persons at variance may be reconciled?* Admit I find the two *significators* representing the two *Adversaries,* in □ aspect; I may then judge, because the aspect is of imperfect hatred, that the matter is not yet so far gone, but there may be hopes of reconciliation between them, the other *significators* or Planets a little helping. But if I find the main *significators* in opposition, it's then in nature impossible to expect a peace between them till the suit is ended, if it be a suit of *Law*; until they have fought, if it be a *Challenge.*

The *Sextile* and *Trine* aspects are arguments of Love, Unity and Friendship; but the △ is more forcible, (*viz.*) if the two *significators* are in ✳ or △, no doubt but peace may be easily concluded.

Conjunctions are good or bad, as the Planets in ☌ are friends or enemies to one another.

There is also a *Partile* or *Platic* aspect: *Partile* aspect is when two Planets are exactly so many degrees from each other as make a perfect aspect: as if ♀ be in nine degrees of ♈, and ♃ in nine degrees of ♌, this is a Partile △ aspect: so ☉ in one degree of ♉, and ☽ in one degree of ♋, make a Partile ✳, and this is a strong sign or argument for performance of anything or that the matter is near hand concluded when the aspect is so partile, and signifies good; and it's as much a sign of present evil when mischief is threatened.

A *Platic* Aspect is that which admits of the *Orbs* or *Rays* of two Planets that signify any matter: As if ♀ be in the tenth degree of ♉, and ♄ in eighteen degrees of ♍, here ♀ has a *Platic* △, or is in a Platic △ to ♄, because she is within the *moiety* of both their *Orbs*; for the *moiety* of ♄ his Rays or Orbs is five, and of ♀ 4, and the distance between them and their perfect aspect is eight degrees; and here I will again insert the Table of the quality of their Orbs, although I have in the Planets several descriptions mentioned them; they stand thus as I have found by the best Authors and my own Experience.

	deg	min		deg	min	
♄	10	0	*According to others*	9	0	I sometimes use the one,
♃	12	0	*As some have wrote*	9	0	and sometimes the other, as
♂	7	30	*All consent*	7	0	my Memory
☉	17	0	*Most say*	15	0	best Remem-
♀	8	0	*Many write but*	7	0	bers them, and
☿	7	0	*All consent only*	7	0	this without
☽	12	30	*Generally but*	12	0	error.

Application of Planets is three several ways: First, *Application* when a Planet of more swift motion applies to one more slow and ponderous, they being both direct; as ♂ in ten degrees of ♈, ☿ five: here ☿ applies to ☌ of ♂.

Secondly, when both Planets are retrograde, as ☿ in ten degrees of ♈, and ♂ in nine of ♈; ☿ being not direct until he has made ☌ with ♂: this is an ill Application and an argument either suddenly perfecting, or breaking off the business, according as the two Planets have signification.

Thirdly, when a Planet is direct, and in fewer degrees, and a retrograde Planet being in more degrees of the Sign, as ♂ being direct in 15 ♈: and ☿ retrograde in 17 ♈; this is an ill application, and in the Air shows great change; in a Question on sudden alteration: but more particularly I express Application as follows.

Application　　It is when two Planets are drawing near together either by ♂ or Aspect, *viz.* to a ✶, △, □ or ☍; where you must understand, that the superior Planets do not apply to the inferior (unless they be Retrograde), but ever the lighter to the more ponderous; as if ♄ be in the 10 degree of ♈, and ♂ be in the seventh degree of ♈ the same Sign, here ♂ being in fewer degrees, and a more light Planet than ♄, applies to his ♂; if ♂ had been in the seventh degree of ♊, he had then applied to a ✶ Aspect with ♄: had ♂ been in the seventh degree of ♋, he had then applied to a □ of ♄; had he been in the seventh degree of ♌, he had applied to a △ of ♄; had ♂ been in the seventh degree of ♎, he had applied to an ☍ of ♄, and the true Aspect would have been when he had come to the same degree and minute wherein ♄ was: And you must know that when ♄ is in ♈ and casts his ✶, □ or △ to any Planet in the like degrees of ♊ or ♋ or ♌, this Aspect is called a Sinister ✶, □ or △, and it is an Aspect according to the succession of the Signs; for after ♈ succeeds ♉, then ♊, then ♋, &c. and so in order. Now if ♄ he in ♈, he also casts his ✶, □, or △ to any Planet that is in ♒, ♑ or ♐, and this is called a Dexter Aspect, and is against the order of Signs; but this Table annexed will more easily inform you.

A Table of the Aspects of the Signs amongst one another.

	✶	□	△	☍		✶	□	△	☍		✶	□	△	☍
Dexter ♈	≈	♑	♐		Dexter ♌	♊	♉	♈		Dexter ♐	♎	♍	♌	
				♎					≈					♊
Sinister ♈	♊	♋	♌		Sinister ♌	♎	♏	♐		Sinister ♐	≈	♓	♈	
Dexter ♉	♓	≈	♑		Dexter ♍	♋	♊	♉		Dexter ♑	♏	♎	♍	
				♏					♓					♋
Sinister ♉	♋	♌	♍		Sinister ♍	♏	♐	♑		Sinister ♑	♓	♈	♉	
Dexter ♊	♈	♓	≈		Dexter ♎	♌	♋	♊		Dexter ♒	♐	♏	♎	
				♐					♈					♌
Sinister ♊	♌	♍	♎		Sinister ♎	♐	♑	≈		Sinister ♒	♈	♉	♊	
Dexter ♋	♉	♈	♓		Dexter ♏	♍	♌	♋		Dexter ♓	♑	♐	♏	
				♑					♉					♍
Sinister ♋	♍	♎	♏		Sinister ♏	♑	≈	♓		Sinister ♓	♉	♊	♋	

The use of the Table aforesaid.

You may see in the 2, 3, 4, and fifth column, in the upper part of the Table, ✶ □ △ ☍.

You may see in the second line and first Column: { *Dexter.* / ♈ / *Sinister.* }

and in the four Columns over against them: { ♒ ♑ ♐   ♎ / ♊ ♋ ♌ }

The meaning is thus; a Planet placed in ♈, and another in ♒ in like degrees, he in ♈ does behold the other in ♒ with a ✶ dexter Aspect.

A Planet in ♈ and another in ♑, he in ♈ beholds the Planet in ♑ with a □ dexter.

A Planet in ♈ beholding another in ♐, casts his △ dexter thither.

A Planet in ♈ beholding another in ♎, casts his opposite Aspect to him.

Again, over against Sinister, and under ♈ you find ♊ ♋ ♌; that is, ♈ beholds ♊ with a ✶ Sinister: ♋ with a □ Sinister, ♌ with a △ sinister: Observe the dexter aspect is more forcible than the Sinister: this understand in the other Columns, *viz.* that Dexter Aspects are contrary to the succession of Signs, Sinister in order as they follow one another.

Signs not beholding one another.

♈	♉	♊	♋	♌	♍	♎	♏	♐	♑	♒	♓
♉	♈	♉	♌	♋	♌	♏	♎	♏	♌	♑	♌
♏	♊	♏	♒	♍	♒	♉	♐	♉	♒	♓	♒
	♎			♑		♈			♋		
	♐			♓		♊					

These are called Signs inconjunct, or such as if a Planet be in one of them, he cannot have any aspect to another in the sign underneath: as one in ♈ can have no aspect to another in ♉ or ♏, or one in ♉ to one in ♈, ♊, ♎ or ♐, so understand of the rest.

Separation. Separation, it is in the first place, when two Planets are departed but six minutes distance from each other, as let ♄ be in 10 degr. and 25 min. of ♈ and ♃ in 10 degr. and 25 min. of ♈: now in these degrees and minutes they are in perfect ♂; but when ♃ shall get into 10 degr. and 31 or 32 minutes of ♈, he shall be said to be separating from ♄; yet because ♄ has 9 degr. allowed him for his rays, and ♃ has also the same number allowed him, ♃ cannot be said to be totally separated or clear from the rays of ♄, until he has got 9 whole degrees further into ♈, or is fully 9 degrees distant from him, for the half of ♃ his orb is 4 degree 30 min. and the half of ♄ his orb is 4 degr. 30 min., added together they make 9 whole degrees; for every Planet that applies is allowed half his own orbs and half the orbs of that Planet from whom he separates: As if ☉ and ☽ be in any aspect, the ☽ shall then be separated from the ☉, when she is fully distant from the ☉ 7 degr. and 30 min. *viz.* half the orbs of the ☉, and 6 degr. the moiety of her own orbs; in all 13 degr. and 30 minutes.

The exact knowledge here is various and excellent: For admit two Planets significators in Marriage at the time of the question, are lately separated but a few minutes; I would then judge there had been but few days before great probability of effecting the Marriage, but now it hung in suspense, and there seemed some dislike or rupture in it; and as the significators do more separate, so will the matter and affection of the parties more alienate and vary, and according to the number of degrees that the swifter Planet wants ere he can be wholly separated from the more ponderous, so will it be so many weeks, days, months or years ere the two Lovers will wholly desist or see the matter quite broke off: The two *significators* in moveable Signs, Angular and swift in motion, does hasten the times; in common signs, the time will be more long; in fixed, a longer space of time will be required.

Prohibition. Prohibition is when two Planets that signify the effecting or bringing to conclusion any thing demanded, are applying to an Aspect; and before they can come to a true Aspect, another Planet interposes either his body or aspect, so that thereby the matter propounded is hindered and retarded; this is called Prohibition. For Example, ♂ is in 7 degr. of ♈, and ♄ is in the 12. ♂ signifies the effecting my business when he comes to the body of ♄ who promises the conclusion, the ☉ is at the same time in 6 degr. of ♈. Now in regard that the ☉ is swifter in motion than ♂, he will overtake ♂, and come to ♂ with ♄ before ♂, whereby whatever ♂ or ♄ did formerly signify, is now prohibited by the ☉ his first impeding ♂ and then ♄, before they can come to a true ♂. This manner of prohibition is called a Conjunctional or Bodily prohibition; and you must know that the combustion of any Planet is the greatest misfortune that can be.

The second manner of Prohibition is by Aspect, either ⚹, □, △, ☍, *viz.* when two Planets are going to Conjunction; as ♂ in 7 degr. of ♈, ♄ in 15 of ♈; let us admit the ☉ in 5 degr. of ♊; he then being more swift than ♂ in his diurnal motion, does quickly overtake and pass by the ⚹ dexter of ♂ (and comes before ♂ can come to ♂) to a ⚹ dexter of ♄. This is called Prohibition by Aspect, in the same nature judge if the Aspect be □, △, ☍.

2.

There's another manner of Prohibition; by some more properly called Refrenation; as thus, ♄ in 12 degr. of ♈, ♂ in 7 degr., here ♂ hastens to a ♂ of ♄, but before he comes to the tenth or eleventh degree of ♈ he becomes Retrograde, and by that means refrains to come to a ♂ of ♄, who still moves forward in the Sign; nothing signified by the former ♂ will ever be effected.

Refrenation.

Translation of light and nature is, when a light Planet separates from a more weighty one, and presently joins to another more heavy; and it's in this manner, Let ♄ be in 20 degr. of ♈: ♂ in 15 of ♈, and ☿ in 16 of ♈; here ☿ being a swift Planet separates from ♂, and translates the virtue of ♂ to ♄. It's done also as well by any Aspect as by ♂. And the meaning here in judgement, is no more than thus; That if a matter or thing were promised by ♄, then such a man as is signified by ☿ shall procure all the assistance a *Mars* man can do to *Saturn*, whereby the business may be the better effected. In Marriages, Lawsuits, and indeed in all vulgar questions Translation, is of great use, and ought well to be considered.

Translation.

Reception. Reception is when two Planets that are significators in any Question or matter, are in each other's dignity; as ☉ in ♈, and ♂ in ♌; here is reception of these two Planets by Houses; and certainly this is the strongest and best of all receptions. It may be by triplicity, term or face, or any essential dignity; as ♀ in ♈, and ☉ in ♉; here is reception by triplicity, if the Question or Nativity be by day; so ♀ in the 24 degr. of ♈, and ♂ in the 16 degr. of ♊; here is reception by term, ♂ being in the terms of ♀, and she in his terms.

The use of this is much; for many times when as the effecting of the matter is denied by the Aspects, or when the significators have no Aspect to each other, or when it seems very doubtful what is promised by □ or ☍ of the significators, yet if mutual Reception happen between the principal significators, the thing is brought to pass, and that without any great trouble, and suddenly to the content of both parties.

Peregrine. A Planet is then said to be Peregrine, when he is in the degrees of any Sign where he has no essential dignity: As ♄ in the tenth degree of ♈, that Sign being not his House, Exaltation, or of his Triplicity, or he having in that degree neither Term or Faces, he is then said to be Peregrine. Had he been in 27, 28, &c., of ♈, he could not be termed Peregrine, because then he is in his own Term.

So the ☉ in any part of ♋ is Peregrine, having no manner of dignity in that Sign.

This is very much material in all Questions, to know the Peregrine Planet, especially in questions of Theft; for ever almost the significator of the Thief is known by the Peregrine Planet placed in an Angle, or the second House.

Void of Course. A Planet is void of course, when he is separated from a Planet, nor does forthwith, during his being in that Sign, apply to any other: This is most usually in the ☽; in judgements do you carefully observe whether she be void of course yea or no; you shall seldom see a business go handsomely forward when she is so.

Frustration. Frustration is, when a swift Planet would corporally join with a more ponderous, but before they can come to a ♂, the more weighty Planet is joined to another, and so the ♂ of the first is frustrated, as ☿ in ten degrees of ♈, ♂ twelve, ♃ in thirteen of ♈; here ☿ strives to come to ☌ with ♂, but ♂ first gets to ☌ with ♃; whereby ☿ is frustrated of the ☌ of ♂: in Questions it signifies as much as our common Proverb, *Two Dogs quarrel, a third gets the Bone.*

Hayz is, when a Masculine and Diurnal Planet is in the day time above the earth, and in a Masculine Sign, and so when a Feminine, Nocturnal Planet in the night is in a Feminine Sign and under the earth: In Questions it usually shows the content of the Querent at time of the Question, when his *significator* is so found. *Hayz.*

Saturn, Jupiter and *Mars* being placed above the Orb of the *Sun,* are called the superior, ponderous and more weighty Planets; *Venus, Mercury* and *Luna* are called the inferior Planets, being under the Orb of the *Sun.* *Superior & inferior Planets.*

A Planet is said to be *Combust* of the ☉, when in the same Sign where the ☉ is in, he is not distant from the ☉ eight degrees and thirty minutes, either before or after the ☉; as ♃ in the tenth degree of ♈, and ☉ in the eighteenth of ♈; here ♃ is *combust*: or let the ☉ be in eighteen of ♈, and ♃ in twenty eight degrees of ♈, here ♃ is *combust*: and you must observe a Planet is more afflicted when the ☉ hastens to ☌ of him, than when the ☉ recedes from him; in regard it's the body of the ☉ that does afflict. I allow the moiety of his own Orbs to show the time of *combustion,* and not of ♃; for by that rule ♃ should not be *combust* before he is within four degrees and a half of the ☉. I know many are against this opinion. *Combustion.*

Use which you find most verity in: the *significator* of the Querent combust, shows him or her in great fear, and overpowered by some great person.

A Planet is said to be still under the Sunbeams, until he is fully elongated or distant from his body 17 degr. either before or after him. *Under the ☉ beams.*

A Planet is in the heart of the Sun, or in Cazimi, when he is not removed from him 17 min. or is within 17 min. forward or backward, as ☉ in 15.30 ♉, ☿ in 15.25 of ♉: here ☿ is in Cazimi, and all Authors do hold a Planet in Cazimi to be fortified thereby; you must observe all Planets may be in Combustion *Cazimi, or in the heart of the ☉.*

of the ☉, but he with none, and that Combustion can only be by personal ♂ in one Sign, not by any aspect, either ⚹, □, △ or ☍, his □ or opposite aspects are afflicting, but do not Combure or cause the Planet to be in Combustion.

Oriental.   ♄, ♃ and ♂, are Oriental of the ☉, from the time of their ♂ with him, until they come to his ☍: from whence
Occidental. until again they come to ♂, they are said to be Occidental; to be Oriental is no other thing than to rise before the ☉: to be Occidental is to be seen above the horizon, or to set after the ☉ is down: ☿ and ♀ can make no ⚹, □, △ or ☍ to the ☉: their Orientality is when they are in fewer degrees of the Sign the ☉ is, or in the Sign preceding; their Occidentality, when they are in more degrees of the Sign the ☉ is in, or next subsequent: for you must know ☿ cannot be more degrees removed from the ☉ than 28, nor ♀ more than 48 though some allow a few more. The ☽ is Oriental of the ☉ from the time of her ☍ to the conjunction, and Occidental from the time of her Conjunction to Opposition; and the reason here is, because she far exceeds the Sun in swiftness of motion, and so presently gets further into the Sign, &c.

Besieging.   Besieging is, when any Planet is placed between the bodies of the two Malevolent Planets ♄ and ♂: as ♄ in 15 ♈, ♂ in 10 of ♈, ♀ in 13 ♈: here *Venus* is besieged by the two infortunes, and it represents in questions, a Man going out of God's blessing into the warm Sun; I mean if ♀ be a significatrix that time in the figure.

There are other accidents belonging to the Planets one amongst another mentioned by the Ancients, but of so little purpose in judgement, that I have clearly omitted them.

Direction is.   When a Planet moves forward in the Sign, as going out of 13 degr. into 14 and so along.

Retrograda-   When a Planet goes backward, as out of 10 degr. into 9,
tion is. 8, 7, &c.

Stationary   When he moves not at all, as the superiors do not 2, 3,
is. or 4 days before Retrogradation.

A ready TABLE whereby to examine the *Fortitudes* and *Debilities* of the Planets

Essential Dignities.

A Planet in his own house, or in mutual reception with another Planet by house, shall have dignities	5
In his exaltation, or reception by exaltation	4
In his own triplicity	3
In his own term	2
Decanate or face	1

Debilities.

In his detriment	-5
In his fall	-4
Peregrine	-5

Accidental Fortitudes

In the Midheaven or Ascendant	5
In the seventh, fourth & eleventh houses	4
In the second and fifth	3
In the ninth	2
In the third house	1
Direct (the ☉ and ☽ are always so, as to them this is void)	4
Swift in motion	2
♄ ♃ ♂ when Oriental	2
☿ and ♀ when Occidental	2
The ☽ increasing, or when she is Occidental	2
Free from Combustion and ☉ Beams	5
In the heart of the ☉, or Cazimi	5
In partile ☌ with ♃ and ♀	5
In partile ☌ with ☊	4
In partile △ to ♃ and ♀	4
In partile ✶ to ♃ and ♀	3
In ☌ with Cor Leonis, in 24 degr. ♌	6
Or in ☌ with Spica ♍, in 18 ♎	5

Accidental Debilities

In the twelfth House	-5
In the eighth and sixth	-2
Retrograde	-5
Slow in motion	-2
♄ ♃ ♂ Occidental	-2
♀ ☿ Oriental	-2
☽ decreasing in light	-2
Combust of the ☉	-5
Under the ☉ Beams	-4
Partile ☌ with ♄ or ♂	-5
Partile ☌ with ☋	-4
Besieged of ♄ and ♂	-5
Partile ☍ of ♄ or ♂	-4
Partile □ of ♄ or ♂	-3
In ☌ with Caput Algol in 20 ♉, or within five degrees.	-5

Positions as of **1 Jan. 2005**

Caput Algol:
26 ♉ 14

Cor Leonis
29 ♌ 54

Spica ♍
23 ♎ 54

I forbear here to explain the Table, because I shall do it better hereafter, upon some Example.

Two necessary TABLES of the Signs, fit to be understood by every Astrologer or Practitioner

Degrees masculine and feminine.	Degr. light, dark, smoky, void.	Degr. deep or pitted.	Degr. lame or deficient	Degr. increasing fortune
♈ *mas:* 8, 15, 30 *fem:* 9, 22	d.3, l.8, d.16, l.20, v.24, l.29, v.30	6 11 16 23 29		19
♉ *mas:* 11, 21, 30 *fem:* 5, 17, 24	d.3, l.7, v.12, l.15, v.20, l.28, d.30	5 12 24 25	6 7 8 9 10	3 15 27
♊ *mas:* 16, 26 *fem:* 5, 22, 30	l.4, d.7, l.12, v.16, l.22, d.27, v.30	2 12 17 26 30		11
♋ *mas:* 2, 10, 23, 30 *fem:* 8, 12, 27	l.12, d.14, v.18, sm.20, l.28, v.30	12 17 23 26 30	9 10 11 12 13 14 15	1 2 3 4 15
♌ *mas:* 5, 15, 30 *fem:* 8, 23	d.10, sm.20, v.25, l.30	6 13 15 22 23 28	18 27 28	2 5 7 19
♍ *mas:* 12, 30 *fem:* 8, 20	d.5, l.8, v.10, l.16, sm.22, v.27, d.30	8 13 16 21 22		3 14 20
♎ *mas:* 5, 20, 30 *fem:* 15, 27	l.5, d.10, l.18, d.21, l.27, v.30	1 7 20 30		3 15 21
♏ *mas:* 4, 17, 30 *fem:* 14, 25	d.3, l.8, v.14, l.22, sm.24, v.29, d.30	9 10 22 23 27	19 28	7 18 20
♐ *mas:* 2, 12, 30 *fem:* 5, 24	l.9, d.12, l.19, sm.23, l.30	7 12 15 24 27 30	1 7 8 18 19	13 20
♑ *mas:* 11, 30 *fem:* 19	d.7, l.10, sm.15, d.19, d.22, v.25, d.30	7 17 22 24 29	26 27 28 29	12 13 14 20
♒ *mas:* 5, 21, 27 *fem:* 15, 25, 30	sm.4, l.9, d.13, l.21, v.25, l.30	1 12 17 22 24 29	18 19	7 16 17 20
♓ *mas:* 10, 23, 30 *fem:* 20, 28	d.6, l.12, d.18, d.22, v.25, l.28, d.30	4 9 24 27 28		13 20

The use of the Table.

Many times it happens, that it is of great concern to the Querent to know, whether a Woman be with child of a Male or Female; or whether the Thief be Man or Woman, &c. When it shall so chance that neither the Angles, or the sex of the Planet, or the Signs do discover it, but that the testimonies are equal; then if you consider the degrees of the Sign wherein the ☽ is, and wherein the Planet significator of the thing or party quesited is, and the degree of the Cusp of the House signifying the person quesited after; and see by the second Column whether they be in Masculine or Feminine Degrees, you may pose your judgement, by concluding a Masculine party, if they be placed in Masculine degrees; or Feminine, if they be in Feminine degrees. You see the first eight degrees of ♈ are Masculine, the ninth degree is Feminine, from nine to fifteen is Masculine, from fifteen to two and twenty is Feminine, from two and twenty to thirty is Masculine; and so as they stand directed in all the Signs.

The third Column tells you there are in every Sign certain Degrees, some called Light, Dark, Smoky, Void, &c., the use here is thus:

Let a Sign ascend in a Nativity or Question, if the Ascendant be in those Degrees you see are called Light, the Child or querent shall be more fair; if the degree ascending be of those we call Dark, his Complexion shall be nothing so fair, but more obscure and dark; and if he be born deformed, the deformity shall be more and greater; but if he be deformed when the light degrees of a Sign ascend, the imperfection shall be more tolerable.

And if the ☽ or the Degree ascending be in those degrees we call Void, be the Native or Querent fair or foul, his understanding will be small, and his judgement less than the world supposes, and the more thou conferest with him, the greater defect shall you find in him. If the Ascendant, the ☽, or either of them be in those degrees we call Smoky, the person inquiring or Native, shall neither be very fair nor very foul, but of a mixed Complexion, Stature or condition, between fair and foul, between tall and of little Stature, and so in condition neither very judicious or a very Ass.

You see the three first Degrees of ♈ are Dark, from three to eight are light, from eight to sixteen are Dark, from sixteen to twenty are Light, from twenty to four and twenty are Void, from four and twenty to nine and twenty are Light, the last degree is Void.

Degrees, deep or pitted   Degrees deep or pitted presented in the fourth Column have this signification, that if either the ☽ or the Degree ascending or Lord of the Ascendant be in any of them, it shows the Man at a stand in the question he asks, not knowing which way to turn himself, and that he had need of help to bring him into a better condition; for as a man cast into a Ditch does not easily get out without help, so no more can this querent in the case he is without assistance.

Called by some Azimene degrees.   Degrees lame and deficient are those mentioned in the fifth Column; the meaning whereof is thus, If in any question you find him that demands the question, or in a Nativity, if you find the Native defective in any member, or infected with an incurable disease, halting, blindness, deafness, &c. you may then suppose the native has either one of these Azimene degr. ascending at his birth, or the Lord of the Ascendant, or the ☽ in one of them: in a Question or Nativity, if you see the Querent lame naturally, crooked, or vitiated in some member, and on the sudden you can in the figure give no present satisfaction to your self, do you then consider the Degree ascending, or degree wherein the ☽ is in, or the Lord of the Ascendant, or principal Lord of the Nativity or Question, and there is no doubt but you shall find one or more of them in Azimene degrees.

Degrees increasing fortune.   These Degrees are related in the sixth Column, and tend to this understanding, that if the Cusp of the second House, or if the Lord of the second house, or ♃, or the Part of Fortune be in any of those degrees, it's an argument of much wealth, and that the Native or Querent will be rich.

A TABLE showing what members in Man's Body every Planet signifies in any of the twelve SIGNS.

		♄	♃	♂	☉	♀	☿	☽
♈		Breast, Arm.	Neck, Throat, Heart, Belly.	Belly, Head.	Thighs.	Reins, Feet.	Secrets, Legs.	Knees, Head.
♉		Heart, Breast, Belly.	Shoulders, Arms, Belly, Neck.	Reins, Throat.	Knees.	Secret-members, Head.	Thighs, Feet.	Legs, Throat.
♊		Belly, Heart.	Breast, Reins, Secrets.	Secrets, Arms, Breast.	Legs, Ankles.	Thighs, Throat.	Knees, Head.	Feet, Shoulders, Arms, Thighs.
♋		Reins, Belly, Secrets.	Heart, Secrets, Thighs.	Thighs, Breast.	Knees.	Knees, Shoulders, Arms.	Legs, Throat, Eyes.	Head, Breast, Stomach.
♌		Secrets, Reins.	Belly, Thighs, Knees.	Knees, Heart, Belly.	Head.	Legs, Breast, Heart.	Feet, Arms, Shoulders, Throat.	Throat, Stomach, Heart.
♍		Thighs, Secrets, Feet.	Reins, Knees.	Legs, Belly.	Throat.	Feet, Stomach, Heart, Belly.	Head, Breast, Heart.	Arms, Shoulders, Bowels.
♎		Knees, Thighs.	Secrets, Legs, Head, Eyes.	Feet, Reins, Secrets.	Shoulders, Arms.	Head, small guts.	Throat, Heart, Stomach, Belly.	Breast, Reins, Heart, Belly.
♏		Knees, Legs.	Thighs, Feet.	Head, Secrets, Arms, Thighs.	Breast, Heart.	Throat, Reins, Secrets.	Shoulders, Arms, Bowels, Back	Stomach, Heart, Secrets, Belly.

	♄	♃	♂	☉	♀	☿	☽
♐	Legs, Feet.	Knees, Head, Thighs.	Throat, Thighs, Hands, Feet.	Heart, Belly.	Shoulder, Arms, Secrets, Thighs.	Breast, Reins, Heart, Secrets.	Bowels, Thighs, Back.
♑	Head, Feet.	Legs, Neck, Eyes, Knees.	Arms, Shoulders, Knees, Legs.	Belly, Back.	Breast, Heart, Thighs.	Stomach, Heart, Secrets.	Reins, Knees, Thighs.
♒	Neck, Head.	Feet, Arms, Shoulder, Breast.	Breast, Legs, Heart.	Reins, Secrets.	Heart, Knees.	Bowels, Thighs, Heart.	Secrets, Legs, Ankles.
♓	Arms, Shoulders, Neck.	Head, Breast, Heart.	Heart, Feet, Belly, Ankles.	Secrets, Thighs.	Belly, Legs, Neck, Throat.	Reins, Knees, Secrets, Thighs.	Thighs, Feet.

The Use and Reason of the former Table.

It was well near four years after I had studied Astrology, before I could find any reason, why the Planets in every of the Signs should signify the members as mentioned in the Table: at last, reading the **88 Aphorisms of Hermes,** I understood the meaning of it, viz. *Erit im-pedimentum circa illam partem corporis quam significat signum, quod fuerit nativitatis tempore impeditum.* There will be some impediment in or near that part of the body, which is signified by the Sign that shall be afflicted at the time of the Birth. The use of all comes to thus much:

That if you would know where any Disease is, I mean in what member of the body, see in what Sign the *significator* of the sick Party is, and what part of man's body that Planet signifies in that Sign, which you may do by the former Table, in that member or part of the body shall you say the sick party is grieved or diseased.

As if ♄ be Significator of the sick party, and at time of your

Question in ♊; have recourse to your Table, and you see ♄ in ♊ signifies a disease in the Belly or heart &c. Do so in the rest.

Now the reason of this signification of every Planet in such or such a Sign is this:

Every Planet in his own House or Sign, governs the head; in the second Sign from his House, the Neck; in the third Sign from his House, the Arms and Shoulders; and so successively through the twelve Signs: as ♄ in ♑ rules the Head, in ♒ the Neck, in ♓ Arms and Shoulders: so ♃ in ♐ rules the Head, in ♑ the Neck, in ♒ the Arms and Shoulders.

The ☽ observes the same order as the rest; yet the *Arabians*, from whom this learning is, do allow her in ♈ the Head as well as the Knees: The Head, because *Aries* signifies so much: The Knees, because *Aries* is the ninth Sign from *Cancer*.

You may observe this in the marks of man's Body, and many other judgements, and make singular use of it; ever remembering this, the more the Sign is vitiated, the greater mole or scar; or the nearer to an *Azimene, Pitted* or *deficient* degree of the Sign, the stronger is the deformity, sickness, &c.

CONSIDERATIONS *before Judgment.*

All the *Ancients* that have wrote of Questions, do give warning to the *Astrologer*, that before he deliver judgement he well consider whether the Figure is radical and capable of judgement; the Question then shall be taken for radical, or fit to be judged, when as the Lord of the hour at the time of proposing the Question, and erecting the Figure, and the Lord of the Ascendant or first House, are of one Triplicity, or be one, or of the same nature.

As for example; let the Lord of the hour be ♂, let the Sign of ♏ ♋ or ♓ ascend, this Question is then radical, because ♂ is Lord of the hour, and of the Watery Triplicity, or of those Signs ♋ ♏ or ♓.

Again, let the Lord of the hour be ♂, and ♈ ascend, the Question shall be radical, because ♂ is both Lord of the hour and Sign ascending.

Let the Lord of the hour be ♂, and let the Sign ♌ ascend, here, although the ☉ is one of the Lords of the fiery Triplicity, and sole Lord of the Sign ♌, yet shall the Question be judged; because the ☉, who is Lord of the Ascendant, and ♂ who is Lord of the hour, are both of one nature, *viz.* Hot and Dry.

When either 0 degrees, or the first or second degrees of a Sign ascend (especially in Signs of short ascensions, *viz.* ♑, ♒, ♓, ♈, ♉, ♊), you may not venture judgement, unless the Querent be very young, and his corporature, complexion and moles or scars of his body agree with the quality of the Sign ascending.

If 27, 28, or 29 degrees ascend of any Sign, it's no ways safe to give judgement, except the Querent be in years corresponding to the number of degrees ascending; or unless the Figure be set upon a time certain, *viz.* a man went away or fled at such a time precise; here you may judge, because it's no propounded question.

It's not safe to judge when the ☽ is in the later degrees of a Sign, especially in ♊, ♏ or ♑; or as some say, when she is in *Via Combusta*, which is, when she is in the last 15 degrees of ♎, or the first 15 degrees of ♏.

All manner of matters go hardly on (except the principal *significators* be very strong) when the ☽ is void of course; yet somewhat she performs if void of course, and be either in ♉, ♋, ♐, or ♓.

You must also be wary, when in any question propounded you find the Cusp of the seventh house afflicted, or the Lord of that house Retrograde, or impeded, and the matter at that time not concerning the seventh house, but belonging to any other house, it's an argument the judgement of the Astrologer will give small content, or anything please the Querent; for the seventh house generally has signification of the *Artist*.

The *Arabians*, as *Alkindus* and others, do deliver these following rules, as very fit to be considered before a Question be judged.

Viz. if ♄ be in the Ascendant, especially Retrograde, the matter of that Question seldom or never comes to good.

♄ in the seventh either corrupts the judgement of the *Astrologer*, or is a Sign the matter propounded will come from one misfortune to another.

If the Lord of the Ascendant be Combust, neither question propounded will take, or the Querent be regulated.

The Lord of the seventh unfortunate, or in his fall, or Terms of the Infortunes, the *Artist* shall scarce give a solid judgement.

When the testimonies of Fortunes and Infortunes are equal, defer judgement, it's not possible to know which way the Balance will turn: however, defer you your opinion till another question better inform you.

CHAPTER XX.

What Significator, Querent and Quesited are; and an Introduction to the Judgment of a Question.

The Querent is he or she that propounds the question, and desires resolution: the Quesited is he or she, or the thing sought and inquired after.

The *significator* is no more than that Planet which rules the house that signifies the thing demanded: as if ♈ is ascending, ♂ being Lord of ♈, shall be *significator* of the Querent, *viz.* the Sign ascending shall in part signify his corporature, body or stature, the Lord of the Ascendant, the ☽ and Planet in the Ascendant, or that the ☽ or Lord of the Ascendant are in aspect with, shall show his quality or conditions equally mixed together; so that let any Sign ascend, what Planet is Lord of that Sign, shall be called Lord of the House, or Significator of the person inquiring, &c.

So that in the first place therefore, When any Question is propounded, the Sign ascending and his Lord are always given to him or her that asks the question.

2ˡʸ You must then consider the matter propounded, and see to which of the twelve houses it does properly belong: when you have found the house, consider the Sign and Lord of that Sign, how, and in what Sign and what part of Heaven he is placed, how dignified, what aspect he has to the Lord of the Ascendant, who impedes your *Significator*, who is friend to him, *viz.* what Planet it is, and what house he is Lord of, or in what house placed; from such a man or woman signified by that Planet, shall you be furthered or hindered; or of such relation to you as that Planet signifies; if Lord of such a house, such an enemy, if Lord of such a house as signifies enemies, then an enemy verily; if of a friendly house, a friend: The whole natural key of all Astrology rests in the words preceding rightly understood: By the Examples following I shall make all things more plain; for I do not desire, or will reserve anything whereby the Learner may be kept in suspense of right understanding what is useful for him, and most fit to be known.

In every question we do give the ☽ as a *Cosignificator* with the querent or Lord of the Ascendant (some have also allowed the Planet from whom the ☽ separated as a *significator*; which I no way approve of, or in my practice could ever find any Verity therein.)

In like manner they joined in judgement the Planet to whom the ☽ applied at time of the question, as *Cosignificator* with the Lord of the house of the thing quesited, or thing demanded.

Having well considered the several applications and separations of the Lords of those houses signifying your question, as also the ☽, the Scheme of Heaven and quality of the aspect of the ☽, and each *Significator* has to each other, you may begin to judge and consider whether the thing demanded will come to pass yea or no; by what, or whose means, the time when, and whether it will be good for the querent to proceed further in his demands yea or no.

CHAPTER XXI.
To know whether a thing demanded will be brought to perfection yea or nay.

The *Ancients* have delivered to us, that there are four ways or means, which discover whether one question or the thing demanded shall be accomplished yea or not.

First, by *Conjunction;* when as therefore you find the Lord of the Ascendant, and Lord of that house which signifies the thing demanded, hastening to a ♂, and in the first house, or in any Angle, and the *significators* meet with no *prohibition* or *refrenation*, before they come to perfect ♂; you may then judge, that the thing sought after, shall be brought to pass without any manner of let or impediment, the sooner, if the *Significators* be in swift motion, and Essentially or Accidentally strong; but if this ♂ of the *Significators* be in a Succedent house, it will be perfected, but not so soon: if in Cadent houses, with infinite loss of time, some difficulty, and much struggling.

Things are also brought to pass, when as the principal signifiers apply by ✳ or △ aspect out of good Houses and places where they are essentially well dignified (and meet with no malevolent Aspect to intervene ere they come to be in perfect ✳ or △; I mean to the partile Sextile or Trine.)

Things are also produced to perfection, when the Significators apply by □ aspect, provided each Planet have dignity in the Degrees wherein they are, and apply out of proper and good Houses, otherwise not. Sometimes it happens, that a matter is brought to pass when the Significators have applied by ☍, but it has been, when there has been mutual reception by House, and out of friendly Houses, and the ☽ separating from the Significator of the thing demanded, and applying presently to the Lord of the Ascendant; I have rarely seen any thing brought to perfection by this way of opposition; but the Querent had been better the thing had been undone; for if the Question was concerning Marriage, the parties seldom agreed, but were ever wrangling and jangling, each party repining at his evil choice, laying the blame upon their covetous Parents, as having no mind to it themselves: and if the Question was about Portion or Monies, the querent did, its true, recover his Money or Portion promised, but it cost him more to procure it in suit of Law, than the debt was worth, &c. and so have I seen it happen in many other things, &c.

Things are brought to perfection by Translation of Light and Nature, in this manner.

When the *Significators* both of *Querent* and *Quesited* are separated from ♂ or ✳ or △ aspects of each other, and some one Planet or other do separate himself from one of the *Significators*, of whom he is received either by House, Triplicity, or Term, and then this Planet does apply to the other *Significator* by ♂ or aspect, before he meets with the ♂ or aspect of any other Planet, he then translates the force, influence and virtue of the first Significator to the other, and then this intervening Planet (or such a man or woman as is signifies by that Planet) shall bring the matter in hand to perfection.

Consider what house the Planet interposing or translating the nature and light of the two Planets is Lord of, and describe him or her, and say to the party, that such a party shall do good in the business of, &c. *viz.* if Lord of the second, a good Purse effects the matter; if Lord of the third, a Kinsman or Neighbour; and so of all the rest of the Houses: of which more shall be said in the following Judgements.

Collection. Matters are also brought to perfection, when as the two principal Significators do not behold one another, but both cast their several Aspects to a more weighty Planet than themselves, and they both receive him in some of their essential dignities; then shall that Planet who thus collects both their Lights, bring the thing demanded to perfection: which signifies no more in Art than this, that a Person somewhat interested in both parties and described and signified by that Planet, shall perform, effect and conclude the thing which otherwise could not be perfected: As many times you see two fall at variance, and of themselves cannot think of any way of accommodation, when suddenly a Neighbour or friend accidentally reconciles all differences, to the consent of both parties: And this is called *Collection.*

Lastly, things are sometimes perfected by the dwelling of Planets in houses, *viz.* when the *Significator* of the thing demanded is casually placed in the Ascendant; as if one demand if he shall obtain such a Place or Dignity, if then the Lord of the tenth be placed in the Ascendant, he shall obtain the Benefit, Office, Place or Honour desired: This rule of the Ancients holds not true, or is consentanious to reason: except they will admit, that when the ☽, besides this dwelling in house, does transfer the light of the *Significator* of the thing desired, to the Lord of the Ascendant; for it was well observed that the application of the *Significators* show inclination of the parties, but separation usually privation; that is, in more plain terms, when you see the principal *Significators* of the *Querent*, and thing or party quesited after separated, there's then little hopes of effecting or perfecting what is desired, (notwithstanding this dwelling in houses) but if there be application, the parties seem willing, and the matter is yet kept on foot, and there is great probability of perfecting it, or that things will come to a further treaty.

In all Questions you are generally to observe this Method following.

As the Ascendant represents the person of the Querent, and the second his Estate, the third his Kindred, the fourth his Father, the fifth his Children, the sixth his Servant or Sickness, the seventh his Wife, the eighth the manner of his Death, the ninth his Religion or journeys, the tenth his Estimation or honour, the eleventh his Friends, the twelfth his secret Enemies.

So you must also understand, that when one asks concerning a Woman or any party signified by the seventh House and the Lord thereof, that then the 7ᵗʰ House shall be her Ascendant and signify her person, the eighth House shall signify her Estate and be her second, the ninth House shall signify her Brethren and Kindred, the tenth shall represent her Father, the eleventh her Children or whether apt to have Children, the twelfth her Sickness and Servants, the first House her Sweetheart, the second House her Death, the third her Journey, the fourth her Mother, the fifth her Friends, the sixth her sorrow, care and private Enemies.

Let the Question be of or concerning a Churchman, Minister, or the Brother of the Wife or Sweetheart, the ninth House shall represent each of these, but the tenth House shall be Significator of his Substance, the eleventh House of his Brethren, and so in order: and so in all manner of Questions the House signifying the party quested shall be his Ascendant or first

House the next his second House, and so continuing round about the whole Heavens or twelve Houses.

If a question be made of a King, the tenth is his first house, the eleventh his second, and so orderly: but in Nativities, the Ascendant ever signifies the party born, whether King or Beggar: These things preceding being well understood, you may proceed to judgement; not that it is necessary you have all that is wrote, in your memory exactly, but that you be able to know when you are in an error, when not; when to judge a question, when not: I should also have showed how to take the *Part of Fortune*, but that I will do in the first Example, the use of the *Part of Fortune* being diverse, but hardly understood rightly by any Author I ever met with: However note, if a King propound an *Astrological Question*, the Ascendant is for him, as well as for any meaner party; and all the houses in order, as for any vulgar person: For Kings are earth, and no more than men; and the time is coming, &c. when.

THE RESOLVTION
of all manner of QUESTIONS
and DEMANDS.

CHAPTER XXII.
Questions Concerning the first House.

If the Querent *is likely to live long yea or not.*

 ANY Men and Women have not the time of their *Nativities*, or know how to procure them, either their Parents being dead, or no remembrance being left thereof; and yet for divers weighty considerations they are desirous to know by a question of Astrology, *Whether they shall live long or not?*, *Whether any sickness is near them?*, *What part of their Life is like to be most happy?* Together with many other such *Queries* people do demand incident to this house.

SIGNS *of Health or long Life.*

In the *Question* you must consider if the Sign ascending, the Lord thereof, and the ☽ be free from misfortune, *viz.* if the Lord of the Ascendant be free from Combustion of the ☉, *Signs of Health.*

from the □, ☍ or ☌ of the Lord of the eighth, twelfth, sixth or fourth house, if he be Direct, in Essential Dignity, swift in Motion, or Angular, especially in the first house, (for in this question he is best placed therein) or tenth, or else in the eleventh, or ninth houses, and in a good aspect with ♃ or ♀, or the ☉, or in the Terms of ♃ and ♀, it's an argument of Health and long life to the *Querent*, for the Lord of the *Signs* Ascendant, or Ascendant itself unfortunate or ☽ in bad houses *contrary,* afflicted, show mischief at hand; the aforesaid *significators* free, *viz. of* argue the contrary: for as you consider the Lord of the Ascendant, *Sickness,* so the Ascendant is to be considered, and what aspect is cast to *Death, &c.* it, *viz.* good or evil, and by what Planet or Planets, and of what *Misfortune* house or houses they are Lords of.

It's generally received, that if the Lord of the Ascendant be under the *Sun* beams, or going to Combustion, which is worse than when he is departing, or the ☽ cadent and unfortunated by any of those Planets who have dominion in the eighth or sixth, and either the ☋, ♄ or ♂ in the Ascendant or seventh House, peregrine or in their detriments, or retrograde, or if there be in the degree ascending, or in that degree of the Sign wherein the Lord of the Ascendant is, or with the ☽, or with that Planet who afflicts any of those; I say, any fixed *Star* of violent influence or nature of the Planet afflicting, or nature of the Lord of the eighth or sixth House, then you may judge the *Querent* is not long lived, but near some danger, or shall undergo some misfortune in one kind or other, according to the quality of the *significator* and signification of that or those houses they are Lords of.

The Time When Any of *These* **Accidents** *Shall Happen.*

You must see if the Lord of the Ascendant be going to Combustion, or to ☍ or ☌ of the Lord of the eighth or fourth, how many degrees he is distant from the ☉, or Lord of the eighth or fourth, and in what Sign either of them are in; if the space between them be eight degrees, and in a common Sign, it denotes so many months; if in a fixed sign, so many years; if in a moveable, so many weeks: this is only for example, and in general; for the measure of time must be limited according to the other *significators* concurring in judgment herein.

Secondly, having considered the Lord of the Ascendant, see how many degrees the ☽ is also distant from any Infortune, or from the Lords of the sixth or eighth, and in what Sign or Signs their Nature, Quality and House wherein they are placed.

Thirdly, consider if there be an Infortune in the Ascendant, how many degrees the Cusp of the house wants of that degree the unfortunate Planet is in, or if the unfortunating Planet be in the seventh, how many degrees the Ascendant wants of his true Opposition, and compute the time of Death, Sicknesses or Misfortune according to the dimension of degrees in Signs moveable, common, or fixed.

If you find the Lord of the Ascendant afflicted most of all by the Lord of the sixth, and in the sixth, or if the Lord of the Ascendant comes to Combustion in the sixth, you may judge the *Querent* will have very many and tedious sicknesses, which will scarce leave him till his death; and the more certain the judgment will be, if the Lord of the Ascendant, and the Lord of the eighth and the ☽ be all placed in the sixth.

If you find the Lord of the Ascendant, the Sign ascending, or ☽ most principally impeded or unfortunated by the Lord of the eighth, or that Planet who afflicts your *significators* out of the eighth, then you may judge that the sickness with which he is now afflicted, or is shortly to be troubled with, will end him, and that his death is approaching for that death is threatened.

But if you find that the Lord of the Ascendant, or Sign of the Ascendant, or the ☽ are chiefly afflicted by the Lords of some other houses, you shall judge his misfortune from the nature of the house or houses whereof the Planet or Planets afflicting are Lords; and the first original thereof, or discovery, shall be signified from something, Man or Woman, &c. belonging to that house wherein you find the Planet afflicting placed, and thereby you shall judge a misfortune and not death: The fixed Stars I mentioned, being of the nature of ♂, show sudden distempers of body, or Fevers, Murders, Quarrels &c. of the nature of ♄, quartan Agues, Poverty, casual hurts by falls &c; of the nature of ☿, they declare Consumptions, Madness, cozenage by false Evidence or Writings; of the nature of the ☽, Tumults, Commotions, Wind-cholic, danger by Water, &c; of the nature of the ☉, envy of Magistrates, hurt in the Eyes, &c.; of the nature of ♃, oppression by domineering Priests, or by some Gentleman; of the nature of ♀, then prejudice by some Woman, the Pox, or Cards, Dice and Wantonness.

Caution.　　You must carefully avoid pronouncing Death rashly, and upon one single testimony, you must observe, though the Lord of the Ascendant be going to Combustion, whether either ♃ or ♀ cast not some ⚹ or △ to the Lord of the Ascendant, ere he come to perfect Combustion, or any other infortune, for that is an argument that either Medicine or strength of Nature will contradict that malignant influence, or take off part of that misfortune; but when you find two or more of the rules asforesaid concurring to death, you may be more bold in your Judgement; yet concerning the absolute time of death of any party, I have found it best to be wary, and have as much as I could, refrained this manner of judgement; only thus much by the Question may be known, that if you find the *significators*, as aforesaid, afflicted, you may judge the man or party inquiring to be no long lived man, or subject to many miseries and calamities, and this I know by many verified examples; the knowledge hereof is of excellent use for such as would purchase any Lease or Office, or thing for Life or Lives, &c. or for those who would carefully in a natural way prevent those casualties their natures or inclinations would run them into.

To what part of Heaven its best the Querent direct his Affairs, or wherein he may live most happily.

You must know that the twelve Houses are divided into the East, West, North and South quarters of Heaven.

The Cusp of the first House is the beginning of the East, and it's called the East Angle, from the Degree of the first house to the Degree or Cusp of the tenth House or *Medium Coeli*, containing the 12, 11 and tenth Houses, are East, inclining to the South: from the Cusp of the tenth House to the Cusp of the seventh house, containing the 9, 8, and 7, is South, verging toward the West; from the degree of the seventh House to the Cusp of the fourth House, consisting of the 6, 5, and fourth houses, is the West, tending to the North; from the Degree of the fourth House to the degree of the Ascendant, containing the 3, 2, and first Houses, is North inclining to the East.

Having viewed the several quarters of Heaven, see in which of them you find the Planet that promises the Querent most good, and where you find ♃, ♀, ☽ or ⊗, or two or more of them, to that quarter direct your affairs; and if you have the part of Fortune and the ☽ free from Combustion and other misfortunes, go that way, or to that quarter of heaven where you find her; for you must consider, that though ♃ and ♀ be Fortunes, yet casually they may be Infortunes, when they are Lords of the 8, 12, or 6. In that case you must avoid the quarter they are in, and observe the ⊗ and the ☽ and the Lord of the Ascendant; and as near as you can avoid that quarter of Heaven where the infortunes are, especially when they are significators of mischief, otherwise either ♂ or ♄ being Lord of the Ascendant or second House, tenth or eleventh, may (being essentially strong) prove friendly. The general way of resolving this Question is thus; If the Querent do only desire to live where he may enjoy most health, look in what Sign and quarter of Heaven the Lord of the Ascendant and the ☽ are in, and which of them are strongest, and does cast his or her more friendly Aspect to the Degree ascending; to that quarter of Heaven repair for Health's sake: If the *Querent* desire to know to what part he may steer his course for obtaining of an Estate or Fortune, then see where and in what quarter of Heaven the Lord of the second is placed, and the ⊗, and his *Dispositor* or two of them; for where and in what quarter they are best fortified, from thence may he expect his most advantage, &c. Of this I shall speak casually in subsequent Judgments.

What part of his LIFE *is like to be best.*

See either in what Angle or quarter of Heaven the
fortunate and promising Planets are placed in; for in this
way of Judicature, we give usually to every house five years,
but sometimes more or less, according as you see the
significators promising Life or Death, (but commonly five
years we give) beginning with the twelfth, and so to the
eleventh, then the tenth, then the ninth, &c. and so to the
Ascendant; as if in your Question you find ♃ or ♀ in the
eleventh or tenth house, you may judge the Man or Woman
to have lived happily from the fifth year of his age to the
fifteenth, or in his youth: if they, or either of them, be in
the eighth or seventh, they declare that from twenty to thirty
he will, or has lived, and may live contentedly: if ♃ or ♀ be
in the 6, 5, or 4, then judge after his middle age, or from 30
to 45 he may do very well: If you find ♃ or ♀ in the third,
second, or first, then his best days, or his greatest happiness
will be towards his old age, or after he is forty five until
sixty; if you find the *significators* of Life very strong, and
signifying long Life, you may add one year to every house,
for it's then possible the *Querent* may live more than sixty
years, or until seventy, or more, as many we know do.

Lastly, you must observe at the time of your Question,
how the Lord of the Ascendant and the ☽ are separated,
from what Planet, and by what aspect; the separation of
those show the manner of Accidents which have preceded
the Question; their next application, what in the future
may be expected; if you consider what house or houses, the
Planet or Planets they separated from are Lords of, it
acquaints you with the matter, nature, person and quality of
the thing already happened: ill, if the aspect was ill; Good,
if the aspect was good; and if you observe the quality of the
next aspect by application, and the well or ill being and
position of the Planet or Planets applied to, it delivers the
quality of the next succeeding Accidents and Casualties, their
nature, proportion, time when they will happen or come upon
the *Querent*.

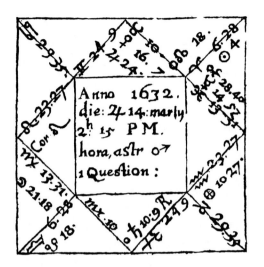

See page
A2

An ASTROLOGICAL Judgment concerning
these demands propounded by the *Querent.*

1. *If he were like to live long, yea or not.*

2. *To what part of the World he were best direct his course of life.*

3. *What part of his life, was in probability like to be most fortunate.*

4. *He desired I would relate (if possible by a Figure) some of the general Accidents had happened to him already.*

5. *What Accidents in future he might expect, good or evil.*

6. *The time when.*

The Stature of the Querent is signified by ♌, the Sign ascending; there is a fixed Star called *Cor Leonis* near the cusp of the first house, *viz.*, in 24.34 of ♌, of the nature of ♂ and ♃, and first magnitude; both the Cusp of the first house and degree of the sign wherein ☉, Lord of the Ascendant is in, are

Position as of 1 January 2005:

Cor ♌: 29 ♌ 54

the terms of ♃; the ☽ is in a △ aspect with both ♃ and ♀, and they in the tenth house; so that the form and Stature of the *Querent's* body was decent, of a middle stature, strongly compacted, neither fat or fleshy, but comely, wanting no gracefulness in its composure; a fair Visage, reddish Hair, clear Skin, some cuts on his right Cheek, (for he was a Soldier;) but certainly the presence of the fixed Star in the Ascendant, which represents the Face, occasioned those hurts or scars.

As the Sign ascending is fiery, and as the Lord of the Ascendant is in a fiery Sign, and by nature is *Hot* and *Dry*, so was this Gentleman's temper and condition, being exceeding Valiant, Choleric, high Minded, and of great spirit; for ☉, Lord of the Ascendant is in his *Exaltation*; yet in regard the ☽ is in △ with the two *Fortunes*, he was sober, modest, and by Education excellently qualified, and thereby had great command of his *Passion*; but as the ☽ was in ☍ to ☿, he had his times of *Anger* and *Folly*, whereby he much prejudiced his Affairs. But to our question.

If live long, &c.

Finding the *Ascendant* not vitiated with the presence of either *Saturn*, who is Lord of the sixth, or of *Jupiter* who is Lord of the eighth.

Seeing the Lord of the *Ascendant* was in *Exaltation*, no ways impeded, pretty quick in motion, in the ninth house, and in the *Terms* of ♃.

Observing the ☽ separated from △ of ♀ applying to △ of ♃, and he placed in the mid heaven, and thereby the malice of ♂ restrained by the interposition of ♃.

Considering the ☉ was above the earth, the fortunate Planets, *viz.* ♃ and ♀ Angular, and more potent than the infortunates, *viz.* ♄ or ♂ : from hence I concluded, that according to natural Causes, he might live many years; and that Nature was strong, and he subject to few Diseases. This has hitherto proved true; he being yet alive this present, *March* 1646.

To what Part of the WORLD, *or of this* KINGDOM,
he might best apply himself to Live in.

The Lord of the *Ascendant* is ☉, who being near the
Cusp of the ninth house, (signifying *long Journeys*) and the
sign thereof Moveable; I intimated he was resolving suddenly
upon a *Journey* Southeast, or to those parts of the World
which lie from *London* Southeast: *South*, because the quarter
of Heaven wherein the Lord of the *Ascendant* is in, is South:
East, because the Sign where ☉ is in is East [*this he confessed:*]
And as the ☉ was but two degrees 10 min. distant from the
Cusp of the ninth, he went away within two months; for ☉
was 4.18 ♈.

I judged those *Countries* subject to the Sign of ♈, might
be suitable and propitious to his Affairs; which you may see
in the nature of ♈, *page* 95, and what their Names are, to
which I now refer you.

Had his resolution been to have stayed in *England*, the ☊
and ☉ being both in ♈, show it might have been good for him, for
England is subject to ♈; I would have advised him to have steered
his course of life towards *Kent, Essex, Sussex* or *Suffolk*, for they
lie East or by South from *London*; but if sometimes you find that
a City, Town or Kingdom subject to the *Celestial* Sign which promises
you good, stands not, as to the *quarter* of Heaven, *directly* as you
would have it, or as the Sign points it out; herein you must observe
this general rule; That if your occasions enforce you, or you shall
and must live in that Country, City, or Town, so directed to you in
Art, that then you must lead your Life, or direct your actions, or
manage your employments to those parts of that City or Country
which lie *East, West, North* or *South*, as in the Figure you were
directed: as for Example; You may see *France* is subject to the
Sign ♈, it lies from *London* Southwest: had this Gentleman gone
into *France*, it would have been best for him to have seated himself
towards the Southeast part, or East part of *France*, &c.

Now because the ☽ applied so strongly to the △ of ♃, and
that he and ♀ were in ♉, and the Sign signifies *Ireland*; I

advised him that *Ireland* would well agree with his Constitution, and that he might get *Honour* there, because the Planet to whom the ☽ applies is in the house of *Honour*.

And verily the *Querent* did go into *Ireland*, and there performed good service and obtained a notable Victory against the *Rebels*; as I could manifest, but that I will not mention the Name of the Gentleman,

What part of his LIFE *would be best.*

Considering the two *Fortunes* were placed in the tenth house, and that ♌ and ☉ were in the ninth, I judged his younger years would be the most pleasant of all his whole *life*; seeing also ♂ in the eighth house, which according to our own direction of time comes to be about 24, 25 or 26 of his age; I judged that about those times he had many crosses, or first of all his afflictions then began; and seeing further no fortunate Planet was either in the seventh, sixth, fifth, fourth or third houses, I judged the remainder of his *life* for many years would be little comfortable to him, but full of labour and trouble; yet I judged those Calamities or Misfortunes should not suddenly come upon him, because the ☽ was in application to a △ of ♃, and wanted almost three degrees of coming to his perfect aspect; wherefore I conceived by means of some man in authority represented by ♃, or some Courtier or person of quality, for almost three years after the proposal of the *Question*, he should be supported and assisted in his affairs, or else get Employment answerable to his desires; had ♃ been Essentially fortified, I should have judged him a more durable fortune.

What general ACCIDENTS *had happened already.*

Although it is not usual to be so nice or inquisitive, yet seeing the Question so radical, I first considered from what Planet or Planets the ☉, who is Lord of the *Ascendant*, had last separated; if you look into the *Ephemeris* of that year, you shall find, that the ☉ had lately, during his passage through the Sign

♓, been first in ☌ with ♂, then in □ of ♄, lately in ⚹ of ♃; now, for that ♂ in our *Figure* is Lord of the fourth house, signifying *Lands*, etc. and was now locally in the eighth, which signifies the substance of *Women*, I judged he had been molested of late concerning some Lands, or the *Jointure* or *Portion* of his Wife, or a Woman: wherein I was confirmed the more, because the ☽ was also applying to an ☍ of ♂, in this Figure placed in the eighth house; for the ☽ being in the *Querent's* house of substance, *viz.* the second, intimated the Quarrel or Strife should be for, or concerning *Money*, for such things as are significated by that house: [*And this was very true.*]

Because ☉ had lately been in □ of ♄, who is *Significator* of the *Querent's* Wife, I told him I feared his Wife and he had lately been at great variance; and because ♄ her *Significator* did dispose of his *Part of Fortune* , I judged she had no mind he should have any of her Estate, or manage it, but kept it to her own use; for ♄ is Retrograde, a superior Planet, and in a fiery Sign, and the Sign of the seventh is fixed; these show her a *Virago*, or gallant spirited Woman, and not willing to be curbed, or else to submit: [*This was confessed.*]

Lastly, because ☉ was lately in ⚹ with ♃, and ♃ was in the tenth; I told him, either some great *Lawyer* or *Courtier* had endeavoured to reconcile the differences between them; and forasmuch as both the ☉ who was his *Significator*, and ♄ who was hers, did now both apply to a △ aspect, there seemed to be at present a willingness in both Parties to be reconciled; nor did I see any great obstruction in the matter, except ☿ who is in □ aspect with ♄, did impede it; I judged ☿ in the general, to signify either some *Attorney*, or *Lawyer*, or *Writings*; but as he is Lord of the *Querent's* second, it might be because the *Querent* would not consent to give or allow such a sum of Money as might be demanded, or that the *Querent's* purse was so weak, he had not wherewithal to solicit his cause lustily; or as ☿ is Lord of the eleventh house, some pretended friend would impede her, or advise the contrary, or some of her *Lawyers*; or as the eleventh is in the fifth from the seventh, a Child of the *Querent's* Wife might be occasion of continuing the Breach. [*I believe every particular herein proved true; however, this was the way*

It was the Lord Coventry

to find the occasion or thing disturbing their unity or concord.]
Observe as ♀ Lady of the tenth, does dispose of ♃ Lord of
the eighth, *viz.* the Wife's Fortune, so she had entrusted her
Estate to a great *Nobleman*.

What ACCIDENTS *in future he might expect; Time when.*

In this *Quere*, I first considered the ☉ Lord of the
Ascendant, who being no ways unfortunated, or in any evil
aspect with any Planet, which might impeach or impede
him, but on the contrary excellently fortified, I judged, he
had the wide world to ramble in, (for a Planet strong, and in
no aspect with others shows a man at liberty to do what he
will;) and that for many years he might (*quoad capax*) live in a
prosperous condition (according to the preceding limitation)
and traverse much ground, or see many Countries; because ♈,
the Sign wherein the ☉ is in, is moveable, placed on the Cusp
of the ninth, signifying long Journeys, which prenoted many
turnings and shiftings, variety of action in sundry parts.

Secondly, I observed the ☽ in the *Querent's* house of
substance, *viz.* the second, did apply to ♃ in the tenth house,
and that ♃ was Lord of the fifth house and eighth: the fifth
house signifies *Children*; the eighth denotes the substance of
the Wife: From hence I gathered, that the *Querent* was very
desirous to treat with some Nobleman (because ♃ is in the
tenth) about the Education of his Child or Children, and
that there might be a Salary payable for their breeding and
education, out of the Wife's Jointure or annual Revenue:
[*Such a thing as this in one kind or other, he did settle before
he went out of* England.]

Thirdly, I found the ☽ in the sign ♍ (*Peregrine*) it being
a Diurnal Question, else she has a Triplicity in that Trigon
by night.

Fourthly, I found ☿ Lord of his second house, *viz.*
signifying his Fortune and Estate, in ♓, which is his
Detriment, yet in his own Terms, afflicted by ♂, from whose
☍ the ☽ lately had separated.

From hence I collected, that he had been in great want of
Money a little before the Question asked; and if we look how

many degrees there is distant between ☽ and ☿, since their ☌ last past, we shall find them to be 6 ᵈ, 21 ᵐ, *viz.* six degrees twenty one minutes which noted, that he had been in some want of Money for about 6 months and somewhat more, or thereabouts, before the time of demanding the Question: [*This was confessed.*]

Fifthly, seeing the ☽ was applying to a △ of ♃, of which signification I spoke before, and then before she got out of the Sign ♍, did occur the ☍ of ♂: I did acquaint the *Querent*, that after some years or times of pleasure, he would be in great danger of losing his Life, Goods, Lands and Fortune. His *Life*, because ♂ is in the eighth: His *Goods* or *Estate*, because ☽ is in the second: His *Lands* or *Inheritance*, because ♂ is Lord of the fourth, now placed in the eighth. For the fourth house signifies Lands, &c.

The Time When.

In this *quere* I considered the application of the ☽ to a △ of ♃, which wanting about three degrees from the true aspect, I judged for some times succeeding the Question, or for three years, he might live pleasantly.

Secondly, seeing the ☉ Lord of his *Ascendant*, during his motion through the Sign ♈, did not meet with any malevolent aspect, and had 26 degrees to run through of the Sign, ere he got into ♉; I gave in this nature of judgment, for every degree one month, and so told him, That for about 26 months following, or until after two years, or much about that time, I judged he should live in a free condition in those parts into which he intended his Journey, &c.

Last of all, I considered how many degrees the ☽ wanted ere she came to the true ☍ of ♂.

Longitude of ♂	28	40
Of the ☽	21	18
Difference	7	22

The difference is seven degrees and twenty-two minutes; which if I proportion into time, and neither give years, because the *Significators* are in Common Signs, and not in Fixed ; or months, because the Signs do signify somewhat more; but do proportion a *mean* between both: the time limited in this way of *Judicature*, will amount to about three years and three quarters from the time of asking the Question, ere the malevolent ☍ of the ☽ to ♂ shall take effect: But in regard his *quere* was general, I might have allowed for every degree one year: After, or about which time, he was in several actions both dangerous to his Person and Fortune; and since that time, til the time of publishing hereof, he has had his *Intervals* of good and ill, but is now under the frown of Fortune, &c.

But as the ☉ at time of the Question was strong, he did overcome all manner of difficulties for many years, and subsisted, and has in our unlucky differences had honorable Employment on his Majesty's part: but as the ☽ is in ☍ to ♂, so it was not without the general outcry and exclamations of the people; nor was it his fortune, though in great Commands, ever to do his Majesty any notable piece of Service; yet is he now forever, by just Sentence of the Parliament, deprived of so much happiness as to end his days in *England*; which, though in some measure, might have been foreseen, by the ☽ her ☍ to ♂, being Lord of the fourth, *viz.* the end of all things.

Yet we must herein admire *Providence*, and acknowledge according to that strong *Maxim of Astrologers*; *That the general Fate of any Kingdom is more prevalent, than the private genitor or question of any Subject or King whatsoever.*

Very little of this Judgment has already failed; I have been herein somewhat large, because young Students might hereby benefit the more; and if my Judgments do vary from the common Rules of the Ancients, let the Candid Reader excuse me, since he may still follow their Principles if he please; and he must know, that from my Conversation in their Writings, I have attained the Method I follow.

CHAPTER XXIII.
Of the Part of Fortune, and how to take it,
either by Day or Night.

Ptolomy does not more consider a Planet than the *Part of Fortune*, thus characterized ⊗; it has no aspect, but any Planets may cast their aspect to it.

The greatest use of it, that hitherto I have either read or made of it for, is thus; That if we find it well placed in the heaven, in a good house, or in a good aspect of a Benevolent Planet, we judge the Fortune or estate of the *querent* to be correspondent to its strength, *viz.* if it be well placed or in an angle, or in those Signs wherein it's fortunated, we judge the estate of the *querent* to be sound and firm, if the ⊗ is otherwise placed, we do the contrary.

The manner either night or day to take it is thus:

First, consider the Sign, degree and minute of the ☽.
Secondly, the Sign, degree and minute of the ☉.
Thirdly, subtract the place of the ☉ from the ☽, by adding twelve Signs to the ☽ if you cannot do it otherwise; what remains, reserve and add to the Sign and degree of the Ascendant; if both added together make more than twelve Signs, cast away twelve, and what Signs, degrees and minutes remain, let your ⊗ be there: For example in our present Figure:

The ☽ is in 21.18 of ♍, or after 5 Signs, in 21 degrees 18 minutes of ♍.

The ☉ is 00 Signs, 4 degrees 18 minutes of ♈.

Set them together thus:

Place of the ☽	5s	21d	18m
Of the ☉	0	4	18

I subtract the ☉ from the ☽ thus: I begin with minutes, 18m from 18m, remains nothing.
Next I subtract degrees, 4 degr. from 21, rests 17 degrees.
Then 00 Signs from 5, remains 5 Signs: All put together, there do rest in Signs and degrees as follows:

5s   17d   00m

To these 5 Signs 17 degrees, I add the Sign ascending,

which is 4 Signs, 23 degrees, 27 minutes, or the 23:27 of ♌.

	Sig	Deg	Min	
Then it is thus:	5	17	00	*distance of ☉ from ☽*
	4	23	27	*Signs and degrees of the Ascendant*
Added together they make: ⎬	10	10	27	

Viz. 10 Signs, 10 degrees and 27 minutes, which direct you to know, that after 10 Signs numbered from ♈, you must place the ⊗, *viz.* in 10 degrees and 27 minutes of ♒, for ♈ ♉ ♊ ♋ ♌ ♍ ♎ ♏ ♐ ♑ are ten Signs, etc. and ♒ the eleventh in order.

Whether your Figure be by day or night, observe this Method; for how many degrees the ☉ is distant from the ☽, so many is the ⊗ from the Ascendant; but because this may not be thoroughly understood by every Learner upon a sudden, let him observe this general rule, the better to guide him.

If the ⊗ be taken upon a new ☽, it will be in the Ascendant.
If upon the first quarter, in the fourth house.
If upon the full ☽, in the seventh house.
If upon the last quarter, in the tenth house.
After the change, and before the first quarter, you shall ever have her in the first, second or third house.
After the first quarter until the full ☽, in the fourth, fifth or sixth.
After the full ☽ until the last quarter, in the seventh, eighth or ninth houses.
After the last quarter, either in the tenth, eleventh or twelfth.

So that if the Learner do mistake, he may by this method easily see his error; ever remembering, that the more days are passed after the change or quarter, &c, the more remote the ⊗ is from the Angle preceding.

Some have used to take ⊗ in the night from the ☽ to the ☉; which if you do, you must then make the place of your ☉ your first place, and add the Ascendant as in the former method. *Ptolomy*, day and night takes it as above directed, with whom all practitioners at this day consent.

Here follows a Table, by help whereof you may examine the strength of the ⊗ in any Figure you erect.

The Part of Fortune is strong and fortunate In the Signs of	♉♓, *wherein if it be, it has allowed dignities*	5
	♎♐♌♋, *in these Signs*	4
	♊, *In this sign*	3
	♍, *so it be in the Terms of* ♃ *or* ♀	2
If in ☌ *with* ♃ *or* ♀, *it has dignities*		5
In △ *with* ♃ *or* ♀		4
In ⚹ *with* ♃ *or* ♀		3
In ☌ *with* ☊		3
⊗ *is strong by being in houses,* viz. *If in*	*First or Tenth, it has allowed dignities*	5
	Seventh, Fourth, Eleventh	4
	Second or Fifth	3
	Ninth	2
	Third	1
In ☌ *with any of these Fixed Stars*	*With* Regulus *in* 24.34 ♌*	6
	With Spica Virginis *in* 18.33 ♎*	5
	Not Combust, or under the ☉ *Beams*	5
The Part of Fortune is weak in	♏♑♒, *being in any of these signs it has debilities*	-5
	In ♈ *he neither gets or loses.*	
⊗ *is weak by* ☌ *or aspect,*	*In* ☌ ♄ *or* ♂, *has debilities*	-5
	In ☌ *with* ☋	-3
	In ☍ *of* ♄ *or* ♂	-4
	In □ *of* ♄ *or* ♂	-3
	In Terms of ♄ *or* ♂	-2
Also by being in Houses, viz.	*In the Twelfth*	-5
	In the Eighth	-4
	In the Sixth	-4
With Caput Agol *in* 20.54 ♉*		-4
Combust		-5

There are many other Parts which the *Arabians* have mentioned frequently in their Writings, of which we make very little use in this Age: I shall, as occasion offers, teach the finding them out, and what they said, they did signify: Sometimes the ⊗ has signification of Life, and sometimes of Sickness; which occasionally I shall teach, as matter and occasion offer, adhering to the true observation of the *Ancients*: but I am little hitherto satisfied concerning ⊗ its true effects; intending to take pains therein hereafter, and publish my intentions.

**Positions as of 1 January 2005:*
Caput Algol: 26 ♉ 14
Regulus: 29 ♌ 54
Spica ♍: 23 ♎ 54

The preceding FIGURE *judged by a more short* METHOD.

1. The *Ascendant* not afflicted, Lord of the *Ascendant* Essentially fortified, the ☽ in △ with both the *Fortunes*; Signs of Long life.

2. ♃ and ♀ in the South Angle, in ♉, a Southeast Sign; ☉ in ♈, an Easterly Sign; ☽ in ♍, a Southern or Southwest Sign; best to travel Southward, or a little East.

3. ♃ and ♀ in the *Midheaven*, ♌ and ☉ in the ninth; his younger years are most full of Pleasure.

4. ☉ Lord of the *Ascendant*, lately separated from good and ill aspects; ☽ also separated as well from ♂ of ☿ as △ of ♀; show both good and ill had happened of late; Good, because of the good aspects: ill, by reason of the malevolent: but the evil aspects being more in number than the good, and signified by superior Planets; augment the Evil and lessen the Good.

5. ☽ applying to △ of ♃ the ☉ Lord of the *Ascendant* in Exaltation; promise Preferment.

☽ weak in the second, and after her △ with ♃ going to ♂ of ♂; shows, after a little time of Joy, great danger.

6. The small distance of degrees between the △ of ☽ to ♃, and he Angular; denotes a present happiness or fortune near to the *Querent*.

Her greater distance from ♂ of ♂, show his miseries to succeed some years after his times of Honour are expired, &c. In such a nature I ever contract my Judgment.

I wish all young Beginners at first to write down their Judgments in length, and the reasons in *Art*, as fully as they can, and afterward to contract their opinions into a narrow compass: by following these directions, they will have the Rules of *Art* perfectly in their memory: I also wish them in delivering their Judgment to the *Querent*, to avoid terms of *Art* in their Discourse, unless it be to one understands the *Art*.

CHAPTER XXIV.

If one shall find the Party at home he would speak with.

The *Ascendant* and his Lord are for the *Querent*, the seventh house and his Lord from him you would speak with; this is understood, if you go to speak with one you familiarly deal with, or are much conversant with, and is not allied to you, &c, but if you would go speak with the Father, you must take the Lord of the fourth; if with the Mother, the Lord of the tenth; if the Father would speak with his Child, the Lord of the fifth, and so in the rest; vary your rule and it serves for all.

If the Lord of the seventh house be in any of the four Angles, you may conclude the party is at home with whom you would speak with; but if the Lord of the seventh, or Lord of that house from whom Judgment is required, be in any Succedent house, *viz.* the eleventh, second, fifth or eighth, then he is not far from home; but if his *Significator* be in a Cadent house, then he is far from home.

If you find the Lord of the Ascendant applying to the Lord of the seventh house by any perfect aspect, the same day that you intend to go visit him, you may assured either to meet him going to his house, or hear of him by the way where he is, for he cannot be far absent; or if any Planet, or the *Moon*, separate from the Lord of the seventh house, and transfer his light to the Lord of the Ascendant, he shall know where and in what place the Party is, by such a one as is signified by that Planet who transfers his light; describe the Planet, and it personates the Man or Woman accordingly: But whether it will be Man or Woman, you must know by the nature of the Planet, Sign and quarter of Heaven he is in, wherein plurality of masculine Testimonies argue a man, the contrary a Woman.

Of a thing suddenly happening, Whether it signifies Good or Evil.

Erect your Figure of Heaven at what time the Accident happened, else when you first heard of it; then consider who is Lord of the Sign wherein the *Sun* is, and the Lord of that Sign wherein the *Moon* is, and the Lord of the house of Life, which is ever the Ascendant, and see which of these is most powerful in the Ascendant, let his position be considered, and if he be in ✶ or △ with the ☉, ♃ or ♀, there will no evil chance upon the preceding Accident, Rumour or Report; but if you find that Planet weak in the Scheme, combust or in □, ☍ or ♂ of ♂, ♄ or ☿, there will some misfortune follow after that accident, in one kind or other; if you consider the Planet afflicting your *Significator*; his posture and nature, it may easily be discovered, in what nature the evil will chance or upon what occasion; as if the Lord of the third, from or by some Neighbour or Kinsman; if the Lord of the second impede them, then loss in substance; if Lord of the fourth, expect discontent with one of your Parents, or about Land or Houses; if the Lord of the fifth, some difference or discord in an Ale house or Tavern, or in Company keeping, or by means of some child, &c. and so of the rest.

What Mark, Mole or Scar the Querent has in any Member of his Body.

I have many times admired at the verity hereof, and it has been one main argument of my engaging so far in all the parts of Astrology, for very rarely shall you find these rules fail.

When you have upon any demand erected the *querent's* Figure, consider the Sign ascending, what member of man's body it represents, and tell the *querent* he has a Mole, Scar or mark on that part of his body represented by that Sign; as if the Sign ascending be ♉, it's on the Neck: if in ♊, on the Arms, &c. See also in which of the twelve Signs of the Zodiac the

Lord of the Ascendant is in, and in that member represented by that Sign, he or she has another.

Then observe the Sign descending on the Cusp of the sixth house, and what part of man's body it personates, for in that member shall you find another; so shall you discover another in that member which is signified by the Sign wherein the Lord of the sixth is.

Last of all, consider what Sign the *Moon* is in, and what member of man's body it denotes, therein shall you also find a Mark, Mole or Scar; if ♄ signifies the Mark, it's a darkish, obscure, black one; if ♂, then it's usually some Scar or Cut if he be in a Fiery Sign, or else in any other Sign, a red mole; and you must always know, that if either the Sign, or the Planet signifying the Mole, Mark or Scar, be much afflicted, the Mark or Scar is the greater and more eminent.

If the Sign be Masculine, and the Planet Masculine, the Mole or Scar is on the right side of the body.

The contrary judge, if the Sign be Feminine, and the Lord thereof in a Feminine Sign.

If the Significator of the Scar or Mole be above the earth, (that is, from the Cusp of the Ascendant to the Cusp of the seventh, as either in the twelfth, eleventh, tenth, ninth, eighth or seventh) the Mark is on the fore part of the body, or visible to the eye, or on the outside of the member; but if the Significator be under the earth, *viz.*, in the first, second, third, fourth, fifth, sixth, the Mole or Scar is on the back part of the body, not visible, but on the inside of the member.

If few degrees of a Sign do ascend, or if the Lord of the Sign be in a few degrees, the Mole, Mark or Scar is in the upper part of the member; if the middle of the Sign ascend, or the Lord thereof in the middle, or near the middle of the Sign, the Mole or Mark is so in the member, *viz.* in the middle: If the latter degrees ascend, or the *Moon*, or Lord of the first or sixth house be near the last degrees of the Sign, the Mole Mark or Scar is near the lower part of the member.

If your Question be radical, the time rightly taken, and the party inquiring be of sufficient age, or no Infant, you shall rarely find error in this rule: I have many times upon a sudden in company, tried this experiment upon some of the company, and ever found it true, as many in this City well know. In *November* and *December*, when Signs of short ascensions are in the Ascendant, you must be wary, for in regard many times the ☉ is not then visible, and Clocks may fail, it's possible you may be deceived, and miss of a right Ascendant, for ♓ and ♈ do each of them ascend in the space of three quarters of an hour, and some few minutes; ♒ and ♉ in one hour and some odd minutes; but if you have the time of the day exact, you need not ever mistrust the verity of your Judgment: which will infinitely satisfy any that are Students herein, and cause them to take great pleasure in the *Art*, and make them sensible, that there is as much sincerity in all the whole *Art* of *Astrologie*, when it is rightly understood and practiced, which at this day I must confess it is by very few.

As these rules will hold certain upon the body of every *querent*, and in every question, so will they upon the body of the *quesited*, (*mutatis, mutandis*;) as if one inquires somewhat concerning his Wife, then the Sign of the seventh house, and the Sign wherein the Lord of the seventh is, shall show the Woman's Marks; so shall the Sign upon the Cusp of the twelfth, for that is the sixth from the seventh, and the Sign wherein the Lord of the twelfth is in, show two more Moles or Marks of the Woman.

Usually an Infortune in the Ascendant blemishes the Face with some Mole or Scar according to his nature, for the first house signifies the Face, the second the Neck, the third the Arms and Shoulders, the fourth the Breast and Paps, the fifth the Heart, &c. and so every house and Sign in order, according to succession; for what Sign soever is in the Ascendant, yet in every Question the first house represents the Face: Many times if the ☽ be in ♂ or ☍ of the ☉, the *querent* has some blemish or the like near one of his Eyes; and this is ever true, if the ☍ or ♂ be in Angles, and either of them have any ill aspect to *Mars*.

Whether one absent be dead or alive.

If a Question be demanded of one absent in a general way, and the *querent* has no relation to the party; then the first house, the Lord of that House and the ☽ shall signify the absent party; the Lord of the eighth House or Planet placed in the House or within five degrees of the Cusp of the 8th House shall show his death or its quality.

In judging this Question, see first whether the Lord of the Ascendant, the ☽ and the Lord of the eighth House or Planet in the eighth house be corporally joined together; or that the ☽, Lord of the Ascendant and the Lord of the eighth are in opposition either in the eighth and second, or twelfth and sixth, for these are arguments the party is deceased, or sick, and very near death.

See also if there be any translation of the light of the Lord of the Ascendant to the Lord of the eighth, especially in degrees deep, lame or deficient; or on the contrary, that there be any translation or carrying the virtue or influence of the Lord of the eighth to the Lord of the Ascendant; or if the Lord of the eighth be placed in the Ascendant, or if the Lord of the Ascendant and the ☽ be placed in the fourth house, these are testimonies the party absent be dead.

If the Lord of the Ascendant be separated from a bad Aspect of the Lord of the sixth, you may say the absent has been lately sick; if from the Lord of the eighth, he has been in danger of death, but is not dead; if from the Lord of the twelfth, he has been lately much troubled in mind, in fear of imprisonment, arrests, &c. if from the Lord of the second, he has been hard put to it for money, or in distress for want; if from the Lord of the seventh, in some quarrel or contention; if from the Lord of the ninth or third, he has been crossed in his journey (if he was at Sea by contrary winds, or Pirates) if at land by Thieves, bad Ways &c. and so of the rest. In judging this question, I have ever found, that if the Lord of the Ascendant be in the ninth, tenth, or eleventh (though many reports went the absent was dead) yet I have found him to live. Now if you find the absent alive, and you would know, when happily

you may hear of him; see in your *Ephemerides* when the
Lord of eleventh and the Lord of the Ascendant come to a △
or ✶ Aspect, and about that time, if not that day, news will
be had of him; or if the ☽ apply to a ✶ or △ of the Lord of the
Ascendant, see how many degrees she wants of the Aspect,
and give days, weeks or months, *viz.* For every degree in
moveable Signs a day, in common Signs weeks, in fixed
Signs months.

A further EXPLANATION *of the preceding Judgments by
the Figure succeeding.*

See page
A3

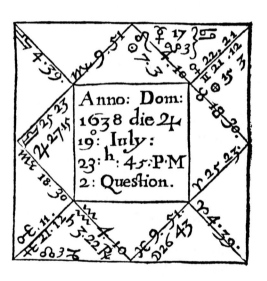

Resolution of these Questions following:

If find the party inquired of at home.
*A thing suddenly happening, whether good or bad is
intended?*
What Moles or Marks the Querent has?
If one absent be dead or alive?

CHAPTER XXV.

Viz. *A Woman being at my House in the Country, demanded*
if her Son were with his Master, or at her own House.

In this Figure ♀ is Lady of the *Ascendant*, and shall
signify her that asked the Question; the matter quesited
after must be required from that house which signifies
Children, and that is the fifth: I considered ♃ who is Lord of
the Sign ♓, for ♓ is the house of ♃, and I found ♃, the
Youth's *Significator*, in the Angle of the East, or *Ascendant*;
one argument, that the Party sought after was at home at his
Mother's house at time of the Question: I observed further,
that the ☽ did apply to a ✶ *dexter* of ♄, Lord of the fourth
house, which signifies the house or dwelling place of the *Querent*:
from which two testimonies, I judged the Youth was at his
Mother's, and that she should find him there at her coming
home, as indeed she did: now had I found ♃, Lord of the fifth,
in the tenth, because that is the house which signifies the
Master, or had the ☽ separated from ♃, Significator of the
Youth, and presently applied to a good or indifferent aspect of
the ☉, and she, *viz.* ☽ been in an Angle, I would have adjudged
him at his Master's house, &c. I did further consider that the
25 of *July* following, at two hours after noon, ♃ and ♀, being
both their *Significators*, *viz.* both the Mother's and the Son's
came to a △ aspect, and therefore I judged she should see him
that very day, but hardly any sooner, or before; (and indeed she
stayed in the country till that very morning; but when the
strength of the influence grew powerful, and as well her
Significatrix, as his, were so near their perfect aspect, she
could not be induced to stay any longer, and so (*volens nolens*)
went away, and it was about three in the afternoon the same
day before she could get home, where she found her Son in her
own house, abiding her coming; for usually about that day
when the *Significators* came to a ✶ or △ aspect (which you
may know by your *Ephemeris*) it's very probable you shall have
a Letter, or news of the Party *quesited* after (if the distance of
places between you can afford it,) but if the Party inquiring, and
Person inquired after be not far asunder, without question they

meet that very day, though neither of them formerly thought any such matter.

Had this Woman inquired, if she should have found a Neighbour or Brother or Sister at home, or not;

You must have taken signification from ♃, who is Lord of the third house; for you may see in the signification of the Houses, *page* 52, that the third house signifies Brethren, Sisters, Kindred and Neighbours; you might safely have adjudged, she should have found any one of these at home, because ♃ their Significator is in an Angle.

But if she had inquired, whether she should have found a Party at home, yea or not, to whom she had no relation, but as to a stranger; then ♂ the Lord of the seventh, had been his *Significator*, whom I find to be in the Sign of ♐, and in the second house of Heaven, for wanting more than five degrees of the Cusp of the third, he is not admitted to have signification in that house. In the first place therefore, I find ♂ in the second house, and in a Northern quarter of Heaven, (for the Cusp of the fourth house to the Cusp of the first, or Ascendant, is so, as you may see *page* 48) next I find ♂, who is *Significator* of the Party with whom she would speak with, is in ♐, which is an Easterly Sign, as you may see *page* 97.

Being ♂ is not in an Angle, I say he is not at home; the second house wherein he is being Succedent, I say he is not far from home.

The quarter of Heaven wherein at present he is, is North-cast, for so Sign and quarter import.

His distance from home may be a Furlong, or a Close or two, because his *Significator* is in a Succedent house,

The quality of the place or ground where you may expect to find him, must be judged from the Sign wherein ♂ his *Significator* is, *viz.* ♐, a fiery Sign; what manner of place that Sign signifies, see in *page* 98, and you shall there find, it represents in the Fields, Hills, or Grounds that rise a little: so that the Party inquired after being absent, you must direct a messenger to find him, in such or such a Ground, or part of the Ground, as is of the nature and quality described, and butting or lying to that quarter of Heaven, as is formerly directed, *viz.* Northeast.

But had it been so, that you were informed, the man was in Town, and not in the Fields, then inquire in the Town near to some Smiths or Butcher's shops, or the like, being Northeast from his house, for you may read ♂ delights in such places, see *page* 68

Of a Thing suddenly happening, whether good or ill, Resolution thereof by the last Figure,

Let us admit the Figure preceding to be set upon such an occasion; the ☉ is the Lord of the Sign wherein he is; ♃ is Lord of ♓, the Sign wherein the ☽ is, ♀ is Lady of the Ascendant, or house of Life; ♀ is most powerful in the Ascendant, ♎ being her house, and she having a Term therein, and casting her △ *Sinister* to the Cusp of the house; as also, being in △ with ♃, and he in the Ascendant; from hence one might have safely judged, had this been the very time of a sudden accident, or thing done, that it could not have rebounded to the *Querent's* disadvantage, but rather good: Now had ♀ been nearer to the ☍ of ♂, he being in the second, which signifies Riches, I should have judged the *Querent* would have received some loss shortly; and so of the rest; or some falling out about Moneys.

What Marks the Querent had.

I find the 25 of ♎ Ascending, and ♃ in the *Ascendant*; which as I acquainted you, signified the Face; this *Querent* had a Wart or Mole on the right side of her Face, near her Mouth, for ♃ is masculine, so is the Sign ♎; and as the later degrees of ♎ ascend, so the *Querent* confessed a Mole on the lower part of her Reins, towards the Haunches; ♈ being the Sign of the sixth, showed she had one on the Forehead, near the Hair, for you see the Cusp of the house is but four degrees; ♂ Lord of ♈, being in a Masculine Sign, *viz.* in ♐ but under the earth, showed a Mole on the right Thigh, towards the middle of it, on the back part, or that part which is not visible; the ☽ being in ♓, *viz.* 26 degrees 43 minutes in a Feminine Sign, and under the Earth, I told her she had one Mole under her Foot, towards the extremity of her left Foot.

The *Quesited* Party being her Son, had ♓ the ninth degree for his Ascendant, which denoted a Mole on the left side of his Cheek; and as ♓ signifies the Foot, so he had one on the left Foot, a little below the Ankle, for you see few degrees ascend. The sixth house from the fifth, is the tenth in the Figure, where you see ♌ 4 degrees, which signified, that near his right Side, below his Breast, he had some Scar, Mole or Mark, &c. Follow these Directions, and they are sufficient Instructions in this kind of Judgment.

Whether one absent be dead or alive, by the preceding Scheme of Heaven.

In the Figure above, let us admit the Question to have been demanded for one absent:

The Ascendant ♎, ♃ therein, ♀ and ☽ are *Significators* of the absent Party.

The ascending Sign manifests his Stature, ♃ gives comeliness to it, ♀, ♃ and ☽ argue his Conditions.

Neither is the ☽ or Lord of the *Ascendant* joined to any Planet in the eighth by ☌ but are all free from the malignant beams and aspects of the Lords of the 8ᵗʰ or 6ᵗʰ, or is the Lord of the *Ascendant* or the ☽ in ☍ with the Lord of the eighth.

Or is there translation of light from the Lord of the eighth to the Lord of the *Ascendant*, or is the Lord of the eighth in the *Ascendant*, but a Benevolent planet, or is ☽ or the Lord of the *Ascendant* in the fourth house: I should therefore pronounce the absent in health; but because ♀ Lady of the *Ascendant*, had not many days before been in ☍ with ♂, who is Lord of the second and sixth; I should adjudge he had been lately discontented for want of Money, and also inclinable to a Fever; but by ♃ his posture in the Ascendant, and his △ to ♀, I should judge *Medicine*, or such a one as ♃ had relieved him: and because ♀ Lord of the eleventh, applies to a □ of ♃

in the *Ascendant*, both of them being in Signs of long ascensions, which is equivalent to a △, I should judge the *Querent* to have news of the absent about ten weeks from the time of the Question, because ☿ wants ten degrees of the □ of ♃; if the absent be known to be at a near distance, I would have said in 10 days they should hear of him, because the Signs are moveable.

CHAPTER XXVI.

Of a Ship, and whatever are in her, her Safety or Destruction.

The *Ancients* do put this Question to those concerning the ninth house, and I conceive for no other reason, than because it must be granted, that all Ships are made for Travel and Journeys: however, in regard the most part of the Judgment concerning its safety or ruin is derived from the Ascendant and his Lord, and the ☽, I thought fit to place this Judgment as belonging to the first house.

Generally, the Sign ascending and the ☽ are *Significators* of the *Ship*, and what Goods are in her, the Lord of the Ascendant of those that sail in her: if in the Question demanded you find all these unfortunate, that is, if a malevolent Planet by position be placed in the Ascendant, he having dignities in the eighth; or if you find the Lord of the Ascendant in the eighth, in any ill configuration with the Lord of the eighth, twelfth, fourth or sixth, or the ☽ combust, or under the earth, you may judge the Ship is lost, and the men drowned, (unless you find reception between themselves) for then the Ship was casually Shipwrecked, and some of the Seamen did escape: but if you find the preceding *Significators* all of them free from misfortune, both Men and Goods are all safe; the more safe if any reception be. But if the Ascendant and the ☽ be unfortunate, and the Lord of the Ascendant fortunate, the Ship is like to be drowned, but the men will be saved: Some for better knowledge and discovery of what part of the Ship was like to be freest from danger, have divided the several parts of the Ship, and have assigned to every of the twelve signs, a part or place of the Ship, by which if any damage was to come to the Ship, they could or might better prevent it.

To Aries *they give the Breast of the Ship.*
To Taurus *what is under the Breast a little towards the Water.*
To Gemini *the Rudder or Stern of the Ship.*
To Cancer *the Bottom or Floor of the Ship.*
To Leo *the top of the Ship above Water.*
To Virgo *the Belly of it.*
To Libra *that part which sometimes is above, and sometimes below the Water, or between Wind and Weather.*
To Scorpio *that part where the Seamen are lodged, or do their Office.*
To Sagittarius *the Mariners themselves,*
To Capricornus *the ends of the Ship.*
To Aquarius *the Master or Captain of the Ship.*
To Pisces *the Oars.*

At the time when the Question is asked concerning the well or ill being of the Ship, see which of these Signs, or how many of them are fortunate, or has the ☽ or the Lord thereof fortunate, it's an argument those parts of the Ship so signified, will have no defect, or need repair thereof, or the Ship will receive any detriment in those parts: but which of these Signs you find unfortunate, or in what Sign you find the ☽ or Lord of the Sign where she is, unfortunate, in that place or part of the Ship assign impediment and misfortune, and thereof give warning.

But when the *Querent* shall demand of any Ship which is setting forth, and the State of that Ship ere she return, and what may be hoped of her in her Voyage, then behold the Angles of the Figure, and see if the fortunate Planets are therein placed, or falling into Angles, and the Infortunes remote from Angles, Cadent, Combust or under the ☉ Beams, then you may judge the Ship will go safe to the place intended, with all the Goods and Loading in her: But if you find the Infortunes in Angles, or succeeding Houses, there will chance some hinderance to the Ship, and it shall be in that part which the Sign signifies where the unfortunate Planet is; if the same Infortune be ♄, the Ship will be split, and the men drowned, or receive hurt by some bruise, or running aground: but if it be ♂, and he in any of his Essential Dignities, or behold a place where he has any Dignity or be in an earthly Sign, he shall then signify the same which ♄ did, or very great danger and damage to the Ship: But if the Fortunes cast their benevolent rays or aspect to the places where ♂ or ♄ are, and the Lords of the four Angles of the Figure, and especially, or more properly, the Ascendant, and the Lord of that house or Sign where the ☽ is in be free, then it's an argument, the Ship shall labour hard, and suffer much damage, yet notwithstanding the greater part both of Goods and Men shall be preserved. But if ♂ do afflict the Lords of the Angles, and Dispositor of the ☽; the Mariners will be in great fear of their enemies, or of Pirates or Sea-robbers, shall even tremble from fear of them: and if there also to this evil configuration chance any other affliction in the Signs, there will happen among the Mariners Bloodshed, Controversies, quarrelling one with another, thieving and robbing each other, purloining the Goods of the Ship; and this judgment will prove more certain if the unfortunate Planets be in the Signs which fall to be in the Division of the upper part of the Ship, towards the height or top of her.

If ♄ in the like nature do afflict, as was before recited of ♂, there will be many thefts committed in the Ship, but no bloodshed; the Goods of the Ship consume, no body knowing which way.

If the unfortunate Signs (*viz.* those which are afflicted by the presence of ♄, ♂ or the ☋) be those which signify the bottom or that part of the Ship which is under Water, it's an argument of the breaking and drowning thereof, or receiving some dangerous Leak: if the Signs so unfortunate be in the Midheaven, and ♂ unfortunate them, it's like the Ship will be burned by fire, thunder or lightning, or matter falling out of the Air into the Ship; this shall then take place when the Signs are Fiery, and near violent fixed Stars.

If that Sign wherein ♂ or the unfortunate Planet be the Sign of the fourth house, it notes firing of the Ship in the bottom of her; but if ♂ be there, and the Sign human, *viz.*

either ♊, ♎ or ♒, that fire or burning of the Ship shall proceed from a fight with Enemies, or they shall cast fire into her, or shall tear the Ship in pieces in grappling with her, and the fire shall in that part of the Ship first take hold, signified by the Sign wherein an Infortune was at time of asking the Question.

If ♄ instead of ♂ do denunciate damage, and be placed in the Midheaven, the Ship shall receive prejudice by contrary Winds, and by leaks in the Ship, by rending or using of bad Sails; and this misfortune shall be greater or lesser, according to the potency of the *significator* of that misfortune, and remoteness of the Fortunes.

If the same Infortune be in the seventh house, and he be ♄, the latter part of the Ship will be in danger of misfortune, and the Stern of the Ship will be broke.

Moreover, if any infortune be in the Ascendant, some loss will be in the fore-part of the Ship, greater of less, according to the quality or strength of the *significator* thereof; or if the Lord of the Ascendant be Retrograde, the Ship will proceed forward a while, but either return or put into some Harbour within a little time after her setting forth; and if the Lord of the Ascendant be in a moveable Sign and Retrograde, and the Lord of the fourth also, *viz.* Retrograde, the Ship will return again crossed by contrary Winds, to the very Port from which she first set out: and if the Lord of the Ascendant have no other impediments than Retrogradation, there will be no loss by the return of it; but if to Retrogradation some other misfortune happen, the Ship returns to amend something amiss, and was also in danger.

Besides, if the Lord of the eighth shall infortunate the Lord of the Ascendant, especially if the Lord of the Ascendant be in the eighth, there will come hurt to the Ship according to the nature of the Planet afflicting: as if the same Planet that is Lord of the eighth house do impede the Lord of the house of the ☽, the Lord of the Ascendant and the ☽, it imports the death of the Master or Governor of the Ship, and of his Mate and principal Officers of the Ship: and if the *Part of Fortune* and the Lord of the second house be both unfortunate, it pronounces loss in sale of those Goods in the Ship, or ill vending of them, or that they will not come to a good Market; but if either ♌ , ♃ or ♀ be in the second house, or Lords thereof, or Dispositors of the Sign the ⊗ is in, there will good profit arise from the Voyage of that Ship, and sale of Goods therein. The more the *Significators* are essentially strong, the more profit may be expected.

If the Lord of the Ascendant and the Lord of the house of the ☽ be slow of course, and those Planets that dispose of them, then it's probable the Ship will be slow in her motion, and make a long Voyage of it: but if the aforesaid *Significators* be quick in motion, the Ship shall make good speed to the Port intended, and will return home again in shorter time than is expected.

And if it happen that there be an ☍ or □ aspect between the Lord of the Ascendant and the Lord of that Sign who disposes the ☽, and this aspect be without reception, then will there be much discord among the *Sailors*, and much controversy between the Merchant and them; wherein, he shall prevail that is most dignified; that is, the Seamen if the Lord of the Ascendant be strongest; the Merchant, if the Lord of the house where the ☽ is be best fortified.

If the Lord of the second be removed from his second (that is, if ♉ be the Cusp of the second, and ♀ further removed than ♊) or if the Lord of the second be removed from the second house wherein the ☽ is in, (as if she be in ♍, and the Lord of the second not in ♎), or if the Disposer of the ⊗ be not with it, then the Shipmen will have scarcity of Provisions of Victuals and Food: if these Planets or ⊗ be in Watery Signs, want of fresh water will most annoy the Sailors: if the *Significators* be in Earthly or Airy Signs, want of Food, Victuals and Fire will oppress them: This is the manner by which the *Ancients* did judge of the good or ill success of a Ship, concerning her Voyage at her first going forth.

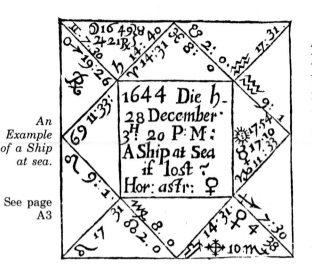

See page
A3

*An
Example
of a Ship
at sea.*

In *December* 1644, a *Merchant* in *London* having sent out a Ship to the Coasts of *Spain* for Trade, had several times news that his Ship was lost or cast away, there having been a little before very Tempestuous weather, in so much that many Ships were sunk and shipwrecked; he would have given 60$^{li.}$ in the hundred for the insurance of her; but so general was the report of her loss, that none of the *Insurance* companies would meddle, no not upon any terms. A Friend of the *Merchant's* propounds the Question to me, *What I thought of the Ship, if sunk or living?* Whereupon I erected the Figure preceding, and having well considered what was requisite in this manner of Judgment, I gave my Opinion. That *the Ship was not lost, but did live, and though of late in some danger, yet was now recovered.* My Judgment was grounded upon the Considerations in *Art* following.

In the first place, the *Ascendant* being the eleventh degree and 33 minute of ♋, showed the Bulk or Body of the Ship; there does also ascend with these degrees of ♋ three fixed Stars in our *Horizon*, wholly almost of the nature of ♄: I find ♄ castes his □ *Sinister* out of the eleventh house, but from a Cardinal Sign to, or very near the Cusp of the ascending degrees, thereby afflicting it: after his □ aspect, I found the ☽ in her Exaltation, casting a ✳ *Sinister* to the degree ascending, interposing her ✳ between the Ascendant and the ☍ aspects of ☿ and ☉ in the seventh, which otherwise had been dangerous, for all opposite aspects to the Ascendant in this Judgment are dangerous.

From the *Ascendant's* affliction both by the □ of ♄, and presence of fixed Stars of his like nature, I judged the Ship was much of the nature of ♄, *viz.* a sluggish, heavy one, and of no good speed, or very sound; and ♋ being a weakly Sign, made me judge the condition, building and quality of the Ship was such; [*and it was so confessed.*]

From hence, and for that ☋ is in the ninth house, I judged the Ship had been in some affliction or distress in her Journey, occasioned from such casualties as are signified by ♄, *viz.* had received some bruise, leak, damage in or near her Breast; because ♈, the Sign wherein ♄ is, represents that part, thereby afflicting it.

But in regard the ☽, who is Lady of the Ascendant, is placed in the eleventh house, and in her Exaltation, is no manner of way impeded, but by a benevolent aspect applying to a △ of ☿ and ☉, and is by bodily presence so near to ♃, and all the *Significators* above the Earth, (a thing very considerable in this Judgment.)

Besides, I observed no *Infortunes* in Angles, which was one other good argument; for these considerations, I judged the Ship was not cast away, but was living, and that the Sailors and Officers of the Ship were lively and in good condition.

The next *Quere* was, *Where the Ship was, upon what Coast, and when any news would come of her?*

Herein I considered the ☽ was fixed, and locally in the eleventh house; ♉ is a Southern Sign, but in an East quarter of Heaven, verging towards the South: her application to a △ of ☿, and he in ♑, a South Sign and West Angle, made me judge the Ship was Southwest from *London*, and upon our own Coast, or near those which lie between *Ireland* and *Wales*; I judged her at that time to be in some *Harbour*, because ♉ wherein the ☽ is, is fixed, and in the eleventh house, which is the house of *Comfort* and *Relief*; and that she was put into some *Harbour* to mend her Defects or Rents: [*It proved true that she was in the West, and in an Harbour.*]

Because the ☽ applied to a △ of ☿ and ☉, and they in an Angle, and was herself as well as they, very swift in motion and did want but a few minutes of their perfect △; I judged there would be news or Letters, or a certain discovery of the Ship in a very short time; the *significators* so near aspect, I said either that night, or in two days; [*and so it proved:*] And you must observe, that it gave me good encouragement when I saw ⊗ disposed by ♂, and ☿ to whom the ☽ applied to be in reception with ♂: as also, that the ☽, by so forcible an aspect, did apply to the ☉, who is Lord of the second house, or of *Substance*, an argument, the *Merchant* should increase his Stock, and not lose by that adventure: You shall also observe, that ♃ has his *Antiscion* in the ninth of ♌, the very Cusp of the second house, and ♂ his *Antiscion* falls upon the very degree ascending: these were good testimonies of safety: ♂ as being Lord of the eleventh, and Dispositor of ⊗; and ♃ as Lord of the tenth, *viz.* of *Trade* and *Commerce*.

Besides, usually when the ☽ applies to a good aspect of a Retrograde Planet, it brings the matter to an end one way or other speedily, and when least suspected: and it's a general Maxim in such like cases, if the ☽ apply to the *Fortunes*, or by good aspect to any Planet or Planets in Angles, then there is reason we hope well, &c.

The Ascendant free from presence of *Infortunes*, a good sign: Lord of the Ascendant above the Earth, and the ☽ and their Dispositors, good signs: Lord of the Ascendant in tenth, eleventh or ninth houses, good: Lord of the Ascendant in △ or ✶ with ♃ or Lord of the eleventh, good.

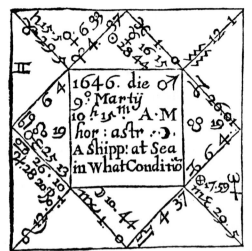

Inside the chart:
1646. die ♂
9ʰ Martÿ
10 ♄ 15 ᵐ A·M
hor : aſtr ⁙ ☽·
A Shippᵗ at Sea
in WhatConditiõ

See page
A4

Example of another Ship.

Here the Ascendant and the ☽ are *significators* of the Ship, and those that sail in her: the ☽ lately separated from a □ of ♄, Lord of the eighth and ninth, then at time of the Question void of course; but afterwards first applied to a △ of ♄, then to ☍ of ☿, Lord of the twelfth and fourth; this showed the Ship had lately been in danger (of Death) *viz.* Shipwreck: and as the ☽ had been void of course, so had no news been heard of her; because the ☽ was last in □ of ♄, in fixed Signs, tortuous or odiously and maliciously aspecting each other, and falling into Cadent houses, and then did not presently apply to the good aspect of any benevolent Planet, but was void of course, and then again continued her application out of the fourth to ♄, who is still Lord of the eighth, although it was by good aspect; and then after separation from him, applied to ☍ ☿, and that ☿ her Dispositor was in his Detriment, and entering Combustion, and ♃ Dispositor of ☿ Subterranean and in ♂ with ♂, and terms of an *Infortune*; and forasmuch as I found ♂ in his Fall, upon or near the Cusp of the second house, I judged loss was at hand to the Merchant; ⊗ being in the sixth house, disposed by ♃, and he Retrograde in the second, not beholding ⊗; the ☽ also casting her □ *Sinister* to the ⊗, and so ☿ his *Dexter* □: by means therefore of so many evil testimonies of receiving loss rather than benefit; I judged that the Merchant should lose much, if not all that was adventured in this Ship, and so consequently I doubted the Ship was cast away; [*and so it proved.*]

Principal Significators under the Earth, ill: worst of all, if in the fourth, for that is an assured testimony of sinking the Ship.

Of the time of receiving any QUESTION.

It has been disputed largely amongst the *Arabians*, who were excellent in the resolution of Horary Questions, what time the *Astrologer* should take for the ground of his Question, whether that time when the *Querent* first comes into ones House or Closet, or first salutes the *Artist*, whether that is to be admitted for the most proper time of erecting a Figure, and giving Judgment thereupon.

Though some have consented to this opinion, yet I could never be satisfied herein either with reason or experience; for let us admit one comes to demand a Resolution of me, and we converse together a good while; but in the end, some occasion intervenes, and we depart: I hope no sound Judgment will allow of this time to be the *Radix* of a Question (when as none is really demanded) *viz.* at what time he first saw me, or entered my house and spoke with me.

Without doubt the true hour of receiving any Question is then, when the *Querent* propounds his desire to the *Astrologer*, even that very moment of time, in my opinion, is to be accepted: for let us suppose a Letter is sent or delivered to me, wherein I am desired to resolve some doubts; perhaps I receive the Letter into my hands at three o'clock in any day of the week, but in regard of some occasions, do not read it until four or five hours after; that very hour and minute of hour when I break it open, and perceive the intention of the *Querent*, is the time to which I ought to erect my Figure, and from thence to draw mine *Astrological Judgment*: This way and manner have I practiced, and found success answerable: And whereas *Bonatus* and some others do give warning that the *Astrologian* judge not his own Question, and say he cannot tell how to accept of a question from himself; this I conceive was his reason, Because he thought the *Artist* would be partial to himself in his judgment: Verily I am of a contrary opinion and have found by many experiments, that at what hour the mind or intention of the *Astrologer* is heavily perplexed with, or concerning the success of any matter wherein himself is really concerned, I say he may with great reason accept of that hour for the true time of erecting his Scheme of Heaven, and he may (if not partial) as well judge of that Figure erected by himself, as of any other; but herein I advise him to lay aside all love and partiality to his own Cause.

JUDGMENTS concerning the second House.

CHAPTER XXVII.

Whether the Querent shall be Rich, or have a competent
Fortune? By what means attain it?
The time when? &c. and if it shall continue?

Whoever interrogates, be his Condition what it will be, *King, Noble, Priest* or *Layman*, the Ascendant, the Lord thereof and the ☽ are his *significators*: and if the question be in general terms, (*viz. Whether he shall ever be rich yea or not?*) without relation to any particular person from whom he may expect a Fortune, the resolution of it is in this nature:

Consider the Sign ascending on the Cusp of the second House, the Lord thereof, the Planet or Planets therein placed, or aspecting the Lord of that house or Cusp thereof; the *Part of Fortune*, the Sign and place of Heaven where it is placed, and how aspected by the Planets, (for ⊗ itself emits no rays, or casts any aspect to any Planet, no more do the ☊ or ☋.)

First, if you find the Planets all angular, it's one good Sign of Substance; if they be in succedent houses, direct and swift in motion, it's a good sign.

If the Planets be in good houses, direct, and but moderately dignified in essential Dignities, it's an hopeful argument of an Estate: Those rules are general:

If the Lord of the Ascendant, or the ☽, and the Lord of the second house, *viz.* of Substance, be corporally joined together, or if they, *viz.* Lord of the Ascendant and ☽, have friendly aspect to the Lord of the second, or if ♃ and ♀ cast their △ or ✶, or be in ♂ with ⊗, or if the Lord of the second be in the Ascendant, or the ☽, or Lord of the Ascendant in the second, or if any Planet transfer the light and virtue of the Lord of the second to the Lord of the Ascendant, or if benevolent Planets cast their ✶ or △ to the Cusp of the Ascendant or ⊗, or any fixed Star of the nature of ♃ and ♀, do ascend with the Cusp of the second or ⊗ be in ♂ with or near to such a fixed Star; or if ♃ who is natural Significator of substance, or ♀ who is naturally a fortune or ☊ be in the second, and no infortune cast his aspect to them, or if you find all Planets direct and swift in motion (*viz.*) if their daily motion be more than what is assigned for their mean or middle motion, which you may perceive by Page 57, 61, 65, 69, 72, 76, 80, the querent shall not fear poverty, for he will be competently rich or have a sufficient fortune to subsist on, and this his estate shall be greater or lesser according to the Major testimonies, which you are carefully to examine of those significators which do naturally resolve the question; and here in this demand you must remember to take notice of the quality of the person inquiring or demanding the question, for (*Quoad capax*) it shall happen to any Interrogant.

By what means attain it.

When you have sufficiently examined your Figure, and perceived that the *Querent* shall have a substance or will come to have riches, it will be demanded, how? by whom, or what means it may be obtained?

Herein you must observe, that if the Lord of the second house be in the second, the *querent* shall obtain an Estate by his own labour and proper industry; if the Lord of the second be placed in the Ascendant, he shall unexpectedly come to a Fortune, or without much labour attain it. If that the Lord of the second or the ☽ do promise substance by any aspect they have to each other, you must consider from what House the aspect is, or of what House the ☽ is Lady of, or if neither of these promise substance; see to the ⊗, what house it is in, and what House of Heaven the *Dispositor* is Lord of.

If the Planet assisting or promising increase of Fortune be Lord of the Ascendant, the *Querent* himself will by his own diligence advance his own Fortune; if he be a mean man or Mechanical that interrogates, then by the sweat and labour of his own hands, his own Invention, Care and Painstaking shall put him into a Fortune: but if the Adjuvant Planet be Lord of the second, he will augment his Estate by advance of his own Stock, and well managing his private Fortune, and adventuring to Buy and Sell in such things as naturally he is addicted to, or falls in his way in the course of his life, or are of the nature of that Planet (the Sign he is in considered.)

If the Lord of the third fortunate the Lord of the second, or the Cusp of the house, or *Part of Fortune*, he will be assisted in procuring an Estate by some honest Neighbour, or some one of his Kindred, Brethren or Sisters, if he have any, or by some Journey he shall undertake, or removing to that quarter of Heaven from whence the Lord of the third casts his good aspect, or is corporally joined with the Significator of Substance.

If the fortunate Planet or Significator be Lord of the fourth, or placed in the fourth, the *Querent* will attain Wealth by means of his Fathers assistance, (if he be living) or by some aged person, as Grandfather, &c. or by taking some Farm or Grounds, or purchase of Tenements, Lands or Hereditaments, or well managing the Stock his *Ancestors* have or shall leave him, or some Stock of Money his Kindred may lend him.

If the Lord of the fifth do promise Wealth, then he obtains means: if a Gentleman (by Play, Cards, Dice, Sports, Pastimes,) if of Capacity, and a Courtier, by some Embassy, Message, &c. If an ordinary man propounds the Question, by keeping a Victualling-house, as Alehouse, Inn, Tavern, Bowling alley, or being a Doorkeeper, Porter to some Gentleman;

or be he who will that inquires, if the Lord of the fifth House be strong, he promises somewhat out of the Estate of the Father, or by making Matches, etc.

If the Lord of the sixth, or Significator, or assistant Planet be in the sixth, and the Sign of the sixth be human, the *Querent* may expect good Servants, and profit by their labour: If a King or Prince propounds the Question (as sometimes they do) you may judge, his Subjects will assist him with many tumbling Subsidies, Privy-Seals, Loans of Money, etc.

If a Nobleman or Gentleman inquire, he shall augment his Estate by Letting Leases, and the discreet managing of his Estate by his Stewards, Bailiffs, and such as undertake for him.

If the Question come from a Countryman, as a Farmer or Husbandman, tell him he may thrive by dealing in little Cattle, as Sheep, Goats, Hogs, Conies, etc.

If a Scholar propound the Question upon the like occasion, advise him to turn Physician, for he shall thrive by his Salary obtained from people infirm and diseased.

If the Lord of the seventh House fortunate the Lord of the second, or the Cusp of the house, or the ⊗, or that Planet which is placed in the second, let the *Querent* expect God's blessing, by means of a rich and good Wife, or the assistance of some loving Woman: As also, if a Gentleman propounds the Question, then by the Sword, or the Wars, or by Law recovering somewhat detained from him, by contracting of Bargains, by the common acquaintance he has in his way of Trade or Commerce, if he be a Merchant.

If the Lord of the eighth be that Planet who fortunates the Significators above named; the *Querent* shall either have some Legacy bequeathed him by Testament of a deceased party, or a further increase of his Wife's Portion, little by him expected at time of his Question, or shall go uncompelled, and reside in some Country, where increase of substance shall happen to him, *viz.* he shall unexpectedly settle himself where formerly he had no intention, and there shall thrive and grow rich.

If the Lord of the ninth gives virtue or fortunate the ⊗ or Lord of the second, or Cusp of the House, the *Querent* may thrive by some Voyage to Sea, if ♋ or ♓ descend on the cusp of the ninth, and the Lord of the same Sign be therein, or one of his Wife's Brothers, or some allied to her, or a near Neighbour, to the place where she did live when he first married her, or some religious man or Minister shall befriend him in the way of his Vocation or Calling, for the increase of his Fortune.

If an Earthly Sign be on the Cusp of the ninth, and the Lord of that house be therein placed, he may thrive by removing to that part of Heaven, or that Coast of the Kingdom or Country signified by the Sign and quarter of Heaven, and by dealing in the native Commodities of that County, City or Country to which the Heavens direct him.

If the Lord of the second be fortunate in the tenth House, or the Lord of the tenth and second be in reception, or the Lord of the tenth do behold the Lord of the second or Cusp of the second house, or a Planet therein, or the ⊗, with any benevolent configuration; let the *Querent* endeavour the service or employment of some King, Prince, Nobleman, Gentleman, Master, or the like, and thereby he shall augment his estate or get a subsistence: if one inquires that is young and of small fortune, let him learn a Mechanical trade, according to the nature of the Sign of the tenth and Planet who is Lord thereof; for the Heavens intimate he shall do well in his Magistery or Trade, if he be capable and fit for it; or if he be a man of any education and desirous of preferment, let him expect an Office or Public employment in the Commonwealth, in one kind or other.

If the Lord of the eleventh be that benevolent Planet who is significator in the premises, *viz.* the Planet fortunating, then some friend shall commend the party inquiring to accept of some employment very advantageous, or some Merchant, Courtier, or servant of a Nobleman, King, or great person shall be the means of raising the *Querent* to a Fortune, and then, shall unexpectedly happen to the *Querent* which he never thought of: and this for good.

If the Fortunate Planet, who casts his Aspect as aforesaid; be in the twelfth, the *querent* shall advance his Fortune by great Cattle, Horse races, by imprisonments, or men imprisoned, if the sign of the twelfth be human; if the Sign be ♉ or ♑ or ♈ by Cattle; if ♍ by corn. And herein mix your judgment with reason.

The most assured testimony in Astrology, and upon a Question only propounded, that the *querent* shall be rich and continue so, is this, If the Lord of the first and second and *Jupiter* be joined together in the second House, first, tenth, seventh, fourth or eleventh; but if they be not in ♂, then that they apply by ✶ or △ with mutual reception: nay, although they apply by □ or ☍, yet if it be with reception, the party will thrive or have an estate, though with much labour, and many intervening difficulties, yet will he ever more abound than want.

Of the Reason, or from whence it proceeds, or what is the Cause, why the QUERENT *shall not obtain Wealth.*

When in any Question you find your Figure signifies the *Querent* shall come to an estate, the resolution following is needless; but if you find that he shall not obtain any great fortune, and the *Interrogant* would know the cause why, or thing impeding, that so he may the better direct his affairs, and be more wary in the course of his life, for better prevention of such difficulties: In this Judgment carefully observe the Planet obstructing, or who does most afflict the Lord of the second, or ⊗, or the Cusp of the second, the ☽, or Lord or Dispositor of the ⊗; if the Lord of the first be that Planet, then the *Querent* himself is the cause; if the Lord of the second do with □ or ☍ behold the ⊗, or the Cusp of the second, then want of Money or a sufficient Stock to set himself in employment is the cause: If Lord of the third, his own Kindred will do nothing for him, or will prove burdensome, or malicious Neighbours will get all the Trade from him, or so undersell him, that he will be much kept under thereby: and so run through the twelve Houses, as in the Chapter before mentioned. I thought good here to give this general caution, that if the Lord of the second House, or Dispositor of the ⊗ be infortunes, yet if they have Essential Dignities where they are, or aspects to good Planets, or be placed in such benevolent houses as I formerly mentioned, they may be

Significators of Acquisition of Substance; and in like nature both ♃ and ♀ being afflicted or impeded, or Significators, as aforesaid, may be the Planets obstructing as well as any other, for every Planet must do the work for which he is by divine Providence assigned to: Do you also ever remember that in what House you can find *Cauda Draconis*, it prenotes detriment and impediment in such things as are signified by that house, as if he be in the second, he denotes consumption of Estate by the *Querent's* own folly or not thriving, by his own proper neglect: in the third, hinderance by evil, beggarly or peevish Kindred, etc., and so judge in all the rest of the twelve Houses.

If the Querent *shall obtain the Substance which he demands, or has lent, or the Goods he has pawned.*

If the Demand of the *Querent* be, *Whether or no he shall procure the Money or Substance from him of whom he intends to demand it?*

The Lord of the Ascendant and the ☽ are his Significators, the Lord of the second of his substance.

The seventh House, and the Lord thereof signify him or her of whom he intends to demand or borrow Money: In proceeding to Judgment,

See if the Lord of the Ascendant or the ☽ be joined to the Lord of the eighth, who is Lord of the Substance of the party quesited after, or see if either of them be joined, or in aspect to a Planet placed in the eighth, if the Planet in the eighth be a *Fortune*, or the aspect itself fortunate, he shall obtain the money desired; or if he would borrow the money required will be lent him: if he have deposited any Pledge, it will be restored, whether the fortunate Planet in the eighth be received or not; yea, if an unfortunate Planet be in the eighth, or Lord of the eighth, and receive either the Lord of the Ascendant or the ☽, the *Querent* shall obtain his desire; but if no reception be, he will hardly or ever procure his demands, and if ever, with so much difficulty and labour, as he would rather wish the thing had been undone.

In like manner, if the Lord of the eighth be in the first, or in the second, and the Lord of the second receive him, it's probable the business will be effected; but if the Lord of the seventh, or of the eighth be in the first or second, and neither have reception of the Lord of the first or second house, or of the ☽, it's an argument he shall not have his desire accomplished, but shall receive a denial or more prejudice in the thing demanded.

If the Lord of the Ascendant and the ☽ be joined to a *Fortune* that has dignity in the Sign ascending, or Sign intercepted in the Ascendant, the matter will be effected; or if any of them be joined to an *Infortune* who has dignity in the Ascendant, and that *Infortune* receive the Lord of the Ascendant or the ☽, the business will be dispatched: Or if the Lord of the Ascendant or the ☽ be joined to a fortunate Planet, and he well placed either in the tenth or eleventh, the matter shall be perfected, though there be no reception: The Judgments of this Chapter shall then have place and prove true, when as the matter in question is amongst ordinary persons, or with such people as with whom there is a community, as Citizens with Citizens, Countrymen with Countrymen, one Tradesman with another; from this Judgment we exempt Kings, Princes, Noblemen and such, who pay Debts slowly, and on whom the Law takes little notice.

If one shall acquire that Gain or Profit, Wages or Stipend of the King or Nobleman, General or Commonwealth, Lieutenant-General, or any great Person which he Expects.

The resolution hereof will serve for any Question of the like nature, where the *Querent* is much inferior to the *Quesited*, or the party or parties from whom he expects the accomplishment of his desires.

The Ascendant, Lord thereof and the ☽ signify him that asks the Question; the tenth House and Lord thereof, signify the *Quesited*, or Person sought after, or from whom the matter is to be required; the second House and the Lord thereof are to be considered for the *Querent*, the eleventh House and Lord thereof shall signify the Estate, Money or Substance of the King, Nobleman, General &c. or Party inquired after: If in the Question you do find the Lord of the Ascendant or the ☽ joined to the Lord of the eleventh house, or if any of them be joined to any Planet in the eleventh house, and that Planet be a *Fortune*, not in any measure impeded, or ill disposed, then you may affirm that the *Querent* shall obtain what Salary, wages, debt or money the great person of what quality soever owes to him; or if it happen that the ☽ and the Lord of the ascendant be joined to an unfortunate Planet, and he receive them into some of his essential dignities, the *querent* shall obtain his Money, Wages, &c., but not without much solicitation, many weary addresses, fears and distrusts; if it happen any Aspect be between the Significators, the one being an infortune and without reception, the *querent* will never obtain what he desires. In this manner of Judgment be very careful to observe the Planets' true essential dignities, and their mutual receptions, and by which of their mutual dignities they receive each other.

Of the time when the aforesaid accidents treated of in this Chapter may happen.

Herein you must diligently observe to what Planet either the Lord of the Ascendant or ☽ applies to, or is joined by body, and does signify the effecting and performance of the matter quesited after, for if that Planet be in ✶ or △ with the Lord of the Ascendant or the ☽, whether he be a Fortune or not, or receive the Lord of the Ascendant or ☽ or not; consider well how both of them project their beams or rays to each other, until they come to their perfect aspect, or see how many degrees at the time of the Question asking, they want of being in true partile aspect or ♂, and you may answer that it shall be so many days as are the number of degrees between the Significators, if they be both in Cadent houses: if they be in Succedent houses of Heaven, it will be so many weeks; if in Angles, the time will be so many months: but herein the Astrologer must use discretion, and consider if it be possible that the matter inquired of may be effected in days, weeks or months; for if it be a business that may require much time, instead of months you may add years, and this especially if the Lord of the Ascendant, the ☽ and other Significators be in Angles; but if one Planet be in an Angle, and the other in Suceedent, then they shall signify Months; if one be in Succedent and the other in a Cadent, then they shall denote weeks; but if one be in an Angle, and the other in a Cadent house, they prenote months.

Some of the Ancients have said, that if at the hour of the Question the Planet which signifies the perfection of the thing demanded be in one Sign with the Lord of the Ascendant, the matter shall then be brought to conclusion when that Planet and the Lord of the Ascendant come to corporal conjunction in Degrees and Minute; if the Lord of the Ascendant be the more ponderous Planet, or whether there be reception yea or not; but if the Lord of the Ascendant be the more light Planet, so that he make haste to the conjunction of the Planet signifying the effecting of the matter, and that Planet receive the Lord of the Ascendant, the matter will be finished. But if that Planet shall not receive the Lord of the Ascendant, then the matter will not be effected, unless the aforesaid significators be in an Angle when the Conjunction shall be, or in one of his own Houses, and especially in that house which is called his joy; as ♒ is the joy of ♄, ♐ of ♃, ♏ of ♂, ♎ of ♀, ♍ of ☿. What I have observed in resolving Questions of this nature, is this, that single reception by exaltation without other testimonies profited not; that reception by essential dignities of House, when benevolent Planets are significators, though by ☐ or ☍ do usually show perfection, yea beyond expectation, and therefore very certainly when by ⚹ or △ aspect it so falls out.

And *for the time when*, I observe, if a fortune, or the ☽ or Lord of the thing quesited be in the Ascendant, and have any essential dignity therein, the number of Degrees between the Cusp of the Ascendant and the body of the Planet, does denote the time when, days if a moveable Sign, and the business capable of being perfected in days, months or years, according to the Sign, its quality and nature of the business.

A Tradesman of this City in the year 1634 propounded these several Demands to me: because I have seen the experience of my Judgment, and his Queries were pertinent for Resolutions of the Demands of this second House; I have inserted his several Queries, with the Reasons in Art of my so judging them. His Queries were;

1. *If he should be rich, or subsist of himself without marriage?*
2. *By what means he should attain Wealth?*
3. *The time when?*
4. *If it would continue?*

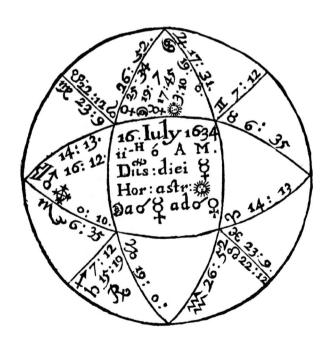

See page A4

CHAPTER XXVIII.

If the Querent Shall be Rich or Poor.

It's first necessary for more exact judgment in this question, that you examine the Diurnal motion of the Planets, which I find here to be as follows:

Viz. ♄ moved in 24 hours, two minutes: and is therefore slow in motion.

♃ 13 min. *Ergo*, he moved more in 24 hours, than his mean motion: which is 4 min. 59 sec. is reputed swift, as you may see page 61.

The Diurnal motion of ♂ is 35 min. this being more than his middle or mean motion, which you see in page 65, is 31 min. 27 seconds. He is reputed swift.

Diurnal motion of the ☉ 57 min. 00 sec. being less than his mean motion; he is slow.

Of ♀	1 degr. 13 min.	very swift
Of ☿	1 degr. 44 min	more swift
Of ☽	11 degr. 54 min.	slow

In the next place I am to examine the fortitudes and debilities of the Planets: by the Table of essential dignities, Page 104, and the other Table of Page 115. I do this more willingly that young Learners may better understand the use of both these Tables, which they will frequently have occasion to use.

True place of ♄ is 15.19 ♐, Essential dignities he has none in that degree of ♐, where he is, as you may observe by the Table of essential dignities, Page 104.

♄ His Accidental Dignities		♄ His Debilities	
In the third House	1	*Peregrine*	5
Free from Combustion	5	*Retrograde*	5
	6	*Slow in motion*	2
		Occidental	2
			14

♃ His Fortitudes

In Exaltation	4
In the tenth House	5
Direct	4
Swift in motion	2
Free from Combustion	5
	20

He has no Debilities, either Accidental or Essential, yet some Detriment it is to him, being in □ with ♂, though the aspect be Platic.

♂ In those degrees of ♎ he is in, has no Essential Dignities

His Accidental Fortitudes.

In the Ascendant	5
Direct	4
Swift in Motion	2
Free from Combustion	5
In ♂ with Spica ♍, *or within five degrees*	5
	21

His Debilities.

In Detriment	5
Peregrine	5
Occidental of the ☉	2
	12

☉ His Fortitudes, Essential and Accidental.

In his own House	5
In Midheaven	5
	10

Debilities.

Slow in motion	2
	2

♀ Her Fortitudes

In the eleventh house	4
Direct	4
Swift in motion	2
Occidental of ☉	2
Free from Combustion	5
♂ with Regulus, *viz. within six degrees of him*	6
	23

Debilities of ♀

Peregrine	5
	5

☿ His Fortitudes		Debilities	
In the tenth house	5	*Peregrine*	5
Direct	4		5
Swift in motion	2		
Occidental	2		
Free from Combustion	5		
	18		

☽ Her Fortitudes		Debilities	
In the tenth house	5	*Slow in motion*	2
Increasing in Light	2	*Peregrine*	5
Free from Combustion	5		7
	12		

⊗ As you may observe, *page* 145, in ♏ has five Debilities, and as it is placed in our Figure, shall rather be admitted to be in the second house, than in the first; and has therefore but three testimonies of strength, which taken from five of Debilities, ⊗ is found weak by two testimonies: and though ⊗ is some minutes more than five degrees removed from the Cusp of the second, yet were it absurd to think it had signification in the first.

The Testimonies of all the Planets collected into one, stand thus.

♄ *Is weak by Testimonies*	8	*And therefore is unfortunate.*	
♃ *Has Fortitudes*	20	*And no imbecility.*	
♂ *Is strong as having*	9	*Dignities: His Debilities subtracted from his Fortitudes.*	
☉ *Has Dignities*	8	0	
♀	18	0	
☿	13	0	
☽ *Has*	5	0	
⊗ *Has Debilities*	2	0	

You must ever consider, whether your Planet have more Fortitudes or Debilities, and having subtracted the lesser number from the greater, make use of what remains, whether they be Fortitudes or Debilities, and so judge.

The Antiscions of the Planets

				Contrantiscions.			
♄ in 14	41	♑		♄ in 14	41	♋
♃	12	29	♊	♃ in 12	29	♐
♂	13	48	♓	♂	13	48	♍
☉	26	50	♉	☉	26	50	♏
♀	4	26	♉	♀	4	26	♏
☿	12	15	♉	☿	12	15	♏
☽	10	53	♉	☽	10	53	♏

If the Querent should be Rich or in a Capacity of substance without Marriage.

Herein first I considered the general disposition of the Planets, and found that the Major number of them (especially the two Fortunes) were swift in their motion, well placed in houses, no manner of ways in a violent way, or by a forcible aspect afflicting each other. I also well considered that ♀ Lady of the ascendant was near to *Cor Leonis*, a Star of great virtue and influence, the ☽ increasing in light, ♃ almost culminating: From hence I collected thus much in general, that he should subsist in the Commonwealth, and live in good rank and quality amongst his Neighbours, &c. (*quoad capax*) according to his calling.

Positions as of 1 January 2005:

Cor ♌: 29 ♌ 54

Secondly, whether he should be rich or not? In resolving this Question, I considered, that the Lord of the second is placed in the Angle of the East, and that the Lord of the second, *viz.* ♂ is Lord of the ⊗ or Dispositor thereof, and is near *Spica* ♍ in 18 of ♎. Then I observed that ♃ a general Significator of wealth, was in his exaltation and Angular, casting his ☐ sinister very near to the degree ascending, which ☐ in signs of long ascensions, we usually repute a △. I also found the ☽ separated

Spica ♍: 23 ♎ 54

newly from a ⚹ of ♂ Lord of the second, and significator of
the thing demanded, and immediately after separated from
♂ of ☿, then instantly applying to the ♂ of ♀ significator of
the *Querent*, transferring thereby both the virtue and influence
of ☿ and ♂ to the proper significator of the *Querent*; the ☽ is
also disposed by the ☉ and he is strong and powerful, and as
she has a general signification in every Question, so being
no ways unfortunate she promised the *Querent* much good.
Lastly, I considered that ⊗ was in a fixed sign and in ♂ his
own terms: from all which testimonies aforesaid, I judged that
the Demandant would acquire an Estate, and have a competent
future in this world, but attain it with labour and care, because
it is signified by an Infortune; so to the day hereof he has; but
because ♂ Lord of the seventh house (which is the house of
Women and Wives) has the most material signification of the
thing demanded, *viz.* Wealth and Riches. I advised to marry,
and acquainted him, that without Marriage he should nothing
so well subsist.

By what Means, or how attain Riches.

Herein you must consider the Planet or Planets promising
Wealth; ♂ in our Scheme being Lord of the second house and
of ⊗ is the Planet we must principally consider; for in the
second house you find no Planet, as he is Lord of the second
and placed in the ascendant, he intimates an estate to be got
by the Querent's own industry, and because the Significator
of the thing demanded is placed in the ascendant, it argues
that an estate or increase thereof would come somewhat
easily or with less labour then expected, but ♂ being an
Infortune something lessens that point in our position at this
time; and as ♂ is Lord of the seventh house, and thereby signifies
(Women, etc.) I acquainted him he would marry a Woman
who would produce him a good fortune, and it fixed, and
more than he could very well look for; which I judged first by
the Lord of the seventh his being in the ascendant and near so
eminent a fixed Star; as also because ♀ who is Lady of his
wife's house of substance, *viz.* the eighth, is so well fortified. I

afterwards considered the ☽ was Lady of the tenth house (which signified his Trade) that she was transferring the light and nature of ☿ and ♂ to the *Querent*; wherefore I advised him to diligence in his profession, and that he should thereby attain a very good or competent Estate. He has, as he informs me, had a good fortune with his Wife, both Money and Land; and for his Trading it has been very good; for ♃ in the tenth is a certain and infallible argument (according to natural causes) that the *querent* shall have plenty of Trading, or exercise a gainful Profession.

The Time When.

All the Significators either in the Ascendant, or Oriental quarter of heaven, and five of the Planets swift in their motion, promise Substance in a small compass of time, after the proposal of the Question. ♂ Lord of the second house, and of ⊗, the principal thing inquired of, being swift in motion argues the same.

The distance of the Ascendant from ♂ being about two degrees, did in this way of judgment signify two years or thereabouts, as what time he had a Portion with his Wife: some may wonder why ♂ being peregrine shall signify any good to the *querent*. I say to that, he being Lord of the second house and of the seventh, and the promising Planet of the thing demanded, shall as well show the time When, as also the performance of what he signifies, (but not without some manner of obstruction;) and herein no question ought to be made, since in civil societies of men, the wicked or ungracious do as well many good offices of love for their Friends, as others better qualified. In the next place, I observed what quantity of degrees the ☽ wanted of her perfect ♂ with ♀, & I found they were six degrees, 27 min.; from hence and the former consideration, I concluded, that about two years after the Question propounded, or sooner, he should sensibly perceive amelioration in Estate by means of a Wife, or by his own proper diligence and industry, and about 1640, which was six years after the Question, he should have very great trading, and live in excellent

repute, have many good Friends and Acquaintance, by whose
means he should improve his Estate: And the reason why I
judged augmentation of his Wealth by means of Friends was,
because ♀ is seated on the cusp of the eleventh house, which
signifies Friendship, &c., for in all Judgments you must warily
consider the nature of the house wherein the application of
your *Significators* are, &c. as also, when you judge in this
nature of things contingent, you must measure out the time
when they shall happen according to reason, and mix Art
and Reason together, and not too much rely upon the general
rules of Art, for *Abs te & a Scientia.*

Of that Planet or Planets impeding the effecting or performance of what is demanded in every Question.

It is considerable in all Demands, that you be careful to
know what that Planet is, who impedes the matter, or hinders
it, that it shall take no effect, and we may justly call him
Strong, Hurtful, Destroyer, Abscissor, because he only destroys
and perverts the nature of the Question, when otherwise it
would come to a good conclusion: We receive judgment herein
from that Planet with whom the Lord of the Ascendant is
joined, or the *Significator* of the thing quesited after, whether
it be the ☽ herself, or that she is partaker with the Lord of
the Ascendant or no, or is *Significatrix* of the thing Demanded.

In resolving this you must consider the Planet to whom
the *Significator* of the *Querent* is joined, or the *Significator*
of the thing required, or the ☽, and observe how that Planet
is disposed, and to whom he is joined; for if the Lord of the
Ascendant, or ☽, or *Significator* of the matter propounded,
is joined to an evil Planet, evil disposed, without reception;
or if he be not ill disposed, but joined to an *Infortune*, and he
ill disposed, and receive him not, it prenotes the destruction
of the thing quesited.

We understand a Planet to be ill disposed, when *Peregrine,
Retrograde, Combust, Cadent*, from the Ascendant or house of the
thing demanded, so that he beholds not the house, or at least the

Lord of the house, in this nature the aspect to the house is better than to the Lord thereof; so any Planet in his Fall or Detriment, may properly be called *Destroyer* or *Obstructor*, or Planet impeding.

Moreover, if the *Significator* of the Querent, or thing sought after, or ☽, or Planet to whom she is joined, whether she is a *Significatrix*, or has participation in the Question, be joined to an unfortunate Planet, *viz. Retrograde, Combust, Cadent,* then observe if *Reception* intervene; which if there be, it signifies the perfection of the matter, though with weariness and much solicitation: If no reception be, the matter will come to nothing, though there have been much probability of its performance.

If the Planet who receives the Lord of the Ascendant, or the ☽, or Lord of the thing Demanded, or the Planet who receives any of them, be free from misfortunes, neither receiving or received, it perfects the matter with facility.

If the Planet to whom the Lord of the Ascendant., or the ☽, or Lord of the matter sought after, be free from the *Infortunes*, and is joined to any benevolent Planet who is in aspect with a malevolent, and he impeded and not receiving the former Planet, the matter will not then be brought to perfection, or come to any good conclusion.

Do you still materially consider if the Planets aspects be without reception, for when they are in reception, things are brought to pass, though with some trouble; ever considering whether any Planet do cut off the light and virtue of the *Significators* before their perfect ♂ with an evil Planet; if such a thing happen, it hinders not, but that the matter may be perfected and accomplished: but if no abscission of light intervene, whereby the malevolence of the *Infortune* may be taken off, the matter is prohibited, and will not be effected.

You must notwithstanding judge if Reception do intervene whether it be not by □ or ♂ aspect, for then if a Planet be evil disposed, then the reception profits nothing; the less when he that is received is impeded: but if reception be by ✳ or △, you may confide the matter will be effected; or if the Planet who receives be at that time well disposed, let the reception be by any manner of aspect, the matter is performed, be the aspect □ or ☍; if the aspect be △ or ✶, it performs the thing, whether the *Significator* be received or not; but provided, the aspect be not separated, but applying; if the *Significator* be joined with a *Fortune* not impeded, the thing will be perfected.

If any Planet translate the light or virtue between one *Significator* and another, and he to whom the light is translated be an *Infortune*, and impeded, the Question or matter is destroyed; unless the *Infortune* be again received.

If the *Significator* of the Querent, or the *Moon*, and *Significator* of the thing looked after, be joined to any Planet who collects the light of both Planets, be he an *Infortune* or unfortunate, he destroys the matter, and permits it not to be accomplished, unless himself receive both the *Significators*; if he receive only one of them, it matters not, the matter will not be performed.

Consider likewise, whether the *Significator* of the Querent be in the house of the thing desired, or going to ♂ of his Lord, this intimates the Querent is going to the thing quesited after; if the *Significator* of the thing demanded be found in the Ascendant, or hastening to the ♂ of the *Significator* of the Querent, it imports the matter inquired of, or thing desired shall come to the Querent, receptions notwithstanding, the ☽ and other aspects remaining in their proper being.

If the Querent should continue Rich.

This I resolved by the cusp of the second, which being a Sign fixed, and ⊗ in it, and ♃ in his exaltation and Angular, and ♀ the Dispositor of ♂, and the ☽ in ♌, a firm and stable Sign, I judged he would continue in a plentiful estate, and that the riches God should bless him with would be permanent; I mean, he would still have a competent fortune, and not be reduced to poverty or want.

The Antiscions of the Planets could be made little use of in this Figure, because none of them fell exactly either upon the cusp of any material house, or with the exact degree of any

Planet; only I observe the Contrantiscion of ♄ falls near to the degree of ♃; from whence I judged, no great unity between him and his kindred, or Brothers and Sisters, for you see ♄ personally in the third, and ♃ Lord of that house, disturbed by ♄ his Contrantiscion, nor did it promise less than prejudice by servants, or some vices or blemishes at least in their behaviour, let their outward demeanour be what it will be; for though ♃ be in his exaltation, yet the foresaid Contrantiscion does afflict him, and leaves a tincture of ♄ with ♃: Here are only two things of which in the course of his life I advised him friendly of, which materially arise out of the Figure, *viz.* because ☉ Lord of the eleventh, beholds ⊗ with a □ *Sinister*, as also, the cusp of the second house, and that the ☉ is Lord of the eleventh, which signifies Friends, I dehorted him from engagements, or confiding in solar men, though of much friendship with him, for in all such cases describe the Planet afflicting, and you give caution enough; what manner of men ☉ signifies; see *page* 71.

Of the third House, *viz. Of Brethren, Sisters, Kindred, Short Journeys.*

Many are the Demands which may be made concerning Questions pertaining to this House; but in effect, the most principal and material of them, and which naturally do arise from hence, concern the Querent's Brethren, Sisters, Kindred, or whether there is like to be Unity and Concord between the Querent and them, yea or no; or if the Querent shall live in peace with his Neighbours, or what are their condition good or bad; or of a short Journey, whether prosperous, yea or not.

CHAPTER XXIX.

If the Querent and his Brother, Neighbour or Sister shall agree or love each other.

The Lord of the Ascendant is for him that asks the Question, the Lord of the third for the Brother, Sister or Neighbour quesited after.

If the Lord of the third be a benevolent Planet, or if he be in the Ascendant, or if a fortunate Planet be in the third, or if the Lord of the third and the Lord of the Ascendant be in ✶ or △ aspect within the orbs of either Planet, or if they be in mutual reception, or if the Lord of the third cast his ✶ or △ to the cusp of the Ascendant, or the Lord of the Ascendant cast his ✶ or △ to the third house; there's then no doubt but unity and concord will be between the Querent and Brother, Sister, Neighbour or Kinsman quesited after; if a *Fortune* be in the Ascendant or the Lord of the Ascendant behold the cusp of the third, and the Lord of the third do not aspect either the Ascendant, or be in aspect with the Lord thereof, you may judge the Querent to be of good condition, and that there will be no default in him, but that the defect will be in the Brother, Sister, Neighbour or Kinsman quesited after; when either ♄ or ♂ or ☋ are locally placed in the Ascendant, it shows the Querent to be evil conditioned, and the fault in him, but if you find either ♄, ♂ or ☋ in the third, unless in their own essential Dignities, it's an assured evidence the Querent shall expect little good from his Brethren, Sister, Kindred or Neighbour, and less if they are Peregrine, Retrograde or Combust, or in any malevolent configuration with any other Planet; for though at the present time of the question, there is appearance of unity, yet will it not continue, but usually mortal hatred or untoward grumbling does afterward arise.

When ♄ is in the third, or ☋, it signifies the Neighbours are Clowns, the Kindred covetous and sparing; if ♂, then Kindred are treacherous, Neighbours thievish; and this most assuredly when either of them are out of their Dignities essential.

Of A Brother that is absent.

The Ascendant and his Lord are the Querent's Significator, the cusp of the third house shall be the Ascendant of the Brother that is absent, the fourth the absent's house of Substance, and so in order.

Consider in what condition the Lord of the third is in, and in what house, and how the Planets do aspect him, and whether he be in the aspect of the good or evil Planets, and what that aspect is they have to each other, or whether they are in corporal conjunction; for if the Lord of the third be in the third and the unfortunate Planets have no □ or ☍ aspect to him, you may judge the Brother is in health; but if the malignant Planets behold him with a □ or ☍, without reception, you may say, the Brother lives, is in health, but he is in great perplexity, discontent and sorrow; but if they behold him with the aforesaid aspects, and be in reception, you may say, the Brother is in great distress, but he will with ease evade it, and free himself from his present sad condition: but if the fortunate Planets behold him with a ✶ or △ aspect, without reception, or with a □ or ☍ with reception, you may judge the Brother is in good health and is well content to stay in the place where he then is: if the fortunate Planets behold him with ✶ or △ and with reception, you may tell the Querent his Brother is in health, and wants nothing in this world to make him happy: But if the Lord of the third be in the fourth, which is his own second house, without the aspect of the malignant Planets, he endeavours to get an Estate or fortune in that Country wherein he is at the time of the erecting the Scheme; but if the Lord of the third be in the fifth house, and is joined with the Lord of the fifth house, with reception of a *Fortune* or not, as long as the Lord of the fifth house is not impeded in any grievous manner, it's an argument the absent Brother is in health, is jocund and merry, and well likes the conversation of the men of that Country where he is: if he be a *Fortune* with whom the Significator of the Brother is in ☌ with, or in ✶ or △ with reception, you may then more safely pronounce the Brother to be in a good condition; yet if the Lord of the third be in the fifth void of course, or in perfect ♂ with any of the unfortunate Planets, without reception, and those unfortunate Planets be themselves impeded, it's an argument the absent Brother is indisposed in health, crazy and not contented in the place where he is: if you find the Brother's significator in other houses which are naturally ill (as the sixth, eighth and twelfth houses are) then he is not well pleased, but yet no hurt will come of it.

If the Brother's Significator be found in the eighth house, and is either corporally or by ✳ or △ aspect joined to a *Fortune*, you may judge the Brother is not very well, yet not so ill, that he need any thing doubt of his well being; however, he is indisposed.

If he be joined to evil Planets by bad aspects, and out of the sixth house, the absent Brother is infirm; the same you may judge if the Lord of the sixth be in the third, unless he have dignities in the Sign, and be in those dignities.

If you find the Brother of the Querent to be ill, see if the Lord of the third be in ♂ with the Lord of the eighth, or is entering Combustion, it's likely then he will die of that infirmity; but if you find his Significator in the seventh, say, he is in the same Country in which he went, and not yet gone out of it, he continues there as a Stranger or Sojourner, is neither well or ill, but so-so.

If the Significator be in the eighth, he doubts himself that he shall die; and the more dubious he is, if his Significator be either combust, or in ♂ with the Lord of the eighth in the eighth, or in aspect by □ or ☍ of the *Infortunes* out of the eighth.

If his Significator be in the ninth, then is he gone from the place to which he first went into a further Country, or if capable, he is entered into some religious Order, or is employed by those that are in Order, *viz.* Religious Men, or possibly according to his quality, is employed in some journey far distant from his former abode.

If his Significator be in the tenth, and joined by ♂ or in aspect with the fortunes by △ or ✳ aspect, especially with reception, he has then got some employment, Office or

Command in the Country where he is, and is in good estimation and lives in a credible way: but if he be joined to the infortunes, or in □ or ☍ of them, or any other ways be impeded by them, or Combust in the tenth; it may be feared he is dead.

If he be in the eleventh House, joined to the Fortunes by any good aspect; or if he be in ☌ with the Lord of the eleventh; he is then safe at the house of a friend, and is pleasant and merry: but if evil Planets afflict him in that House, or cast their malevolent beams to him; then is he malcontented, and not well pleased with his present condition.

If he be in the twelfth House, joined to the Fortunes with reception, and that or those Fortunes not impeded; he then trucks for Horses, or great Cattle, is turned Grasier, or is Master of a Horse, an Hostler, a Drover of Cattle, or one that drives Cattle to Market, according to the quality of the person inquired after.

If he be unfortunate in the twelfth, or in bad aspect with the infortunes, or in aspect with the Lord of the eighth, or Combust; the man is discontent, and doubts he shall never see his Country again; and well he may, for it's probable he will die there.

If he be in the first, the absent Brother is frolic and merry, and extreme well pleased where he is; and they much love and respect him where he is.

If he be in the second, it's probable the man can by no means come away; either he is detained as prisoner, or has done some such act as that he is not capable of coming away; yet if the Significator be Retrograde, he will make hard shift to escape whenever opportunity is offered.

I have been somewhat more tedious in this judgment, because it is as a Key to all the rest: For if any ask of their Father being absent, let the fourth house be the Ascendant of him, and so run round the twelve Houses in your judgment for the Father as you have done for the Brother, ever having this Consideration, that the second House from the Ascendant of your Question, is the substance of the quesited; the third from that shall signify his Brethren; the fourth his Father: If inquiry be made for a Child, or Son, or Daughter absent, the fifth house is their ascendant; the sixth their second House, then the seventh their third, &c.

If one ask of a Servant, the sixth House is his first House or Ascendant; the seventh his second or House of Substance, and so orderly as is before specified: and you must understand that although every House has his sixth, eighth House and twelfth House, yet in every one quesited after, the sixth House of the Figure shall signify his infirmity, the eighth his death, the twelfth his imprisonment; only you must know how to vary your Rules, wherein principally consists the Masterpiece of the Art.

Of Reports, News, Intelligence, or Fears, Whether true or false, or in what sense it's best to take them? Whether they signify good or evil?

The manner of understanding this Question, and taking it in its proper sense, is diversely related by the Ancients; for some would make these like Questions to belong to the fifth house; others, to certain Lords of triplicities, having dominion in the Signs ascending or descending on the Cusps of the third or fifth House. That which I have found true by experience (in our woeful late sad times of War) was this; that if I found the ☽ in the ascendant, tenth, eleventh, or third House, separated by a benevolent aspect from any Planet (be he Lord of what House soever) and then applying by ✶, △ or ☌ to the Lord of the ascendant; I say, I did find the report or rumour true, but always tending to the good of the Parliament, let the report be good or ill; but if at the time of erecting the Figure, the ☽ applied to the Lord of the seventh by any good aspect, I was sure we had the worst, and our enemies the victory: if the ☽ was void of course, the News proved to be of no moment, usually vain or mere lies, and very soon contradicted: if the ☽ and ☿ were in ☐ aspect or in ☍, and did not either the one or other, or both cast their favorable ✶ or △ to the degree ascending, the News was false, and reported of purpose to affright us. For the time when to take the Question, I ever observed the hour when I first heard the news of the rumour, and took that moment of time for the ground of my question; but if another propounded it, then that very particule of hour when it was proposed: however, if at any time upon the like occasion you hear some speech or have some intelligence or report of anything, and would know whether it will be prejudicial to you, yea or no, then see whether ♃ or ♀ be in the Ascendant, or the ☽ or ☿ in any of their essential Dignities, in △ or ⚹ to the Lord of the eleventh; you may then judge, the news is such as you or the party inquiring shall receive no detriment thereby: but if you find the Lord of the sixth, eighth or twelfth houses in the Ascendant, or in bad aspect to the Lord of the Ascendant, or ♂ or ♄ *Retrograde* in the Ascendant, or in an evil aspect with the Lord of the Ascendant, or casting their □ or ☍ rays to the degree ascending, then the Querent shall receive prejudice by the news he hears, if it concern him or herself; or if it concern the Commonwealth, some damage has happened to their Ministers or Parties: If ♄ signify the mischief, their poor Country-friends have been plundered, lost their Corn and Cattle; if ♂, then some straggling parties of theirs is cut off; if ☿, some of their Letters have miscarried, or been intercepted; if the ☉ be the Significator, their principal Officer or Commander in chief is in some distress, &c. if ♃ or ♀, the mischief falls on some Gentleman, their friends, or such as take part with them. Herein vary your rules according to the Question.

If Rumours be true or false, according to the ANCIENTS.

Consider the Lord of the Ascendant and the ☽, and see which of them is in an Angle, or if the Dispositor of the ☽ be in an Angle, and a fixed Sign, or if any of these be in any succedent house and fixed Sign, or in good aspect with the fortunate Planets, *viz.* in ⚹ or △ of ♃, ♀ or ☉, you may then judge the Rumours are true and very good; but if you find the Lord of the Ascendant afflicted by the *Infortunes*, or cadent in house, you must judge the contrary though he strong in the

Sign wherein he is. Rumours are for the most part true when the Angles of the Figure are in fixed signs, *viz.* ♉, ♌, ♏, ♒, and the ☽ and ☿ in fixed Signs, separating from the *Infortunes* and applying to a fortunate Planet, placed in any Angle. Ill Rumours hold true, if the Angles of the fourth and tenth house be fixed, and the ☽ received in them; I say, they will be in some sort verified: If you hear evil news or bad reports, or have unlucky intelligence, yet if either of the *Fortunes* be in the Ascendant, or the ☽ unfortunate, it's a strong argument the Rumours are false, and that they will turn rather to good than evil: The Retrogradation of ☿, or he any other way afflicted, or of that Planet to whom the ☽ applies, or to whom ☿ applies, and above all, if either of those two be Lords of the Ascendant, do signify the ill Rumours shall vanish to nothing, and shall be converted to good; if the Lord of the Ascendant be under the ☉ Beams or Combust, the matter is kept secret, and few shall ever know the truth of them.

Of Counsel or Advice given, whether it be for Good or Evil.

Sometimes a Neighbour, Kinsman or Friend takes occasion to come visit their Friends, with intention and pretension to give them good advice, or persuade them to such or such a matter, &c. if you would know, whether they intend really, yea or no, erect your Figure for the moment of time when first they begin to break their minds to you; then consider if there be in the *Medium Coeli* or tenth house a fortunate Planet, *viz.* ☉, ♃ or ♀, or else ☊, or the ☽ applying to the Lord of the Ascendant, then judge they come with an honest heart, and the advice they give is intended for your good: If an *Infortune*, *viz.* ♄, ♂ or ☋, they intend deceitfully, and are liars. *Haly* does further affirm, that if the Sign ascending be a moveable Sign, and the Lord of the Ascendant, and the ☽ in moveable Signs, he is a treacherous fellow, and comes with deceit to entrap thee.

Whether the Querent have Brethren or Sisters.

Although this is better resolved from the proper Nativity of the Querent, than the Question; yet you may observe these rules, which I have found true by experience.

Viz. If you find upon the cusp of the third house a fruitful Sign, as ♋, ♏, ♓ (♒, ♐ or ♊ , though these are not so fruitful as the other) yet you may judge he has Brethren or Sisters; Brother or Brethren, if a Masculine Sign be there, and the Lord thereof in a Masculine Sign or house, or in aspect with a Masculine Planet: Sister or Sisters, if the Feminine Sign and Planet be in the third, or the *Significators* in Feminine Signs or Houses, and in ♂ or application to Feminine Planets; some say, so many Planets as are in the house, or that the Lord of the third is in aspect with, so many Brothers or Sisters the Querent has; but I ever held it too scrupulous to require such particulars from a Question: the unity amongst Brethren or Kindred, either in the present or future, is discernible by the last aspect the Lord of the third, and the Lord of the Ascendant were in, or by the happy position of Benevolent or malignant Planets in the Ascendant or third; for where the *Fortunes* are placed, from thence it may be expected all unity and concord from that party: from the Querent, if they be in the Ascendant: from the Brother, Sister or Kindred in general, if the *Fortunes* be in the third. The ill position of ♄ or ♂ out of their essential Dignities in the third, or ☋ therein, is a strong argument of untoward and cross Brethren, Sisters or Kindred, and of no unity between them, but continual discord, wrangling and jangling, &c.

Of a short Journey, if good to go, yea or no; which way intended.

By a short Journey I intend, twenty, thirty or forty miles, or so far from one's home, as he may go and come in a day, or at least on the next; now if you would know whether it will be best for you to go, yea or not: herein consider the Lord of the Ascendant at the time of propounding the Question, and see if he be swift or slow in motion, or in any of the Dignities of the Lord of the third, or placed in the third, or in ✶ or △ or ☌ either with the Lord of the third, or with a Benevolent Planet placed in the third, or if the ☽ apply to the Lord of the third, or to any Planet placed in the third, or be in the third, or cast her ✶ aspect to the Sign ascending, or her □ in Signs of short ascensions, in any house whatsoever, or if she be swift in motion, all, or any of these are arguments, that the party shall go his short Journey, and with good success; and if you would know to what part of Heaven the place lies whether he would go, consider the Sign of the third house, the Sign wherein the Lord of the third is, and wherein the ☽ is, and judge by which of them is strongest in essential Dignities where he is; if the principal Significator be in a Northern Sign, then his Journey is intended North, and so of the rest, with their due limitations.

Where an absent Brother was?

See page
A5

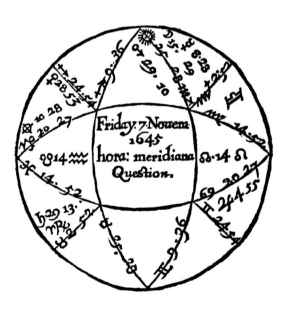

In *November* 1645, a Citizen of *London* being gone into the West of *England*, and no news for many weeks had where he was, his own Brother with great importunity moved me to give my judgment concerning these Particulars.

1. *If living or dead? If dead, whether killed by soldiers? For at this time our miserable Kingdom was full of soldiery.*
2. *If living, when he should hear of him? And where he was?*
3. *When he would come home?*

CHAPTER XXX.

Judgment upon the preceding Figure.

The Ascendant does here represent the shape and form of him that asked the Question, with consideration had to ♄ Lord of the Sign; and as both the Sign ascending and Lord thereof are of a dry quality and nature, so was the *Querent*, lean, spare of body, and a real Saturnine man, &c.

♉ Is the Ascendant of the third House, and ♀ being Lady of the sign, did represent the absent Brother, or party inquired after: the ☽ in regard she neither applied to one significator or other, had not much to do in this Question, I mean in description of the parties.

For as much as ♀ significatrix of the Quesited is no manner of way afflicted either by ☿ who is Lord of the eighth in the figure, or by ♂ who is Lord of the eighth as to the ascendant of the quesited, and that the separation of the ☽ was good, *viz.* from a △ dexter of ♃, and her next application to a ♂ of ☉, upon the Cusp of *Medium Coeli*, I judged the absent Brother was alive and had no manner of casualty happened to him, but was in good health. Having judged the man to be alive, there needs no proceeding to judgment of the rest of the first *Quere.*

When hear of him.

You see ♀ is Lady of the third, and ♄ is Lord of the Ascendant; if you consider the Signs they are in, and the several degrees of each Planet in the Sign; you shall observe, that as well the Significator of the absent Brother, who is ♀, as ♄ Lord of the Ascendant do apply to each other by a friendly △; for ♄ though a ponderous Planet, yet being Retrograde and in more degrees of the Sign than ♀, does by Retrogradation apply to meet her: a very good argument that the Querent should hear news of his Brother very suddenly; and if you look into the *Ephemeris of Eickstadius 1645, November* 7, you shall find the true time of the △ aspect between ♄ and ♀ to be at five of the clock the same day the Question was asked in the afternoon; but with reduction to our *London Meridian* a little after four: I therefore advised the Querent to go to the *Carriers* of those Countries where he knew his Brother had been, and ask of them when they saw the quesited; for I told him, it was probable he should hear of him that very day; upon the reason only because the Significators of both parties met by a friendly △. *He has since confidently affirmed, that about the very moment of time,* viz. *about four, a Carrier came casually where he was, and informed him his Brother was in health and living.*

Where he was.

His Journey was into the *West;* at time of the question I find ♀ the quesited his *Significatrix,* leaving ♐ a Northeast Sign, and entering ♑ a South Sign: whereupon I judged he was in the Southeast part of the Country to which he went; and because ♀ was not far removed from the Ascendant, but was in the *Oriental* quarter of Heaven, I judged he was not above one or two days journey from *London;* and because ♀ was departing the Sign ♐, and entering the Sign ♑, wherein she has essential Dignities by *Triplicity* and *Term,* I judged the man was leaving the Country and place where he last was, and wherein he had no Possessions or Habitation, and was coming to his own house in *London*, wherein he had good propriety; in regard that ♀ wanted one degree of getting out of ♐, I judged he would be at home in less then one week; for ♐ is a *Bicorporeal, Common* Sign, and one degree in that Sign, and in the nature of this question, might well denote a week.

But he came home the *Tuesday* following, when the ☽ came to the body of ♀, she being then got into ♑ to her own *Terms*, and into her *diurnal Triplicity*.

There being an amicable aspect between the two Brothers' Significators, *viz.* ♄ and ♀, these two Brothers always did, and do agree lovingly: This which has been said is enough concerning the judgment of this question; vary your judgment according to the position of your Significators and matter propounded, and by this method you may judge of anything propounded belonging to this third house.

CHAPTER XXXI.

If a Report or common Rumour were True or False.

In the year 1643, His Majesty's Army being then *Rampant*, several Reports were given out, that his Majesty had taken *Cambridge*, &c. a well-affected person inquires of me, if the News were true or false? Whereupon I erected the Figure ensuing, and gave Judgment, *All that we heard was untruth, and that the Town neither was, or should be taken by Him or his Forces.*

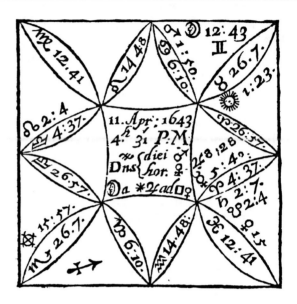

See page
A5

A Report that CAMBRIDGE *was taken by the King's Forces; if true?*

First, I considered that the Angles were all moveable, and that ♂ did vitiate the cusp of the tenth, and ♄ the cusp of the seventh, one argument the Report was false.

Secondly, I found the ☽ cadent, and in Ⅱ, a Sign wherein she nothing delights; a second strong evidence of a false Rumour.

Thirdly, I found ♌ on the cusp of the Ascendant, a Sign of good to the Parliament, for the first house signified that honorable *Society*: I found ♀ Lady of the Ascendant, and our *Significatrix*, in her Exaltation; but ♂, Lord of our Enemy's Ascendant, *viz.* the seventh, entering his Fall, *viz.* ♋, and afflicted by □ of ♄; I saw the ☽ separating from ♃, placed in the seventh and transferring his light and virtue to ♀, which gave me reason to expect, that there would come good to us or our side from this report or Rumour, and no benefit to our Enemies: I saw ♂ and ♄ in a □, which assured me our Enemies were so full of division and treason, and thwarting one another's Designs, that no good should come to them upon this Report; and so in short, I judged *Cambridge* was not taken, and what we heard of its taking were lies.

Had this question been propounded, *Whether the Querent should have Brothers or Sisters?* Then you should have converted the Judgment thus:

♏ The Sign of the third is a fruitful Sign.

♋ Wherein the Lord of the third is placed, is a fruitful Sign.

☽ Applies to ♀ who is placed in a fruitful Sign, as you may see *page* 89, where all these Signs are noted Prolific, or Signs arguing fruitfulness; from hence you might have assured the Querent, he might have expected both Brothers and Sisters, or a plentiful numerous Kindred; but more Sisters than Brothers, because all the Signs are Feminine, as you may see *page* 88, and ♂, Lord of the third, is in a Feminine Sign; yet in regard the ☽ who is Dispositor of ♂, is in ♊, a Masculine Sign, and in ♓ platic with ♃, a Masculine Planet, Angular, and in a Masculine Sign and House, it's an argument of the *Demandant's* having a Brother or Brethren.

It were too nice a point in *Art*, to predict of the certain number, since we only intend to satisfy our self in general, leaving the disposing and determination of their certain number to divine *Providence*.

The third house no ways afflicted, or any ill aspects between ♀, *Significatrix* of the Querent, and ♂ Lord of the third, both being in Signs of the same nature, and ☽ applying by a □ *dexeter* in Signs of short ascensions, to ♀; ☽ having been lately, and yet being within Orbs of the ✶ of ♃; these argue an agreement, concord and unity between this Querent's Kindred and him, and between him and such Brothers or Sisters as he should in future have.

**Of the fourth House, and the JUDGMENT
depending thereupon.**

**This is the House of Parents, of Lands, Tenements,
Hereditaments, Cities, Towns, Villages, Farms,
Manors, Castles, Treasure-trove, or of anything
hid in the ground, &c.**

CHAPTER XXXII.

To find a thing hid or mislaid.

B e careful to take your Ascendant exactly, and consider
the nature of the Question, *viz.* whose Goods, or to whom
the thing missing, or lost, or inquired after did appertain; if
the Goods be the Querent's own Commodity, then see to the
Lord of the second; if it belong to the Brother or Sister, then
have regard to the Lord of the fourth; if to the Father, the
Lord of the fifth; if to the Mother, the Lord of the eleventh,
&c. and so in order, according to the nature of the Party who
proposes the Question.

If you find the Lord of the second in any Angle, you may
judge the thing lost, hid or missing, is within the house of
him that demands the Question; and if the Lord of the second
be in the Ascendant, or in the Sign wherein the Lord of the
Ascendant is, or in one of his houses, you may judge the
thing is in that part of the house which he himself most
frequents, or wherein he does most abide, or is conversant,
or where himself lays up his own Commodities, or such
things as he most delights in; but if the Lord of the
second be in the tenth house, it's then in his Shop, if he
be a *Mechanic*; if a *Gentleman*, in his Hall or Dining-
room; if a Husbandman, in the ordinary common room of
his house, or first room after entrance into his house: If the
Lord of the second be in the seventh, it's in that part of
the house where his Wife, or his Maidservants have most to

do in: If the Lord of the second be in the fourth, it's where the most aged of the house does lodge, or formerly did most frequent, or in the middle of the house, or in the most ancient part of the house, where either his Father or some ancient man lodged: The nature and quality of the place is known by the Signs the *Significators* are in; for if the Sign of the second be airy, or the greater number of the *Significators* and Sign wherein ⊗ is, does concur, the thing is hid in the Eaves or top, or upper part of that house or room where it is, or on high from the ground: and if the thing hid be in the Field, or in a Garden or Orchard, it's higher than the ordinary ground, or upon the highest hill or part of that ground, or hangs upon some stalk of a Plant or Tree.

If the former *Significators* be strong, and in watery Signs, it's in the Buttery, Dairy or Wash-house, or near Water.

If in fiery Signs, it's near the Chimney, or where Iron is, or in, or near the Walls of the house.

If in earthly Signs, the thing hid is on the ground or earth, under or near some Pavement or Floor, and if you find the thing to be mislaid out of the house in any ground, it notes near the Bridge or Stile where people come into the ground.

If your *Significator* be going out of one Sign and entering another, the thing is behind something or other, or is carelessly fallen down between two rooms, or near the Threshold, or joining together of two rooms, and is higher or lower in the place, according to the nature of the Sign, &c.

The *Ancients* have delivered many rules, and do say, *What part* that to judge in what part of the house or ground the thing *of the house* is in, you must see to the Lord of the hour, and if he be in *or ground.* the tenth house or eleventh, you may say the thing is in the South part of the house, towards the East; and if he between the fourth house and Ascendant, then Northeast: if between the fourth and seventh, then Northwest; if between the tenth house and the seventh, then Southwest.

This is and was the opinion of the former *Astrologians*, however, I have not found this judgment very exact, therefore I laboured to find a more certain manner, and a more exact way for the ready discovery or finding out anything mislaid or missing in a house, and not stolen: and it was thus:

First, I considered the Sign ascending, it's nature, the quarter of Heaven it signified.

Secondly, what Sign the Lord of the Ascendant was in.

The Sign of the fourth house.

The Sign the Lord of the fourth was in.

What Sign the ☽ was in.

The Sign of the second.

The Sign the Lord of the second was in.

The Sign ⊗ was in.

I considered the quality of the Sign, as to show what part of the house it was in; I mean, what quarter, whether East, West, North or South, according to the greater number of testimonies: and you must know, for things lost, mislaid, or fugitives, these are the true quarters of Heaven the Signs signify.

♈ *East,* ♌ *East and by North,* ♐ *East and by South.*
♎ *West,* ♊ *West by South,* ♒ *West by North.*
♋ *North,* ♏ *North by East,* ♓ *North by West.*
♑ *South,* ♉ *South by East,* ♍ *South by West.*

Having found the quarter of Heaven, the nature of the Signs showed me also the quality of the place in the house, *viz.* airy Signs, above ground; fiery Signs, near a Wall or Partition; earthly Signs, on the Floor; watery, near a moist place in the room, &c. A few experiments I know may better this Judgment: I have sometimes in merriment set a present Figure, and by that discovered in what part of the house the Glove, Book or anything else was hid, and found the rule very true.

CHAPTER XXXIII.

Of Buying and Selling Lands, Houses, Farms, &c.

Give the Ascendant and Lord thereof, and Planet from whom the ☽ is separated to the *Querent* or *Buyer.*

Give the seventh house the Lord thereof, and the Planet to whom the ☽ applies to the *Seller.*

Give the fourth house, the Planet therein placed, and the ☽ and Lord of the fourth house to the *House, Ground* or *Manor* to be bought or purchased.

Let the tenth house, a Planet or Planets placed therein, and Lord of that house signify the *Price*, that is, *Whether it will be sold cheap or dear.*

If you find the Lord of the Ascendant and Lord of the *If Agree.* seventh in any amicable aspect, the Lord of the seventh applying to the Lord of the Ascendant, you may judge the *Seller* has good will to *sell* and to deal with the *Querent* or *Buyer*: and if the *Significators* be in any essential Dignities upon this their application or translation of light; or their application be by ♂, it's then probable they will agree and conclude upon the *Purchase* with little labour: if the application or translation of light be by □ or ☍, the two Parties will at last bargain, but with many words and probabilities of breaking off, and after much expense of time.

Consider also, if the Lord of the Ascendant or the ☽ apply to the Lord of the fourth, or the Lord of the fourth or the ☽ to the Lord of the Ascendant, and whether only the Lord of the fourth apply to the Lord of the ascendant, and he receive him in any of his Dignities, or if the Lord of the ascendant be in the fourth, or the ☽, or the Lord of the fourth in the ascendant, then shall the Party inquiring buy the House or Inheritance at that time in question,

But if this dwelling in houses be not, yet if the ☽ transfer the virtue or light of the Lord of the fourth to the Lord of the ascendant, the *Bargain* will be concluded, but rather by Messengers or Brokers, than by the personal treaty of the two principal *Agents.*

If there be no application or translation, or transferring the light of one Planet to another, it's not like there will be any *Bargain* concluded.

Of the goodness or badness of the Land or House.

If you find in the fourth house the two *Infortunes*, very *House or* potent, or peregrine, or if the Lord of the fourth be Retrograde *land, good or ill.*

or unfortunate, or in his Fall or Detriment, 'twill never continue long with your Posterity.

But if either ♃, ♀ or ☊ be in the fourth, or the Lord of the fourth in his own house, *viz.* in the fourth, the *Purchaser* may expect good success in the Land or House now in buying, and that it may continue a long time with his Posterity, and it's an argument he shall have good increase for his Money by that Bargain.

Quality of the ground. If it be arable Land, and you would know the nature of it, make the ascendant the *Significator* of the Tenants, Husbandmen and Farmers occupying it.

The fourth house shall signify the condition and nature of the Soil, its form and condition; or of a House or Houses, when the Question is for them.

The Angle of the West shall signify the Herbage thereof, and the quality and quantity, but the *Medium Coeli* is signifier of the Wood, Trees and Plants growing thereupon.

Tenants good or ill. If an *Infortune* possess the Ascendant, the Tenants or Occupants are ill, deceitful and unwilling the goodness of the ground should be discovered: if a *Fortune* be in the Ascendant judge the contrary, *viz.* the Tenants are honest men, and do give, and will give the Landlord content, and will love him besides, and are content to hold what they have already, and to occupy the Land still; but if an unfortunate Planet be in the ascendant, and direct, the Tenants will purloin the Woods, or wear out the virtue of the land; but if he be retrograde, the Tenants will put the land upon the Landlord, or will run away or throw up their Leases.

Wood on the Ground. If a Fortunate Planet be in the *Midheaven*, and direct, say, there is good Timber upon the ground, and good store; if the *Fortune* be Retrograde, judge there are many Trees, but little Timber, and those lopped, or that of late the *Seller* has sold many, or made much spoil thereof, or that the Trees are much decayed, &c. If an *Infortune* be in the *Medium Coeli*, direct, there's then but few Trees; if he be retrograde, say, the Country people have stolen, or made great waste thereof.

But if no planet be in the *Midheaven*, see to the Lord of that house, if he behold it with a good aspect, and be in any of his own Dignities, say, there is some Wood on the ground; if he do not behold the Midheaven, either there is little or no Wood, or it is worth nothing; if the Lord of the tenth be *Oriental*, and behold his own house, the Trees are young ones, or the Wood of small growth, or there are Copses: but if the Lord of the tenth be *Occidental*, and in the condition beforesaid, the Trees are of more growth, and the Wood is ancient; and if the Lord of the tenth be then direct, the Trees are sound, and will continue so a long time; but if retrograde, there's many Trunks and hollow Trees among them.

Having considered what precedes, consider the Angle of the West, or the seventh house, which will declare to thee the state and quality of the Herbage, or smaller Plants of the ground, for if you find either ♃ or ♀, or the Lord of the seventh in the seventh, it's an argument the Land yields plenty of Grass, Corn, or what is reasonably required from it, if an *Infortune* be there, judge the contrary, &c.

In consideration of the property of the earth, have respect *Quality of* to the fourth house and Sign of the fourth, for if ♈, ♌ or ♐ be *the ground.* on the cusp of the house, it's hilly, mountainous, dry and hard piece of ground, or a great part of it is so; if either ♉, ♍ or ♑ be on the cusp of the fourth, the ground is plain, champion, and excellent Pasturage, or good for Grazing or Tillage.

If ♊, ♎ or ♒, it's neither very hilly or very plain, but there is grounds of both sorts, and in nature part of it is good, and part not so: if ♋, ♏ or ♓, then there is no doubt but there is some pretty River, Rivulet, or good store of Water.

You must for the perfect knowledge of the quality and nature of the Soil, observe this general rule, That if an *Infortune* be in the Sign of the fourth, Retrograde, or in his Fall or Detriment, the land shall partake highly in the infelicity that Planet signifies; as if ♏ be the cusp of the fourth, and ♄ is place therein, and is either Retrograde or afflicted by some other Misfortune, you may confidently aver, the ground is troubled with too much Water, or it's Boggy and unwholesome, full of long rushy Grass, &c.

And if the Land lie near the Sea, you may fear the excursion of the Sea, or a decay in the Sea-banks, or it is subject to be overflowing with the River or Water, &c. If ♄ afflict a fiery Sign in the fourth, the Land is barren, stony hungry, mountainous, yields no profit without infinite labour, wants water, for it's naturally barren, produces little Grass: If ♄ afflict the sign of Ⅱ, by his presence there, or any of the human Signs, *viz.* ♎ or ♒, by his retrogradation, that Sign being the cusp of the fourth, there's yet defect in the goodness of the Land, and ill Husbands have formerly managed it unthriftily: If he be unfortunate in an earthly Sign, upon the Sign of the fourth, the Land is good, but the present Occupiers give it not its due Tillage, or are not in the right way in their managing it, they are idle, lazy, slothful, penurious, and unwilling to bestow cost upon it; besides, it's an heavy clay ground, and the *Farmers* understand not the nature of the Soil, &c.

Cheap or dear   This is known by the Lord of the tenth, for if he be Angular, Direct, and strong in essential Dignities, the price will be high, and the *Seller* will put it off at dear rates; but if the Lord of the tenth be cadent, combust, retrograde, slow of motion, afflicted, then the price will not rise high.

If it be good to hire or take the Farm, House or Land desired.

Give the Ascendant and his Lord to the person of him that would hire a House, or take Lands.

Let the seventh house and his Lord signify him or her that has the letting or selling of this House or Farm.

Let the tenth house and the Lord thereof signify the Profit which may arise by that undertaking.

The fourth house, and Planets therein placed shall show the end which shall ensue upon taking, or not taking the House, Land or Farm, &c. be it what it will be.

If the Lord of the ascendant shall be in the ascendant or Sign ascending, or shall have a ✶ or △ aspect to the Sign ascending, but more properly to the degree ascending, within the moiety of his own Orbs, or if in the ascendant there be a *Fortune*, whether essentially dignified or not, or if ⊗ be therein placed, and not impeded, it's an argument or testimony the

Farmer shall take the House, Land or Farm, and is full of hopes to do good thereby, or that it will be a good Bargain, and he obtain much profit thereby, and that he has much liking to the thing, and is well pleased therewith.

But if an *Infortune* be in the Ascendant (it's no matter which of them) if the man have taken the thing ere he come to you, it now repents him; if he have not taken it already, he has no will thereunto; or if he do take it, he will presently post it off to some other party, for he nothing at all cares for the Bargain.

Having considered what belongs to the party intending to buy or take a Lease, have now recourse to the seventh house, and Lord thereof, for him that shall let it: If you find the Lord of the seventh in the seventh, or casting a benevolent aspect to the cusp of the house, or find a fortunate Planet therein, the man will keep his word with you, you shall have what you bargain with him for, but he will profit by the bargain.

If an *Infortune* be in the seventh, and not Lord of the seventh, have great care of the Covenants and Conditions to be drawn between you, the Landlord will be too hard for you, he minds nothing but his own ends in dealing with you.

Consider the tenth house afterwards, and if a fortunate Planet be therein, or behold the tenth house, the parties notwithstanding some rubs, will proceed in their Bargain, and the House, Farm or Lands will be let to the *Querent.*

But if you find an unfortunate Planet in the tenth, or behold that house with an ♂ or □ aspect, there will be no house or Lands taken; and if it be Land that is in agitation to be let, it's probable they differ about the Wood or Timber on the ground, or upon the new erecting of some houses or building upon the ground; or if it be a house, they differ upon the repairs thereof.

As to the end of the business, see to the fourth house, and let that signify the end thereof; if there be a *Fortune* therein, or if the Lord of the fourth be there, or behold the house with ✷ or △, there will come a good end of the matter in hand, both parties will be pleased: but if an *Infortune* be there, in conclusion, the Matter, bargain or thing demised will neither please the one party or other.

CHAPTER XXXIV.

If the Querent shall enjoy the Estate of his Father.

You must in this Question give the Ascendant and Lord thereof to the Querent; the fourth house, Lord thereof and Planet placed in the fourth for the *Significator* of the Father; the personal Estate or Goods moveable of the Father, are signified by the fifth house, his Lord, and any Planet accidentally placed in the fifth; if in this Question you find the Lord of the second and Lord of the fifth in reception, the Lord of the fifth being in the second, and the Lord of the second in the fifth, there's no doubt to be made but the Querent shall have a competent fortune out of the Estate of his Father; but if it happen that the Lord of the fifth house be Retrograde, or in some bad aspect of any malevolent Planet, then some part of that Estate the Father intends for the Querent, will be wasted or otherwise disposed of by the Father; and if you inquire wherefore or upon what grounds, or who shall be the occasion of it? then see what Planet it is that impedes the Lord of the fifth, either by □ or ☍, or if it be the ☉ by Combustion, what house he is Lord of; if it be the Lord of the sixth, it's probable it is one of the Father's Brothers or Sisters, or some of his Tenants or Neighbours that will persuade the Father to alter his intention, and to diminish part of what he did formerly intend to do: If it be the Lord of the seventh, it is some Woman or Sweetheart, or one the Querent has been sometimes at variance with, that will withdraw the Parent's intention: If it be the Lord of the twelfth, it's some sneaking *Parson* or Parish *Priest*, or some or other of the Mother's Kindred; now if upon the description of the Party, the Querent is well informed of him or her who it is, and he is desirous to obtain this party's favour or good will, that so he may be less malicious to him, let him then observe, when the Planet who impedes, and the Lord of the ascendant, are approaching to a ⚹ △ or ☌, and that day that in the *Ephemeris* he shall find the ☽ separating from the one, and applying to the other, let him, I say, about or at that time endeavour a reconcilement, and it's not to be doubted that he may obtain his desires, as I have found many times by good experience.

If the Lord of the fifth dispose of ⊗, and be in the Ascendant or second, the Querent shall obtain his desires which he expects from his Father.

If ♃ or ♀ out of the fifth house cast their benevolent aspects to any Planet in the Querent's second, it argues the same.

If the ☽ separate from the Lord of the fifth, and either have presently after a ✶ or △ to the Lord of the second, or of the ascendant, it shows strong and assured hopes of acquiring the thing demanded of the Father.

If you find an *Infortune* in the fourth, not having Dignities there, then you may say the Father has little wish to part with his Money, nor will it be good to move him much, until that unfortunate Planet be transited out of that Sign; but if you cannot stay so long, observe when that unfortunate Planet is Direct, swift in Motion, Oriental, and in ✶ or △ with ♃ or ♀, or with the Lord of the ascendant, and then let the Father be moved in the business: This I write, where the Querent would have present means, and cannot conveniently stay the Father's leisure: nor do I write, that the observation of those times do themselves enforce the mind or will of the Father, but that then at those times there's more benevolent inclinations.

If you find the Lord of the second and of the fifth, applying by Retrogradation to any good aspect, the Querent will receive some Estate from his Father suddenly, ere he be aware, or when he least thinks of it: now to know, whether the Father loves the Querent better than any of his Brothers or Sisters, you must observe, whether the Lord of the third, or any Planet in the third be nearer to, or in better aspect with the Lord of the fourth, than the Lord of the ascendant is, or if there be any reception between them, *viz.* the *Significators* of Brethren and Sisters, or translation of light, and none between the Lord of the Ascendant and the Lord of the fourth. You may then be assured, the Father's affection stands more to another than to the Querent; the Planet nearest in aspect to the Lord of the fourth, shows the party or person beloved, so do the most powerful reception of *Significators*.

CHAPTER XXXV.

If good to remove from one house or place to another,
or to stay or abide in any place or not?

See to the Lords of the ascendant, the fourth house and seventh house, for if the Lord of the fourth be in the seventh, and be a good Planet, and the Lord of the first and seventh be good Planets, or strong in that part of Heaven where they are, or in the whole Figure, if they be Direct, and of swift motion, and in aspect with good Planets, it is good then to abide still and not remove from the place where the Querent is; but if the Lord of the seventh be with a good Planet, and the Lord of the fourth with an evil one, it is then not good to stay, for if he do, he shall receive much damage there: That which I have observed in this manner of Judgment was this; That if the Lord of the ascendant did lately separate from the □ or ☍ of the Lord of the sixth, eighth or twelfth, and the ☽ also did concur in judgment, *viz.* if she did separate from any evil aspect of the *Infortunes*, they being Lords of either the seventh or fourth &c. and not Friends or Significators in the person of the Querent; or if I found an *Infortune* in the ascendant, Peregrine or Retrograde, or if a Peregrine or unfortunate Planet was in the fourth, or if the Lord of the second was weak or ill placed, I advised the Querent to remove his Habitation, and gave him reason why he should; for if I found the Lord of the sixth house in the ascendant, or afflicting the Lord of the ascendant, I judged he had his health very bad there, was sickly, or was tormented with ill servants, by whose means he did not thrive in his Vocation.

If the Lord of the twelfth afflicted the Lord of the ascendant or the ☽, I said he had backbiting, evil or slanderous Neighbours, or people that lived not very far from him did scandalize him: if the Lord of the second was unfortunate, or in □ or ☍ to the Lord of the ascendant, or if ⊗ was in the twelfth, eighth or sixth, I judged he went back in the world, and his Estate consumed.

If his Significator, *viz.* if the Lord of the ascendant was afflicted by the Lord of the tenth, I acquainted him, his Reputation was lost, his Trade decayed, or had no Trading; and if the Lord of the fourth was unfortunate, or the fourth house itself, I judged the house was unlucky, and few that had lived therein did thrive, or that the Repairs of the house had much weakened him*: If the Lord of the seventh afflicted the Lord of the ascendant or second, his overthwart Neighbours had all the Trade, were better furnished with Commodities, &c. Now in giving direction which way to steer his course, in hopes of better Trading, I observed what Planet in the Scheme was most fortunate and strongest, and had the most friendly aspect to either the Lord of the ascendant or Lord of the second, look what quarter of Heaven the Sign that Planet was in did signify, to that part did I ever advise the Querent to remove; and I remember not, that any ever repented their following my advice; many have afterwards returned to me thanks and rewards.

*Or the house stood not conveniently for his Trade.

And whereas I mention these words [*perhaps the house was unlucky*] some may cavil at the words, and say, *God's blessing is alike in all places, and it's superstitious to judge, a house that is not a living thing, can be made unsuccessful,*‖ &c.: Let these enjoy their opinion still; there's not a man in this world less superstitious than myself, yet what I have found by experience, I freely communicate, and do remain of this opinion; That in what house any execrable facts are committed, the ministering Angels of God seeing the villainy done in that house, and the dishonor done to God therein, do accurse that place or house; which continues so long, as there is not a full expiation made by some godly person, for the sins committed in that house; or until the time limited by the angry Angel be expired, the house shall remain a most unfortunate house for any to live in: And this which I write, and is inflicted upon houses which are insensible, I assuredly know is performed to the full upon the great and smaller Families of this world, &c. How in a natural way to discharge these curses, *Sunt sigilla & Lamina quae nec scripta sunt, & ego novi.*

‖Or unfortunate.

But some for resolution of this Question, say, if the ☽ separate at time of the Question from ♃ or ♀, then stay; if she separate from an *Infortune*, remove; or a *Fortune* in the ascendant bids you stay; an *Infortune* remove: This heedfully considered with the preceding Judgment, will instruct any indifferent *Astrologer* to resolve the preceding Question concerning removing from one place to another.

CHAPTER XXXVI.

Of turning the course of Rivers, or bringing Water into one's Ground or House, either by Conduit or Pipes.

In this manner of judgment, you must principally consider the position and strength of ♄ and the ☽, and in what aspect they or either of them are in, either with ♃ or ♀; for if you find ♄ Direct, swift in Motion, Oriental, and the ☽ in the third, eleventh or fifth house, without any aspect either good or evil to ♂, it's an argument, the Work that is to be undertaken will have good success, be brought to a good conclusion, and that the Querent will have prosperity and credit by it, and the matter easily performed; and this the rather, if the ☽ apply to that Planet who is Lord of the Sign wherein she is, and he receive her in any of his Dignities; and if that Planet who is receiver of the ☽ be a *Fortune*, and is ascending in his latitude, and in a fixed Sign, the Querent shall not need to fear, but that there will be water enough, and that it will run plentifully, and the Watercourse will long continue: if there be in the tenth house either ♃ or ♀, but especially ♃, it's a sure argument the River, Channel, Conduit, Pipe or Waterwork shall remain many a year.

In further consideration of this judgment, if you find ♄ in the eleventh, very strong and potent, and the ☽ in ✶ or △ to him, and the Dispositor of the ☽ in a fixed Sign, or a common one, or the ☽ herself in one of those Signs producing Rain, which are ♋, ♌, ♒, ♓.

All these arguments, that in the work you are in hand with, you shall have a good Current, and plenty of Water; but if you find an unfortunate Planet in the tenth, it's probable your Pipes will break, your Watercourse be subject to ruptures or breaking down of the Banks, the Water will not run currantly, that the Plot is ill laid, nor is there any success promised to the undertaker or undertakers, by that present employment.

CHAPTER XXXVII.

Of Treasure lying hid in the Ground, or to be dug out of the Earth.

The resolution of this Question is various, according to the nature of its proposal, or according to the nature and quality of the thing inquired after, *viz.* whether Money, Plate or Jewels, or things easily movable, or for Treasure long since obscured or hid, the Querent not knowing what it is: or if it be, Whether there be any Mine of Gold, Silver or Iron, or any other Minerals in the Ground, Manor or Lordship now questioned; then it is requisite to know whether the Querent did hide or obscure this Treasure now inquired after, or whose it was, or what relation the party that did so had to him, or whether that he ask in a general way of Treasure hid, not being able to discover either when, where, or whose, or what it is?

If the Querent did hide his own Plate, Money or Jewels in any part of his Ground, or in his house, and has forgotten whereabouts, you must herein observe the Sign of the second house, the Lord thereof, what Sign and quarter of Heaven he is in, as also, the Sign of the fourth and his Lord, and what quarter of Heaven they signify: the Lord of the second and of the fourth in Angles, the Plate is still in the house, or in the ground, and not removed; but if these Planets be not in Angles, but an *Infortune*, without dignities, be either in the fourth or seventh, there's then either part of it, or all removed and made away; and if your Figure promise, that your Goods are not removed, to find in what part they are, have recourse to the first Chapter of this house concerning things hid, &c.

If the question be concerning Treasure absolutely, without

knowledge whose or what it was, *viz.* whether there be any in the place or ground suspected, yea or no; observe in the Figure whether ♃ or ♀ or ☊ be in the fourth house, there's then probability of Treasure being there; if they be there and in their own houses, the matter is without dispute, and you may be sure there is Treasure, or something of value in the house or ground suspected; or if you find either ♄ or ♂ in any of their own houses, Direct, and without Impediment, and in the fourth, there is also Treasure, or if you find ♀ in ♉ in the fourth, not labouring with any misfortune, it's probable there is Treasure there, for you must know there is no Planet unfortunate, when he is in his own house, or essentially dignified, and a Significator.

If you are ignorant of the nature and quality of the Treasure, or thing obscured, then see to the Planet who signifies the Treasure, and consider if he be Lord of the seventh house and examine his nature and property, if he be so; if he be not Lord of the seventh, join the Lord of the seventh in judgment with him, so frame a mixture for the quality of the thing.

But if that Planet who is Significator of the Treasure be not Lord of the 7ᵗʰ or have affinity with him, then absolutely take the Lord of the seventh to signify the nature and *Species* of the Treasure; who if he be the ☉, and he in his house or exaltation, there is Gold there, or precious Stones or Jewels of that colour, or near to the colour of the ☉.

And if the Question were, Whether there were a good Mine yea or not? the place considered, it's like there is; if the ☉ be not so well dignified, and yet signify the Treasure, it's then somewhat very precious, and near to Gold in goodness.

If the ☽ be in her own house or exaltation, and be Lady of the seventh, the Treasure is Silver, Plate, Crystal or Jewels &c. of the colour she is of, &c.

If ♂ be the Lord of the seventh, and so dignified, he shows, the thing sought after may be Brass or Glass, or some Curiosities or Engines of Iron &c. but if he be weak, perhaps you may find some old rusty Iron, Candlesticks, Kettles &c. If the Question were about Ironstone, it's probable it will prove good Ironstone, and make good Iron. If ♄ be Lord of the seventh, and fortified as before specified, there's some *Antiquities* of great account, or ancient Monuments of men long since deceased, some *Urn*, &c. or there are some things wrapped up in old black Cloths, or old wooden Boxes: and if the Question were concerning any Mine or quarry of Stone, then it's very probable there is a rich Mine of Coal, if the Question were concerning Coal, or of good Stone, if the Question were of it: but if ♄ be weak, and ill dignified, then neither is the Mine a rich one, or can it be wrought without much expense of Treasure; whether it be full of water, or what may be the impediment, you must require from the Sign he is in, well considering what was formerly said in this Chapter.

If ♃ be Lord of the seventh and essentially fortified, there is Silver or very rich Cloth, and great store of it, or Tin, &c.

If ♀ be Lady of the seventh, she intimates curious Household stuff, costly Jewels, or that fine Linen is there hid.

If ☿ be Significator, he prenotes some Pictures, Medals, Writings, Books, some pretty Toys are obscured, or are the Treasure looked after.

If the Querent shall obtain the Treasure hid.

If the Planet who Signifies the Treasure or thing hid, does apply to the Lord of the ascendant, or if there be mutual reception or translation, or collection of light and nature between them, it's probable the Querent shall obtain the matter sought after; if the aspect be by □ or ☍, then not without difficulty and much labour; the ☌ of both Significators best of all performs the business, and the more assuredly, if they be in a fixed Sign, and placed in the Querent's second house, or in the ascendant, either of the *Luminaries* placed in the ascendant and not unfortunated, gives great facility in the Work; but if neither of them be in the ascendant, or behold it, but be both in cadent houses, there remains little hopes in the matter: When ⊗ is in the ascendant, and also his Lord or Dispositor, it promises acquisition of the Treasure: but if the Lord of ⊗ be cadent, and both the Lights, especially the ☽, and have no aspect to the

⊗, or the Lord of the ascendant behold not the ascendant, I can give the Querent then no hopes of obtaining the Treasure or thing hid: *Alkindus* gives this general rule concerning Treasure, or anything obscured in the ground; Erect your Figure aright, consider the several aspects of the Planets, if there be in the ascendant, or in any Angle a *Fortune*, say, there is Treasure in the ground, and that the thing hid is still in the ground, the quality, price, esteem thereof, shall be according to the potency, virtue or debility of the *Fortune*.

If you find the thing hid to be unremoved, then he proceeds and says, behold the Lord of the ascendant and the ☽, if there be any good aspect between them, and that *Fortune* which signified the Treasure to be there, *viz.* a good aspect and reception, he that demands the question shall then have the thing inquired after, &c. He further says, that fixed Signs show the thing is hid in the Earth, common Signs in or near a Wall, moveable Signs on high, or in the covering of houses: whether it lie deep in the earth or not, consider if the Planet Significator, be in the beginning, middle or near the end of the Sign; if he be newly entered the Sign, the Commodity is not deep, but shallow, near the upper part of the earth; the further the Planet is in the Sign, the deeper, &c. when you would dig, let not the *Infortunes* be angular, but if possible, the Significators applying by ✶ or △ to the Lord of the second house, or the ☽ separating from the Significator of the Treasure, and applying to the Lord of your ascendant

CHAPTER XXXVIII.

If I should purchase Master B. his houses.

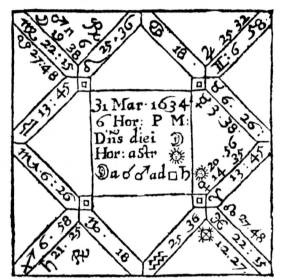

See page
A6

    The Inheritance of the house wherein at this present
1647, *I live, and some others being proffered me to*
buy **1634.** *I had a desire to know if I should deal*
with the seller and procure Moneys in convenient time
to pay for the Purchase, (my own Money being in
such hands as I could not call it in under six months
warning) being desirous, I say, to purchase the said
houses, and fully resolved upon it, I took my own
Question myself, at what time I found my mind was
most perplexed and solicitous about it; the time of my
Quere to myself fell out according to the position of
Heaven aforesaid.

The Sign ascending is ♎, the degree of the Sign is the same wherein ♃ was in my *Radix*; I looked upon that as a good *Omen* in the first place.

♀ Is for myself, the ☉ locally placed in the seventh is for the Seller; the ☉ receives ♀ in his Exaltation; besides, ♀ is near the cusp of the seventh, and no other Planet in the seventh ☉ excepted, which signified, there was at present no other purchaser about it but myself: the ☉ so exalted and angular prenoted the Seller to be high in his Demands, [*and so he was*] nor was he necessitated to depart with it: finding, I say, my Significator received of ☉, and so near to the cusp of the Angle of the West, it was an argument I should proceed further in the matter, notwithstanding ♀ her many Debilities; for as I found ☉ Lord of the seventh, so also was he Lord of the eleventh, signifying my hopes should not be frustrated: besides, ♀ was applying to a △ of ♄, Lord of the fourth, *viz.* the houses inquired after, and had no abscission or frustration ere the perfect aspect; a main strong argument I should buy the houses: and indeed both *Significators* strongly applied to a △ aspect *viz.* ♄ and ♀, for ♄ is Retrograde: I also considered the ☉ was in perfect △ with ♄, the ☉ being, as I said, Lord of my eleventh, and he of the fourth; ♄ has also signification of me, as Querent, because he beholds the ascendant, and therein has exaltation: now whether you consider him, as having Dignities in the ascendant, or as Lord of the fourth, the Lord of the eleventh and he applying to each other by a △, argued, assuredly I should proceed further in the matter, and in the end conclude for them: The ☽ in the next place translating the influence of ♂, who has Dignities in the seventh, to ♄, having virtue in the ascendant, though by a □ aspect (yet out of Signs of long ascensions) did much facilitate the matter, and argued my going on, and probability of contracting, but with some leisure, and slowly, because of the □ aspect; for as the ☽ is afflicted, and ♀ unfortunate, so had I much to do, and many meetings about it; the Seller not abating one penny of the five hundred and thirty pounds, being the first penny he demanded: As the ☉ is near to a ⚹ aspect of ♃, so did a jovial man endeavour to procure the purchase to himself* ; but ♃ is cadent, and in

This was after I begun, and before I concluded.

detriment, showing he should not prevail, ♀ angular and in aspect with ♄ Lord of the thing sought after; and as ☉ is Lord of the eleventh, which is the fifth from the seventh, so a Daughter of the Seller's was my very good friend in this business, and suffered no interloper to intervene, though some offered fair*; for ♂ Lord of my second house Retrograde, argued I should get none of my own Moneys to supply my occasions; nor did I: ♃ Lord of ⊗ in ✶ with ☉ no ways impeded, but by being in detriment, in ✶ platic with ♀ Lady of my Ascendant, shortly entering his exaltation, gave me such hopes as I doubted not of procuring Moneys when he entered ♋, and ♂ became direct, which he did 12 days after, at what time a friend lent me £ 500. The qualities of the Houses are signified by ♑ the Sign of the fourth, and ♄ Lord thereof, who having no material debilities, except Retrogradation and Cadency, being also in △ with ☉; the Houses were really old, but strong and able to stand many years. When ♀ and ☉ came to ♂ in ♉, that day I bargained, *viz. die* ♀ 25 *April* following: the seventeenth of *May* ♀ and ☽ in ♂; I paid £ 530, and my Conveyance was Sealed. So that as ♀ wanted six degrees of the body of the ☉, so was it six weeks and some days from the time of the Question ere I perfected what the Figure promised; as to the Moles and Scars of my body it does exactly agree: for as ♀ is in ♈, which represents the face, so have I a Mole on my cheek about the middle of it; and as ♎ ascends, I have one on the reins of my back, the ☽ in ♍ afflicted by ♂, I have a red Mole below my Navel, ♃ Lord of the sixth in ♊ a Masculine Sign, I have a Mole near my right hand visible on the outside; so have I on the left foot, as ♓ the Sign of the sixth does represent. Many things might be considered herein, besides what is written; but I fear this Book will increase beyond my first intention: *Ergo.* The truth of the matter is, I had a hard bargain, as the Figure every way considered does manifest, and shall never live to see many of the leases yet in being, expired: and as ♀ is in ♈, *viz.* opposite to her own House, so did I do myself injury by the Bargain, I mean in matter of Money; but the love I bore to the House I now live in, wherein I lived happily with a good Master full seven

*To hinder me.

years, and therein obtained my first Wife, and was bountifully
blessed by God with the Goods of this World therein, made
me neglect a small hinderance, nor now, I thank God, do I
repent it; finding God's blessing in a plentiful measure upon
my Labours: yet was I no Tailor or Scrivener, as *Wharton*
affirms, or indeed any profession at all; nor was my Master
a Tailor, or my Wife a Scrivener's Widow.

Of the fifth HOUSE, and its Questions

CHAPTER XXXIX.

If one shall have Children, yea or no?

When this question is demanded by a man or
woman, long before marriage, or by some
ancient Bachelor, or Maid, *Whether they shall
ever have any Child or Children, yea or not?*
herein generally you are to consider, whether the Sign upon
the fifth, or ascending, be of those we call Fruitful, yea or no,
(*viz.* ♋, ♏, ♓) and whether the Lord of the ascendant (be the
Sign what it will) or the ☽ be in aspect with the Lord of the
fifth house, and that aspect be either ♂, ✶, △ or □ (though ♂
is not properly an aspect) which if it be so, and the Planet to
whom the Lord of the fifth does apply, or is in aspect with, be
free from Combustion, and other Accidental or Essential
misfortunes, it's an argument the good old Bachelor or stale
Maid, or whoever propounds the Question, shall have Children
or Issue ere they die; In like case judge, if the Lord of the fifth
be in the ascendant, or else the ☽, or the Lord of the ascendant
in the fifth, for this is a strong argument of having Issue or Children;
but if neither the Lord of the ascendant or the ☽ apply to the
Lord of the fifth, yet if there be rendering of virtue or light one
to another, or translation or collection by or from the principal
Significators, you may still continue your judgment, that

the Querent shall have issue, but not so soon, as if it had been foreseen by the first manner of judgment. After all this, have respect to the Planet who is receiver of the Disposition of the Significators; who if he be clear from misfortune or affliction, *viz.* from Retrogradation, Combustion, or Cadency in House, it gives great hopes of issue. See also if that Planet from whom the ☽ is separated be Lord of the fifth Sign from the Sign wherein the Planet is to whom the ☽ applies, and both these Planets have any aspect to each other; that also does testify the party shall have Children or a Child. If no Aspect happen between them, it's not then likely he will have any; and yet some say, that if the above named Planets or Significators be not in any Aspect, yet if the Planet to whom the ☽ applies be in an Angle, the Querent may have Issue.

If a Woman ask, whether she may conceive?

Many times a Woman married, having been long without Children, may inquire, whether she is like to Conceive, yea or no? In this Question you are to consider:

If the Lord of the Ascendant be in the seventh, or the Lord of the fifth in the first, or the Lord of the first in the fifth, or if the Lord of the fifth be in the seventh, or the Lord of the seventh in the fifth, or the ☽ with him, or good Planets in the Ascendant, or with the Lord of the fifth, or in any of the Angles; she may then conceive: but if none of these testimonies concur, and you find barren Signs and ill Planets to be in the former places, she neither is at present conceived, or will hereafter conceive. If good and bad Planets be mixed together, she may perhaps conceive or have children, but they will not live: If ♋, ♏ or ♓ be in the Ascendant or fifth, she may have children; but if ♌ or ♍ be there, she neither is at present, or hardly after will be with Child. When women have been long without children, and propound such a question, see if their Nativity did not originally deny children.

At what time, or how long it may be before she have a Child?

If you find that according to natural causes she may have a Child or Children; and the Querent is desirous to know near what time: See then where thou findest the Lord of the fifth house, *viz.* if in the Ascendant or first house; then judge the first year; if in the second house, the second year; if in the tenth house, the third year; if in the seventh house, the fourth year; if in the fourth house, the fifth year. And herein you must be careful in considering what sign the Lord of the fifth house is in; for the swiftness of a Planet in a moveable sign does somewhat hasten the time; a double bodied Sign does not manifest so soon; fixed Signs prolong the matter; however, this is worthy of your consideration, that let the Significator be in what Sign he will be, yet if he be swift in motion and direct, he does make the more haste in performance of the business he is a Significator in, and causes the matter sooner to be accomplished.

Whether the Querent shall have Children, be he Man or Woman that asks?

Behold the Ascendant, and if fortunate Planets behold the same, and the Lord thereof be in the Ascendant, or in the tenth, eleventh or fifth house, and you find ♃ also well placed together with that Planet who is Lord of the Triplicity ascending, and he be not Combust or Retrograde; judge then, if the Man ask the Question, he may have Children, or is capable of getting them. If a woman inquire, say, she may Conceive, and is not naturally barren. If the Lord of the ascendant be in the fourth or seventh, and ♃ in a good House of heaven, do you say, the party shall have a Child a long time after the asking of the Question.

But if you find the Ascendant afflicted, or infortunated by the Malevolent Planets, and the Lord of the Ascendant in an evil place or House of heaven, and ♃ Cadent, or in the eighth or Combust, or not fully elongated from the Sun-Beams; then you shall judge he will have few Children, and they sickly, hardly any to live. It's also a great Sign of non-conception, or no capacity to conceive, when the ☽ is unfortunate. If you find a fortunate Planet in the fifth House, or having a benign aspect to the Cusp thereof; it gives hope and strong testimony of having a Child in a little compass of time; but if an infortune be in the fifth ill dignified, Combust, Retrograde, slow of motion, &c. the Querent will have no Children; but if the Infortune be direct and swift, Oriental, and in any of his essential dignities, he shall signify Children; the more Children if ♃, ♀ or ☉ be in ✶ or △ with him out of good houses: you must ever remember, that the nearer a Fortune is to the Ascendant, the sooner the Querent may expect Children, the more remote the longer time must be allowed. Others observe this rule following, That if ♃ be in the Ascendant or fifth, and in a Sign which is not barren, it's an argument the Querent may have a Child; there is also much strength in the Lord of the house; for if he be angular with reception of the Lord of that Angle where he is, or in the eleventh or fifth with the like reception, it is a sure testimony of having Children. In all Questions concerning Children, be careful of the age of the Querent, or some other natural or hereditary infirmity incident to the Querent, and seldom conclude without two testimonies.

If a Man shall have Children by his Wife yea or not, or of any other Woman whom he nominates.

When it is demanded of you by any Man, *Whether he shall have any Children by the Wife he has, or the Woman he mentions*; or if a Woman ask if she shall have Issue or Children by such a Man. Behold the Ascendant, his Lord and the ☽, and if the Lord of the Ascendant or the ☽ be joined to the Lord of the fifth, you may judge he or she shall have Issue by the party inquired of; if this be not, then see if any translation be from the Lord of the fifth to the Lord of the ascendant; that's an argument of having Children after some space of time: If the Lord of the ascendant or the ☽ be in the fifth House, he or she may have children, or the Lord of the fifth in the ascendant: if none of these be, consider if the Lord of the ascendant, the ☽, and the Lord of the fifth be not joined to a Planet more ponderous than themselves; for he collecting both their lights, shall be the receiver of their disposition, and shall signify whether the Child or Children (if any be) shall live or not; if he be not impeded the Children then shall live, but if he be Retrograde, Combust, Peregrine, or otherwise unfortunate, neither will the Children live long, or will the Parents take comfort of these Children. After this, consider ♃, who naturally signifies Children, if he be in the ascendant, third, fifth, ninth or eleventh house, free from all manner of misfortune; you may affirm the Woman shall shortly conceive, perhaps upon the first congress or coition after the asking of the question, or a little after, and the matter seems as good as done.

If ♀ be in the fifth no way impeded, and some other *Fortune* be there besides, it hastens the time, and she will conceive very suddenly. But if ♃ be in the aforesaid places impeded, say, that either she is not conceived, or if she be, it will not come to perfection, for the Woman shall suffer abortion. In like manner if ♀ be unfortunate by ♄ or ♂, or be under the ☉ beams, or Combust, the Woman is not conceived, unless a *Fortune* be in the fifth house, and then she is more assuredly with child, or shall be shortly; yet you may justly fear she will suffer mischance ere the birth.

If either ♄ or ♂, or especially ☋ be in the fifth, or the two former malevolents cast their ☍ to the fifth, it seems the Woman is not with child; and verily the □ of the *Infortunes* to the fifth house seems to hinder conception.

Whether she is with Child or not.

She is.   A woman mistrusting herself to be with Child, and desirous to know the truth; if she ask the Question of thee, then give Answer, having well considered your Figure, erected according to the time of her demand, *viz.* as these following rules direct you.

The Lord of the ascendant or ☽ behold the Lord of the fifth with any aspect or translation.

If the Lord of the ascendant and the ☽ be in the fifth house, free from the malevolent aspect of the *Infortunes* and direct; and herein you must not wholly rely upon ♄ and ♂ or the ☋ to be the only *Unfortunate* Planets,* you must consider the position of

*I mean ♄ and ♂ for Planets, not ☋.

heaven at the time of erecting your Scheme, and take any evil aspects of the Lord of the sixth, eighth or twelfth, be he what Planet he will, to be an affliction, if he have □ or ☍ to the Lord of the fifth, or Lord of the ascendant, or the ☽.

♃ generally in the first, fifth, eleventh or seventh, not in aspect to ♄ or ♂, they being slow in motion or Retrograde.

The Lord of the ascendant, or Lord of the fifth house aspecting a Planet in an Angle with reception, and rendering up his virtue to him; if the ☽ be in reception with any Planet in an Angle, that is, essentially Fortified, else not; for accidental dignities in this manner of judgment, gives hopes, but not real assurance.

If the Lord of the Ascendant behold the Ascendant with an amicable aspect, out of any good House; or if the ☽ be in the seventh, and behold the Lord of the seventh in the eleventh, or if the ☽ be in the eleventh, and behold the Lord of the seventh in the seventh.

The Lord of the Ascendant received in either House, Triplicity or Exaltation, and the receiver of the Lord of the Ascendant having alike dignity in the House, *Triplicity*, *Exaltation*, or Term of the received, *viz.* Lord of the Ascendant.

The ☽ giving virtue, or rendering her light to a Planet in the fifth house, or having essential dignities in the fifth.

The ☽ applying to the Lord of the ascendant or Lord of the fifth in the first or tenth house, and he not Cadent from his own House or exaltation;* where you must understand this general rule concerning a Planet his being Cadent from his own House, is this, *viz.* if ♂ be in ♈, it being his own House, let him then be in any of the twelve Houses, he shall be said to be Angular as to his being in ♈: if ♂ be in ♉ he is succeeding or in a succedent House in that way: if ♂ be in ♊ he is then Cadent as from his own House; and so do in the rest: for ever a Planet is Angular in any of his own Houses. *A Planet cadent from his own house.*

*The *Dispositor* of the ☽ and the Lord of the hour in Angles; ♂ in the Sign of the seventh House, she is newly conceived (this is to be understood if he be well Fortified:) ♄ in the seventh, the party is quick, or her Infant moves: ♃ in the seventh, she is impregnated of a male child: ♐ or ♓ in the *These added to other testimonies.*

seventh, she is with child of a Girl; this must be understood when all the rest of the Significators are equal, and balance not the judgment, then if you find ♐ or ♓ in the seventh, you may judge the party shall have a Girl. Besides, the ☽ in the fifth applying to ♃ or ♀ argue the same. You may ever predict true Conception, if the Sign ascending be fixed, and a Fortune therein placed, or the Lord of the fifth strong in the Ascendant or tenth House.

If the Man ask unknown to the Woman.

She is. If the Lord of the fifth behold a Planet in an Angle with reception, or if the Lord of the Hour, Lord of the fifth, ♃, ♀, ☉, ☽, ☿ or ☊ be in the fifth Fortunate; or if the Lord of the fifth be in the seventh, or Lord of the seventh in the fifth.

She is not. If ♃ or ♀ be impeded, if ♀ be joined to ♄ or ♂, and they either Combust, Retrograde or slow in motion, or in ♌, ♍ or ♑, ♄ or ♂ in the fifth, in □ or ☍ to the Lord of the fifth, denotes no conception, or danger of abortion, if other significators be more prevalent then they, and give testimony of conception.

The Lord of the ascendant joined to a Retrograde Planet; or one in a Cadent House, or received by a Retrograde or Combust Planet, no aspect or translation of light between the Lord of the fifth and Lord of the ascendant; judge by the major testimonies.

Male or Female. The Lord of the Ascendant, Lord of the fifth, Lord of the Hour Masculine, and the ☽ in a Masculine Sign, degrees, or quarter, do note a Male, the contrary a Female.

The Lord of the fifth Retrograde, Combust, or Cadent from his House or Exaltation, is a presage of Death, &c. *e contra.*

Whether it shall live? The Lord of the Ascendant, Lord of the Hour, Lord of the fifth, all or most of them unfortunate, is an argument of death; ♄, ♂ or ☋ in the first or fifth house, and Retrograde, denote the same.

Where suspicion is had of Twins: if upon that Question you find the Sign ascending Common, and a Fortune in it, or the fifth or first house, and ☉ and *Luna* in common Signs, or the Sign of the fifth one, and Lord of the fifth in a common Sign, you may judge Twins.

Other Judgements concerning Women being with child or not.

CHAPTER XL.

Whether a Woman be with Child or not.

When a Woman asks this Question, have respect to the Lord of the ascendant and the ☽ who shall signify the person of the *Querent*, the fifth house and Lord thereof shall show the Conception, if any be: If the Lord of the ascendant be in the fifth, or Lord of the fifth in the ascendant, free from all manner of impediments, it argues the Woman is conceived with child; so also if the Lord of the ascendant his virtue or disposition be translated to any Planet in an Angle, the more certain you may judge; if he to whom the Lord of the ascendant commits his Disposition, be received of the Lord of the ascendant by him, or the Lord of the ascendant by him; but if the Planet to whom the Lord of the ascendant has committed his Disposition, be in a cadent house, it notes the Woman has taken grief; and whereas she thinks she may be conceived of a Child, it's more like to be a Sickness; and if the Conception should hold, 'twil come to no good end, especially if the ascendant be ♈ or ♋, ♎ or ♑, or if any of the malevolent Planets be in an Angle, or else ☋, for usually ☋ in the fifth, shows abortion, in the ascendant extreme fear and mistrust of it; but if the ponderous Planet to whom the Lord of the ascendant commits his Disposition be in a good house, *viz.* in the second, eleventh or ninth, not in ♂ with the *Infortunes*, and the ☽ be free, it notes the Conception shall come to a good end, and the Woman safely delivered: so as also if the Lord of the fifth, who is natural *Significator* of children, be in the Ascendant free from misfortune, *viz.* Retrogradation or Combustion, or not with ☋.

If a Woman do Conceive with Child of more than one?

To resolve this Question, see if either ♊, ♍, ♐ or ♓ be ascending, then see if both ♃ and ♀ be in the Sign ascending, or in the Sign of the fifth, or be in any of the twelve Signs (except ♌) it's probable she goes with two children; and if the ☊ be with ♃ and ♀ in the ascendant or fifth, it's possible she may have three; but if none of these be in the ascendant or fifth, behold if these Planets cast their ✳ or △ to the degree ascending, or to the cusp of the fifth house; it's also probable she may conceive, or is with child with more than one: but if a fixed Sign possess the ascendant or fifth house, or any moveable Signs, and the ☉ and ☽ be therein, *viz.* either in fixed or moveable Signs, and in the fifth or first house, it's a certain argument the Woman is with child but with one: The *Astrologer* must not rashly adventure his Judgment without well considering his rules, or without knowledge had, whether it be not natural or usual for some of her Family to bring at one Birth more than one.

If Male or Female.

See to the ascendant, the Lord that Sign, the Sign of the fifth and Lord of the fifth, and whether the Signs be ♈, ♊, ♌, ♎, ♐, ♒; these Signs import a Male, the other six Signs a Female: If the Lord of the ascendant be in a Masculine Sign, and the Lord of the fifth in a Feminine, then have recourse to the ☽, and see what Sign she is in, and if she apply to the Planet in a Masculine Sign, then she gives her testimony to that *Significator* who is in a Masculine Sign, and you may judge the party is with child of a Boy or Man-child.

Masculine Planets.   Masculine Planets are ever ♄, ♃, ♂ and ☉; ♀ and the ☽ are Feminine, and ☿ as he is in aspect or ☌ with a Masculine or

Feminine Planet, so is he of either sex accordingly; but when he is *Oriental* of the ☉, he is reputed Masculine; when *Occidental*, then Feminine.

How long the Woman has been Conceived?

In this case have regard to the ☽ and the Lord of the fifth and the Lord of the hour, and see which of all these is nearest from the separation of any Planet, and well consider him, and from what manner of aspect this separation is; if he be separated by a △ aspect, say, she is in the fifth month of her Conception, or the third; if the aspect was a ✶, say, she is in the second or sixth month of her conception; if the separation was by a □ aspect, she is in the fourth of her Conception; if it was by an *Opposition*, she has been Conceived seven months; if it were by a *Conjunction*, then she has been Conceived one month.

Of the time when the Birth will be?

In judging about what time the *Querent* may be delivered, you are to consider, When ♂ and ☉ are in ♂ with the Lord of the fifth, and with the ☽ and Lord of the hour, or the more part of them, and that time of their ♂ shall show the hour of Birth; help yourself herein by that *Fortune* which in the Question shall behold the *Part of Children, viz.* when he shall apply to that Quarter of Heaven where the *Part of Children* is, and direct that *Part of Children*, by the ascensions to the degree of the fifth house, and to the degree of ♃, and to his aspects, especially if ♃ be between the *Part of Children* and the fifth house, because when that *Part* does apply itself to the degrees of ascensions, and when it is within the *Orbs* of those degrees, is the time of delivery, giving to every degree one day.

Behold also the Disposition or application of that Planet to whom the *Part of Children* is directed, before the ♂ of the Lord of the fifth with the Lord of the ascendant, in the ascendant or in the fifth house, because about that time will be the time of birth. See also when the *Significator* of the Question does change his form, *viz.* when he removes out of one Sign into another, then is also like to be the time of the Birth: or behold the Lord of the fifth, how far he is removed from the cusp of the fifth, and give to every Sign one month, and help yourself with your other testimonies, and judge according to the major part of those *Significators* that do most nearly concur.

The *Part of Children* is taken day and night from ♂ to ♃ and projected from the ascendant

Whether the Birth shall be by day or by night?

In this manner of Judgment, behold the ascendant and his Lord, the *Moon*, Planet in the ascendant, Lord of the fifth, Sign of the fifth; if the major part of the *Significators* be in Diurnal Signs, the Birth will be by day; if the contrary happen, then in the night. If the *Significators* disagree amongst themselves, take him that is Essentially most strong, and judge by him; or else consider the number of degrees that the Planet you judge by is distant from the cusp of the fifth house, so many degrees as is their distance each from other, do you project from the degree ascending, and see where your number determines; and if it end in Diurnal Sign, she will be brought to bed by day; if contrary then in the night: by this means also you may judge of the quality of the Sex, by considering the Lord of the fifth, the *Moon*, the Lord of the Hour, and the Part of Children before mentioned, and his Dispositor; if the major part hereof be in Masculine Signs, it's a Male the Woman goes with, and the birth will be by day; but if the testimonies be equal, the birth will be by twilight.

Some say, if the Question be, *Whether a Woman be with Child or not*; consider the Lord of the Ascendant, Lord of the fifth, and Dispositor of the *Moon*, and the *Moon* herself; if any application be between these Planets, and the *Moon* be in a common Sign, and the ascendant one, and the *Significators* in Angles, or if in the Ascendant or second there be a fortunate Planet, she is with child, otherwise not.

Or if by chance a Planet Direct be in ♂ with the *Moon,* it

shows the same; ♃ or ♀ in the fifth, or ☽ in the fifth, applying to ♃ or ♀, or a Planet in *Cazimi* of the ☉, the Planet being a *Fortune*, is a strong argument of being with Child; but if instead of *Fortunes* you find the *Infortunes* so placed as abovesaid, it's no sign of Conception; or if there be assurance of Conception before the Question be asked, it's a pregnant proof of abortion, and if you find ♂ to be the unfortunate Planet afflicting, she will miscarry by a Flux of blood; if ♄ afflict, then by Sickness, Fear, Frights, or by too much abundance of wind and water.

If you are demanded of the state of the Mother, and how, or in what case she shall be in after the Birth? behold the ☽, and observe to what Planet she applies, and according to the last application she has before she go out of the Sign she is in, it shall be with the Mother; so observe that Planet she last applies to, his Nature, place in the Heaven and Fortitude, so shall it be with the Mother after Birth: I have in my practice observed this concerning the safety of the Mother, and her condition at the Birth, if it were evident she were with Child; and if I found the ascendant free, and the Lord of the ascendant neither separated from a bad aspect of the Lord of the eighth or fourth, or applying to any bad aspect of the Lord of those two houses, or if I found the ☽ fortunately applying to either of the *Fortunes*, or to the ☉, or indeed to any good aspect of the *Infortunes*, I never doubted the life of the Mother, and I remember not that I ever failed.

If the Lord of the fifth were in the eighth, and had no essential dignities in the Sign, and had any aspect good or ill to the Lord of the eighth or fourth, I usually judged the *Infant* would not live long after the Birth, and I ever found the prediction true; and you shall very seldom observe any Infant born upon the very change of the ☽, but he dies shortly, seldom outlives the next full ☽; or if he or she be born at the moment of the full *Moon*, it's very probable the Infant dies upon the next new *Moon*; for as there is no light in earth but what these two Planets give, so neither do I believe any life can be permanent, when both these at the time of birth are either of themselves, or by *Infortunes* afflicted, &c.

Whether Unity is like to be between the Infant and the Parent, or between the Parent and any of his Children of elder Years.

This were better resolved from the Nativity, but because few among us are capable of judging one, I adventure somewhat by an *Horary Question*: The *Question* being then demanded as aforesaid, behold the Lord of the ascendant, the *Moon*, the Lord of the fifth; if you find reception and application between the Lord of the fifth, and Lord of the ascendant, and this in the tenth, eleventh, fifth, third, ninth, first or second houses, there will be Love and Unity between them; or if ♃ or ♀ do behold the cusps of both houses, there will be Unity and Concord between them.

I do in these manner of demands observe only thus much; I presently consider if either ♄, ♂ or ☋ be in the fifth, for if those two Planets, or any Planet who is placed in the house be Peregrine; I say, that the Child will be untoward, very averse, and not easily regulated by his Parent's directions, and that the fault is wholly in the Child, or young Man or Maid, according to the Question propounded. If I find ♄, ♂ or ☋ in the ascendant, I tell the Parents that inquire, the fault is their own, that the Child is not more observant to them; and if ♂ be there, I say, they are too much lordly over him or her, or their Children, and overawe them, and keep them in too much subjection; if ♄ be the Planet impeding, I say, they are too austere, dogged, and too much close fisted, and expect more service, duty, obedience or attendance from them than is fitting in a Christian liberty, that they give their Children no encouragement, or show them any countenance, &c. If ☋ be there in the ascendant, I blame the Parent inquiring, and tell him, he is too jealous, and too mistrustful of the actions of his or their Children, that he believes lies and calumnies against his or their Children, that simple people fool him in his humour, and besot him with vain reports, &c.

You may apply the last part of Judgment to any other Question as well as this, with very good success, as I have done many times, and thereby have reconciled the father or mother and their Child.

But by all means I desire all *Astrologians* to deal fairly and really, let the fault be where it will be, &c.

CHAPTER XLI.

Of Ambassadors or Messengers.

The Lord of the fifth shall represent the person of the *Ambassador*, the *Moon* shall herein be admitted to have signification, that Planet to whom either the Lord of the fifth house or the *Moon* do apply to, shall show the cause of his Embassy, or you may take judgment from both those Planets to whom they apply.

If you find the application is from a *Fortune* by a □ or ☍ or ☌, and if there be reception between them, or collection or translation of light by any Planet, and that Planet be either Lord of the tenth, or in the tenth, you may say, the cause of his Embassy is to the King upon a mere point of honour, or upon some high and great Business, or concerning a very great and urgent occasion: If the Planet who is received, or who collects or translates the virtue of one to another, be Lord of the eleventh, he comes to renew the League of Friendship between the two Nations: If the Lord of the fifth be unfortunate in the seventh, and the Lord of the ascendant and he be in □ or ☍, and ♂ have any malicious aspects to them both, or to either of them, there is then no likelihood of Unity, or to be any content in the Embassy to be delivered, or both parties will find trivial means to discontent one another, so that no solid peace may be expected from any act performed or to be performed by this Treaty or Embassy, rather probability of falling at variance; whether the Ambassador will deal fairly or prove false, or shuffle in his Undertakings, you must know that Judgment from the well or ill affection of the Lord of the fifth house, and from that aspect he shall cast to the ascendant or Lord thereof, or to the Lord of the eleventh; observe also in what house the Lord of the fifth is in, for if he be in the tenth, and there dignified essentially, the *Ambassador* will stand too much upon the Honour of his own Prince, and has an overweening conceit of his own abilities: If ☿ and the Lord of the fifth be in □ or ☍, the *Ambassador* has not a *Commission* large enough, or shall be countermanded or contradicted either by some Missive from his Prince, or the Secretary plays the knave with him, &c. or his Message will be ill taken.

Observe this generally, if the *Significator* of the *Ambassador* have any ✶ or △ aspect (or be he well dignified or not) either to the Lord of the ascendant, or Lord of that Sign under which the Kingdom you are in is subject, the *Ambassador* himself wishes well to the Kingdom, and will perform his trust with much sincerity.

Of a Messenger sent forth upon any Errand for Money.

Herein give the ascendant and his Lord to him that sends, the seventh house and his Lord to him to whom the *Messenger* is sent, the Message to the ☽, the Lord of the fifth to the Messenger and managing of the Business: If you find the Lord of the fifth separated from the Lord of the seventh, and applying to the Lord of the ascendant, you may judge the *Messenger* has effected the thing he went about, is departed from him, and returning home again: If the Lord of the fifth be separated from the Lord of the second house, he brings Money with him, whether a *Fortune* or *Infortune* be Lord of that house; and you must understand, that the answer which the *Messenger* brings is of the nature of that house, whose Lord is the Planet from whom the Lord of the fifth is separated, and of the Planet himself; so that if you find his separation from a good Planet, it gives hopes of a good Answer, the contrary when separation is from the *Infortunes*: If the *Significator* of the *Messenger* do apply by □ or ☍ to an *Infortune*, before he is separated from the Lord of the seventh, you may then acquaint the *Querent*, the his *Messenger* has some impediment in effecting his Business by the party to whom he was sent, and that he also sustained some hinderance in his Journey, ere he came to the place to which he was sent: but if this application to an *Infortune* happen after that the Lord of the fifth was separated from the Lord of the seventh, the *Messenger* will have delays or misfortune in his returning home again; if you find an *Infortune* in the ninth, he will hardly travel safe for Thieves; if a *Fortune* be in the ninth, judge his going and returning will be safe.

Concerning the sending of *Foot-Posts, Lackeys,* &c. about any Message or Errand, whether they shall come to their Journeys end, or safe to the place to which they are sent, behold the Lord of the ascendant and the ☽, and if either one or the other be in the seventh, or one or both apply to the Lord of the seventh, he then went safe to his journey's end; ever judge in this manner of Question according to the nature of the *Fortune* or *Infortune*, and how he is dignified in the Heavens, what is his Virtue, what his Debility, and accordingly frame your judgment according to *Fortunes*, or they dwelling or being in Significant Houses, portend good, the *Infortunes* the contrary.

If there be reception between the Lord of the fifth and seventh, and any amicable aspect, your *Messenger* was well received and entertained by him to whom he went, yea though the application be by □ or ☌, yet he was well received; but the party sought after, framed some excuse, or framed some matter in his own defence, concerning the thing sent to him for. For your Messenger's return when it shall be; behold if the Lord of the fifth be receded from the Lord of the seventh, or applying to the Planet who is his Dispositor, say, he comes; the time when, is found out thus; according to the number of degrees of the application, give Days, Weeks or Months, according to the nature and length of the Journey, and according to the nature of the Signs, *viz.*, either Fixed, Common, or Moveable; if the *Significator* be Retrograde, the Messenger will return when he comes to be Direct, or according to the number of degrees he wants ere he prove Direct. I do usually observe this general rule, when the Lord of the fifth comes to a ✶ or △ of the Lord of the ascendant, that day, or near it, the Messenger is heard of; or when the ☽ separates from the Lord of the fifth to the Lord of the ascendant, the *Querent* shall have intelligence of his Messenger: You must know, the application of the *Significator* to a ponderous Planet, shows more certainly the day; use discretion in knowing the length or brevity of the Journey, and by what precedes you may be satisfied.

If The Querent should ever have Children?

See page
A6

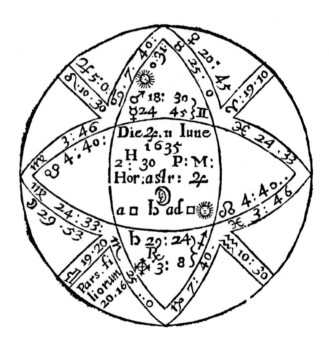

CHAPTER XLII.

Judgment upon the preceding Figure.

The ascendant is here ♍ a barren Sign, as you may see *page* 89 and 96. The Sign of the fifth is ♑, a Sign of indifference in this nature of judgment; the ☽ is in a barren

Sign; ♄ Lord of the fifth house is Retrograde, and in ♐; ☿ Lord of the ascendant in Ⅱ; both ♄ and ☿ being in Signs rather barren than fruitful: the ☽ in the Terms of ♂, in □ of ♄ Lord of the fifth, ☿ Lord of the ascendant in the Terms of ♄, afflicted by the presence of ♂, and going to ☍ of ♄, who is Lord of the sixth, as well as of the fifth; ☋ also possesses the ascendant; a strong argument of barrenness: for these reasons in *Astrologie* above recited, I delivered this Judgment, *viz.* That the *Querent* neither had been ever yet conceived, or for any reason in *Art* that I could find, ever would conceive, and that she was naturally barren; for finding the fifth, tenth and fourth houses, being the principal Angles of the Figure, afflicted, I was certain, the evil impeding her Conception had been long upon her, and would also continue.

Had I found ♃ either fortunating the cusp of the fifth house, or in any aspect to the Lord of the ascendant, or to ♄, or if any reception had been between ♄ and ♃, or ♃ and ☿, or any collection of light from ☿ to ♄, and that Planet so collecting had received ♄ or ☿, I would not have been so peremptory; but when I found no one promising testimony, I gave my judgment in the negative, *viz.* she should not conceive or ever have any children; for whoever considers the position of Heaven exactly, shall find it is a most unfortunate Figure for having children: as the ☽ was in □ of ♄, Lord of the sixth, and ☿ Lord of the ascendant, applying to his ☍, so was the *Querent* very sickly, and extremely afflicted with the Wind and Colic in her Belly and small Guts; the ☋ in the ascendant showed very great pain in the Head, so did ☿ in Ⅱ, being afflicted by both the Malevolents, represent extreme grief in the Head, for ☿ in Ⅱ signifies the Head, *vide page* 119.

She affirmed, that the Moles of her Body did correspond exactly to the Figure of Heaven, *viz.* one Mole close by the Navel, one upon the right Ankle, signified by ♒ on the cusp of the sixth; one towards the right Knee on the inner side of the Thigh, represented by ♄, Lord of the sixth in ♐; one in or near the member signified by the ☽ in ♍; and as ☿ Lord of the ascendant is in Ⅱ, so had the *Querent* a Scar or Mole on her right Arm, on the outside thereof, &c.

When you find a Question that is so peremptory in the negative, you shall deal discreetly to inquire the time of Birth, and set the Figure thereof, and see what correspondence there is between the *Radix* and the Question propounded, and help yourself in your judgment by discretion; for if the *Radix* affirm Barrenness, it's impossible any promising Horary Question can contradict its signification: and usually I have found, that whoever propounds a Question to the *Astrologer*, I mean in their first Question, they have a Sign of the same Triplicity ascending in their Question, agreeable to the nature of the ascendant in their Nativity, and many times the very self same Sign and degree is ascending upon an Horary Question which was ascending in the Nativity, as I have many times found by experience; for if ♊ ascend in the Nativity, it's probable upon an Horary Question, either ♎ or ♒ may ascend, which are Signs of the same Triplicity.

If one were with Child of a Male or Female, and about what time she should be delivered.

See page
A7

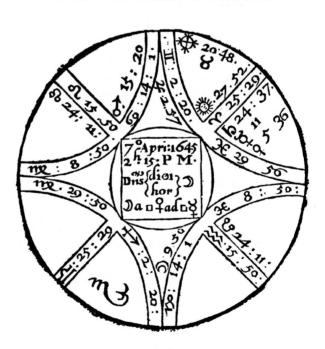

CHAPTER XLIII.

Judgment upon the Figure beforegoing.

You may see in the judgments appertaining to this house how to judge of this question; however, I did follow the Method succeeding, and considered only the plurality of testimonies, Masculine or Feminine, of the proper *Significators*, and thereby gave resolution.

Arguments of a Girl

♍ Sign of ascending,*Feminine*
♑ Sign of fifth,   *Feminine*
☽ In a Sign   *Feminine*
☿ Lord of ascendant ⎱
   with ♀, a Planet ⎰   *Feminine*

Significations of a Male Child

☿ Lord of ascendant⎱
   in a Sign   ⎰   *Masculine*
♄ Lord of fifth a Planet   *Masculine*
♄ Lord of the fifth in a Sign   *Masculine*
☽ in a house   *Masculine*
♄ in a house   *Masculine*
♃ Lord of the Hour   *Masculine*
♃ In a Sign   *Masculine*
☿ Applying to ♂ his □, ⎱
   and ♂ a Planet   ⎰   *Masculine*

You see here are eight testimonies of a Male Conception, or of Being with child of a Son, and but four of a Female; I therefore affirmed, that the *Lady* was impregnated of a Man child, [*and so it proved.*]

How long ere she should be Delivered.

The Sign of the fifth, *viz.* ♑, is moveable, so is ♈, wherein both the Lord of the ascendant and fifth are placed; these argued but a short time: but because ♄ Lord of the fifth is a ponderous Planet, and of slow motion, I much valued him in this Judgment, so did I the ☽, because she was placed in the Sign of the fifth; I took their proper difference in degrees and minutes each from other:

$$\left. \begin{array}{l} \textit{Locus } ♄ \textit{ in } 24 \quad 37 \quad ♈ \\ \textit{Locus } ☽ \textit{ in } 9 \quad 50 \quad ♑ \end{array} \right\} \textit{Both Cardinal Signs}$$

The distance of the ☽ from the □ aspect of ♄ is, as you may find by subtraction of the ☽, from ♄ 14 degrees, 47 minutes.

I then subtracted ☿ his distance from the body of ♄, because he was Lord of the ascendant, and ♄ Lord of the fifth.

$$\begin{array}{lll} ♄ & 24 \quad 37 & ♈ \\ ☿ & 11 \quad 00 & ♈ \end{array}$$

Distance 13 degr. 37 min. so that finding no greater difference between the distance of the ☽ to the □ of ♄, and the ♂ of ☿ with ♄, than one degree and ten minutes; I gave for every degree one week, and so judged, that about fourteen weeks from the time of the Question, she should be delivered.

The truth is, she was delivered the eleventh of *July* following, at what time ♂ transited the degree ascending, and ☿ Lord of the Ascendant, the opposite place of the ☽, *viz.* the ninth of ♋: You may further observe that the ☉ the same day is in 27.48 ♋, *viz.* in perfect □ to his place in our Figure, and the ☽ in ♋ in ♂ with ☿.

Of The sixth House, and its
Questions.

Viz. Sickness, Servants, small Cattle.

CHAPTER XLIV.

Judgment of Sickness by ASTROLOGY

That which I hold convenient to write of *Sicknesses*, is thus much:

That in the first place, we ought to carefully take the exact time of the party's first falling sick, *viz.* the hour as near as can be had, not that moment when first the Patient felt a snatch of it, but that very time when first he was so ill, or so extremely oppressed, that he was enforced to take his Bed, or to repose.

Secondly, if that cannot be had, then accept of that time when the sick party's *Urine* was first carried to somebody, to inquire of the Disease, whether the party inquired of was a Physician or not.

Thirdly, if no such thing can be had, let the Physician take the time of his own first speaking with, or access to the Patient, or when first the *Urine* was brought to him, let a Figure be erected accordingly, and the place of the ☽ exactly rectified to the very hour; and then to know where the Disease is, let him carefully observe:

First, the ascendant, what Planet or Planets are therein placed. Secondly, the sixth house, and what Planet or Planets are therein placed. Thirdly, the Sign and house wherein the ☽ is. Fourthly, how she is affected or afflicted, by what Planet, in what house that Planet is, what house of the Figure that Planet is Lord of.

What part of the Body is afflicted; wherein you consider:

If the first house be afflicted by the presence of an evil Planet and he Retrograde, Combust, Peregrine, slow in motion, or in □ or ♂ to any Planet who is Lord of the fourth, sixth, eighth or twelfth, the Disease is then in the Head, or in that or those parts of the Body which the Planet or Planets signify in that Sign then ascending, which you may see by the Table beforegoing *page* 119. As if the Sign ascending be ♋, and ♄ therein, you may judge, the sick party is afflicted in the Head, or such Diseases as are incident to the Head, because that first house signifies in man's Body the Head, and is now afflicted by the position of ♄ in that house: but you shall also judge the sick party is Diseased with a Looseness or Flux in the Belly, or an imperfection in the Reins or Secrets, or troubled with cold, raw Matter in his Stomach, because ♄ in ♋ does signify those members, or else with some rotten Cough; and your Judgment herein shall be more certain, and I dare say infallible, if either the Lord of the ascendant, the ☽, or Lord of the sixth be in a Sign, and therein signify that very member which ♄ does, or if the Sign of the sixth represent that member.

The same course and manner which I have directed in the ascendant, I would have observed in the sixth house, *viz.* the Sign of the sixth, the Planet or Planets therein placed, what member of man's Body they represent in the Sign wherein they are placed, from whom the Lord of the sixth last separated, to whom he next applies: Together with these, observe carefully the Sign and house wherein the ☽ is, her separation and application, and you may then descend to give judgment in what part of the Body the sick party is grieved, and of what nature and quality the Sickness is of, or what humour is most predominant and ill.

From what cause the Sickness is. Generally observe:

The *Significators* in Signs fiery, and the Signs ascending in the first, and descending in the sixth of the same nature, show Hectic Fevers, and that Choler is predominant in this Sickness.

The *Significators* in earthly Signs, argue long and tedious Agues, or Fevers of great continuance, or such Diseases as may occasionally proceed from Melancholy, Consumptions, &c.

The *Significators* in airy Signs, show the Blood putrefied or corrupted, Gouty Diseases, Leprosies, the Hand and Foot Gout.

The *Significators* in moist Signs, declare the Disease to proceed from some cold and moist cause or causes, and shows Coughs, rottenness in the Stomach, and that those parts are disaffected, &c.

Diseases signified by the Houses.

House

1 The Head, the Eyes, the Face, Ears, stinking Breath, sore Mouth, and *Noli me tangere.*

2 The Throat, Neck, Kings-Evil

3 Shoulders, Arms, Hands.

4 The Stomach, Breast, Lungs.

5 The Back, hinder part of the Shoulders, Stomach, Liver, Heart, Sides.

6 Lower part of the Belly, Guts, Liver and Reins

7 Hams, Flank, small Guts, Bladder, Womb, members of Generation.

8 The Backbone, Arse, Groin.

9 The Huckle-Bone, *or*, the Hips.

10 The Knees, the Ham of one's Leg behind the Knee.

11 The Shank, Leg from the Knee to the Ankle, Shin-Bone.

12 The Feet, and all Diseases incident to them.

Diseases signified by the Signs.

♈ All Diseases incident to the Head (as in the first house is signified) and such as proceed or have origin from Choler, Smallpox, Pushes, Pimples.

♉ Diseases in the Neck and Throat, having their beginning from Melancholy, as in second House.

♊ Shoulders, Arms, Hands, proceeding from Blood distempered.

♋ Scabbiness, Cancers in the Breast, Hurts in the Breast, ill Digestion in the Stomach, Spleen, Lungs, upper part of the

Belly, Cold and Moisture being the cause, Surfeits, &c.

♌ Backbone, Sides, Ribs, Heart, lower part of the Breast, such infirmities as proceed from Choler and excess of Blood.

♍ Shows Melancholy, Diseases in the Guts, and Bellyaches, Fluxes, &c. impediments in the Miseraicks, Wind-colic.

♎ Great Heats in the Back, or the Stone in the Reins or Kidneys, Surfeits by drinking or eating, or from too much Venery, Diseases in the Buttocks, Joints, Hams and Haunches.

♏ The Groin and parts about the privy Members, the Arse, Bladder, Piles, Stone in the Bladder, Strangury.

♐ The Hips, Hams, Buttocks, Fistulas, Itches, Sciaticas.

♑ The Knees, back part of the Hams, Scurfs and Itches in and about the Knees, proceeding of Melancholy.

♒ The Legs, Shinbone and Calves of the Legs, with the Ankles.

♓ The Anklebone and Feet, Gouts, Swellings in those parts.

Diseases Of The Planets.

♄ Is Significator of these Diseases; of noise or rumbling in the right Ear and Head, Deafness, the Toothache, pain in the Bones, in the Bladder, all cold Diseases proceeding from a deflux of the Humours, the Gout, Scab, Melancholic infirmities, Leprosy, Palsy, Consumption, black-Jaundice, quartan Agues, the Iliac-passion, Dropsy, Chin-coughs, Catarrhs of Rheums falling upon the Lungs and Pectorals.

♃ The Lungs, Ribs, Grissels, Liver, the Pulse, the Seed, Arteries, Apoplexies, Pleurisies, wringings at the Heart, Convulsions, Inflammations of the Liver, Diseases in the Head, prickings and shootings near or upon the Ridgebone, all windiness in the Veins and Body, or any Diseases arising from putrefaction in the Blood, &c.

♂ The left Ear, Gall, Reins, Privates and Stones, the Plague, wounds in the Face, Imposthumations, burning-Fevers, yellow-Jaundice, Carbuncles, Fistulas, Epilepsies, bloody-Flux, Calentures, St. Anthony's Fire.

☉ The Brain, Heart, Eyesight, right Eye of a man, left of a woman, Cramps, Swoonings or sudden tremblings at the Heart, the Cardiac Passion, Fluxes in the Eyes, Catarrhs, red Choler.

♀ The Matrix, Genitals, Paps, Throat, Liver, Sperm, or Seed in man or woman, Suffocations or Defections in the Matrix, Pissing Disease, Gonorrhea, Debility in the Act of Generation, Strangury, weakness of Stomach and Liver, French or Spanish Pox, imbecility or desire to vomit, or that Disease when presently after eating, all comes up again.

☿ The Brain, Spirit, Fancy, Imagination, Speech, Tongue, Fingers, Hands, privation of Sense, Madness, Lethargy, Stammering, Hoarseness, Coughs, falling Evil, abundance of Spittle, &c.

☽ Left Eye of man, right Eye of a woman, the Brain, the Intestines or small Guts, the Bladder, Taste, falling Sickness, Palsy, Colic, Menstrues in women, Apostems, Fluxes of the Belly, *viz.* Looseness, and all coagulated, crude Humours in any part of the Body

From what proceeds, it's easy to discover both the member afflicted, quality of the Disease, its cause and original rise; which being well considered, it's requisite you be able to acquaint the sick party of the length or shortness of his Disease, and its time of access or recess, the better to comfort him if life be ordained, or to make him more penitent and prepared for Heaven, if you see apparent testimonies of death.

Whether the Disease will be long or short.

Herein you must have respect to the time of the year in the first place, and to consider, that Sicknesses happening in the Winter are usually more long, and of long continuance; in the Summer more short; in the Spring they are reputed healthful; in the Autumn, for the most part Diseases mortal and pernicious are stirred up.

Also cold and dry Diseases which proceed from ♄, or which

he stirs up, or is the Author of, are more permanent and long, and generally are regulated by the ☉: hot and dry Diseases, which are procreated from the influence of ♂ and the ☉ are but short, and are determined by the motion of the ☽: ♄ produces chronic Infirmities; ♃ and ☉ short; ♂ more short, violent and quick; ♀ a mean between both; ☿ divers and inconstant; the ☽ such as do again revert, as the Falling-sickness, Giddiness, Swimming of the Head, Gouts, &c.

Signs of a long or short Sickness.

If the Sign of the sixth be fixed, expect a long Disease; a moveable Sign, short continuance, a common Sign, a mediocrity, neither too long or short, but for the most part, an alteration of the Disease, and return of it again.

The last degrees of any Sign being upon the cusp of the sixth house, the Disease is almost at an end, or is either altering for better or worse: fixed Signs do argue the humour not to be expulsed without much time and difficulty.

When the Lord of the sixth is of evil influence, and placed in the sixth, it's an ill *Omen,* or an unlucky sign of a durable and great Sickness: but if in the like nature a *Fortune* be there, the Disease will soon be cured, nor is it mortal: When the Lord of the sixth is stronger than the Lord of the ascendant, the Disease is like to increase, advise the Patient to take fit remedies, for Nature is weaker than the Disease; but if the Lord of the sixth house be more weak than the Lord of the ascendant, then be assured nature will be able to overcome the malignity of the Disease, without much assistance of the Physician: When ♄ is Lord of the sixth house, and fixed in the Sign he is in, he extremely prolongs the Disease; if he be Retrograde or slow in motion, he performs the same; but if he be in a moveable Sign and in any of his Terms, or swift in motion, he is not then much unfortunate, or will he greatly prolong the Disease: a moveable Sign in the sixth, and the ☽ likewise, and no impediment otherwise appearing, the Disease continues but a while; common Signs do more long continue any infirmity, except ♓, for that being upon the cusp of the sixth, I ever found it equivalent to a moveable Sign: If the ☽ apply by ill aspect to the Lord of the ascendant, the Disease increases; if the ☽ be in the sixth in ill aspect with ♀, the sick may thank himself for his Disease, he is a disorderly fellow, and of ill Diet; and if ♀ be in ♏, &c, he has got a clap of some unclean woman; if a woman asks, she has too great Flux of Whites or Reds, or the Disease is occasioned by her own Folly, &c,

If the Lord of the sixth apply to the Lord of the ascendant by □ or ☍, the Disease is increasing, and is not yet at his height or full growth; so also the Lord of the sixth in the eighth or twelfth, is an ill argument and great presumption, that the party sick must be more afflicted ere his Disease leave him: If an unfortunate Planet be in the sixth, and is removing out of one Sign into another, the Disease will speedily alter: if it's desired, *When, or how long it may be before it do so?* then see how many degrees the malevolent Planet wants ere he can get out of the Sign, and thereby judge so many Month, Weeks or Days according to the nature and quality of the Sign: if the Lord of the sixth be Retrograde, Combust in the eighth or twelfth, and in □, ☍ or ☌ with ♄, ♂, or Lord of the eighth or fourth of the Figure, he prenotes much infirmity, a long continued and sudden alteration of the Disease from better to worse, if not Death itself; the Lord of the sixth in the eighth, and the Lord of the eighth in the sixth, there being also a ✶ or △ aspect between both *Significators*, you shall not doubt of the death of the Patient at that time, for the Heavens do declare, that Nature is not yet so overcome, or so weak, but that the sick shall overcome it: if there happen any △, ✶ or ☌ between the Lord of the sixth and ♃, and he in the ninth, and the ☽ separate from the Lord of the sixth to ♃, so in the ninth house placed, it's an assured argument, that the Medicines which the Physician proscribes, or which the Patient has already taken, have caused the party to be very sick at time of their taking, and while they operated, and that the Medicines wrought effectually in the outward parts of the body, but afterwards the sick felt great comfort, and has found great emendation in the parts of his Body, afflicted at time of his first being ill; either ♄ or ♂, or any unfortunate Planet in the sixth, threatens great danger in the Sickness, yet if he be well affected or essentially fortified, he hurts little; and you may rather judge, the Disease is happened casually and suddenly, than upon any prepared matter in the Body beforehand, therefore let the sick be of good comfort: so likewise when you find a Benevolent Planet well fortified in the sixth, and he not author of the Disease, you may safely judge, the Disease is not, or will be permanent.

Many times it happens that in some Country towns, people are afraid of *Witches*; If the Lord of the twelfth be in the sixth when mistrust is had by any such Querent, it's a strong argument the supposition is true, that the party is vexed by an evil Spirit, or by Fascination; when you find in the Question of a sick party, the Lord of the sixth in the ascendant, and the Lord of the ascendant in the sixth, you may give judgment the Disease has been of long continuance, and will continue until one of the *Significators* get out of the Sign wherein he is; and if it happen, at the time of the Planets transit out of one Sign into another, he meet with the □ or ☍ of the Lord of the fourth or eighth, or with the oppressing or malicious aspect of ♄ or ♂, and they slow in motion, in Signs odiously beholding or aspecting another, it's a very great Sign the sick will then depart this Life; when you find the Lord of the sixth afflicted by the □ or ☍ of the Lord of the ascendant in *Azimen* degrees, a sign for the Physician, the Disease is incurable, and the sick party continually pained: When the Lord of the sixth is in the ascendant, the Disease will continue, but the pain does slacken and seems quite removed at some times, or the Patient sometimes is not sensible of the pain: but if he be in a Cadent house, the Disease is neither very grievous, or will it endure any long space of time; so also good Planets in the sixth do promise a good end of the Disease; evil the contrary: Usually a malignant Planet in the sixth, show the Disease unsettled, so does also the Lord of the sixth if he be in the sixth, eighth or twelfth, denotes a Disease not easily curable; if the Lord of the ascendant and ☽ be free from the □, ☍, or ☌ of ♄ or ♂, or any unfortunate Planet, and be Direct, free from Combustion, swift in Motion, not Peregrine, or in his Fall or Detriment, or in the eighth or sixth, or in any aspect with the Lord of the twelfth, sixth or eighth, it's a fair signification of health and recovery; when the Lord of the ascendant is in the fourth or eighth, and is not afflicted, he shall not signify death, but recovery; but if he be unfortunate in the fourth, it notes great difficulty ere the party be cured; but if the Lord of the ascendant be himself unfortunate, either in his house, or by Retrogradation, Peregrination, Combustion, or be in his Fall or Detriment, it's possible be may be cured, but within a short time after he will relapse, die or fall into some desperate infirmity; when also the Lord of the ascendant is infortunated by the Lord of the sixth or twelfth, and in a bad aspect of the ☽, there's danger in the Disease threatened; above all, have a care if ♄ be Lord of the ascendant, and in his Dignities, slow, diminished in light, Retrograde, for then the Patient or Querent will be long sick; judge contrary of the signification of ♄ when otherwise qualified.

The Lord of the ascendant in an Angle, having no configuration to any malevolent Planet, but being in a benevolent house of Heaven, and not under the ☉ beams, or Retrograde, you may judge the *Querent* is in no danger at this time: when the Lord of the ascendant is swift in motion, and entering into another Sign, or going out of his own house into another, so it be not into the Sign of the sixth or twelfth, the Disease will quickly determine: if the Lord of the ascendant be not afflicted in himself, or by any ill aspect of the malevolent Planet, or Planets of a contrary nature to himself, but is swift in motion, and in some good aspect with the fortunate Planets, it's a strong argument that the nature of the Diseased or *Querent* is nothing diminished, but is able to overcome the malignity of the Disease, and that in a very short time; but if the *Significator* of the sick be afflicted powerfully, it's a Sign of a strong fit of sickness; the greater it will be, when the *Significator* of life is more weak then the Planet afflicting: if all the *Significators* of the Disease be in Signs fixed, it prenotes a great space of time ere the Patient can be cured, nor will the cure be easily perfected; when the Lord of the ascendant is applied to by a malevolent Planet, it retards the cure, prolongs the infirmity, though at present great hopes appear; so does also the ☽

when she is slow in motion, and goes in twenty-four hours less than her mean motion, and be in any aspect or ♂ with the Lord of the ascendant; but if she be swift the cure is performed presently, or effected in a little time; for the most part when the ☽ decreases in light and motion, and comes to the ♂, □ or ☍ of ♄, unless the disease be in its decrease and leaving the Patient or *Querent*, it's I say, very mortal and dangerous: When the ☽ is in ♂ with a Planet that is Oriental, Direct and Swift, expect a short Sickness; joined to a Retrograde or Planet Occidental, look for the contrary.

When you find ♏ ascending, you may for the most part judge, the party was cause of his own infirmity, either by peevishness, folly, choler or the like; and your judgment will be more firm, if ♂ be then placed in ♏: If both the *Luminaries* be in Cadent houses, and the Planet or Planets that are their Dispositors be unfortunate, the *Querent* may expect a terrible Sickness; if the *Fortunes* assist in judgment, yet will the Sickness be of long continuance, and of a sharp Disease, prove chronic, yet beyond all expectation, the sick party will recover; and the more confident be in your judgment, by how much more strong the *Fortunes* are dignified above the *Infortunes*; when you find ♂ Lord of the ascendant and placed in the sixth house, in ⚹ or △ with ♀, nay, if he be in □ or ☍ of her, there's no great danger.

If the Lord of the sixth be Combust or Retrograde, in his Fall or Detriment, and in the eighth, in ♂, □ or ☍ of ♄ or ♂, you may doubt, and not unjustly, that the Disease will never leave the sick party till death; and if the ☽ have equal testimony to the former *Significators*, *viz.* if she also apply to the □, ☍ or ♂ of the Lord of the eighth, your former judgment will be very certain; If either the ☽ or Lord of the ascendant be in □, ♂ or ☍ to a benevolent Planet, Retrograde, the sick will recover, but not in haste, for it's an argument of the prolongation of the Disease, and relapsing out of one Disease into another: When you find the ☽ receded from ☍ of the ☉, to be swift in motion, and hastens to the □ or ☍ of ♂ it will come to pass, that the Disease which the *Querent* now undergoes, will be grievous and mortal; but if she salute at the same time the ✶ or △ of ♃ or ♀, the sick shall recover. There's usually no danger if the ☽ at time of the Question be strong, and the Lord of the ascendant free from misfortune, and in no aspect to the Lord of the sixth, yet when the ☽ at time of the Question applies to ♄, or is impeded, it's an ill *Omen* and sign of a sickness at hand, and that the *Querent* mistrusts his own health, is sick, but knows not where to complain, or in what part of the Body the infirmity is placed.

At the time of one's first lying down, if the ☽ be placed in the ascendant, in ♂, □ or ☍ of ♄ or ♂, or of any other unfortunate Planet, it's a sign of ill, & shows ill, unless the ☽ be in reception with the Planet or Planets so afflicting: It's very considerable to observe at the time of the Question, what Sign the ☽ is in: if in a fixed, expect a long fit of sickness; in a moveable Sign, quick dispatch; in a Common or Double-bodied Sign, the Disease will not be very difficult to cure, but somewhat long in curing: and thus much more you must consider, that if there be translation of light (from that Planet who is Dispositor of the ☽, and he unfortunate) to the Lord of the ascendant, or Sign ascending, it gives great suspicion that the *Querent* will have a sharp sickness, according to the nature of the Signs and Planets signifying the infirmity.

Testimonies that the Querent shall live and not die of the infirmity now afflicting.

When it is demanded seriously, if you conceive the *Querent* shall escape the Sickness he now languishes under, or shall live, you must carefully have recourse to your Figure erected, and therein observe these rules following: That if the ☽ be separated from a malevolent, weak Planet (that is ill dignified) and is applying to a *Fortune* powerfully strong, the sick party will be restored to former health; where ♄ is Oriental of the ☉, and *Significator* of the Disease, it proceeding from Cold (which is the true nature of ♄ without mixture) the Patient will recover; if you find in like case, that ♄ is Occidental, and the general *Significators* do incline or manifest, that the Disease is more of Heat than Cold, the sick will also be recovered; yet you must ever understand, that ♄ is unlucky when he is Occidental &c. For the Disposition of ♂, you shall find, that after his ☍ with the ☉, that is, when he is Occidental, he is not so much to be feared (*viz.* his evil influence) as when he is Oriental; for the ♂ of the ☽ with ♂ is dangerous, and an argument of a strong sickness at hand, his ☍ or ☐ aspects do less mischief; the ☽ does more hurt in her increase than in her decrease, so does ♂ being Oriental, more than when Occidental.

When you find there is any reception between the Lord of the ascendant and the Lord of the eighth, and neither of then infortunated by the malignant Planets, after desperation, there will be recovery: The Lord of the ascendant in reception of the Lord of the eighth by House or Triplicity, the *Fortunes* afflicting either with their △ or ✶ the degree ascending or of the sixth house, or the ☽ herself, there's no danger of death, but the sick will perfectly recover; so also, when the Lord of the ascendant shall happen to be a benevolent Planet, and placed in the first, tenth, eleventh, fifth or third house, being no ways endangered by the ☐ or ☍ configuration of the Malevolents, it prenotes sanity: so does also the position of the *Fortunes* in the Midheaven or first house, at what time the sickness first assaulted the sick person, nothing is a more sure argument of health, or that the party sick shall live, than when you find the ☉, ♃, ♀ or the ☽ in the ascendant of the Question, not any ways damnified by the hateful aspect of the Lord of the eighth or sixth; and this argument is more certain, if the aforesaid *Significators* be in good Signs, that is, in either of ♃ his houses, or in ♋ or ♌, ♎ or ♉: When the *Moon* is in her own house, or in the house of ♃ or ♀, and there in either of their aspect, free from any ill aspect of ♄ or ♂, she signifies health and life.

It's a good argument of recovery, when in your Question you find the *Moon* in ♂ with ♃, let ♃ be in what Sign he will it denotes good, but less in ♑ than in any other Sign, for neither the *Moon* or ♃ have any delight therein, that Sign being the Fall of ♃ and Detriment of the *Moon*; in very deed, no Planet delights to be in the Sign wherein he Falls, or is he able therein to express the strength of his influence. When the ☽ is applying to the Lord of the ascendant by a △ or ✶ aspect, and she be clear of all misfortune, or not impeded by the Lord of the eighth, or sixth especially, health and life are promised: Safety is also to be expected, when the *Moon* shall be well affected and placed in a Succeding house, provided, she be increasing in light and motion, and not near the bodies of ♄ or ♂, or infected with their Rays: The *Moon* either in the first, tenth, eleventh, ninth, second, third or fifth, in △ or ✶ with the Lord of the ascendant, or with his Antiscion, yea; if he be a malevolent Planet, so that neither the Lord of the ascendant or the *Moon* have any other impediment, it does argue life.

When at the first falling sick of the infirm Body, the *Moon* is void of course, and at her next *Crisis* meets with a ✶ or △ of ♃ or ♀, in that very degree which makes a perfect *Crisis*, the sick shall recover, be he never so much pained or grieved at the time of demanding the Question or access of the *Urine*: when in the first beginning or approach of a Disease, the *Sun, Moon* and Lord of the ascendant are free from the ill aspects of the *Infortunes* or Lord of the eighth, there needs no fear or suspicion to be made of the death of the then sick party, or when the Benevolent Planets are more potent then the Malevolent, they give assured hopes of life, and invite the infirm person to confide of his escape.

Arguments Of Death.

When the ascendant at time of first falling sick, shall be the seventh house at the Birth, you may fear death, unless the Profection of that year be the same Sign: What Profection is, you shall know in my Treatise of *Nativities*; those Signs which are adverse in a Nativity are the Signs of the sixth, seventh, eighth and twelfth.

When the five *Hylegical* places at the hour of Birth, at time of *Decumbiture* of the sick, as also the Lord of the ascendant, are oppressed, judge death immediately to follow, unless reception intervene between the *Infortunes*, and the *Fortunes* interject their comfortable aspects; for then, by a divine miracle as it were the sick party may escape.

He will be infinitely oppressed who in the hour of ♂ shall first get an hot Disease, and in the hour of ♄ a cold one.

The Lord of the ascendant and of the Figure Combust, do undoubtedly declare death, unless there be some reception between the ☉ and them, such a chance happening, and the *Moon* proving Fortunate, after a fear of danger, a little hope remains.

The Lord of the ascendant and the *Moon* in ♂ with the Lord of the eighth, without the interposing aspects of the *Fortunes*, threatens death.

The Lord of the eighth in an Angle, the Lord of the ascendant in a Cadent, is always mortal; the rather if he be an *Infortune*.

The application of the *Moon* to a Planet in the eighth, is always dangerous: The application of the Lord of the ascendant to the Lord of the eighth or to malevolent Planets therein, the *Moon* being any manner of way corrupt, denotes death.

The *Moon* transferring the light and influence of the Lord of the ascendant to the Lord of the eighth, brings usually death: So also when the Lord of the eighth is in the ascendant, the Lord of the ascendant and the *Moon* being both afflicted: It also proves fatal when the Lord of the ascendant is unfortunate in the eighth, the *Moon* being then corrupted or very weak, and in no essential Dignity: The Lord of the ascendant being Subterranean, and in any aspect to the Lord of the eighth in the eighth, or if he be in the fourth, and the Lord of the eighth in the fourth, and they both in ♂, argue death: It's a very ill Sign of life when the Lord of the ascendant is corporally joined with the Lord of the fourth, sixth, seventh or twelfth, it seldom succeeds well with the sick person then.

Have special consideration to the *Luminary* of the time, for according to the well or ill affection thereof you may improve your Judgment. The Lord of the ascendant afflicted of an evil Planet in the eighth, without the benevolent aspect of the *Fortunes*, the *Moon* also then vitiated, shows great peril of death, and usually by reason of ill government of the sick party, or some error in his ordering or course in Physic: It's a powerful argument that the sick person will die, when at time of his first Question to his Physician, you find the Lord of the ascendant Combust in the ascendant

The Lord of the Ascendant and of the eighth unfortunate, prenote death.

The Lord of the eighth in the tenth house, and Lord of the ascendant in the fourth, sixth or seventh, afflicted of the malevolent Planets, argue death.

A Planet very strong, and placed in the ascendant, if he be Lord of the hour and of the eighth, portends death: If the Lord of the eighth be Retrograde, and in ♂, □ or ☍ of the ☽, it shows death: The Lord of the eighth in the seventh, the *Moon* and Lord of the ascendant in cadent houses, infested with the ill aspects of *Infortunes*; and more certain, if one of the malevolents be Lord of the eighth, or placed in the eighth; some say, if the *Moon* be in ♂ with ♄ or ♃, the sickness will have little good thereby, nor will he escape, unless ♄ be Retrograde and ♃ Direct.

When the Lord of the Ascendant is in ♂ with the Lord of the eighth, or in □ or ☍ of a Planet placed in that house, or in the Antiscion of the Lord of the eighth, without the benevolent ⚹ or △ of ♃, and at the same time the ☽ be anyway afflicted, it's probable the sick will die; but if the Lord of the ascendant be in reception with the Planet in the eighth, it's possible he may avoid death; however, let him be assured a very long and grievous Disease he cannot: If the ☽ be with ♄ or ♂, without the assistance of some good aspect from ♃ and ♀; and if ♄ be slow in motion, or is going Retrograde, it's so much the worse, and it's one argument the sick will die at that time; if other testimonies concur, it's more certain. The Lord of the ascendant in the seventh, in his Fall, or under the earth in the fourth or sixth, or in other Cadent houses, afflicted by the malevolents, and the Lord of the eighth in the seventh, these are testimonies of death. A malevolent Planet near to the degree ascending, or a violent fixed Star, *viz. Antares* in the fourth degree of ♐, *Lans Australis* about the ninth degree of ♏, *Palilicium* in four of Ⅱ, *Caput Medusae*

Positions as of 1 January 2005:

Antares 9 ♐ 49

Lance Australis 15 ♏ 08

Palilicium aka Aldebaran: 9 Ⅱ 52

Caput Medusae (*Algol*): 26 ♉ 14

in twenty ♉, these prenote death. The Lord of the ascendant in ♌ or ♒, in any bad configuration of the Lord of the sixth or twelfth, shows little hopes of recovery. Both the Lights afflicted of ♄ in Angles, give testimony of a tedious long sickness; so do both the Lights, being ill dignified and under the earth, signify the same. When as also the ☉ from the beginning of the Disease shall be corporally afflicted, or by the □ or ☍ of ♄ or ♂ impeded, or be in the perfect Antiscion of a malignant Planet, or shall apply and not separate, either death, or an extraordinary long sickness succeeds: The ☽ after the beginning of the Disease coming to ☍ of the Lord of the ascendant, and he Retrograde or Combust, argues death, or a sharp disease, not easily curable: ♄ in ☍ with the Lord of the eighth, the ☽ in the fourth with ♂, or ☽ in the ascendant, and near the degree ascending, are arguments of death: The ☽ besieged by the *Infortunes*, or between ☉ and ♂, or between ☉ and ♄, are ill *Omens* of health: Who falls sick while the ☽ is under the ☉ Beams, *viz.* departing from Combustion, his Disease shall increase till she has passed the ☉ his ☍; but then if she prove ill affected, and come to an ill aspect of the Lord of the eighth, it threatens death, otherwise he or she will escape.

Position as of 1 January 2005:   Any malevolent in the sixth, or any Planet peregrine and unfortunate in that house, show great danger in the Disease; the Combustion of the ☽ in the eighth house, and *Pleiades:* in ♌, or in ♎, in □ or ☍ to ♄ or ☿, or in ♂ with the *Pleiades* 0 ♊ 04 in 24 ♉, or other violent fixed Stars, argues death: The ☽ being Lady of the sixth, or of the ascendant in Combustion, and the Lord of the eighth at the same time afflicted by ♂, or ill aspect of ♄ or ♂, show death.

DARIOT *Abridged.*

In regard I have ever affected Dariot his Method of judgment in sicknesses, I have with some abbreviation annexed it, in a far more short way and method heretofore published.

If the Party be sick of whom the Question is Demanded.

The *Significator* of the *Querent* in the Sign contrary to *Dariot.*
his own nature, as ♂ being Lord of the ascendant, and
naturally hot and dry, if he be in ♋, which is cold and moist;
or if the Lord of the ascendant be in a Cadent house, chiefly
in the sixth, he is sick.

A diurnal Planet being *Significator*, and he under the
earth, ill affected, Combust, Retrograde, in his Fall or
Detriment, weak, or in Terms of malevolents, or with violent
fixed Stars, or besieged by the two *Infortunes*, these things
happening, the party is sick. What was spoken of a diurnal
Planet, must be understood of a nocturnal one. (*consideratis,
considerandis.*)

When a Question was asked of me upon any *Urine*, or *Lilly.*
without it, having erected my Figure, I observed this method,
to know whether the *Querent* was ill or no.

If the ascendant were not afflicted, or the Lord thereof
out of his essential Dignities, or in any evil aspect of ♄ or ♂,
or Lord of the sixth.

Or if no Planets afflicted the sixth house by presence, or
that the ☽ were not afflicted in the eighth or twelfth; or if
I found ♃ or ♀ or ☊ in the ascendant, or the ☉ in the sixth,
or the ☽ and the Lord of the ascendant in any good aspect, or
♃ or ♀ casting a △ or ✶ to the cusp of the ascendant or
sixth house, I would directly acquaint the party they were
not sick, or that no sickness would succeed upon this *Quere*,
but that their mistrust of a sickness was grounded upon
some sudden distemper of Body, which would presently be
rectified.

Cause Of The Disease Inward or Outward.

The inward cause and condition of the Disease we require *Dariot.*
from the ill disposition of the *Significator*, in Sign, House and
place of Heaven, his good or ill configuration with the malevolent
Planets: where generally observe, any Planet may in

this case be malignant, if he be the Lord of the eighth, twelfth or sixth, &c.

The outward cause is required from those *Infortunes* that do afflict the Lord of the ascendant, or from the principal *Significators* in the Figure, or the ☽; for if you find the Lord of the ascendant sufficiently strong in essential Dignities, swift in motion, in a good house of Heaven, you may then judge the *Querent* is not naturally ill, but accidentally and outwardly afflicted, and if you find notwithstanding the strength of the Lord of the ascendant, that either ♄ or ♂ have some □ or ☍ aspect to him, and neither of them be Lords of the sixth, or Dispositors of the ☽, you may judge some outward cause has happened to the party, whereby it comes to pass he is not well, yet not perfectly sick; do you then observe in what house that Planet is, or of what house he is Lord, and from the judgments belonging to that house, require satisfaction in *Art*; as for example:

If you find the Lord of the ascendant casually afflicted by *Saturn* or *Mars* , &c. and either of them are Lords of the second house, and there appears no inward cause of a Disease, then do you judge the *Querent* is in some want of money, (if the *Significators* apply) or has had lately damage, if the *Significators* are separated; the greatness or smallness of his loss judge according to the strength of the Planet afflicting, and quality of the aspect; where note, *Oppositions* herein are worse then □ aspects or *Conjunctions*. If it be the Lord of the fifth, be the Planet good or ill, that afflicts, or has evil aspect to the Lord of the ascendant, either by evil Diet, Surfeit, &c. or by loss at Dice, Tables or Sports (if *Querent* be capable) or that the Father comes not off freely with his Pension; (this is when young people demand a Question, or are distempered) if it be the Lord of the seventh that oppresses the Lord of the ascendant, the party has had lately some difference with his Wife (and so a Woman, on the contrary, with her Husband) or some Lawsuit, or willful Neighbour, contention, or Partner is the outward cause of his evil indisposition. In Youth, if the like configuration be upon the Question from the Lord of the seventh to the Lord of the ascendant, it's a Love-melancholy, his Friend, or the Maid he affects, or the man she longs after is unkind, and discontent for that occasion is the outward cause of this ill affectedness in the Body, yet will no sickness follow it. *This is the Method which I ever observed, which I freely communicate to the world, and which, if well understood, will give knowledge sufficient to this way of judicature.*

Of the quality and nature of the Disease.

Although formerly I have briefly given directions herein, yet now I hold it fit to be more copious, and desire the Learner that he will contract what I write into such a Method as may best please his own Fancy; and be enabled to make the best use of it for his own advantage. When therefore you have erected your Figure, consider what Planet is significator of the Disease; and if you do find ♄ to be significator, he produces continued and tedious Sicknesses, quartan Agues, Coughs, consumptions, &c. If he be in ♌ or in ♏ with ☊ or ☋, or Combust, or if ♄ be with violent fixed Stars, he afflicts the sick party with pestilent and dangerous Fevers, and it may be doubted (where suspicion of Poison is) that the Sick has been endeavoured to be Poisoned, or has taken some potion equivalent to Poison.

When ♄ is in Signs of the fiery Triplicity, as ♈, ♌, ♐, he usually signifies Hectic-Fevers; If he be in ♋, ♏ or ♓, the cause and matter of the Disease grows from some cold and moist cause or matter, or distemper; and this more assuredly if ♀ or ☽, who are moist Planets, have together with him any signification in the Disease, the matter then afflicting or cause of the disease is more gross and vicious with long Paroxysms, with ebbing and flowing of the Disease; the sick party is almost overwhelmed with horror, dread, and fearful imaginations, with extreme chilliness or coldness.

When ♄ is in fixed Signs, as in ♉, ♌ or ♒, he afflicts the Patient with durable and long continued Agues and Fevers, pectoral rottenness, or dry coughs, the joint Gout, Leprosy, or general Scabbiness all over the Body, all manner of Gouts.

♄ being in moveable Signs, as ♈, ♎, ♋, ♑, prenotes a general Flux of humours all over the Body, principally the Dropsy or Tympanical humours. Being in common Signs, the Disease proceeds not from the disaffection of one humour alone, but has many changings, receding and reverting, and yet the Disease continues a long time.

♃ When he is author of the Sickness, he demonstrates ill affection of the Liver, and a corruption of the blood either by inflammation, or other causes of nature agreeable to the Sign wherein he is placed, as if in ♋, or in a moist Sign the blood is waterish, or too thin, &c. If in ♈, ♌ or ♐, it's overheated by some extravagant excess of heat or choler, if in ♒, ♎ or Ⅱ the Blood over flows, there's too much, breathing of a Vein is necessary or Sweating, if in ♉, ♑ or ♍, the blood is infected with Melancholy, too gross, and not fluent. ♃ in fiery Signs he causes Fevers proceeding from blood, yet without rottenness or store of putrefaction.

When ♂ is joined with the ☉, it prenotes a distempered Fever procreated, by putrefaction of the blood.

If ♂ be significator of the Disease and in fiery Signs afflicting the Luminaries or the Ascendant or Lord of the Ascendant, he procreates hot burning Fevers, some mixture of Melancholy; If *Saturn* be mixed in the Judgment, that is, if he have anything to do in the Signification of the Disease, or ♂ in any of his dignities.

When ♂ is in common Signs, the disease will not easily be discovered, it will come and go, and be at no certainty, yet at what time it seems to leave, if *Saturn* have any signification and be in aspect with good Planets, the disease will quite go away, but if then *Saturn* be with the Lord of the eighth or sixth, the Sick may expect death: Usually when ♂ is in common Signs the Patient is vexed with many infirmities and they acute, returning when expectation is of amendment; The symptoms hereof are sudden motions, and more quick and speedy Critical days, either to good or ill, according to the nature of the Significator: ♂ under the beams of the ☉ in the sixth or in the twelfth, in fiery Signs, brings scorching or burning inflaming Fevers, that is, Fevers exceeding, especially in heat, and as it were boiling the blood.

♂ being the cause of a Fever and in ♌, shows ebullition or a boiling of the humours, continual burning Fevers, whose original cause springs from the great Veins near the heart: When the ☉ at first lying down of the Sick party, is in ☌, □ or ☍ of ♄, or in *Saturn* his Antiscion, the Disease then afflicting is merely Melancholy; If the ☉ be afflicted of or by ♂ with the aforesaid Aspects, the Disease is from Choler: ♀ being Significatrix of the Disease, shows it proceeds of intemperance, too much Gluttony of some Surfeit, disaffection in the Belly, or in or near the privy parts, or by some Womanish trick, &c. ♀ in fiery Signs, shows a Fever but of one day's continuance, but if ♂ join in signification, it notes rotten Fevers arising from Phlegm.

When ☿ is unfortunate and is author of the Disease, the sick party has his Brain disaffected, is disturbed with an unquiet Fancy or Mind, with a Frenzy, Falling-sickness, Cough, Ptissick, or the like. When the Lord of the ninth is in the sixth, the Disease is from some Poison, Witchery or Fascination, Charm, or by or from some occult cause; this is, when mistrust is of such like chances.

Whether the Disease be in the right or left side or part of the Body of him that demands the Question or is Sick.

When you find the Lord of the sixth unfortunate or afflicted above the earth (that is in the 12, 11, 10, 9, 8, 7 houses) the Disease is in the right side of the Body, and in the upper part thereof; If the Lord of the sixth be under earth, *viz.* in the 1, 2, 3, 4, 5, 6 houses, or vitiated in a diurnal Sign, the Disease is in the superior and fore-part of the body, as in the forehead, stomach, &c. If in a nocturnal Sign, the infirmity is in the back part of the Body.

If the Significator of the Disease be in a Feminine Sign, and in Aspect to a Feminine Planet in a Feminine Sign or House, the Disease is in the left side of the Body. I ever find this general rule to hold true, *viz.* if the Lord of the sixth be a Masculine Planet and above the earth, the right side of the Sick is pained, and if the Significator be in few degrees of the Sign, the upper part of that Member is pained or grieved; If the Significator be in the middle of the Sign, the middle part of the Member is distressed, and so the lower part of the Member, when the significator possesses the lower degrees of the Sign.

Whether the Disease be in the Body, Mind or both.

You must understand in the first place, that the Sign ascending the ☽ and the Lord of that house wherein the ☉ is, do show the Spirit of Man, and that the Lord of the Ascendant, the Planet who is dispositor of the ☽, does denote both the external and internal Members. Wherefore in giving judgment herein, you may consider if the Ascendant ☉ and ☽ be all vitiated or afflicted, the Disease is then through the whole Body, or no place is free: But if those Planets who dispose of the ☉ and ☽, or he that is Lord of the Ascendant, or two of them at least be afflicted, the Disease is in the Spirits together with some indisposition of Mind; The reason hereof is, because the Lord of the Ascendant and Dispositor of the ☽ are properly the Significators of the Animal faculties and infirmities in Man, or which may chance to him; as deprivation of Sense, Madness, Frenzy, Melancholy, &c.

If the Ascendant, the ☽ and Lord of the House of the ☉ are all or but two of them impeded, the infirmity rests in the Mind but not in the Body.

If the Ascendant and the ☽ be both unfortunate, and the Lord of the Ascendant and Dispositor of the ☽ free, the indisposition is in the Mind and not in the Body. This general rule many Astrologians observe, *viz.* that ♄ naturally foreshows or causes Melancholy, all manner of distempers from Melancholy, and by consequence the disturbed Mind; wherefore wheresoever you find ♄ Lord of the Ascendant or of the Hour, or twelfth House, or sixth, or if the ☽ separate from him, or if ♄ be in the sixth house, or in the Ascendant, or in ♂, □ or ☍ of the Lord of the Ascendant, the sick-party labours with some affliction of Mind, or with some vexatious care wherewith his mind is much troubled; now the contrary hereof ♃ effects, for he never oppresses the Mind but the Body. If the Lord of the House of the ☽ and of the Ascendant are unfortunate by the ☉, or Combust, or under his beams, the infirmity is Bodily.

If that Planet who rules the Sign wherein the Lord of the Ascendant is in, and he who is Dispositor of the *Moon* be unfortunate in their fall, detriment or otherwise very much afflicted, the Disease reigns more in the Mind than in the Body.

If a Planet in the Ascendant, or the Ascendant, or if the Lord of the House of the *Moon* be oppressed in the twelfth by a ⚹, ☐ or ☍ of ♂, the Disease is both in Body and Mind. A Planet being by nature malevolent, beholding the Ascendant and not the *Moon*, and together with this, if the Lord of the Sign where the ☉ is be afflicted, the party is grieved in Mind, but not sick in his Body. Also, if the degree ascending and degree of that Sign wherein the ☽ is be more afflicted than the Lords of those Signs, the Disease ranges more in the Mind than the Body, and so the contrary when the Lords are more afflicted than the parts of the Signs before mentioned. If the Lord of the Ascendant and the ☉ be in their exaltations, and the dispositor of the ☽ in his detriment or fall, &c. the Disease reigns in the Body, not the Mind. When the Lords of the places of the ☽ and of the ☉ be in their detriments, falls, or Peregrine, Retrograde, Combust, and the degree ascending in ☐ of the ☽; and free from the ill aspects of ♄ and ♂, then is the Patient vexed with a tormented Soul. Usually when the ☉, the Lord of the Ascendant, or hour, or of the twelfth house are significators of the party inquiring, these show a Mind vexed with haughtiness, vainglory, self-conceitedness, Pride, &c.

Venus argues luxury, a lascivious desire to Women, wherewith both Body and Mind are disturbed. ☿ shows doting fancies, and fearful imaginations, wheresoever you find him a Significator and afflicted: as also, that he is stirred to mistrust upon vain fears, his own jealous fancies, or upon some flying reports. Over and above the many Directions formerly prescribed, you must well consider whether the degrees wherein the Lord of the Ascendant, the ☉ or ☽ at time of the Birth (if you have the Patient's Nativity) do fall to be the degrees of a Sign wherein a present Eclipse is, at time of the sickness or near it, or of some eminent great Conjunction; for I must tell you, these are all unfortunate.

The sign of the Eclipse or of a great Conjunction threatening evil, or the Sign of the eighth House of the yearly revolution of the World, falling in any of the Angles of the Nativity, especially in the ascendant, proves very dangerous.

When a Sign ascends upon the first falling sick, or demand of the Patient, wherein an *Infortune* was in the Nativity, it most fearfully torments the sick party, *viz.* it shows he shall have a hard fit of Sickness. The ♂ of the ☽ with the ☉ is a very ill sign, when there's not above six degrees distance between them, and the ☽ not yet passed by the ☉, that is, not having been yet in ♂ with him: however, upon the ☉ and ☽ their being in ♂ in ♈ or ♌, this misfortune is lessened; when the ☽ is twelve degrees from the ☉, she shows little danger.

Of the Crisis, or days Critical.

Sundry *Astrologians* have handled this part of *Medicinal Astrology* so learnedly, that I shall only refer them to their excellent Works, which are publicly to be had; only thus much I have ever observed, that to find the true *Crisis*, you must as near as can be obtained, get the hour wherein the Patient first took to his Bed; which if it cannot be had, then take the hour when first Judgment was required of the Physician, and rectify the *Moon* her motion to that very hour; if the Disease be not chronic, but acute, you shall find great alteration in the Disease and party infirm, near upon those times when the *Moon* comes to be distant from that her first place, 45 degrees; so also when she is 90 degrees from that place; and again, when distant 135. For discovering whether the *Crisis* will be good or ill, you must note what Planet she is in aspect withal at those times, whether with a friendly Planet or an *Infortune*, if she be in a good aspect at those times with a benevolent Planet, it does promise ease, and a better condition in the Disease; but if she then meet with an ill aspect of the Lord of the eighth or sixth, the Patient will be worse, his pain increase, and the Medicine do little good. I usually observe, and I do not remember that I have failed, *viz.* that as oft as the *Moon* came to □, ♂ or ♂ of that Planet who did any ways either afflict the ascendant, the Lord of the ascendant or the *Moon*, or when she came to the like aspect of the Lord of the sixth or any Planet that was placed in the sixth, I say, then I did ever observe the Patient to be much distempered, the Disease high, and Medicines given about those times to work little or no good effect; when I observed *Moon* to come to a △ or ✶ of the Lord of the ascendant, or Lord of the eleventh, or Lord of the ninth or tenth, I use to pronounce to the Infirm, comfort and some relaxation or an interval of ease; so also, when the Lord of the ascendant came to any good aspect of the ☉ (if he had not power or domination in the disease,) I found the Patient's mind much enlightened.

When I find, that by God's blessing the sick party shall *How long* recover, and it be demanded, When or about what time it is *ere the sick* like to be? I usually observe, who is the Lord of the ascendant, *recover.* and which of the benevolent Planets he is in aspect with, and how many degrees there are distant between them, in what house they both are in, *viz.* whether in Angles, Succedent or Cadent, what Signs they possess, whether Moveable, Fixed or Common, and according to discretion and quality of the Disease, so I frame my measure of time; yet ordinarily if the aspect be in moveable Signs, I judge, in so many days the party will amend, the more certainly, I determine, if the *Significators* be swift in motion, angular. If the application be in common Signs, I neither judge months, weeks or days, but according as I can with discretion frame my judgment, having first observed the nature of the Disease, and possibility of determining in such or such a time, the *Ancients* did say:

> *Moveable Signs show Days.*
> *Common Signs, Weeks or Months.*
> *Fixed Signs, Months or Years.*
> *Angles are equivalent to moveable Signs.*
> *Succedent to common Signs.*
> *Cadent to fixed Signs.*

Together with the principal *Significators*, consider the quick or slow motion of the ☽, the Sign she is in, and its quality, mix all together, and your judgments will be more rational: I many times find, when the Lord of the ascendant moves out of the Sign he is in at the time of the Question, and has essential Dignities in the Sign he is going into, the party recovers then, or sensibly feels an alteration for the good in himself; and so if the later degrees of a Sign are on the cusp of the sixth, *viz.* if I find 28 degrees, and the Sign common, I say, the Disease will vary in less time than 2 weeks: I might give infinite rules, but in the judgment of a Figure or two subsequent, I shall better be understood in the practical part of it, and deliver the method I always observed; but because, together with what I write, the *Reader* might have more variety of judgment; and because nothing in this life is more irksome then Sickness, or more delightful than health, I have endeavoured to English the *Iatromathematics* of *Hermes*, much esteemed in all Ages, and here to insert them, as being necessary to the Judgments of this House.

Hermes Trismegistus *upon the first Decumbiture of the Sick.*

The heavenly Rays or Influences proceeding and emitted from the seven Planets are multiplied and dispersed into the several members of man, even whilst the conception in the Mother's Womb, does first begin to cleave together: neither verily does it happen otherwise when the Child first sees the light of this world, but even according to the position of the twelve Signs of Heaven, so do we assign the Head to the Sign ♈.

The *Sensitive* Parts or Instruments of Man's Body are
thus attributes to the seven Planets.

The right Eye to the ☉, the left to the ☽.
The sense of Hearing and Ears to ♄.
The Brain to ♃, Blood to ♂.
Smelling and Tasting to ♀.
The Tongue, the Windpipe of a man's Throat or
Lung-pipe to ☿.

That member suffers a defect or imperfection, of which
either at conception or birth an afflicted Planet had dominion
or did signify the same.

There are also in Man four more principal and general
parts; the *Head*, the *Breast*, the *Hands*, and *Feet*.

If the Planet who governs any of those principal parts be
unfortunate and ill affected, either at the time of Conception
or Birth, the same Planet afflicts or disfigures all those parts
so attributed to himself, or some particular or principal part
of those members.

As when the ☉ or *Moon* be ill disposed or vitiated, either
the one or both, the eyes receive prejudice; if ♄ the ears,
teeth or sense of hearing. When ☿ is oppressed, we find a
defect in the tongue, or stammering in speech. And in the
same manner we may apprehend, whether any part of the
Breast, Lungs, Liver, Spleen, Heart, or any of the intestines
or inwards of the body be corrupted and infected, radically
from the Birth or Conception.

In consideration of the Hands and Feet we shall observe,
whether the Fingers, Nails or any of these are imperfect or
vitiated by the affinity of some predominating malignant Planet.

To such defects and imperfections as are within the
compass of cure, convenient Medicines are to be applied, and
we must resist the Disease proceeding from the influence of
the Planets, by other Planets of contrary nature and power
to the Planet afflicting.

To ♄ are assigned such Medications as do cool or
refrigerate, extenuate with dryness and siccity.

To ☿ such as congeal, are flatulent and windy.

To ♂ such as are calefactory, warm and impletive, as to a Planet being a very sharp heater and procurator of blood.

To ♃ and ♀ things conglutinating, mollifying and are effective to assuage and cure all Ulcers.

The *Moon* helps that Planet, or lends assistance to him, be he good or bad, to whom she applies.

To him therefore that would either cure the Sick or heal the Lame, the position of Heaven ought to be well considered and known, set or erected for the hour of his first falling sick, or lying down; the Planets and their respective disposition and mutual habit to and amongst themselves, is carefully to be respected; for without the congress and influence of these in human and worldly affairs, nothing is either infirm or sound. No Patient can possibly be cured by the industry of his Physician, be he never so learned, without the benevolent configuration of the Stars, and happy position thereof; but he shall either perish, being destitute hereof, or recover and be preserved by their kind influence.

If the certain hour of the party's first falling sick cannot exquisitely be known, then carefully take the position of Heaven at that given time when judgment is required of the Physician: therein observe from whom the ☽ is separated, to whom she applies, with what Planets she is in □ or ☍ to, or with whom in ♂; if she be in configuration with the malevolents, she intimates the Disease will extend almost to death; but with the *Fortunes*, the sick will obtain remedy more speedily: Observe if she be swift in motion, and increasing in light, or whether both of them happen at once, or neither of them: for if after her ♂ with the ☉, when she begins to grow great, and as it were, to swell with the increase of light and motion, she shall then be afflicted by the □ or ☍ of ♂, before she come to ☍ of ☉, and no intervening aspect of a benevolent Planet chance between, she signifies mortal and pernicious Diseases; but if conjoined, or in good aspect of beneficial Stars, the infirm Body shall recover, though he were absolutely persuaded he should not live or escape that Disease; but if the ☽ be decreasing in light and motion, and afflicted either by the □

or ☍ of ♄ (unless presently after ☍ with ♄ the vigor of the Disease remit) the Disease is not curable but Mortal; but if she apply to benevolent Planets, the Disease will soon be cured: This is further to be considered, that during the increase of the ☽ in number and light, the Disease increases: when the ☽ grows slow in motion, the sickness diminishes: this ought carefully to be regarded upon the first insult of every Disease.

Those who are at the time of their first lying down are oppressed by the malignant influence of ♄ or ☿, they are commonly heavy and drowsy, unwillingly moving their diseased Members, stupefied or benumbed with immoderate cold, or molested with unnatural defluxions: The Disease by little and little steals upon the sick party, nor is he easily awakened though moved thereunto: He is silent in speech, fearful, desires such Plasters or formentations as are very hot, and enforce heat; they delight to be without light, as to be in darkness; he sighs continually, and gently draws in his breath, or sucks it up, or is short winded; the Pulse is swift and painful; warm things applied gives them great comfort; they have feeble Pulses; the outside of their bodies are cold and dry whereby it comes to pass, that in curing such people, that the Physician ought to apply such Medicines as are naturally hot, do mollify and constringe.

Who fall sick upon any malevolent configuration of the ☉ or ♂, become disturbed in their Minds, perplexed in their Fancies, are troublesome and very rugged in their deportment; the superficial parts of their bodies being inflamed with a fiery heat. They are prone to anger, make much clamour or noise, look peevishly, lie staring, always thirsty by reason of the roughness of their parched tongues; desirous of Wine, cold Drink, importuning the use of Baths: no manner of Meat whets their appetite; they freely squander out their virulent language against every man; they have a short, depressed and inordinate Pulse; red rubicund faces, oppressed with fullness of body. For recovery of these Men, it conduces much to let Blood until the fifth day, or prescribe such Medicines as evacuate and Purge the foulness of their bodies, and to administer such other Remedies as the necessity of nature further requires. What Medicines are agreeable to the nature of ♂ are repugnant to ♄ as not calefactory, emollient or mollifying and dissolving obstructions.

Medications which naturally are concurring with ♄, prove contrary to those of the nature of ♂; as those which are refrigerating or cooling, astringent or binding, and repercussive.

All infirmities or passions, or tremblings of the heart, and such as proceed from the mouth of the Stomach, Diseases and pains in the Arteries, Veins and Joints, have origin from the evil influence of ♂ and ☉.

Continued Fevers, Frenzies, Exulceration and inflammation of the Lungs and Lights, and such like Diseases, draw their origin from ♄ and ☿: against such Diseases, Medicines that refrigerate are most proper, of which sort are these:

Nightshade	*The stone Hematites*	*Alum*
Coriander	*Purcel* and	*Flower of the Field-*
Endive	*White of an Egg*	*Vine*
Juice of Poppy	*Flaxseed*	*The Fruit of both*
The Bark of the	*Reed*	*Palm Trees*
root Alkakenge	*Leaves of Mallows*	*The Myrrh-Tree*
Knotgrass	*Pomegranate*	*Sumac*
Sengreen	*Hypocistis*	*Fresh Roses*
Fleawort	*Cypress Tree*	*Bull-rushes*
Lentils	*Blackberry*	*Ladanum*
Vine-leaves	*Acacia*	*Saffron*
White Lead	*Quinces*	*Patomagitum*
Silver-froth	*Pirapirastra*	

Such medicines as are naturally calefactive or hot, are assigned to the dominion of *Mars* and the *Sun*; whereof some are as follows:

Oleum Cyprinum	*Unguentum Irinum*	*White Daffodil*
All things smelling	*Cinnamon*	*Fenugreek*
sweet, and being	*Sweet Majoram*	*Spikenard*
fragrant.		

Myrrh	*Cassia Odorata*	*The foam of the*
Bdellium	*Frankincense*	*Sea indurate,*
Storax calmita	*Ammoniacum*	*or made hard*
The Root Sera	*Rue, or Hearbgrace*	*Helleborus*
Ocymun	*Mirabolans*	*Pyethrum*
Cumin	*Dry Figs*	*Chrysocalla*
Pix Liquida, & Solida	*The foam of Saltpetre*	*Onions*
Fat	*Granum Gnidium*	*Garlic*
Marrow	*Stavesacre*	*Leeks*
Galbanum	*The Stone Asius*	*Radish Roots*
Flower de Luce	*Galangal*	*Chick Peas*

To expulse and recover those Diseases which have their original rise and cause from ♄ or ☿ (which afterwards you shall have discovered by the course of the ☽) such manner of Medicines as these must be administered, which do naturally heat and mollify; but in repressing Solar and Martial Diseases, the learned Physician must apply such Remedies, as by nature are refrigerative, cooling and repercussive.

Of the signs and conjectures of the Disease, and of life or death by the good or ill position of the ☽ at time of the Patient's first lying down, or demanding the Question.

Whoever shall first lie down of their sickness, the ☽ decreasing in light and motion, in any of the twelve Signs, and afflicted by ♄ his □, ☍ or ♂, shall in part or in all, be partaker of such Diseases as follows, during the time of the continuance of their Disease.

Viz. With Headache, or heaviness of the Head, or Rheum, ☽ *in* ♈ *in* falling down into the Nostrils, singing in the Ears, stuffing ♂, □, ☍ in the Head, weariness or dullness of the Eyes, distillation of *of* ♄ Rheums and corrupt humours falling from the head into the Throat and Windpipe, weak Pulses and inordinate, drowsiness of mind, loathing of the Stomach, intemperate or unseasonable Sweats, hot within, cold without, more afflicted by night than day; if ☽ be not favoured by the aspect of any good

Planet, without doubt the sick party will die, God sending no extraordinary remedy. To loosen the Belly represses the grief, to let blood is ill.

☽ *in* ♉   Fevers proceeding from obstructions and distemper of
in ♂, ☐,   the Praecordiacs and Arteries, *viz.* of the inward parts near
☍ *of* ♄   the Heart, Liver and Lungs, occasioned by too much Luxury, or from Surfeits or inordinate Repletion; their Pulses are lofty and high, but immoderate, an inflation or puffing up of the Body, ulceration of the Lungs; if the ☽ be not supported with some gentle aspects of the *Fortunes*, the party will hardly live fourteen days; but if the ☽ be, as beforesaid, in any good aspect, beyond expectation the sick may recover. Those Medicines which purge or dissolve gross Humours, and Phlebotomy are good.

☽ *in* ♊   Who fall sick, the ☽ in ♊, afflicted of ♄, by ♂, ☐ or ☍,
in ♂, ☐,   have the origin of their Disease occasioned by weariness of
☍ *of* ♄   the mind, and overburdening it with multiplicity of affairs, or some weariness in travel, or overmuch exercise of body, fear of a small Fever, the pain disperses itself all over the body, but principally in the Arteries or Joints.

I ever find the Vitals much afflicted when ☽ is in ♊, at the time of any one's *Decumbiture*, and the sick inclinable to a Consumption; with such the Pulse is rare and little, afflicted with frequent sweatings, Symptoms of the Spleen, and the Disease more troublesome in the night than in the day; if ♂, together with ♄, at the same time afflict the ☽, most Authors hold, the sick will not live above ten days, unless the favorable aspect of ♃ or ♀ intervene, and then after a long time, the sick may recover.

☽ *in* ♋   Who falls sick the ☽ afflicted of ♄ in ♋, is much afflicted
in ♂, ☐,   in the Breast with tough melancholy Matter, or with slimy,
☍ *of* ♄   thick Phlegm, is vexed with Coughs, or abundance of Spittle and moisture, Catarrhs, Hoarseness, distillation of Rheums, or descending of Humours into the Breast, their Pipes are narrow and obstructed, small Fevers, and many times fear of a

Quotidian Ague; but usually a Quartan Ague follows, holding a long time, Bellyache, or some infirmness in the Reines or Secrets. If the ☽ be decreasing and near the Body of ♄, the sickness will continue a great space of time; and if together with her affliction, the Lord of the ascendant be impeded by the Lord of the eighth, there's small hopes of recovery.

Those who lie down or first complain, the ☽ being impeded of ♄ in ♌, the sickness shall proceed of ill melancholy Blood, the sick will be oppressed with unkindly heat in the Breast, intension of the Heart-strings, with violent Fevers, the Pulses are troubled, external and internal Heats do much annoy the sick, sometimes they are taken with a fit of the Stone, or faintness of Heart, or Swooning, and if the disease do continue long, the sick is in danger of the Black-jaundice. *☽ in ♌ in ♂, □, ☍ of ♄*

Such things as gently moisten and heat, are good for the Diseased; when the ☽ comes to the ☍ of ♄, if the ⚹, △ or ♂ of ♃ or ♀ assist not, many times the sick dies.

The ☽ in ♍ afflicted by ♄, the Sickness proceeds from Crudities and evil digestion in the Stomach, and from too much viscous Phlegm obstructing the Bowels and Entrails, pricking or shooting under the Ribs, inordinate Fevers, many times I find the sick afflicted when the ☽ is in ♍ in aspect of ♄ with the Wind-cholic, with extreme Melancholy, with the Gout or aches in the Thighs and Feet, &c. Things which mollify heat and dissolve, are most proper for the sick; when the cause of the Disease originally rises from this configuration of the ☽ in ♍, unfortunated by ♄, I seldom find by experience but that the Diseased continues sick a great while; for ♍ is an earthly Sign, and ♄ is slow. *☽ in ♍ in ♂, □, ☍ of ♄*

The ☽ in ♎ by ♄ afflicted, the Disease has its origin from some Surfeit of Wine, Gluttony, or Meat not fully digested, or too many Venery, the Breast is disaffected, so also the Head, no appetite to eat, a loathing in the Stomach, the Cough, Hoarseness, distillation of Rheums afflict him: I have found the sick party, upon this aspect of the ☽ to ♄, to have been troubled *☽ in ♎ in ♂, □, ☍ of ♄*

with great pains in their Joints, Knees and Thighs, and an itching in those parts, they fearing a Sciatica.

☽ *in* ♏   ♄ afflicting the *Moon* in ♏, the Disease is in *Ano* or
in ♂, ☐, *Anglice* [Arse-hole] usually an Ulcer there, or the Hemorrhoids
☍ *of* ♄ or Piles, or some Exulceration or Bubo, [*Anglice*] a botch in the Privy-members.

I find by experience, if a man or woman inquire upon the *Moon* her affliction by ♄ in ♏, there's no retention of Urine, the party is vexed with the Stone in the Bladder, or with a swelling dropsical Humour, offending and swelling about their Knees and Legs; as also sometimes they have a Flux, if a man then the Gonorrhoea; if a woman, too much abundance of Menstrua's.

☽ *in* ♐   ♄ afflicting the *Moon*, the diseased party is sensibly
in ♂, ☐, oppressed with Deflux of subtle, thin, sharp Humours, griefs
☍ *of* ♄ in the Arteries or Joints, fear of a Fever, extremities of heat and cold, many times a double access of a Fever; what mitigates heat gently, and moistens, is good for such people as fall sick under this aspect.

I find by experience, that the *Moon* in ♐, afflicted by a ♂ of ♄, does cause the Disease to proceed from Blood infected with choler and melancholy, and many times by too great painstaking, or violent exercise, and cold thereupon taken; upon the ☍ of the *Moon* and ♄, for the most part the sick has a spice of the Gout, or some Tumour or Swelling in his Hands, or Thighs, or Feet, &c. If ♂ have any ill aspect to the *Moon* as well as ♄ at time of first falling sick, it proves a violent burning Fever.

☽ *in* ♑   The Disease proceeds from Cold or Melancholy, with
in ♂, ☐, subtle, thin Distillations, heaviness of the Breast and Stomach,
☍ *of* ♄ difficulty of breathing, dry Coughs, the Lungs oppressed, intended Fevers, more pained in the night than in the daytime: Medicines that heat and moisten moderately do avail in this Disease.

I find the party still complaining of the Headache, or pain

in the left Ear, or of a Rumbling or Noise in his Head.

The Sickness has beginning, or is occasioned from too much labour, wearisomeness or toiling the Body and Mind, want of sleep and due refreshment of nature: the Malady ceases on him unequally, with remission and intension, until the ☽ have past the ☍ of her own place, then if the fortunes have any good Aspect to the *Moon*, the sick is recoverable. ☽ *in* ♒ *in* ♂, ☐, ☍ *of* ♄

I find the sick complaining or lying down under the preceding malevolent Aspect, to be grieved with wind or noise in the head, with faint fits or passions of the heart; or many times they have either a sore throat, or are troubled with a rising there, and in danger of suffocation.

The Malady its cause, is from cold distillations; the party is afflicted with continual Fevers, oft and continual sighings, pricking or shootings under the Paps, extensions of the precordiacs and heart-strings. ☽ *in* ♓ *in* ♂, ☐, ☍ *of* ♄

I find the Sick have surfeited by some extremity of cold, that their throat is oppressed with thick phlegm, and their breast is troubled with a rotten cough and abundance of watery matter lodging there.

Those Medicines that heat and gently calify are good in these cases.

As we have treated of such Diseases as may afflict any one upon their first falling Sick or Decumbiture, the ☽ being in any of the 12 Signs and oppressed by ♄, or indeed by ☿: So now we will endeavour to show the quality of the Disease from the ☽ her affliction from ♂ or the ☉ through the 12 Signs of the Zodiac.

Who fall sick the ☽ in ♂, ☐ or ☍ of ♂ in ♈, their disease shall proceed from a distempered affection of the Membranes or Pellices of the brain, continual Fevers, no rest or quietness; an hot thirsty mouth, extreme thirst, dryness of the tongue, hot Liver or inflammation thereof, much heat in the Breast, high and sublated Pulses, keeping no order, a Frenzy may be feared, or ☽ *in* ♈ *in* ♂, ☐, ☍ *of* ♂

deprivation of Senses: letting of Blood and such things as do cool and nourish are very helpful.

If the ☽ next after her separation from the Malevolent beams or aspect of ♂ do also apply to ♂ or ☍ of ♄, and she decreasing in light and slow in motion, there's small hopes of life; let the sick prepare for God. I find, usually the ☽ being in ♈ afflicted of ♂, the party is almost ready to run mad, or has some extreme pain or grief in his Belly or small guts occasioned by choleric obstructions.

☽ *in* ♉   The party falling sick, has too much abundance of ill
in ♂, □,   Blood, continual Fevers, the whole frame of the body
☍ *of* ♂   obstructed, inflammation of the throat, neck and hinder-part thereof, ache of the bones, ungentle slumbers, but no sleep, a foolish longing after Wine and cold water. Blood letting and such things as moderately cool or allay heat are necessary.

I find ☽ in ♉ afflicted by ♂, the Patient is afflicted with the strangury, or stone, or gravel in the Reines and Kidneys, with pestilent sore throats, or hoarseness, or some malignity there in that member.

☽ *in* ♊   Who takes his or their Bed the *Moon* in ♊ afflicted by ♂,
in ♂, □,   usually shall undergo a violent and dangerous Fever,
☍ *of* ♂   obstructions; high and inordinate Pulses attend such; the blood is too hot, and a necessity there is of emission of blood, the whole body being near corruption, by reason of the rankness of blood.

I find those falling sick the *Moon* in ♊ afflicted by ♂, to be pained all over the body, the Disease in no place settled, their Blood extremely windy, corrupted, and what not, some lameness or grief in their Arms or joints, and afflicted with the stone or heat in the reines, and sometimes spitting of blood.

☽ *in* ♋   The *Moon* afflicted by ♂ in ♋, the Sick is sensible of
in ♂, □,   great abundance of sweet phlegm in his stomach, has too
☍ *of* ♂   much ingurgitated, or taken some surfeit, oft vomits or desires so to do, with eversion or turning of the ventricle.

I find, usually it's a mere surfeit gotten by riot and excess, and most that I have seen thus afflicted have been cured by Vomit; many times it turns to a looseness, or a rotten filthy cough, sometimes spitting of blood.

In this case too much blood abounds and thereby strong Fevers, very weak Pulses, raving and strong raging fits, a disturbed Brain, deprivation of appetite, heaviness and drowsiness all over the body, many distempers of the heart; the body in danger of a Consumption; usually they die about the ninth day after the first falling sick, if other configurations of heavens accord. *☽ in ♌ in ♂, □, ☍ of ♂*

I find the Blood overheated, the party almost stark raging mad, choler in excess abounding, the body over-dried, a probability of the Pleurisy; faintness and swooning, or the heart very much afflicted; I evermore fear this dangerous ♂ or ☍ of ♂ and the *Moon* in this Sign, more than in any of the Zodiac.

Usually in alteration or flux in the Belly, or miseraicks follows this unlucky position, small Fevers, the original choler and melancholy, the Pulse remiss, eversion of the ventricle, loathing of food; death within thirty days, if the fortunes assist not. *☽ in ♍ in ♂, □, ☍ of ♂*

I have by experience found, the afflicted upon this aspect or aspects, to be tormented with the wind, cholic, many times weakness in the legs or near the ankles. Yet I did never find any Disease easily removable, if the *Moon* at time of the decumbiture, or first falling ill, was afflicted by ♂ in ♍.

The Patient is grieved with plenitude of Blood, and from that cause has intended Fevers, high Pulses, abstains from sleep, has no natural rest, an inflammation all over the body. *☽ in ♎ in ♂, □, ☍ of ♂*

I observe in this kind, sick people upon this kind are oppressed with Blood overheated, have taken some surfeit by disorder in diet; many times have the stone or gravel in their kidneys, or great heat therein.

Glister, and such things as gently cool, are best in this nature; many times the Disease is all over the Body, in every part; and most violent burning Fevers follow. Blood letting is good.

☽ *in* ♏   It's neither better or worse with the party inquiring, but
in ♂, ☐,   that he or she has some grievous infirmness in his or her privy
☍ *of* ♂   parts. There's usually some exulceration, the Pox small or French (or Measles, if children) the Hemorrhoids or Piles.

I observe the Sick offended with sniffling in the Head, or some grievous colds or rheums in that member; if the party look like a wanton, the French Pox or Gonorrhoea or burnt Prick, without more words I do judge: many times I find the party scabby and oppressed with breakings out, &c.

This is corruption of Blood, &c. such things as heat and comfort, are now necessary; the Disease usually is a scandalous one. Let a modest party propound the Question; there's cause to distrust foul play, &c. If a Man propound, the Wife may be faulty, &c. *in Contrario*.

☽ *in* ♐   Such an affliction of the *Moon* in ♐ intimates, the sick
in ♂, ☐,   party is grieved with a very desperate Disease, occasioned from
☍ *of* ♂   surfeiting or gluttony, or too much repletion; he is tormented with high Fevers, with choleric passions, with the Flux or Lask: the Pulses are few and faint, or beat slowly and weakly. If the Sick escape the seventh day, or know properly that day when the *Moon* comes to a true ☐ of the place she was in at first lying down, there's then hopes of recovery.

I daily find by experience, the sick party his Blood is overheated by some inordinate exercise, that he burns extremely, sometimes the malignancy of the pestilent Fever is such, he is twice or thrice let Blood; they are besides many times offended with the Hand and Foot-gout, or Itches and breakings out, and sometimes with sore Throats, &c. at other times sharp Rheums offend their Eyes.

☽ *in* ♑   Here appears no perfect concoction, Choler abounds, the
in ♂, ☐,   sick desires to vomit, there's inappetency of the Ventricle, a
☍ *of* ♂

swelling or puffing up the Sinews, a Flux of the Belly follows immediately, continual or oft returning Fevers, inflammation of the Breast, some Exulceration offends the party, or a choleric humour his Hands or Joints of his Fingers. Obstructive and constringent Medicines are useful, their Pulses are remiss and slow.

I find the sick inclinable to the Yellow-jaundice, their Countenance meagre, and their Persons exceeding lean, and that the Blood all over the body is disaffected, and the Disease is very hard to be cured by the most Learned; such usually have very little Blood, or their Blood is corrupted to purpose, or in the highest measure.

If the ☽ be slow in motion, and decreasing in light, *☽ in ♒ in* when a Disease first takes the party, and is afflicted of ♂, the *♂, □, ☍* Infirmity proceeds from most sharp and violent affections, or *of ♂* vehement passions; any favorable Planet casting his good aspect to the ☽, either at her first □ to her own place, or when she comes to ☍ of that degree of the *Zodiac* she was in at the first lying down, gives present remedy after twenty days.

Experience has informed me that upon the preceding aspects, especially upon the ☍, the sick has been pained at the Heart, troubled with swooning fits, had a most desperate Fever, the Blood swelling in all the Veins, high Pulses; sometimes they complain of great pain in their Breast, and draw their Wind with great difficulty.

When the ☽ is afflicted of ♂ in this Sign ♓, and is *☽ in ♓ in* increasing in light, and swift in motion, the Body is full of *♂, □, ☍* gross Humours, the Disease proceeds from too much *of ♂* ingurgitation, swilling and drinking, the Disease is most prevalent in the nighttime; the party is vexed with a frenetic Outrage or *Delirium*, has sharp burning Fevers, vehement thirst and is desirous of Wine.

Usually I find, the party sick or inquiring, when the ☽ is of ♂ in ♓ so afflicted, oppressed with violent Looseness, and grievously complaining of pain in their Bellies, or an extraordinary rotten Cough, and continual defluxion of Rheum from the Head into the Throat, the party almost suffocated therewith, their Bellies swollen, and they in danger of a Dropsy.

Astrological APHORISMS beneficial for PHYSICIANS.

*I*n *Questions concerning sick People, give the ascendant and his Lord and the Lord of the Figure for Significators of the sick party.*

2. *From the Sign of the sixth, the Lord of that House, Planets therein placed, and place of Heaven and Sign wherein the* ☽ *is, require the Disease or part afflicted, with relation to the ascendant.*

3. *The seventh house represents the Physician, the tenth his Medicine; if the Lord of the seventh be unfortunate, the Physician shall not cure; if the tenth house or Lord thereof, his Physic is improper.*

4. *The fourth house signifies the end of the sickness, and whether it will terminate quickly, or endure long: fixed Signs prolong, common Signs vary the Disease, moveable ones show an end one way or another quickly.*

5. *That Physician that first visits his Patient in the hour of* ♄*, his Patient shall either be long sick, or long in curing, and suffers much torment in his cure; nor shall be cured, until almost both Physician and Patient despaired.*

6. *He that first enters upon a cure in the hour of* ♂*, shall find his Patient disaffected to him, and partly disdain or reject his Medicines, his pains ill rewarded, and his person slighted.*

7. *He that first visits his Patient in the hour of* ♃ *or* ♀*, shall have good words of the sick, be well esteemed and paid for his pains; though he fail of the cure, yet shall he receive no prejudice thereby; I mean, in point of estimation.*

8. *When a Urine is brought, let the ascendant represent the sick Party, whether the Querent come with consent or no, for the Urine was sometimes of the essence of the sick.*

9. *If no Urine or consent of the sick party come to the Physician, then*

the Ascendant presents the Querent; but the person and sickness must be required according to the relation the Querent has to the sick party: A man for his servant, the sixth shall show his person, not his Disease, that must be from the sixth to the sixth, which is the eleventh, &c., sic. in aliis where no consent is.

10. But in every Disease have care to the place of the ☽, for she is a general Significatrix in all things.

11. The sick party is in great danger of death, when at the time of the Question asked, or when the sickness first invaded the sick party, both the ☉ and ☽ are under the Earth.

12. As no light is in this World without the presence of the ☉ or ☽, so no safety, or hopes of recovery in the sick, when they are obscured or subterranean at first lying down of the sick, and it's a greater argument of death, if either of them be then afflicted.

13. The □ or ☍ of the Fortunes, as it destroys not, so neither does the benevolent aspect of the Infortunes profit, unless that aspect be with Reception.

14. If the ☉ and ☽, or Lord of the Figure, or Lord of the ascendant be free from affliction, and have no affinity with the Lord of the eighth, without doubt the sick party will recover; if two of these Significators be so affected, it will go well with him, otherwise he dies.

15. The Lord of the ascendant in his Fall, unfortunate or Combust, or else the Lord of the Figure, it's doubtful the sick party will die of that Infirmity.

16. When the Significator of the sick is feeble, and the Lord of the eighth strong and afflicting him, it's much feared the sick party will die of his then infirmness, nature being weak, and the Disease prevalent.

17. If the Lord of the ascendant be placed in the eighth, and received of the Lord of the eighth by some essential Dignity, though the Lord of the ascendant receive not him again, the sick party recovers beyond expectation.

18. The Physician may justly fear his Patient, when the Lord of the ascendant and the ☽ do both apply by ill aspect to a Planet under the Earth; the contrary is to be expected, if they apply to a Planet above the Earth: the twelfth, eleventh, tenth, ninth, eighth, seventh houses are above the Earth, the rest under.

19. The Lord of the eighth being on the cusp of the tenth, and the Lord of the ascendant under the Earth, there's great fear of recovery.

20. *If the ☽ be swift in course, and increasing in light, and by a ✶ or △ apply to the Lord of the ascendant, though under the earth, it hastens the cure, the more easily if any Reception be; the cure must needs be sooner if the application be above the Earth to the Lord of the ascendant.*

21. *If the Lord of the ascendant be in the sixth, or the Lord of the sixth in the ascendant, it protracts the Disease, and is an argument of much affliction therein; so also does the □ or ☍ of the Lord of the sixth to the Lord of the ascendant.*

22. *If the two benevolent Planets ♃ and ♀ be most powerful in the Figure, judge well to the sick, or hope well; if the Infortunes be most strong, judge the contrary.*

23. *The application of the Lord of the fourth, to the Conjunction of the Lord of the eighth, prolongs the Infirmity, and also signifies Death, if the Lord of the fourth be an Infortune; if a benevolent expect the contrary.*

24. *A Retrograde Planet Significator of the Disease, shows the continuance of it, and argues the Body's Consumption, Backsliding and Relapses.*

25. *The Significator being stationary, shows aptness and desire to vomit, and the oft change and variation of the Disease; but if he be Combust of the ☉, for the most part the sick dies: and the reason is, a Planet stationary has time to work mischief, because he moves not.*

26. *A Significator in his Fall or Detriment, shows ill and much danger, and argues much distrust and fear in the sick party.*

27. *The ascendant and the ☽ being afflicted, and the Lord of the one and Dispositor of the other not so, the Disease is in the Body, not in the Spirits:*

28. *But the ascendant and ☽ free from misfortune, and their Lords unfortunate, the grief lies in the Spirits, not in the Body; but if both be afflicted, both Body and mind are tormented: so also, if a malevolent Planet behold the ascendant and not the ☽, the Disease is in the Animals, not the Body, and so on the contrary.*

29. *The Lord of the sixth in the ascendant, ninth, eleventh or tenth house, the Disease is manifest; in the seventh or fourth, it lies occult and not known, and so in the twelfth or eighth.*

30. *Moveable Signs easily cause the Disease to vary; fixed Signs make it long and permanent, and not without much difficulty; removable, common, show recidivation, or that it's now here, now*

there, or that the sick party is much better at one time than at another.

31. *In the beginning of Diseases, ever fear the ill position and affliction of the ☽, mix the signification with the well or ill being of the Lord of the ascendant, and so judge of the good or ill attending the sick.*

32. *If the Nativity of the sick may be obtained, observe if the ☽ at the time of the first Decumbiture or Question asked, be then in a place where an Infortune was in the Radix, or in □ or ☍ thereof, the cure will go on the more hardly, and be more difficult to overcome.*

33. *If in the beginning of a sickness the ☽ be in the sixth of the Nativity, fourth, seventh, eighth or twelfth, and both times therein happens to be an Infortune, it does manifest death, unless a Fortune at one of those times cast thither his benevolent Beams.*

34. *When the ascendant of the sickness is opposite to that of the Nativity, and is either the fourth, sixth, eighth, twelfth, or seventh, the ascendant of the Revolution being not the same, it shows hardly any recovery.*

35. *When the Lord of the second does infortunate the Lord of the ascendant the sick shall not be cured without much expense of his money; or if he die, he spends most part or much upon his cure to no purpose.*

36. *The ☉ in the ascendant brings usually health immediately; if in the sixth, the sickness presently changes; if the Lord of the eighth be combust, the sick shall recover and not die at that time.*

37. *The ☉ is the candle or light of Heaven, and that Spirit which clarifies and beautifies those Signs he is in, destroying nature's enemies.*

38. *Fear not the death of thy Patient if ♃ be in good aspect to the ☉, although the Lord of the ascendant apply to the Lord of the eighth.*

39. *When a sickness takes one first, at what time the ☽ separates from combustion, the sickness will increase until the ☽ does come to Opposition of the ☉.*

40. *The Lord of the ascendant being unfortunate in the eighth, the Patient will much increase the Disease and retard the cure by his ill government and carelessness.*

41. *The Significator of the sick, Occidental, denotes chronic Diseases; but Oriental, new Sickness: consider the separation of the ☽, and as she separates or applies, so will the Disease decrease or increase, &c.*

42. *If ♄ be author of the Disease, it proceeds of Cold; if ♂ or the ☉,*

it proceeds of Heat and Dryness; and so do in the signification of the rest of the Planets.

43. The ☽ is more afflicted of ♂ when she is increased in light, and more oppressed by ♄ in her wane: beware in the beginning of a sickness when the ☽ is thus unfortunated, and understand ♂ does more mischief when he is in masculine Signs, Oriental and above the Earth: do the contrary in the judgment of ♄.

CHAPTER XLV.

A sick Doctor, what was his Disease?   If curable?

See page
A7

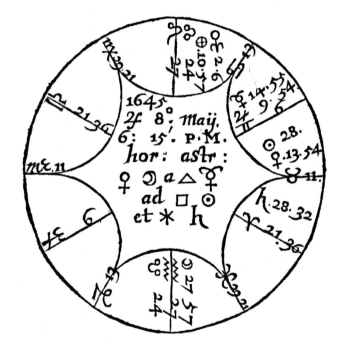

Positions as of
1 January
2005:

Chelea:

North Scale
19 ♏ 26

South Scale 15
♏ 08

What part of the Body was afflicted.

The Sign ascending in the Question is ♏, the *Chelae* notable fixed Stars near to the Ascendant, yet it is not afflicted by the evil position or presence of any evil Planet; therefore I must next look to the sixth house, and see if it be afflicted, wherein I find ♄ in his Fall, who thereby afflicts that house, which naturally signifies Diseases by his unlucky presence; from whence I concluded, that from thence and from that house I must require the part or member of the Body afflicted or most grieved, as you may read *page* 244.

♈ represents the Head, as you may see *page* 245.

♄ in ♈ signifies the Breast, as *page* 119.

♂ Lord of the ascendant in ♌ does signify the Heart.

The Lord of the ascendant is ♂, and him you may find but lately separated from a □ *dexter* of ♄, both of them in Cardinal Signs, ♂ at time of that □ in ♋, which presents the Breast and Stomach: from hence I positively concluded, as to the parts of Body grieved, they were the Head, Breast, Heart and Stomach, and that there lodged in the Breast or Stomach some melancholic Obstruction, the cause of all his disease and Misery.

From what Cause the Sickness was.

♄ Being principal *Significator* of the Infirmity, in his own Terms, and the ☽ in his house applying to him, did prenote Melancholy, and such dry Diseases as are occasioned from melancholy distempers, and might abide in the Head and Breast: what Infirmities ♄ naturally signifies , see *page* 244. How to make a right mixture, your Physicians best know, and what Diseases man may be subject to in those parts, and may proceed from such causes as abovesaid.

♂ Lord of the ascendant was also in the Terms of ♄, and the ☽ out of his Terms, applied to a □ of ☉, and he in ♂ his Terms; so that Choler was a secondary cause of this Doctor's sickness; and indeed when I came to speak with him, he was afflicted with great pain and rumbling in his head, very silent, dull and melancholy, slept very little, had a very dry Cough, and complained of great weakness and pain in his Breast, and at the Heart; his Complexion was between black and yellow, as if there was inclination to the Jaundice; he had besides these, a lingering Consumption and great weariness all over him, and in every joint, for the ☽ is in an airy Sign; and as ♏ does ascend, which signifies the Secrets, Stone in the Bladder; so does also the ☽ in ♒ signify the Secrets and Diseases therein, &c. so had he difficulty in making Urine, voided red gravel, and was greatly pained in those parts, &c. Having myself little judgment in Physic, I advised him to prescribe for himself such Physical Medicines as were gently hot, moist and cordial, whereby he might for a while prolong his life; for the ☽ in the fourth in ♓ with ♄, argued sickness until death: *He died the fourteenth of August following.*

Whether the Disease would be long or short?

♄ Being author of the Disease, showed it would be permanent, or of some continuance, as *page* 248, for he is a ponderous, slow Planet: besides, the Angles of the Figure are all fixed, the ☽ and ☉ both in fixed Signs, and in □, out of Angles, both in the Terms of an *Infortune*; ♂ Lord of the ascendant and sixth in a fixed Sign; all these portended the longitude of the Disease: Besides, the Antiscion of ♂ falls near the ☉, and thereby afflicts him, being the *Luminary* of the time.

CHAPTER XLVI.

Whether the Sick would live or die,
and what his Disease was?

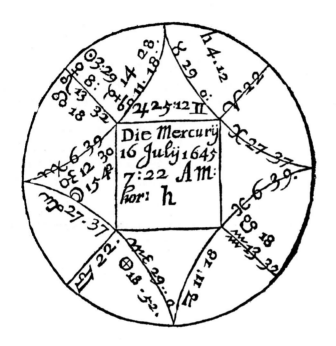

See page
A8

Judgment of the Figure aforesaid.

The Sign Ascending, *viz.* ♍, is in the Figure most afflicted
by the corporal presence of ♂, who is partly Lord of the
eighth house, therefore from that house and Sign must we
require the Disease, cause, and member grieved: ♒ being the
Sign of the sixth, is fixed, afflicted by ☋, and ♄ who is Lord of
the sixth house is in ♉, a fixed Sign, earthly and melancholy,
of the same nature and Triplicity that ♍, the Sign ascending,
is of; the ☽ a general *Significatrix* in all Diseases, being
afflicted by her proximity to ♂ and placed in the

ascendant, in an earthly, melancholy Sign, together with the other *Significators*, did portend the Patient to be wonderfully afflicted with the Spleen, with the Wind-cholic, and melancholy obstructions in the Bowels or small Guts, small Fevers, a remiss Pulse; and as the Sign ♍ is the Sign ascending, and ☽ and ♂ therein, it argued, the sick was perplexed with distempers in his Head, slept unquietly, &c. [*All which was true.*]

I persuaded the man to make his peace with God, and to settle his house in order, for I did not perceive by natural causes, that he could live above ten or twelve days.

And my reasons were, because all the *Significators* did promise no less than death: for first, ☉ who was the temporal light at time of the *Quere*, and is (*fons vitalis potentiae*) was in perfect □ of ♄ Lord of the sixth in Signs fixed.

Position as of 1 January 2005:
Secondly, the ascendant was extremely afflicted by the presence of ♂, he being naturally ill, and accidentally almost Lord of the whole eighth house.

Cauda Leonis: 21 ♍ 41
Thirdly, the ☽ was near *Cauda Leonis*, and afflicted by the cross influence of ♂, in that house which signifies Life, *viz.* the ascendant

Fourthly, the ☽ did separate from the ⚹ of ☿, Lord of the ascendant, in Signs of long ascensions (which is more properly a □ aspect) and did transfer his virtue to ♃ Lord of the eighth.

The sick died the 28th of *July* following, ☿ coming to the degree of the ☉ in the Question, and therein to the □ of ♄ Lord of the sixth, the day preceding; and the ☽ to an ☍ of the ☉, the ☽ that day transiting the degree of the sixth house at the time of the Question, *viz.* 14 of ♒, and ☉ the cusp of the twelfth.

CHAPTER XLVII.

Of the CRISIS in Diseases.

Crisis is no other thing than a duel or contention between nature and the infirmity; if nature at time of the

Crisis overcome the malignity of the Disease, it's a good *Crisis*; if the sickness prevail, it's a pernicious and ill *Crisis*. Or

CRISIS is no more than this, *viz.* A sudden alteration of man's body when he is sick, tending either to health or further sickness; for when this *Crisis* is, there's a sharp fight, as it were, between nature and the Disease, which of them shall overcome.

Days *Critical, Decretory* and *Chrysmall* are all one, and intend no more than a certain and more sure judgment of the infirmity afflicting, either more powerfully, or in a less measure at those times when the true *Crisis* is.

The true *Crisis* is best of all taken from that moment of time when first the sickness invaded the Infirm; which if it cannot be had, then it may be taken (but not so certainly) from the very hour when first the Water is brought to the Doctor to advise for recovery: but if no Urine come, then when the Doctor first speaks with the sick party, and is demanded by the *Infirm* what he thinks of his sickness, and what course he would advise for cure thereof.

Every sudden and vehement motion of the Disease may be called a *Crisis* as *Galen* says; or it is, not a local motion altogether, but an alteration of the Disease.

Or *Crisis* imports judgment in the Disease afflicting, and which way it will terminate, *viz.* for good or evil.

Hippocrates will have *Crisis* to be an acute or swift reportation in diseases, either to recovery or death: *But,* say some, *in regard there are more Diseases to terminate in health than in death* (except pestilential Diseases) *where the matter and cause is so malignant and poisonous, that nature many times does not attend a fight or combat with the Disease, whereby it cannot properly be called a* Crisis; *that definition of* Hippocrates *will not well hold, unless it be in such diseases as do determine in a recovery of the sick party:* So some say.

Avicenna, in *Canticis,* agrees with *Galen,* and says, *Crisis (est velox motus morbi ad salutem vel ad mortem.)*

There are some that have contended, *That although in diseases there is a* Crisis, *yet is it not caused by influence of the Celestial bodies, but from inferior causes.*

Now if this were granted that *Decretory* or *Critical-days* did proceed from inferior causes, then according to divers sickness and variety of humours, the several *Critical-days* were to be assumed, after a different way in tertians, quartans and continued Fevers: But this, as many learned say, cannot be, therefore it is more generally received and concluded, That in regard of the great dominion and influence the ☽ has upon our inferior Bodies, whereby she does excite and stir up the humours, that she by her motion does declare the true *Crisis* of the disease, and that it is required from the time of the sick party's first falling sick, and her recess and access forward and backward to and from that place or degree of the Zodiac, wherein she was at the exact time of falling sick; or if that time cannot be procured, then as beforesaid, take her true place exactly rectified to the hour of the Patient's first asking advice. I have hereunto inserted a Table, wherewith if you enter with the place of the ☽ in Sign and degree, you shall easily discover when she comes to an *Indicative* day, when to a *Semi-quadrate* (or half *Crisis*) when to a true □, when to an ☍ (which is called a full Crisis), and so for all the *Indicative* and *Critical* days during the sickness, &c. As for example; let the place of the ☽ in the later Figure of the 16th of *July* 1645 be supposed the true period or beginning of a Disease, the place of the ☽ is 15.42 ♍; because 42 minutes do almost make one degree, I enter with 16 degr. under the Sign of ♍ in the eighth column, so that 16 degr. of ♍ is my *Radix*, or true place of the ☽; over against 16. degr. to the right hand, I find 8.30 over the head thereof ♎, so that when the ☽ came to 8 degr. and 31 min. of ♎, it was the first *Indicative* day, wherein the Physician might expect how the Disease then would show itself; upon every *Crisis* or *Indicative* day, have consideration with what Planet the ☽ is in configuration; if with a benevolent, expect some remission in the disease; if with a malevolent, a bad indication, &c.

Next on the right hand to 8.30 ♎, you find 1 ♏, *viz.* when the ☽ came to the first of ♏, she was then in *Semi-quadrate* to her first place, and this is, as it were, half a *Crisis*, at what time the Disease might more or less manifest itself according to that aspect the ☽ found at her being in that first degree of ♏. In the next column on the right hand, you see 23.30 over it ♏, it tells you, when the ☽ came to the 23 and 30 min. of ♏, it was a second *Indicative* day, whereby the Physician might further judge of the increase or decrease of the Disease: In the next column you find 16 over it ♐, when the ☽ came to the 16th of ♐ there was then a true *Crisis*, at what time the Disease assuredly might be more fully discerned in one kind or other, and then, according to the aspects the ☽ in that degree had to the Planets, good or ill, so might the Patient or Physician expect a better or worse *Crisis*: and so in the same continued line or column, you run round the Heavens, ever observing the ☽ her coming to those places of the Zodiac, wherein she makes the *Indicative* or *Critical* day, and what Planets she is then in aspect with, and whether in the Figure they promise good or ill: Besides this, you shall observe what days she transits the cusps of the sixth, seventh and eighth houses, and how then she is aspected of the benevolent or ill Planets.

The Table Follows.

♈		♈	♉		♊	♋		♋	♌		♍	♎		♎	♏		♐	♑		♑	♒		♓
0	30	23	15	30	8	0	30	23	15	30	8	0	30	23	15	30	8	0	30	23	15	30	8
1	30	24	16	30	9	1	30	24	16	30	9	1	30	24	16	30	9	1	30	24	16	30	9
2	30	25	17	30	10	2	30	25	17	30	10	2	30	25	17	30	10	2	30	25	17	30	10
3	30	26	18	30	11	3	30	26	18	30	11	3	30	26	18	30	11	3	30	26	18	30	11
4	30	27	19	30	12	4	30	27	19	30	12	4	30	27	19	30	12	4	30	27	19	30	12
5	30	28	20	30	13	5	30	28	20	30	13	5	30	28	20	30	13	5	30	28	20	30	13
6	30	29	21	30	14	6	30	29	21	30	14	6	30	29	21	30	14	6	30	29	21	30	14
7	30	30	22	30	15	7	30	30	22	30	15	7	30	30	22	30	15	7	30	30	22	30	15
8	30	1♉	23	30	16	8	30	1♌	23	30	16	8	30	1♏	23	30	16	8	30	1♒	23	30	16
9	30	2	24	30	17	9	30	2	24	30	17	9	30	2	24	30	17	9	30	2	24	30	17
10	30	3	25	30	18	10	30	3	25	30	18	10	30	3	25	30	18	10	30	3	25	30	18
11	30	4	26	30	19	11	30	4	26	30	19	11	30	4	26	30	19	11	30	4	26	30	19
12	30	5	27	30	20	12	30	5	27	30	20	12	30	5	27	30	20	12	30	5	27	30	20
13	30	6	28	30	21	13	30	6	28	30	21	13	30	6	28	30	21	13	30	6	28	30	21
14	30	7	29	30	22	14	30	7	29	30	22	14	30	7	29	30	22	14	30	7	29	30	22
15	30	8	1♊	30	23	15	30	8	1♍	30	23	15	30	8	1♐	30	23	15	30	8	1♓	30	23
16	30	9	2	30	24	16	30	9	2	30	24	16	30	9	2	30	24	16	30	9	2	30	24
17	30	10	3	30	25	17	30	10	3	30	25	17	30	10	3	30	25	17	30	10	3	30	25
18	30	11	4	30	26	18	30	11	4	30	26	18	30	11	4	30	26	18	30	11	4	30	26
19	30	12	5	30	27	19	30	12	5	30	27	19	30	12	5	30	27	19	30	12	5	30	27
20	30	13	6	30	28	20	30	13	6	30	28	20	30	13	6	30	28	20	30	13	6	30	28
21	30	14	7	30	29	21	30	14	7	30	29	21	30	14	7	30	29	21	30	14	7	30	29
22	30	15	8	30	30	22	30	15	8	30	30	22	30	15	8	30	30	22	30	15	8	30	30
23	30	16	9	30	1♋	23	30	16	9	30	1♎	23	30	16	9	30	1♑	23	30	16	9	30	1♈
24	30	17	10	30	2	24	30	17	10	30	2	24	30	17	10	30	2	24	30	17	10	30	2
25	30	18	11	30	3	25	30	18	11	30	3	25	30	18	11	30	3	25	30	18	11	30	3
26	30	19	12	30	4	26	30	19	12	30	4	26	30	19	12	30	4	26	30	19	12	30	4
27	30	20	13	30	5	27	30	20	13	30	5	27	30	20	13	30	5	27	30	20	13	30	5
28	30	21	14	30	6	28	30	21	14	30	6	28	30	21	14	30	6	28	30	21	14	30	6
29	30	22	15	30	7	29	30	22	15	30	7	29	30	22	15	30	7	29	30	22	15	30	7

You must observe, that upon any *Critical* day (but especially upon the first Quartile) when ☽ meets with the body or aspect of a fortunate Planet, it's very probable (if the party be ordained for life) that nature will be fortified above the disease; and this her good aspect or application is a good indication of health, and that the Physician now employed shall restore the sick party to former health by most easy Medicines; but if she meet at that time with the unlucky aspect of an *Infortune*, it gives the Physician little hopes at present; the *Crisis* is then ill, and the Physician must more warily proceed, &c. Formerly men did repute the seventh, fourteenth and one and twentieth days for *Critical* days; but in regard that the ☽ her motion is sometimes more slow, at other times more quick, the precise day cannot be had without compute or calculation of her true motion; which how to do, I have given sufficient direction in my *Introduction*.

In giving Medicines, observe the motion of the ☽, for she

being in
- ♈,♌,♐, the *Attractive* virtue is strengthened in the *Phlegmatic*.
- ♉,♍,♑, the *Retentive* is fortified in *Sanguine* people.
- ♊,♎,♒, the *Digestive* in the *Melancholic*.
- ♋,♏,♓, the *Expulsive* in the *Choleric*.

☽ in ♋, ♏, ♓, in ✶ or △ to:
- ♃ Purge Melancholy.
- ♀ Purge Choler.
- ♂ ☉ Purge Phlegm.

The virtue retentive is stirred up from ♄, *by reason of his frigidity.*

Vegetative & Digestive		♃
Attractive & Irascible		♂
Vital & Natural potency	by	☉
Appetitive & Concupiscible		♀
Cogitative & Imaginative		☿
Expulsive		☽

Fiery Signs stir up red choler, *viz.*	♈, ♌, ♐
Earthly Signs, Black melancholy, or *Atram Melancholiam*	♉, ♍, ♑
Airy Signs, Blood	♊, ♎, ♒
Watery, Spittle and Phlegm	♋, ♏, ♓

I once intended a more large Discourse of Sickness, but

Master BOOKER having promised to undertake that labour, I forebear.

CHAPTER XLVIII.

If a Servant shall get free from his Master?

The first house, the Lord thereof, and the ☽, shall signify the Servant; the tenth house and the Lord of that Sign shall denote his Master, let this condition be what it will be in this judgment; consider if the Lord of the ascendant be joined to the Lord of the tenth house, and whether it be a perfect ♂, whether by body or aspect, whether with reception or not: if it be a ♂ by degree and minute, the Servant shall be freed easily, and in a short time; but if the Lord of the ascendant be separated from the Lord of the tenth some few minutes, it's an argument he is as good as freed already from his Master: if no such ♂ or aspect be between the Lord of the ascendant, and the Lord of the tenth, then have recourse to the ☽, and judge the same of her, as if she had been Lord of the ascendant, &c. I mean if she be so aspected as abovesaid.

But if neither the ☽ or Lord of the ascendant be separated from the Lord of the tenth, consider if either of them be separated from the ☉, or joined with him, judge in the like nature of them as you would have done with the Lord of the ascendant and the Lord of the tenth, the same aspects considered: But if the Question be determinate and not absolute, *viz.*, if he demand, *Shall I be freed from the service or slavery of this man my Master, in which I now live, or shall I ever be freed from his power?* then see if the Lord of the ascendant be cadent from an Angle, and have no aspect to the ascendant, or is in aspect with any Planet in an Angle, or with a Planet that does behold the ascendant, or if he be in the third or ninth, or joined to a Planet in them; then say, he shall be freed from his service, and shall depart from his Master: say the same if you find the like aspects or have the same occasion, from the aspects of the ☽.

But if the ☽ or Lord of the ascendant be in the ascendant,

tenth, seventh, or fourth house, or if either of them be joined
to a Planet being in those angles, and that Planet be Direct,
he shall not be delivered from his Master; but if the aforesaid
Planet be Retrograde, it argues freedom, but with slowness
and difficulty: If the Lord of the ascendant be impeded in
the ascendant, tenth, seventh or fourth, by corporal ♂ of any
ill Planet, or by his □ or ♂, or if he be entering combustion,
he shall not be freed from his service, &c.

Finis sexae Domus

The Significations of the seventh House

It signifies Marriage, open Enemies, Lawsuits, Controversies, Contracts, Wars, Bargains, Fugitives, Thefts, &c.

Because the Demands which do naturally appertain
to the seventh house, require more consideration, and
are more difficult to judge than of any other house, I
have been enforced to be more large in delivering the
opinions of the Ancients, as of some modern
Practitioners; and have also published forty-three
significant Aphorisms; which, if well understood, will
give great light, not only for better understanding what
concerns this house, but the whole body of *Astrology*.

APHORISMS and Considerations for better judging any HORARY QUESTION.

1. **S**ee *the Question be radical, or fit to be judged; which is, when the Lord of the ascendant and hour be of one nature or Triplicity.*

2. *Be not confident of the Judgment if either the first degrees or later of any Sign be ascending: if few degrees ascend, the matter is not yet ripe for judgment: if the later degrees arise, the matter of the Question is elapsed, and it's probable the Querent has been tampering with others, or despairs of any success: however, the Heavens advise you not to meddle with it at that time.*

3. *The position of ♄ or ♂ in the tenth, and they peregrine or unfortunate, or the ☋ in that house, the Artist hardly gets credit by that Question.*

4. *Judge not upon every light motion, or without premeditation of the Querent, nor upon slight and trivial Questions, or when the Querent has not wit to know what he would demand.*

5. *Have special regard to the strength and debility of the ☽, and it's far better the Lord of the ascendant be unfortunate than she, for she brings to us the strength and virtue of all the other Planets, and of one Planet to another.*

6. *Behold the condition of ♄ in every Question, he is naturally ill by his excess of cold; ♂ is of ill influence, because of his too much heat: in very truth, neither of them is cold or dry, but signify so much in their virtue and operation, and therefore in all Questions they show tardiness and detriment in the Question, unless the ☽ and they receive each other in the signification.*

7. *See the condition of ♃ and ♀ be observed, who naturally are Fortunes and temperate, and never import any malice, unless by accident: where they are Significators without reception, they put forward the matter, but they best preform the matter in question when they apply by △ or ✶, and to purpose when in Essential Dignities.*

8. *In every Question where Fortunes are Significators, hope well; but if the Infortunes, then fear the worst, and accordingly order your business.*

9. *Generally consider the state of the ☽, for if she be void of course, there's no great hopes of the Question propounded, that it shall be effected; yet if she be in ♋, ♉, ♐ or ♓, your fear may be the less, for then she is not much impeded by being void of course.*

10. *See from what Planet the ☽ is separated, that Planet shows what has already been done: if from a Fortune good; if from a malevolent, ill; according to the nature of the house, &c.*

11. *The application of the ☽ shows the present condition of the thing demanded, viz. her applying by a good aspect, and in a good house, to a good Planet, intimates the strong hopes of the thing intended.*

12. *The application of the ☽ to a Planet in his Fall, signifies anguish, trouble and delays in the thing demanded.*

13. *A Retrograde Planet, or one in his first station, Significator in the Question, denotes ill in the Question, discord and much contradiction.*

14. *We ought warily to consider if evil Planets be Significators in anything, for if they predict evil in the thing quesited, the vengeance is more heavy; if they foretell of any good, it's less than what is expected, it's imperfect, and nothing therein comes, without infinite solicitation and affliction, &c.*

15. *A Planet that is slow in motion, prolongs the thing quesited after, so that it's hardly performed; the nature of the Sign wherein the Planet is, does herein much advantage the judgment.*

16. *When Infortunes are Significators of any evil, do you well consider if the Fortunes, viz. ♃ or ♀, cast not any aspect to them, then the evil intended formerly is lessened; do so when the Fortunes are Significators.*

17. *If the Fortunes signify anything, and are cadent, or ill placed in Dignities, or behold not the ascendant, or are Retrograde, then are they impeded, and shall perform little, if not received.*

18. *Notwithstanding Reception, if he be an Infortune, he performs but little; but if the same happen when the Fortunes are Significators, the thing is perfected.*

19. *A Planet Peregrine, viz. having no essential Dignities where he is, he is malicious beyond expression; if he be in essential Dignities, the less; for then he is like a noble soul that has his enemy in his clutches, but scorns to hurt him.*

20. *And yet generally, if ♄ or ♂ be in House, Exaltation, Triplicity*

and Angles, and then have signification in a Question, they perform the thing desired.

21. *Confide not too much in the assistance a Fortune lends, unless he be in essential Dignities; for then he performs matters wholly, else but by halves.*

22. *When in a Question wherein both the Fortunes and Infortunes are either weak or equally ill placed, promise no success upon that demand; defer the Judgment until the Heavens have a better Position.*

23. *Beware in all Judgments, when the Significator of the question is either Combust, or in Opposition to the ☉, he will then signify nothing of the matter, no good, nor is he able to bring anything to perfection.*

24. *One Infortune joined to another, if good be signified by their aspect, yet will it have no effect, or come to any thing: If they signify evil, it's probable that it may fall out with more malice then expected.*

25. *The Lord of the ascendant out of his essential Dignities, Cadent, &c., shows the Querent is out of all hopes in his business.*

26. *A Planet within twelve degrees of the ☉, is said to be under his Beams, and then has no fortitude, let it be in what Sign it will; when a Planet is within sixteen minutes of the ☉, he is said to be in Cazimi, or heart of the ☉, and then it's an addition of fortune, and he is wondrous strong.*

27. *See to what Planet the Significator commits his disposition, and if Oriental or Occidental; if it be to ♄, ♃ or ♂, and they Oriental, the matter is sooner performed; later, if Occidental, do the contrary in ♀ and ☿.*

28. *Observe if the Planet that is Significator of the thing desired, be in a fixed Sign, moveable or common: fixed Signs show stability, and that the thing shall continue, whether it be begun, or is to be begun: common Signs show the oft probability of perfecting the thing, and yet not its conclusion: moveable Signs show a sudden resolution or conclusion of the matter one way or other. From hence we begin Foundations of Houses and Towns when Significators are fixed; short Journeys when they are in moveable: but in things wherein we desire a mediocrity, we elect common Signs.*

29. *The Lord of the ascendant or the ☽ with the Head or Tail of the*

Dragon, brings damage to the Question propounded; see in what house they are in, and receive signification from thence.

30. *Look whether the degree of the ascendant, or place of the Sign the Significator is in, be the then place of any Eclipse at hand; though the matter propounded be in a fair way to be concluded, yet shall it insensibly receive prejudice when least is expected, and hardly be concluded.*

31. *If you find the ☽ impeded in any Question, be it what it will, there will be the like stay, demur or hinderance in the thing quesited; and indeed there's seldom good end comes of a Question where the ☽ is impeded; if it be in going to War, you may fear the life of the Querent; if in a Journey, ill success; if Marriage, an ill end of Wooing, &c.*

32. *If the Lord of the question or the ☽ be in a Sign opposite to his own house, as ☿ in ♐ or ♓, &c., the Querent has no good hopes of his demands, he despairs, nor does he delight in it, nor does he care whether it be performed or not.*

33. *Consider diligently the Planet impeding the Signifier of the thing demanded, and what house he is either Lord of, or is placed in; from the nature or person of that house require the cause obstructing.*

34. *The nearer your Significator is to an Angle, the more good you may expect; less, if placed in a Succedent house; little, if in a Cadent.*

35. *In all Questions, know there's not so great an affliction to the ☽, as when she is in ♂ with the ☉; the ill aspects of the Infortunes does much afflict her, but none so powerful as her Combustion.*

36. *In any question, see if an Infortune aspect your Significator, and whether they be both Peregrine, Retrograde, Cadent, or in Signs contrary to their own nature, it may then be doubted they infer such a mischief in the question, as is inevitable, according to natural causes.*

37. *Planets that are Significators in any thing, if they are in ♂, and in a Sign agreeing to their own nature, then the thing quesited after is brought to perfection with much ease and facility, else not.*

38. *Have special regard to the Significators, and whether any frustration or prohibition be before the perfect aspect: the Planet frustrating describes the party or cause hindering the matter demanded.*

39. *Ever consider the ⊗, which if well dignified in any house, the querent gets by men, or things denoted by that house; and so, if ill dignified, damage from thence.*

40. *In questions of Marriage, an unfortunate Planet in the seventh threatens ill agreement in Marriage, unless the same Planet be a Significator at the Birth.*

41. *If the Lord of the eighth be impeded or unfortunate in the eighth, the Querent shall receive prejudice by the death of some woman, or concerning some debts due to him from men deceased.*

42. *In what house you find* ♃ *and* ♀ *well dignified, you may expect benefit from such men and things as are signified by that house; as if in the third, from Kindred; in the fourth, from Father, or by Lands, &c. in the fifth by Play, &c. and so in other houses.*

43. *Beware of men and things appertaining to that house wherein* ☋ *is in; it seldom fails, but the querent shall receive damage, scandal or slander from men and matter signified by the house he is in.*

CHAPTER XLIX.

Of Marriage.

If a Question be asked of *Marriage*, behold the ascendant and the Lord thereof, and the ☽, and the Planet from whom the ☽ is separated, and give those for the *Significators* of the *Querent*; and the seventh house, and the Lord thereof, and the Planets to whom the ☽ applies, for the Signifiers of him or her concerning whom the Question is asked: and if it be a man that asks the Question, join the ☉ and ☽ with his *Significators*, and make him partner in the signification; and if it be a woman, join ♀ and ☽, and make them partners: afterwards, behold what application the Lord of the ascendant or ☽ has with the Lord of the seventh, and what application that Planet has from whom the ☽ is separated, with the Planet to whom she does apply, or ☉ with ♀; for if the Lord of the ascendant or the ☽ apply to the Lord of the seventh house, it does signify the *Querent* shall have his or her desire, yet with many petitions, solicitations and prayers: and if the application be by □ or ☍, and with reception, it signifies that it shall be brought to pass with a kind of slowness, labour and travail: but if the Lord of the seventh apply to the Lord of the ascendant, or the Planet to whom the ☽ does apply, to the Planet from whom she is separate; or if the Lord of the seventh be in the ascendant, the matter shall be brought easily to pass, with great good will of the man or woman quesited after; chiefly if there be an application by △ or ✶ aspect.

Aphorisms of ALKINDUS Touching
MARRIAGE

When the Lord of the ascendant does apply to the Lord of the 7ᵗʰ house,* it's an argument the Marriage shall be performed and done. Also, if the ☽ do apply to ♀, and she strong, increasing in her motion, and in some of her own Dignities, and the ☽ likewise, the Marriage shall be concluded: if ♀ do behold the ☉, and the ☉ have any dignity in the ascendant, and behold the Lord of his house, *viz.* of the Sign wherein he is, it does signify likewise the Marriage shall be concluded; but if the Planet applying, and he to whom he does apply, be both cadent from the angles, and especially if their Lords do not behold them, it does signify there shall be good hopes at the first, but by dallying and tracting the time, there shall be trouble, and no Marriage at all performed: Also if ☽, ☉, ♀ and Lord of the seventh, and Lord of the ascendant be in angles, and they beholding one another, or if their Lords behold them, though with ☐ or ☌, yet it signifies the matter shall be first in despair or suspended, but afterwards it shall by the will of God, be brought to pass, and finished by the consent of all parties.

* Or if the Lord of the seventh apply to the Lord of the Ascendant.

Of Marriage, whether it shall take effect or no?

Give to the *Querent* the Lord of the ascendant, the ☽ and the Planet from whom the ☽ is separated; and to the party inquired, the Lord of the seventh, and the Planet to whom the ☽ does apply; and if the *Querent* be a Man, then add the ☉, but if a Woman then add ♀; and then behold what application there is between the Lord of the ascendant and the Lord

of the seventh; for if the Lord of the seventh be in the
ascendant, or apply to the Lord thereof, it will unwillingly
be consented to by the party desired; but if the Lord of the
ascendant or the ☽ apply to the Lord of the seventh, or be in
the seventh, the Querent shall obtain his purpose by his own
labour; but if none of these happen, yet if there be translation
of light between them, then it shall be effected by the means
of Friends or Acquaintance; also the ☽ in the tenth signifies
the same, also, the application of the ☽ with ♀ effects the
matter, but by mediation of Friends: also the application of
the ☉ and ♀, especially when ☉ has dignity in the seventh,
idem: if the Lord of the ascendant be in the seventh, or with
the Lord thereof, or behold him with a good aspect, or if the
Lord of the seventh be in the ascendant, or with the Lord of
the ascendant, or behold him with good aspect, it does give
great encouragement for effecting the matter.

Of Marriage.

If a man ask, his *Significators* are, first, the Lord of the
ascendant: secondly, the ☽; thirdly, the Planet the ☽ is
separated from; fourthly, ☉, the natural significator of men.

The *Significators* of the woman are; the Lord of the
seventh, the Planet the ☽ applies to, the Planet in the seventh,
♀ the natural significatrix of women: the like judge for the
woman if she ask the Question, (*mutatis mutandis*) that is,
the ascendant and other *Significators*, and ♀; the question
asked by the woman, the seventh and his Lord, the Planet the
☽ applies to; these are for the man, the ascendant and his
Lord, the Planet the ☽ is separate from, the ☽ and ♀, so the
querent has three *Significators*, the party desired has also three:
It shall be. It shall be, if the Lord of the ascendant or ☽ be in the seventh;
Viz. one secondly, if the Planet the ☽ separates from, applies to the
in Terms, Planet the ☽ applies to, thirdly, or the ☉ and ♀ apply to each
the other other; fourthly, the Lord of the first in the seventh, or seventh
in the in the first; fifthly, any translation of light from the *Significators*,
Triplicity or Reception of the *Significators*, or any collection by a More
of the weighty Planet, the *Signifiers* in interchangeable Dignities,
Significator,
or the like.

the ☽ in the seventh giving virtue to the Lord of the ascendant, or Lord of the seventh.

The Lord of the seventh in the ascendant, the party *Which love* desired loves best: The Lord of the ascendant in the seventh, *most, or* the Querent loves best; and so of the other Significators, for *desire it* those that apply argue most love, &c. The Lord of the seventh *most.* in the seventh, especially in one of his own houses, the party desired is free from love, has little mind to Marriage, and her Portion is known, or the man's.

The Significators of the party desired, not beholding the Significators of the Querent, notes the love of some other more than the Querent, or an aversion to the party now inquiring.

The application of the *Significators* frustrated, notes the Marriage to be broken off, by such a person or thing as that *Signifier* notes, which you may know by the house he is in & Lord of, *viz.* if by the Lord of the 2nd house, want of Riches; if Lord of the 3rd, by the Brother, &c. contrariwise, the Marriage being presaged by translation of light, or collection, it shall be furthered by such a one (as above mentioned) *viz.* if by the Lord of the second, by some friend promising Dowry; third, a Brother; tenth, a Mother; fifth or eleventh, a Friend; sixth, an Uncle, Aunt, or a Servant: Where note, that Marriages promised by ♂ □ or ☍, note performance with much ado; △ or ✶, easy; with Reception, best of all.

What shall be the occasion of hindering the Marriage.

Having carefully observed, that although there seem great probability of effecting the Marriage inquired of, yet you find just cause to judge, it shall not either really be acted, or much obstruction will be before it can be done; and you are desirous to know from whence the impediment shall come, the better to prevent it; consider what evil Planet it is who does hinder the Reception of the disposition of the *Significators*, *viz.* of the man and woman, or who frustrates their aspect, or prohibits them, or interjects his Rays between the *Significators*; if he be the Lord of the second, they break off on the Querent's behalf,

Money or Fortune being wanting on that side, or poverty objected: if it be the Lord of the third, the Querent's Kindred, Brethren or Sisters, or some untoward Neighbour, or some Journey &c. if the Lord of the fourth, the Parent will not agree, he will part with no Lands, no House, Houses or Tenements, will settle no Estate: if the Lord of the fifth, Children may be the occasion (if either party have any;) or if a Bachelor propounds, perhaps it's objected, he either is not capable of getting a Child, or that he has had a Bastard, or is scandalized about such a thing, or that it's feared the party will be wanton, or given to luxury, too much to his pleasure and pastime, &c. vary your rule, and it serves if a woman propound, &c. If it be the Lord of the sixth, either some of his Father's Kindred, *viz.* some Uncle or a Servant, or the like, or some infirmity or sickness in the *querent* may be the cause impeding.

If it be a Planet in the seventh, some other he or she Friend will impede, or a public Enemy, or one he or she have formerly had variance with, or a Lawsuit, &c.

If it be the Lord of the eighth, it may be feared Death will bereave the *querent* of Life ere the Marriage, or the *quesited* has not a sufficient Portion, their Estate is disliked, it gives no content, it will not be accepted.

If the Lord of the ninth, one or other of the *quesited's* Kindred or difference in Religion, or some busy-headed Priest, or by reason of some long Journey to be undertaken by the *querent*, &c.

If the Lord of the tenth the Father of the *quesited*, or Mother of the *querent*, or some principal man, Officer or Magistrate.

If the Lord of the eleventh, the Friends of both parties dislike the Match, or such as at first brought on the matter, will now endeavour to dissolve the Match.

If the Lord of the twelfth, then there is some underhand dealing and much juggling in the business, the matter shall be much retarded, and the *querent* shall never know by whom; the *querent* is much slandered, or some scandal privately insinuated does much wrong, and will quite break the matter.

As you have notions whereby you may understand what

may be the obstacle in any Marriage, so by the same rules, rightly varied, you shall find who will afflict or befriend the *querent* in his suit, or will endeavour to do him good therein; I have herein dealt very candidly, and expressed the whole truth.

Whether a man shall Marry.

If the ☽ behold the ☉ or ♀ by a good aspect, or the Lord of the ascendant be in the seventh, or the Lord of the seventh in the ascendant, or either of them behold other with a good aspect, it signifies Marriage to the Querent.

I observe, if the *Significators* be in Prolific Signs, or Dignities of ♀, the party inquiring does marry.

The time of Marriage.

The degree of the application of ☽ to ☉ or ♀, or Lord of the ascendant to the Lord of the seventh, or Lord of the seventh to the Lord of the ascendant; if it be in moveable Signs, Days; in common Signs, Months; in fixed Signs, Years; according to that time the Marriage shall be performed.

This must be understood when you find strong testimonies of Marriage, and that the *Significators* are swift.

How many Husbands a woman shall have.

Behold from the degree of the tenth house to the degree of ♂, and so many Planets as you shall find between them, so many Husbands shall she have; but if ♂ be in the eleventh house, then look from ♂ to ♃, and judge accordingly: some judge from ♂ to the Lord of the tenth; these rules are *Arabic*: plurality of Husbands is best adjudged from the Lord of the seventh and from ☉ and ♂ being in common Signs, or many Planets in the seventh, or ☉ in ✶ or △ to many Planets in the seventh, argues plurality, or more than one.

From what part one shall Marry.

If the Lord of the seventh be in the ninth, he shall marry a Stranger, &c. If the Lord of the seventh and of the ascendant be in one quarter of Heaven, or in one house or Sign, usually the party marries one near to the place of their own abode: consider the Sign of the seventh, the Sign and quarter of Heaven the Lord of the seventh is in, and judge by the major testimonies, from what part of Heaven the party shall live whom the *querent* shall marry; as if most concur in South testimonies, the South; mix the quarter of Heaven and Sign, preferring the Sign before the quarter: but this will be best explained upon an example.

What manner of person he or she is.

For the man, note the Planet the ☽ is with; as if with ♀, say she is fair, slender and pleasant; and for the woman, judge by the Planet the ☉ beholds; ☉ in △ or ✶ of ♄, wise and painful; ☉ aspecting ♃, honest; and so of the rest: the ☉ and ☽ in □ or ☍, note contention, separation and discords.

Whether man or woman be more noble.

If the Lord of the seventh be in an angle, and the Lord of the ascendant in a succedent house, the woman is best descended; and so if the Lord of the ascendant be in an angle, judge accordingly; in like manner one may judge of two Companions, or any one else: A more assured way is, by observing whether of the *Significators* is most superior, and most potential in essential Dignities; if no such thing be, who is best placed in an angle, is most noble; and this will not fail.

Who shall be Master of the two.

Behold the Lord of the ascendant and the ☽; if the ☽ or the Lord of the ascendant be received in an angle, and he that is the receiver be an heavy or ponderous Planet, the *querent* shall be Master; and whether *Significators* shall be found weak, ill dignified, or in cadent houses, that party shall be subject.

Whether she be rich or not.

If a man ask, see the Lord of the eighth, or Planet in the eighth, for if they be strong, or ☽ applying to the Lord of the eighth by a good aspect, then she is wealthy (& *e contra*, poor;) if the woman ask of the man, and of his estate, judge after the same manner, for (*eadem est ratio.*)

Whether the MARRIAGE be Legitimate.

If the *Significators* of them, either of the man or woman be vitiated or joined to ♄ or ♂, and they not *Significators* in the Question, or if they be with ☋, it shows unlawful Marriage, *viz.* there has been some wrangling or claim laid to the party by some former man or woman.

How they shall agree after Marriage.

If the Figure perform Marriage, note if the Lord of the ascendant and Lord of the seventh aspect each other with △ or ✶, they agree well: ☽ beholding her Dispositor, or Lord of the Exaltation of the house wherein she is, with good aspect, *idem*: The Lord of the seventh more weighty, and in an angle, she will be Master, or strive for it: if neither the Lord of the ascendant, or of the seventh be in angles, then note the weightier, for that party signified by him, shall be master; ☉ impeded, worst for the man; if ♀ be impeded, worst for the woman; if the ☽ be impeded or unfortunate, is ill for them both.

Disagree.

The Lord of the ascendant and Lord of the seventh in □ or ☍, Lord of the ☽ impeded beholding the Ascendant, or ♄,

♂ or a Retrograde or Combust Planet in the ascendant, does note contention ever by the *querent*; & *e contra*, judge the like if the Lord of the seventh suffer the same afflictions, that then the *quesited* shall be the occasion of strife: the ☽ in her fall, or at □ or ☍ with ♄ or ♂, or any Retrograde Planet, if the ☽ then behold the ascendant, notes brawling ever moved by the woman; ♄, ♂, ☋ in the ascendant, *idem*, if the question be asked by the man.

Who shall be the cause of their Strife, or the author of their Good.

If the Lord of the third be that Planet who does afflict or impede, and be in the ascendant or seventh house, it shall be by Brethren or Kindred; an *Infortune* in the tenth, notes brawling, and continual chiding and wrangling: In the fourth, either a Divorce or a willingness to it, or hinderance in Dowry; the ☽ unfortunate beholding the ascendant, note brawling, separation and dishonest living: ill Planets in the tenth or fourth, ill persons make contention, or their Parents; no application between the Planet the ☽ separates from, and the Planet to whom she does apply, notes contention always: if the ☽ do aspect, or be in ♂ with ♄ or ♂, one of them shall die quickly, or have some misfortune; if this ♂ be in the tenth or fourth, in a masculine Sign, the man shall suffer; if in a feminine Sign, the woman: The ☽ in △ or ✶ of good Planets, declares gifts from Friends; ☽ in □ of good Planets, by dead men; ☽ in ♂ of good Planets, promises good by their own industry and labour; if the ☽ aspect ♄ or ♂, or be in the twelfth or eighth, or void of course, they shall have both troubles, griefs and sickness; in angles, notes a probability of separation or long disagreements.

That the Marriage shall be broken, and the cause thereof.

Behold the Planet who receives the light of the *Significators*, if he be a heavy Planet, and be hindered by □ or ☍ of an ill

Planet, or be Cadent, the intended Marriage shall be broken off again, though at present it is very feasible.

Behold whether parties *Significator* is strongest, that party shall first marry after this dissolution.

If the ill Planet that hinders the Marriage be Lord of the second or eighth house, it is for matter of Dowry; if Lord of the third, Brother; if Lord of the fourth or tenth, it is the Father or the Mother, or such like; and so judge of the rest.

If there be an ill Planet that carries the light between the *Significators*, it shall be by means of a Messenger; describe that Planet, and you may notify the party.

That woman who does depart from her Husband or become a Widow, the ☽ being between the seventeenth degree of ♐, and the first minute of ♑, shall never return or marry. *An Arabic Aphorism, not overmuch to be credited without consent of other Significators.*

Whoso is Espoused to a Wife the ☽ being in the twelve first degrees of ♑, shall lose her before marriage, or die within six months, or live in discord with her.

Whether a Man or his Wife shall die first, and the time when.

Behold the Lord of the ascendant and the Lord of the seventh, and see which of them goes first to Combustion, and if the Lord of the ascendant, the *querent* shall die first; if the Lord of the seventh, *e contra*: The Lord of the ascendant Retrograde or Combust, or in his Fall, or near the Lord of the eighth, the Man; the Lord of the seventh in the like case, the Woman: ☉ unfortunate, the Man; ♀ unfortunate, the Woman.

Usually I observe, whose *Significator* is first Combust, and in what Sign; if he be Combust in Tropic Signs, as ♈, ♋, ♎, ♑, it portends death in a short time; If in common Signs, *viz.* ♊, ♍, ♐, ♓, the time is longer: in Signs fixed, *viz.* ♉, ♌, ♏, ♒, it will be a longer time ere the party die, &c.

Which of the two shall live longest?

Behold the Lord of the ascendant, and of the seventh, which

of these two are in the best place of heaven, best dignified, and in good aspect with *Fortunes*, and more remote from the presence or ill aspect of the Lord of the eighth house, that person shall live longest: Where you must observe, as to the Lord of the seventh, the Lord of the second in the Figure is his eighth house, and so Lord of, or *Significator* of death.

Whether she be a Maid, or Chaste, of whom the quere is.

Look if the Lord of the ascendant ♀ and the ☽ be found in fixed Signs, good Planets beholding them, then say, she is a Maid, and chaste: But if in place of the *Fortunes* there be *Infortunes*, say she is neither a Virgin, nor chaste: especially if ♂ be there, and he in the house of ♀ without Reception: Also, if ☽ and ☉ behold themselves and ♂, she is no Maid; but if the *Significators* be in moveable Signs, *Infortunes* beholding them, say then she desires a man very much, and that she refrains and restrains her concupiscence very much, and casts off her Suitors; yet, it is no good to trust always to this judgment, because the nature of women is changeable.

The *Significatrix* of the woman in her own essential Dignities, or in △ to the ☉ or ♃ with any Reception, or the ☽ and the *Significatrix* in △ or ✶, in Reception, out of any mutual Dignities, or ♀ in ♌ not afflicted, or the ☽ in ♒, free from □, ♂, ☍ of ♂, I judged honesty, and I found it ever true.

Whether A Damsel be a Maid or not.

Behold the ascendant and his Lord, and the ☽, and if thou findeth them fixed and well disposed, it signifies she is a Virgin; but if they be in common or moveable Signs, or evil Planets be in fixed Signs beholding them, or aspect them any way, it is a doubt of *Legerdemain*; also ♏ ascending, argues she is, or would be too familiar.

In many things I dissent from the *Ancients*, and so in this; for if ♂ be in ♌, and ♏ ascend, the *querent* is suspected and tempted, but yet is honest.

Whether a Woman be honest to her Husband.

The Lord of the ascendant, the ☽ or ♀ in fixed Signs, in aspect of the *Fortunes*, she is chaste; these being in aspect of the *Infortunes*, not chaste, chiefly with ♂; ☉ or ☽ beholding ♂, she is *meretrix*; ☉ and ☽ in no aspect, nor ♂ with them, she is suspected a privy Harlot, rather privately wanton; but not yet come to the act.

The Moon in ☍ to ♂, he in ♉, she in ♏ or he in ♎ she in ♈, ill in this case.

I must charge all sons of Art to be sparing in delivering judgment upon these queries, rather to be silent; for as men we may err, and so by delivering an unlucky judgment, be authors of much mischief.

Of a woman whether she be corrupt, or has a Lover besides her Husband or Sweetheart.

Behold the ascendant and his Lord, and the ☽, and see if they be both in angles or fixed Signs, then say the Maid is a Virgin, and they lie of her, or what is reported is false: if the Lord of the ascendant and the ☽ be in fixed Signs, and the angles be moveable Signs, she was tempted, but gave no credit or admittance to the *Tempter*. If the ☽ be joined to ♄, ♃, ♂, ☉ corporally by aspect, so that there is between them but 5 degrees or less, she is tempted of someone who has the effigies of that Planet to whom she is joined; but if the ☽ be joined to ♀ or ☿, she is tempted by some woman for a man, but she makes not reckoning of the old or young Bawd's words, but laughs her to scorn: If the angles be fixed Signs, and the Lord of the ascendant or ☽ in moveable or common, (for in this judgment the common are of less importance) she has been attempted, and is still tempted, but she is honest; and has been formerly deluded, if she be with the ☊; but if then the ☽ be with ☋, she has formerly offended, and is still guilty, nor will she amend hereafter; the same may be said of ♂, if he be in place of the ☋; yet ♂ imposes not so much malice on the woman as ☋: generally the ☽ in any Question with ☋, imports mis-reports of the woman, you may call them slanders.

Whether a woman is honest.

The ☽ in the last face of ♊, the woman seems to be corrupt, if the ascendant be a moveable Sign, or common, or *This* if the Lord of the ascendant or ☽ be in moveable or common *where* Signs she is no Virgin; The Lord of the ascendant combust *suspicion* in a moveable Sign, the woman has been tempted and made *is of the* a harlot by violence, or she was unwillingly drawn to lewdness; *quesited's* the Lord of the ascendant in a fixed Sign, and the ascendant *honesty* *will hold* fixed, though the ☽ be in a moveable Sign, she is still a *true.* Virgin, and honest; the ☽ in the ascendant with ♄, the woman was abused by force, and not by her consent: If the ascendant be a fixed Sign, and the Lord of the ascendant in the fifth, or the ☽ in the fifth, or the Lord of the fifth in the ascendant, or both of them corporally joined in one Sign, it seems the woman has newly conceived, or was lately tempted; but if they be separated asunder by three degrees, it seems the woman is delivered, or free from the party she was lately in fear of.

Whether a woman trades with any but her Husband.

These Behold the ascendant, his Lord, the ☽, and Planet from *judgments* whom the ☽ is separated, these are *Signifiers* of the *querent*; *must be* *carefully* the seventh house and his Lord, the Planet to whom the ☽ is *observed* joined, are the *Signifiers* of the woman: see to whom the ☽ *and well* and Lord of the seventh is joined, which if they be both *considered* *before* joined to the Lord of the ascendant, whether with Reception *judgment* or ♂, say, the woman is not faulty, but honest: but if the *be* Lord of the seventh, or the ☽ or either of them is joined to *propounded* *in the* the Lord of the Triplicity of the ascendant, *viz.* to him that is *negative,* Lord of the Diurnal or Nocturnal Triplicity then ascending, *viz. that* or if any of them is joined to the Lord of the seventh, and ☽ *she is not* *honest.* is separated from the Lord of the ascendant, it then seems she has a Friend that she loves besides her Husband: the Lord of the seventh void of course, the woman has no Friend.

The Lord of the seventh, the ☽, or both, separate from any other Planet but the Lord of the ascendant, and he not separated above three degrees, the woman did love another, but she has now left him: the Lord of the seventh with the ♌, the Woman is blameless, without he be in ♂ with some other Planet, then she is worthy to be blamed now, was also in times past, and in times to come will be; for if she be not faulty in act, she is in her desires and affections.

The Lord of the seventh or ☽ joined with ♂, if the ☋ be there, it seems the woman has a Sweetheart whom she loves, and that uses her company: If ♂ be with ☋, and the Lord of the seventh be joined as beforesaid, it diminishes the malice, and though the woman love some martial man, yet he cannot bring her under his Yoke, yet is she hard put to it, and much persuaded

If ♂ be with the Lord of the seventh, or with ☽, or in one Sign in ♂, or with ☋, the woman has a Sweetheart in contract, not far from her house; and if they be in one degree, then he is in the house, and one of the familiars of the man that asks the Question, or of her own Husband.

If the ☽ or Lord of the seventh separate from ♂, or ♂ from him, or that they be separated, perchance the woman had a Lover before she knew her Husband, but now they have one forsaken the other, or they have forgot each other.

♂ Lord of the seventh, or ☽ Lady of the seventh, in ♈ or ♏, and ♂ beholding any of them, *viz.* either of the Signs, or ☽, or in Reception with one or other, *viz.* ☽ and ♂, for if ♂ did receive the ☽, she did a long time love one, but she has little to do with him now: ☽ Lady of the seventh, in ♂ with ♂ or ♃ in any Sign whatsoever, the woman has loved a certain man, a *Nobleman* or a *Bishop*, *viz.* a man of better quality than herself, &c. but if there be a mutual Reception between them, they still love one another, or still some acts of kindness pass between them, and there wants naught but opportunity.

The Lord of the seventh or ☽ joined to ☿, the woman seems to love a young Clerk, or a Merchant, or witty, nimble Fellow.

The Lord of the seventh joined to ♀ with Reception, with or without any aspect, or else by a △ or ✶, or □ without

Reception, the Woman cares not for men, but has a friendship with women, or speaks wantonly, but is not naturally lewd or vicious.

The Lord of the seventh or ☽ in ♂ with ♄, the woman loves an Old man, or a Religious man, or a Countryman or a man of plain sober carriage.

The Lord of the seventh joined to the ☉, she loves at present, and did love a certain great person, according to the quality of the *Demandant*; if it be with Reception, he has or may have, if he please, to do with her; but if it be without Reception, he cares not for her, but has quite forsaken her: But if more Planets do behold the ☉ as well as the Lord of the seventh, especially ♄ or ☿, more men have had to do with her, nor is she yet amended, but somewhat tardy, &c.

If one's Lover or Wife has a Sweetheart besides himself.

See if ♂ be in the seventh house, so that he be not in his own house, then she has one; if ♄ be there, she loves one but lies not with him; if ♃ be there, she has much ado to be honest; if ♀, she is a merry wag, and is thought to be wanton, but is not: if ☿, she had a Friend but has not now; if ☽ be in the seventh, she as yet has none, but she will have, and will be common: if ☉ or ☊ be there, she is chaste and has no Friend: After the same manner you may judge of Friends, or of the man, when the woman propounds the Question.

Has she a Lover.

Any Planet in the seventh, (so he be not the Lord of the seventh) she has one of his complexion, (if none be in the seventh, none;) thus do for the man, but have relation to the eleventh house: The Lord of the seventh void of course, she has none; or with the ☊, *idem*: the Lord of the seventh or ☽ joined to ♂, she has a Sweetheart, or one whom she is familiar with, that she does much respect, but I say not in any dishonest way.

If a Marriage shall be perfected or no.

Consider the Lord of the ascendant and the ☽, these are properly *Significators* of the *querent*; the seventh house and his Lord are for the *quesited*.

If the Lord of the ascendant or ☽ be joined to the Lord of the seventh, in any of the dignities of the Lord of the seventh, and in the ascendant, eleventh or tenth, hardly in the seventh, the *querent* shall obtain the party desired.

If both *Significators* behold each other with ✶ or △, out of the ascendant and eleventh, or ninth and seventh, or seventh and fifth houses, with or without Reception, no prohibition, frustration or abscission, or Retrogradation of the principal *Significators* intervening, the Match will be concluded if the *querent* please, (for we do suppose a freedom of will in this nature) if a □ or ♂ be between the *Significators* (and no Reception) the matter will come to nothing.

A □ aspect with Reception of *Significators*, perfects the matter, but with a little difficulty; if no Reception be, there's only hopes, no grounds whereby to judge the thing shall be effected really.

Contrary to all the rules of the *Ancients*, I have ever found, that when the Lord of the seventh has been in the ascendant, the *querent* has loved most, and when the Lord of the ascendant was in the seventh, the *quesited* loved best.

If the *Significators* aspect not one another, but some Planet transfers their influence one to another, and this with a benevolent aspect, then shall the matter be brought to pass by one signified by that Planet, whose description you may frame according to the Sign wherein he is, and his quality from the house he is Lord of: A masculine and diurnal Planet denotes a man; a feminine, nocturnal Planet, or a man of a feminine construction, & *sic e contrario*.

If a Planet transfers the *Significator's* disposition, observe who that Planet is, and to whom he commits his disposition, and whether he be not Retrograde, Combust or unfortunate or Cadent from his own house, or in the figure, or in ♂ or □

aspect to an *Infortune*, without Reception; for then if no such thing be, the matter will be effected and continue, especially if he be a *Fortune*, and the Matrimony will take well, and the people love together.

Whether the Child conceived is the Son of him who is reputed his Father.

Behold the Lord of the ascendant and the ☽, who signify the *Interrogant*; then observe the Sign of the eleventh and his Lord, these signify the issue in Conception; if these *Significators* behold one another by △ or ✳, with Reception or not, the Conception is legitimate; if they behold one another with ☐ or ☍, with mutual Reception, and perfect aspect, or the Lord of the ascendant or the ☽ in the fifth, or if the Lord of the fifth be in the ascendant, without evil aspect of the *Infortunes*, or if the *Fortunes* one or both do behold the fifth house or his Lord, the Child conceived is legitimate and true begotten, &c. but if none of these things be, but that ♄, ♂ or ☿ behold the fifth house, or Lord thereof, there may be just suspicion the Child is conceived in adultery, and the Mother was stuprated.

Of a woman living from her Husband, whether she shall ever live with him again or not, or be received into favour.

This Question will as well resolve the doubt concerning a Mistress, &c. or Sweetheart.

If the woman herself propound the Question, who is absent from her Husband or Friend, &c. *Whether she shall be received into favor or not again?*

Consider herein the Lord of the seventh, which is the ascendant of the woman in this case, for the seventh is ever given to the banished or expulsed party; see if the Lord of the seventh behold the ascendant so partilly, or with so true and good an aspect as himself does, then without doubt she shall again return and come into favour; if the Lord of the seventh behold not the ascendant, but another Planet who is not impeded, yet beholds the ascendant, the woman shall be received again by the mediation of some person who shall interpose his friendship with the Husband or Friend, and reconcile them; if none of these things be, then have recourse to the ☉, the natural *Significator* of man, or the Husband, and of ♀, the natural *Significatrix* of the woman; and if the ☉ be above the Earth, and ♀ behold the ascendant with a pleasant ✶ or △ the woman shall return to her house or Sweetheart with ease or without any great noise.

If the ☉ be under the earth, and ♀ above, and behold the ascendant with ✶ or △, the woman or wife shall be received, but with some importunity and delays, with much ado, and a great deal of labour, and all her Neighbours shall take notice of it.

If the ☽ be increasing in light, and in any good aspect to the ascendant, she shall return, but with much solicitation.

If the ☽ be decreasing in light, and in her second or last quarter, and not near the ☉ beams, but beholding the ascendant, she will return with much ease and quickly.

Behold if ♀ be Occidental, Retrograde and hastening to Combustion, then of her own accord the woman will return to her Husband, fearing by her absence she shall offend him, and she is sorry she ever departed from him; but if she be lately separated from the ☉ beams, then it repents the man that he gave occasion to his Wife to absent herself, or that he abused her; but the woman will be angry and malapert, and seems sorry that she shall return, nor will she much respect her Husband after that time.

CHAPTER L.

Of Servants fled, Beasts strayed, and things lost.

The *Signifier* of the thing lost is the ☽, wherefore if you find the ☽ applying to the Lord of the ascendant, or to the Lord of the twelfth from the ascendant, or to the Lord of the house of the ☽, the thing missing shall be found again;

This principally concerns Cattle strayed. but if the ☽ apply to none of these, nor abide in the ascendant nor in the second house, the thing lost or miscarried shall not be found: if the Lord of the house of the ☽ be in the third, or in a ✶ to the ascendant, there is some hope of finding the thing again, during that aspect with the degree ascending: And again, if he separate himself from the Lord of the twelfth, eighth, or sixth house, and apply to the degree of the house of Substance, (what aspect soever it be) there is hope to find it again; or if the Lord of the house of the ☽ do behold ☽; but if you find these Constellations contrary, judge the contrary; if the ☽ be fortunate by any of the two *Fortunes*, the thing that is lost chanced into the hands of some trusty body, which keeps the same, and would fain restore it again; or if that *Fortune* apply to the ascendant, or behold the same, or the ☽ behold the ascendant, that faithful person will restore the same again to the owner.

The place where the thing is that is lost.

The *Signifier* of the place where the thing is at time of the Question, is the place of the *Moon* according to the nature of the Sign she is in, for if the Sign be Oriental, it is in the east part; if it be Occidental, it is west, &c. Behold also the place of the *Moon* in the Figure, for if she be in the ascendant, it is in the east, &c. if the Lord of the house of the *Moon* be in human Signs, it is in a place where men use to be; if in Signs of small Beasts, as ♈ and ♑, it is where such kind of Beasts be: Also, look to the ☽, and see if she be in a fiery Sign, it is where fire is; if in a watery Sign, where water is &c. if the ☽ be with the Lord of the ascendant in one quarter, and there be not between them more than one Sign, the thing lost is in the house of him that lost it, or about it; but if there be between them more than thirty degrees, and less then seventy degrees, the thing is in the Town where the owner is, but if they be not in one quarter, it is then far from the owner.

How the things or Goods was lost.

If you will know how and in what manner they were lost, behold from whom the Lord of the ascendant did last separate, and if he did separate from ♄, the cause of the lost thing was through forgetfulness of the owner, who knows not where he laid it, or it is forgotten by reason of some cold or sickness which afflicted the loser, especially if ♄ be Retrograde, if he be separated from ♃, or in the house of ♃, then through fast or abstinence, or ordering of Laws, or by his excess of care of governing of things, or managing the affairs of the house, or else by some trust put upon him that carried it away or mislaid it.

This was Frierly Astrology and supposes somewhat lost in an Abbey or Nunnery.

If he be separated from ♂, or in the house of ♂, it was lost through fear, or by some sudden passion, provoking the loser to anger, fury, fire, or for enmity, or upon a quarrel. If from the ☉ or in his house, then by the means of the King, study of hunting or pastime, or by means of the master of the Family, or a Gentleman. If from ♀ or in her house, then by drinking, Cards or Dice, or making merry in an Alehouse or Tavern, or by pastime, or singing and dallying with women, &c. If from ☿ by reason of writing, or sending, or dictating of Letters, or going on a Message: If from the ☽, or in the house of the ☽, it was lost by too frequent use, and showing the Commodity or thing lost, or the party made it too common, or some Messenger, Widow or Servant lost the same. If the thing lost or missing be a Beast, and not a thing moveable, the signification in knowing the place, and the state thereof, is as the said significations of things not having life, but that it is needful to seek whether it fled away of itself, or some other drove him away, whether it lives or no? and to find the cause of the death of it, if it be dead.

Whether it be stolen or no.

If you would know if the Beast fled away by itself, or some body took it, behold if you find the Lord of the house of the ☽

This concerns Cattle.

separating himself from any Planet, say then, that he fled away of his own accord; but if the lord of the house of the ☽ be not separated from any Planet, but that another Planet is separating himself from him, say that some one or other took it and fled away; but if the lord of the house of the *Moon* be not in any of these two we speak of, behold what you see by the position of the Lord of the second house, and judge by him as you judged by the Lord of the house of the *Moon,* and her separation; and if you find of these two no separation, say that the Beast is still in his place, or near it, and that he fled not away.

Whether it be alive.

If you will know whether it be alive or not, behold the *Moon* and if you find her in application to the Lord of the eighth house from her, say it is dead; and if you find no such thing, behold her Lord, and if you find him applying to the Lord of the eighth house from the *Moon,* say likewise that it is dead, or it shall die very shortly; but if in none of these you find application, take the signification from the Lord of the eighth house after the same manner.

Whether the thing missing be stolen, or fled of itself.

Stolen.   If the *Significator* of the Thief be in the ascendant, or gives his virtue to the ☽, or the ☽ to him, it is stolen, or the Lord of the ascendant to the *Significator* of the Thief, or the *Signifier* of the Thief apply to the Lord of the ascendant by □ or ☍, or the ☽ by ♂, □ or ☍, or the Lord of the house of the ☽, or of her Term, or the Lord of the second house, or ⊗ or his Lord, or if any Planet be in the ascendant, and give his power to the *Signifier* of the Thief, or the *Signifier* to him by □ or ☍, if some of these constellations be not, it is not stolen, except there be an *Infortune* in the ascendant or second, or the Lord of the house of the ☽, or her Term be unfortunate, or the ⊗ or his Lord, or the Lord of the ascendant, or the Lord of the second house be unfortunate, these signify losing.

Not Stolen.   Or of you find the Lord of the house of the ☽ separating from any Planet, it is fled of its own accord; if he separate not, but some other from him, it is driven away; the like in either by the Lord of the second, if he be in no such state or position, the thing abides still, and it is not stolen.

For Beasts strayed, or Fugitives, or any thing lost.

The *Significator* is ☽, wherefore the ☽ applying to the *If found.* Lord of the ascendant, or second house, or to her Dispositor, it shall be found, otherwise not; ☽ in the ascendant, or her Dispositor in a △ or ✶, gives hopes to find it; the Dispositor of the ☽ separating from the Lord of the sixth, eighth or twelfth, and applying to the Lord of the ascendant, or to the degree of the second house, good hopes also; ☽ in aspect to her Dispositor, good; ☽ unfortunate of the Lord of the sixth, eighth, or twelfth house, it is in the hands of an ill person that will not depart from it, chiefly if the *Infortune* behold the ascendant or his Lord.

☽ Beholding ♃ or ♀, it is in the hands of an honest man *Restored.* that will restore it again; if ♃ or ♀ have any aspect to the ascendant, or ☽ apply to the ascendant; ☽ in the ascendant, it is restored with trouble or pain; or the Lord of the twelfth *Fugitive in* in the twelfth house, the Lord of the seventh in the twelfth, *restraint.* the Fugitive is imprisoned.

The place: ☽ in the tenth, it is south; in the seventh, *The place.* west; in the fourth, north; in the ascendant, east, &c. the Dispositor of the ☽ in a human Sign, it is in a place where men use; in ♋, ♏ or ♓, a place of Water or Wells; ☽ in the last face of ♑, it is amongst Ships; this must be when things are lost near a Harbour.

☽ In ♈, ♌, ♐, in a place of fire; ☽ or her Dispositor being in movable Signs, it is in a place newly broken up.

☽ Within thirty degrees of the Lord of the ascendant the *Strayed.* thing is with the Loser, or near him; ☽ more than thirty degrees from the Lord of the ascendant, it is far off; the Dispositor of the ☽ separating from another Planet, it is strayed; another Planet separating from the Dispositor of the ☽, it is stolen.

☽ Or her Dispositor applying to the Lord of the eighth, or eighth house from the ☽, it is dead or will die shortly.

☽ In the ascendant, or △ to the Lord of the ascendant; ☽ in △ to ☉, found.

The Lord of the second in the tenth or ninth, it is in the house of the *Querent*, or in the power of a familiar friend; ☉ in the ascendant (unless in ♎ or ♒) found; the Lord of the second in the eleventh or twelfth, far off.

Of Beasts or Strays.

If the Lord of the sixth be in the sixth, the Beasts be small: if the Lord of the twelfth be in the twelfth, the Beasts be great: if the Lord of the sixth be in the sixth or twelfth, they be in a Pound; if the lord of the sixth be in fiery Signs, they shall be under fetters and locks; if the Lord of the ascendant and Lord of the hour be one Planet, then it is true they are in pound; if the *Moon* be in common Signs, they are in rushy grounds; if in an angle, they be in Closes or Grounds, if in a succedent, they be within Closes, or about them, on the right hand of the owner; if the *Moon* be in a cadent house, they are in common Fields; if in ♋, where Dens and water-beasts be, or some little Rivulet, if ♒ or ♓ in watery or fishing places, or near Fishponds, in the last moiety of ♑, in a place of Ships, or some Wood or Wood-yard.

This concerns Goods immovable. Behold the Sign where the ☽ is, if in fiery Signs, in a place where fire is, or about a fire, or where fire has formerly been made; the *Moon* in watery Signs, where water is, or about waters; the *Moon* in airy Signs, in a place of many windows, or open places, as Garrets, and such like; *the *This has relation to Beasts strayed.* Moon* in earthly Signs, in an earthly place, where houses are made of earth, or near mud walls or clay; the *Moon,* or the Lord of the house where she is, be in a movable Sign, in a place new peopled, or a house new built, or where are hills, and in other places level grounds; the *Moon* in a fixed Sign, in a plain Country or champion; the *Moon* in a common Sign in a place of much water, according to the nature of the place where the thing was lost or missing.

Another Judgment

Common Signs, as Ⅱ, ♍, ♐ or ♓, do signify within the house, if it be dead things, as rings &c. but if it be quick or living things, or Cattle, it signifies watery grounds, Ditches, Pits, Rushes, a Marketplace; fixed Signs, the Goods are hid, or laid low by the earth, or near it, in walls, or in hollow Trees; movable Signs, high places, Roofs, or Ceiling of houses; watery Signs, in water, or under the earth, a Pavement, Foundations of houses, &c.

That the Beasts are lost.

The Lord of the sixth unfortunate by ♄ or ♂, the Beasts be lost, chiefly if the Lord of the sixth be cadent, or that the Cattle are driven away or stolen; if any Planet do separate from the Lord of the house of the ☽, it is driven away or sold; if the Planet separate from the Lord of the second, *idem*; if you find none of these, the Beasts are not far off.

Dead or alive.

If the ☽ apply to the Lord of the eighth, it is dead, or to the eighth house; if the Lord of the house of the ☽ apply to eighth, *idem*; or if the *Significator* of the Beast be in the eighth, in □ to any infortune in the fourth.

In Pound or not.

If the Lord of the sixth or twelfth be in the ninth or tenth, then are the Beasts with some Justice or Officer, as Bailiff or Constable, or under Lock, or are commanded to be safe kept; for the most part Lord of the twelfth or sixth in the twelfth or sixth, they are kept close.

That the Cattle shall be found again.

If the Lord of the sixth be fortunate by ♃ or ♀, and if they be found in the second, fifth or eleventh houses, the Beasts will be had again; if the Lord of the Term of the *Moon*, or the Lord of the Cusp of the fourth house be with the Lord of the ascendant, *idem*; or if the Lord of the sixth or twelfth be in △ of ☉ out of angles.

How far off a thing lost is from the owner.

The *Moon* in the same quarter with the Lord of the ascendant if there be but one Sign between them, the lost thing is in the house, or about his house that lost it; if there be more than thirty degrees to seventy, the thing lost is in the Town, and in the same limits and bounds where the owner is; and if it be not within ninety degrees, the thing lost is far distant from the owner; for usually when the *Significator* of the thing lost is in the same Quadrant, or the *Moon,* the goods are in the same Town or Hundred where the *querent* lives.

Beasts stolen or strayed.

If the Lord of the house of the *Moon,* or Lord of the second do separate from their own houses (if the goods be fixed) it is stolen; if moveable, fled of his own accord.

In what place they are.

If the Lord of the sixth be in an angle, the Beasts be of small growth and in Pounds, Closes or houses; in cadent, in a Common, and are going wayward; in succedent, in some Pasture near hand.

Which way.

If the Lord of the sixth be in fiery Signs, eastward in Woods or where Bushes, Brambles or Ferns have been burned; but in angles in fiery Signs, in Closes or Pound, or under lock.

The Lord of the sixth in earthly Signs, South on dry lands, or grounds, but if in an angle, in a Pound, or close Pound with a thing that earth is about it, *viz.* a mud wall; if succedent, it is about Closes on the right hand of the *querent.*

The Lord of the sixth in an airy Sign, they are most in plain ground, if he be in an angle, they be in Pound or housed west from the place where they were lost; In succedent, on the right hand westward; in cadent, on the left and going away-ward, *viz.* Straying further from their right Owner.

If the Lord of the sixth be in watery Signs, North, in a low place; if in an angle, in Close-ground, northward; in succedent, on the right hand of you northward; in cadent, in the Common on the left hand, where water is, or Meadows, going away-ward, or where people water their Cattle.

In what ground they be.

If the Lord of the sixth be in movable Signs, they are in hilly grounds.

If the Lord of the sixth be in fixed Signs, in plain ground where is new building, or some grounds new plowed or turned up.

Common Signs, where water is, rushy grounds, ditches.

If the Lord of the Term of the *Moon* be in a fixed Sign they are in a plain ground newly taken in, or nigh a new building.

In movable, in new land, or ground full of hills.

In common Signs, in a watery place, rushy or a marshy ground, nigh ditches and pits.

The Cattle shall to Pound.

If the *Moon* be in the twelfth, they shall be had to Pound or be pounded, what signification soever, if the *Moon* be unfortunate, they shall to Pound; if the Lord of the twelfth and principal *Significator* be unfortunate, they shall to pound, or be kept obscurely in some private or close place.

Long in Pound.

If ♄ be in the twelfth, or in the first (when the *querent* comes to know of you what is become of the Cattle) or the *Moon* in the twelfth, any of them unfortunate, than shall they be long in pound; if ♂ aspect ♄ or the *Moon* in the twelfth, with ♂, □ or ☍, they will be killed in Pound, or die there, or be very near starving.

From hence the movable, fixed or common Signs may easily

be known, when Sheep be stolen, whether and where they are killed or not? if ♄ be in the ascendant, fourth, eighth or twelfth, long in pound.

Escape the Pound.

If the Lord of the ascendant be in a movable Sign, in the third, ninth or tenth, they shall escape Pound; if the Lord of the ascendant be in the twelfth, though good, yet sick and ill in Pound.

If the Lord of the ascendant be in the eighth, it's probable they die in pound.

If the principal *Significator* of the ascendant be Retrograde they die in Pound.

If the Lord of the sixth behold the Lord of the ascendant with ✶ or △, they will be had again; if he behold him with ☐ or ☍, then they will be stopped: if he behold the *Moon* or the Lord of the house of the *Moon,* with ✶ or △, had again; with ☐ or ☍, stopped or stayed in some Village or Town.

Whether the Fugitive shall be taken.

Give the ascendant and his Lord and the ☉ to the *Querent,* and the seventh and his Lord to the *Fugitive* or thing asked for, and behold what aspect is between them, and so judge; for if the Lord of the ascendant apply to the Lord of the seventh with ♂, ✶ or △, or that the Lord of the ascendant be in the seventh, it betokens the *Querent* shall recover the things lost or Fugitive, gone away. Also, if the Lord of the seventh be in the ascendant, or apply to the Lord thereof, or there be any translation of light between them, it shows the same with more facility.

Of the Moon.

For Fugitives, have respect to the *Moon,* being natural Significatrix of them, by reason of her quick motion, for if she be in the ascendant, or apply to the lord thereof with a good aspect, or that the lord of the seventh or the *Moon* separate from the *Fortunes,* and be immediately conjoined to the *Infortunes,* all these show, that the Fugitive shall return and be recovered, or shall be so hindered, that he shall come again.

The ☽ increasing in light and number, he shall be long in search; decreasing, soon found, and with less labour: also, the ☽ separating from the Lord of the seventh, and joined with the Lord of the ascendant, the *Fugitive* is sorry he went, and will send some to entreat for him; the Lord of the seventh Combust, signifies the *Fugitive* will be taken, willy-nilly; behold in what quarter the ☽ is, that way the *Fugitive* draws, or intends to go.

Whether he shall be taken.

The Lord of the seventh joined to an *Infortune* in an angle, upon good search, the *Fugitive* will be taken; but if both be not in an angle, he shall be detained or stayed by the way, but not imprisoned; if the Lord of the ascendant behold that *Infortune* who afflicts the *Fugitive*, the *querent* shall find the *Fugitive* detained by someone, to whom he ought to give money, or who will demand money before he do restore the *Fugitive* to him: if the *Infortune* be in the ninth, he shall be stayed in his journey and taken; the Lord of the seventh with a Planet stationary, in his first or second station, in an angle or succedent, he knows not which way to fly but shall be taken.

If a Fugitive shall be found, or come again.

If the Lord of the seventh be in the ascendant, the *Fugitive* will return of his own accord; ☽ separating from the Lord of the ascendant, and joined immediately to the Lord of the seventh house, or to the seventh house, one will shortly bring news of him; the Lord of the seventh combust, or entering combustion, the *Fugitive* shall be found (*volens, nolens*;) the ☽ separating from the Lord of the seventh, and joined immediately to the ascendant, or Lord thereof, the *Fugitive* repents his departure, and will send some to entreat for him; ☽ joined to *Infortunes*, viz. ♄, ♂ or ☋, or to a Planet Retrograde, he shall be found or come again, and has endured much misery since his departure; the Lord of the seventh beholding an

Infortune from the seventh, the *querent* shall find him that is fled with some to whom he must give money before he can have him; ☽ separating from ♃ or ♀, he shall quickly come back again, or, a thing lost shall suddenly be found; ☽ aspecting her own house with ⚹ or △, the *Fugitive* returns within three days; or, according to probability, the *querent* shall hear where he is within three days, if the distance be not too great.

Distance.

Behold the Lord of the seventh, and the Lord of the hour, and look how many degrees are between them, so many miles he is off from the place he went from.

The former rule I do conceive not so perfect as this which follows; see what distance there is between the ☽ and *Significator, viz.* their aspect and what Signs they are in; give for every degree in a movable Sign seventeen houses or Furlongs, at discretion; in common Signs, give for every degree five Furlongs or distance of five houses; in fixed Signs, for every degree give one Furlong, or one house, &c. having relation to the thing lost, and whether it be in a Town, or in the Fields.

Of a Woman flying from her Husband.

The ☉ under the earth, ♀ Occidental and Retrograde, she will return of her own will; ♀ Oriental, she comes, but not willingly; Lord of the ascendant, the ☽, and Lord of the seventh in △, she returns, with a □ or ☍ without Reception, never; ♂ in an angle, and giving the ☽ strength, and the ascendant movable, they shall be contented to be separated forever.

Of a Thief and Theft.

Haly says, you must know that the ascendant is the *Significator* of the *querent*, the Lord of the second is *Significator* of the thing that is stolen or taken away, and the seventh house is the *Significator* of the *Thief*, if there be no peregrine Planet in an angle or second house; the tenth house is the *Signifier* of the

King, and the Sign of the fourth the *Signifier* of the place where the thing is, that is, or was taken away; whose proper significations you must know from the Lords of those houses, whereby you may know the condition and state of what is missing, and if you find in the ascendant a Planet peregrine, put him as the *Significator* of the *Thief*, and especially if he be Lord of the seventh house; but if no Planet be in the ascendant, look if there be any in the other angles, and give him to be *Signifier* of the *Thief*.

This shall be more copiously handled in some Chapter following. A most certain rule.

Of the SIGNIFICATOR *of the Thief.*

The Lord of the seventh commonly signifies the *Thief*, but especially if he be peregrine in the ascendant, or in any other angle; but if he be not so, then behold if any other Planet be peregrine in any of the angles, call him the *Thief*; if none be peregrine in any of the angles, take the Lord of the hour, and call him the *Thief*, and if it happen that the Lord of the hour be Lord of the seventh, then it is more radical; if the Lord of the seventh be in the ascendant, the *querent* is Thief; this will hold where just suspicion is made of the *querent's* fidelity, or most cause above all others, whose complexion and condition is according to the Planet, Lord of the seventh, and Sign thereof.

*A Planet is then peregrine when he is neither in his House, Triplicity, Term, Exaltation or Face.
I rather and more assuredly prefer the Lord of the seventh, as more rational and consentanious to reason.*

The SIGNIFICATOR *of the thing stolen.*

*The *Significator* of the thing stolen is the Lord of the Term the ☽ is in; when thou hast found the *Significator* of the *Thief*, and understand the nature of his disposition by the significant Planet and his aspects, know that the ascendant is *Signifier* of the *question*, or *Demandant*, and if thou see the Lord of the ascendant draw towards the Lord of the seventh, or to the Lord of the hour, or be in the seventh, it signifies that the Thief shall be taken anon after, or it gives hopes of discovery of the thing lost.

*This rule is vulgar, and not of any credit.

Of THEFTS.

The first house, which is the ascendant, is for the *querent*, and his Lord for him that has lost the Goods, and signifies the place from whence the Goods was taken; the seventh house and his Lord, and the peregrine Planet in an angle, and the Lord of the hour, signifies the Thief, or party that took away the Goods.

The second house and the Lord of the second house and the ☽, shall signify the Goods or thing that is lost, stolen or missing; the fourth house and his Lord shall signify the place where it is laid, put or done, or conveyed to, and is in at that instant of time.

The aspects of the ☉ and ☽, of the Lord of the ascendant, of the Lord of the second house, and of the Lord of the house of the ☽, to the lord of the ascendant, and their application and aspects one to another, shall tell and show whether the Goods shall be found or had again or not: If the lord of the second and the ☽ be in the seventh, in the Sign of the seventh, and the Lord of the seventh house behold them both by △ or ✶ aspect (though long out, *viz.* if the aspect be by many degrees distance) then is the Goods taken away by somebody, *viz.* they are not simply lost: if the ☽ be *Lady* of the second, and in the house of the lord of the hour, going to ♂ of the lord of the seventh house, then has the party lost the thing or Goods in some place where he was, and has forgot it, and it is neither lost nor stolen, but carelessly mislaid.

If the ☽ be Lady of the ascendant, and in the fourth, and the Lord of the second in the seventh, or in the sign of the eighth house, in a ✶ or △ to the second house, at a ✶ or △ to the ☽, the thing is not stolen, but taken away in jest.

If the ☽ be Lady of the ascendant, and in the ascendant, not far remote, and the ☉ Lord of the second in the tenth with the Lord of the seventh house, and the Lord of the seventh oppress the ☽ with a □, then is the Goods stolen and taken away; if the ☽ be in the third, oppressed with the Lord of the seventh house by his □ aspect, and Lord of the second also being Lord of the ascendant, and in the seventh, in the Sign of the seventh, then it is stolen, but first it was taken in jest, and it will be hard to get it again, except the ☉ and ☽ behold the ascendant.

If ☽ be in the seventh in the Sign of the Lord of the hour, the Lord of the hour being Lord of the seventh, then is the Goods not stolen or taken away, but overlooked and mistaken. If ☽ be in the fifth house and in ♑, and be Lady of the hour, and ♀ Lady of the second in the tenth, in the Sign of the tenth, and ☽ in ☍ to the Lord of the seventh, then has the party lost the Goods as he went by the way, or was in someplace where he left them: If the ☽ be Lady of the hour, in ♋, in the eighth, and the Lord of the second in the fifth, and neither of them behold the Lord of the seventh, but the Lord of the seventh be in the seventh, then is the Goods taken away in jest by the Master of the house, and he will deny it: If the ☽ be lady of the hour in the fourth, in ☍ to the lord of the seventh, and the lord of the second in the twelfth, in a ⚹ to the lord of the seventh, then has somebody taken the things away in jest: If ☽ be in the Sign of the lord of the seventh, and not beholding the lord of the seventh, but ☽ in the twelfth, and lord of the second in the sixth, then is the Goods taken away in jest, if the lord of the second did last separate from the lord of the house of the ☽, then the Goods is stolen in jest, but will scant be had again. If the ☽ do separate from the lord of the second by □, the Goods is taken away and stolen by somebody: sometimes the ☽ is lady of the second and does separate from the lord of the house wherein she is, then it is stolen: If the lord of the ascendant do separate from ♃, or from the lord of the second house, then did the *Querent* lay it down and forget it, and so it was lost: but when the lord of the ascendant and lord of the second do separate from ♃, it is the surer: and sometimes it falls out, that the ☽ is *Lady* of the ascendant, and separates from ♃, and does apply to the lord of the second house, which did also last separate from ♃, and sometimes the lord of the ascendant, as ☉ is also lord of the second, and does separate from ♃, yet if it be so, it gives all one judgment as aforesaid: If the lord of the second or ♃ do separate from the lord of the ascendant, then did the party lose the Goods by the way as he went, or in some place where he was, or else it tumbled out of his pocket privily into some secret place where it is not stolen or found: But if there be none of these separations aforesaid, then see if the peregrine Planet or lord of the seventh or ☿, who is also for the Thief, do apply to ♃, or the lord of the second; if they do, then is the Goods absolutely stolen, and the Thief came with intent for to steal: If the lord of the second or ♃ do apply to the peregrine Planet, or to the lord of the seventh, or to ☿, who is for the Thief, then the Goods or the thing lost did offer itself to the Thief, or he came easily by them without trouble; for he that stole them, came not with intent for to have stolen it, but seeing the thing did lie so open, and so carelessly, he took it and carried it away. If the ☽ be lady of the ascendant, and also lady of the second, and be in ♉, and apply by ♂ to the ☉, within one degree, and ☉ be the Lord of the third house, and ♂ be the peregrine Planet, and in the tenth, and ☿ apply to ♂, none of the abovesaid separations or applications impeding, or the lord of the seventh in the third, then the *Querent* did lose the thing by the way as he went, and it is not stolen from him.

Whether it be stolen or no.

For this, behold if the *Signifier* of the Thief be in the ascendant, or give his virtue to the ☽ or the ☽ to him, it is stolen; if the lord of the ascendant give his virtue to the *Signifier* of the Thief, it is stolen; if the *Signifier* behold the lord of the ascendant by □ or ☍, or the ☽ by ♂, □ or ☍, or the lord of the house of the *Moon*, or the lord of the Term of the *Moon*, or the lord of the second house, or the ⊗ or his lord, the thing is stolen.

And if any Planet be in the ascendant, and give his power to the *Signifier* of the Thief, or the *Significator* to him by □ or ☍, it is stolen: and if some of these constellations be not, the thing is not stolen, except there be an *Infortune* in the ascendant or second house, or the Lord of the house of the *Moon*, or of the Term of the *Moon* is unfortunate, or the ⊗ or his lord be unfortunate, or the lord of the ascendant, or the lord of the second house be unfortunate, all these signify loss or losing.

That the Goods are stolen.

If any Planet be in the ascendant peregrine, it is stolen; or the peregrine Planet give virtue to the ☽, or the ☽ to him, it is stolen; the Lord of the ascendant peregrine, it is stolen; if the Thief be peregrine, that is, if he have no dignities where he is, it is stolen; if the *Significator* be with the Lord of the ascendant or in ☐ or ☍ to the Lord of the ascendant, it is stolen.

If any Planet do separate from the Lord of the house of the ☽, it is stolen; if any Planet have respect to the Lord of the Term of the ☽, with ♂, ☐ or ☍, it is stolen: if any Planet be separate from the Lord of the house of Substance, it is taken away: if the Thief have respect to the Lord of the house of the ☽, with ♂, ☐ or ☍, it is taken away.

Not stolen.

If neither the Lord of the house of the *Moon* or lord of the second separate not themselves from one another, or any other Planet from them, then what you look for is in his own place; if the *Moon* give virtue to ♄ or ♂, or to any Planet in cadent houses, or to the Lord of the eighth, not stole, but missing, or else negligently thrown aside.

It will be (or is intended to be stolen.)

If the *Moon* be lady of the seventh, and give her virtue to a Planet in the second, or in the eleventh or fifth, having herself neither ⚹ or △ to the cusps of the houses, or if any Planet in the seventh give virtue to a Planet in the second, fifth or eleventh, and have no ⚹ or △ to the Planet in the seventh, it will be, or if the Lord of the tenth be in ♂, ☐ or ☍ with the Thief, it will be stolen.

It is Lost or Stolen.

If a Planet do separate himself from the lord of the house of the ☽, or from the Lord of the second, then it is taken away with hands and stolen: If the ☽ be Lady of the seventh, and give virtue to the Lord of the ascendant, it is stolen: if the Lord of the ascendant give virtue to the *Moon* in the seventh, it is stolen.

If any Planet in the ascendant give virtue to the *Signifier* of the Thief, it is stolen, or the Thief to the Lord of the ascendant, it's stolen, but the Thief gives so much of the Goods to the owner again, according to the virtue or light that the Thief gives to the Lord of the ascendant; if any Planet in the ascendant be peregrine, it is stolen, and the Thief shall escape.

If the peregrine Planet give virtue to the *Moon,* or the *Moon* to him, if the Thief aspect the *Moon* with ♂, □ or ☍, or aspect the Lord of the Term of the *Moon,* it is stolen.

If the ☽ give virtue to ♄ or ♂, or if she give virtue to any Planet in a cadent house, or if the *Moon* give virtue to the Lord of the eighth, and he in a movable Sign, the things are stolen, but in fixed Signs, taken away.

If the Lord of the house of the *Moon* separate from any Planet, or the Lord of the second do separate from any Planet, stolen.

If the Lord of the house of the *Moon* or second be in his own house, and have virtue of ♄ or ♂, gone away by itself, and not stolen.

Of the age of the Thief.

The age is taken from the Planet that is *Significator* of the Thief, if he be Oriental, he is young; in the midst of his Orientality, then of middle age; if he be in the end of his Orientality, he is old, says *Haly.*

To judge by the distance of the Planets from the ☉, for by the ☉ the Planets are Oriental and Occidental, by which the signification of age is taken, after *Haly,* and other Writers.

If together with this, you consider in what degrees of the Sign the *Significator* is in, you shall do better, for a Planet Oriental and in a few degrees, denotes youth, or younger; in more degrees, more age; frame the age according to an exact mixture.

If ♄, ♃ or ☌ be significators, then behold the distance of them from the ☉; from their ☌ with the ☉ to the □ aspect, signifies the age of 18 years, and the nearer the ☉ the lesser in age, and from the □ to the ☍ signifies the age of 36. From the ☍ to the next □ signifies the age of 45. From that last □ to the ☌ signifies the age of 72. And so to the end of life.

Guido Bonatus says, the ☉ being significator, and being between the ascendant and Midheaven or tenth house (which is all one) signifies the thief to be young, and so increasing till he come to the angle of the earth.

And if ♀ or ☿ be significators, the age is taken by their distance or elongation from the ☉, from their ☌ with the ☉, being direct to the midway of their ☌ in their Retrogradation, signifies the age of the thief to be about 18, and the nearer the ☉ the younger, and from the midway to their ☌ in their Retrogradation, signifies the age of 36, or near that age, the nearer to the ☌ the elder, and from the ☌ in the Retrogradation, to the midway of their ☌ in the direction, signifies the age of 45, and from the midway to their ☌ in direction, signifies the age of 72, and so to the end of life; and if the ☽ be signifier judge as by ♄, ♃ and ♂, as before is said.

The same *Guido* says, ♀ signifies the thief to be young, a woman or a Maid, ☿ of less age than ♀, ♂ signifies full age, or in prime of his youth, ♃ more of years than ♂, and ♄ signifies old age or decrepit, or well in years, the ☉ signifies as before said; the ☽ being significatrix in the beginning of the Month to the first quarter, signifies to be young; and if she be near to the full ☽, it signifies the middle age or perfect man; and if she be in the end of the Month, it signifies the Thief to be aged, or of greater years.

The age of the Thief.

If the ☽ increase, he is young; if decrease he is old; if the significator be in the house of ♄, or aspected by him, or in the last degrees of a Sign, it signifies old age; ♄ signifies the same; ♂, ☉, ♀, ☿ from the Ascendant to the tenth, signify young years, especially if they be in the beginning of Signs: from the tenth to the seventh, middle years; if the significator be a superior Planet and direct, then he is of good years, if Retrograde elder or very old, and so judge of inferior Planets; for if they be Retrograde or joined to Planets Retrograde, it augments the age: thus if you mingle your signification, you may the better judge. The ☉ between the Ascendant and midheaven argues a child, between the *Meridian* and *Occident*, accuses a young Man, between the *Occident* and *Septentrional angle*, a Man grown; and from the *Septentrional* to *Oriental*, accuses a very old Man; Lord of the ascendant in the East quarter, or ☽ in the Ascendant, a young Man; ☿ always signifies a Child or a young Man, especially being in the *Ascendant* and *Oriental*: any Planet, except ♄, signifies young Men; or if the signifier be joined to ♀, ☽ increasing in light, or in the first ten degrees or middle of the Sign, or the significator in the beginning of the *Oriental* quarter, signifies a Child, or a young Man, or Woman, &c.

Whether the Thief be a Man or Woman.

Behold the Sign ascending and the Lord of the hour; if both be Masculine, the Thief is Masculine; and if the Lord of the hour and Ascendant be both Feminine, the Thief is Feminine; if the Sign Ascending be Masculine, and the Lord of the hour Feminine, it is both Masculine and Feminine, *viz.* there were two Thieves, both a Man and a Woman.

Also the Significator Masculine and ☽ in a Masculine Sign, signifies a Man-kind, *& e contra*. If the Lord of the Ascendant and the Lord of the hour be both in the Ascendant in Masculine Signs, it is a Man; in Feminine Signs, a Woman.

If the Lord of the Ascendant and the Lord of the hour be the one in a Masculine, and the other in a Feminine Sign, both a Man and a Woman had a hand in the Theft.

The Angles of the Figure Masculine, a Man; Feminine, a Woman.

♀ Significatrix aspecting ♂ with □, notes impediment in hearing, principally in the left ear.

♀, ☿, ☾ denotes Women, ♄, ♃, ♂ and ☉ Men; respecting the Sign and quarter wherein they be.

If one Thief or more.

Behold the Significator of the Thief; if he be in a fixed Sign, and of direct Ascensions, or a Sign of few Children, or of few shapes and likeness; it signifies to be one and no more. If the Sign be of two bodies, *viz.* a common or bicorporeal Sign, it signifies more than one, and more likely if there be in the Sign many Planets peregrine: also when the ☉ and ☾ behold themselves by a □ in the Angles, it signifies more than one: Signs that signify many Children are ♋, ♏ and ♓; few Children are ♈, ♉, ♎, ♐, ♑ and ♒. Divers shapes or forms, ♊, ♋, ♐, ♒: barren Signs are ♊, ♌ and ♍; Signs of direct Ascensions ♋, ♌, ♍, ♎, ♏ and ♐; Signs of oblique Ascensions are ♑, ♒, ♓, ♈, ♉, ♊. If the ☾ in the hour of the Question be in the Angle of the Earth, in a common Sign, there is more than one; if she be in any of the other Angles, in a fixed Sign, there is but one Thief. Look how many Planets are with the Thieves' significator, so many Thieves; the ☾ in a common Sign more than one. Lord of the Ascendant in a Male Sign, and Lord of the hour in a Female, Man and Woman (as aforesaid;) look to which the ☾ does agree, *viz.* to whom she applies, that person is the principal actor; the Angles moveable especially the first and seventh, or the Significator being in ♋, ♏ or ♓, more than one. The Sign wherein the significator of the Thief is in, if it be immoveable, or a double bodied Sign, more than one. Both the Luminaries beholding one another from Angles, more than one; ☾ in the Ascendant, and it a double bodied Sign, does demonstrate there were more Thieves than one.

Of the Clothes of the Thief.

You must know the colour of the Clothing by the Planets, Signs and degrees, and the House the Significator is in; and after the mixture the one with the other, accordingly judge the colour of their Clothes. If there be signification of many Thieves, judge them by the Lord of the triplicity the significators are in. The Significators of the Colours of the Planets after *Alcabitius* are these, ♄ Black, ♃ Green, Spotted, or Ashy, or such like; ♂ Red; ☉ Tawny or Saffron, I rather conceive an high Sandy colour. The Colours by mixing the Planets one with another are these; ♄ and ♃, a dark Green, or deep spotted with Black; ♄ and ♂ a dark Tawny, ♄ and ☉ a Black-yellow and shining, ♄ and ♀ a White gray, ♄ and ☿ a Black or Bluish, ♄ and ☽ a deep Tawny, or deep Gray or Russet. ♃ and ♂ a Tawny, somewhat light spotted, ♃ and ☉ much after the mixture of the *Sun* and *Mars* but more shining, ♃ and ♀ a Greenish-gray, ♃ and ☿ a Spotted Green, ♃ and ☽ somewhat a high Green. ♂ and ☉ a deep Red shining, ♂ and ♀ a light Red or Crimson, ♂ and ☿ a Red or a red Tawny, ♂ and the ☽ a Tawny or light Red.

They who are conversant in judging many Thefts might much perfect this judgment; I have known it hold true very many times; my greater employments keeps me from further observations.

You must mix the colour of the Signifier with the colour of the House he is in, and thereafter judge the colour of their Clothes; or judge the Colour by the Signs and the Degrees the Signifier is in; as if he be in the Sign, or House, or Term of ♄, judge after ♄ as before; and if he be in the House of ♄ and Term of ♃, judge after the mixture of ♄ and ♃, and so of all other as before.

For Names.

♃, ☉ and ♂ in Angles signify short Names and of few Syllables, and being near the Midheaven do begin with A or E: ♄ or ♀ Significator, the Name is of more Syllables, as *Richard* or *William*, for the most part if the Querent's Names be short, so is also the Quesited.

Names of Thieves or Men, as Astrologers write.

To know the Names by the Lord of the seventh house; or the Planet in the seventh House, or the Planet joined with them, as follows:

Men's names

The principal Significator	The Planet joined	
☿	♂	Matthew
☽	☿	Simon
☉	♃	Laurence
☿	☉	Clement
☿	♄	Edmund
♃	☉	John
♄	♀	William
♂	☉	Robert
♂	☉	Peter
♂		Anthony
☉	☿	Benjamin
♃	♄	Thomas
☉		Roger
☉		Phillip
♄	☉	George
☉	♄	Andrew
☽	☉	Henry
☽	♄	Nicholas
♃	☉	Richard
☉		James
☉		Stephen

Women's Names

The Significator	The Planets	conjoined	
♂	☿		Katherine
☿	♂	☉	Christine
♄	☽	♀	Joane
♀	♄		Isabel
♄	☉		Elizabeth
♄	☉		Julianne
☽	♂	☉	Mary
☽	♀		Ellen
♀	☿		Agnes
☉	☿		Margaret
☉	♀		Alice
☉	☿		Edith
☉	♀		Maud
☉	♃		Lucy
☉			Anne
♃			Rachel
☽			Nell, Eleanor

Some modern Professors, have endeavoured to give a probable conjecture what Christian name the Thief is of, or party inquired after, whether man or woman. First, they consider if the Planet who is principal *Significator* of the party inquired of, whether he be angular or no, and then whether he be in aspect (it matters not what aspect, good or ill) with any Planet or Planets: if he be in no aspect, then in whose Dignities he is, and from hence they make their mixture; for example; let us admit ☿ to be Lord of the seventh, and *Significator* of a Maid's Lover and he in aspect, or in the dignities of ♂, I shall then have recourse to the Table before, and there I find in the first line over against ☿ and ♂ *Matthew*, I shall then say the man's name is *Matthew*, or of a name equivalent in length, or same number of letters: for my part I never use this way, nor yet have much credited it; yet I believe, were it well practiced we might find out very pretty conclusions, and go near to find the very name, or somewhat near it.

Whether the Thief be of the house or not.

If both the Lights behold the ascendant, or be in their own houses, the Thief is one of the Family, the Lord of the seventh in the ascendant, *idem*; the Lord of the sixth in the second, it is a Servant; if either of the *Luminaries* behold the ascendant, it is no stranger; ☉ opposite to the ascendant, it is an overthwart Neighbour; the Lord of the seventh beholding the ascendant with a friendly aspect, *idem*.

A Stranger or Familiar.

☉ and ☽ beholding the ascendant or the Lord of the ascendant in the first, or joined to the Lord of the seventh, it is one of the house, or one that frequents the house; the *Luminaries* in their proper houses, or in the house of the Lord of the ascendant, the same; in the Triplicity of the Lord of the ascendant, a Neighbour; in the Terms of him, a Familiar; ☽ in the ninth in ♂, □ or ☍ to ♄ or ♂, brings back the Thief; without fail if they be Retrograde.

Another.

If the ☉ and ☽ aspect the Lord of the ascendant, and not the ascendant, the Thief is known to the owner; the *Significator* of the Thief strong in the ascendant, notes a Brother or Kinsman; *Zael*, Lord of the seventh in the ninth from his own house, it is a Stranger; ☉ and ☽ beholding each other, a Kinsman; the Lord of the ascendant in the third or fourth, accuses thine own household-Servant; this I have oft proved true by experience.

Rules by the Lord of the seventh house.

The Lord of the seventh in the ascendant or fourth, notes one of the house, or of the household, or frequenting the house, and is in the City or Town, and is one whom the *querent* least mistrusts, and one which will hardly confess the fact.

The Lord of the seventh in the second, notes one of the household, or an acquaintance (if it be in a masculine Sign,) but if it be in a feminine Sign, it is his Wife, perhaps a Sweetheart or Maid of the house, and is within the power of the Loser, or some of his house, and may be recovered by money.

The Lord of the seventh in the third, one of the Kindred, Brother, Sisters, Cousins, or his only Fellow by way of service, or some Neighbour often in his sight, or his Disciple, Messenger or Servant, &c.

The Lord of the seventh in the fourth, it is his Father, or some old Body, or of his Father's Kin, or one dwelling in the Heritage or house of his Father, and the Thief has given it to his Wife, or the woman to her Husband, or it is the good man or good Wife of the house, or else he is a Tiller or Labourer of the Land for the *querent*.

The Lord of the seventh in the fifth, the Son or Daughter of him, or the Son or Daughter of his Cousin or Nephew, (if the Sign be a masculine) or of the household of his Father, or else his very Friend.

The Lord of the seventh in the sixth, A Servant, a Disciple or Labourer to the *querent*, or one conversant with some Churchman, a Brother or Sister of the Father, a sick body or unsteadfast, or grieved person.

The Lord of the seventh in the seventh, his Wife or Lady, or a Harlot, or a woman that used to be suspected for such matters, or a Buyer or Seller in Markets; if it be a feminine Sign, the Taker is an utter enemy to the Loser, by some cause formerly happened between them, and dwells somewhat far from him, and the things are in his custody still, and hard to be recovered. *This must be warily understood.*

The Lord of the seventh in the eighth, a Stranger, yet seems to be one of the household, or one of his open enemies, or of his near Kinswoman, for some cause of offence done, or some evil disposed person (and of the Livery of the Man) and he used to come to his House, and either is kept by him, or else does some servile acts, as a Butcher or Labourer does, otherwhiles to kill Cattle, and it seems the thing lost will not be had again but by either fair words, or dread of death, or by reason of some threats, or else the thing is lost by some Man absent, the which is not now had in the mind at this time, but seems to be quite forgotten.

The Lord of the seventh in the ninth, an honest person, a Clerk, or a Churchman, and the Thief is out of the way or Country, a Disciple, or Governor to some Master of some privileged Place, or a poor vagrant person, hard to be recovered but by some religious person as aforesaid.

I ever find it to signify one lodging in the House, when the thing was lost, or using the House. The Lord of the seventh in the tenth, a Lord, or Master, or Governor in the King's House, or of his Household; or some Lady or Gentlewoman, if the Figure be Feminine, & *e contra*; or some crafts-Master; usually it's some person that lives handsomely, and is not necessitated to this course of life.

The Lord of the seventh in the eleventh, a Friend or one known by some service done; or of the household of some man of the Church, or Neighbour, or Servant in the place where the Querent has some Lordship, and is put in trust, or is of the Household of the Querent his Mother, and by such a one or his means to be recovered again.

The Lord of the seventh in the twelfth, a Stranger, envious a false person, and enthralled, encumbered or oppressed with poverty, and has no riches; wherefore he has visited many Regions, as some Enemy or Beggar does, and he joys in it; judge his quality by the Sign and Place, and co-mix all these with the other testimonies of the Signs and Planets.

Whether the Thief be in the Town or no.

Behold the Significator of the Thief, if thou find him in the end of the Sign direct, or separating from Combustion, or applying to a Planet in the third or ninth House; say, he is gone or going out of the Town, for the removing of the *Significator* out of one Sign into another, denotes change of Lodging or removing; if it be a superior Planet, the rule is infallible.

If the Lord of the ascendant and the ☽ be not in one quarter but above ninety degrees asunder, it notes departure, or a great distance between the Goods and the Owner; but if they be in angles, and applying to Planets in angles, it notes no far distance, especially if the ☽ and the Lord of the ascendant be in one quarter.

Distance between the Owner and the Thief.

If the Thief, *viz.* his *Significator*, be in a fixed Sign, account for every house between the Lord of the ascendant and him, three miles; in common Signs, every house between the ascendant and Thief, one mile; in movable Signs, for every house between the ascendant and the Thief, account that so many houses on the earth are between the Loser and the Thief. *These judgments best agree from the Country.*

If the Sign ascending be a fixed Sign, for every house give three miles; if a common Sign, then for every house give one mile; if a movable Sign, for every house reckon one half mile.

If his *Significator* be in an angle, he is still in the Town; in a succedent, not far off, in a cadent he is far gone.

Where the Thief is.

☽ In an angle, at home; succedent, about home; if in cadent, far from home. *These are still for the Country.*

The *Significator* of the Thief in an angle, in a house; ☽ in an angle, in his own house; in a succedent, he is in Closes; ☽ in a succedent, in his own Closes.

The *Significator* of the Thief in a cadent house, he is in a Common; ☽ in a cadent, in his own Common, or that which belongs to the Town he lives in.

If the *Signifier* of the Thief be within thirty degrees of the Lord of the ascendant, then is the Thief near him that lost the

Goods; if within seventy degrees, within the Town or Parish of him that lost the Goods, the more degrees between them, the farther off they are from each other.

If the *Significator* be in a ☐ aspect to the Lord of the ascendant, he is out of the Town; if the Lord of the seventh be strong, & in an angle, the Thief is not yet gone out of the Town or Parish where the Theft was acted; if he be found weak in an angle, he is gone, or departing.

Another.

It sometimes holds true, the Lord of the seventh in the ascendant, the Thief brings the Goods home willingly. If the Lord of the seventh be in the ascendant, tell the *Querent* the Thief will be at home (before him) or before he get home, *probatum est.*

If the Lord of the seventh be in the seventh, he is hid at home and dare not be seen.

If the Lord of the sixth be in the first, or second with any of their Lords, the Thief is of the house of the *Querent.*

If the Lord of the ascendant and the *Significator* of the Thief be together, the Thief is with the *Querent, probatum est*; the very truth is, he cannot be far from him.

Towards what part the Thief is gone.

These things shall be more fully explicated in the succeeding sheet. If you would know to what part he is fled, after he is gone out of Town, behold the Planet that signifies his going out of Town, and in what Sign he is; and if he be in a fiery Sign, say he is in the east part of the Town or Country; if he be in a watery Sign, he is in the North; if in an Airy Sign, he is in the west; if in an earthly Sign, he is in the south: Behold also in what quarter of Heaven he is in, and judge accordingly; if the *Signifier* be in the west, he is in the west; the east part is from the Midheaven to the ascendant, &c. mix the signification of the Sign with the signification of the quarter, and thereafter judge, preferring the Sign before the quarter, only making use of the quarter to balance your judgment when other testimonies are equal.

Which way the Thief is gone.

Behold the significant Planet, in what Sign he is, and also the quarter, and accordingly judge; others judge by the place of the ☽; others behold the Lord of the seventh, and the Lord of the hour, what Sign and quarter they are in, and if they agree, then they judge thereafter; others regard the *Significator* to whom he does apply, or render his power; others by the Lord of the fourth, I always judge by the strongest, either of the *Significator* or the ☽.

If the *Significator* of the Thief be in a fiery Sign, he went east; earthly, south; airy, west; watery, north; see what angle ☽ is in, there is the Thief; in no angle, look for the Lord of the house of the ☽, to that part he went.

See what Sign the Lord of the seventh is in; if in ♈, eastward; in ♉, in the South against the east; and so of the rest.

The peculiar quarter of heaven every Sign naturally signify does follow hereafter.

Of the house of the Thief, and the mark thereof.

If you will know the quality of the house the thing lost is in, and the sign and token thereof, and in what place the thing is, behold the Sign the *Significator* of the Thief is in, and in what part of heaven he is, and say in that part of the Town the thing is; if it be in the ascendant, it is in the point of the east; in the seventh, just in the west; in the fourth, just in the north; in the tenth, it is south; and if it be between these angles, judge accordingly; as southwest or northwest; give the place of the ☉ to be the house the Thief is in, and the place of the ☽ to be the door of the house; if the ☉ be in an Oriental Sign, the house is in the east part from the Master, or from him that lost the Goods.

The Door of the house.

To know in what part of the house the Door is, behold the place the ☽ is in, whether in the angles, succedents or cadents, and judge as it is said in the parts of the house, the which part is taken of or from the Sign the ☽ is in one way; if the ☽ be in a fixed Sign, say the house has but one door; in a movable Sign, say the door is high above the earth, and it may be there is one other little one; and if ♄ have any aspect to that Sign, the door has been broken and after mended again, or else it is black or very old.

If ♂ have any aspect thereunto, the gate or door shall have some token of burning or fire; and if ♄ and ♂ have a *Or is well* friendly aspect to the same Sign, the gate is Iron, or most *Barred* part of it, or a good strong one; and if the ☽ be unfortunate, *with Iron.* the gate or door is broken or bruised; and if the ☽ have small light, the house has no door opening to the highway, but opens on the back part of the house.

Tokens of the Thief's house.

If the ☽ be in □, ♂, or ☍ to ♂, the door is burned with iron, fire or candle, or has been cut with some iron instrument; if the ☽ be in △ or ✶ to ♂, say the door of the Thief's house is mended with iron; if the ☽ be but newly increased in light, his gate or door is part under the earth, or under a Bank side, or they go down by a step, ☽ in a fixed or movable Sign, he has but one door outwardly, in common Signs more than one.

Or men ☽ In a fixed Sign, the gate is under the earth, *viz.* if in *go down* ♉, or the house stands on the Bank-side, if in ♒; ☽ in *by steps.* movable Signs, the gate or door is above the earth, and a step to go up into it (*probatum est.*) or one ascends somewhat in going into the house.

☽ Infortunate, the gate is broken, and note what part of heaven ☽ is in, that part of the house the door stands in; if ♄ aspect the ☽ with ♂, □ or ☍, the door or gate is broken down, old or black; if with ✶ or △, the door is mended again.

Of the house where the Thief remains or dwells.

Behold the Sign wherein the *Signifier* is in, and in what

part of heaven he is, & say the Goods so taken are in that quarter of the Town, as if in the ascendant, east; the place of the ☽ shows in what part the gate is in; for if she be in an easterly quarter, the gate is on the east-side of the house; if in a westerly quarter, on the west; and if the ☽ be fixed, the house has but one door, near the ground; if in a moveable Sign the gate is up some steps; if ♄ behold the Sign, the gate is, or has been broken, and is very ancient, or is black; if ♂ behold it, it does increase the signification, *viz.* that it is rent or cracked, or torn, or needs repair; if at such an aspect the ☽ has but then small light, say there is no great appearance of ironwork.

Several men, several minds.

Are the Goods in the Owner's hands.

Lord of the Ascendant in an Angle, the Goods are in his hands; the Lord of the hour in an Angle the same: if the Lord of the House of the ☽ be with the Lord of the hour in an Angle, the Goods are in his hands, and are Goods moveable; if the Lord of the hour and the Lord of the term of the ☽ and the Lord of the second be in an Angle with the Lord of the Ascendant, they are in his hands and fixed goods; if any of these Lords be in an Angle, with □, △ or ✶ to the Lord of the Ascendant, the Owner shall have his Goods again.

If the Lord of the Ascendant and Lord of the hour be in a succedent House, the Goods are about the Owner, ☽ or the Lord of the House of the ☽ in a moveable Sign, they are not far from the Owner; if the Lord of the term of the ☽, or the Lord of the second be in a succedent House, then the things are about the Owner, and not much elongated.

The Planets last before spoken of, or rehearsed, placed in cadent houses, show the Goods far from the Owner.

Whether the Goods be in the custody of the Thief.

Behold the signifier of the Thief or Thieves; and if he or they give their power to another Planet, the things stolen are not in the keeping of the Thief or Thieves; if he or they give not their power to another, it remains in his own power, custody or possession.

Behold the Lord of the term wherein the *Significator* of the Thief is, and by him judge the estate of the Thief; if an unfortunate Planet be in a fortunate term, he was of a wild stock, and now is in good state: If a fortune be in the term of an infortune, say the contrary.

If he carried all with him,

Behold the Lord of the seventh and eighth, if the Lord of the seventh be in an Angle, he was willing to have carried all away, but could not; if in a succedent, and the Lord of the eighth with him strong, he had all; if both the Lord of the seventh and eighth be in cadent Houses, he neither carried it away or had it.

The distance of the thing from the Owner.

These rules are much followed by those that practice in the Country. Behold how many Degrees are between the *Significator* and the ☽; and whether the Signs be fixed, movable or common; in fixed Signs account for every Degree a Mile; in common Signs so many tenths of Miles; in Movable Signs so many Rods. How many Degrees between the Lord of the seventh and the Lord of the hour, so many thousand Paces between the Querent and the Fugitive.

Look what distance is between the Ascendant and his Lord, such is the distance between the place where the thing was lost and the thing itself.

Look how many Degrees the *Signifier* is in his Sign, and so many Miles are the Cattle from the place where they went, and in that quarter or coast where the Lord of the fourth is.

How far the thing is from the Querent.

Behold the Lord of the Ascendant and the Ascendant, and see how many Signs and Degrees are between the Lord of the Ascendant and the Ascendant; and if the Lord of the Ascendant be in a fixed Sign, then give for every Sign (between him and the Ascendant) four Miles; and if he be in a common Sign, give for every Sign a Mile and a half; and if he be in a moveable Sign, give for every Sign (between them) half a Mile, and the overplus of the Degrees, according to the Sign the Lord of the Ascendant is in: *As for example;*

A Question was asked, and the seventh Degree of ♑ ascended, and ♄ in ♏ four Degrees; so there is between the Ascendant and ♄ three Signs, and ♄ in a fixed Sign; therefore I must give for every Sign four Miles, three times four is twelve, and there is three Degrees more to the which belong half a Mile; so the whole sum is twelve Miles and a half.

The Place where the Goods stolen are.

If you will know the place where the thing stolen is in; take Signification of the Place from the Sign the *Significator* of the Thief is in, and from the place of the Lord of the fourth House; if they be both in one Signification it is well; if not, behold then what place is *Signified* by the Lord of the fourth House, and judge by that Sign the nature of the place where the thing stolen is. If he be in a moveable Sign, it is in a place high from the ground; if in a fixed Sign, it is in the Earth; and if in a common Sign, it is under some Eaves of a House; and help your judgment in these by the Term of the Signs, as if the *Significator* be in ♈, it is in a place where Beasts do use that be small, as Sheep, or Hogs &c. if he be in ♌, it is in a place of Beasts which bite as Dogs, &c. if he be in ♐, it is in a place of great Beasts that are ridden; as in a Stable of Horses, or such like: if in ♉, ♍ or ♑, it Signifies a House or place of great Beasts, as Oxen, Kine or such other Cattle: ♍ or ♑ Signifies a place of Camels, Mules, Horses, Asses, and such like: ♍ has the Signification of a Barn, and of such places as be under the Earth, or near to the Earth, or Granaries, such as they put Corn in: ♑ Signifies a place of Goats, Sheep, Hogs, and such like. If he be in ♊, ♎, ♒, it is in the House; in ♊ it is in the Wall of the House; ♎ near a little House or Closet; ♒ it is near a Door that is above a Door or Gate, in some place on high. If ♋, ♏ or ♓, the thing is in Water, or near Water, and these do Signify a Pit or Cistern: ♏ it is near a place of unclean Water, or where they use to

More certainly by the Lord of the fourth. This is where things are hid in grounds.

cast out filthy Water, as a Gutter: ♓ shows a place always moist.

The place where the thing lost or stolen is hidden.

Behold the place of the *Significator* of the Thief, and the Lord of the fourth, if they be both in one *Signification* and well agreeing, if not, behold the Lord of the fourth; if he be in a moveable Sign, it is in an high place; if in a fixed Sign, it is on the Earth; if in a common Sign, in a covered place. Herein behold what Sign the ☽ is, or whether in the Ascendant or Midheaven, or about it, behold the form or Sign that Ascends with her, and say the thing is in that place which the form thereof represents.

Where the Goods are.

Look to the Lord of the second and his *Almuten*, (*viz.* he that has most dignities there) there are the Goods: if the Lord thereof and the Lord of the fourth be both in one Sign, judge the things to be where they are, and the Thief and Theft both together; if they be not together, judge by the fourth, &c.

If the Lord of the fourth be found in a fixed Sign, the Goods are in the Earth, or in a House having no Chamber.

If the Lord of the fourth be in a moveable Sign, the Goods are in a Chamber above another, or in an upper Loft or Room.

This is, when Goods are certainly known to be out of the House. If in a common Sign, in a Chamber within another Chamber. If the Goods be found in a fiery Sign, they are East; in an Earthy, South; in an Airy, West; in a Watery, North.

If the Lord of the term of the ☽ be in an angle, and in a moveable Sign, the Goods are in Closes where are both Corn and Grass.

If in a succedent and fixed Sign, in Woods, Parks, or in closed Grounds that lie from the Highway-side: if in a cadent and common Signs, in a Common of divers Men, or Pasture or Meadow of divers Men.

Haly says, it was asked him one time when ♌ was Ascending

and ♀ therein; and he says, the thing was under a Bed near a Robe or Covering; because ♀ was in the Ascendant, the which is Significatrix of a Bed, and after these considerations judge.

Lost or stolen in what part of the house.

If the thing is lost or stolen be in the house, & you would know the place where it is, behold the Lord of the fourth, and the Planet which is therein; if it be ♄, it is hid in a dark place or part of the house, or in a desolate or stinking place and deep, be it a siege-house or Jakes, where people seldom come.

The true quality of the place every Planet and Sign does signify, I have exactly set forth from pag. 57 to page 100.

If it be ♃, it signifies a place of Wood, Bushes or Briars.

If it be ♂, it is in some Kitchen, or in a place where fire os used, or in a Shop, &c.

If it be ☉, it signifies the Cloister or Hall of the house, or the Place or Seat of the Master of the house.

If it be ♀, it signifies the place of the Seat of a woman, or Bed or Clothes, or where women are most conversant.

If it be ☿, it is in a place of Pictures, Carving or Books, or a place of Corn, and chiefly in ♍.

If it be ☽, it is in a Pit, Cistern or Lavatory.

The form or likeness of the entering of the house.

Behold the place of the ☉, from him is known the form and likeness of the opening of the house; from ☽ is known the Cellar, and the place that holds the water, or a Pit; by ♀, the place of Mirth, Play and women &c. from the place of the ☊ is known the place of height, or highest Seat, Stool, Stairs or Ladder to climb by; and from the place of the ☋ is known the place the Wood is in, or the house the Beasts be in, or a Pillar in the house; and if ☿ be in a common Sign it is in a little Cell within another Chamber; if he be in a movable Sign, it is within a little Cell that has another Chamber about it; if in a fixed Sign, it is in a house that has no Cellar nor other Chamber, as many Country houses have not.

This has relation as well to any other thing as to Thefts, and may be made good use of for several Discoveries.

And if ♃ or ♀, or both of them be in the tenth house, the door has a fair opening; if ♄ be in the tenth, the opening of the door is near some Ditch or Pit, or deep place; if ♂ be there, near to the opening of the house is the place of making a fire, or killing of Beasts, or heading; if ☿ be in the tenth, say in the opening of the house, is a place where the Master of the house keeps his things in, *viz.* his instruments or Tools he uses about his Beasts; and if ☉ be in the tenth, in the opening is some Stool or Seat to sit on, or a bed; if the ☽ be in the tenth house, say that in the entering of the house is a door under the ground, or some other necessary thing that a man has much occasion to use in his house, as a Furnace or Quern, or such like.

What is stolen by the Lord of the second or tenth House.

More properly by the Lord of the second. ♄ Lead, Iron, Azure, black or blue colour, Wool, black Garments, Leather, heavy things, labouring tools for the Earth: ♃ Oil, Honey, Quinces, Silk, Silver: ♀ white Cloth, and white Wine, Green-colour.

♂ Pepper, Armour, Weapons, red Wine, red Clothes, Brass, Horses for War, hot things: ☿ Books, Pictures, implements: ☉ Gold, Oranges, Brass, Carbuncles, yellow Clothes: ☽ ordinary and common Commodities.

The quality of the Goods stolen.

These Judgments are more proper for the Country than City. Behold the Lord of the second; if he be ♄, it is Lead, Iron, or a Kettle, something with three feet; a Garment or some black thing, or a Hide or Beast's skin.

If ♃ be Lord of the second, some white thing; as Tin, Silver, or mixed with veins, as it were with yellow and white, or Broadcloth, &c.

☉ Signifies Gold and precious things, or things of good value. ♂ those which be fiery belong to the fire, Swords, Knives. ♀ Such things as belong to Women, Rings, fair Garments, Smocks, Waistcoats, Petticoats.

☽ Beasts, as the Horse, Mules, Cows, or Poultry in the

Country of all sorts; ☿ Money, Books, Paper, Pictures, Garments of divers colours.

A sign of recovery.

The ☽ in the seventh Aspecting the Lord of the Ascendant with a △, ♀ or the Lord of the second in the Ascendant, ♃ in the second direct, ♀ Lady of the second in the Ascendant, ☽ in the tenth in △ to a Planet in the second: ☽ in the second, with a △ to the Lord of the second: ☽ in the second, to a □ of ☉ in the twelfth: the Lord of the Ascendant in the second, ☉ and ☽ aspecting each other with a △, ☉ and ☽ aspecting the cusp of the second with a △: Lord of the second in the fourth, or in the House of the Querent, *viz.* in the Ascendant.

These are excellent and approved rules.

This must be in signs of short ascensions.

If it shall be recovered.

To know if it shall be recovered or not: For resolution hereof, behold the Lord of the term of the ☽, the which is *Signifier* of the substance stolen to be recovered. If the Lord of the term of the ☽, and the Lord of the house of the ☽ be increasing both in motion and number, and free from infortunes; it shows it shall be recovered whole and sound, and nothing diminished thereof.

Consider also the Lord of the hour, and take his testimony, as you did from the Lord of the term of the ☽; behold also the application of the Lord of the Ascendant, to the Lord of the term of the ☽, or to the Lord of the second House; or if that they apply to him, for when he does apply to one of them, or to both, and the ☽ apply to them both or to the Lord of her House, or if the ☉ do apply to the Lord of his House, and the ☽ be diminished in light; I mean if the Lord of his House, the Lord of the term of the ☽, and the Lord of the House of the ☉, do apply to the ☉; for the state of all these do Signify that the thing stole shall be found, and especially if the Planet *Signifier* be in an angle or succedent.

To increase in motion is, when as lately a Planet had moved slowly, and now increases his motion, or moves more quick; to increase in number is, when the day subsequent he is found to have moved more minutes than the day or days preceding.

Also if the Lord of the term of the ☽, or the Lord of the House of the ☽, or the Lord of the second house apply to the

Lord of the Ascendant, the Master of the thing lost shall recover the same. Also if the ☽ or Lord of the Ascendant apply to the Ascendant, or one of them apply to the Lord of the second House, or to the Lord of the term of the ☽, the thing stolen shall be had again through inquisition and diligent search.

And if the Lord of the House of the ☽, and the Lord of the Term of the ☽ be both diminished in their motion or number, say the more part is lost and shall not be recovered.

If the Lord of the term of the ☽, and the Lord of the house of the ☽ be increasing in number and motion, and safe from ill fortunes, the thing shall be restored whole and nothing diminished; for if those *Signifiers* be not cadent from angles, it *Signifies* the things shall be soon recovered; but if they be in angles, it *Signifies* meanly, *viz.* neither very soon nor very late, *viz.* the recovery.

In what time it shall be recovered.

Behold the application of the two Planets that *Signify* the recovery, and number the Degrees that are between them, or from the one to the other, and determine days, weeks, years, or hours, in this manner; Behold the place they are in, or the place of their application; for if they be in moveable Signs, the shorter time is required, or it shall be in weeks, or in months; in fixed Signs it *Signifies* Months or Years; in common Signs a mean between both: help yourself from these judgments: or if the *Significator* be quick in motion, they Signify it shall be recovered quickly, or lightly: which *Significators*, if they be falling from angles, signifies a time more short, wherein the Goods shall be recovered: These Judgements are made properly for this Chapter; you must not judge in other things by these, or by this Method.

Aphorisms concerning Recovery.

The Lord of the eighth in the Ascendant, or with the Lord

thereof, signifies the recovery of the theft. The Lord of the second in the eighth, denies recovery.

♄ also, or ♂, or ☋, signifies dividing and loss of the thing, and that all shall not be recovered.

The Lord of the second in the Ascendant shows recovery.

The Lord of the Ascendant in the second, signifies recovery after long search.

If the second House be hindered or the Lord thereof, it cannot be that all shall be found and recovered.

When the Lord of the Ascendant and the ☽, with the ☉, or the Lord of the tenth, or the Lord of the House of the ☽; or if the Lord of the seventh be with the Lord of the Ascendant, or have good aspect to him; or if the Lord of the seventh be in combustion; or at least the Lord of the tenth, and the Lord of the house of the ☽ agree well together, upon such a position it is probable the thing lost shall and may be recovered. When both the Luminaries are under the earth it cannot be recovered.

Whatsoever is lost, the ☉ together with the ☽, beholding the Ascendant cannot be lost but will, shortly be discovered.

Behold when the body of the ☽ and the body of the Lord of the Ascendant, *viz.* when one of them applies bodily to the Planet that signifies recovery; the thing stole shall then be recovered; and if the application of the Significators be by Retrogradation, the recovery shall be sudden, if the application be by direction, the recovery shall be before it be looked for.

Behold also the Lord of the term of the ☽, if he do apply to the same term, and the Lord of the house of the ☽ applies to the same house, or when the Lord of the second applies to his own house: or when any of them apply to the Ascendant; all these do signify the time of recovery.

Look also if the ⊗ have any testimony with the Lord of the Ascendant, or with the ☽, because when any of them apply to each other, or the Lord of the house of the ☽ to the ☽, there is the time of the recovery in hope; and when the Lord of ⊗ applies to the Lord of the Ascendant, or to the second house, or to the place in which the ⊗ is, or to the ☽; all these signify recovery: Behold also how many degrees is from the planet which signifies recovery, to the angle he goes first to, and the number of those degrees is the time of recovery.

When both the lights behold themselves in angles, it signifies recovery of the thing at length, but with labour and pain; and it signifies more than one thief; if the aspect be a △, it signifies the lighter recovery.

The ☽ in the Ascendant with any Fortune, it signifies recovery: If the ☽ be *sub radis*, or combust, it signifies the thing lost shall not be recovered, if it be, it shall be with much pain and labour; ☉ and ☽ in the tenth, sudden recovery.

If both ☉ and ☽ be nearer the Ascendant than any other angle, it signifies recovery of the thing with much trouble, anxiety, strife, bloodshed, or quarreling.

When ☉ is in the Ascendant, the thing stolen shall be recovered, except the Ascendant be ♎ or ♒; for therein the ☉ is weak. The ☽ in the Ascendant and ♃ with her, it shall be recovered.

Of the discovery of the thief, and recovery of the goods.

If the ☽ be in the Ascendant, or in a △ aspect to the Lord thereof, thou findest the thief.

If there be a △ aspect between ☉ and ☽, it signifies recovery. If ☉ and ☽ be joined to the Lord of the seventh, or beholding him by aspect, he cannot hide himself.

If the Lord of the Ascendant apply to the second, or the Lord of the second to the Ascendant; if there be any application or translation of light between the Lord of the 8th, and the Lord of the second; or the Lord of the eighth be in the second, it signifies recovery.

☽ in the second with one of the Fortunes, or applying with a good aspect to her own house, or the Lord of the sign wherein she is, shows recovery.

The chief signs of no recovery are if ♄, ♂ or ☋, be in the second, or the Lord of the second in the eighth, or combust, or when the Lord of the second applies to the Lord of the eighth with any aspect, all or any of these are signs of no recovery. If the Lord of the second be in his exaltation, there is a great hope of recovery, especially if there be any other testimony of the recovery.

Of Theft.

If the Lord of the seventh be in the Ascendant, the theft shall be restored again; if the Lord of the ascendant be in the seventh, it will be found after much enquiry; if ☽ be in the ascendant, or with the Lord of the ascendant, it will be found or may be found; if the ☽ be in the fifth, with the Lord of the ascendant, it may be had; or if ☉ and ☽ be in the fifth, and the Lord of the eighth be with the Lord of the ascendant in the ascendant, it will be found. *Thefts recoverable or no.*

If the Lord of the second be in the eighth, it cannot be had; if ♄ or ♂ or ☋ be in the second, it will not be had; if the Lord of the second be in the ascendant, it will be had again, and none shall know how; if the Lord of the ascendant be in the second, with great labour it may be had; if the Lord of the second be cadent, it will not be had; but if he be in his exaltation, it will be quickly restored; the sooner if ☽ apply to him.

Other Judgments of Thefts.

Lord of the ascendant and Lord of the seventh joined, it shall be got by searching of the *querent.*

Lord of the ascendant in the seventh, or the lord of the ascendant joined to the lord of the eighth, or Lord of the seventh in the ascendant, the Thief comes of his own accord before he goes any farther; very many times I have found it so.

If ☽ be separated from the lord of the ascendant, and be joined to the lord of the seventh, he shall be found, *viz.* the Thief.

The lord of the seventh joined to an *Infortune* in an angle, he shall be taken: the Lord of the seventh joined to a *Fortune*, he shall not be taken, unless that *Fortune* be under the ☉ beams, or impeded; if he go to combustion, it signifies his death.

☽ joined to an unfortunate Planet, he shall be found; the ☽ joined to a retrograde Planet, he returns of his own *I have oft found this true.*

accord, if he went; if the same Planet be stationary, he shall not remove from his own place until he be taken.

Whether the Thief shall be known or not.

Most Planets in cadents, he shall be known: ☉ in ♂, ☐ or ☍ to the *Significator* of the Thief, known; ☉ in ✶ to him, he is suspected, but not openly known.

Whether the Thief be suspected of the Owner or not.

If the Thief be in ☐ or ☍ to the lord of the ascendant he is suspected, a △ or ✶, not; if the Thief's *Significator* be in ♂ with the ☽, the Owner suspects one with him, or using his own company.

If the ☽ be in ☐ or ☍ to any Planet in the tenth or seventh, say he suspects one far from him, except the *Almuten* of the tenth or seventh house be in ☐ or ☍ to the ☽.

If ☽ have ♂, ☐ or ☍ to a Planet in the seventh, or to the *Almuten* thereof, the Owner suspects him; but if ☽ aspects another Planet, he suspects another, and not the Thief: if the ☽ be joined to, or received of an evil Planet, the suspected is the Thief; look to the lord of the ascendant and the ☽, and take the strongest of them, who if he have received any virtue from evil Planets, *viz.* separated from them, he has played the Thief; and so much the more being received of the Lord of the second: Lord of the ascendant in an angle, applying or separating to a Planet in a cadent house, truth is said of him; or ☽ conjoined to a Planet in an angle, especially in the tenth, signifies the same.

Who did the Deed or Theft.

This where the querent is suspected a Knave. Lord of the ascendant in the second, or seventh, it is the Owner himself; or lord of the second in the ascendant, the owner. If ☉ and ☽ be with the Lord of the 3ʳᵈ, it's the Owner's Kinsman; ☉ and ☽ in the fourth, Father or Mother, or a Friend; ☉ or ☽ in the fifth, a Son or Daughter of the Owner; ☉ or ☽ in the sixth, a Servant; ☉ or ☽ in the seventh his Wife or a Woman.

☉ and ☽ together conjoined, beholding the ascendant, the Owner's acquaintance; or if either of them behold the ascendant, *idem*.

☉ or ☽ in their proper houses, or in the ascendant, the Owner may be justly suspected.

If ☉ or ☽ be not together, but one of them behold the ascendant, it was one was born, or formerly lived in the house where the robbery was done.

If ☉ or ☽ be in their own Triplicity, the Thief retains *A Familiar of* him that lost the Goods; they having but a Face where they *the house.* are, then he is not one of the house, but Kin to him.

If ☉ or ☽ behold the ascendant, and not the Thief, the Thief entered not the house before he took it.

If the Thief have any great Dignities in the ascendant, the Thief is Kin to the *Querent*, or a very near acquaintance.

♂ being *Significator* of the Thief, and placed in the tenth, the *querent* is the Thief, or very negligent.

The Lord of the seventh in the ascendant, he is suspected to be the Thief.

Whether it be the first fact the Thief has committed.

If ☉ and ☽ do behold the Lord of the house where the ☽ is from an angle, he has played the Thief more then once.

If ⊗ or Lord of the seventh be free from misfortunes, or ♃ *Significator* alone of the Thief, it is the first fact he has committed.

♂ separating from the Lord of the seventh, or ♄ Oriental, it is not the first; ♂ *Significator*, he breaks in* ; ♀, under **Viz. By* the cloak of love; ☿, by subtlety and flattery. *violence.*

Of Theft by Astrologie, or LILLY'S *best experienced Rules.*

Many Thieves, if Peregrine Planets be in angles. *Number.*

The *Significator* in a Sign of Fruitfulness, *viz.* ♋, ♏, ♓; or in a Bicorporeal, *viz.* ♊, ♐, ♍, ♓; or beholding many peregrine Planets.

The angles fixed, or the ☽ or Significator in Signs of *One.* direct ascension, which are ♋, ♌, ♍, ♎, ♏, ♐; or in Signs not fruitful, *viz.* ♈, ♉, ♊, ♌, ♎, ♐, ♑.

The Sex.

Masculine, if the Lord of the hour, Lord of the seventh and his Dispositor be masculine, or if the Dispositor of the ☽ and the Planet to whom she applies be masculine; or if the *Significator* be in the masculine part of Heaven, *viz.* in the first, twelfth, eleventh or seventh, sixth, fifth, and Oriental.

Feminine, if the contrary to this happen.

Age.

Old, or in years, the *Significator* being ♄.

A man, if ♃, ♂ or ☉.

Not so old, if ☿ or ♀ be *Significators*.

The ☽ for her age, *viz.* young, she in her first quarter; more than if in her second quarter; and so in her third quarter more aged; in her last quarter of greater years.

Where note, the ☽ or any Planet Oriental, denotes the Thief more young; Occidental, more aged. Or thus; observe in what house the *Significator* is in, give for every house five years from the ascendant.

Or observe the degree descending in the seventh house, and give for every degree two years.

Or see the age of the Planet to whom the ☽ applies, or the *Significator* of the Thief, or consider the day of the month the Question is asked, give for every day elapsed to the day of the Question two years.

The best way, and most sure is, to consider most of these ways, and pitch upon the greatest number.

Form and Stature.

Proportion great, if the *Significator* have much Orientality, and be in ♌, ♏ or ♐.

Proportion little, if his Occidentality be much, or the *Significator* in ♋, ♏ or ♓.

The upper part of his body is thick and strong, if the *Significator* be in ♈, ♉, ♌; his lower parts if in ♐, ♊, ♏.

Fat.

If the *significator* have much latitude from the *Ecliptic*, be Retrograde, or in his first station, or in the first part of ♈, ♉, ♌, or in the last part of Ⅱ, ♏, ♐.

It's probable he inclines to tallness, the ☽ in ♋ or ♓.

♎, ♍ or ♒ give fleshy bodies, and well proportioned.

Lean

The *significator* having small latitude, or direct, or in his second station, or in the beginning of Ⅱ, ♏, ♐, or in the summit of his Eccentricity.

☉ beholding the *Significator*, gives a handsome shape and fatness; the ☽ Beholding, gives temperature and moistness.

The Thief's strength.

Significator in South Latitude, the party is nimble; in North latitude, slow in motion.

A Planet in his first station gives strong bodies; going out of one Sign into another, weak and feeble.

Where the Knave is.

He flies, or is running out of one place into another, or removing his Lodging, if the *significators* be going out of one Sign into another; or if his *significator* be leaving combustion, or the Rays of the ☉; or if the Thief's Dispositor separate from the Lord of the first, and apply to a Planet in the sixth, eighth or twelfth.

He flies, or is far distant if the *significator* of the Thief and thing sought after be not in one quarter of heaven, or apply to the Lord of the third or ninth, or if the *significators* be in the third or ninth.

He remains.

If the Lord of the first be joined to a Planet in a cadent house, and behold the ascendant.

Who the Thief is.

A Familiar if ☉ and ☽ at one time behold the ascendant, or if the Lord of the first be joined to the Lord of the seventh in the ascendant.

Or if ☉ and ☽ be in ♌ or ♋, or in the ascendant itself, or in the house of the Lord of the ascendant, and beholding him, or the Lord of the seventh house in the twelfth or eighth, the ☉ or ☽ in their exaltation, note one well known, but not of the Family.

The *Luminaries* in their Terms or Faces, the party is known to some of the household, but not of the Family; Lord of the seventh in the seventh he is of the Household.

A Stranger.

If the Lord of the seventh be in the third or ninth from his house.

Lord of the ascendant and Lord of the seventh not of one Triplicity.

If you see the Thief is domestic, then

☉ Signifies Father, or Master.
☽ The Mother, or Mistress.
♀ The Wife, or a Woman.
♄ A Servant, or a Stranger lying there by chance.
♂ A Son, or a Brother, or Kinsman.
☿ A Youth, Familiar or Friend.

Whither is the Thief gone, or Fugitive.

Where you are principally to observe, that the ascendant or a *significator* in the ascendant, signifies the East; but this Table expresses the quarters of Heaven more fully.

First house East.	*Seventh house West*
Second house Northeast by East	*Eighth house Southwest by South*
Third house North Northeast	*Ninth house South Southwest*
Fourth house North	*Tenth South*
Fifth house Northwest by North	*Eleventh Southeast by South*
Sixth house West, Northwest	*Twelfth East, Southeast*

The Signs.

Aries *East.*	♈ *East.*	*This small*
Taurus *South and by East.*	♌ *Northeast by East.*	*difference*
Gemini *West and by South.*	♐ *East Southeast.*	*breeds no*
Cancer *is full North.*	♎ *West.*	*error, let*
Leo *East and by North.*	♊ *Southwest by West.*	*every one*
Virgo *South and by West.*	♒ *West, Northwest.*	*use what he*
Libra *full West.*	♋ *North*	*finds most*
Scorpio *North and by East.*	♏ *North, Northeast.*	*true.*
Sagittarius *East and by South.*	♓ *Northwest by North.*	
Capricornus *Full South.*	♑ *South.*	
Aquarius *West and by North.*	♉ *Southeast by South.*	
Pisces *North and by West.*	♍ *South, Southeast.*	

The flight of the Thief.

It's swift, if his *Significator* be swift in motion, or joined to Planets swift in motion, or being himself in Signs movable or of short ascensions.

His flight is uncertain.

If his or their *Significators* are in their second station, or joined to stationary Planets in angles or succedents.

He makes slow haste.

If his *Significator* is slow in motion, or joined to Planets of slow motion, or in Signs fixed or of long ascensions.

He shall be taken.

If the Lord of the ascendant be in the seventh, or in ♂ to the Lord of the seventh; or the Lord of the seventh in the first, or joined to the Lord of the first, or a Retrograde Planet; or if the ☽ separate from the lord of the seventh, to the ♂ of the lord of the first; or from the ♂ of the lord of the first to the lord of the seventh; or if ☉ and ☽ be in ♂ with the lord of the seventh, some say, if they behold him; or if the lord of the seventh be going to ♂, *viz.* Combustion; or if the lord of the ascendant be in ♂ in the ascendant, tenth or seventh, or an unfortunate Planet in the seventh.

Not taken.

If the lord of the seventh be in aspect with a *Fortune*, if in aspect to ♃ or ♀ in the eleventh, he escapes by friends; if in the third, by strangers.

The Goods restored.

If the lord of the first or second are in ♂ with the lord of the eighth, or in any strong Reception:

Or if the lord of the second depart from Combustion; or *Sol* or ☽ in the ascendant or tenth house, it notes recuperation; the most part, if they are strong; less, if they be weak.

There's hopes of restitution when the Lights behold themselves with any aspect, chiefly in angles; or the lord of the seventh or eighth.

No Restitution.

If the lord of the second be Combust or the lord of the seventh in ♂ with the lord of the eighth; or if the lord of the second behold not the first house, or his lord; or the *Sun* and ☽ not aspecting themselves, or the ⊗, or when both are under the earth.

Other Rules that the Thief shall be taken.

☽ In the seventh, applying to the lord of the eighth.
  Lord of the first in the ascendant.
☽ in the seventh applying to a □ of ♂.
☽ separating from a □ of ♄ or ☿, applying to a □ of *Sol*.
☽ In the sixth, eighth or twelfth.
☽ Separating from a ♂ of ♄, applying to a □ of ☿,
  Lord of the seventh in the first.
☽ In the eighth, in ☍ to ♂ in the second.

CHAPTER LI.

Of Battles, War, or other Contentions.

If one demand, whether he shall overcome his Adversary or not; give to the Querent the Lord of the ascendant the ☽, and the Planet from whom she is separated; and to the

Defendant the seventh and his Lord, and the Planet to whom the ☽ applies; and behold whose *Significator* is in Angles and with better Planets, and so judge.

If evil Planets be in the Ascendant, and Fortunes in the seventh, the Adversary shall overcome, *& e contra*. The Lord of the seventh in the Ascendant, betokens victory to the Querent, *& e contra*.

Whether one shall return safe from War, or any dangerous Voyage.

Behold if the Lord of the Ascendant be strong, and with a good Planet, and well disposed; it is a great testimony of security, *& e contra*. Behold also the seventh and the Lord thereof, and if they be Fortunate (although the first be not so) yet shall the Party return, though not without great crosses and lets, *& e contra*. Behold also the ☽ how she is disposed; for her application with the good is Fortunate, *& e contra*. Evil Planets also in the eighth, are no small Signification of fear, and terror, or death. ♄ signifies ruins or bruises, ♂ or the ☋ wounds by Weapons.

If one shall return safe from War.

If the Lord of the Ascendant be with good or good himself, or a good Planet in the Ascendant, he shall return safe. If the ☉ be with the Lord of the Ascendant in any part of the Question, he may not go; because the ☉ burns him. If the Lord of the seventh be with a good Planet, and the Lord of the Ascendant with an evil, he shall have some impediment in his way, yet shall not die.

If an evil Planet be with the Lord of the first, and a good one in the first; if he then go, he shall suffer great loss, but not death; but questionless he will be sorely wounded.

If ♄ be in the first, or with the Lord of the first, let him not go; because loss will happen to him by one whom he meets: If an ill Planet be with the Lord of the first, and ♄ in the ascendant, or with his Lord, he shall be wounded with Wood or Stone. If ♂ or the ☋ be in the Ascendant, or with the Lord thereof, or evil Planets in the first, or with the Lord thereof, he shall receive a wound, and go near to die thereof. Also if an evil Planet be in the eighth, it is to be feared, death will ensue; if the ☉ be with the Lord of the seventh, or in the eighth, it is ill to go; and so of the tenth and seventh.

What will ensue of the War.

Behold the Lord of the seventh and first, and their Lords: the first House signifies the Querent, the seventh his Adversary; if good Planets be in the first, and malevolent in the seventh, and the Lord of the Ascendant good, and the Lord of the seventh ill; the Querent overcomes: but if an Infortune be with the Lord of the Ascendant, and an evil Planet in the Ascendant; and the Lord of the seventh good, and a good Planet there, the Querent shall be overcome, and shall be taken or slain.

If both the Lord of the Ascendant and seventh be in the Ascendant, and on the behalf of the Lord of the Ascendant, there be good Planets casting their benevolent aspects to the cusp of the second; then the Querent will do well in the War and obtain money thereby; he shall have victory of his Adversary, or they will endeavour to be reconciled.

Any Planet in the 10, 11, 12, 1, 2, 3, is conceived a friend to the Querent. So all Planets in the 9, 8, 7, 6, 5, 4, are reputed for the Quesited. If both Lords, *viz.* of the first and seventh, be in the Ascendant, and good Planets be on the part of the Ascendant, and evil on the part of the seventh; both Parties shall suffer loss; but the Querent shall have the better in the end. If the Lord of the seventh be in the Ascendant, of his Question, it shows the Fortitude of the Actors; the contrary notes the contrary.

If the Lord of the Ascendant be in the eighth, or with the Lord of the eighth, or the Lord of the eighth in the Ascendant; it notes the death of the Querent.

If the Lord of the seventh be in the second, or with the Lord thereof; or the Lord of the second in the seventh, or with the Lord of the seventh; it notes the death of the Adversary.

CHAPTER LII.

Who shall do best in a suit of Law.

If the Lord of the Ascendant and seventh be in angles, neither shall overcome: see which is joined to an evil Planet in a cadent house, that Party shall be overcome: If both be joined to Infortunes, both Parties will be undone by the Suit, or receive infinite prejudice. If the one be strong and the other weak, and he that is strong be not cadent, nor joined to an Infortune; and he that is ill dignified, or in a weak quarter of Heaven or House, I say, if he be not in his own House, or Exaltation, or with a good Planet; then the strongest in the Scheme overcomes. *This shall be more copiously handled, ere I conclude the judgements of this seventh house.*

He that is but meanly strong in the Figure, seems very fearful; for sometimes he hopes to win, at other times to loose: and observe this in Questions, concerning Wars and *Kingdoms*, the Fortitude of a Planet is greater in his Exaltation than in his House, in all other Questions quite contrary.

Of Partnership, Society or Fellowship between two, if it shall be, or not.

If good Planets be in the seventh and first, the Society shall be, and good will come of it: the continuance of it, whether for years, days, or months, is known by the Lord of the seventh. If you will know when it shall be, see if a good Planet be in the seventh, then the Society or Partnership shall be that year. If the Lord of the Ascendant and seventh agree in nature and quality, the Parties will agree; if not, they will disagree, and there will be perpetual (or at least often) jangling.

Of two Partners, which shall gain or do best.

The Lord of the ascendant and seventh are to be considered, and in what state they be, and so judge; for if the *Significator* of the *querent* be in better dignities then the *quesited*, the *querent* prospers; & *e contra*. If evil shall come on the business, then he whose *Significator* is in a cadent house, that party does the worst; if anyone's *Significator* be exalted, he gains.

See the second and his Lord, and the eighth and his lord, and in which of these houses the best Planet, or the Lord thereof in the best place, or joined to the best Planet, he shall gain most. The second house shows the *querent's* substance, the eighth the riches of the Companion or Partner; if both be good, both shall gain. If both ill, both shall lose; if one good and the other ill, he that has the good Planet shall gain, the other shall lose.

Of familiarity between Neighbour and Neighbour.

Whether Society or Friendship shall endure, behold if a good Planet be in the seventh, then he pretends thee or the *querent* good fellowship and means really, especially if the same Planet or the lord of the seventh behold the ascendant, or the lord thereof, with a △ or ✳ aspect; also it shall endure so many Months, Days or Years, as he has Degrees to go in the same House, or Sign, fixed, common, or moveable.

Of removing from place to place.

Behold the fourth and seventh houses, and their lords, and if they be good and strong, and well affected, and good Planets in the said houses, it is very good, & *e contra*.

Another.

The Lord of the ascendant stronger than the lord of the seventh, abide; if not, remove; if both be evil disposed, go; both indifferent and better aspected of good than evil, stay; & *e contra*. ☽ separating from Infortunes, go; from Fortunes, abide. Note, the ascendant is for the Journeyer (or the place he goes from,) the seventh the Place whither he would go. Also if the Lord of the ascendant separate from Infortunes and apply to Fortunes, go; If from Fortunes, and applies to Infortunes, stay: and if the Lord of the ascendant and ☽ agree, the judgement is more certain.

Of removing from one place to another; or of two
Businesses, which is best.

Consider the first and second houses, and their lords, and the lords of the places to which thou wouldest go, and lord of the substance thou thinkest for to attain there, see the seventh and eighth houses and their lords, which of them is best and strongest, thither go and remove. Or see the lord of the ascendant or the ☽, whom if thou findest to be separated from evil Planets, and joined to *Fortunes*, it is better to go than stay, and do any business thou intendest. If the Lord of the ascendant be separated from fortunes, and apply to infortunes, neither move or do the business thou intendest; see if the planet to whom the ☽ applies be better than that she separated from, for then thou mayest remove, else not: &c.

If it be best to remove or stay in any place, whether
Village, Territory, City or House.

See the lord of the ascendant, fourth and seventh house; if the lord of the fourth be in the seventh, and be a good planet, and if the lord of the first and seventh be good, and with good planets, it is good to abide still: but if the lord of the seventh be with a good planet, and the lord of the fourth with an evil one, it is then not good to stay; for if he do, he shall receive much damage by abiding there.

CHAPTER LIII.

Of Hunting.

You shall know the lord of hunting by the ascendant, the ☽, and from the lord of the term of the degree of the ☽ and from the lord of the hour; for the lord of the hour is of great force and strength, when he is in the ascendant, and the ascendant a sign of four footed beasts: in case of hunting see if the ascendant be a sign of four footed beasts, or an earthly sign, for these are good for hunting amongst mountains, and hills; see the lord of the ascendant, and the lord of the hour, if they be fortunate or unfortunate; and if either do behold other, or separate one from another, and if one be falling from another, *Since the Ancients have taken notice of such trifles, I must consent.*

note this. Consider after if the seventh be a sign of four footed beasts, and if you do find in the same the lord thereof, or the lord of the hour; or the lord of the angle fortunate, judge that the beast you seek for shall be found and taken. But if the lord of the seventh be an Infortune, and the ☽ unfortunate, the good planets falling from her, after much search something shall be found, and little shall be taken, and that with weariness of the body; which shall be the truer, if the lord of the ascendant be ♄, and in the seventh house a sign of four footed beasts. If you find ☽ in the seventh or in any of the angles, or the lord of the seventh, and she be fortunate, say that he shall speed in his *hunting*.

Of a Lawsuit or Controversy between two, who shall speed best, or whether they shall compound, or have the matter taken up or not before they do go to Law.

Behold the ascendant, his lord and ☽, these signify the *querent*; the seventh house and his lord are for the *Adversary*.

If the lord of the ascendant or the ☽ be joined to the lord of the seventh, or be in ⚹ or △ aspect with mutual Reception, the parties will easily of themselves accord, and compose all differences without mediation of any, or with a little entreaty.

But if one receive the other, and he that is received, receive not the other *Significator*, they shall agree without Suit of law, but not without intermission of a third party or more; and those that intercede, for the most part shall be his Friends or Acquaintance that did receive the other Planet.

If they, *viz.* the lord of the seventh and ascendant are in a □ aspect, or in ☍, with mutual Reception, or in a ⚹ or △ without Reception, they will be reconciled, but first they will have one little combat at law: and you must observe, that unity shall proceed from that party whose *Significator* is less ponderous, and commits his disposition to the other; and this concord shall be the more firm, if both *Significators* receive one another: If the lighter Planet be joined to the more weighty, and receive him not, but the superior Planet receive him, it argues, he that receives would accord whether his Adversary will or not.

Having considered the former *significators*, do you observe the *significator* of the *Judge*, who is ever the lord of the tenth house, and whether he aspect either of the *significators*, *viz.* whether the lord of the ascendant or seventh, or be in ♂ with either of them; see if the lord of the ascendant hastens to the ♂ of the lord of the seventh, or the lord of the seventh to him, and that the lord of the tenth house does frustrate their ♂, it's then an argument they shall not agree before they have been at law, and herein the *Judge* or *Lawyer* seems faulty, who will not permit the parties to compose their differences: see if the ☽ transfer light between the lord of the ascendant and seventh; if she do not, see if any other Planet carry their influence or light to each other; for if it be so, it's like some or other interpose their pains, and reconcile the parties though they be in law.

See after this, whether the lord of the ascendant or seventh be strongest, for he whose *significator* is most powerful, ought to have the victory; he is strongest, who is in an angle, and in some of his essential Dignities; the greater his strength is, how much greater the essential Dignity is wherein he is; and if he be also received by any other Planet, it's an argument that party is able, and that he has the more Friends to assist him: if you do find that they will compound, the first mover thereunto, will be on the part of the lighter Planet, who commits his disposition to the other; for if the lord of the ascendant be more light, and the lord of the seventh more ponderous, the first motion of peace shall come from the *querent*, and so *e contrario*: A Planet in a cadent house is more weak, if not received or assisted by the aspect of some other; if the lord of the seventh house be in the ascendant, then the *querent* without doubt overcomes, and the *Adversary* will yield; the like happens to the *querent*, *viz.* that he shall be overcome: and this happens not only in law *When he is* Suits, and for more Moneys, but also in Fights, Duels and *in the same* War: see further if the Lord of the ascendant or seventh be *condition.* retrograde, for if the lord of the ascendant be retrograde, it argues the weakness of the *querent*, and that he will not stand to it stoutly, that he will deny the truth to his *Adversary* nor will he believe that he has any right to the thing in question; if the lord of the seventh be retrograde, it argues the same things on the *quesited's* part.

Behold the *significator* of the *Judge* who is to give sentence in the Cause, which is the Lord of the tenth house, whether he be direct, and behold them, for then he will proceed according to order of law in the Cause, and will endeavour to shorten and determine it; but if he be Retrograde, it's an argument the *Judge* will not go on or proceed according to order of law, nor will he care to end it; nay it's rather probable he will prolong it a longer time then he ought by law: judge the same if the Lord of the ascendant be separated from the Lord of the seventh, or the Lord of the seventh from the Lord of the ascendant.

See if the Lord of the ascendant be in aspect with the ☉ or ☽, or either of them joined to him, so that no other Planet hinder their aspect, beware it be not a corporal ♂, for that signifies an impediment, unless the Planet were in the heart of the ☉, for then the Planet was fortified thereby; so is he in like nature, if the Planet be in either of the houses of the *Luminaries*, or if the ☉ and ☽ be in the ascendant, these argue the potency of the *querent*: if the Lord of the seventh be dignified or qualified as before I mentioned of the Lord of the ascendant, you must judge in like nature on the behalf of the *quesited*: If the Lord of the ascendant be joined to the Lord of the tenth, he that is the *querent* will acquaint the *Judge* himself, or make means to acquaint him with his Cause, and it may be he will endeavour to bribe the *Judge*, that so he may judge on his side: if the lord of the tenth receive the lord of the second, the *Judge* will have Money for his pains; but if the lord of the tenth receive the lord of the ascendant, the *Judge* hears the *querent's* importunities, otherwise not.

If the lord of the tenth be more light than the lord of the ascendant, and joined to him, he will do the *querent's* business, though he never speak to him; if the lord of the second be joined to the lord of the tenth, then the *Adversary* makes means to the *Judge*; and if the lord of the tenth receive the lord of the seventh, he will assist him; but if he receive the lord of the eighth, he will take his Money.

If the lord of the tenth receive both *significators* the *Judge* will compose the matter ere it do come to a full Trial.

If the Lord of the tenth be in the tenth, in his own house, the *Judge* will then do justice, and judge the cause for his honour, unless that Planet be ♄: if the Lord of the tenth be only in his own Terms or Triplicity, it's true the *Judge* will determine the Cause, but makes no matter which way it goes, if a Planet be in the tenth house that has no dignity, or is not in Reception with the Lord of the tenth, it argues the parties will not be content, or stand to that Sentence, they both fear that *Judge*, and had rather have another *Judge* his Sentence, with which they would be content: If ♄ be *Judge*, he will not judge as he ought; if at that time ♃, ♀, ☉, ☿ or ☽ be in any aspect to ♄ but ☍, the *Judge* will be ill reported of, but in a little time will be cleared, and the aspersion taken off; but if any of those be in ☍ to ♄, there will go a hard report on the *Judge* for that his Sentence, and it will continue long; the *Judge's* defamation will be great if ♂ be in ☍ to ♄, unless ♂ be with ♄ in ♑, then the scandal will be the less.

But to be short, in these like Judgments observe this method; the *Querent* is signified by the Lord of the ascendant, the *Adversary* by the Lord of the seventh, the *Judge* by the Lord of the tenth, the end of the matter from the Lord of the fourth; consider well the Lords of the houses, their Fortitudes, and whether they be in Angles, Succedents or Cadents, Fortunate or not Fortunate; for the Planet that is most strong, and best placed, is the best man, and most likely to carry the victory, and has the best Cause.

If more Planets be in the ascendant and second, the *Querent* shall have most Friends & *sic e contario*: if both *Significators* give their virtue to one Planet, there will be one who will intercede between them: if the Sign ascending and seventh be fixed, both *querent* and *quesited* are resolutely bent to proceed in the Suit or Controversy; if movable Signs be there, it's like they have no great stomach to the business, but will end it very shortly; if common Signs be there, they will continue the Suit long, and have the Cause out of one Court into another; on whose part you find the *Infortunes*, that party shall receive most prejudice, sorrow and trouble by the Contention.

You are to consider in this manner of Judgment the ☽ from whom she is separated, and the Planet to whom she applies are equally significant, as the ascendant and seventh house, &c.

CHAPTER LIV.

Of Buying and Selling Commodities.

The *Buyer* is signified by the Lord of the ascendant and the ☽; the *Seller* by the Lord of the seventh, see if the ☽ be joined with the Lord of the seventh, the *querent* may then buy the thing or Commodity he desires, and this quickly; if the Lord of the ascendant be a more light Planet than the Lord of the seventh, the *querent* will occasion the sale of it, & *e contra*, if the Lord of the seventh be the lighter Planet: if the preceding *Significators* have no aspect to each other, behold if the ☽ or some other Planet transfer not the light of the one to the other, a Friend shall then appear who will drive on the bargain for them both, so that the matter will be done: In this manner of Judicature, you must distinguish what you are to buy; as if a Servant or Sheep, Hogs, Coneys, &c. the sixth house and his Lord are then considered: if it concern Horses, Asses, Camels, Oxen or Cows, Judgment must be drawn from the twelfth house and the ascendant: if a House, Town or Castle, then the fourth house and his Lord, and so consider in any other Commodity.

If the Lord of the seventh be in the ascendant, the *Seller* will importune the *querent* to buy; the contrary if the Lord of the ascendant be in the seventh, for then the *querent* has most mind to buy: if either ♃ or ♀ be in the ascendant, the *Buyer* performs his work suddenly without any labour; so if the ☉ be in the ascendant, and not corporally joined to any other Planet; if ☿ or the ☽ be in the ascendant, not infected with the evil aspect of an *Infortune*, they fortunate the *Buyer*, and he performs what he intended; ♄, ♂ or ☋ in the ascendant, argue labour and difficulty, and that the matter will not be had without much labour, & that the *Buyer* is a cunning companion, and means deceitfully, and will deceive the *Seller*, if possible: if the *Infortunes* be in the seventh, have a care of the *Seller*, he will find out one trick or other to delude the *Buyer*; he is a crafty Fellow, &c. If the ☽ be void of course, unless the *Significators* apply strongly, there's seldom any Bargain concluded, or Commodity at that time bought, and yet both parties wrangle, and have some meetings to no purpose: If the Planet from whom the ☽ separates enters Combustion, he that sells his Land or House at that time, shall never recover them again: but if the Planet from whom the ☽ did last separate, be free from misfortune, and beholds the Lord of that Sign from whence the Judgment, or thing in question is required; it's then possible the *Seller* may in time repurchase the Lands or Commodities again, or others of as good value.

CHAPTER LV.

Of Partnership.

The Lord of the ascendant is for the *querent*; Lord of the seventh for the *Partner* intended: but herein be careful that you observe what Planet is in the seventh, and near the cusp of the seventh, and whether the party inquired of be more like to the description of the Planet placed in the seventh, or to the Lord of the seventh; take that Planet for his *Significator* who is nearest to his description, and consider him as you would otherwise the Lord of the seventh, and as you ought to do of the Lord of the seventh, no other Planet being in the seventh.

Let the ☽ be partner in signification; the tenth house shall show what credit there may come of the Partnership: but whether the Partnership will extend to good or ill, you must expect that from the fourth house and his Lord, and the Planet therein placed, and the Planet to whom the ☽ applies.

If the Lord of the ascendant and the ☽ be in movable Signs without Reception by House or Exaltation, or Triplicity or Term, then there will happen Contention, and they will disagree, but matters will again be reconciled, and the Partnership will hold, but still they will be mistrustful of one another, nor will much good come of it: but if the *Significators* be in fixed Signs, their society will continue long; but if no Reception be, little profit will from thence accrue to either party; if they buy anything, the Commodities will lie long on their hands; if the *Significators* be in common Signs, it promises a gainful Partnership, and that they will be faithful to each other: If one *Significator* be in a movable Sign, and the other in a fixed, the disturbance arising will be less than at first may be feared: If ill Planets aspect both the *significators, viz.* Lord of the ascendant and Lord of the seventh, the Partnership will be ill for both, neither the one party or other will deal fairly; see where, and in what house or houses the evil Planets are placed, and from thence you may discern the cause: I have oft acquainted you with the signification of the houses: an evil Planet in the ascendant, the *querent* is a false companion; judge the like if an evil Planet be in the seventh.

If the ☽ separate from one *Fortune* and apply to another, they will begin well and end well, though neither of them get any Wealth; but if she be separated from a good Planet, and apply to an ill, they begin well, but end in strife and hatred; and so the contrary: but if the ☽ be separated from an ill Planet and apply to another, they will begin Partnership with muttering and repining, continue it with fears and jealousies, end it with Lawsuits.

A good Planet in the tenth, shows they will obtain reputation, and will rejoice and delight in their mutual Society.

A good Planet in the second, best for the *querent*; in the seventh for the *Partner*.

An ill Planet in the second, or ☋, the *querent* will get little, but be cheated, or entrust much, and get in few Debts.

If the Lord of the fourth apply to the Lord of the eleventh by ✶ or △; or if a good Planet be in the fourth, or if the Lord of the eleventh and fourth be in Reception, or if good Planets cast their ✶ or △ to the Lords of the ascendant and seventh, a good end may be expected by the Partnership intended: observe the ⊗, how dignified, how aspected; if the Lord of the seventh or of the eighth cast a □ or ☍ to it, the *querent* must expect no great good from his Partner, for it's like he will embezzle the Estate, or their common Stock.

CHAPTER LVI.

Whether a City, Town or Castle, besieged, or to be besieged, shall be taken or not.

The ascendant and his Lord are for the *querent*, and those that do or shall besiege; the fourth house shall signify the *Town, City* or *Fort* besieged, or to be besieged, the Lord thereof the *Governor*; the fifth house, Planets therein, and his Lord, the *Ammunition, Soldiery* and *Assistants* the *Governor* and *Town* may expect to relive or assist them*: If **in the* you find the Lord of the first strong and fortunate, or joined *Town and* to the Lord of the fourth in the first, or with the ☽ or Lord *are in* of the tenth, or in any house except the twelfth, eighth, and *Garrison* sixth, conditionally, that the Lord of the first receive the Lord of the fourth, or the ☽ receive the Lord of the fourth, though she be not received again, it's an argument, the *Town, Fort* or *Castle* shall be taken: or if the Lord of the fourth be in such houses as behold not the fourth, (except the Lord of the seventh be in the fourth, then it will not be taken;) if the Lord of the fourth be with the ill *Fortunes*, and impeded, it's probable the City shall be taken, and the Governor wounded, or if *Infortunes* be in the fourth without some strong aspect of the *Fortunes*, It will be taken, or can it hold out long, or there may be treason in Town: If ☋ be in the fourth, it will be taken, and there will be some go about to betray or deliver it, or some principal Work or Fort therein; the Sign shows which part of the Town; nor does the Governor think himself able to preserve it.

If none of these Accidents or Configurations before rehearsed be, then have regard to the Lord of the fourth; if he be in the fourth strong and fortunate, and not Retrograde or Combust, or besieged of the *Infortunes*, or if the Lord of the seventh be there, free from all impediments, or if ♃ or ♀ or ☊

be therein, and no reception between the Lord of the ascendant and fourth, then the City, Fort or Town at that time surrounded or besieged, shall not be taken or delivered to the Army now besieging it; nay, if there be both a *Fortune* and an *Infortune* in the fourth, the Town shall not be taken, if the *Fortune* be nearest to the cusp of the house, or first of the two Planets which shall transit the degree of the fourth; and this you may aver with greater confidence, if the Lord of the ascendant be anything weak, or a light Planet and unfortunate; but if the Lord of the ascendant be fortunate, and a *Fortune* therein, and he or the ☽ behold the fourth house, it notes surrendering or taking the City, Town or Castle besieged: but if he be unfortunate and otherwise impeded, and an *Infortune* in the second, or the Lord thereof Retrograde, or in □ or ☍ to the Lord of the ascendant, it signifies the *querent's* Soldiers will desert him, and will not continue the Siege, they have no mind to the work, or the *querent* wants to fit instruments or materials for a Siege, or his Ammunition will not come opportunely, or the Soldiers will depart discontented for their pay, or their duties are too hard, so that he may expect no honour at this Siege.

CHAPTER LVII.

Of COMMANDERS *in Armies, their abilities, fidelity, and whether by them Victory may be had yea or not, &c.*

Again, consider well all the twelve houses and their proper *Significators*, and make the ascendant *Significator* of the *querent*, and his Lord; let the seventh & his Lord show the opposite parties or *Adversaries* who may come to relieve the Besieged; let the eighth be their Seconds or Friends, and the ninth their third house, and so all the other houses in order.

An *Infortune* in the ascendant, or beholding the house with □ or ☍, it notes, the *querent*, or that side he takes part with, will not manage their matters well, or prosecute the War discreetly: an *Infortune* in the ascendant, or being Lord of the ascendant, argues no great justice on the *querent's* part, or that he has no cause to begin the War or quarrel, but if either a good Planet be in the ascendant, or behold the ascendant with ⚹ or △, it signifies a good ground or cause on the *querent's* behalf; if an *Infortune* be in the second, and be not Lord of the second (or have Exaltation in the Sign,) if he, I say, behold the second with a □ or ☍, it's like there will be no War, but if any be, the *querent* shall have the worst; a *Fortune* in that house, or aspecting it, shows the contrary, &c. If an *Infortune* be in the third, and ♂ be that Planet, and he strong, the *querent* is like to have good warlike Provisions; say the same if ♃ be there: but if ♂ be therein unfortunate, his Army is like to be composed of Thieves, Highwaymen, vagrant Fellows, seditious, and such as will obey no commands.

If an *Infortune* be in the fourth, the place where the War is like to be, or where the Armies may engage, is like to be unfit for the *querent's* Army: if it be mountainous, the places are rough, inaccessible not habitable, full of Woods, no passage for Armies; if the place seem to be described moist, it's mirey, dirty, full of standing waters, Bogs, Rivers or Brooks, not fit to marshal an Army in, or wherein an Army can do any service: If ♂ be in the fifth, well dignified, or the good aspects of the *Fortunes* irradiate that house, or a *Fortune* be therein placed, then it's like the Army or Soldiers on the *querent's* part, will be good Soldiers, apt for fight, and obedient to their Officers; the *Infortunes* placed therein show contrary qualities.

If either of the *Fortunes* or ☊ be in the sixth, the Carriage-Horse attending the Army, seem serviceable, high prized, and fit for the employment.

If ♂ be therein well dignified, the Horse entertained or employed will be fierce, impatient and hard to be governed.

But if ♄ be in the sixth without dignities, the Horse are old, rotten jades, unserviceable, tired, overspent, slow, not fit for this service, diseased, &c.

If a *Fortune* be in the seventh, the instruments of War and Fortification, the Cannons and great Guns of the Army are fair, sound, well cast, and will perform their work: and this position of a *Fortune* in the seventh, denotes, the Enemy is no fool; if an *Infortune* be there, or have the before-named evil aspects to the house, the enemy is weak, the *querent's* instruments are nought, will perform no service, the Enemy will rather fight by policy, craft and treachery, than manhood.

If a *Fortune* be in the eighth, it's an argument no mortality or much destruction of men will follow, or will there be many men wounded, or their wounds difficult to cure; no great slaughters, fights, flights, or any set Battles will be between the Armies on either part: but if ♄ be therein Retrograde, many prisoners will be taken, much ruin and destruction, much poverty and plundering will succeed.

If a *Fortune* be in the ninth, or have aspect to the house, the enemy is in a good posture, hopes to benefit himself by some false reports, or by some false alarms or sallies, and that he intends to act much by such like reports, and by witty inventions, for the Enemy is politic.

If a *Fortune* be in the tenth or cast his ⚹ or △ thither, it's an argument, the Commander in Chief is a discreet man, understands what to do in his place, and that the Officers of the Army are expert men, every one in his place being capable of what he undertakes: but if ♄ or ☋ be therein, or ♂, any ways unfortunate, the Officers and Captains are very asses and buzzards, have no judgment, simple Fellows, the whole design is like to be overthrown by their knavery, and want of discretion and judgment; I mean, the greater part of the Officers, &c. they are more fit for hanging, than to Command.

If a *Fortune* be in the eleventh, it shows, the Conductors of the Army are men of good discretion and sound judgment, expert men in the art of War, know how to command and order their affairs, are valiant and careful, and understand in every particular when to charge or retreat; in a word, the Officers seem men of approved integrity and judgment.

If an *Infortune* be in the eleventh, the Conductor or Conductors may be men of fidelity, and assured Friends and Well-wishers to the cause they undertake, but they are inexpert, and not fit to undertake such a weighty employment in hand, for they nothing understand the stratagems of War, whereby the whole cause is like to suffer.

If a *Fortune* be in the twelfth house, those against whom the Army is to go, are well provided, and resolve to defend themselves; they agree well, fear nothing, will stand it out to the last: but if an *Infortune* be there, they suspect their own abilities, are not capable of resisting, disagree amongst themselves, fear surprise every moment: It is, notwithstanding, ever considerable, that if ♂ be in the twelfth house, the *querent* may justly suspect treachery, and indeed you have just cause to fear the same if ☋ be in the twelfth. Now as you have considered the whole twelve houses on the behalf of the *querent*, so must you observe the same method and manner of judgment on the behalf of the *Adversary*, only considering what house for the *querent* is the ascendant, the opposite house is the same for the *quesited*, and so every house in order: Which judgments rightly understood, will give great light to any manner of question propounded in this nature by any prime *Officer* or *Commander*.

If the Armies shall fight.

Behold herein the ascendant and his Lord, the ☽ and Lord of the seventh, see if they be corporally joined in any angle, then it seems the Armies will fight: if there be no ♂ of the Lord of the ascendant and seventh, see if they behold one another by □ or ☍, they will also then fight: if this happens not, see if any Planet transfer the light of one to the other by □ or ☍ aspect, with or without Reception; if such an aspect be, there will be a fight between them: but if the more ponderous of the two receive that Planet who transfers their light, no fight will be, but all things will be composed lightly.

CHAPTER LVIII.

If the Querent have open Enemies, or any Adversaries, or many that do envy him.

This is a difficult Question, and yet by *Astrologie* responsible, but you must justly consider whether the querent do demand thus much, viz. *Have I enemies or not?* Or, *Whether is such a man my adversary?* &c.

But if the querent doubt his Brother, Father, or Servant; then take Signification from each particular House signifying them.

If any be nominated, require judgment from the seventh house and Lord thereof: if the Lord of the seventh aspect the Lord of the ascendant, with □ or ☍, or be in like aspect with the ☽, it's then very probable, the party inquired after does envy the Querent, and wishes him no good: if the aspect be separated, they have lately been in some contest, or some difference has been between them; but if they are then applying to a □ or ☍, the enmity, difference or controversy is approaching, is not yet over, will grow to a greater height than now it is, and the party inquired after, does what in him lies to thwart and cross the occasions of the *querent*. In like manner, consider if the Lord of the seventh be in the twelfth from the ascendant, or in the twelfth sign from the place wherein the Lord of the ascendant is in, or from the place wherein the ☽ is, or if the Lord of the seventh be in ♂ with any Planet, or in any aspect with a Planet who is in ☍ or □ to the Lord of the ascendant or the ☽, without Reception, then the Quesited, or man or woman nominated, is averse, and an enemy to the Querent, but if it be not so, then he or she inquired after is no enemy.

If the Question be absolute, (as thus) *Whether have I enemies yea or no?* you must require judgment herein from the twelfth house, and see if the Lord of that house be in □ or ☍ to the ☽ with or without Reception; if so, then he has enemies that watch for an opportunity against him, but they do all things clandestinely and cunningly, and desire to play their part when they can do it without noise or rumour of evil, that so they may still go under the notion of Friends, when as in truth they are treacherous, false and deceitful: Consider also where and in what house the Lord of the twelfth is, say confidently such people, men or women of such a quality or condition, are the Querent's adversaries: Many Planets in the seventh, denotes many enemies,* many Planets in the second, much want of money, if they are ill dignified, &c. and so do in all the rest, observing how many Planets there are in the seventh, and of what houses they are Lords of, or from the houses whereof

*Often and ever by me found true.

they are Lords, from thence do you require the quality of the people who are enemies, &c. remembering, that the □ aspect shows envy and malice, yet possible to be reconciled, ♂ aspects without Reception, never, &c.

CHAPTER LIX.

A LADY, *if marry the* GENTLEMAN *desired?*

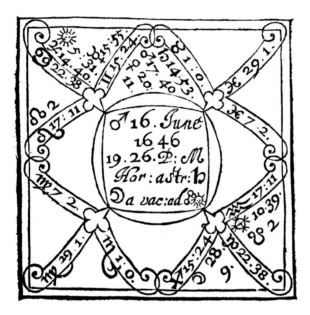

See page
A8

Judgment upon the Figure abovesaid.

The true state of this Lady's cause stood thus: *A Gentleman had been a long time an earnest Suitor to her for Marriage, but she could never master her affection so much as to incline to Marriage-thoughts with him, but slighted him continually; and at last, to the great discontent of the Gentleman, she gave him an absolute denial: After which denial so given, she became passionately affectionate of him, and did sorely repent of her folly, and so churlish a carriage, wishing she might again have former opportunities.* This was her condition at what time she propounded the Question to me.

The ascendant and ☉ are for the *querent*; ♄ Lord of the seventh, is for the man *quesited* after. The *querent* was moderately tall, of round visage, sanguine complexion, of a cheerful, modest countenance, gray eyed, her hair a light brown, occasioned, as I conceive, by ☉ Lord of the ascendant, in the Terms of ♂, she was well spoken, and sufficiently comely.

Finding ♄ in an angle of the South, and in ☌ with ♂, and both in ♉, a fixed, earthly Sign, I judged the corporature of the quesited party to be but mean, and not tall, or very handsome, his visage long and incomposed, a wan, pale or meagre complexion, dark hair, or of a sad, chestnut colour, curling and crisp, his eyes fixed, ever downward, musing, stooping forward with his head, some impediment in his going, as treading awry, &c. [*this was confessed.*] Finding ♄ so, as abovesaid, elevated, and in ☌ with ♂, I judged the Gentleman to be sad, angry, much discontented, and scorning his former slights, (as ever all Saturnine people do;) I judged him much incensed by a Kinsman or Gentleman of quality, signified by ♂, Lord of the third, in part, from the seventh, and of the fourth, being the tenth from the seventh; and that this Gentleman and he lived either in one house, or near one another, because both *significators* are angular and fixed, [*and so it was.*] I said, the Gentleman had no inclination or disposition to her, finding the ☽ separated from void of course, and applying to ☍ of ☉, Lord of the ascendant, it did argue there was small hopes of effecting her desire, because she herself, by her own perverseness, had done herself so grand a mischief. Whereupon she told me the truth of all, and not before, and implored my directions, which way, without scandal to her honour, it might be brought on again, if possible: and indeed she was lamentably perplexed, and full of heaviness. Hereupon, with much compassion, I began to consider what hopes we had in the Figure: I found ☉ applying to a ⚹ of ♄; this argued the woman's desire, and the strength of her affections towards the *quesited*, because she is signified by the lighter Planet; but there was no Reception between the *significators*, therefore that application gave little hopes: but finding Reception between ♃ and the ☽, and between ☉ and ☽, she in his Triplicity, ☉ in her House; observing also, that the ☽ did dispose of ♄ in her Exaltation, and of ♃ in her House, and that ♃ was very near a ✶ *dexter* of ♄, still applying, and not separated; as also, that ♃ was in his Exaltation, and a fortunate Planet ever assisting nature and the afflicted, and that he was able by his strength to qualify and take off the malice of ♄: besides, the nearness of ♃ to the ✶ of ♄, made me confident that the *quesited* was intimately acquainted with a person of quality and worth, such as ♃ represented, whom I exactly described, and the *Lady* very well knew: To him I directed to address her Complaints, and acquaint him fully with her unhappy folly: I positively affirmed, in the Gentleman described she should find all honour and secrecy, and I doubted not but, by God's blessing, he would again revive the business (now despaired of) and bring her to her hearts content: But finding that ♄ and ☉ came to ✶ aspect the 27th of the same month, I advised to hasten all things before the aspect was over; and also gave direction, that the nineteenth of *June* near upon noon, the Gentleman should first move the *quesited* in the business: and my reason was, because that day ♄ and ♃ were in perfect ✶ aspect.

My counsel was followed, and the issue was thus: By the Gentleman's means and procurement the matter was brought on again, the Match effected, and all within twenty days following, to the content of the sorrowful (but as to me unthankful) Lady, &c. In *Astrologie*, the true reason of this performance is no more than, first, an application of the two *Significators* to a ✶, *viz.* the Lord of the seventh and first: Next, the application of the ☽ to the Lord of the ascendant, though by ☍, yet with Reception, was another small argument; but the main occasion, without which in this Figure it could not have been, the application of ♃ to ✶ of ♄ Lord of the seventh, receiving his virtue which ♄ did render to him, and he again transferred to the ☉ Lord of the ascendant, he, *viz.* ♃, meeting with no manner of prohibition, abscission or frustration until his perfect ♂ with the ☉, which was the 29th of *June*, so that no difficulty did afterwards intervene. I did acquaint this Lady, that very lately before the erection of this Figure, her Sweetheart had been offered a Match, and that the Gentlewoman propounded, was such a one as is signified by ♀, one not only of a good fortune, but excellently well descended: I bade her follow my directions, with hope and expectation of a good end, and told her she should not fear his marrying of ♀: Which judgment I gave, by reason ♂ was nearer ♀ than ♄, and so interposed his influence, or kept off ♄. I judged ♂ to be some Soldier, or Gentleman that had been in Arms: this I did the more to enlighten her fancy, which I found apprehensive enough. She well knew both the Gentlewoman and man, and confessed such matters were then in action.

Had the *Quere* been, *Who should have lived longest?* certainly I should have judged the woman, because ☉ is going to ♂ of ♃, and ♂ afflicts ♄ by his presence.

Had she demanded, *Whether the Quesited had been rich?* I must have considered ♃ Lord of his second house, whom I find in his Exaltation, Direct, Swift, &c. only under the Sunbeams; I should have adjudged his Estate good.

For Agreement, because ☉ and ♄ are applying to ✶, I should have conceived they would well accord; yet doubtless ♄ will look for much observance, for as he is ill by nature, so is he vitiated by ♂, and made thereby choleric as well as melancholy, so will he be naturally jealous without cause; yet the gentle ✶ of ♃ to both ♂ and ♄, seems by education, to repress that frowardness naturally he may be subject to.

If it be demanded, *Will the querent be honest?* I answer, her *significatrix, viz.* ☉, is no way afflicted by ♂: her Sign ascending being ♌, and Reception between ♃ and ☽, are arguments of a virtuous woman.

In this nature you may examine any Figure for discovery of what is necessary, &c.

CHAPTER LX.

If she should marry the man desired?

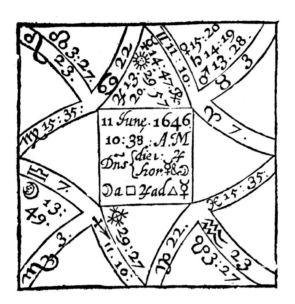

See page
A9

The Judgment.

The *querent* was of tall stature, ruddy complexioned, sober, discreet and well spoken, &c. The *quesited* was very tall, slender, lean, and of a long visage, black hair: His tallness I attribute to ♃, as being in the Terms of ☿, and the cusp of the seventh being also in his Terms: and indeed the being of a *significator* in the Terms of any Planet, does a little vary the party from his natural temper and constitution, so that he will retain a small or great tincture from that Planet according as he is dignified: The sadness of his hair, I conceive to be from ♃ his aspect to ♄, and the ☽ her □ to him, being herself subterranean.

☿ Is here *Significatrix* of the *querent*, Retrograde, under the

Sunbeams, was in some distress and fear that the *quesited* would not have her; and she might and had some reason for it, for ♃ was in his Exaltation, and near the ✶ of ♀, an argument the man stood upon high terms, and had been tampering with another; yet were both *Significators* in a *Semisextile*, and in good houses, from which I gathered hopes, that there was some sparks of love between them; but when I found the ☽ separating from □ of ♃, and carrying his light by a △ aspect to ☿ the Lord of the ascendant, and he in an angle, receiving willingly, by his Retrograde motion, that her virtue which she brought from ♃. I was confident the Match would suddenly be brought to pass by such a one as ☽ was, or represented by her, who did much interpose in the business, and who at last, with a little difficulty, produced the Marriage to effect, to the content of both parties.

CHAPTER LXI.

A Fugitive Servant, which way gone, when return?

This chart set for February 26, 1645 (OS)

See page A9

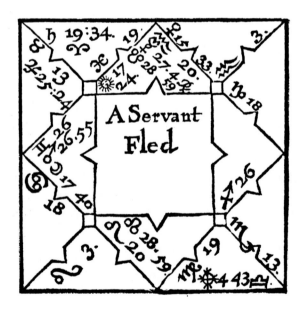

Judgment upon the Figure beforegoing,

The ascendant, and ☿ in ♒, together with ♂ placed in the ascendant, did signify the *Master* of the *Servant,* who was short of stature, corpulent, of a good complexion, and ruddy, fresh countenance; his fatness I conceive from the north latitude of ☿, which was about one degree; as also, that the degrees ascending were in the Terms of ♂, in an airy Sign, and in the Face or Decanate of ☉, now placed in a watery Sign, and in partile △ to ☽, both in moist Signs, which argues a phlegmatic, full body, &c.

The *Significator* of the Servant was ♂ peculiarly in this Figure, although many times ☿ shall signify a *fugitive* Servant: The Servant was a young Fellow of about nineteen, a well set Fellow, short, big jointed, broad and full faced, dark brown hair, his teeth growing ill favoured, a Sunburnt, obscure complexion, yet the skin of his body clear.

I observe that he went away from his Master the Sunday preceding, at what time the ☽ was in ♊, a Western Sign, and that now ♂, the *Significator* of the Fellow was in the same Sign; as also, that ☿ the common *Significator* of Servants, was in ♒, a Western Sign, but South quarter of Heaven; it is true that ♊ has some relation to the South quarter, and ♒ to the North.

I judged from hence that the Servant went westward at his first departing, and that at the time of the Question, he was West from the *querent's* house; and this I judged because ♂ was angular, and every way as strong as the ☽, otherwise I should have judged by the ☽: Forasmuch as ♂ the *Significator* of the Servant, and ☿ Lord of the ascendant, were suddenly hastening to a △ out of angles, I judged, that within a day or two he should have his Servant again: I found the ☽ in the second, in her own house; the Servant being a part of his Master's Estate, I judged from hence also, that the Master should not lose, but recover forthwith his lost Goods; and the rather, for that the ☽ was in the second, and in perfect △ of the ☉ in the eleventh, both of them in the Mediety ascending: the nearness of ♂ to the degree ascending, made me judge the Servant was not above three or four houses Westward from his Masters house.

The truth is, that upon Friday following betimes in the morning, he came home, and said he had been at *Kingston* upon *Thames*: which if true, then he was full West, or a little to the South, and near a great Water, *viz.* the *Thames*, as ☽ in ♋ did or might signify.

CHAPTER LXII.

A Dog missing, where?

See page A10

Judgment upon this preceding Figure.

Living in *London* where we have few or no small Cattle, as Sheep, Hogs, or the like, as in the Country; I cannot give example of such creatures, only I once set the Figure preceding concerning a Dog (who is in the nature of small Beasts) which Dog was fled and missing. The *Quere* to me was, *What part of the City they should search, next if he should ever recover him.*

The *querent* was signified by the Sign ascending and the Lord thereof; and indeed in his person he was *Saturnine*, and vitiated according to *Cauda* in the ascendant, in his stature, mind or understanding; that is, was a little deformed in body, and extreme covetous in disposition, &c.

The Sign of the sixth and his Lord signifies the Dog; so must they have done if it had been a Sheep or Sheep, Hogs, Conies, &c. or any small Cattle.

The Sign of ♊ is West and by South, the quarter of heaven is West; ☿ the *significator* of the Dog, is in ♎ a Western Sign but Southern quarter of heaven, tending to the West; the ☽ is in ♍, a Southwest Sign, and verging to the Western angle: the strength of the testimonies examined, I found the plurality to signify the West, and therefore I judged, that the *Dog* ought to be Westward from the place where the Owner lived, which was at *Temple-barre*, wherefore I judged that the *Dog* was about *Long-acre*, or upper part of *Drury-lane*: In regard that ☿ *Significator* of the Beast, was in a Sign of the same Triplicity that ♊ his ascendant is, which signifies *London*, and did apply to a △ of the Cusp of the sixth house, I judged the *Dog* was not out of the lines of Communication, but in the same quarter; of which I was more confirmed by ☉ and ♄ their △. The Sign wherein ☿ is in, is ♎, an airy Sign, I judged the *Dog* was in some chamber or upper room, kept privately, or in great secrecy: because ☽ was under the Beams of the ☉, and ☿, ☽ and ☉ were in the eighth house, but because the ☉ on Monday following did apply by △ *dexter* to ♄ Lord of the ascendant, and ☽ to ✶ of ♂, having exaltation in the ascendant; I intimated, that in my opinion he should have his *Dog* again, or news of his *Dog* or small Beast upon Monday following, or near that time; which was true; for a Gentleman of the *querent's* acquaintance, sent home the Dog the very same day about ten in the morning, who by accident coming to see a Friend in *Long-acre*, found the *Dog* chained up under a table, and knowing the Dog to be the *Querent's*, sent him home, as abovesaid, to my very great credit. Yet notwithstanding this, I cannot endure Questions of *Fugitives* or *Thefts*, nor ever would have done anything, but with intention to benefit Posterity.

Usually I find, that all *Fugitives* go by the ☽, and as she varies her Sign, so the *Fugitive* wavers and shifts in his flight, and declines more or less to East, West, North or South: but when the Question is demanded, then without doubt you must consider the strength both of the *Significator* and the ☽, and judge by the stronger; if both be equivalent in Fortitudes, judge either by the *Significator*, if he best personate the *Fugitive*, or by the ☽, if she most resemble him; with relation to either of them that comes nearest in aspect to the cusp of the house, from whence signification is taken.

CHAPTER LXIII.

Of Theft.

It was the received opinion of Master *Allen* of *Oxford*, a man excellently versed in *Astrologie*, that the true *Significator* of a *Thief* is that Planet who is in an Angle or second house, and beholds the seventh house: if no peregrine Planet be in an angle or the second house, then the Lord of the seventh shall be *Significator* of the *Thief*, if he behold the seventh house: otherwise that Planet to whom the ☽ applies, if he behold the seventh house; the rather, if the ☽ separate from the Lord of the ascendant. And he says further, that a peregrine Planet in what angle soever, shall not be *Significator* of the *Thief*, unless he behold the seventh house, or have any dignity in the degree of the seventh; yet if one and the same Planet be Lord of the hour and of the ascendant, he shall signify the *Querent*, though he behold not the ascendant: The truth is, I have ever found that if a peregrine Planet were in the ascendant, he was *Significator* of the *Thief*: next to the ascendant, I preferred the angle of the South, then the West angle, then the fourth house, last of all the second: many peregrine Planets in angles, many are or may be suspected, justly if they are in ♂, ⚹ or △; not consenting, if in □ or ☍: ever prefer that peregrine Planet for your *Significator*, who is nearest to the cusp of the angle he is in.

Money lost, who stole it? If recoverable?

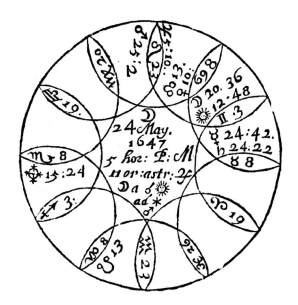

See page
A10

Judgment upon this Figure.

♏ Here ascends, and partly represents the *querent's* person, ♂ his mind and disposition, who being in □ with ☿ and ♄ gave sufficient intimation to me of the inclination of the *querent*, who was sufficiently ill conditioned, arrogant, proud, wasteful, &c.

♂ Is here in the 25 degr. and 2 min. of ♌, is angular, and but two minutes entered his own Terms, yet being in his Decanate I refused him for *Significator* of the *Thief*, and that justly, nor indeed was he.

In the next place, although ♄ was in the angle of the West, yet did I find him in his own Terms, and Decanate; I also passed by him.

In the next place, I found ☿ in 24.42 ♉, lately separated or rather in ☐ of ♂, and now almost in partile ♂ with ♄; him I found truly peregrine, *viz.* having no essential Dignity where he is, therefore I adjudged ☿ to be *Significator* of the *Thief*.

But whether ☿ signified Male or Female, was the dispute, as also the corporature, quality, &c.

The angles are part Masculine, part Feminine, no certain judgment could therefore arise from thence, the ☽ was in a Masculine Sign, applied to a masculine Planet in a masculine Sign, and ☿ usually is convertible in nature, according to the nature of the Planet he is in aspect with: he is now in aspect with ♂, and in ♂ with ♄; from hence I judged the Sex to be Male.

And said it was a young Youth of some fifteen or sixteen: young, because ☿ ever signifies Youth; but more young, because the ☽ was so near the ☉, and scarce separated from him, I said he was of reasonable stature, thin visaged, hanging Eyebrows, a long Forehead, some blemish or scars in the Face, because ♂ cast his ☐ dexter to ☿; bad Eyesight because ☿ is with evil fixed Stars, of the nature of ♂ and ☽; a sad Hair, because of his nearness to ♄; but of a scurvy countenance, one formerly a Thief or suspected for such knaveries: in regard ☿ the Youth his *Significator* was in ♂ with ♄ Lord of the third & 4ᵗʰ, I judged he was some Neighbour's child; and as the ☽ was in ♊ and ☿ in ♉, I conceived he dwelt either opposite to the *querent* or a little Southwest; and because ⊗ was in the ascendant, and disposed by ♂ Lord of the ascendant in the tenth, and the ☽ applied to his ✶ aspect, and was within four degrees of the aspect: I judged he should not only hear of, but have his Money within four days after the Question. He believed not one word I said, but would needs persuade me, that a Woman-servant signified by ♂, was one Thief, and ♄ was another; but I stood firm to the true rules of Art, and would not consent to it, because both those Planets were essentially dignified. The event proved directly true as I had manifested, both as to the person described, and to the day of the money returned, which was within three days after.

CHAPTER LIV.

Fish Stolen.

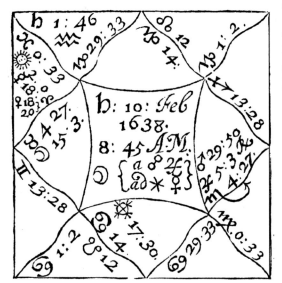

See page
A11

Living in the Country 1637, I had bought at *London* some Fish for my provision in Lent, it came down by the Barge at *Walton,* on Saturday the 10 of *February* one of the Watermen, instead of bringing my Fish home, acquainted me, their warehouse was robbed last night, and my Fish stolen: I took the exact time when I first heard the report, and erected the Figure accordingly, endeavouring to give myself satisfaction what became of my goods, and, if possible, to recover part or all of them again.

I first observed, there was no peregrine Planet in angle but ♃ whom I found upon the cusp of the seventh house, the thing I lost was Fish, therefore any Gentleman would scorn such a course Commodity; I considered the signification of ♃ in ♏, a moist Sign, and the *Significator* of my Goods, *viz.* ☿ that he was in ♓, a moist Sign, and that ⊗ was in ♋, a moist Sign. Discretion, together with Art, assisted me to think he must be a man whose profession or calling was to live upon the Water, that had my Goods, and that they were in some moist place, or in some low room, because ⊗ was in ♋, and the ☽ in ♉ an earthly Sign.

I was confident I should hear of my Goods again, because ☿ Lord of my house of Substance, was applied to by a ✶ of ☽, who was Lady of my ⊗; and yet without hopes of recovering them, because ☿ Lord of my second, was in his fall and detriment, but as he was in his own Terms, and had a △ aspect to ⊗, there was hopes of some of my Goods,

There being never a Waterman in that Town of *Walton* near to the description of ♃ in ♏, I examined what Fishermen there was of that complexion; and because ♂ Lord of the 7ᵗʰ was departing the Sign ♏, *viz.* his own, and entering another Sign, I examined if never a Fisherman of ♂ and ♃ his nature had lately sold any Land, or was leaving his proper house, and going to another habitation; such a one I discovered, and that he was much suspected of thievery, who was a good fellow, lived near the *Thames* side, and was a mere Fisherman, or man conversant in water; for all *Significators* in watery Signs, argued, he must needs live near the water, or a watery place, that stole the Goods, or be much conversant in waters.

The man that was the Thief was a Fisherman, of good stature, thick and full bodied, fair of complexion, a reddish-yellowish hair.

I procured a Warrant from a Justice of peace, and reserved it privately until Sunday the eighteenth of *February* following, and then with a Constable and the Bargeman, I searched only that one house of this Fisherman suspected; I found part of my Fish in water, part eaten, part not consumed, all confessed. This jest happened in the search; a part of my Fish being in a bag, it happened the Thief stole the bag as well as the Fish; the Bargeman, whose sack it was, being in the same room where the bag was, and oft looking upon it (being clean washed) said to the woman of the house, Woman, so I may have my sack which I lost that night, I care not: the woman answered; she had never a sack but that which her husband brought home the same night with the Fish. I am persuaded the Bargeman looked upon the sack twenty times before, and knew it not, for the woman had washed it clean: I as heavily complained to the woman for seven *Portugal Onions* which I lost; she not knowing what they were, made pottage with them, as she said.

The remainder of my Fish I freely remitted, though the hireling Priest of *Walton* affirmed I had satisfaction for it, but he never hurt himself with a lie.

So that you see the peregrine Planet in an angle describes the Thief, and that neither the ☉ or ☽ in the ascendant, and in essential Dignities, gives assured hopes of discovering who it was; the application of ☽ to the Lord of the second, argues recovery; a full recovery, if both the ☽ and the Lord of the second be essentially dignified; part, if accidentally fortified; a discovery, but no recovery, if they apply and be both peregrine.

CHAPTER LXV.

A Figure erected to know whether Sir WILLIAM WALLER *or* Sir RALPH HOPTON *should overcome, they being supposed to be engaged near* Alsford, ♀ 29th *of* March, 1644.

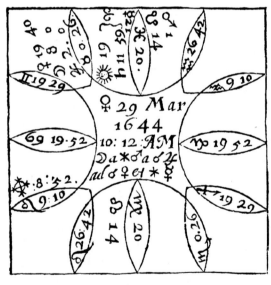

The ascendant is for our Army, the ☽, ♃ and ♀ for our Generals, *viz.* Sir *William* & Major General *Browne,* a valiant & prudent citizen of *London,* who may justly Challenge a large share of honor in that day's service: Sir *Ralph Hopton* is signified by ♄ Lord of the seventh, his Army by ♑, in the descending See page A11 part of heaven, which is usually given to the Friends and Assistants of the Enemy; there is only ♂ and ☋ in the ninth, so that by this it appeared Sir *Ralph* had no supplies ready to attend that day's success, &c.

From the existence of the ☽ in her exaltation, and in the eleventh house with ♃, she being Lady of the ascendant, and having principal signification for us and our Army, engaged for the Parliament, I concluded all was, and would be well on our side, and the victory ours: by her separation from ♃, I said, I did verily conceive we had gained already from them some ammunition, or performed some service against them, which judgment was more strengthened by ☉, Lord of our assistants and substance, placed in the tenth house, in the very degree of his Exaltation; and though I did imagine, by reason of the proximity of ♄ to ☉, we should not game the whole, or have a perfect victory without diminution of some part of it, yet I was confident we should obtain a considerable proportion of their Ammunition, and obtain a complete victory, the only thing inquired after; for that the ☽ did apply to ♀, and then to a ⚹ of ☿, he angular, I acquainted the *querent* that within eleven or twelve hours after the question we should have perfect news, and it pleasing and good; for considering the fight was within fifty miles of *London*, I ordered my time according to discretion, not allowing days for the time, but hours; for you may see the ☽ is distant from ♀ eleven degrees, but withall is in her swift motion, and increasing in light, all which were arguments of our success, and the Enemy's routing; as it did appear the same Friday by a Letter that came from the Army, certifying, that our Generals took the Thursday before, one hundred and twenty Commanders and Gentlemen, five hundred and sixty common Soldiers, much Ammunition. That according to natural causes in Art, the Enemy should be worsted, I had these reasons; first, because ♄ the Lord *Hopton's* Significator is *sub radiis*; next, he is in his Fall; thirdly, in no aspect of any Planet, but wholly peregrine and unfortunate, beholding the cusp of the seventh with a □ dexter, arguing loss to his Army, and dishonour to himself by the fight, &c.

CHAPTER LXVI.

If his Excellency ROBERT *Earl of* ESSEX *should take*
Reading, *having then surrounded it with his*
ARMY.

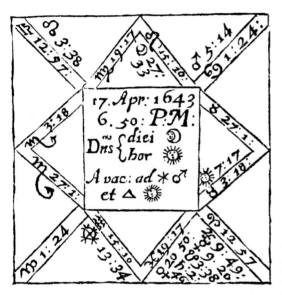

T he most
honorable
of the *English*
nation, *viz.* ESSEX
the Kingdom's
General, is here
signified by ♂ Lord
of ♏, the Sign
ascending: his
Majesty by the ☉
Lord of the tenth;
the forces that
were to relieve
Reading, or to
oppose and hinder
his Excellency, by ♀
in ♓, and ☉ in ♉.

See page A12

The Town of *Reading* by ♒ the Sign of the fourth, the
Governor Sir *Arthur Aston,* reputed an able Soldier, by ♄
Lord of the fourth, their Ammunition and Provision in the
Town by ♃ Lord of the fifth, and ♀ locally therein.

We have ♂ his Excellency's *Significator* excellently fortified,
labouring under no one misfortune (except being in his **Fall**)
and of how great concernment it is in War, to have ♂ the
general *Significator* of War, friendly to the *querent,* this Figure
well manifests; the ☽ separated (*a vacuo*) and indeed there
was little hope it would have been gained in that time it
was; she applied to a ✶ of ♂, being in Signs of long ascensions,
the aspect is equivalent to a □; which argued, that his

Excellency would have much difficulty, and some fighting, ere he could get it: but because ♂ and the ☽ were in Reception, *viz.* ♂ in her house, the ☽ in his Terms and Face, and near *Cor* ♌, placed also in the tenth, I judged his Excellency should obtain and take *Reading*, and get glory and honour thereby.

Finding the ☉ his Majesty's *Significator* in the seventh, in a fixed Sign, I acquainted the *querent*, his Majesty would oppose what he could, and send Forces to relieve the Town with all vigour and resolution, but I said he should not prevail, for ♂ is better fortified than ☉.

I considered ♒ for the Town, and in regard I found not the Sign afflicted, I judged the Town strong, and capable of holding out; when I considered ♀ to be in the fifth, I was confident they wanted not Ammunition. Having thoroughly considered all particulars, and well weighed that ♄ Lord of the fourth, signifying the Governor, was in his Fall with ☋, and that ♀ and ♃ were not far from ☋, and that ♂ did with his ☐ aspect behold ♄, I said and sent somebody word, the most assured way, & which would certainly occasion the surrender of the Town, was, to set division amongst the principal Officers, and to incense them against their Officer in Chief, & that about eight days from the time of the Question, I believed his *Excellency* would be Master of the Town, yet rather by composition than blood, because ☉ and ♂ were separated from their ✶ aspect, and ♂ was in like manner separated from the ☐ dexter of ♄ from Cardinal Signs; as also, because the application of the ☽ was so directly to the ✶ of the Lord of the ascendant, without any frustration or prohibition.

The Town was delivered for the Parliament's use the 27ᵗʰ of *April*, 1644, three days after the time limited by me was expired: But it's observable, the very Monday before, being eight days after the Figure set, they began to treat.

The truth of this Siege was thus, that his Majesty in person did come, and was worsted and beaten back at *Causham-bridge*.

That Sir *Arthur Aston* the Governor, was hurt in the head, as ♄ in ♈ with ☋ well denotes: nor did they want ammunition, as ♀ in the fifth signifies.

It was delivered by Colonel *Fielding*, a very valiant

Gentleman, a good Soldier, and of noble Family, not without jealousy and mistrust of underhand dealing in the said Colonel by the King's party; for which he was brought to some trouble, but evaded: And I have since heard some of his Majesty's Officers say thus, They did believe that *Fielding* acted nothing but what became a man of honour, and that it was the malice of his Enemies that procured him that trouble, &c.

A person of honour demanded this Question, and was well satisfied with what has been spoken.

Had this very Question been of a Law suit, *Who should have overcome?* you must have considered the Lord of the ascendant for the *querent* or *Plaintiff*, and the ascendant itself, together with the ☽: for the Enemy or *Defendant*, the seventh and his Lord and Planets therein placed. In our Figure, in regard the ☽ applies to a ⚹ of ♂, the *querent* therefore would have had the victory, by reason of the Verdict given by the *Jurors*, who ever are signified by the ☽; but because the ☉ is locally in the seventh, opposite to the ascendant, and is Lord of the tenth, *viz.* of the *Judge*, there's no doubt but the Judge would have been adverse to the *Plaintiff*, as his Majesty was to his Excellency and to the Parliament.

In this case I should have judged the *Defendant* a man of good estate, or able to spend well, because ♀ Lady of the eighth, *viz.* his second, is in Exaltation; and yet the ☉ and ♂ in ⚹, might give strong testimonies that the Judge would labour to compound the matter between both parties; the Dispositor of the ⊗ in his Fall, *viz.* ♄ in ♈ with the ☋, would have shown great expense of the *querent's* or *Plaintiff's* estate and money in this Suit; and that such a man as ♄ would herein be a great enemy to him, because ♄ and ♂ are in ☐. As ♄ is Lord of the third, he may show an ill Neighbour, or a Brother or Kinsman; but as the third house is the ninth from the seventh, it may argue some pragmatic Priest, or one of the *Defendant's* Sister's Husbands; wherefore the *Plaintiff* must either take such a one off, or else compound his matter, or he must see whether his Enemy's *Attorney* be not Saturnine, then shall he receive prejudice by his extreme rigid following the Cause: If ♄ signify his Lawyer, the damage is by him, or by some aged man, perhaps the *querent's* Father or Grandfather, or else some sturdy Clown or ill Tenant, &c. for according to the nature of the Question, you must ever vary the nature of your rules; by exact knowledge whereof, you may attain the perfection of the whole *Art.*

The eighth HOUSE, and those QUESTIONS properly belonging to it.

Of Death, Dowry, Substance of the Wife, &c.

CHAPTER LXVII.

If the absent party be alive or dead?

The true resolution of this Question depends much upon a right understanding, what relation the *querent* has to the party inquired of, for you have oft to read in the preceding judgments, that in every Question great care is to be taken, that the intentions of the *Demandant* and *quesited* party may be carefully apprehended, that thereby one *Significator* be not mistaken for another; wherefore for better satisfaction of this part of judgment we now are handling, you must inquire whether he, *viz.* the *querent*, inquire of the death of a Friend, or of his Wife, or a Father, or a Child, or of a Servant, &c. Give the first house and his Lord for the *significator* of the *querent*; but for the party *quesited*, give the Sign of that house he is signified by, the Lord thereof and the ☽ for his *Significators*: if you find the Lord of his ascendant in the fourth or eighth, either from his own ascendant, or of the Figure, that configuration is one argument that man or woman inquired after, is deceased; (this must be judged where the party has been long absent, and in remote parts, and strong intelligence concurring therewith.)

Together with this, consider if the Lord of his ascendant or the ☽, be in the twelfth from his own house, with any evil Planet, or if he be in the twelfth, in aspect of any unfortunate Planet, either by ☐ or ⚻, or if the ☉ be unfortunate or afflicted, or the ☽ in like manner, for then the absent is dead: If the *Significator* of the absent man or woman be in the sixth from his own house, or sixth of the Question, or in any ☐ or ⚻ or affliction of the Lord of the sixth, without Reception, or the benevolent aspect of a *Fortune*, the absent is then sick: but if he be but going to, and is not separated from the aspect, he has not been, but he will be suddenly ill, or very shortly: but if he be going from the ♂ of evil Planets, either by body or aspect, so that he be surely separated from them, or is departing from Combustion, it argues the party inquired of has lately escaped a danger or sickness, or peril equivalent; the greatness of the disaster or infirmity you shall judge to be according to the quality of the Signs the *Significators* are in, and manner of aspect afflicting, having relation to the house from whence the aspects are.

It's considerable, that you poise in your judgment, whether the *Significator* of the absent party be in the sixth, and not joined to the Lord of the sixth, or to any unfortunate Planet afflicting him, or whether he be in any amicable aspect with either of the *Fortunes*, or if he be strong in the Sign, you must not then judge the man sick, but rather weary or drowsy, or perhaps he has let blood of late, &c. or taken some Physic for prevention of a disease which he feared.

I do only observe, if the *Significator* of the absent be strong, and separated from a *Fortune*, and in a good house, the absent lives; if he be afflicted, or was lately in ☐ or ⚻ of the *Infortunes*, he was perplexed, or suffered much misery, according to the nature of the house from whence afflicted; but I judge him not dead, unless together with that mischance, the Lord of the eighth do unfortunate him.

Whether one absent will return or not, and when?

Consider by what house the absent party is signified, and what Planet is his *significator*; then see if his *significator* be in the first house (let his Journey be whither it will,) yet if it be a long Journey, and beyond Seas, then see if he be in the ninth, or if in the twelfth, if a very long Journey was undertaken; or if he be in the fifth, if a moderate Journey was intended, or in the third, if a short Journey: If he be in any of these houses, or do commit his disposition to any Planet in any of these houses, it signifies the absent will not die in that Voyage, but return: if he be in the seventh, he will return, but not in haste; nay, he will tarry long; and he is at time of the Question in that country to which he first went, nor has he hitherto had any thoughts of returning; however, now he has: If he be in the fourth, he will stay and abide longer than if he were in the seventh: if his *significator* be in the third or ninth, and in any aspect with any Planet in the ascendant, the absent is preparing to come home, and is fully resolved thereof; or if he be in the second, in aspect with a Planet in the 9th, he is endeavouring to provide moneys for his Voyage homewards, nor will it be long ere he be at home; but if he be in a Cadent house, and not behold his own ascendant, he neither cares for his return, or has any thoughts thereof, nor can he come if so be he would: if he be cadent and also afflicted, and behold not the ascendant, but is otherwise impeded, there's no hopes of his return, nor will he ever come; but if either his *significator* be Retrograde, or the ☽ be joined to a Retrograde Planet, and behold the ascendant, it imports his sudden return when not expected: if you find his *Significator* impeded, see what house he is Lord of that does unfortunate him; if it be the Lord of the fourth, the man is detained and cannot have liberty; if it be the Lord of the sixth, he is ill; if the Lord of the eighth, he fears he shall die by the way, or before he gets into his own Country; if the Lord of the twelfth, he is as a prisoner and cannot procure liberty: such configurations as these seem to impede his return.

Having considered the *Significator* of the absent, now have recourse to the ☽, the general *Significatrix*, for if she be in ♂ or good aspect of the absent's *Significator*, or commit her disposition to him, and he placed in the ascendant, it argues his return; the nearer the aspect is to the degree ascending, the sooner he returns; the more remote, the longer it will be.

The *Significator* only placed in the eighth, without other impediments, prolongs his return, but at last he will come: but if unfortunated therein, he dies and never returns: ☽ separating from the Lord of the fourth, seventh, ninth or third, or any Planet under the earth, and then joined to the Lord of the ascendant, or a Planet above the earth, the absent will return.

The time when he will return.

You are herein with discretion to consider, first, the length of the Journey; then the Lord of the ascendant and *Significator* of the party absent, and to observe, whether they are of the superior Planets or not, or whether the Journey was long or short, or according to discretion, in what space of time a man might come and go, or perform by water or land, such or such a Journey or Voyage; if you find both the *Significators* applying by ✳ or △ aspect, observe in your *Ephemeris* when the day of the aspect is, and then much about that day or near to that time, shall you hear some news of the party, or have a letter from him, or concerning him; this supposes the party so near, that a possibility thereof may be, for if the distance be very far, then you may judge within a fortnight or more of the day of the aspect: But if you be asked, *When he will come home, or when the Querent shall see him?* then it is very probable, when both the *Significators* come to ♂, he will come home and the Querent shall be in his company; if the *Significator* of the absent be in any Sign preceding one of his own houses, observe how many degrees he wants ere he gets out of that Sign and enters his own house, and put them into days, weeks, months or years, according to discretion, and the nature of the Sign and place of heaven he is in; for movable Signs argue a short stay in the place; common ones, more long; fixed do prolong and show long time.

Of the death of the Querent, *or space of his own life.*

If one is fearful of death, or feels himself ill, or would be resolved, Whether, according to natural causes, he may live a year, two, three or more, the better to dispose of some matters concerning his own private affairs, and shall demand such a Question of you, give the ascendant, his Lord and the ☽ for his *Significators*, and see in what houses they are in, and how dignified essentially, to whom they apply, or with what Planets associated: if the Lord of the first be joined with any of the Fortunes, and commit his virtue to him, and that Planet is well dignified and commit his disposition to no Planet, then see if that Fortune be Lord of the eighth; for if he be not, then assuredly the Querent outlives the year, or two or three, or time by him propounded; but if the Planet to whom the Lord of the ascendant is in ♂ with, or commits his disposition to, be Lord of the eighth, then whether he be a good or an ill Planet, he kills (for every Planet must do his office,) and signifies, that the Querent shall die within the compass of time demanded; and this judgment you may aver with more constancy, if the ☽ be then impeded, unless some other Planet be joined with the Lord of the ascendant, who receives either him or the ☽, for then he shall not die in that space of time inquired of by him.

Consider if the Lord of the ascendant be joined to an Infortune, who receives him not either by House or Exaltation, or by two of his lesser Dignities, and the ☽ also at that time unfortunate, it signifies the Querent's death.

If in like manner you find the Lord of the first joined to the Lord of the eighth, unless the Lord of the eighth receive him, and so notwithstanding, as that the Lord of the first receive not the Lord of the eighth, though he receive the Lord of the first; because if the Lord of the eighth receive the Lord of the first, and the Lord of the first the Lord of the eighth, whether Fortune or Infortune, you may justly fear the Querent's death; but if the Lord of the eighth receive the Lord of the ascendant, so there be not mutual Reception, it hinders not.

Having considered judiciously that the *Querent* shall not die, behold when or in what time it will be ere the Lord of the ascendant is joined to that Planet who receives him with a complete ♂, until that time and year or years signified by that ♂, the Querent shall be secure, and so may ascertain himself, that at this time he shall not die.

But if you find upon just grounds in Art the *querent* shall die, behold when and at what time the Lord of the first is joined to the Lord of the eighth, or to the abovesaid *Infortune*, who receives him not, but afflicts him, and is the interficient Planet; for when their perfect ♂ is, whether by body or aspect, at that time he is like to die.

But if the Lord of the first is so disposed, or he in such a condition, as you conceive that by him alone, without other testimonies, you cannot sufficiently judge of his death or life, then do you consider the ☽, and judge by her position, as you did of the Lord of the first: but as I related before, if the Lord of the eighth and the Lord of the first be joined together and each receive other, or at leastwise, the Lord of the first receive the Lord of the eighth, it prenotes his death, as aforesaid: when the interficient Planet comes to the degree wherein the two *Significators* were in ♂, or if they were in □ or ☍ aspect, then when the malevolent *Interfector* comes to the degree of the *Zodiac* wherein the Lord of the ascendant was at time of the Question; or when the unfortunate *Anareta* transits the degree ascending, and there meets with the malevolent aspect of the Lord of the sixth, or when an *Eclipse*, or its opposite place falls to be either the degree ascending or the degree of the Sign wherein the Lord of the ascendant was, or of the ☽, if you judged by her, and not by the Lord of the ascendant.

When, or about what time the Querent may die?

When the Question is absolute, and without limitation, and the *querent* shall propound to you, being an *Astrologian*, his Question in this manner of way, viz. *When shall I die, or how long may I live?* In this demand, you are to behold the Lord of the

ascendant, the ascendant itself, and the ☽, the Lord of the
8th or unfortunate Planet in the eighth, and that Planet to
whom either the Lord of the first or the ☽ is joined by body
or malevolent aspect, and you shall determine the death of
the *Querent* according to the number or distance of degrees
which are between the Lord of the first and the Lord of the
eighth, or of that Planet to whom either the Lord of the
ascendant or ☽ is joined, for those number of degrees shall
show either months or years: If the Lord of the first be in ♂
with the Lord of the eighth in an angle, it notes so many
years; for in these judgments, angles do not accelerate death,
but show that life and nature are strong, and a possibility of
overcoming the malignity of the humour afflicting: if the
abovesaid ♂ be in a succedent house, it notes so many months;
but note, if the Sign be fixed, it gives half years, half months:
if in a cadent house, so many weeks: you must understand this
Question with mature judgment, and well consider whether
the *Significators* are extremely afflicted, or have sufficiently
manifested that according to natural causes, the *Querent* cannot
long live, or that death is not far from the *Querent*.

If the *Significators* do not presage death at present,
then acquaint him, it's possible, he may live so many years
as there are degrees between the ♂ of the Lord of the
ascendant and the Lord of the eighth, or of that Planet at
time of the Question afflicting him. The *Ancients* have ever
observed, that the Lord of the ascendant is more in this
judgment to be considered than the ☽, and therefore his
affliction or ♂ with the Lord of the eighth, or Combustion
with the ☉ is especially worth consideration, and most to be
feared; for naturally the Lord of the first does signify the life
and body of the *querent*, and not by accident.

If the Lord of the ascendant be separated from the Lord
of the eighth, or the Lord of the eighth from him, or from that
Planet who did afflict him, it's not then probable the *querent*
shall die, in so many years as there are degrees between them,
viz. from that their separation: where observe, the ♂ of the ☽
with the Lord of the eighth, does not much hurt, unless the
Lord of the first be also joined with him; for let the ☽ be

afflicted, yet if the Lord of the ascendant be strong, it's no great matter; but if the ☽ be well Fortified, and the Lord of the ascendant be weak and afflicted, the strength of the ☽ assists nothing for the evasion of the *querent*; for although in the *querent's* affairs she has much to do, yet in this manner of judgment little, where life or death are in question.

Whether the Man or Wife shall die first?

This does more nearly depend upon the Nativity of either party, than upon an horary Question, and therefore I would advise in the resolution of this Question, that first the *Artist* do demand of the *querent*, his or her age, or if they have it, the time of their Birth, and that he erect the Figure thereof, and see what possibility there was in the *Radix*, of the length or shortness of the *querent's* life if time give you leave, see if the ☉ or ☽ in the *Radix*, or the ascendant of the Nativity, do near the time of the Question, come to any malignant direction, or whether the *querent* be not in or near a Climacterical year or years, which are the seventh, fourteenth, one and twentieth, 28, five and thirtieth, two and fortieth, &c. or whether you find not malefic transits of the unfortunate Planets either by their near ♂ to the degree of the ☉, ☽ or ascendant in the *Radix*, or whether they cast not their □ or ☍ aspects to the degrees of the ☉, ☽ or ascendant of the *Radix*, now at this instant time of the Question; this I would have well considered: and then erect your Figure according to the time of the day given, and behold who asks the question, and let the Lord of the ascendant be for him or her, the Lord of the seventh for the quesited party; see which of them is weakest, or most afflicted in the Figure, and whether the ascendant or seventh house has any malevolent Planet placed therein, or whether there arise with the ascendant, or descend with the cusp of the seventh, any malefic fixed Stars; for in this manner of judgment they show much: Behold whether the Lord of the seventh, or of the ascendant go to combustion first, or to the affliction of any malignant Planet, or to the Lord of the eighth; for it is an assured rule, that if the Lord of the ascendant be most afflicted, or first go to combustion, and the first house itself be unfortunated by the presence of an *Infortune*, that then the *querent* dies first: and so judge for the *quesited*, if the same misfortunes befall to the seventh house, and his Lord, &c.

What manner of death the Querent shall die.

In this manner of judgment observe the Lord of the eighth, if he be therein placed, or what Planet is nearest to the cusp of the house, and has Dignities therein; for you must take signification of the quality of death from either of these, or from that Planet who afflicts the Lord of the ascendant, and have Dignities in the eighth: If the Planet signifying death is either ♀ or ♃, you may assure the *querent*, he or she shall die a fair death: and observe what Diseases they or either of them in the Sign they are in do signify, and what part of man's body they represent in that Sign, and you may certify the *querent*, that the disease or infirmity he or she shall die of, will be of the nature of the Planet, and in that part of the body they signify in that Sign. Usually, good Planets in the eighth, a fair, gentle death; malevolent ones, either strong Fevers, or long continued Sicknesses, and much afflicting.

CHAPTER LXVIII.

Whether the Portion of the Wife will be great, or easily obtained, or whether is the Woman inquired after rich or not.

Herein vary your ascendant, and then the Question as well resolves the demand concerning the estate of a man as of a woman. The *querent* is still signified by the Lord of the ascendant and first house, his substance and Estate by the second house, Lord thereof, Planet or Planets placed in the house, and the Lord of ⊗ and place of heaven, and Sign wherein it is found.

That which is the occasion of this Question, is, if a man propound the Question, Whether the Woman he inquires after be rich, &c. Behold in this judgement the Sign of the eighth house, the Lord thereof, the Planet placed therein.

The cusp of the eighth in the Terms of ♃ or ♀ give good hopes of Wealth, or ♃ or ♀ placed in that house; plenty of Wealth if they are essentially dignified, direct, and free from Combustion; not so much, if they or either of them be Retrograde, Combust, or slow in motion: for though in essential dignities and so qualified, they express a sufficient and large proportion, yet with some kind of trouble it will come to the *querent*.

The Lord of the eighth in the eighth no ways impeded, gives good hopes of some Inheritance or Land to fall to the wife or woman, or by some Legacy, some Estate; the more certain if either the Lord of the fourth in the figure, or the Lord of the tenth and the Lord of the eighth be in any benevolent aspect out of Angles or succedent houses, or out of the eleventh and eighth. ⊗ in the eighth and in ♒ or ♌, or any of the houses of ♃ or ♀, they casting their △ or ✶ aspect to ⊗: you need not fear but the estate of the quesited party is sufficient, and if the dispositor of ⊗ do but cast his ✶ or △ to it, or else is in a good aspect of ♃ or ♀: these argue the Woman inquired after to be a good Fortune, and you are not to make doubt of his or her Estate.

♄ or ♂ Peregrine in the eighth, either poor or little of what is promised will be obtained, or extreme contention about it.

The Lord of the eighth Combust, slow performance, scarce ability in the Parents to perform what is promised.

☋ in the eighth, no fortunate Planet being there, there's cheating intended, or more will be promised than performed.

Lord of the eighth in the second, or in △ or ✶ to the Lord of the second, the *querent* shall have what is promised, in □ with difficulty, in ☍ never, without much wrangling; if no reception hardly at all. It's impossible to give such general Rules as will hold ever certain, therefore I advise every Practicer to well weigh the *querent* his Condition, and the possibility the Figure promises, and so frame his conjecture.

CHAPTER LXIX.

If one be afraid of a thing, Whether he shall be in danger of the same or not.

Behold the ascendant and his Lord, and the ☽; if you find the ☽ unfortunate, or if the Lord of the ascendant be unfortunate, and falling from an angle; or especially in the twelfth and ☽ with him; it signifies the same Fear is true, and certain that there is cause for it, or that great labour and grief shall molest him, and that many things shall be demanded of him, or he charged with many matters not appertaining to him, or of which he is guilty. If the Lord of the ascendant does ascend from the twelfth into the eleventh or tenth, or shall be joined to Fortunes; it signifies the thing feared shall not appertain to him, or he be molested thereby, or that he need not be afraid, nor shall the matter do him ill, but he shall escape that fear. When the Lord of the ascendant shall be in one degree with Fortunes, no ill is towards the *Querent;* if the Fortunes to which the Lord of the ascendant does apply, or which apply to him be in the midheaven, and the ☽ apply to those Fortunes, and she be in an angle or elevated above him, it signifies he that is afraid shall easily be delivered from fear; nor has he any grounds for it.

The signifier of the question applying to infortunes, it is true; to a fortune, and not received of an infortune, it is false. Many have judged, that if the ☽ be in the eighth, sixth or twelfth, and apply to any Planet in a Cadent house, the Suspicion is not true, or the report will hold long, but that it will be smothered and vanish to nothing: the ☽ in △ to ☉ discovers all suddenly.

CHAPTER LXX.

Whether Man or Wife shall die first?

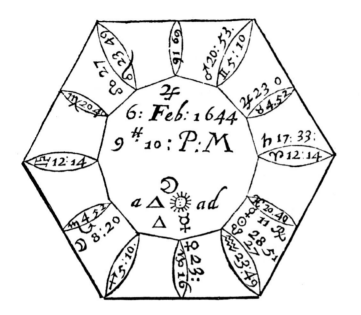

See page
A12

Judgment upon this Figure.

For many weighty Reasons one desired me to consider, whether himself or wife should die first; Whereupon I erected the figure of heaven, as above placed.

Finding the seventh house afflicted, which signifies the Wife by the position of ♄ in ♈ his fall, and that ♂ Lord of the seventh was cadent in ♊ and the ninth house, and disposed by ☿ Lord of the sixth from the seventh, and he Retrograde and in his fall, and the ☽ in ♏, but the eighth house from the seventh. These considerations moved me to inquire of the *querent*, whether his Wife was not very sick, and in a Consumption (for so it appeared to me) and also infirm (*in Secretis.*) For if you observe all those *Significators* which have relation to her, are wholly unfortunate and out of their essential dignities. I inquired her age, her exact Nativity I could not obtain, only I understood she was now in her 42 year of age, *viz.* her *Climacterical* year, which is usually dangerous; and the more to her, she meeting with an untoward Disease near or in that time.

I considered the seventh house which was her ascendant whereby I judged her Corporature to be small, or her Person incurvating, her visage long and lean, her complexion dark and pale, her conditions very waspish, or she very froward, &c. which was confessed, and I afterwards found. Because ♄ shows long lingering Diseases, and ☿ Lord of the sixth house was Retrograde; I judged she would relapse out of one Disease into another, partly by her own obstinateness, and partly by the error of the Physician: By her own willfulness, because that the Lord of her ascendant was also Lord of the eighth; and partly by neglect of the Physician, who was signified by ♀ who was in □ with ♄ in *Equinoctial* and *Tropical* Signs and in Angles, arguing his or their small care of the miserable Gentlewoman: All things seriously considered, I concluded the Woman would die first; for the *Significator* of the Man has no manner of affliction, *viz.* ♀ she being in her *Hayz*, and free from the least manner of misfortune, and so was the Man from all infirmities. For the time when she should die, I observed when ♄ and ♂ came to an ill aspect; for ♄ did most of all represent her in person and condition; and I found that about the latter end of *September* following ♂ came to an ☍ of ♄, ♂ then being near the place of the ☽ at time of the Question, *viz.* in 2 degrees of ♏, and ♄ in two of ♉, the ☽ at that moment in the place of ♂, *viz.* in 20 degrees of ♊ or thereabouts. From thence I concluded, that it was probable she would die or be in great danger of death about the latter end of *September* or beginning of *October*; and in truth she died the eighth of *October*, upon which day ♂ and ☿ were in ♂ in the eighth degree of ♏; the one in the Question being Lord of the ascendant, and the other of the sixth, the degree itself the very same of the ☽ in the question, and ☽ to the 12 of ♎ the opposite degree to her ascendant in the Question.

CHAPTER LXXI.

A Woman of her Husband at Sea, if alive, where, when return?

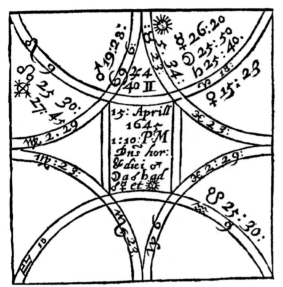

☿ Lord of the ascendant does personate the *querent*, and as ☿ is in ♂ with ☽ and ♄ in ♈ which does signify the Face, so was she e x t r e m e l y disfigured therein by the small Pocks, had weak Eyes, &c. was full of grief & sorrow for her Husband occasioned by ♄ *This question has as much relation to the ninth as eighth house.*

See page A13

his affliction of ☿; she also had a lisping in her speech, and spoke but ill; for usually ♄ afflicting ☿ in mute or bestial Signs, causes impediment in speech.

The *quesited* was signified by ♃ Lord of the seventh, who *Alive.* being placed in the tenth house, and lately separated from the ✳ of ♀ now in the ninth, she being Lady of the third, argued the man had been lately some voyage Southeast; and because both ♀ and ☽ are in ♈, and ♃ in the South angle, and that ♃ of late had been with ✳ of ♀, he being now no way afflicted, but swift in motion, made me judge the man was alive and in health: but as ☿, who disposes of ♃, is Lord of the second, *viz.* the eighth from the seventh, and as the ☽ is so exceedingly afflicted by ☿ and ♄, I judged he had been in much danger and peril of his life, by treachery and the cunning plots of his adversaries, and had suffered many afflictions in his absence;

for ☿ is Lord of the seventh from his ascendant, and ♄ of the twelfth from the seventh: besides, ♃ is accidentally Fortified, but not essentially, and in his Detriment, with *Oculus* ♉ a violent fixed Star, intimating, the man had endured many sudden and violent chances.

Where.   Finding ♃ more Fortified then the ☽, she almost entering ♉ a Southerly Sign, and ♃ in ♊ a Western Sign, and South quarter; I judged the man absent was in the Southwest of *England*, in some Harbour, because ♃ was Angular.

When return or hear of him.   The ☽ separates from ♄ & does apply to the ♂ of ☿ *Significatrix* of the *querent*; an argument after much expectation & longing, the Woman should hear of him in two or three days, because the distance of ☽ from the body of ☿ is about one degree and no more, and the Sign movable, [*so she did.*] But as ☿ is in a movable Sign, and ☽ is corrupted by him and ♄, the report she heard of her Husband was false (for she heard he was in Town,) but it was not so. Considering that ☿ and ♃ did hasten to a ♂ in ♊, ☿ being therein very potent, and that this ♂ was to be the fifth of *May* following; I judged from thence that about that time she would have certain news of her Husband, if happily he came not then home. The second week in *May* the Woman did hear certain news from her Husband, but he came not home till the second week in *July*, he had been several Voyages in the West parts, was taken prisoner by the King's Forces, and at time of the Question asked, was at *Barnstable*, &c.

CHAPTER LXXII.

What manner of Death CANTERBURY *should die?*

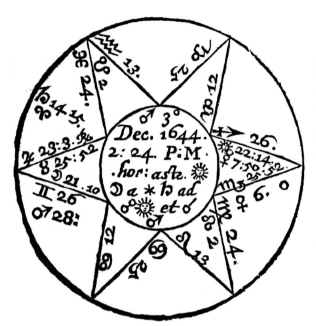

See page
A13

It may appear to all indifferent minded men, the verity & worth of *Astrologie* by this Question, for there is not any amongst the wisest of men in this world could better have represented the person and condition of this old man his present state and condition, and the manner of his death, than this present Figure of heaven does.

Being a man of the Church, his ascendant is ♑, the cusp of the ninth house; ♄ is Lord of the Sign, now in ♈ his fall; a long time Retrograde, and now placed in the twelfth of the Figure, or fourth from his ascendant; so that the heavens represent him in condition of mind, of a violent spirit, turbulent and envious, a man involved in troubles, imprisoned, &c. ♃ a general *Significator* of *Churchmen*, does somewhat also represent his condition, being of that eminency he was of in our Commonwealth: ♃, as you see, is Retrograde, and with many fixed Stars of the nature of ♂ and ☽; an argument he was deep laden with misfortunes, and vulgar Clamours at this present.

The ☽ is Lady of the fourth in the Figure, but of the eighth as to his ascendant; she separates from ♄, and applies to the ☍ of the ☉ near the cusp of the eighth house; ☉ in a fiery Sign, applying to an ☍ of ♂, the Dispositor of the aged *Bishop*; ♂ being in an Airy Sign and human, from hence I judged that he should not be hanged, but suffer a more noble kind of death, and that within the space of six or seven weeks, or thereabouts; because the ☽ wanted seven degrees of the body of ♂. He was beheaded about the tenth of *January* following.

I write not these things as that I rejoiced at his death; no, I do not; for I ever honoured the man, and naturally loved him, though I never had speech or acquaintance with him: nor do I write these lines without tears, considering the great uncertainty of human affairs: He was a liberal *Maecenas* to *Oxford*, and produced as good Manuscripts as any were in *Europe* to that University, whereby the Learned must acknowledge his bounty: let his imperfections be buried in silence, *Mortuus est, & de mortuus nil nisi bonum*. Yet I account him not a *Martyr*, as one Ass did; For by the Sentence of the greatest Court of *England*, *viz.* the *Parliament*, he was brought to his end.

CHAPTER LXXIII.

If have the Portion promised?

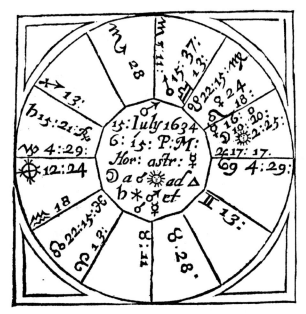

♄ is here *Significator* of the *querent*, Retrograde, and in the 12th house, as if the *querent* had been in some despair of it, *and so he confessed.*

See page A14

The Woman is signified by ♃ and ☽; ♃ in his Exaltation, and ☽ in ♌, a fixed Sign argue the Woman to be well conceited of herself, confident, yet virtuous and modest: the ☽ her *Significatrix* near the ☉, she had a scar near her right eye, for the ☽ signifies in Women the right Eye.

That which is pertinent to the resolution of the thing demanded is this; That finding ♀ in the eighth house, which is the woman's second, and the ☉ to be Lord thereof, in his own house, and that ☽ did separate from the ♂ of ☉, and transferred his virtue to ♄, who is Lord of the ascendant and Dispositor of ⊗, and also Lord of the *querent's* second house, I did from hence cheer up the dull *querent*, and assured him he had no cause to fear the non payment of his Wife's Portion, but that it would really be performed, whatsoever was or had been promised; and that, to his further comfort, she would prove a chaste virtuous woman, but somewhat proud; all this proved true, as I experimentally have it from the *querent's* own Mouth.

The ninth HOUSE, and those QUESTIONS properly belonging to it.

Long Journeys, Religion, Pilgrimage, Dreams, &c.

CHAPTER LXXIV.

Of good or ill in questions concerning this House.

I f in this house good Planets have either government, or are in possession thereof, or aspect the same without the testimonies of the *Infortunes*, it signifies good, or is an argument thereof in all questions concerning this house.

Of a Voyage by Sea, and success thereof.

Look to the ninth house, if it be good and strong, and aspected of good Planets, or good Planets in the said house, especially if the Lord of the ascendant and the tenth be well affected, it is very good: but if thou findest ♄, ♂ or the ☋ there, then is the way evil, if the Lord of the ninth be with an evil Planet, it is evil, and he shall not speed well in the way, or get any wealth by that Voyage: ♂ in the ninth, intimates danger by Thieves or Pirates; ♄ threatens loss of Goods, or sickness; the ☋ does import the same that ♂ does, but most part with cozenage and deceit.

The substance of the Journey is from the tenth, because it is the second from the ninth: *Fortunes* there, expect Wealth;

Infortunes, loss: the ninth unfortunate, many hardships in the Voyage; *Fortunes* there, a happy passage. Together with this, see to the Lord of the eighth, or eighth house; for if he or it be strong there is Wealth to be got; ♄, ♂ or ☋ in that house, nothing to be had, or not worth labour.

What wind you shall have.

Behold the Lord of the ascendant, if he be with a good Planet or Planets, and they strong, and in friendly aspect, it signifies good winds; but if with evil Planets, or they in cadent houses, the contrary; if the *Significators* be in ☍ out of fixed Signs, and near violent fixed stars, the Traveller may expect impetuous storms, sudden blasts, contrary winds often driving the Passenger this way, and sometimes that way; as also, that he shall await many days, weeks or months for a comfortable wind before he shall gain it: Gentle gusts of wind are signified when the *Significators* are in △ aspect out of Signs airy, *viz.* ♊, ♎ or ♒.

Of him that takes a Journey, and the success thereof.

Behold what Planets are in the angles, if you find in the ascendant a good *Fortune*, judge then that he shall have good success, before that he removes from the place he is in, or in the beginning of his Journey; if that good *Fortune* be in the Midheaven, he shall have much happiness in his Journey, and after his entering the Ship, or upon the way as he goes on his Journey: but if the *Fortune* be in the seventh, he shall have content in the place whereunto he goes: if that Planet which is the *Fortune* be in the fourth, it shall be at his return, or when he shall come to his own place or home back again.

If that *Fortune* be ♃, the benefit he expects, or the Means to advance him, shall come from or by means of a religious person, or Judge, or Gentleman, in quality and kind according to the power, quality and nature of the Lord of the house of that *Fortune*, or by a person of that description; as if it be the house of the ☉, it shall be by the King, a Magistrate, or some noble Person, or by a Solar man of noble disposition. If ♄ be *Significator*, it shall consist in things and Commodities of his nature, or else in things of antiquity, or Ground, Corn or Tillage; or by means of an ancient man: describe ♄ exactly, and let the man apply to such a one in his Affairs. If ♀, it shall be as touching Women, Joy and Sport, or by means of Women, Friends, or in Linen, Silks, Jewels, or pleasant things. If ☿, it shall be by writing, or by wit and discretion, or Merchandise, Accounts or Letters testimonial, or by the Merchant. If it be the ☽, it shall be by Services or Masteries, much employment by some Woman or Widow, or Sailor, or by carrying News, or playing at Dice, Sports or Pastimes, Tables, or such like.

Example.

If the *Fortune* in the tenth house, is ♀, he shall have good, or make great benefit in his Journey, by dealing in such things as bring joy, or cause delight and pastime, by Jewels or Silks which are of the nature of ♀: If the Lord of that house be ♄, and he strong, say then of ♄ as in the preceding part, and so of the rest: If a Planet who is an *Infortune* be Lord of the twelfth and he be ♄, it is to be feared there shall happen to him some sickness coming of a cold and dry cause, or by much treachery, but if ♄ be in a Sign Bestial, it is to be feared, some ill fortune or mischance shall happen to the Traveller by means of some Four-footed Beast; if he be in a human Sign, it may be by some deceitful men; if that ill *Fortune* instead of ♄ be ♂, it is to feared he may incur some sickness that is of a hot nature, or fall into the hands of Thieves, and shall have fear of himself touching hurt to his body, &c. and so of the rest.

Of the short or slow return of him that takes a Journey.

Behold the Signifier of the Journey, if that Planet be swift in Course, Occidental, and ☽ and he in movable Signs, it signifies his Journey to be short, and not much tarrying from home, or a quick, speedy passage, yet with trouble and pain; but if he be swift, (*viz.* the *Significator*) in motion and Oriental, it shall be quick, short, and without any labour or much trouble: when the Lord of the ascendant does apply to the Lord of the house of Journeys, or when the Lord of the Journey applies to the Lord of the ascendant, or any Planet carries light of one to the other, or when the Lord of the house of Journeys is in the ascendant, or when the Lord of the seventh is in the ascendant, or the Lord of the ascendant in the seventh; all these do signify short return, or good speed according to the length of the Voyage: But if none of these be, or the greater part of the said *Significators* be in angles, especially in fixed Signs, it signifies either destruction of his Journey, or else slow, or to be a great while absent: If a *Fortune* be in the house of Journeys, it signifies health of body; a good *Fortune* in the midheaven signifies mirth and jollity, or gladness in his journey, or that he shall have good company: in the seventh and fourth, it signifies prosperity, and a good end of the Journey or Voyage.

If the Lord of the house of Journeys be in a fixed Sign, it signifies continuance and long tarrying: in a common Sign, it signifies he shall change his mind from his first intended thoughts, or remove from one journey to another.

If the ☽ in questions of Journeys, be in the sixth, or in ☌ to the Lord of the sixth, it shows sickness to him that travels, and impediments in his occasions, and that his business shall be for the most part feeble, weak and slackly handled, his endeavours and designs shall be much crossed; yet if the Lord of the ascendant be fortunate, or in the house of trust, or not opposite to the same, it signifies success and prosperity, and the accomplishing of his business, though with many difficulties and obstructions.

When he shall return that is gone a long Journey.

Behold the Lord of the ascendant, if you find him in the ascendant or midheaven, or giving his power to another Planet being in any of those places, it signifies that he shall return, and is thinking of it; but if the Lord of the first be in the seventh, or in an angle of the earth, it signifies, that his return *You must ever have regard to the proper Significator.*

is prolonged, and that as yet he is not gone far from the place he went to, nor has he yet any desire thereunto.

If the *Almuten* of the first be in the ninth or third from the ascendant, applying to a Planet in the ascendant, it signifies he is in his journey homewards: the same also does the Lord of the ascendant signify if he be in the 8th or second, applying to any Planet in the tenth; yet notwithstanding, if the Lord of the ascendant be cadent, and do not apply to any Planet in an angle, or behold the ascendant, it is a token of tarrying.

But if at any time the Lord of the ascendant or the ☽ do apply to a Planet Retrograde, or the Lord of the ascendant himself be Retrograde, (*viz.* the *Significator* of the absent) and do behold the ascendant, it is a token he is coming: but if the Lord of the ascendant be unfortunate, it does signify some let or hinderance which makes him to tarry, or that he cannot come: If you find not in the house of the ascendant any of those things which I have said, behold the ☽, and if she do give her power or light to the Lord of the ascendant, being in the ascendant or near the ascendant, it signifies that he shall come shortly, or intends it: also, if the ☽ be in the seventh, ninth or third, applying to the Lord of the ascendant, it signifies that he comes: If the ☽ be separate from a Planet which is in the left side of the ascendant (that is, under the earth) and applies to another Planet on the right hand of the ascendant, (that is, above the earth) it does signify that he comes.

If the ☽ be on the right hand of the ascendant, and apply to a Planet in the midheaven, it signifies that he comes, yet with slowness, for the ☽ being on the right hand of the ascendant, does show so much; which if she had been on the left hand, she had showed his coming sooner. If the Lord of the house of the ☽ be unfortunate, it signifies tarrying, and let or hinderance in coming home.

You must ever consider for whom the question is asked, for if he that demands the question ask for a Son, then from the fifth house look for the *Significator*: If for a Brother, then to the third: If for a Father, the fourth, &c. Behold the Fortunes and *Infortunes* casually placed in those places, and by them and their position, judge the estate of him that is absent in his journey, both for health and hinderance, for according to the estate or place of the *Fortunes* or *Infortunes* in the Figure, and their dignities or imbecilities, so you may judge.

When the Lord of the ascendant is in the ascendant, or in the second, entering or arising towards the ascendant, or if he be Retrograde, or the Planet which was the signifier of the Journey be Retrograde, or the Lord of the ascendant apply to the Lord of the tenth, or the Lord of the midheaven apply to the Lord of the ascendant, or if the Lord of the ascendant be in the midheaven, or the Lord of the midheaven be in the ascendant, or the ☽ received of the Lord of the tenth, or the Lord of the ascendant received of him; all these do signify that he that is absent is coming, and that he returns speedily and shortly. *Still you must keep to the Lord of your proper ascendant.*

The Planet from whom the Lord of the ascendant of the question is separated, is the *Signifier* of the state and condition in which he lately was, and of those actions which are past; and the Planet to whom the Lord of the ascendant does apply, is the *Signifier* of the state he is now in; and the Planet to whom he applies after him, is the *Signifier* of the state of him to whom he shall come, or intends to come.

If a question be asked for one that is in a journey, and you find his *Significator* going out of one Sign and entering into another, judge that he went out of the place he was in, and is entered another, or taken another journey in hand; and behold in which of those Signs he was stronger, more fortunate, or better received and so judge his success the better, and corresponding thereto.

Note that Combustion in a question of one that is absent is ill, for that signifies captivity, imprisonment, or some great let: if the Combustion be near the house of death, or the ☉ Lord of the house of Death, it signifies death except God do miraculously deliver him.

If in the question of him that is absent, you find in the ascendant or midheaven ☿ or the ☽, judge that Letters shall come from him, or some News very shortly, for ☿ is the *Significator* of Letters or News.

If you would know whether the News or Letters which are to come be good or ill, look from whom ☿ and ☽ are separate; if the separation be from a *Fortune*, it notes good news, and joyful; but if from ill *Fortunes*, judge the contrary.

If a Question be asked of a Letter, whether it be true or not, behold ☿, if he be in a movable Sign, beholding ♄ or ♂, say it is a lie; if in a fixed Sign, judge it is true; in a common Sign, part true and part false.

The cause of a Journey, and the success thereof.

Behold if the ☽ apply to the ☉, he goes to Kings or States, or in service of such men, *viz.* of such as are able to maintain him, &c.

If ☽ apply to ♄, he is directed by old men, or men of gravity and years.

If ☽ apply to ♃, Religious persons or Gentlemen do employ him.

If ☽ apply to ♂, men of War, Captains, or such like are the cause.

If to ♀, Women-kind, or desire to purchase such things as Women love.

If to ☿, Merchants, Scholars, or he travels to see variety of Countries, and to learn the languages.

If ☽ herself signify the cause, it seems he is hired, or that he is publicly employed.

The cause is usually required from the house wherein the Lord of the ninth is; or if a Planet be therein, see what house he is Lord of; the Lord of the ninth in the ascendant, he goes of his own accord; the Lord of the ninth in the second, for gain; the Lord of the ninth in the third, purposely to travel, &c.

Success thereof.

Behold the four angles, if a fortunate Planet be in the ascendant, the beginning of his journey shall be fortunate; if the midheaven be fortunate, the rest of his journey shall prove in like manner; if the seventh, it shall also happen well when he is arrived to the place he intends, or is at his journey's end: If

Fortunes be in the fourth, all shall happen well in his return homeward, & *e contra*: a most happy journey is intended.

Also for the success of a journey, behold the Lord of the ascendant, the ninth house and the ☽, and if they be all well affected, it shows a fortunate Journey.

Length thereof.

If the Lord of the ninth be in the ascendant, or the Lord of the ascendant in the ninth, it hastens the journey; the Lord of the ascendant in the seventh, *idem*; the *Significators* in cadent houses, or in movable Signs, or the angles movable, *idem*: But if the angles be fixed, and the *Significators* placed therein, it prolongs the journey: the Lord of the ninth in the ascendant, hastens the journey, and being fortunate therein, fortunates the same Voyage, the *Significators* and ☽ slow in motion, a tedious Journey.

CHAPTER LXXV.

If one shall profit by his Knowledge, be it in what kind it will; Chymistry, Surgery, &c. or if he be perfect.

Give to the *querent* the ascendant, his Lord and the ☽; the ninth house, Planet therein placed, and the Lord thereof for the *Science* endeavoured to be attained: See if the Lord of the ninth be fortunate or not, *Oriental* or *Occidental*, cadent from an angle, in an angle or succedent house, and whether he behold the Lord of the ascendant or not with ✶ or △; if he be a *Fortune* and behold the Lord of the first, the man has good knowledge in him, and what is reported of the man is true, and he will do good by his knowledge; and the more if it be with Reception: if the aspect be by □ or ☍, the man knows much, but shall do no good thereby; if an *Infortune* aspect either the Lord of the ninth or first, the man has wearied himself, and will do, but to no purpose, for he shall never attain the perfection of the knowledge he desires.

Of Science, Cunning or Wisdom in a man,
whether it be true or not.

You must give the ascendant to him of whom it is asked, and the ninth house to the *Science*; and if there be *Fortunes* in the ninth house, or the Lord of the ninth fortunate, and behold the Lord of the ascendant, judge there is Science in that man: But if in the ninth house there be *Infortunes*, or the Lord of the ninth unfortunate, and behold not the Lord of the ascendant, it does signify the contrary, and that there is none, or little knowledge in him.

Behold in what condition the ☽ is, with the Lord of the ninth; if they both apply to *Fortunes*, it signifies that there is knowledge in the man; but if the apply to *Infortunes*, it signifies the contrary.

If the ninth house, and the Lord thereof be unfortunate, nor behold the Lord of the ascendant, it signifies no knowledge in him, or such as by which he will never do himself good, if it concern the *querent*: if another body, then the party *quesited*.

Of many Persons absent or travelling,
in what Condition they are.

It happens sometimes that four or five or more are travelling together in a company beyond Seas, or are at places far distant, and the *querent* is willing to hear news of every one of them: In this case you must desire the *querent* to set down all their names in order, one after another; then observe the ☽ her application first of all, and that Planet to whom she applies; shall signify the state and condition of the first Man in order as he is writ down; observe in what condition that Planet is in, how placed, how dignified, how and by whom or what Planet aspected, from whom he last separated, to whom he next applies; accordingly judge of the state and condition, health or welfare of the first Person inquired after. Having performed that work, then behold the ☽ her second application, be it good or ill, and to what Planet, the second Man in order shall partake in his affairs according to the well or ill being of that Planet to whom she does the second time apply; and so in order, do for all the rest remaining, ever considering the *significators'* Retrogradations, Directions, Combustions of the Planets; and in this manner run them all over by turns again, if the Men inquired after be more than seven. In the same order you may do by a Man inquiring after many Women, *& e contra,* &c.

To what part of Heaven the Traveler had best direct his Journey.

Although we have in some measure handled this judgement in the Chapter of the first house, yet I shall again briefly mention some further judgements herein, pertinently belonging to this House. If therefore the *querent* who is desirous to Travel or take a Journey, shall make this demand, *To what part of the World is it best for me to Travel?* Do you herein consider in what quarter of the Figure the fortunate Planets are placed, and where most fortified, you may safely direct the *querent* to travel, sojourn or direct his voyage to those parts, as if the fortunate Planet promising happiness to him be in the East Quadrant, then direct him Eastward, if in the South Quarter Southward, in the West Westward, in the North Northward, and observe where the most or greatest number of fortunate Planets are placed, to those parts it's best to Travel; and as you will elect that part of Heaven for best where the Fortunes are, so dissuade from travelling or journeying to those parts where the Infortunes are. In the number of Infortunes; put the ☋; in all Journeys have a special care of the second and eighth Houses; for an Infortunate Planet in the eighth portends or signifies little gain, or small success in the Country the Traveller is going to; but a malevolent Planet in the second, intends no great success in the Country, wherein after the voyage is performed the Traveller intends to settle himself. Hence it is, that when elections of times are made for the happiness of a party in the Country he is going to, that we always put a good Planet in the eighth house. But if we expect to live happily after our return, then we ever set forth or begin our Journey when a good and fortunate Planet is in the second. Beware of *Cauda* in the second when you return, or in the eighth when you set forward.

CHAPTER LXXVI.

If an idle covetous Priest upon his Question propounded shall Obtain a good Parsonage, yea or no?

Since the Clergy are as Covetous and vicious as other men, I give them leave to make their demand as well as others, provided always, it be not to hinder themselves from enjoying a lusty Benefice, or impeach them in preferment; if therefore the Lord of the ascendant who is significator of the Minister (it matters not whether he be Protestant, Presbyter or Papist) that would have a Church-living, or other Ecclesiastical preferment, or the ☽ or both be joined to the Lord of the ninth who signifies the thing sought after, *viz.* a Benefice: for if the Lord of the 9th be in the 9th, or behold the house, it argues the Clerk or Priest shall obtain the Benefice desired, but with Labour and industry, and his own very much painstaking, which I confess they do willingly; but if neither the ☽ or Lord of the ascendant be joined to the Lord of the ninth, or he with them; see if either the ☽ or Lord of the ascendant be in the ninth, for that argues the attaining of the thing sought after: if he be not Retrograde, or otherwise unfortunate or Combust, or in □ aspect of an infortune without reception, for then it argues a destruction of the matter after it seems to be in a good forwardness, or near accomplishing; but if the Lord of the ninth be in the first, whether the Lord of the first behold him or the ☽ or not, in what condition soever the disposition of the Lord of the ascendant or the ☽ are in, or if the Lord of the ninth be the lighter Planet, and apply to the Lord of the first, it's a pregnant testimony of procuring the thing sought after without much seeking on the *querent's* behalf.

The Lord of the ascendant in △ or ✶ to ☉ or ♃, and either of them in the ascendant, argues the acquisition of the *Benefice* or Preferment.

The ♂ of the Lord of the first and ninth, or their aspects, with Reception, gives the preferment without bribing, freely, perhaps upon a desert or merit; for some of that Tribe are black Swans: If the aspect be by □, it comes not so lightly; yet if Reception be, it comes at length, perhaps a fish with 20d. is presented to the Patron.

After this, see if any Planet transfer the light of the Lord of the ninth to the Lord of the ascendant, the Benefice is obtained by some interloping person, unless the more ponderous Planet to whom the Translator does afford virtue, commit that influence to some other Planet, and that Planet have no signification in the Question, for such an action intimates destruction of the matter, after it is hoped to be near perfecting: If the Lord of the ascendant hasten to the ♂ of the Lord of the ninth, and meet with no obstructive aspect before, it's not then to be doubted but the *Parson* obtains his preferment, but not without solicitation: many Planets *Significators* in this or the like Question, either many Competitors in the thing, or many contentions and much labour to obtain it.

Lord of the ascendant in ♂ with an *Infortune*, and he not Lord of the ninth, or in Reception with him, or not committing his disposition to any Planet who receives the Lord of the first or the ☽, the matter will not be performed: If that *Infortune* commit his virtue to any *Fortune*, who is strong in the Figure, the thing will be perfected; for the ♂ of the *Infortunes* without Reception, performs nothing; with Reception, they perform with difficulty: a Planet signifying the effecting of anything, being placed in an angle; hastens the matter, in a succedent, it retards the thing; in a cadent, quite destroys the matter, or suddenly, beyond expectation, when all men despair, by some secret trick, perfects it; but this is very rare.

If any malevolent Planet aspect the Lord of the ascendant or the ☽ with □ or ☍, without Reception, the *querent* seems much troubled, is displeased with the manner of prosecuting the matter, and believes he is either negligently or knavishly dealt with, by such as endeavour to negotiate in the matter: if the Lord of the first and ninth both of them commit their disposition to any Planet, by whatsoever aspect, who is not impeded, or becomes Retrograde before he go out of the Sign he is in, it argues performance of the business: The ☽ well dignified, shows many Friends: if the Lord of the ninth be joined to the Lord of the fourth, or the Lord of the fourth apply to the Lord of the ninth, without much labour the matter will be effected: But to know whether the *Benefice* be a lusty one or not, or worth acceptance, (a thing considerable;) consider the tenth house, the Lord thereof, and Planet or Planets therein placed; Planets well dignified and angular, show hopes, and are sure testimonies of a good thumping Benefice.

And now I wonder why some wooden Clergy should so preach against me and Astrology; I never either countenancing or maintaining one heretical position, or persuading any person to attain a Benefice by Symony, or professing more than Astrology, of which these men are as ignorant (the most of them as Asses;) witness *Astrologo-Mastix*, a most absurd Coxcomb, to meddle with what he knows not.

CHAPTER LXXVII.

Of Dreams, whether they signify any thing or not.

BONATUS in judging this Question far exceeds HALY, in many others he is not so judicious; when therefore any shall demand, *What the effect of his Dream shall be?* Behold the ninth house, and give it to signify the *Dream*, if any of the seven Planets be therein placed, he shall have signification of the *Dream*: If ♄ be therein, he dreamed of some things that frightened or terrified him, & it was some inordinate matter, not really natural, as it is believed by the *querent*: If ☋ be in the ninth, he beheld somewhat in his Dream more terrible, and which more affrighted him; he was afraid some prosecuted him, and would have killed him, and that he had much ado to escape: Behold in what house ♑ and ♒ fall, they being the houses of ♄, for from some matter signified by either of those houses shall this horror proceed, or disturbance by dream: If either of those Signs ascend, the fear proceeds from himself; if they be on the cusp of the second, Money or personal Estate occasioned that Dream; if ♑ or ♒ be on the cusp of the third, the matter proceeded from some occasion concerning his Kindred or Brethren, or ill Neighbours, or bad reports: you must run all the houses in order in the same nature, as I have formerly both in the second and third house acquainted you, &c. and from thence find the occasion.

If you find no Planet in the ninth, consider the tenth house and see if any Planet be therein, and judge as formerly by the ninth house; for whatsoever Planet is in the tenth, the signification of the Dream has signification thereof, either for good or evil: If no Planet be in the tenth, see if any be in the ascendant, he shall signify the matter of the Dream; if no Planet be in the ascendant, behold if any be in the seventh, he shall then manifest the Dream; if no Planet be there, see to the fourth, for a Planet therein shall demonstrate the quality and effects of the Dream; if no Planet be in the fourth, see to the third; if none be there, see to the second, fifth, sixth, eighth, 11th or 12th, all which have signification of the vanity of the Dream, and that it has no effects to follow it: The very true way of judging whether Dreams, how terrible soever, have or shall have any influence upon the *querent*, is by observing whether the Lord of the ninth, or any Planet placed in the ninth, does behold the Lord of the ascendant with □ or ☍, for then assuredly the *querent* shall receive prejudice thereby in one kind or other; usually crosses or afflictions to his person: But if the Lord of the ninth afflict the Lord of the second, he receives some prejudice by one or other in point of Estate, &c. and so do in all the other houses, (*consideratis considerandis*.)

A good Planet in the ninth, no ill shall happen by the Dream; a good Planet in the ascendant signifies the same; or the Lord of the ascendant in △ of ☉, ♃ or ♀ argues the same, the *Infortunes* the contrary. I hold it vain to be more large upon this Discourse.

CHAPTER LXXVIII.

Terrible Dreams.

See page A14

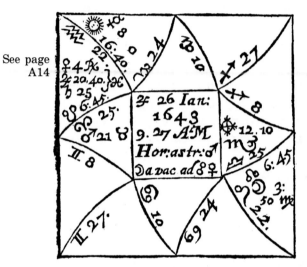

♃ and ♄ are Lords of the ninth accidentally placed in the twelfth casting a □ aspect to the cusp of the ninth: their position in the twelfth according to the best Authors, intimates the vanity of the Dream, and rather a Person or fancy oppressed with various perturbations and worldly matters, than any other matter: But according to our judgment, ♂ being the only Planet in an Angle, shall best express the cause of the Dream, and whether it will tend to good or evil; if we observe what house ♂ is Lord of, we shall find he is Lord of the ascendant and disposer of ⊗, it being angular. I therefore acquainted him that the occasion of his Dreams might be construed two ways; one, by his too great care of his Estate and Fortune entrusted out, and now desperate; because ♂ was in ☍ to ⊗; and that his mind ran so much thereupon, that his Fancy was disturbed, so that he could not enjoy that quiet and rest by night which nature affords all Creatures. In the next place, because ♄ is Lord of the tenth, which signifies Office, Command, &c. and did afflict ♃ Lord of the ninth, or did impede him at least; I told him I doubted he had lost the benefit of some good Place in the Commonwealth, and that now he was solicitous how to live in that credit he formerly did:

howsoever, because ♃ and ♂ were in ✶, I judged no matter
of peril to his person should come thereby, only some damage
in Estate; and this really proved true.

CHAPTER LXXIX.

If he should obtain the Parsonage desired.

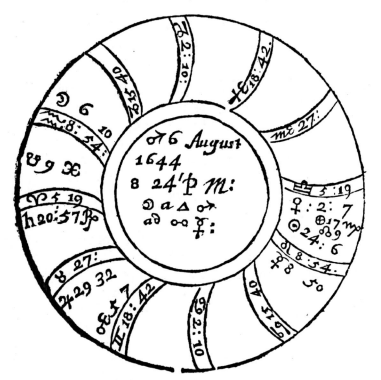

See page
A15

Judgement upon this Figure.

The *querent* is signified by the sign ascending, ♄ therein
placed, and ♂ Lord of the ascendant in Ⅱ, an Airy Sign,
and ☽ in ♒, of the same triplicity. The ninth house and ♃

Lord thereof are *Significators* of the *Benefice*. In the first place I find no ♂ between ♃ Lord of the ninth, and ♂ Lord of the ascendant, or is the ☽ in any aspect with ♃.

2. I find neither ♂ Lord of the ascendant, or ☽ placed in the ninth.

3. There is no weighty Planet that translates or collects the light of ♃ (who signifies the preferment) to ♂.

4. There is no reception between ♃ and ♂.

5. ♄ is impeded in the ascendant, and by his presence infortunates the question, causing the *querent* to despair in the obtaining it.

6. The ☽ separates from a △ of ♂, and applies to an opposition of ☿, Lord of the third: which intimated in my judgment, that some neighbour of the *querent's*, either with letter, words, or cross information would wholly destroy the *querent's* hopes, and that *Mercurial* men, *viz.* Scholars, or Divines would be his enemies: and because I found ♀ in ♎ and seventh house, opposing the ascendant; I judged some Women would inform against him, or prejudice him in his suit.

By all what has been collected, I dehorred him from proceeding after the matter any further, as not to be obtained; but the Parson being covetous would proceed further in the matter; and so he did, and when he thought to have the matter absolutely on his side; Behold, a scurvy Letter revealing some manifest truths concerning a Female, dashed the good Man's hopes, &c. *exit*. The *querent* was ♄ and ♂ exactly, had wit and volubility of tongue; and as ☿ and the ☽ are in ☍, he under the Earth, she in the twelfth, he could never discover which of his neighbours it was that thus affronted him, nor would he ask me; if he had, it must have been ♄ Lord of the twelfth, *viz.* some Farmer, or dealer in Cattle, living Northeast from him about fifteen Furlongs; a covetous repining Miser, Sickly, &c.

CHAPTER LXXX.

If Presbytery shall stand?

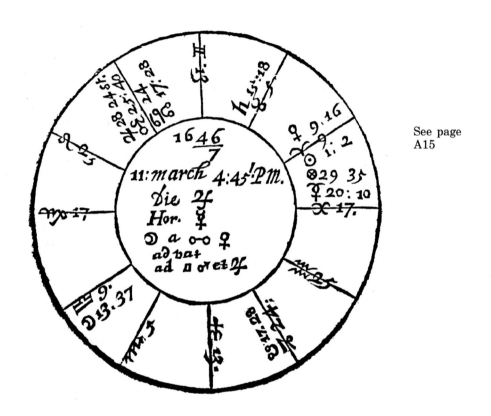

See page
A15

Judgment upon the Figure abovesaid.

The angles of the Figure are common, and not fixed, but the Sign of the ninth, from which at present judgment must be naturally deduced, is ♉, a fixed, stable Sign, and from ♄ in the Terms of ♃, who is therein placed, a slow and ponderous Planet; a general *Significator* in Religion, Religious Rites and Ceremonies is now standing to Direction; and is departing out of his Exaltation, having been a long time Retrograde therein, and now at present impeded by ♂: after his transit out of ♋, he enters the fixed Sign ♌, and into the Terms of ♄; but in the first six degrees thereof he meets with several obnoxious fixed Stars, and thence passes into the Terms of ☿, who is now in the Sign ♓ his Fall; yet angular, entered into the Decanate of ♂.

We find ♀ Lady of the ninth house in ♈ her Detriment, and in the eighth of the Figure, but twelfth house from her own *viz.* ♉, now the cusp of the ninth: and if you observe ♀ well, she has one and twenty degrees to pass through the Sign of ♈, and these degrees all in the eighth house, ere she get into ♉ where she may possible fix, or at least would; but before she fully gets out of this movable Sign ♈, she first has occurse to the sinister □ of ^a ♃, then of ^b ♂, all three in the Terms of ♄: this might have produced some material effects, if ♄ had been essentially Fortified where he is, or if Presbytery had any relation to Monkery, or if it had been the first beginning of a Religious Order.

Let us take all the Planets as placed, and there's not a Planet fixed except ♄, nor any essentially dignified but ♃, and he impeded by ♂; the ☽ is entering *via combusta*, ♂ is in his Fall, ☿ in his, ♀ in her Detriment.

We have the ☽ separating from ♀ in the eighth, then going to be *vacua cursus*, afterwards she squares with ^c ♂, then with ♃: From those configurations we shall naturally frame our judgment, not positive or affirmative, but conjectural, only out of a desire that posterity may see there's some verity in Astrology, and the Clergy's just cause to carp at the Art if I lie: and we hope herein, that we shall no more offend in writing the Astral intention of the heavenly bodies, (deduced from reasons in Art) than those who daily (*pleno ore*) and publicly deliver amongst hundreds their conceptions, though repugnant to the opinion of very many now alive. The placement of ♄ in the ninth who is naturally of a severe, surly, rigid and harsh temper, may argue, the Presbytery shall be too strict, sullen and dogged for the English Constitutions, little gentle or compliant with the natures of the generality, and that there

^a *The Gentry of England will oppose it.*

^b *Lord of the ascendant of England, the generality or whole Kingdom will distaste it.*

^c *The Presbytery will struggle hard, and wrangle stoutly.*

shall spring up amongst themselves many strange and fearful opinions and distractions even concerning this very Presbytery now mentioned, that they shall grow excessive covetous, contentious, and desirous of more than belongs to them, worldly, envious and malicious one against another; that amongst them some Juniors represented by ♀, shall be but of light judgment, wave and decline the strictness of this Discipline; that the Elder, represented by ♄, shall not be respected by reason of their too much rigidness, or shall their Orthodox opinions be consented to.

♄ is Peregrine, Occidental, &c. fortified by no essential Dignity, or supported with the favourable aspect of either of the *Fortunes*; there's Reception between the ☽ and him, but no aspect: ☿ Lord of the tenth signifying Authority, is separated and separates apace from ♄, as if the Gentry, or supremest people of this Kingdom, do in part decline from the severity of the too too austere Clergy or Presbytery, mistrusting a Thraldom rather than a Freedom to ensue hereupon.

If you would know who shall most afflict, or who shall begin the dance, or most of all oppose it? ♄ represents the Countryman, for he afflicting the house properly signifying Presbytery shows the cause; this in few words expresses, it will not stand or continue (*status quo*:) Remove ♄, *viz.* Covetousness, Rigidness, Maliciousness, &c. then there may be more hopes that it might, but yet it will not stand (*ita in fatis.*) *The Soldiery will distaste it.*

Three whole years from hence shall not pass, ere Authority itself, or some divine Providence inform our understanding with a way in Discipline or Government, either more near to the former purity of the primitive times, or more beloved of the whole Kingdom of *England*, or Authority shall in this space of time moderate many things now stiffly desired: For some time we shall not discover what shall be established, but all shall be even as when there was no King in *Israel*, a confusion among us shall yet a while remain: the Soldiery then, or some men of fiery Spirits will arise, and keep back their Contribution from the Clergy, and will deny obedience or submission to this thing we call Presbytery; it will then come to be handled by the Magistrate, and taken into consideration by the grand Authority of the Kingdom; yea, and by the plurality of the Clergymen of *England*, or men of very sound judgments, it will be contradicted, disputed against, disapproved; and these shall make it manifest, this very Presbytery now maintained, is not the same the Commonwealth of *England* will entertain, as a standing rule, for it to live under, or be governed by.

From what I do find by this Figure, I conclude, that Presbytery shall not stand here in *England* (*status quo*) without refining and amending, and demolishing many scrupulous matters urged at present by the Clergy; for if we consider ♃ as Lord of the fourth, we find the ☽, in plain language, (after a little being void of course) run hastily to the □ of ♂ and ♃; intimating, the Commonalty will defraud the expectation of the Clergy, and so strongly oppose them, that the end hereof shall wholly delude the expectation of the Clergy.

CHAPTER LXXXI.

If attain the Philosopher's Stone?

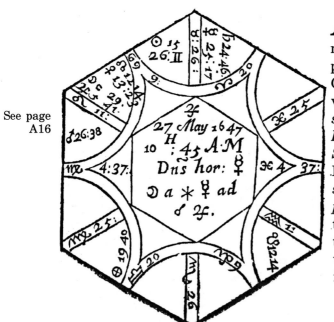

See page
A16

An ingenious man with much seriousness propounded the Question above, viz. *Whether he should obtain the Philosopher's Stone? or, that Elixir by which such wonders are preformed?* That there is such a thing in being I verily believe; that it may be attained

I am as confident: but as it is a blessing beyond all blessings upon earth, so I hold, that it is given but to very few, and to those few rather by revelation of the good Angels of God, than the proper industry of man. This Question must admit of this manner of proposal; *Whether the Knowledge of the querent is so able, or he so cunning, as to produce to effect by his Art what he desires?*

The *querent* is signified by the ascendant, and ☿ Lord thereof; his knowledge by ♂ Lord of the ninth, and the aspects which may be cast to him from other Planets.

I find ♂ Lord of the *Querent's* Science in a cadent house, but in his own Term and Face.

♂ is in a □ aspect both of ☿ and ♄, and they and he in fixed Signs, they in the Terms of ♄, falling into the ninth house; I find ☿ lately Retrograde, and in □ of ♂, now moving slowly in his direct motion, and applying again to a second □ of ♂: From hence I judged, the *querent* had formerly spent some time in the search of this admirable Jewel the Elixir, but in vain and to no purpose; his second application by □ happening not long after, while ☿ was in Ⅱ, and in his own Terms, intimated a stronger desire, greater hopes and resolution to endeavour once more the attaining of the *Philosopher's Stone*, but I advised the *querent* to decline his further progress upon that subject; and in regard of the former reasons, advertised him how incapable he was, and the improbability of the thing he intended, according to natural causes, and advised him to desist: I also said, that he erred in his materials or composition, working upon things terrene or of too gross and heavy a substance; part of which judgment I collected by ♄ his □ to ♂, part by the affliction of ☿, his intellective part by the proximity of ♄, both cohabiting in an earthly Sign, for in any operation where ☿ is corrupted, there the fancy or imaginative part is imbecile; but where the Lord of the Work itself is unfortunate (as here ♂ Lord of the ninth is,) there the groundwork or matter itself of the principal part of the operation is defective, as here it was: and that the Gentleman should think I spoke not in vain, I acquainted him, he had more necessity to cure himself of a Consumption, he was entering into (nay entered) than of advancing his pains further in the scrutiny of this Labyrinth.

For seeing ☿ Lord of the Ascendant, and ♄ in ♂ in ♉, ♄ being Lord of the sixth, of evil influence naturally, and finding ♂ afflicting ☿ out of the twelfth, and ☿ not receded from, but applying to a further evil □ of ♂, no *Fortune* interjecting his benevolent aspect between ☿ and the two *Infortunes*, but that he stood single of himself without any assistance, and thereby was incapable of resisting their malevolent influence. I advised to have a care of his health speedily, &c.

The tenth HOUSE, and those QUESTIONS properly belonging to it.

CHAPTER LXXXII.

Of Government, Office, Dignity, Preferment, or any place of Command or Trust, whether attainable or not?

The first house and his Lord are given to the *querent*, the tenth house and his Lord shall signify the *Place, Office, Preferment, Command, Honour,* &c. inquired after; if the Lord of the ascendant and the ☽ be both joined to the ☉, or to the Lord of the tenth, or either of them, and the Lord of the tenth behold the tenth, or be personally therein, the *querent* shall then have the thing sought after, but not *gratis*; nay, he must bestir himself, and use all the friends he can about it: if none of the *Significators* be joined to the Lord of the tenth, see if the Lord of the first or ☽ be in the tenth, he shall then attain what he desires, if that Planet be not impeded: The Lord of the tenth in the first, so he be a lighter Planet than the Lord of the first, though no aspect be between them, yet shall he attain the Place or Office desired; but with more ease and less labour when the Lord of the tenth is in the ascendant, and is either going to ♂, ✶ or △ aspect with the Lord of the first.

If the Lord of the tenth be joined to ♃ or ♀ by any aspect,

and the Lord of the tenth be in the ascendant, it argues obtaining of the Office with ease and facility: If the Lord of the tenth be joined to ♂ or ♄, and they or either of them in the ascendant, in their own house or exaltation, and themselves Oriental and Direct, and not one opposite to another, this does argue obtaining the Preferment, though with much importunity.

If the Lord of the tenth receive the Lord of the first or the ☽ by any reception, or in any house, the matter will be effected with much content and profit.

If any Planet transfer the virtue of the Lord of the first to the Lord of the tenth, then the thing will be perfected, or Office obtained by means of another that labours in the matter, and not by himself: In this case, it's best that he who would acquire the Dignity, observe if he know such a man as the Planet describes, that in probability is active, or of near acquaintance to the person of whom he would have the Office, and let him employ such a one in the business, for by his means it's very like he may attain the place desired.

If the Lord of the tenth do not desire the ♂ of the Lord of the first, but the Lord of the ascendant his, and does really come to ♂ of the Lord of the tenth, without the abscission of any other Planet before ♂, the Office will be obtained, but the *querent* must labour hard for it.

No ♂ being between the Lord of the first and tenth, or either of them joined to a *Fortune*, but to a malevolent Planet, and that malignant joined to another malevolent, and this malevolent joined to a *Fortune*, and this *Fortune* joined to the Lord of the tenth; if the ♂ of the first *Infortune* be with the Lord of the first, or the last Planet is joined to the Lord of the first, or if their first ♂ be with the Lord of the tenth, yet it imports acquisition of the Dignity, but with infinite perplexities, and solicitation of many and several persons: you may easily distinguish the persons of those to be employed, by the Planets before mentioned, and the houses they are Lords of; those Planets that are in ✳ or △ to the Lord of the tenth are great with him: Let application or means be made to such, for those men may be great Friends to the *Querent*.

Behold if any of the preceding Planets be in the first, or in the tenth; if he be a *Fortune*, it notes obtaining the Dignity, whether he be in Reception or not: if the Planet so placed do receive the ☽ or Lord of the first, the matter will be perfected, but without Reception, not.

If the tenth house be the house or exaltation of that evil Planet, and he placed in that house, he performs the business, whether he receive the Lord of the ascendant or the ☽: In every Question you must observe, that what Planet soever is *Significator* of anything, if he be in an angle, he hastens to effect the matter; in a succedent, the matter goes on slowly; in a cadent house, the matter goes backward and backward, yet at last is performed.

See if an ill Planet behold the Lord of the ascendant or the ☽, with □ or ☍, without Reception, for unless he then commit his disposition to another, he hinders and disturbs the *querent* by means of that person who is to solicit the cause or business, and it's probable they will fall out about it: if a △ or ✶ be between them, he will not be angry with him, although he perform not what he expects.

If the Lord of the ascendant and tenth commit their disposition to any Planet by any aspect, with or with no Reception, whether the Receiver be a *Fortune* or *Infortune* (so that he be not Retrograde, Combust or Cadent, or go out of that Sign wherein he is before the ☌ of the Lord of the first and tenth with him) and if the ☽ be joined to the Lord of the first or tenth, the *querent* shall achieve the preferment expected.

It's generally concluded by all *Astrologers*, that if the Lord of the ascendant and Lord of the tenth be joined together, and the ☽ apply to either of them, the matter will be effected, but best of all when ☽ separates from the Lord of the tenth, and applies to the Lord of the ascendant.

Behold if the Lord of the first be joined to the Lord of the fourth, or the Lord of the fourth to the Lord of the ascendant, it argues their perfecting of the thing: but if the Lord of the ascendant be joined to the Lord of the fourth, and the Lord of the fourth be joined to the Lord of the tenth, the matter shall be effected, but with so much struggling and delaying, that it was absolutely despaired ever to be effected, yet at last it was perfected.

If one shall continue in the Office or Command he is in.

Behold herein the Lord of the first and the tenth, and see if they be in any aspect, or near to a corporal conjunction; and see if the more ponderous Planet of the two, that is, the receiver of the Disposition be in any angle but the fourth; say then, he shall not be removed from his Office until his appointed time comes out: but if that Receiver of the Disposition be under the earth, or in the descending part of heaven, it imports he shall depart from his Office, or for a time loose it; but shall return thither again more confirmed in his Place: and if the receiver of the Disposition be received again, then he returns with more honour than before, and also very speedily.

You may judge in the same manner, if the Lord of the ascendant be joined to the Lord of the third or ninth, or to a Planet therein, and after separation from him, be joined to a Planet in any Angle except the fourth.

But if they are separated from each other, then he returns not again to his government, but shall depart from it.

If the Lord of the first or tenth, or ☽ commit their disposition to any Planet in an Angle (except he be in the fourth) and that Planet be slow in motion, he shall not be removed from his Office or place of trust, until that Receiver become Retrograde or approach to Combustion, or go out of the Sign wherein he is; for much about that time will he be removed. If the Lord of the first be joined to any Planet who is in a Sign opposite to the exaltation of the Planet who now disposes him, the Officer will then carry himself ill in his place, and it may be feared he shall die for it (but this is to be understood according to the quality of the place he has.) If the Lord of the opposite house to the exaltation of the Lord of the first be joined to him; the men of that Kingdom, or people of that City or Country shall report ill of him, shall produce false witnesses against him; the ignorant shall believe those false reports, nor will they be easily beaten into any other opinion.

But if the Lord of the tenth be joined to the Lord of the opposite house of his exaltation; the Country where he governs or governed, shall suffer great detriment, *viz.* by the said Governor.

If the ☽ be joined to the Lord of the tenth, and he in the tenth, the Governor or Officer shall not be put from his Office or Dignity.

If the Lord of the first or the ☽ be joined to the Lord of the tenth or either of them, and he more weighty than either of them, and be in a good place of heaven, *viz.* either in the tenth, eleventh, or fifth free from all manner of impediments, though he behold not the tenth, yet not withstanding if the *querent* be then in any Command or Office, he shall be transferred to some other place of trust or Command: But if he behold the tenth house, then he shall continue where he is. If the Lord of the ascendant and the ☽ be in Angles, and the Angles moveable Signs and ☽ not joined to the Lord of the exaltation of that Sign she is then in, it argues he shall go from this present Command or Government: or if the ☽ be joined to any Planet who is not in any of his essential dignities, though he be received, unless it be from a fortune by ✶ or △, and that fortune in the third or ninth, the *querent* shall leave his Government or Office. In like manner the same thing will happen to him, if either the Lord of the fourth or the ☽ be in the fourth, and the Sign of the fourth be ♈, ♋, ♎, ♑, the judgement will hold more certain if the ☽ be then joined to the Lord of the fourth, and he Peregrine: and again, the same will come to pass, if the ☽ be joined to a Planet, who is in the ☍ to the Sign of the exaltation or house of herself; or if she be in ♑, or if the ☽ be void of course.

CHAPTER LXXXIII.

Whether a King expulsed his Kingdom, or an Officer removed from his government shall return to his Kingdom or Office.

In these sad times of our Civil Distempers, many of the Gentry have propounded such *queries*; *Whether they should return and enjoy once more their former estates, &c.* that Question falls not to be judged by this house; the matter of this Question is of greater concernment; For Kings and Princes are now in this Chapter upon the Stage; and all manner of principal men cast out from former honours or preferments.

The first house in this Question and Lord thereof, are for the Querent, be he King, or other Officer, &c. Lord, Marquess, Duke or Gentleman.

Do you well observe if the Lord of the first be in ♂ with the Lord of the tenth, and see if the more ponderous of them who receives the disposition of the more light Planet behold the tenth house, then the King, Gentleman or Officer, shall return and have power, or rule in the Kingdom or place he formerly had, and from whence at present he is suspended.

If that receiver of the disposition of the other *Significator* do not aspect the tenth house, then observe the ☽, a general *Significatrix*, and see if she be joined to any Planet who is placed in the first or 10ᵗʰ, that signifies his returning or restoring: see if the ☽ be in ♈, ♋, ♎, ♑, he returns the sooner: But if the Lord of the tenth be so joined to a Planet in the tenth, it signifies the return of a King to his Kingdom, or of one ousted from his Office, to his place or command again.

If the Lord of the tenth be more light than the Lord of the fourth, and be separated from him, these argue the same: If the Lord of the tenth be more light than the Lord of the first, and be joined to him, he shall return and continue; so also, if the ☽ be joined to the Lord of the tenth, and she behold the tenth house, unless she commit her disposition to a peregrine Planet under the earth: if the Lord of the first be received of a Planet not impeded, he returns: if not received, no return.

The ☽ joined to a Planet in the ninth, signifies the King so expulsed,* recedes from his Kingdom, unless the Planet be a *Fortune*: if the Planet to whom the ☽ is joined be a *Fortune*, and be in ♈, ♉, ♋, ♌, ♎, ♏, ♑, ♒, the forlorn King or dejected Officer returns: if the Planet to whom the ☽ is joined, be in ♊, ♍, ♐ or ♓, the King obtains Sovereignty in another place, or the abjected a Command or Office in some other Country.

*Or has little desire to return.

If you find the Lord of the tenth and the ☽ impeded in any angle, by the corporal ♂ of any *Infortune*, it imports that neither the distressed King, or expulsed Governor, or removed Officer, shall return again to their former Dignity, Rule or Command.

CHAPTER LXXXIV.

Of the Profession, Magistery or Trade any one is capable of.

Country people many times have not the time of their children's Nativities, yet being desirous to know what profession such or such a Son is fittest for, they may repair to the *Astrologian* for satisfaction herein: Upon the time of their demanding the Question, erect your Figure, and therein consider the ascendant and his Lord, the Lord of the 10th and 10th house, and especially the places of ♂ and ♀; for these Planets are the *Significators* of Magistery, Trade or Profession: take which of the two you find most powerful, and see in what Sign he is, if he be in ♈, consider the four angles, and whether you find a Planet in either of them, and if that Planet be in a fiery Sign, or of the nature of ♈, you may say, the Boy will prove a good Cart-maker, Coach-maker, Shepherd, Grasier or Drover to deal in Cattle, a good Groom, or Master of Horse, or Farrier, successful to deal in four-footed Beasts, or a good Butcher, Brick-maker, Smith, &c. but if ♂ have any dignity in the place of the *Significator*, or the ☉, he will prove excellent in any Profession where fire is used, or of its nature: if the *Significator* be in his Exaltation, it's pity the Child should be of any servile Trade, as aforesaid, he may do better in serving the King, some Nobleman or Gentleman: After this manner consider in all those Signs which represent the shape of four-footed Cattle, according to the Angles, ♈, ♉, ♌, ♐, ♑, for these five signify Cattle: ♊, ♎, ♒ represent men, yet sometimes ♊ presents flying fowl; ♋, ♏, ♓ when they are in angles, signify Fish and Waterfowl, or such like; but if no Planet be therein, then they import anything of the nature of water.

But to the purpose, observe if the *Significator* of one's Profession be in ♉, then Husbandry may be best for him, or planting Trees, Gardening, buying and selling Corn, or grazing Cattle, dealing in Oxen, Cows, Sheep, Hogs, or he may be of such a Trade as has affinity in Women's matters, or Housewifery, he would prove a good Soap-maker, a Fuller of Cloth, a Whitster, &c.

If the *Significator* be in ♊, he will make a Scrivener, Clerk, Arithmetician, a Bailiff to gather Rents, a Geometrician or Surveyor, Astronomer, Astrologer, Painter, &c.

If the *Significator* be in ♌, he will make a good Serving-man, or to be of any Trade that uses fire or hot things, a good Huntsman, a good Leech for Cows or Cattle, a good Rider or Horse-courser, or Coachman, or a Smith, Watchmaker, Glass maker.

If the *Significator* be in ♍, he will make a good Secretary to a King or Nobleman, a Schoolmaster, an Accountant, a Stationer, or Printer, he will be an excellent Politician, a good Astrologer, and of a divining Soul.

If the *Significator* be in ♎, he will be a good Poet, a good Orator, a Song-man or Musician, a Silkman or Linen-Draper, a good Pedagogue, or fit to redeem Captives.

If the principal *Significator* be in ♏, he may prove a good Surgeon, Apothecary or Physician, a Brazier or Founder, a Brewer, Vintner, Waterman or Maltster.

If the *Significator* be in ♐, he will make an excellent man to buy and sell Cattle, to study Chymistry, or to make a Churchman, or he may be a good Cook or Baker.

If the *Significator* be in ♑, he will prove a good Chandler, Victualer, Farrier, Cow-leech, Jeweler, Farmer, dealer in Wool, Lead or Country-commodities, a good Husbandman.

If the *Significator* be in ♒, he may be an excellent Ship carpenter; and if any Planet out of a watery Sign aspect him, he may prove an excellent Sailor, or Master of a Ship, a Trimmer or Painter of Ships, a good industrious Merchant.

If the *Significator* be in ♓, he may be a Jester, Singer, a Gamester, a Brewer or Fishmonger; but for the most part in such like cases, the Genius is dull, and the child proves a mere Sot.

CHAPTER LXXXVa.

If Prince RUPERT *should get honour by our Wars, or worst
the Earl of* ESSEX? *What should become of him?*

See page
A16

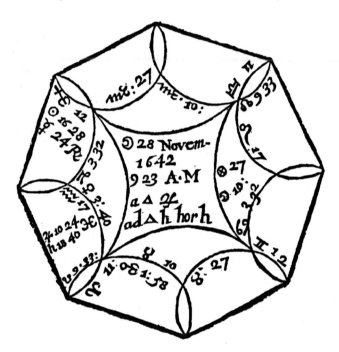

Resolution of this Figure.

This Question falls not under the notion of vulgar rules,
or must the *Astrologian* expect particular Rules to govern
his Fancy in every Question; it was well said, *Ate & a scientia*, for
I do daily resolve such Questions as come not into the vulgar
Rules of *Guido* or *Haly*, and yet I was never to seek a sufficient
reason in Art, whereby to give a good and satisfactory answer
to the *Proponent*, &c. as many hundreds in this Kingdom well
know, &c. He that propounded the Question was a very great

well-wisher to the Parliament, and involved himself and
Fortune amongst us, therefore the ascendant and Lord thereof
shall signify the *querent*; but in regard Prince RUPERT is a
noble Man, or person of eminency, he is signified by the
tenth house and Lord thereof; the Sign is ♏, the Lord thereof
♂: I must confess, at first finding the ☽ in ♋, to cast her △
sinister to the cusp of the tenth; I judged, the person of the
man would be in no very great danger, and that many vulgar
people, and some of better quality, would much honour him,
and he find great respect amongst them, and have a special
care of his own person: and verily ♃ does also cast his △
dexter to the cusp of the tenth house, whereby I judged, that
we should not destroy his person, for the heavens by this
Figure intimated the contrary: The very truth is, I was
twenty four hours studying the resolution of this Question,
for much may be said in behalf of the Prince, and the hopes
might be expected from him; at last I came to this resolution,
that he should gain no honour by this War, because neither
of the *Luminaries* were in the tenth house, or in perfect
aspect with his *Significator*, but at last fall into the hatred
and malice of all or many, by his own perverseness and folly,
and in the end should depart without either honour, love or
friendship, but should not be killed: The Lord of the tenth in
his Detriment, argue his depraved Fancy; and being in a
fixed Sign, shows his obstinateness, self-opposition,
conceitedness and continuance in his erroneous judgment,
for let all the Planets assist in a Question concerning War or
Soldiery, if ♂ himself, who is *Significator* thereof, be unfortunate,
or not strongly supported by the *Luminaries*, it's as good as
nothing, the party shall be preserved, but do no glorious work
or action in War, though he be never so valiant.

If he should worst the Earl of ESSEX?

ESSEX is here signified by ♀, because she is Lady of ♉,
the opposite house to the Prince's; we find ♀ in ♒, in the
Terms of ♄, and he Lord of the ascendant; in Reception with ♄,
for as she receives him in her Exaltation, so does he her in

his Joy and Term: the ☽ transfers the influence of ♃ to ♄, by a forcible and strong aspect, *viz.* a △; ♀ is in □ of ♂, but separated; as if not long before there had been some fight or war between them, (for you must understand we are now upon point of war;) [*and so there had:*] For *Edge-hill* fight was above a month before, wherein *Essex* had the better; and this I prove because he kept the ground where the Battle was fought, when both the *King* and Prince *Rupert* left the Field. I know Posterity will believe me, since I write now as an *Artist*, and upon a subject which must be left to Posterity: This I know by the testimony of many of the King's own Officers who have confessed as much to me &c. But let it suffice, I positively affirmed, *Rupert* should never prevail against the valiant *Essex*, &c. nor did he.

What should become of him?

His *Significator*, viz. ♂, being peregrine, and in the third, I said, it should come to pass, he should be at our disposing, and that we should at last have him in our own custody, and do what we like with him: this I judged, because the gentle Planet ♀, *Essex* Significator, did dispose of *Rupert*: an error in part I confess it was, yet not much to be blamed, for (*in totidem verbis*) it was very near truth, for in 1646, he was besieged in *Oxford*, and after surrender thereof, having unadvisedly repaired to *Oatlands*, contrary to Agreement and Covenant, he was then at the mercy of the Parliament, and in their mercy: but they of that house looking on him rather as an improvident young man, than any worthy of their displeasure or taking notice of, let him depart with his own proper fate, heavy enough for him to bear; and so he escaped. So that the general fate of this Kingdom, overcame my private opinion upon Prince *Rupert*. However, I am glad he escaped so, being questionless a man of able parts, but unfortunate, not in himself, but in the fate of his Family.

CHAPTER LXXXVB.

If his MAJESTY *should procure Forces out of* **Ireland** *to harm the Parliament?*

If the QUEEN, *then in the* **North**, *would advance with her Army? If she would prosper? When She and his Majesty should meet?*

In the original, both this & the previous chapter were numbered 85 - *Ed. note.*

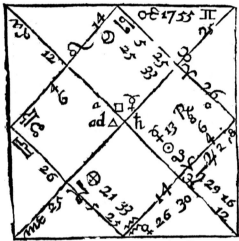

His Majesty is here signified by ☽ in ♋ in the tenth house, who increasing in light, elevated and placed in her own house, void of all infelicity, except slowness in motion, did manifest at the time of the erecting of this Figure, his Majesty to be in an able condition, as indeed he was.

March 18, 1643, 6 pm, (OS) See page A17

In this Judgment we find ☉ Lord of the eleventh (which house signifies assistance or aide in this manner of Judgment) placed in the seventh, in his Exaltation, and applying to the cusp of the eleventh with a △ aspect, but wants six degrees of being partile; forasmuch as the ☽ being in her own house, and ☉ so well fortified, I did judge his Majesty should have aid of Commanders out of *Ireland* (for ☉ represents Commanders) and men, or common men, besides; because both ☉ and ☽ are friendly to him: that they should harm us, I judged because ☉ Lord of that assistance, was in the seventh, in direct ☍ to the ascendant, which represented the Parliament and their party: but because the ☉ is so near ☋, and beholds the cusp of the tenth with a □ sinister, I did in the end less fear them, and judged they should produce much scandal, to his Majesty and his Party, and that they would cause many ill and heavy reports to fall upon his Majesty by their means: I also then judged, that his Majesty was likely to improve his Forces, and augment them for some certain time, but that it should not continue very long, for that neither the ☉ or ☽ were fixed. The truth is, he had *Irish* Forces come over, which much hardened the hearts of the *English* against him, but time cut them off, &c. as we do all well know, at the Siege of *Namptwich*, by valiant FAIRFAX.

Her Majesty's *Significatrix* is ♄ Lord of the fourth, for that is the seventh from the tenth, removing out of one Sign into another: ♄ being a ponderous Planet, made me more confident her Majesty would move forwards with her Army, with intention to meet his Majesty, which I said she should do about three or four months from the time of the Figure, because the ☽ wanted three or four degrees of the △ of ♄. I intimated a great desire in his Majesty to see her, because his *Significator* applied. The truth is, she met him about the 14 of *July* 1643 in *Warwickshire*. I judged that she would not prosper but decline, because ♄ her *Significatrix* was going into ♈ his Fall, and that ♃, viz. *good Fortune*, was separated, and did separate from ♄. Besides, I observed that ♂ made haste to a □ of ♄ in ♋, as if our Soldiery would quite destroy and bring to nothing her Army; and that she would be crossed at or near the time of that aspect, which was the 11th of *April*, when about *Nottingham* she lost some Forces, and more had, but that we had ever either some knaves or fools in our Armies.

CHAPTER LXXXVI.

If attain the Preferment desired?

At the same time within four or five minutes thereof, a Gentleman desired to know if he should obtain an Office or place he looked after.

The ascendant and ♀ are for the *querent*, the tenth house for the Office or place of preferment he expects.

Finding the ☽ placed in the tenth, which is in the house of the thing looked after, viz. *Preferment*, it was one argument the *querent* should have it.

In the next place, the ☽ applied to a △ of ♄, who has Exaltation in the ascendant, and who receives ♀, and is received of her again.

Besides, the ☽ applying to ♄, who is Lord of the fourth, argued, that in the end he should obtain the Office: but because ☉ was in the seventh house in ♂ to the ascendant, and with ☋, and was Lord of the eleventh, I judged he did employ as a Friend, a *Solar* man, who was false, and did rather envy than affect him. I concluded for the reasons above-named, that with some difficulty he should obtain the Dignity, notwithstanding the opposition a pretended Friend did make; and so it came to pass within less three weeks, and he then discovered that his Friend was false, who had a great scar in his Face, was not of bright or yellow Hair, but of a blackish dark colour, occasioned by ☉ his nearness to ☋: the separation of ☽ from a □ of ☿, argued, he had delivered many Petitions about it, but hitherto without success.

The eleventh HOUSE, and those QUESTIONS properly belonging to it.

It is the House of Friends, Hope, Substance or Riches of KINGS.

CHAPTER LXXXVII.

Of good or ill questions concerning this House.

If the Lord of this house be strong, fortunate, and well aspected of the Lord of the ascendant, it foreshows the obtaining of the thing at present hoped for; as also, love and concord of Friends and Acquaintance, if the Question be thereof.

If a man shall have the thing hoped for?

Behold if there be any good aspect between the Lord of the ascendant and the eleventh, or Reception or translation of light, or that the Lord of the ascendant be in the eleventh, or the Lord of the eleventh in the ascendant: all or any of these gives hope of obtaining the same. If there be none of those, behold ☽, and if she be not qualified with the Lord of the eleventh, aforesaid, judge the contrary,

Another Judgment concerning the former Question.

When anyone asks for a thing he hopes to have of his Prince, Lord, Master or Nobleman, as some Dignity, &c. behold if the Lord of the eleventh house do apply to the Lord of the ascendant, or the Lord of the ascendant to the Lord of the eleventh, say then he shall have the thing hoped for; and if the aspect be by △ or ✶, he shall obtain the same with great ease and speed: but if the aspect be with □ or ☍, he shall get it with much labor and tediousness; yea, although there be Reception of *Significators*.

If you find the Lord of the eleventh in an angle received, judge the thing shall come to pass as he would wish.

If you find the Receiver of the disposition of the ☽ in a common Sign, judge he shall have but part of the thing hoped for: If the same Receiver be in a movable Sign, he shall only have the name, or a probability of having thereof, or else very little of it: but if the same Receiver be in a fixed Sign, he shall have the thing whole and complete: but if the Receiver of the ☽ be unfortunate, the matter shall receive damage or hurt, after that he has the same, or is in possession thereof.

If you find the Receiver of the ☽ received, he shall likewise obtain the same, and more than he looked for: if you find the Lord of the ascendant received, he shall obtain whatsoever he hoped for: this must be understood in things feasible and possible.

CHAPTER LXXXVIII.

Of the agreeing of Friends.

If one ask, *If he shall join, and be at Concord and Unity with his Friend, or not?* behold the Lord of the ascendant and ☽, if you find them applying to the Lord of the eleventh house, say they shall both join and agree together; if the application be by ⚹ or △ they shall agree and join together with respect, desire, joy and love: but if the application be by □ or ☍, in their joining there shall be brawling and strife, and the one shall be irksome to the other; and note, that the application which is by ☍, is worse than that which is by □.

Note, if anyone ask for a thing secretly, saying, *Look I pray you for me, If I shall obtain the thing I hope for, or not*: consider if you find the Lord of the ascendant and the ☽ applying to *Fortunes*, and in angles or Succedents, then he shall obtain it, otherwise not. But if the *querent* shall manifest the thing and name it, then you must behold the thing in its own proper place pertaining to the same House, and so judge of the hopes or not hopes thereof.

Of Love between two.

If it be asked of the love of two, viz. *If the one do love the other or not?* behold the Lord of the eleventh, seventh and third, and if the Lords of these houses do behold the Lord of the ascendant with a ⚹ or △ aspect they love one another: but if the aspect be by □ or ☍, they love not, or but teeth outward; chiefly if one of them be Lord of the twelfth house; if neither of them shall have aspect thither, *viz.* to the twelfth house or Lord thereof, the love of the two persons shall be the more firm and strong: if all three be there, *viz.* either in the eleventh, seventh, or third, or do behold each other out of those houses, their love shall be the stronger, especially if the aspect be in fixed Signs.

❖❖

Of the twelfth HOUSE, and those QUESTIONS which properly appertain to it.

Viz. *Of Imprisonment, great Cattle, Witchery, private Enemies, Labour, banished Men, &c.*

CHAPTER LXXXIX.

Of Secret Enemies, not named.

If a Question be asked, concerning Enemies, and none named, see to the Lord of the twelfth; but if any be named, then to the seventh house and the Lord thereof; diligently considering their applications to and with the Lord of the ascendant, and by what aspect, and out of what houses; for if the Lord of the twelfth behold the Lord of the ascendant with □ or ☌, out of the eighth, sixth or twelfth, or out of those houses which have a □ aspect to the ascendant, or no aspect at all, then there is some that privately and secretly wish him ill, and do him mischief, or is a secret enemy to him.

To know some secret Enemy who he is.

If any man demand the state of a secret Enemy, behold the Lord of the twelfth house, and how he is affected, and whether he be with good or evil Planets, and behold the ascendant or Lord thereof, for if he be in the sixth, or joined to the Lord thereof, it shows the secret Enemy is afflicted with some secret Disease or Malady; as also, if the Lord of the sixth be in the twelfth: but if he, *viz.* Lord of the twelfth, be with the Lord

of the tenth, he is in favour with the King, or is a man of
good quality, or lives with some man of quality, and it is not
good for the *querent* to meddle with him, especially if at such
time he behold the Lord of the ascendant with □ or ♂: but
if the Lord of the twelfth be in the fourth or eighth, or with
the Lord thereof, judge him sickly, or near to dying, or ever
pining and repining. Consider and judge with discretion in
such like cases, according to former Directions.

CHAPTER XC.

Any man committed to Prison, whether he shall be soon Delivered?

Behold the ☽, if she be swift or slow of course: if she be *You must*
swift, it shows short tarrying in prison; the contrary if *know your
ascendant*
she be slow of course: if she give her strength to a Planet in *exactly, and*
the third house or ninth, this shows he shall soon come forth *what relation*
of prison; if she give power to the Lord of the ninth or third, *the party
inquired of*
and be not in one of the angles, *idem*: and as you judge by *has to the*
the ☽ so judge by the Lord of the ascendant. *querent, &c.*

You shall also note, that the Quarters of Heaven in the Figure,
are of great strength and force; for the *Significators* in Quarters
feminine, do signify a swift going out, the other more slow: so also
common Signs show a time between both; for if the *Significator* be
in one of them, it signifies he shall be imprisoned again.

If you find the Lords of the angles in angles, he shall not
come out of prison; and so much the worse, if the Lord of the
ascendant be in the fourth, or that he give power to the Lord
of the twelfth, or the Lord of the twelfth to the Lord of the
ascendant; and yet worse, if the Lord of the ascendant give
power to a Planet being in an angle; which if he be an ill
planet, it's so much the worse; if it be the Lord of the eighth
house, he shall die in prison: If the ☽ give power to the Lord
of the ascendant, it's an evil Sign; and the worse, if a Planet
being in an angle, and slow in motion; if he be swift, it
diminishes part of the evil, and shortens the time.

Every Planet that is Retrograde, shows slowness: If the Lord of the ascendant be Combust, he shall never come out; or if he be not then received of the ☉, he shall die in prison.

Of the Imprisoned.

☽ and ☿ in movable Signs, aspecting a *Fortune*, or ☿ in aspect of a *Fortune*, notes enlargement: this is when ☿ is Lord of the ascendant.

♃ in the ascendant, or ♂ or ☽ at time of Arrest, or ♀ in the ascendant with the ☽, or ☿ with ♃, aspecting the ☽, or ☽ applying to ♃ or ♀ notes enlargement.

The Dispositor of ☽ in aspect with a *Fortune*; any of these note he shall be delivered in a short and convenient time.

If a Question be asked for a Captive or Prisoner.

Behold the Lord of the ascendant, and if he be separate from the Lord of the fourth house, or the Lord of the fourth house from him, it signifies he shall quickly go out of prison: if the Lord of the ascendant in separating himself from the Lord of the fourth do apply to a *Fortune*, and he himself remove from an angle, it is a more sure and certain sign that he shall escape and come forth of prison; when the Lord of the ascendant shall be in Cadents from the Angles, it is likewise a sign of escape.

If the Lord of the ascendant do separate himself from the ☉, or if the ☽ shall be existent under the Beams, it signifies escape and that especially if he be in the King's Prison.

If at any time any of the ill Signs, *viz.* fixed, be ascending at the hour of Imprisonment, or when the Question is taken for the Prisoner, or the Lord of the ascendant or ☽ be unfortunate in any of these Signs ♉, ♌, ♒, ♓, it signifies long time of imprisonment; if she be unfortunate in the two first Signs, and in ☍ of ♂, it signifies he shall be slain with the sword after long imprisonment, or in danger thereof by quarrelling: If the same *Infortune* be ♄ it signifies great Tortures, Irons, and grievous punishments, amongst us it notes wants, hard measure, small or no mercy, sickness: If an *Infortune* be in the two latter Signs, it signifies long endurance in prison, but shortest time if in ♓. If the Lord of the ascendant be cadent from his House or his Exaltation, and ☽ in ♒, it signifies long imprisonment: The Lord of the ascendant or the ☽ in the eighth, do signify the same. If ☿ be with any of the *Infortunes*, he adds evil and misery to the Incarcerated, and an ill end to the Prisoner.

To be short, there can be nothing better to be wished for the Prisoner, than if the ☽ be in her wane, descending to her Septentrional part, and applying to *Fortunes*, and the ascendant and his Lord fortunate.

Note also, that ♀ is more to be wished for the Prisoner than ♃, and delivers sooner out of Prison; especially if she be joined in signification with the ☽ or ☿: If the ☽ be with ♄, and ♃ behold them with a □, and ♂ with a △, it signifies that after long imprisonment and misery, he shall break prison and escape.

CHAPTER XCI.

Of a Captive or Slave.

Behold the sixth house or twelfth, and if any Planet be therein, he is the *Signifier* of the Captive, because those houses are the houses of Captives or imprisonment. If you find none there, behold the Planet which is under the Sunbeams, he is the *Signifier*.

Behold the hour at what time the Captive is taken in, and if the Lord of the hour be an *Infortune*, it signifies long imprisonment; but if he be a *Fortune*, it signifies short imprisonment or Captivity.

The *Ancients* say, he that is taken in the hour of the ☉, shall escape within a month; in the hour of ♀, in forty days; in the hour of ☿, long imprisonment; in the hour of the ☽, his state shall change according to the applications the ☽ has with the Planets, fortunate or unfortunate; according to which you shall judge easy or slow deliverance: he that is taken in the hour of ♄, shall be long in prison; in the hour of ♃, he shall soon go out, but he that is taken in the hour of ♂, much trouble shall happen to him in prison, for he shall be put in Fetters or beaten; this you must understand of Felons, or Soldiers, or men that break Prison, or of madmen, &c.

CHAPTER XCII.

If one be Bewitched or not.

If the Lord of the twelfth be in the sixth, or the Lord of the sixth in the twelfth, or the Lord of the ascendant in the twelfth, or the Lord of the twelfth in the ascendant, or the Lord of the eighth in the ascendant, or the Lord of the ascendant in the eighth, in a Question where suspicion of Witchcraft is, it is probable; otherwise not so: But the Judgment succeeding I have found more certain.

It's a received, general Rule amongst those *Artists* that know the *Cabalistic Key of Astrologie*, that if one Planet be Lord of the ascendant and twelfth house, that then the Sickness is more than natural: When ♄ is Lord of the ascendant and twelfth, and in the twelfth Retrograde, or in the seventh or eighth house in the same condition, and the ☽ being Lady of the sixth, apply to ♄, we constantly judge the party inquiring is Bewitched or Forespoken, or that an evil Spirit has power over him, and that the Infirm will be sore oppressed and disturbed in his Fancy, if not distracted.

If the Lord of the ascendant be Combust, or unfortunate in the twelfth, or joined to the Lord of the twelfth house, there may be great fear, that the party inquiring or inquired for is Enchanted or Bewitched, or else some evil Spirits do haunt him. If the Lord of the ascendant be Lord of the twelfth, and Combust, you must observe of what house the ☉ is Lord, and in what Sign and quarter of Heaven he and the Lord of the ascendant are, and judge the Witch lives that way; describe the ☉ in Sign as he is, and it represents the person.

If the Lord of the ascendant be Lord of the twelfth, Combust, or unfortunate by the Lord of the third, it's a Neighbour has procured some *Witch* to do this act, or one of the Kindred; see in what house the Lord of the ascendant falls to be in, and in what house the Lord of the third is in, and infortunates him, you may judge the cause of the malice to proceed from something of the nature of that house; as if either of them be in the sixth, it's for Pasturage of Cattle, or some difference about small Cattle, or for one hiring the other's Servants, &c. and in like manner consider all the twelve houses.

If the Lord of the ascendant be unfortunate, as aforesaid, by the Lord of the fifth, it's some Alewife, Nurse, or some drunken companion that occasions it, or has procured this Witchery.

If the Lord of the tenth afflict the Lord of the ascendant in the twelfth, it's doubtless the hand of God, or by some supernatural power or cause.

If the Lord of the ascendant be an unfortunate Planet, as ♂ or ♄, and be in the twelfth house, Combust and infortunated by the Lord of the twelfth, it imports the man is bewitched by a common Witch.

If the Lord of the twelfth be in the ascendant it argues Witchcraft, or that some evil Spirit does molest the party, or that some that are near him or about him have evil tongues, or in plain terms, have bewitched him.

In places where people are troubled with Witches, as in many places of this Kingdom they are, these Rules will hold: as also, if the ☽ be in the twelfth, in ☍ to the lord of the ascendant or twelfth. If people suspect their Cattle Bewitched, if they be great Cattle, make the twelfth house their ascendant, and the eleventh their twelfth house, and vary your Rules with Judgment.

Natural *Remedies* for WITCHCRAFT.

H aving by the Figure discovered and described the Party, either by that Planet who is Lord of the 12th, or placed in the 12th, and does behold the Lord of the ascendant with a malicious aspect, you must let one watch the party suspected, when they go home to their own house, and presently after, before anybody go into the house after him or her, let one pull a handful of the Thatch, or a Tile that is over the Door: and if it be a Tile, make a good fire and heat it red hot therein, setting a Trivet over it, then take the party's water, if it be a man, woman or child, and pour it upon the red hot Tile, upon one side first, and then on the other, and again put the Tile in the fire, and make it extremely hot, turning it ever and anon, and let nobody come into the house in the mean time.

If they be Cattle that are bewitched, take some of the Hair of every one of them, and mix the Hair in fair water, or wet it well, and then lay it under the Tile, the Trivet standing over the Tile: make a lusty fire, turn your Tile oft upon the Hair, and stir up the Hair ever and anon: after you have done this by the space of a quarter of an hour, let the fire alone, and when the ashes are cold, bury them in the ground towards that quarter of heaven where the suspected Witch lives.

If the Witch live where there is no Tile but Thatch, then take a great handful thereof, and wet it is the party's water, or else in common water mixed with some salt, then lay it in the fire, so that it may molter and smother by degrees and in a long time, setting a Trivet over it.

Or else take two new Horseshoes, heat them red hot, and nail one of them on the Threshold of the Door, but quench the other in Urine of the party so Bewitched; then set the Urine over the fire, and put the Horseshoes in it, setting a Trivet over the Pipkin or Pan wherein the Urine is; make the Urine boil, with a little salt put into it, and three Horse-nails until it's almost consumed, viz. the Urine; what is not boiled fully away pour into the fire: keep your Horseshoe and nails in a clean cloth or paper, and use the same manner three several times; the operation would be far more effective, if you do these things at the very change or full Moon, or at the very hour of the first or second quarter thereof. If they be Cattle bewitched, you must mix the Hair of their Tails with the Thatch, and moisten them, being well bound together, and so let them be a long time in the fire consuming. These are natural experiments, and work by sympathy, as I have found by several experiments: I could have prescribed many more, *Multa creduntur ratione experintia, non quod videntur vera vi rationis.*

CHAPTER XCIII.

A Horse lost or stolen near Henley, if recoverable or not?

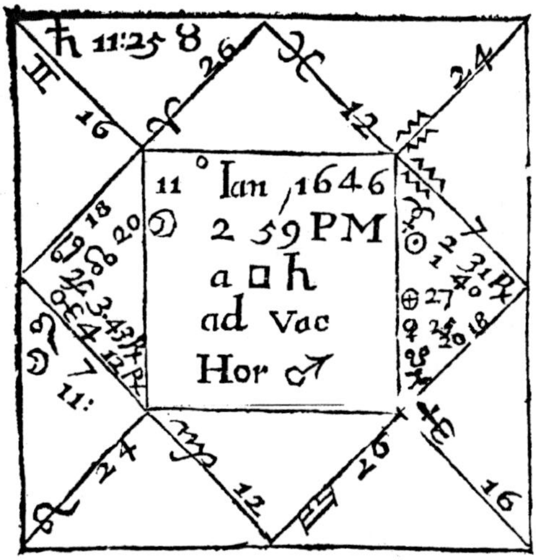

☿ Here Lord of the twelfth signifies the See page A17 Horse, whom you see Retrograde, & hastening to a ☌ of the ☉, Lord of the *Querent's* House of Substance; forasmuch as ☿ did by his Retrograde motion apply to the Lord of the *querent's* house of Substance, and that the ☽ was locally in the second and both ♃ and ♂ Retrograde, near the cusp of the second, I judged the *Querent* should have his Goods or Horse quickly and unexpectedly, within a day to two from the time of the Question asked; and because the seventh house was afflicted by ☋, I judged the Thief could not keep him.

I was asked, *Which way he went?* I considered the Sign of the twelfth was ♊, *viz.* West; the Sign wherein ☿ Lord of the twelfth was in, was ♒, *viz.* West; though the quarter of Heaven was South, but much inclining to the West; the ☽ was in ♌, a Northeast Sign. Besides, ☿ as he was Lord of the fourth, was in a West Sign. From whence I concluded, the Horse was gone Westward; but because ☿ was Retrograde, I judged the Horse would not proceed far, but return again to his proper owner; [*and indeed the Horse did come home three days after, and had been full West.*] However, I judged the Horse would have been at home a day sooner; but who shall more exactly consider of the Scheme, shall find, the ☿ *Significator* of the Horse, although he came to the body of ☉ Lord of the Querent's house of

Substance, the same night the Question was asked, yet because the ☉ had no Dignities where he was, the Horse came not home until Wednesday or Thursday the 13ᵗʰ or 14ᵗʰ of *January*, at what time ☿ and ♀ came to a partile ♂.

I must confess, here were many good significations that the *querent* should recover his lost Horse: first, ♌ in the ascendant: next, ☽ in the second, arguing he should be discovered: thirdly, ☿ Lord of the thing lost Retrograde, importing a returning of the thing again casually: fourthly, two Retrograde Planets upon the cusp of the second, which usually shows quick and unexpected recovery; ♃ and ♂ peregrine, I took them for those that rode away the Horse, ♃ especially; [*and it was very true.*]

CHAPTER XCIV.

If Bewitched.

See page
A18

Anno 1646
13 Martij 7
h 8 ʒ A·M
Hor ♂
a □ ♃
ad ☍ ♄

We must first consider if ♂ Lord of the twelfth afflict ☿ Lord of the ascendant, or if ♂ afflict the ☽; or whether ☿ be Lord of the ascendant and twelfth, or if ♄ Lord of the eighth do mischieve the ascendant; for without the Lord of the ascendant or ascendant itself, or the ☽ be afflicted by the Lord of the twelfth, there's no strong Witchcraft: Here finding the ☽ going to ☍ of ♄, both Planets in the sixth and twelfth houses, it gave suspicion of Witchcraft, and there seemed to those that asked for the *Querent* some reason for it, in regard the *Physicians* had prescribed much Physic, and it wrought no effect, but the Patient was worse and worse: I positively affirmed he was not bewitched, because ☿ was in △ to ♃ and ♂, and ♀ in the twelfth, and ♄ much elongated from the cusp of the house, the ☾ applying, after her ☍ of ♄, to ☿ Lord of the ascendant, he above the earth, ascending towards the *Meridian*.

I directed them again to advise with the Doctors, and civilly to acquaint them, that the Disease peccant was occult, and lay in the Reines and Secrets, and occasioned by too much Venerian sports, &c. That it was so, ♎ is on the cusp of the sixth; ♀ Lady of the Sign in the twelfth; *ergo*, an occult secret Disease, and Venerian,

☾ in ♏ in the sixth, in ☍ to ♄ in the twelfth; this argues a Female Disease, closely obtained; for as it was a deed of darkness, so do neither ♄ or ☾ behold the ascendant: I judged he was itchy, because ☿ was in ♓, a moist Sign, and because ♎ the Sign of the sixth, and ♊ are airy Signs, the Disease was all over his Bones, and in his joints, and in his Blood, that being corrupted: I did not say it was a perfect *Lues Veneria*, but I gave caution to prevent it. This advice was followed, the course of Physic altered, and the afflicted party in or about three weeks perfectly recovered.

CHAPTER XCV.

A Prisoner escaped out of Prison, which way he went, If Recoverable?

See page
A18

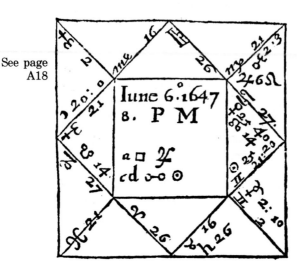

The person of the Prisoner is represented by ♐ the cusp of the twelfth, and ♃ in ♌.

The way he went and intended to go, is from the Sign of the twelfth, *viz.* ♐, and the Sign ♌ wherein ♃ is.

Quarter of Heaven & Sign where ☽ is in.

All of them considered, they signified unanimously that the Prisoner would go Eastward, or Full East; [*and so he did.*] The nearness of ☽ to the ascendant, showed he was not yet out of Town, but Eastward from the Prison he broke out of; at least, that he could not be far from Town: and as ♃ is in the eighth house, so I judged he lay obscurely for a while, *viz.* a night, but then would go away; [*so he did.*]

I confidently affirmed, he should be recovered again, and taken by some man of authority; for the ☽ separated from △ of ♃ his *Significator*, and applied to ☌ of ☉, both in angles; for it never fails, but if either the ☽ or *Significator* of the Prisoner or Fugitive be afflicted by an unfortunate Planet out of the seventh, but that the Fugitive or Prisoner is again taken.

In the next place I found ♃ and ☿ in ✶; ☿ in his own house, and applying to ♃, therefore I judged the *Querent* should have news of the Prisoner by Letter, or by some young

man within six or seven days, or when the *Significators*
came to a ✶ aspect, which was six days after. The truth is,
the Friday after, he had a letter where he was, and the
Sunday after apprehended him again by authority, &c. This
manner of judgment is the same with that of Fugitives,
(*Consideratis, considerandis.*)

CHAPTER XCVI.

A LADY *of her Husband imprisoned, when he
should be delivered?*

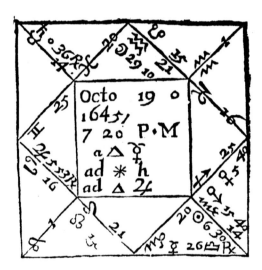

See page
A19

Judgment upon this Figure.

This Question belongs to the twelfth house; ♃ Lord of
the seventh signifies the Lady's Husband, in ♋ Retrograde,
lately, or the day before, in △ with the ☉, the ☽ applying to
a ✶ of ♄, Retrograde, then to a △ of ♃, with a most forcible
Reception; from hence I made not many words, but told the
Lady, she should neither care to make Friends to his

Majesty or any else for delivery of her Husband, for I was assured he either was or would within three days be discharged of his imprisonment, by means of a *Solar* man, Commander, who would release him and furnish him with what was convenient for his necessity. The very truth is, he was released, and the Garrison where he was prisoner taken the same day before the Question was asked, by an honest Parliament-Colonel, who plentifully relieved him with Money, and all convenient necessities.

♃ In Exaltation Retrograde, in a movable Sign, in △ to ☉, short imprisonment, because ☉ is Lord of the fourth, and in so perfect a △.

The time of his Excellency's, ROBERT Earl of *Essex*, last setting forth into the *West*

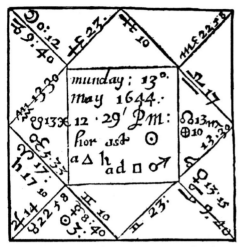

Here ≈ the ascending Sign, well represents his form of body, for it was comely, &c. ♄, ☿ and ♀ his mind; ♃ has also much to do in his qualities, as being Lord of ♓ an intercepted Sign in the ascendant.

See page A19

I first considered that the ☽ separated from a △ of ♄, & applied to a □ of ♂ Lord of his Substance, Assistants and Friends, and also of the 9th house, viz. his *Journey, which intimated, he should have slender success, and much loss by this his present March: Finding* ☋ *in the ascendant, I judged he would be betrayed in his Counsels; and seeing* ♄ *Lord of the ascendant Peregrine, and in his Fall in the second, and* ☽ *in her Detriment, and* ⊗ *disposed by* ☿ *a Significator of his Enemies, and that* ♃ *did even partially with a dexter* □ *behold the degree ascending, I only gave this Judgement, that his Excellency must expect no success from this employment, that he would have no honour by the Journey, that he would be extremely crossed by men of great power here at* London, *that pretended friendship to him; that he would be betrayed wholly, and be in danger to lose all; that I was heartily sorry he had made the choice of so unlucky a time to set forth in;* cum multis aliis. *The issue was thus, (for I write to Posterity) he prospered in the beginning, and daily men of good quality and of authority jeered at me, and derided my former prediction: I was well content to have been abused all to pieces, conditionally he might have had the better: But behold the eighth of* September *following came sad news, that the second of* September *this worthy man had surrendered all his Ammunition to his Majesty, having only Quarter for his Soldiers, with some other Articles, which were dishonourably performed, to the eternal shame of the royal Party.*

(1)

Place of the ☉	The Sun's rising.	A Table whereby to find the Planetary hour — Hours before Noon.						Place of the ☉
		1	2	3	4	5	6	
S.D.	H.M.	H.M.	H.M.	H.M.	H.M.	H.M.	H.M.	S.D.
♈ 0	6 0	7 0	8 0	9 0	10 0	11 0	12 0	♍ 30
3	5 54	6 55	7 56	8 57	9 58	10 59	0	27
6	47	47	51	54	56	58	0	24
9	41	44	47	51	50	57	0	21
12	35	39	43	48	50	56	0	18
♈ 15	5 28	6 33	7 39	8 44	49	10 55	12 0	♍ 15
18	22	28	35	41	47	54	0	12
21	16	23	31	38	45	53	0	9
24	10	18	27	35	43	52	0	6
27	3	13	22	32	41	51	0	3
♉ 0	4 57	6 8	7 18	8 29	9 39	10 50	12 0	♍ 0
3	51	3	14	26	37	49	0	27
6	45	5 58	10	23	35	48	0	24
9	40	52	7	20	33	47	0	21
12	34	48	3	17	31	46	0	18
♉ 15	4 28	5 42	6 59	8 14	9 29	10 45	12 0	♌ 15
18	23	39	55	12	28	44	0	12
21	18	35	52	9	26	43	0	9
24	12	30	48	6	24	42	0	6
27	8	27	45	4	23	41	0	3
♊ 0	4 2	5 23	6 42	8 2	9 21	10 41	12 0	♌ 0
3	3 59	19	39	0	20	40	0	27
6	55	16	37	7 58	18	39	0	24
9	51	13	34	56	17	39	0	21
12	48	10	32	54	16	38	0	18
♊ 15	3 45	5 8	6 30	7 53	9 15	10 38	12 0	♋ 15
18	43	6	29	52	14	37	0	12
21	41	4	27	51	14	37	0	9
24	40	3	27	50	13	37	0	6
27	9	2	26	50	13	36	0	3
♊ 30	3 38	5 1	6 25	7 49	9 13	10 36	12 0	♋ 0

Place of the ☉	A Table whereby to find the Planetary hour Hours after Noon.						Place of the ☉
	7	8	9	10	11	12	
S.D.	H.M.	H.M.	H.M.	H.M.	H.M.	H.M.	S.D.
♈ 0	1 0	2 0	3 0	4 0	5 0	6 0	♍ 30
3	1	2	3	4	5	6	27
6	2	4	6	9	11	13	24
9	3	6	10	13	16	19	21
12	4	8	13	17	21	25	18
♈ 15	1 5	2 11	3 16	4 21	5 27	6 31	♍ 15
18	6	13	19	25	32	38	12
21	7	15	22	29	37	44	9
24	8	17	25	33	42	50	6
27	10	19	29	38	48	57	3
♉ 0	1 11	2 21	3 32	4 42	53	7 3	♍ 0
3	12	23	35	46	58	9	27
6	13	25	38	50	6 6	15	24
9	13	27	40	53	7	20	21
12	14	29	43	57	12	26	18
♉ 15	1 15	2 31	3 46	5 1	6 17	7 31	♌ 15
18	16	32	49	5	21	37	12
21	17	34	51	8	25	41	9
24	18	36	54	12	30	48	6
27	19	37	56	15	33	52	3
♊ 0	1 20	2 39	3 59	5 18	6 38	7 57	♌ 0
3	20	40	4 1	21	41	8 1	27
6	21	42	3	23	44	5	24
9	22	43	5	26	48	9	21
12	22	44	6	28	50	12	18
♊ 15	23	2 45	4 8	5 30	6 53	8 15	♋ 15
18	23	46	9	31	54	17	12
21	23	46	10	32	56	19	9
24	23	47	10	33	57	20	6
27	24	47	11	34	58	21	3
♊ 30	1 24	2 47	4 11	5 35	6 58	8 22	♋ 0

(2)

These tables may be used, unmodified, for those in the London/Oxford area. Times are GMT. - *Ed. note*

(3)

Place of the ☉	The Sun's rising.	A Table whereby to find the Planetary hour Hours before Noon.						Place of the ☉
		1	2	3	4	5	6	
S.D.	H.M.	H.M.	H.M.	H.M.	H.M.	H.M.	H.M.	S.D.
♎ 0	6　0	7　0	8　0	9　0	10　0	11　0	12　0	♓ 30
3	6	5	4	3	2	1	0	27
6	13	11	9	7	4	2	0	24
9	19	16	13	10	6	3	0	21
12	25	21	17	13	8	4	0	18
♎ 15	6　32	7　24	8　21	9　16	10　11	11　5	12　0	♓ 15
18	38	30	25	19	13	6	0	12
21	44	37	29	22	15	7	0	9
24	50	42	33	25	17	8	0	6
27	57	48	38	29	19	9	0	3
♏ 0	7　3	7　53	8　42	9　32	10　21	11　10	12　0	♓ 0
3	9	58	46	35	23	11	0	27
6	15	8　3	50	38	25	12	0	24
9	20	7	53	40	27	13	0	21
12	26	12	57	43	29	14	0	18
♏ 15	7　32	8　17	9　1	9　46	10　31	11　15	12　0	♒ 15
18	37	21	5	49	32	16	0	12
21	42	25	8	51	34	17	0	9
24	48	30	12	54	36	18	0	6
27	52	33	15	56	37	19	0	3
♐ 0	57	8　38	9　18	9　59	10　39	11　20	12　0	♒ 0
3	8　1	41	21	10　1	40	20	0	27
6	5	44	23	2	41	21	0	24
9	9	48	26	4	43	22	0	21
12	12	50	28	6	44	22	0	18
♐ 15	8　15	8　53	9　30	10　8	10　45	11　23	12　0	♑ 15
18	17	54	31	9	45	23	0	12
21	19	56	33	10	46	23	0	9
24	20	57	33	10	47	23	0	6
27	21	58	34	11	47	23	0	3
♐ 30	8　22	8　58	9　35	10　11	10　47	11　24	12　0	♑ 0

(4)

Place of the ☉ S.D.	A Table whereby to find the Planetary hour — Hours after Noon.						Place of the ☉ S.D.
	7 H.M.	8 H.M.	9 H.M.	10 H.M.	11 H.M.	12 H.M.	
♎ 0	1 0	2 0	3 0	4 0	5 0	6 0	♓ 30
3	0 59	1 58	2 57	3 56	4 55	5 54	27
6	58	56	54	51	49	47	24
9	57	54	51	47	44	41	21
12	56	50	48	43	39	35	18
♎ 15	0 55	1 49	2 44	3 39	4 33	5 28	♓ 15
18	54	47	41	35	28	21	12
21	53	45	38	31	23	16	9
24	52	43	35	27	18	10	6
27	51	41	31	23	13	3	3
♏ 0	0 50	1 39	2 29	3 18	4 8	4 57	♓ 0
3	49	37	26	14	3	51	27
6	48	35	23	10	3 58	45	24
9	47	33	20	7	53	40	21
12	46	31	17	3	48	34	18
♏ 15	0 45	1 29	2 14	2 59	3 43	4 28	♒ 15
18	44	28	12	55	39	22	12
21	44	26	9	52	35	18	9
24	43	24	6	48	30	13	6
27	41	23	4	45	27	8	3
♐ 0	0 41	1 21	2 2	2 42	3 23	4 3	♒ 0
3	40	20	0	39	19	3 59	27
6	39	18	1 57	36	15	55	24
9	39	17	56	34	13	51	21
12	38	16	54	32	10	48	18
♐ 15	0 38	1 15	1 53	2 30	3 8	3 45	♑ 15
18	37	14	51	28	5	43	12
21	37	14	51	27	4	41	9
24	37	13	50	27	3	40	6
27	37	13	50	26	2	39	3
♐ 30	0 36	1 13	1 49	2 25	3 2	3 38	♑ 0

(5)

Place of the ☉	The Sun's setting.	A Table whereby to find the Planetary hour Hours before Midnight.						Place of the ☉
		1	2	3	4	5	6	
S.D.	H.M.	H.M.	H.M.	H.M.	H.M.	H.M.	H.M.	S.D.
♈ 0	6 0	7 0	8 0	9 0	10 0	11 0	12 0	♍ 30
3	6	5	4	3	2	1	0	27
6	13	11	9	7	4	2	0	24
9	19	16	13	10	6	3	0	21
12	25	21	17	13	8	4	0	18
♈ 15	6 32	7 24	8 21	9 16	10 11	11 5	12 0	♍ 15
18	38	30	25	19	13	6	0	12
21	44	37	29	22	15	7	0	9
24	50	42	33	25	17	8	0	6
27	57	48	38	29	19	9	0	3
♉ 0	7 3	7 53	8 42	9 32	10 21	11 10	12 0	♍ 0
3	9	58	46	35	23	11	0	27
6	15	8 3	50	38	25	12	0	24
9	20	7	53	40	27	13	0	21
12	26	12	57	43	29	14	0	18
♉ 15	7 32	8 17	9 1	9 46	10 31	11 15	12 0	♌ 15
18	37	21	5	49	32	16	0	12
21	42	25	8	51	34	17	0	9
24	48	30	12	54	36	18	0	6
27	52	33	15	56	37	19	0	3
♊ 0	57	8 38	9 18	9 59	10 39	11 20	12 0	♌ 0
3	8 1	41	21	10 1	40	20	0	27
6	5	44	23	2	41	21	0	24
9	9	48	25	4	43	22	0	21
12	12	50	28	6	44	22	0	18
♊ 15	8 15	8 53	9 30	10 8	10 45	11 23	12 0	♋ 15
18	17	54	31	9	45	23	0	12
21	19	56	33	10	46	23	0	9
24	20	57	33	10	47	23	0	6
27	21	58	34	11	47	24	0	3
♊ 30	8 21	8 50	9 35	10 11	10 47	11 24	12 0	♋ 0

(6)

Place of the ☉	A Table whereby to find the Planetary hour Hours after Midnight.						Place of the ☉
	7	8	9	10	11	12	
S.D.	H.M.	H.M.	H.M.	H.M.	H.M.	H.M.	S.D.
♈ 0	1 0	2 0	3 0	4 0	5 0	6 0	♍ 30
3	0 59	1 58	2 57	3 56	4 55	5 54	27
6	58	56	54	51	49	47	24
9	57	54	51	47	44	41	21
12	56	52	48	43	39	35	18
♈ 15	0 55	1 49	2 44	3 39	4 33	5 28	♍ 15
18	54	47	41	35	28	22	12
21	53	45	38	31	23	16	9
24	52	43	35	27	18	10	6
27	51	41	32	22	13	3	3
♉ 0	0 50	1 39	2 29	3 18	4 8	4 57	♍ 0
3	49	37	26	14	3	51	27
6	48	35	23	10	3 58	45	24
9	47	33	20	7	53	40	21
12	46	31	17	3	48	34	18
♉ 15	0 45	1 29	2 14	2 59	3 43	4 28	♌ 15
18	44	28	12	55	39	23	12
21	43	26	9	52	35	18	9
24	42	24	6	48	30	13	6
27	41	23	4	45	27	8	3
♊ 0	0 41	1 21	2 2	2 41	3 23	4 3	♌ 0
3	40	20	0	39	19	3 59	27
6	39	18	1 57	36	15	55	24
9	39	17	56	34	13	51	21
12	38	16	54	32	10	48	18
♊ 15	0 38	1 15	1 53	2 30	3 8	3 45	♋ 15
18	37	15	51	28	5	43	12
21	37	15	51	27	4	41	9
24	37	14	50	27	3	40	6
27	37	13	50	26	3	39	3
♊ 30	0 36	1 12	1 49	2 25	3 2	3 38	♋ 0

(7)

Place of the ☉	The Sun's setting.	A Table whereby to find the Planetary hour Hours before Midnight.						Place of the ☉
		1	2	3	4	5	6	
S.D.	H.M.	H.M.	H.M.	H.M.	H.M.	H.M.	H.M.	S.D.
♎ 0	6 0	7 0	8 0	9 0	10 0	11 0	12 0	♓ 30
3	5 54	6 55	7 56	8 57	9 58	10 59	0	27
6	47	47	51	54	56	58	0	24
9	41	44	47	51	54	57	0	21
12	35	39	43	48	52	56	0	18
♎ 15	5 28	6 36	7 39	8 44	49	10 55	12 0	♓ 15
18	23	28	35	41	47	54	0	12
21	16	23	31	38	45	53	0	9
24	10	18	27	35	43	52	0	6
27	3	13	23	32	41	51	0	3
♏ 0	4 57	6 8	7 18	8 29	9 39	10 50	12 0	♓ 0
3	51	3	14	26	37	49	0	27
6	45	5 58	10	23	35	48	0	24
9	40	53	7	20	33	47	0	21
12	34	48	3	17	31	46	0	18
♏ 15	4 28	5 43	6 59	8 14	9 29	10 45	12 0	♒ 15
18	23	39	55	12	28	44	0	12
21	18	35	52	9	26	43	0	9
24	12	30	48	6	24	42	0	6
27	8	27	45	4	22	41	0	3
♐ 0	4 3	5 23	6 42	82	9 21	10 41	12 0	♒ 0
3	3 59	19	39	0	20	40	0	27
6	55	16	37	7 58	18	39	0	24
9	51	13	34	56	17	39	0	21
12	48	10	32	54	16	38	0	18
♐ 15	3 45	5 8	6 30	7 53	9 15	10 38	12 0	♑ 15
18	43	6	29	52	14	37	0	12
21	41	4	27	51	14	37	0	9
24	40	3	27	50	13	37	0	6
27	39	2	26	50	13	36	0	3
♐ 30	3 38	5 1	6 25	7 49	9 13	10 36	12 0	♑ 0

(8)

Place of the ☉ S.D.	A Table whereby to find the Planetary hour — Hours after Midnight. 7 H.M.	8 H.M.	9 H.M.	10 H.M.	11 H.M.	12 H.M.	Place of the ☉ S.D.
♎ 0	1 0	2 0	3 0	4 0	5 0	6 0	♓ 30
3	1	2	3	4	5	6	27
6	2	4	7	9	11	13	24
9	3	6	10	13	16	19	21
12	4	8	13	17	21	25	18
♎ 15	1 5	2 11	3 16	4 21	5 27	6 31	♓ 15
18	6	13	19	25	32	38	12
21	7	15	22	29	37	44	9
24	8	17	25	33	42	50	6
27	10	19	29	38	48	57	3
♏ 0	1 11	2 21	3 32	4 43	53	7 3	♓ 0
3	12	23	35	46	58	9	27
6	13	25	38	50	6 3	15	24
9	13	27	40	53	7	20	21
12	14	29	43	57	12	26	18
♏ 15	1 15	2 31	3 46	5 1	6 17	7 31	♒ 15
18	16	32	49	5	21	37	12
21	17	34	51	8	25	41	9
24	18	36	54	12	30	48	6
27	19	37	56	15	33	52	3
♐ 0	1 20	2 39	3 59	5 18	6 38	7 57	♒ 0
3	20	40	4 1	21	41	8 1	27
6	21	42	2	23	44	5	24
9	22	43	5	26	48	9	21
12	22	44	6	28	50	12	18
♐ 15	23	2 45	4 8	5 30	6 53	8 15	♑ 15
18	23	46	9	31	54	17	12
21	23	46	10	32	56	19	9
24	23	47	10	33	57	20	6
27	24	47	11	34	58	21	3
♐ 30	1 24	2 47	4 11	5 35	6 58	8 22	♑ 0

CHAPTER XCVII.

To find out what Planet rules every hour of the Day or Night by the preceding Table.

You must understand that as there are seven days of the Week, viz. *Sunday, Monday, Tuesday, Wednesday, Thursday, Friday, Saturday*; so there are seven Planets, viz. *Saturn, Jupiter, Mars, Sol, Venus, Mercury, Luna*: We appropriate to each day of the Week a several Planet; as to *Sunday*, ☉; to *Monday*, ☽; to *Tuesday*, ♂; to *Wednesday*, ☿; to *Thursday*, ♃; to *Friday*, ♀; to *Saturday*, ♄: and the first hour of every day we assign to that Planet assigned for the day, beginning at Sunrise ever, the second hour we give to the next Planet, the third hour to the third Planet from him; as if upon any *Sunday* I would know what Planet governs the first, second, third, fourth, fifth, sixth hour of that day, I say ☉ governs the first, ♀ the second, ☿ the third, ☽ the fourth, ♄ the fifth, ♃ the sixth, &c. and so in order successively during that day and night subsequent: and if you account in order, you shall find by this continual account, that ☽ falls to rule the first hour upon *Monday*, ♄ the second, ♃ the third, ♂ the fourth, &c.

It is very true, some of the *Ancients* have Winter and Summer, made the day and night to consist of equal hours, I mean every hour to consist of sixty minutes equally; but *Astrologians* do not so, but follow this method, *viz.* according to the motion of the ☉ both Summer and Winter, so do they vary their hours in length or shortness; for all that space of time which is contained from Sunrise to Sunset, they divide into twelve equal parts, whereof the one half contains the hours before Noon, the rest the hours after Noon; so also, what space of time is from Sunset until Sunrise again the next day after, is equally divided into twelve parts; whereof every twelfth part contains the space or time of one hour Astrological; and we do ever begin to number from Sunrise, and continue until the next Sunrise, accounting 24 hours, beginning evermore at Sunrise, with that Planet who is assigned to the day, and so numbering successively in order until the next day; so that your Astrological hours are called unequal hours, as all the year long consisting of more or less than sixty minutes for the space of one hour, unless it be the day of the ☉ his entrance into ♈ or ♎, at what time an Astrological hour is just sixty minutes and no more.

Use of the Table.

Be the ☉ in ♈, ♉, ♊, ♋, ♌, ♍, and you would know the Planetary hour of the day, first and second Pages serve your turn.

If you would know the Planetary hour of any day, the ☉ being in ♎, ♏, ♐, ♑, ♒, ♓, the third and fourth Pages will serve you.

If you would know the Planetary hour of the night or after Sunset, while the ☉ is in ♈, ♉, ♊, ♋, ♌, ♍, then you must be directed by the fifth and sixth Pages of this Table.

If you would know the Planetary hour of the night, the ☉ being in ♎, ♏, ♐, ♑, ♒, ♓, the seventh and eighth Pages will satisfy you.

An Example.

If you would know when the ☉ rises, being in the third, fourth or fifth of ♈, see to the first Column of the first Page, and there you find, *Place of the* ☉, under it, *S.D. viz*, Signs, Degrees, under these two letters, ♈ 0, then under, 0 3 on the right hand, 5 54 over it *H.M. viz.* Hours and Minutes; so that it tells you, the ☉ being in three degrees of ♈, rises at 54 minutes after 5. Proceed in the same line, and you see the Planetary hour; as, admit I would know at half an hour after nine in the morning, upon *Monday* the 15 of *March* 1646/7, the ☉ at noon that day being in 4 degrees 47 min. of ♈, which wanting so few min. of 5 degrees I enter with five whole degrees under the Sign ♈, and in the fourth line of the first Column I find 6. For the whole *Table* of Signs goes by the continual addition of three, and if I had entered with four or five degrees of ☉ in ♈, I might have taken either three or six, and it had bred little difference. But to the purpose, over against 6 on the right hand, I find, as aforesaid, 5 47 for the time of Sunrising, then 6 47, then in order 7 50, then 8 54, then 9 56. My hour was 9 30, so then I begin and say, the ☽ being the Planet of the day, begins to rule at 47 min. after 5 and governs until 47 min. after 6. Then ♄ he rules the 2ⁿᵈ hour of the day, until 51 min. after 7. Then ♃ rules the 3ʳᵈ hour, *viz.* til 54 min. after 8. Then ♂ the fourth hour, until 56 min. after 9 which is the hour sought for, I say ♂ rules at that hour; and so you must do either day or night: And you must remember, that as you see only in the first Column ♈, ♉, ♊, and in the ninth Column of the said first page, ♍, ♌, and ♋, so when you enter with the place of the ☉ in ♍, ♌ or ♋, you must enter upward contrary to the former side; for the ☉ being in 15 of ♉, rises at the same moment of time as he does being in the 15 of ♌: or when in the 15 of ♍, as when in the 15 of ♈. The length of the Planetary hour is thus known, let the ☉ be in the sixth degree of ♈, he rises then, as you may see, at 47 min. after 5.

In the third Column you find 6 47, which if you subtract from the next number on the right hand in the same line, *viz.*

7 51   ⎰ 7 51 ⎱   rests one hour and four minutes for
             ⎱ 6 47 ⎰   the length of the hour that day,

and so as your day-hour is more than sixty minutes, so much the nocturnal hour must want of 60 min. and this is a general rule.

The above named 15 of *March* 1646/7, the ☉ being in 4:47 of ♈, I would know what Planet reigns at 20 min. past 5 in the afternoon; I enter the first Column of the second Page, under the title of the ☉, in the fourth line under ♈ I find 6 and accept of that without error, because the place of ☉ is 4:47 of ♈, and so is nearer 6 than 4. Over against 6 on the right hand, I find 1 2, then 2 4, then 3 6, then 4 9, then 5 11, then 6 13. These tell me, the first Planetary hour after noon ends at 1 2, that is, two min. after one, the second at two min. after two, the third at six min. after three, the fourth at nine min. after four, the fifth at eleven min. after five, the sixth at thirteen min. after 6. Now my hour inquired after was 20 min.

past 5, which falls to be the last hour of the day; and if you look over the head of 6 13, you may see the number 12 *viz*, it's the twelfth hour of the day; now if you begin in the morning at Sunrise, accounting ☽ the first, and so proceed,

☽ ♄ ♃ ♂ ☉ ♀ ☿ ☽ ♄ ♃ ♂ ☉
1 2 3 4 5 6 7 8 9 10 11 12

You shall find, that ☉ begins his rule at eleven min. past five, and ends at thirteen min. past six. I need not be more copious in a thing so plain and obvious to the eye; I shall only propound one example more, *viz*.: the said 15 of *March* 11 hour 10 min. after noon, I would know what Planet rules; the ☉ being in 4 47 of ♈, I now enter the fifth Page of the Table, I look to the 6 of ♈, against it on the right hand I find 6 13, then 7 11, then 8 9, then 9 7, then 10 4, then 11 2, then 12 0.

My hour is ten min. after 11, in the seventh column you have 11 2. My hour is included in the next; so then I conclude my hour is the last hour before midnight, and consequently the sixth hour after Sunset, but the eighteenth hour of the day, and being accounted as we formerly instructed, you shall find it the hour of ♂. Either in giving Physic, or performing many natural conclusions, without exact knowledge of the Astrological planetary hour, no worthy work can be done, with it wonders, either in collecting Herbs, framing *Sigils*, *Images*, *Lamens*, &c.

So now by the blessing of Almighty God, without whose providence we can perform no worthy act, I have produced to an end the second part of my intended Work, and could have willingly acquiesced until a further opportunity had been offered: but such is the desire and importunity of several well-affected to this study, that beyond my first intentions I again adventure upon the succeeding *Tractate of* NATIVITIES, wherein the pitiful and merciful God of all the faithful, whose brightness shines in our frail understandings, assist me, that I may perform this Work with judgment and understanding, for the good of all honest-hearted *English*, my most beloved Countrymen. Assist me O glorious God, for my Task is difficult, and thy servant is of little understanding! Few, nay none at all are the helps I expect from any man living (having hitherto had no assistance) but what thy pleasure is, by the universal *Anima Mundi*, to infuse into my obtuse intellective part, that will I candidly deliver without deceit or fraud; and as my former two Parts have had neither the Head, Hand, Heart or assistance of any man, so neither now will I beg or begin to distrust that Providence, whereby I have waded through the former Treatises, but will like a valiant Champion enter the fields of Defiance, against all the world of Detractors, and perform what my present weakness is able, &c. not doubting but there will some arise in all Ages, who will either amend my failings, or defend my sayings so far as they may with modesty.

June 11 1647.

WILLIAM LILLY.

Appendix 1:

Modern Charts for Lilly's Christian Astrology

Christian Astrology was handsomely produced for its day. Lilly made lavish use of tables and had his charts engraved in many different styles.

A careful comparison of Lilly's original charts with the ones I pulled from the computer convinced me that modern charts are not a replacement for Lilly's originals. Use the ascendant of the modern versions as your key. Find the same ascendant on the originals and begin your study.

On Dates. Until 1752, the calendar used in England (and America) was the **Julian**, or **Old Style** (OS). In Lilly's day, this differed from the modern **Gregorian** (**New Style**) calendar by ten days. In other words, Lilly's February 10, 1638 (pg 397, *Fish Stolen*) is our February 20. This ten-day shift is why the sun's position in Lilly's charts appears ten degrees ahead of where we ordinarily would expect it.

In England in Lilly's day, the year changed on March 25th, not January 1 as it does now. There was a convention that dates in March were written in both years, as 1646/7, as shown in one of Lilly's charts. *Beware!* In transferring from Julian to Gregorian, this changes the year on several charts.

In the charts that follow, I have left Lilly's dates as he gave them, adding the modern dates as footnotes. If it's of interest, Lilly uses Regiomontanus houses, mean node and calculates the Part of Fortune by day, in both day and night charts.

With these caveats, the charts. Enjoy.

Page 35
1646 Tuesday
January 6, 1646
1:30 pm
☽ separating ☌ ♂
applying ☌ ☉
and □ ♄

Computed as:
January 16, 1646
1:44:20 pm
London

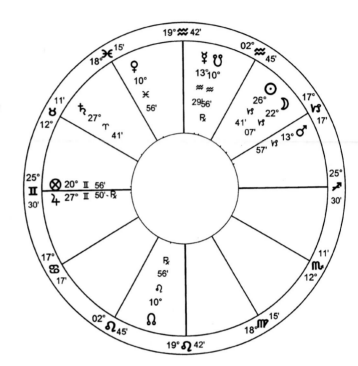

Pg. 135:
If he were like to live
long, etc.
March 14, 1632
2:15 pm
♃ day
♂ hour

Computed as:
March 24, 1633
2:22:30 pm
London

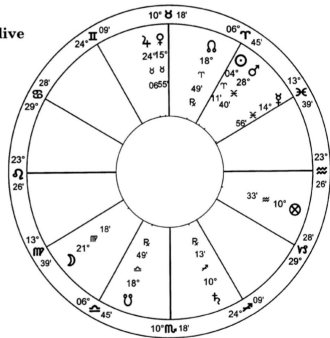

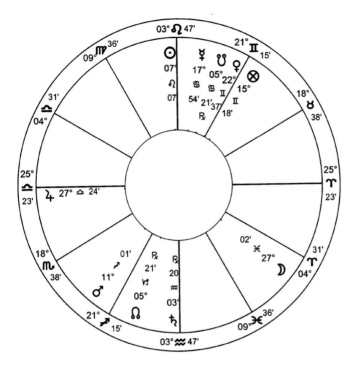

Page 152:
**If find the party
inquired of at
home, etc.**
*July 19, 1638
23:45 pm*
♀ day
♂ hour

*Computed as:
July 30, 1638
11:52 am*
London

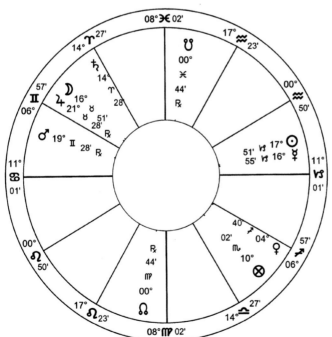

Page 162:
**A Ship at Sea,
if Lost.**
*December 28, 1644
3:20 pm*
♄ day
♀ hour

*Computed as:
January 7, 1645
3:28:50 pm*
London

Page 165:
**A Ship at Sea,
in what
Condition.**
*March 9, 1646
10:15 am*
♂ day
☽ hour

*Computed as:
March 19, 1647
10:27:50 am
London*

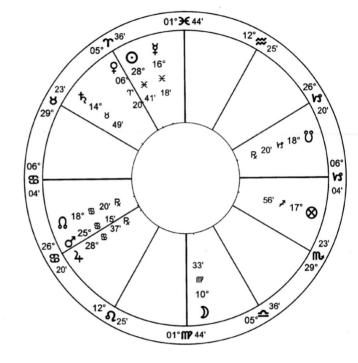

Page 177:
**If he should be
rich, etc.**
*July 16, 1634
11:00 am*
☿ day
☉ hour
☽ separating ♂ ☿,
applying ♂ ♀

*Computed as:
July 26, 1634
11:04:20 am
London*

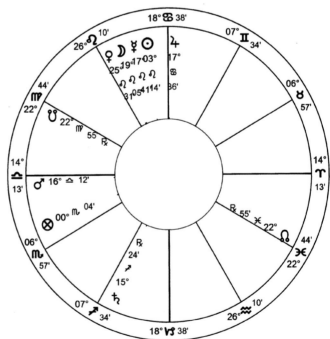

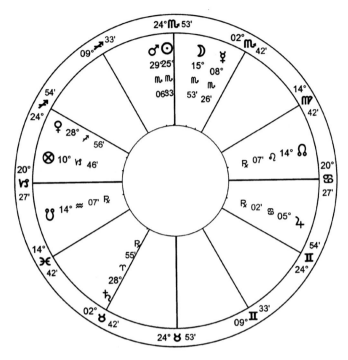

Page 196:
**Where an absent
Brother was?**
*November 7, 1645
Noon*
♀ day
♂ hour

Computed as:
November 17, 1645
11:42:48 am
London

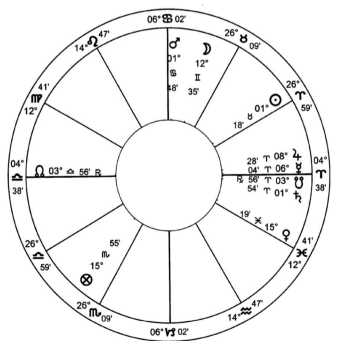

Page 200:
**A Report that
Cambridge was
taken by the
King's Forces, if
true?**
*April 11, 1643
4:31 pm*
♂ day
♀ hour
☽ separating ⚹ ♃ ,
applying □ ♀

Computed as:
April 21, 1643
4:28:10 pm
London

Page 219:

**If I should
purchase Master
B. his houses.**

March 31, 1634

6:00 pm

☽ day

☉ hour

☽ separating ♂ ♂,
applying □ ♄

Computed as:
April 10, 1634
6:02:25 pm
London

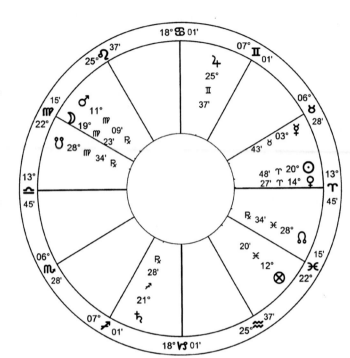

Page 238:

**If the Querent
should ever have
Children?**

June 11, 1635

2:30 pm

♃ hour

☽ separating □ ♄,
applying □ ☉

Computed as:
June 22, 1635
9:29:35 am
London

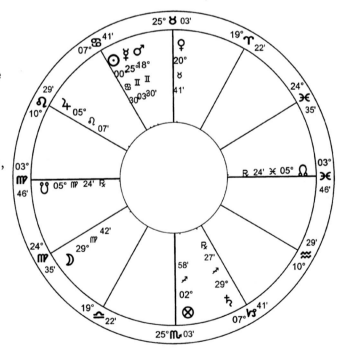

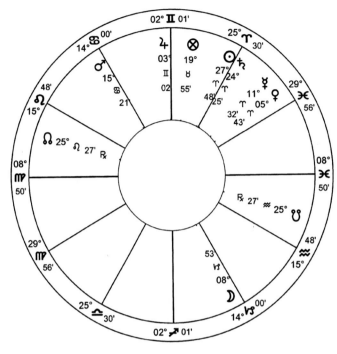

Page 240:
**If one were with a
Child of a Male or
Female, etc.**
April 7, 1645
2:15 pm
☽ day
☽ hour
☽ separating □ ♀,
applying □ ☿

Computed as:
April 17, 1645
2:15:40 pm
London

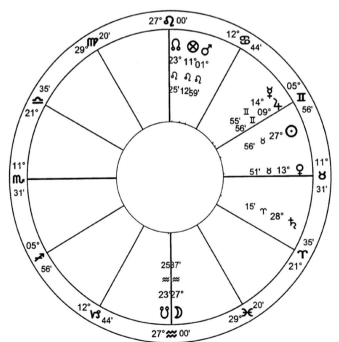

Page 286:
**A sick Doctor,
what was his
Disease?**
May 8, 1645
6:15 pm
♃ day
♀ hour
☽ separating △ ☿
applying □ ☉
and ⚹ ♄

Computed as:
May 18, 1645
6:10 pm
London

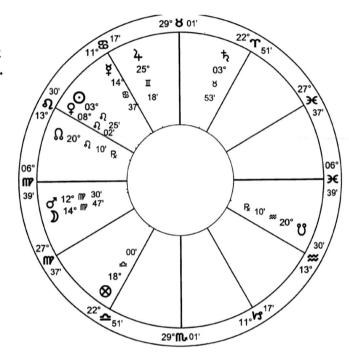

Page 289:
Whether the Sick would live or die.
July 16, 1645
7:22 am
☿ day
♄ hour

Computed as:
July 26, 1645
7:30 am
London

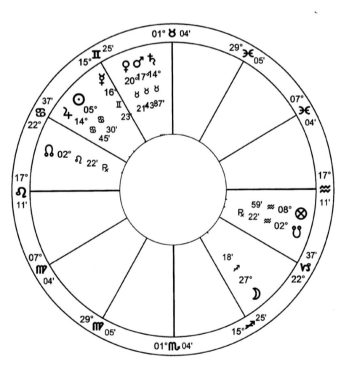

Page 385:
A Lady, if marry the Gentleman desired?
June 16, 1646
19:20 pm
☿ day
♄ hour
☽ void of course
applying ♂ ☉

Computed as:
June 27, 1646
7:33:50 am
London

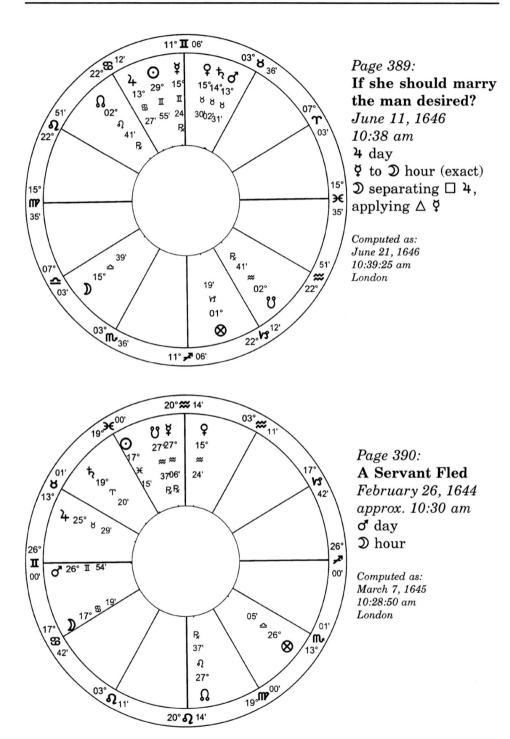

Page 389:
**If she should marry
the man desired?**
June 11, 1646
10:38 am
♃ day
☿ to ☽ hour (exact)
☽ separating □ ♃,
applying △ ☿

Computed as:
June 21, 1646
10:39:25 am
London

Page 390:
A Servant Fled
February 26, 1644
approx. 10:30 am
♂ day
☽ hour

Computed as:
March 7, 1645
10:28:50 am
London

Page 392:

**A Dog missing,
where?**

August 29, 1646

4:05 pm

♄ day

♂ hour

☽ separating □ ♄,
applying ⚹ ♂

*Computed as:
September 8, 1646
4:00:40 pm
London*

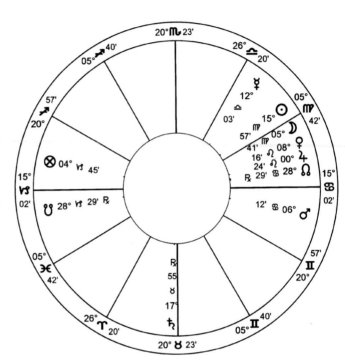

Page 395:

**Money lost, who
stole it? If
recoverable?**

May 24, 1647

5:00 pm

☽ day

♃ hour

☽ separating ♂ ☉,
applying ⚹ ♂

*Computed as:
June 3, 1647
4:49 pm
London*

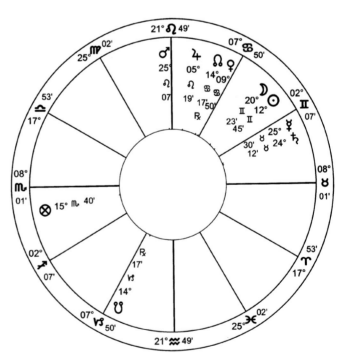

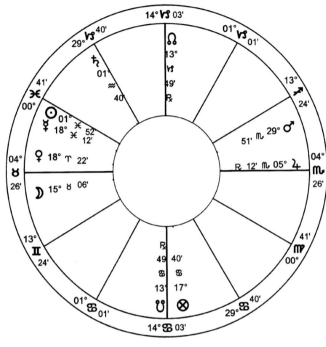

Page 397:
Fish Stolen.
February 10, 1638
8:45 am
♄ day
♂ hour
☽ separating ☍ ♃,
applying ⚹ ☿

Computed as:
February 20, 1638
9:01:20 am
London

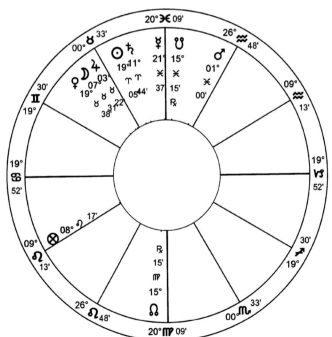

Page 399:
Sir William Waller
vs: Sir Ralph
Hopton.
March 29, 1644
10:12 am
♀ day
♃ hour
☽ separating ⚹ ♂,
separating ☌ ♃,
applying ☌ ♀ and ⚹ ☿

Computed as:
April 8, 1644
10:15 am
London

Page 401:

If his Excellency Robert Earl of Essex should take Reading?

April 17, 1643
6:50 pm
☽ day
☉ hour
☽ void of course
applying ✶ ♂ and
△ ☉

Computed as:
April 27, 1643
6:47:40 pm
London

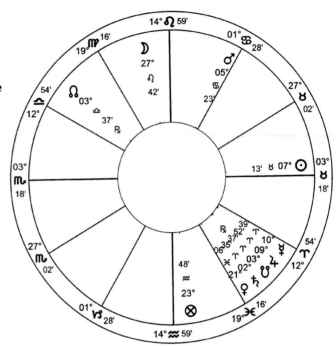

Page 415:

Whether Man or Wife shall die first?

February 6, 1644
9:10 pm
♃ day
♂ hour
☽ separating △ ☉
and △ ☿

Computed as:
February 16, 1645
9:20:50 pm
London

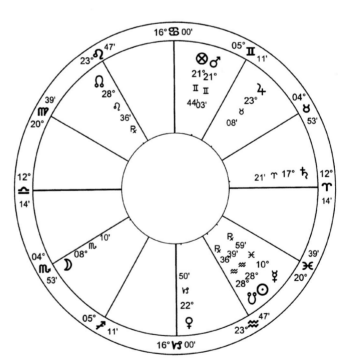

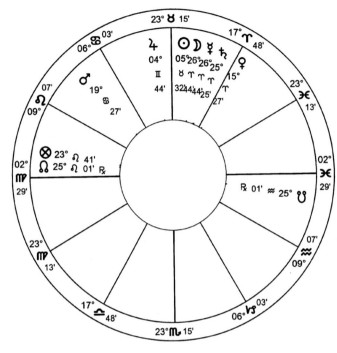

Page 417:
A Woman of her Husband at Sea, if alive, where, when return?
April 15, 1645
1:10 pm
♂ day
♃ hour
☽ separating ♂ ♄,
applying ♂ ☿ and ☉

Computed as:
April 25, 1645
1:08 pm
London

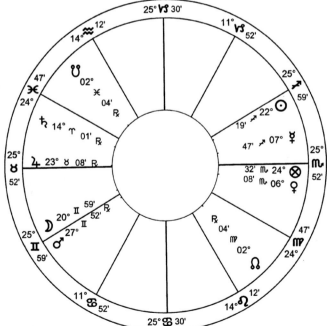

Page 419:
What manner of Death Canterbury should die?
December 3, 1644
2:24 pm
♂ day
♀ hour
☽ separating ⚹ ♄,
applying ☍ ☉
and ♂ ♂

Computed as:
December 13, 1644
2:18:42 pm
London

Page 421:

If have the
Portion promised?
July 15, 1634
6:15 pm
♂ day
☿ hour
☽ separating ♂ ☉ ,
applying △ ♄, ✶ ♂
and ♂ ☿

Computed as:
July 25, 1634
6:17:47 pm
London

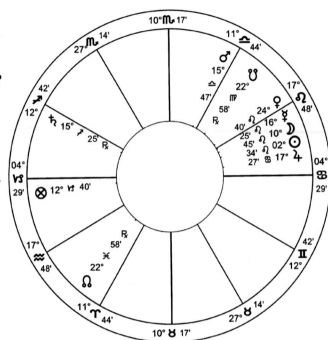

Page 436:

Terrible Dreams
January 26, 1643
9:27 am
♃ day
♂ hour
☽ applying ☍ ♀

Computed as:
February 5, 1643
9:41:50 am
London

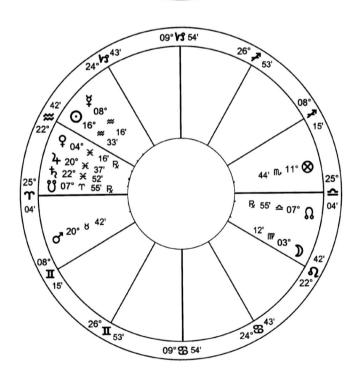

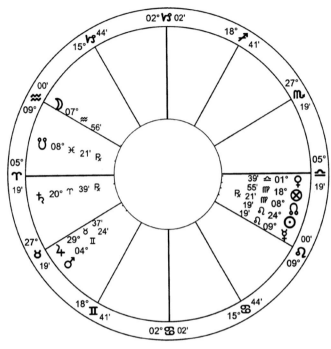

Page 437:
**If he should obtain
the Parsonage
desired.**
August 6, 1644
8:24 pm
♂ day
♃ hour
☽ separating △ ♂,
applying ☍ ☿

Computed as:
August 16, 1644
8:25:50 pm
London

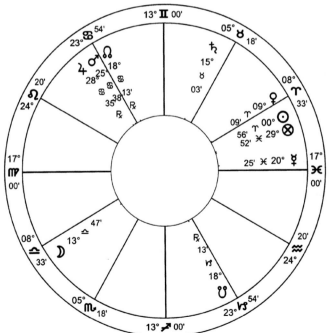

Page 439:
**If the Presbytery
shall stand?**
March 11, 1646/7
4:45 pm
♃ day
☿ hour
☽ separating ☍ ♀ ,
applying □ ♂ and ♃

Computed as:
March 21, 1647
4:50:10 pm
London

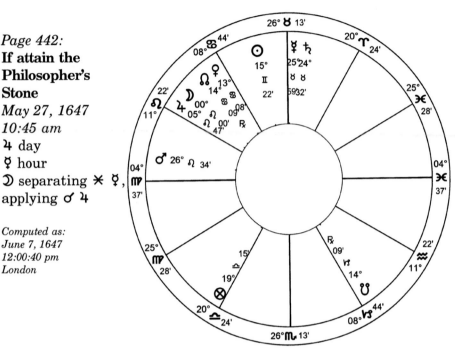

Page 442:
**If attain the
Philosopher's
Stone**
*May 27, 1647
10:45 am*
♃ day
☿ hour
☽ separating ⚹ ☿,
applying ♂ ♃

*Computed as:
June 7, 1647
12:00:40 pm
London*

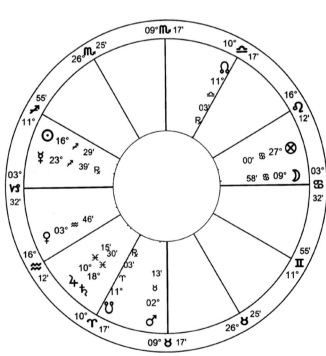

Page 452:
**If Prince Rupert
should get
honour by our
Wars?**
*November 28, 1642
9:23 am*
☽ day
♄ hour
☽ separating △ ♃,
applying △ ♄

*Computed as:
December 8, 1642
9:18:53 am
London*

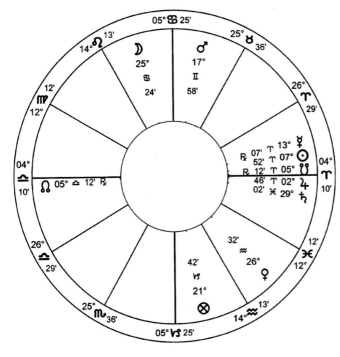

Page 455:

If His Majesty should procure Forces out of Ireland to harm the Parliament?
March 18, 1643
6:00 pm
♄ day
♀ hour
☽ separating □ ☿, applying △ ♄

Computed as:
March 28, 1643
5:59:53 pm
London

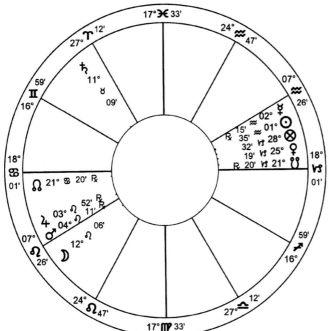

Page 467:

A Horse lost or stolen near Henley, if recoverable or not?
January 11, 1646
2:59 pm
☽ day
♂ hour
☽ separating □ ♄, and then void of course.

Computed as:
January 21, 1647
3:11 pm
London

Page 468:
If Bewitched
March 13, 1646
8:03 am
♄ day
♂ hour
☽ separating □ ♃,
applying ☍ ♄

Computed as:
March 23, 1647
8:11:37 am
London

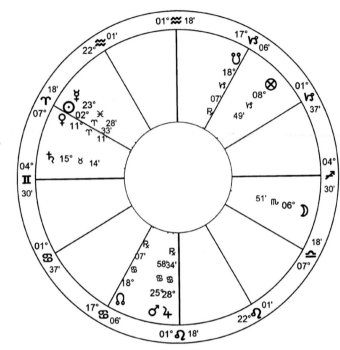

Page 470:
**A Prisoner
escaped out of
Prison, which
way he went?**
June 6, 1647
8:00 pm
☉ day
♄ hour
☽ separating △ ♃,
applying ☍ ☉

Computed as:
June 16, 1647
7:55 pm
London

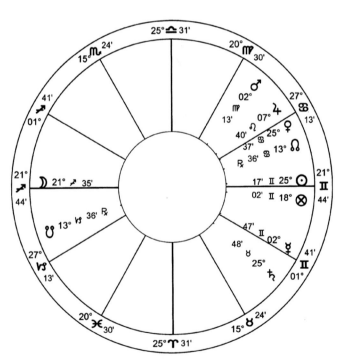

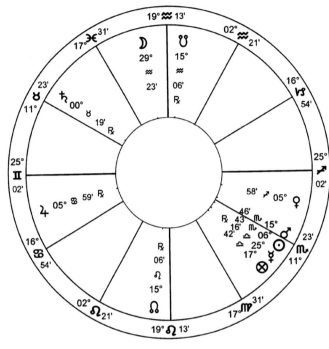

Page 471:
**A Lady of her
Husband
imprisoned, when
he should be
delivered?**
October 19, 1645
7:20 pm
☉ day
♂ hour
☽ separating △ ☿,
applying ✶ ♄
and △ ♃

Computed as:
October 29, 1645
6:53pm
London

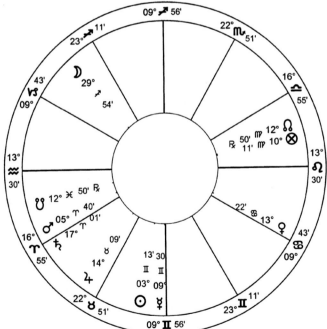

Page 473:
**The time of his
Excellency's Robert
Earl of Essex, last
setting forth into
the West.**
May 13, 1644
12:29 pm
☽ day
☉ hour
☽ separating △ ♄,
applying □ ♂

Computed as:
May 24, 1644
12:24:35 am
London

Glossary

We are as distant from William Lilly as he was from Geoffrey Chaucer. We fool ourselves to think Lilly's English is identical to ours. It is not. While archaic spellings and verb tenses can (and should) be exchanged for their modern counterparts, there are three classes of words that should be glossed: Nouns that refer to obscure things and techniques (*jake*); words, such as *clown*, which have changed their meanings; and words, such as *image*, which have additional meanings to Lilly.

Below, a glossary of some of them. For the most part, these do not include astrological terms, which are in Book 1. Other astrological terms can be found in standard references, such as de Vore's **Encyclopedia of Astrology**. I have omitted glossing herbs and plants as I have not the necessary knowledge. Suggestions for these, as well my mistakes, and the words I've overlooked, will be much appreciated. Numbers at the end refer to a page where the entry can be found (some appear on more than one). A list of the principal references consulted will be found at the end.

1646/7 - In addition to using a different calendar, in England, up to 1753, New Year's was the 25th of March. Dates in March were customarily marked as, for example, 1646/7. 483

A vacuo - Void of course. 401

Abs te & a Scientia - From yourself as well as from science. 184

Abscissor - That which cuts off. 184

Advowson - The right in English ecclesiastical law of presentation to a vacant benefice. 55

Agues - A condition with alternating periods of chills, fever and sweating. 59

Alcabitius - Arabic astrologer, died 967. 340

Alsace - A former province in eastern France, bordering the Rhine. 97

Anareta - Killing planet. 409

Apoplexy - A cerebral hemorrhage; a stroke. 59

Apostem - Abscess. 82

Apulia - A region of southeast Italy bordering on the Adriatic Sea, Strait of Otranto, and Gulf of Taranto. Its southern portion forms the heel of the Italian "boot." 96

Arles - A city in Provence, southern France, on the Rhone River delta. 97

Ate & a scientia - From yourself as well as from science. 452

Augustia - A city in eastern Sicily. 94

Avicenna - Arabian physician and philosopher, born at Kharmaithen, in the province of Bokhara, 980; died at Hamadan, in Northern Persia, 1037. Famous for his Canon, or Canticis, written about 1001. 291

Bamberg - A city in Bavaria, Germany. 94

Barbary - The North African states of Algeria, Tunisia, Tripoli, and Morocco. 97

Basil - Now known as Basel, in Switzerland. 96

Basilisk - A legendary serpent or dragon with lethal breath and glance. 60

Batavia - Probably Jakarta, Indonesia. Houlding says it's the old Roman name for the Netherlands, but I think it unlikely Lilly would use such an obscure word for a well-known & nearby country. 68

Bear-wards - Keeper of bears. 67

Benefice - A church living held by a parsonage or vicar. 432

Bergamo - A city in Lombardy, northern Italy. 94

Betimes - Early. 392

Black Jaundice - A more serious version of yellow jaundice. 59

Black Moors - Generally speaking, natives of the northwest African coast. Specifically, one of the various native groups of Mauritania. 84

Bloody flux - Dysentery, eg, a disease in which the flux or discharge from the bowels is mixed with blood. 67

Bonatus - Guido Bonatti, called Bonatus in Latin, c.1210 - c.1295. He was one of the most famous astrologers of the late Middle Ages. 166

Botcher - Tailor or cobbler. 67

Brabant - A former duchy, today divided between Belgium and the Netherlands. Louvain, Brussels, and Antwerp were its chief cities. 94

Brandenburg - A region of eastern Germany, surrounding but not including Berlin. 98

Brazier - Craftsman who works in brass. 451

Breast (of a ship) - The bow. 158

Bremen - A city in northwest Germany, its second largest port. 99

Brescia - A city in Lombardy, Italy. 94

Bruges - A city in northwest Belgium. 94

Brundusiam - Brindisi, in Italy. 96

Bubo - An inflamed, tender swelling of a lymph node, especially in the area of the armpit or groin. 276

Buda - Part of the modern city of "Budapest". Independent cities, lying on either side of the same river, are usually notably distinct. 98

Cadiz - A city in Andalusia, southwest Spain. 95

Calabria - The toe of the Italian boot. 99

Calenture - A furious delirium accompanied by fever, among sailors, which sometimes led the affected person to imagine the sea to be a green field, and to throw himself into it. 246

Campana - A low-lying area surrounding the city of Rome. 76

Capua - A town north of Naples, Italy. 94

Carbuncle - An acute inflammatory nodule of the skin caused by bacterial invasion into the hair follicles or sebaceous gland ducts. Actually a boil, but one that has more than one focus of infection. 246

Cardiac passion - Heart attack. 247

Carter - One who drives a cart. 59

Casarea - Casarea Philippi, ancient city in Palestine. 94

Catalonia - A region of northeastern Spain. 97

Catarrh - A head cold. 247

Cauda - Old name for the south Node. 393

Cesena - A city in north central Italy, on the Savio River. 94

Chaldea - Properly speaking, the southernmost portion of the valley of the Tigris and the Euphrates rivers, in present-day Iraq. Sometimes is extended to include Babylonia and thus comprises all southern Mesopotamia, as in the Bible. 72

Champion - A common, unenclosed area of land. 207

Chandler - One that makes or sells candles. 59

Chelae - Claws of Scorpio. 286

Choler, Choleric - One of the four humors of ancient and medieval physiology, thought to cause anger and bad temper when present in excess. Associated with yellow bile, summer, fire & gall bladder. 136

Chymistry - Alchemy. 429

Cleves - A German duchy, bordering the Netherlands, straddling the Rhine. Or the capital city, also known as Cleves. 98

Climacterial Periods - Every seventh year in a nativity (some say every seventh & ninth), from the moon. By transit, the moon squares her position every seven days, by secondary progression, she squares herself every seven years. When evil directions coincide, the result is said to be potentially fatal, especially in the later Climacterial periods. (*Adapted from de Vore.*) 411

Close - An area partially or entirely enclosed with walls. If Lilly has linear measurement in mind, I cannot find reference to it. 154

Clown - A country oaf. 59

Collier - Coal miner. 59

Cologne - Lilly's original has Cullen. 65

Common-Council - Nowadays the Guildhall, in London. 56

Commons - As in, "a few of the Nobles and Commons", Commons are representatives from towns. 56

Composition - There is this: "*Law:* A settlement whereby the creditors of a debtor about to enter bankruptcy agree, in return for some financial consideration, usually proffered immediately, to the discharge of their respective claims of receipt of payment which is in a lesser amount than that actually owed on the claim." (*from Bartleby.com*) 402

Compostella - Santiago de Compostella, in Spain. 99

Concupiscence - Lust. 312

Consentanious - Agreeable. 331

*Consideratis, considerandi*s - With the necessary considerations. 471

Constantia - A seaport on the Black Sea, Romania. 61

Constellation - A set or configuration of related items, properties, ideas, or individuals. 334

Consumption - Tuberculosis. 59

Contemner - To have contempt, to despise. 58

Conys, Conies - Rabbits, rabbit fur. 376

Cor Leonis (Leo) - Fixed star Regulus. 402

Coral tree - Any of various mostly deciduous trees or shrubs of the genus Erythrina in the pea family, native to and widely cultivated in warm regions, having trifoliolate leaves, showy red or orange flowers, and pods containing often brightly colored seeds. 64

Cordial - Serving to invigorate; stimulating. 288

Coxcomb - A conceited dandy; a fop. 434

Cozenage - Trickery, fraud, deceit. 422

Cremona - A city in northern Italy, famous for musical instruments. 96

Crudity - Raw foods. 275

Cum multis aliis - With many others. 473

Currier - One who cures or tans hides. 67

Dalmatia - Formerly the Yugoslav Adriatic coastline. Now the Croatian coastline. 98

Dariot, Claude - A French astrologer who lived from 1533 to 1594. 258

Deflux - A discharge or flowing of humors or fluid matter, as from the nose in catarrh; sometimes used synonymously with inflammation. 246

Dehor, dehort - To urge to abstain or refrain. 438

Demised - Transferred, conveyed. 209

Desert - Merit. 433

Distemper - To upset the balance of the humors. 59

Ditcher - One who digs ditches. 59

Divine - A cleric or theologian. 78

Dog hunger - Ravenous hunger, the reason is unclear. 59

Doubt - Suspicion. 312

Dropsy - Edema, or swelling, especially in the lower legs. 59

Drover - One that drives cattle or sheep. 450

Drury Lane - A street in Soho, London. 393

Eadem est ratio - The reason is the same. 309

Ebullition - A sudden, violent outbreak. 263

Eccentricity, summit of his - Greatest distance from the sun, aphelion. 363

Enlargement - A setting at large, release from confinement. 462

Epistle - A literary work in the form of a letter, eg, a letter intended for public consumption. St. Paul's are the best known examples. 52

Est velox motus morbi ad salutem vel ad mortem - [Crisis] is a rapid movement from sickness to health or death. 291

Etesia - A northerly Mediterranean wind,

rising about the dog-days of summer, lasting about forty days altogether. 76

Eversion - Turned outward, turned inside out. 278

Falling evil - Epilepsy. 247

Fancy - Faculty of forming mental images. 464

Farrier - One who shoes horses. 450

Ferrara - Italian city, southwest of Venice. 94

Fez, Kingdom of - Morocco. 97

Firmament - The universe beyond Saturn. 57

Fistula - An ulcer opening on to the skin. When arising from stillbirth, results in uncontrolled discharge of urine or feces. 67

Flank - The side of a person or an animal between the last rib and the hip. 245

Flux - Flow. 59

Fons vitalis potentia - The source of vital power. 290

Formentation - Hot, wet compress or bandage. 271

Forum Julii - Frejus, now in SE France. Founded by Julius Caesar, 49 BC. 97

Frankfurt an der Oder - The "other" Frankfurt, in eastern Germany. 97

French or Spanish Pox - Syphilis. One notes with wry amusement how this disease always bears the name of some other country. 247

Frenzies - A state of violent mental agitation or wild excitement, temporary madness or delirium. 67

Fribourg - A canton & city in western Switzerland. 97

Frowardness - Stubbornness. 388

Fuller of cloth - Cloth worker who shrinks, beats and presses cloth. 451

Fundament - Buttocks or anus. 55

Furlong - A unit of measurement equal to one-eighth mile, or 201 meters. 154

Galen - A Greek doctor who lived from 131 - c.200 AD. Holden says his astrological writings are "apocryphal", which might have been a surprise to Lilly. 291

Gall - Presumably gall bladder, a small pear-shaped sac that stores and concentrates bile. 246

Gaunt - Ghent, Belgium. 97

Genitor - One who produces or creates. 142

Gentleman - A man of gentle or noble birth or superior social position. 449

Glister - Glitter. 280

Gothland - A region of southeast Sweden comprising several islands in the Baltic Sea, including Gotland Island. 68

Gout - A disturbance of uric-acid metabolism occurring chiefly in males, characterized by painful inflammation of the joints, especially of the feet and hands, and arthritic attacks resulting from elevated levels of uric acid in the blood and the deposition of urate crystals around the joints. The condition can become chronic and result in deformity. 59

Grasier - A person who grazes cattle. 450

Grissels - Cartilage. 246

Groom - A person in charge of horses or a stable. 450

Hall - A large room, suitable for banquets, feasting, entertainments, etc. 353

Haly - Haly Abenragel (d. after 1037), court astrologer to the Tunisian Prince al-Mu'izz ibn Badis. Best known for his comprehensive book on astrology, *The Outstanding Book on the Judgments of the Stars*. 194

Hams - The buttocks. 245

Hasford - Hassfurt, Germany. 94

Hassia - Hesse, in Germany. 98

Haunch - The hip, buttock, and upper thigh in humans and animals. 155

Hawking - Falconry, which is the use of trained falcons or eagles to hunt birds & small animals for sport. 96

Hayz - A masculine diurnal planet above the earth in a day figure, or below the earth in a night chart; a feminine nocturnal planet above the earth in a night figure, or below the earth in a day. (from al-Biruni) 417

Heart strings - Angina pectoris. 275

Hectic - A fever that fluctuates during the day. 244

Heidelberg - A city in Baden-Wurttemberg, southwestern Germany, situated on the Neckar River. 96

Hemorrhoids - Veins liable to discharge blood. Piles refer specifically to veins in the anus. 59

Herbipolis - Now known as Wuerzburg, in northern Bavaria. 94

Hereditament -   Property that can be inherited. 169

Hermes Trismegistus - A mythical early Egyptian leader. Said to be the author of many books & treatises, all of which are lost. Many others have been attributed to him. (Hermes thrice-blessed.) 268

Hermetical - Conjuring, eg, to summon spirits, devils or winds by magical means. Also said of things or processes which are completely sealed. 82

Hogherd - One who herds hogs. 53

Hostler - The valet who parks your horse while at the inn. 59

Houses of Offices - Public toilets. 60

Huckle-bone - The hip bone. 245

Humour - One of four basic fluids in the body, influencing health & character. 53

Hundred - In England, a subdivision of a shire, first mentioned in the 10th century, surviving as a unit of local government into the 19th century. 326

Hylegical places, five - 1st, 11th, 10th, 9th & 7th houses. 255

Iliac-passion - Sciatica. 246

Image - An apparition, or possibly a magical charm. 485

Imposthumation - The act of forming an abscess; state of being inflamed. 246

In totidem verbis - In so many words. 454

Inappetency - Lack of desire. 280

Incurvating - Curved inwards.   416

Ingolstadt -   A city of southeast Germany on the Danube River, north of Munich. 99

Inland countries - Areas without access to the coast. 95

Inland journeys - "Inland" in the UK, refers to things inside England itself. 52

Intension - Stress. 275

Interficient - Killing planet, or Anareta. 409

Ironstone - Iron ore. 216

Ita in fatis - So it is fated.   441

Itch, the - Caused by one of a number of subcutaneous, parasitic mites. 98

Jake - Latrine, outhouse, privy. 353

Journier - He who undertakes a journey. 370

Karlstadt - A city in Bayern, Germany. 94

Kine - Plural of cow. 351

King's evil - Scrofula; so called from a notion which prevailed from the reign of Edward the Confessor to that of Queen Anne, that it could be cured by the royal touch. 82

Knave - Rogue. 360

Koblenz - Lilly's original is Confluentia. 96

Lamen - A magical knife. 485

Lask - Diarrhea or flux. 280

Leech - Physician. 451

Legerdemain - French, literally, light of hand, eg, deceit. 312

Leipzig - A city in east central Germany. 94

Let - Hindrance. 427

Limner - Illuminator of books, painter or drawer. 74

Linsie-woolsie - Literally, part linen, part wool, eg, part this, part that, a mixture. 79

Linz - The capital of upper Austria, in northwest Austria, on the Danube. 96

Livery - Servant's uniform. Perhaps in this instance, a servant himself. 344

Livonia - A region of north-central Europe in southern Estonia and northern Latvia. 97

Lombardy - A region of northern Italy, bordering on Switzerland. Capital, Milan. 94

Lords Major - The plural of Lord Mayor, itself now a largely ceremonial post. 56

Lorraine - A former province in eastern France. 94

Louvain - A city in central Belgium. 94

Lues Veneria - Syphilis. 469

Lyons - A city in east central France, at the confluence of the Rhone & Saone Rivers. 96

Maecenas - Roman statesman and patron of letters. Born c.70 BC, died 8 BC. 420

Magazines - "imports their magazines" - Eg, military supplies. 52

Magdeberg - The capital city of Saxony-Anhalt, Germany, on the Elbe River. 95

Malapert - Arrogant. 319

Malster - Brewer, maker or seller of malts. 59

Mantua - A city in Lombardy, Italy. 94

Mastery, masteries - A thorough knowledge or skill. 424

Matches, making - To arrange introductions between young men & young women. 170

Matrix - The womb. 247

Mechanic - A tradesman, of any sort. 81

Media - An ancient Asian country in what is now western Iran and southern Azerbaijan. 99

Mediety - Half. 391

Melancholic - One of the four humours, cold & dry. Associated with black bile, autumn, earth & spleen.

Mercer - Cloth seller. 74

Meretrix - Prostitute. 313

Mesopotamia - The territory about the Tigris and Euphrates rivers, included in modern Iraq. 96

Messina - A city in northeastern Sicily. 97

Mirey - Swampy, boggy (from mire). 381

Miseraicks - The veins of the mesentery, or peritoneum, the membranes that hold the digestive tract in place. 96

Molter - A process where the outer layer(s) peel away. 466

Monkery - Monastic life, monks in general. 440

Mont - Mont Saint Michel, off the coast of Normandy, France. 94

Montferrat - A region of Piedmont, Italy, south of the Po River. 99

Moravia - A region in the eastern Czech Republic. 98

Mortuus est, & de mortuus nil nisi bonum - He is dead, and say naught but good of the dead. 420

Multa creduntur ratione experintiae, non quod videntur vera vi rationis - Many things are believed by reason of experience, not because they are truly seen by the force of reason. 466

Muscovy - Also known as the Grand Duchy of Moscow, the ancient area around Moscow itself. 99

Mutatis, mutandis - With the necessary changes. 150

Nantes - A city in western France, on the Loire River. 94

Narbonne - A city in southern France, near Montpellier. 98

Neatherd - Cowherd. 53

Necromancy - Communicating with the dead in order to predict the future, a form of black magic. 77

Night-farmer - Sewer worker. 59

Noli me tangere - Touch me not: A name formerly applied to several varieties of ulcerous cutaneous diseases, but now only to Lupus exedens, an ulcerative affection of the nose. 93

Novgorod - A city in northwest Russia, on the Volkhov River. 94

Occult - Hidden or undiscovered. 469

Occurse - Runs into, collides. 440

Office - The kitchen & laundry of a ship. 158

Orcades, Isles - Orkney Islands. 98

Ordinaries - Inns and taverns that served, at a common table, one meal a day at a fixed time and price. 79

Pace - A unit of length equal to 30 inches (0.76 meter). 350

Padua - Also known as Padova, a city in northern Italy. 94

Palermo - The largest city & chief seaport of Sicily. 94

Palsy - Uncontrollable trembling. 59

Papist - Roman Catholic. 432

Paps - The nipples. 277

Parish - A political subdivision of a British county, usually corresponding in boundaries to an ecclesiastic parish. 346

Park - Clearly, to Lilly, not an area of grass & trees in the middle of a city. A broad, fairly level valley between mountain ranges, or perhaps a tract of land attached to a country house. 95

Paroxysm - A violent, excruciating seizure of pain. 261

Parthia - An ancient Asian country, southeast of the Caspian Sea. 94

Peccant - Morbid. 469

Pellicle - A thin skin or film. 277

Philosopher's Stone - Like Lilly, I also believe. The Stone is said to be a stable super-heavy element with an atomic weight of about 135. This places it beyond the unstable radioactive series known to science. The Stone has at least two interesting characteristics: It can be created by extraordinary, though nonradioactive, means, and, among its other properties is the ability to transmute base metals to gold. It has also long been prized for its ability, taken as an elixir, to prolong human life. Lilly's time saw a renaissance of interest in the Stone, and in Alchemy in general. 442

Phlebotomy - Opening a vein, bloodletting. 274

Phlegmatic - One of the four humours, cold & moist. Associated with phlegm, winter, water, brains/lungs. Having or suggesting a calm, sluggish temperament; unemotional. 87

Phoenicia - An ancient seafaring country where Lebanon is today. 72

Phrenetic - Wildly excited or active; frantic; frenzied. (Variation of frenetic.) 77

Phthisis - Any illness of the lungs or throat, such as asthma, cough, or, in extreme cases, tuberculosis. 78

Physic - Medicine, or purge. 405

Pipkin - A small earthenware pot. 466

Pisaurum - An ancient city in Umbria, Italy. Now known as Pesaro. 99

Pissing disease - Diabetes. 247

Placentia - A city of northern Italy on the Po River southeast of Milan. 97

Plaster - A medical dressing, bandage. 271

Plate - A sheet of hammered, rolled, or cast metal, often silver. 215

Pleno ore - Copiously. 440

Pleurisy - Inflammation of the membrane that covers the lungs and lines the chest cavity. It is sometimes accompanied by pain and coughing. 246

Polonia - Poland. 94

Portion - A right or a legal share in something. 183

Praecordiacs - Vessels of the heart. 274

Privy Parts - External sex organs. 54

Probatum est - It has been proved. 346

Ptissick - Houlding suggests pertussis, or whooping cough. 263

Pushes - Eczema. 245

Pye - Magpie. 68

Quartan - Occurring every fourth day, counting inclusively, or every 96 hours. Said of a fever or illness. 59

Quern - Stone handmill for corn. 354

Quinces - Hard yellowish fruit with sharp flavour. 354

Quoad capax - According to capacity. 140

Ratisbon - Regensburg, in Bavaria. 99

Ravenna - A city in north central Italy, near the Adriatic. 96

Reims - A city in northeast France, the center of the Champagne region. 99

Reins - The kidneys, loins, or lower back. 155

Rent - The inflected form of rend: To tear or split apart. 349

Repletion - A state of excessive fullness. 274

Rheum - Mucous discharge from membranes of nose, throat or mouth. 59

Rhodes - A Greek island in the Aegean Sea, near Turkey. 96

Ridgebone - Backbone. 246

Rod - A linear measure equal to 5.5 yards or 16.5 feet (5.03 meters). 350

Romandiola - A region of northern Italy. Ravenna was once its capital. 61

St. Anthony's Fire - Any of several inflammatory or gangrenous skin conditions. 246

Saint Lucas - Possibly Lucca, or its famous hospital, in Tuscany, Italy. 95

Sanguine - One of the four humours, warm & moist. Associated with blood, spring, air, liver.

Sarmatia - The territory along the Danube and across the Carpathians. 68

Savoy - Once the extreme NW corner of Italy, it is now the extreme SE corner of France. 97

Saxony - A region in east central Germany. Capital, Dresden. 61

Scab, the - Scurvy. 98

Schismatical - Referring to those who broke away from the main church of the day. 63

Sciatica - Pain along the sciatic nerve usually caused by a herniated disk of the lumbar region of the spine and radiating to the buttocks and to the back of the thigh. 246

Science - Art, skill, or expertness, regarded as the result of knowledge of laws and principles. 430

Scurf - Scaly or shredded dry skin, such as dandruff. 246

Sectarist - One belonging to a (generally unaccepted) religious group, eg, belonging to a sect. 55

Sedge - Grasslike and rushlike herbs found in marshes. 95

Seed - Semen. 246

Sic in aliis - And so in other cases. 283

Siccity - Dryness. 269

Sienna - Siena, in Tuscany, Italy. 94

Sigil - A sign or image considered magical. 485

Silesia - A region of central Europe primarily in southwest Poland and the northern Czech Republic. 94

Slavonia - Part of Croatia. 98

Smith - A metalworker, especially one who works metal when it is hot and malleable. 450

Soil - As in, "where soil is laid": manure. 98

Species - Coins. 216

Speed - Prosper, succeed. 372

Spires - In German, Speyer, a city of the Rhineland-Palatinate, southwestern Germany. 97

Spoil - "to spoil his estate". Lilly's original phrase was, "to fool his estate." 77

Sport - Perhaps Lilly meant the same competitive, athletic behaviors as we know sport now, he may also have had lovemaking in mind. 97

Squinzies - As quinsy, tonsillitis. 63

Stargard - A town in what was Pomerania, now part of Poland, today known as Stargard Szczecinski. 98

Strangury - Slow, painful urination, caused by muscular spasms of the urethra and bladder. 54

Stuprated - Ravished or debauched. (Ravish = rape.) 318

Styria, Stiria - Province of modern Austria, capital, Graz. 98

Sub radiis - Under the rays. 358

Sublated - Literally, to negate or deny. In relation to pulse, weak or none? 277

Sunt sigilla & Lamina quae nec scripta sunt, & ego novi - There are sigils & lamens which have not been described, and I myself have knowledge of them. 213

Surfeit - Overindulgence. 246

Sweathland - Given elsewhere as Sweden, but I am unable to confirm. If "Swevia" is Sweden and Aries, does it make sense that Sweathland, Taurus, is also Sweden? 94

Swevia - Sometimes given as Sweden, but possibly Suabia, in Germany. 94

Swoon - Faint, black out. 281

Symony - The crime of buying or selling Church preferment, profiting from religious privileges. Also as Simony. 434

Sympathy - A relation between parts by which a condition in one induces an effect in the other. 466

Syracuse - A city in southeastern Sicily, on the Ionian sea. 96

Tapster - Bartender. 81

Tartary - China, or the Mongol empire. 99

Terrene - Of the earth. 443

Tertian - Recurring every third day. 67

Thrace - An area occupying the southeastern tip of the Balkan Peninsula, comprising NE Greece, S Bulgaria, and European Turkey. 98

Toulouse - A city on the Garonne River, in southern France. 96

Treat - Engage in negotiations in order to reach an agreement; "they had to treat with the King". 402

Trent - A city in northern Italy, on the Adige River and the road to the Brenner Pass. 99

Turing - Thuringia, a state in central Germany. 76

Tympanic - Referring to the eardrum. 262

Urbino - A town in central Italy. 97

Utrecht - A city in central Netherlands. 94

Vacua cursus - Empty course, said of the moon after it makes an aspect early in a sign, with the next aspect towards the end of it, eg, many hours in a sign with no aspect. 440

Valencia - A city in eastern Spain, on the Turia River. 97

Venery - Indulgence in or pursuit of sexual activity. 246

Ventricle - The chamber on the left side of the heart that receives arterial blood from the left atrium and contracts to force it into the aorta. 278

Verona - A city in northern Italy on the Adige River, west of Venice. 94

Vienna, Vienne - Lilly gives "Vienna" under both Libra & Scorpio. It is presumed the Scorpionic Vienna is Vienne, in Isere, southern France. 97

Virago - A nag or scold. 139

Virtue - Strength. 111

Volens nolens - Willy-nilly. 153

Walachia - An area of southern Romania. 99

Warrener - One who owns or keeps rabbits, or other small animals. 53

Waspish - Easily irritated or annoyed. 416

Waterman - Boatsman. 451

West Indies - The Americas, both North & South. 98

Westphalia - A region of western Germany, including the Ruhr valley. 99

Whitster - One who bleaches cloth. 451

Wind cholic - Gastric distress. 246

Windiness - Flatulence. 63

Wittenberg - A city in Saxony-Anhalt, eastern Germany, on the Elbe River. 95

Worms - A city on the Rhine River, in the Rhineland-Palatinate, in southwestern Germany. 99

York - A city in northern England. 95

Zael - Also known as Zahel, a Jewish astrologer named Sahl ibn Bishr, lived in the first half of the 9th century. He was a master of horary astrology. 342

Zealand - An island of eastern Denmark, now known as Sjaelland. 95

References:

My thanks to John Frawley for his suggestions & corrections.

Christian Astrology, by William Lilly. Regulus Publishing, London, 1985.

Bartleby.com, an amazing on-line assortment of reference works, including **The Columbia Encyclopedia, American Heritage Dictionary of the English Language, Roget's Thesaurus** & a dozen others.

A History of Horoscopic Astrology, by James Herschel Holden, AFA, 1996

Encyclopedia of Astrology, by Nicholas de Vore, Astrology Classics, 2002

The Penguin English Dictionary, by G.N. Garmondsway, 1977.

http://cpcug.org/user/jlacombe/ terms.html, a list of archaic occupations.

http://www.books.md/index.html, medical dictionary search engine.

Hyperdictionary.com, Webster's 1913 dictionary.

Christian Astrology, books 1 & 2, by William Lilly, as retyped & annotated by Deborah Houlding, Ascella, 1999.

Le Petit Robert 2, by Paul Robert, SEPRET, Paris, 1975.

Various webpages.

A Catalogue of moſt ASTROLOGICAL AUTHORS now extant, where Printed, and in what yeer.

Albumazar — **Flores**, quarto, Augustae, 1488.
Albumazar — **Introductorius Liber in Astronomiam**, quarto, Augustae, 1489.
Albumazar — **De Magnis Conjunctionibus**, quarto, Augustae, 1489.
Alfraganus — **Compilatio Astronomica**, quarto, Ferrariae, 1493.
Albubater — **De Nativitatibus**, quarto, Norrimbergae, 1540.
Alkindus — **De Pluviis & Aeris Mutatione**, quarto, Venetiis, 1507, *printed since in folio*
Alcabitus — **Judicionum Astrorum Isagoge cum Commentario Johannis Saxionii**, quarto, Parisiis, 1521.
Abano, Petrus de — **De Mutatione Aeris**, quarto, Venetiis, 1485.
Allen, Thomas — **Commentarium in 2 & 3 libr Ptolomei**, *never printed*.
Agrippa, Cornelius — **De Oculta Philosophia**, octavo, Lugduni.
Albinius, Constantinus — **De Magia Astrologica**, octavo, Parisiis 1611.
Aitsingerus, Michael — **Pent Plus Regnorum Mundi**, quarto, Antwerpiae, 1579.
Alhohali — **De Nativitatibus**, quarto, Norimbergae, 1546.
Allatius, Leo — **Paraphrasis in 4 Libros Ptolomei**, octavo, Lugduni Batavorum, 1635, **De Syderum Affectionibus**.
Alstedius — **Thesaurus Chronologiae**, octavo, Herbonae Nassavorum, 1637.
Alliaco, Petrus de — **De Concordia Astronomiae cum Theologia**, quarto, Augustae, 1490.
Angelus, Johannes — **De Nativitatibus**, quarto, Venetiis, 1494.
Angelis, Alexander de — **Libri Quinque in Astrologos**, quarto, Lugdum, 1615.
Albertus — **Speculum Astronomicum**, 24⁰, Lugduni, 1615.
Aratus — **Prognostica**, octavo, 1589.
Alkindus — **De Judiciis, Amanusor Pt.** folio, *translated 1272 per Ro. Anglicum*, **Iatromathematico**, octavo, Rostochi, 1629.
Assuerus, Johannes — **De Scientia Stellarum**, quarto, Norrumbergae 1537.
Albategnius — **Methodus Mathematica Curandorum Morborum per Anonymum**, quarto, Frankford, 1613.
Argolus, Andreas — **Primum Mobile de Directionibus**, quarto, Romae, 1610, *lately new printed. His* **Ephemerides**, quarto, *in 3 Tomes*, Patavii 1638. **De Diebus Criticis**, quarto, Patavii, 1639. **Pandofion Sphericum**, quarto, Patavii, 1644.
Avenaris, Abraham — **Principum Sapientiae**, quarto, Venetiis, 1507.

Bartholinus, Gasper — **De Stellarum Natura**, 12⁰ Wittenberga, 1609.
Baranzanus, Redemptus — **Uranoscopia**, quarto, 1617.
Bonaventura, Federicus — **De Affectionibus Ventorum**, quarto, Urbin, 1593.
Bricot, Thomas — **De Coelo & Mundo**.
Bariona, Laurentius — **Cometographia**, quarto, Londini, 1578.
Boderius, Thomas — **De Ratione Dierum Criticorum**, quarto, Parisiis, 1555.

Baker, Humphrey — **Introduction to Judicial Astrology**, octavo, London.
Brahe, Tycho — **De Disciplinis Mathematicis**, 4⁰, Hamburgi, 1621.
Beds — **De Natura Rerum & Temporum**, folio, Basiliae, 1529.
Bellantius, Lucius — **De Astrologica Veritate**, folio, Basiliae, 1554.
Bonincontrus, Laurentius — **De Rebus Coelestibus**, folio, Basiliae, 1575.
Bonatus, Guido — **De Astronima Tractarus 10**, folio, Basiliae, 1550.
Booker, John — **Of the Conjunction of Saturn and Mars**, 4⁰, London, 1646, *besides many excellent judgments in his annual* **Prognostication**.

Carion, Johannes — **De Affectibus Directionum**, 16⁰, Frankford, 1611.
Cardanus, Hieronomus — **De Judiciis Geniturarum**, quarto, Norimbergoe, 1547. **In Quadripartitum Ptolomei**, folio, Basiliae, 1578. *All other editions are defective; in this you find at the end* **Conrad Dasipodius upon Ptolomy**.
Campanella, Thomas — **Medicinalium Opus**, quarto, Lugdoni, 1635. *Idem,* **Astrologicoum Libri 7**, 4⁰, Frankford, 1630.
Censorinus — **De Die Natali**, octavo, Lugduni Batavorum, 1642.
Codronchus, Baptista — **De Annis Climactericis**, octavo, Coloniae, 1623.
Celoestinus, Claudius — **De Influentiis Coelorum**, quarto, Paris, 1542.
Camerarius, Rudolphus — **Centuriae Duoe Geniturarum**, quarto, Amsterodami, 1633.
Claudinus, Caesar — **De Diebus Criticis**, octavo, Basiliae, 1620.
Chambers, John — **Against Judicial Astrology**, 4⁰, London 1601.
Curtius, Joachimus — **De Certitudine Matheseos**, 4⁰, Hamburgi, 1616.

Dariot, Claudius — **Judgement of the Stars**, 4⁰, London, 1598.
Dee, Johannes — **120 Aphorismi**, quarto, Londini, 1558.
Dietericus, Helvicus — **Elogium Planetarnm**, 8⁰, Argentorati, 1627.
Duret, Natalis — **Novae Ephemerides**, quarto, Parisiis, 1641.

Eichstadius, Laurentius — **Ephemerides ab an. 1636 ad 1665**, quarto: Stetini impressis 1634, 1636. **Ab anno 1650 ad 1605** Amsterodami, 1644.
Erastus, Thomas — **De Astrologia Divinatrice**, quarto, 1569.
Etzlerus, Augustus — **Physico-Magico Medica**, octavo, Argentinae, 1631.
Escuidus, Johannes — **Summa Astrologiae Indicialis**, folio, Venetiis, 1489. *It's miserably printed; he was Student of Merton College in Oxford.*

Ferrier, Oger — **Judgment of Nativities**, quarto, London, 1642.
Ferrerius, Augerius — **De Diebus Decretoriis**, 24, Lugduni, 1549.
Forsterus, Richardus — **Ephemerides Meterographica**, octavo, London, 1575.
Frytschius, Marcus — **De Meteoris**, octavo, Norimbergae, 1563. *Idem* **Catalogus Prodigiorum**.
Fromundus, Libertus — **De Cometa 1618**, octavo, Antwerpae, 1619. *Idem* **Meteorologieorum Libri Sex**, octavo, Oxoniae, 1639.
Frischlinus, Nicodemus — **Astronomica Artis Congruentia cum Doctrina Coelsti & Naturali Phylo, Ophia**, octavo, Frankfurt, 1586.
Finaeus, Orontius — **De 12 Coeli Domiciliis**, quarto, Lutetiae, 1553.
Firminus — **Repertorium de Mutatione Aeris**, folio, Parisiis, 1540.
Ficinus, Marsilius — **De Vita Coelitus**, quarto, Venetiis, 1584.
Fage, John — **Speculum Aegrotorum**, 4⁰, London, 1638.

Fludd, Robert — **Medicina Catholica**, folio, Francofurti, 1629, *and in several other pieces of his Works, has wrote much of Astrology, he may justly be accounted the mirrour of our times, and of the Welsh Nation.*

Field, John — **Ephemerides**, quarto, Londini, 1558.

Gallenus, Claudius — **De Diebus Decretoriis**, in sixteen, Lugduni, 1553.

Ganivetus, Johannes — **Amicus Medicoru**, 16, Frankfurt, 1614.

Gassendus, Petrus — **Coelestes Observationes**, 8⁰, Paris, 1630.

Goclenius, Rodolphus — **Generalis Astrologiae**, 4⁰, Marpurgi, 1614.

Goclenius, Rodolphus — **Uranoscopi**, 16, Frankfurt, 1608.

Golcenius, Rodolphus — **Synopsis Astrologiae**, octavo, Frankfurt, 1620.

Gauricus, Lucas — **Tractatus Astrologiae**, quarto, Norimbergae, 1540. *Idem* **De Geniture Civitatum & Virorum Illustrium**, 4⁰, Venetiis, 1552. **De Diebus Criticis**, 4⁰, Romae, 1546. **Super Tabulis Directionum Joannis Regiomontani**, 4⁰, Romae, 1560. **De Tota Astrologia Predictiva & Aliis**, *in 2 Tom.* folio, Basil, 1575.

Gordonius, Bernardus — **Lillium Medicine**, 8⁰, Frankford, 1617.

Gaphar — **De Mutatione Temporis**, quarto, Venetiis, 1507.

Goclenius, Rodolphus — **Acroteleution Astrologicum**, quarto, Marpurgi, 1618.

Guarimbertus, Matthei — **De Radiis Planetaru**, quarto, Norimbergae, 1535.

Goclenius, Rodolphus — **Pro Astromantia Discursus**, quarto, Marpurgi, 1611.

Gluffus, Antonius — **De Eclipsibus**, quarto, Neapoli, 1621.

Garcaeus, Johannes — **Astrologiae Methodus**, folio, Basiliae, 1586.

Gaudentius, Paganinus — **De Prodigiorum Significatione**, quarto, Florentiae, 1638.

Harvey, John — **Problematical Discourse**, 4⁰, London, 1588.

Haghen, Theodoricus — **Prognosticum Stellare**, 4⁰, Ultrajecti, 1553.

Hasfurtus, Johannes — **De Medendis Morbis ex Corporum Coelesticum Positione**, **lib. 3, 4**, Venetiis, 1584.

Hermetis — **Centum Aphorismi cum Comentationibus Thaddaei Haggecii**, 4⁰, Pragae, 1564.

Hispalensis, Johannes — **Epitometotius Astrologiae**, 4⁰, Norimbergae, 1548.

Hemings, Sextus — **Astrologiae Refutatio**, 4⁰, Antwerpiae, 1653.

Hopton, Arthur — **Concordancy of Yeers**, 8⁰, London, 1635.

Heydon, Sir Christopher — **Defence of Astrology**, 4⁰, Cambridge, 1603. *A most learned work in the English tongue.*

Herlitius, David — **Prognosticon Astrologicum**, quarto, Stetini, 1619.

Hartgill, George — **Astronomical Tables**, folio, London, 1594. *A most accurate piece for by the **Table of Houses** in his book the fixed Stars are discovered upon the cusp of every house.*

Haly, Albohazen — **De Judiciis Astrorum**, folio, Basiliae, 1571. *All other Editions are defective.*

Hewes, Robertus — **De Globis**, 26⁰, Frankfort, 1627.

Hyginus — **Poeticon Astrohomicum**. *Idem*, **Opus Aureum**, quarto, Parisiis, 1412.

Hyppocrates — **De Medicorum Astrologica**, quarto, Venetiis, 1485.

Hermes — **De Revolutionibus Nativitatum**, folio, Basiliae, 1559.

Junctinus, Franciscus — **Speculum Astrologiae**, 4⁰, Lugduni, 1573.

Judeus, Abraham — **De Nativitatibus**, 4⁰, Coloniae, 1537.

Junctinus, Franciscus — **Speculum Astrologiae**, *in two Tomes*, folio, *he comments upon the third and fourth of Ptolomey, and upon Sacro Bosco, was printed* Lugduni, 1583.

Keplerus, Johannes — **Epitomes Astronomiae**, octavo, Frankford, 1621. *Idem* **Ephemerides Novae ab anno 1617, ad 1636,** quarto, Lincii, Austriae.

Leonarde, Camilli — **Speculum Lapidum, & Simpathia Metallorum ad Planets**, 8⁰, Parisiis, 1610.

Lavaterius, Ludovicus — **De Spectris**, octavo, Genevae, 1580.

Lemnius, Levinus — **De Astrologia**, twelves, Frankford, 1608.

Laurentius, Andreas — **De Crisibus**, octavo, Lugduni, 1605.

Leupoldus — **De Astrorum Scientia**, 4⁰, Venetiis, 1520.

Lindhout, Henricus — **Speculu Astrogiae**, 4⁰, Francofurti, 1608.

Leovitius, Cyprianus — **De Magis Conjunctionibus**, 4⁰, Laugingae, 1564. *Idem* **Tabulae Directionum**, 4⁰, Norimbergae, 1552. **De Eclipsibus**, folio, Augustae Vindelicorum, 1556. **Ephemerides**, folio, Augustae Vindelicorum, 1557.

Licetus, Fortunius — **De Comeri**, quarto, Venetiis, 1623.

Longomontanus, Severinus — **Astronomia Danica**, quarto, Amsterodami, 1622.

Lalamantius, Johannes — **De Diebus Decretoriis**, 4⁰, Lugduni, 1560.

Lilly, William — *Author of this Work, has wrote* **Anglicus**, 1644. **Anglicus**, 1645. **Anglicus**, 1646, 1647. **Of the Conjunction of Saturn and Mars**, 1644. **Of the Conjunction of Saturn and Jupiter, 1642/3**, London, 4⁰, 1644. **The Starry Messenger**, 4⁰, London, 1645. **World's Catastrophe**, 4⁰, London, 1646.

Manginus, Antonius — **Nova Dirigenii Ars**, 8⁰, Bononiae, 1616.

Murer, Wolfgangus — **Meteorologica**, quarto, Lipsiae, 1588.

Manfredus, Hieronimus — **De Medicis & Infirmis**, 12⁰, 1530.

Maples, John — **Dial of Destiny**, octavo, London, 1582.

Manilius, Marcus — **Astoonomicon Repurgatum a Jo Scaligero**, quarto, Lugduno Betavae, 1600.

Merula, Gaudentius — **Memorabilia**, octavo, Lugduni, 1556.

Messahala — **De Revolutione Annorum Mundi, de Nativitatibus**, &c., quarto, Norimbergae, 1549. *Idem*, **de Oribus Coelstibus**, 4⁰, Norimbergae, 1549.

Mizaldus, Antonius — **Ephemeridum Aeris Perpetuarum**, 16⁰, Amberga, 1604. *Idem*, **Cometographia**, 4⁰, Parisii, 1549. *Idem*, **Planetologia**, 4⁰, Lugduni, 1551.

Montulmo, Antonius de — **De Judiciis Nativitatum**, quarto, Norimbergae, 1540.

Mizaldus, Antonius — **Harmonia Macrocosmicum Macrocosme**, quarto, Lugduni, 1550. **Ephemeris 1555**, octavo, Lutetiae.

Michael, Johannes — **Almanack Perpetuum**, 4⁰, Venetiis, 1502.

Morshemius, Mercurius — **De Judiciis Astrologicis**, 8⁰, Basiliae, 1559.

Mollerius, Elias — **De Eclipsibus**, 4⁰, 1607.

Mullerius, Nicholaus — **Institutionum Astronomicarum Libri Due**, 8⁰, Groningae, 1616.

Muller, Phillip — **De Cometa**, 8⁰, Lipsiae, 1619.

Minerva, Paulus — **Prasagitura Temporu**, folio, Neapoli, 1620.

Maginus, Johannes — **Tabulae Nova**, 4⁰, Bononiae, 1619, **De Directionibus**, *idem*. **Die Diebus Criticis**, 4⁰, Venetiis, 1607. **Ephemerides**, quarto, Francofurti, 1610. **Primum Mobile**, folio, Venetiis, 1604.

Montebrunus — **Ephemerides per Tabulas Lansbergianas ab 1645 ad 1660**, 4⁰, Bononiae, 1645.

Modronus, Ludovicus — **De Directionibus per Novas Tabulau Domorum**, 4⁰, Bononiae, 1641.

Moletius, Josephus — **Ephemerides**, 4⁰, Venetiis, 1564.

Naibod, Velentinus — **De Coelo & Terra, lib. 3**, 8⁰, Venetiis, 1573. *Idem*, **Enarratio in Alcabitum**, 4⁰, Coloniae, 1560.

Niphus, Augustinus — **De Diebus Criticis**, 4⁰, Marpurgi, 1614.

Origanus, David — **Ephemerides**, 4⁰, Frankford, 1609, *in 3 Tomes.*

Offusius, Jofrancus — **De Divina Astrorum Facultate**, 4⁰, Parisiis, 1570.

Obitius, Hippolitus — **Iatrastronomicum**, 4⁰, Vicentiae, 1618.

Olaus, Elias — **Diarium Astrologicum**, 4⁰, Uraniburgae, 1586.

Omar — **De Nativitatibus**, folio, Basiliae, 1551.

Paracelsus — **De Meteoris**, 8⁰, Basiliae, **De Summis Naturae Mysteriis**, 8⁰, Basiliae.

Paduanius, Johannes — **De Rebus Astronomicis**, 4⁰, Venetiis, 1563.

Partlicius, Simeon — **De Influentiis**, 16⁰, 1623.

Pucer, Gasper — **De Astrologia**, octavo, Witinbergae, 1572.

Pleierus, Connelius — **Medicus Criticus Astrologicus**, 16⁰, Norimbergae, 1627.

Picolhomineus, Alexander — **De Sphera lib. 4**, quarto, Basiliae, 1568.

Pitatus, Petrus — **Ephemerides**, quarto.

Pontanus, Jovianus — **Urania**, octavo, Basiliae, 1556. *Idem*, **De Rebus Coelestibus**, quarto, Basiliae, 1530. **In Centum Ptolomei Aphorismes Commentatio**, quarto, Basiliae, 1531.

Porta, Baptista — **Physiognomonia Coelestis**, octavo, Argentorati, 1606.

Puteanus, Erycus — **De Cometa 1618**, 24⁰, Coloneae, 1619.

Pezelius, Christopherus — **De Genethliacis**, quarto.

Pererius, Benedictus — **De Magia & Astrologica Divinationie**, octavo, Coloniae, 1598.

Piso, Carolus — **Physicum Cometae Speculum**, octavo, Ponte ad Montionem, 1619.

Ptolomeus, Claudius — **Quadripartitum**, folio, Basiliae, 1551.

Proclus — **In Quadripartitum Ptolomei**, folio, Basiliae, 1559.

Porphirius — **In Ptolomeum**, folio, Basiliae, 1559.

Radinus, Thomas — **Syderalis Abissus**, quarto, Lutetiis, 1514.

Ranzovius, Henricus — **Tractatus Astrologicus**, octavo, Frankforti, 1615. *Idem*, **Opusculum Astronomicum**, quarto, Witinbergae. **Catalogus Imperatorum Qui Amarunt Astrologiam**, octavo, Antwerpiae, 1580.

Regiomontanus, Johannes — **Tabulae Directionum**, quarto, Witinbergae, 1606.

Rockenbach, Abrahamus — **De Cometis**, octavo, Witinbergae, 1619.

Rotmannus, Johannes — **Meteorologiae Synopsis**, Frankford, 1619.

Rothmannus, Johannes — **Concordantia Genethliaca cum Chryomatia**, quarto, Erphordiae, 1595.

Regiis, Ludovicus de — **Aphorismi Astrologici**, quarto, Norimbergae, 1535.

Ricciolio, Baptista — **Crux Geographica**, folio, Bononiae, 1643.

Regiomontanus, Johannes — **Kalendarium**, quarto.

Roflin, Helisaeus — **Hypotheses de Mundo**, quarto, Francofurti, 1587.

Haly, Rodan — **Commentarium in Quadripartium Ptolomei, & Centum Aphorismos**, folio, Venetiis, 1493, *with which is printed* **The 100 Aphorisms of Bethen, Almanso and Hermes**; *as also, Zael* **De Interrogationibus**; *and of Messahalah*, **De Annorum Revolutionibus**.
Ryff, Gualter — **De Diebus Criticis**, sixteens.

Satlerius, Wolfgangus — **Dianoia Astrologica**, octavo, Montisbelgardi, 1605.
Schylander, Cornelius — **Medicina Astrologica**, Antwerpiae, 1577.
Stanhusius, Michael — **De Meteoris**, octavo, Witibergae, 1562.
Savanorola, Hieronomus — **Adversus Divinatricem Astronomiam**, octavo, Florentia, 1581.
Smoll, Godfridus — **Philosophica & Medica Pryncipia**, quarto, Lubecae, 1609.
Scholl, Jacob — **Canones Astrologicae ad Medicinam**, quarto, Argentorati, 1537.
Stoeflerus, Johannes — **Ephemerides**, quarto, Parisis, 1533.
Stadius, Johannes — **Ephemerides**, quarto, Coloniae Agrippinae, 1570. **Tabulae Bergenses**, Coloniae Agrippinae, 1560.
Siderocrator, Samuel — **De Distantiis Locorum**, quarto, Tubingae, 1562.
Schonerus, Johannes — **Opera Mathemateca**, folio, Norimbergae, 1551. *A good book, but not methodical.*
Sempilius, Hugo — **De Mathematicis**, folio, Antwerpiae, 1635.

Taisnier, Johannes — **Astrrologiae Isagogica**, 8⁰, Colonia, 1559.
Tanner, Robert — **Of the Conjunction of Saturn and Jupiter 1583**, octavo, London, 1583.
Tanstetter, Collimitius — **Canones, Astronomici**, octavo, Argentorati, 1531.
Thurnhesserus — **Kalendarium & Ephemeris**, quarto, Berlini, 1582.
Tentzelius, Andreas — **Medicina Diastatica**, 16⁰, Jehnae, 1629.
Theophrastus — **De Ventis**, quarto, Urbini, 1593.
Torporleius, Nathaniel — **Valvae Astronomicae**, 4⁰, London, 1602.
Trapezuntius, Georgius — **In Centum Ptolomei Aphorismos**, octavo, Coloniae, 1544.
Thurneisse, Leonardus — **Virtutes Plantarum Influentiales**, folio, Berlini, 1578.
Tyardeus, Pontus — **Ephemerides 8⁰ Spherae**, Lugduni, 1562.

Valla, Georgius — **Commentationes in Ptolomeum**, folio, Venetiis, 1502. *A most pitiful Commentary.*
Vernerus, Johannes — **De Mutatione Aurae**, 4⁰, Norimbergae, 1546.

Welperus, Eberhardus — **Compendium Astronomiae**, octavo, Argentori, 1634.
Wicknerus, Abdias — **Tabulae Ascensionum**, 4⁰, Tubingae, 1561.

Zinckius, Johannes — **De Crisibus**, sixteens, Francofurt, 1609.
Zobolus, Alphonsus — **De Directionibus**, folio, Vincentiae, 1620.

[Argentori, Argentorati, etc.: Strasbourg. Entries are as ordered by Lilly. Almost all these books are out-of-print, most have never been translated into English. Only a few can be found in Gardner's **Catalogue Raisonne of Works on the Occult Sciences, Volume 2, Astrological Books** (1913, reprinted 1977 as **Bibliotheca Astrologica**), which makes Lilly's bibliography a useful annex to Gardner. - *Ed. note.*]

There may happily be many more Authors extant who have written of *Astrologie*, but no more have as yet come to my hands; these I mention are all my own, &c. Many of these perhaps have since been printed at other places: Indeed *Ptolemy* has been printed in *folio*, in *quarto*, in *octavo*, in *sixteens*, and has been translated several times out of *Greek* into *Latin*: That lately printed at *Leiden* I conceive to be the most exact, it was performed by *Allatius*, &c. In a word, some may blame me that I write in the *English* tongue; yet I trust I have offended no man, since I write in my own Language; and to such as speak as I speak; nor do I know that it is forbid unto man to write in his own Language, or is any man bound to read or hear that contents him not: If this Book do generally please, I shall account him good, and think him worthy to live: But if he displease, I then believe the memory of it shall soon perish, and myself shall count it ill: If notwithstanding this, mine Accusers will not be satisfied with this common judgment, let them content themselves with the judgment of the time, which at length discovers the privy faults of everything: Which because it is the Father of truth, it gives judgment without passion, and accustoms evermore to pronounce true sentence of the life or death of Writings. *Finis; Deo gloria. October 1, 1647.*

LILLY

An Alphabetical T A B L E, ſhewing the
Contents of the principall matters in every
Page of this B o o k.

[Lilly's original entries were not strictly alphabetical. I have made them so. *Ed.*]

F I N I S.

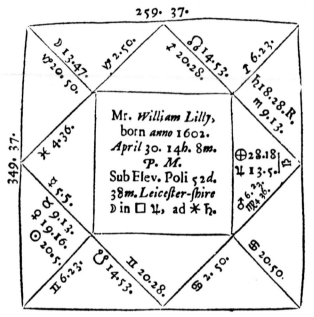

From **Collectio Genitorum**, *by John Gadbury (London, 1662)*

The Latitude of
the Planets.

	d.	m.	
♄	2	44	} North
♃	1	56	
♂	1	27	
♀	0	40	} South
☿	2	47	
☽	2	33	North

The Person whose Geniture this is, (to puzzle the Understandings of the inquisitive) has pretended himself to have two several Nativities. (1.) In his Almanac 1645, he tells his Reader (in the Epistle thereunto) that he had the Moon in *Pisces*, which makes him a piece of a good Fellow, &c., which, (if true) he must be born the fifth or sixth of *May* 1602. (2.) In his Introduction under his Effigies, he says he was born on *May* 1, 1602, and then the Moon will not be in ♓, but in ♑, as in this Figure. I am of Opinion, he has not the moon in ♓, but in ♑, and therefore believe this to be his right Nativity: the rather, because my loving Friend Mr. *James Blackwel*, has proved it so to be, by 13 several Arguments or Accidents; printed a year and a half since by itself. In which little Tract, the ingenious Artist may meet with a concise Method for the Calculating and judging a Nativity; and unto which, I refer the desirous Reader for further satisfaction in his Geniture. The reason why I am no larger herein, is, Because I would not be esteemed either Envious or Partial.

CPSIA information can be obtained at www.ICGtesting.com
Printed in the USA
LVOW102030261012

304558LV00003B/1/A